COLLEGE AND UNIVERSITY LAW

By

KERN ALEXANDER

Professor
University of Florida

AND

ERWIN S. SOLOMON

Attorney at Law
Member of Virginia Bar

THE MICHIE COMPANY
Law Publishers
CHARLOTTESVILLE, VIRGINIA

PREFACE

This book is intended to provide students and practicing administrators with a comprehensive discussion of the law governing colleges and universities. At a time when students want instructors to "tell it like it is"; when non-student activists use the campus as a forum for their ideology; when professors join students and non-students in protests against the administration; when the drug culture infiltrates the colleges and universities; when new sexual mores replace an older code, the college administrator must have more than superficial acquaintance with the law governing higher education.

At any time the courts may modify or broaden the law. Thus, the law is not static, and one cannot assume that change will not occur. In actuality the law is constantly in a state of flux, especially where free speech, due process and constitutional guarantees are interpreted in relation to colleges and universities. The very fact that a budding administrator recognizes that a change is inevitable, is the beginning of awareness of the problems he will face An era of rapid change is present in education. The college official who has empathy with those who are seeking change will be successful—others needless to say, will fail. If this volume gives some additional understanding and in some degree enhances the operation of colleges and universities then the authors' time will be well invested.

The book is a combination textbook and casebook. The textual material of the chapters relates the legal precedents of hundreds of cases forming the parameters of the law of higher education. Legal definitions, historical development, and current status of the law are revealed through the text. The case materials are compiled from carefully selected decisions of both state and federal appellate courts. The cases were individually selected to identify substantive issues which in sum illustrate the judicial actions, procedures and attitudes of the courts in educational matters. The authors have attempted to maintain objectivity in preparation of the text and the selection of all cases and materials, but it should be admitted that personal knowledge and values probably cannot be entirely neutralized in any book. It is hoped that the materials presented will give the reader as fair an assessment as possible of the law as it governs the various aspects of higher education. Notes are appended at the end of the principal cases in all chapters citing precedents and exceptions to precedents in other jurisdictions.

Organizationally, the chapters of the book focus on the primary elements of the law which bear directly on the daily operation of colleges and universities. Chapter 1 of the book familiarizes the reader with legal processes including sources of the law, descriptions of the courts, and a brief analysis of judicial procedure. Other chapters include the basis for higher education, constitutional law as it affects both students and teachers, legal aspects of financing, and tort liability as it impacts on employees, officials, and the institutions. In each of the chapters throughout the book terms are defined by legal precedent as established by the courts. Where diversity of terminology exists more than one definition may be given depending on the jurisdiction of the courts. The terms college and university are for the purposes of this book generally used interchangeably, unless otherwise specified by the courts.

While legal issues involving both public and private higher education are discussed, the main thrust of the book is toward public colleges and universities. Much attention is given to the relationship between the state and the institution as well as among the institution, the student and the teacher.

All contributions to research and literature are dependent on their predecessors. This book is no exception; great reliance is placed on prior works of scholarship giving form and substance to the topics discussed in the chapters of this book. Surprisingly, few authors have written books which attempt to encompass the entire realm of the law of higher education. However, one name stands out as undisputed leader in this field. Anyone writing in this area must acknowledge his dependence on the massive contributions of M. M. Chambers. His books form the basis for any inquiry into higher education in the United States. We have relied either directly or indirectly on the works of Chambers, the most notable being his recent benchmark study *Higher Education in the Fifty States* along with *The Colleges and the Courts Since 1950*, and *The Colleges and the Courts 1962-1966*. Other works of scholars of particular note which were helpful in the preparation of this book were Thomas E. Blackwell's *College Law* and Leo Pfeffer's outstanding book *Church, State and Freedom*.

PREFACE

No book can be completed without the behind-the-scenes assistance and cooperation of many individuals. The authors wish to give special acknowledgment to Mrs. Betty Taylor, Law Librarian, College of Law, University of Florida, for providing the authors with a convenient and quiet place to research and write. Appreciation should also be extended to Mrs. Nelda Cambron of the University of Florida and Miss Elsie Dunn of The Michie Company for their devotion to the editorial tasks so important in preparation of the manuscript for publication. We are also indebted to University of Florida graduate students Carl Daeufer, Jack Fisher, Scott Rose, and David DeRuzzo for their assistance in proofreading the manuscript and galleys.

Of course, we cannot forget to acknowledge our wives, Ruth and Joyce, for their consistent patience and understanding from the beginning to the end of the entire endeavor.

KERN ALEXANDER
ERWIN S. SOLOMON

TABLE OF CONTENTS

[Table contains principal cases and major notes.]

TABLE OF CONTENTS

TABLE OF CONTENTS

xi

TABLE OF CONTENTS

TABLE OF CASES

[The principal cases are in Italic type. Cases cited in the footnotes and textual notes are in Roman type. References are to Pages.]

COLLEGE AND UNIVERSITY LAW

CHAPTER 1

NATURE OF THE LAW

To embark on the study of college and university law requires some basic understanding of the American legal system. Knowledge of the sources of our law and the function and structure of the courts is a logical starting point. This chapter is designed to give the reader the background necessary to properly understand and interpret the succeeding chapters.

The study of higher education law is only one small cross-section of American Jurisprudence, but its principles emanate from the basic sources of law which govern our nation generally. Essentially, the law is based on three sources: constitutions, statutes and court law. Constitutions, federal and state, are the primary law giving form and substance to the legal system under which the people choose to govern themselves. Within this structure the branches of government possess certain roles which predetermine the nature of the law. The legislative branch enacts, the judicial branch interprets and the executive branch implements and administers the law. This broad governmental framework, which is common knowledge to all Americans, is the logical point of embarkation on our study of the fundamental legal concepts which have such important bearing and impact on higher education in the United States.

SOURCES OF LAW [1]

CONSTITUTIONS

A constitution is a body of precepts providing a framework of law within which orderly governmental processes operate. The constitutions of this country are characterized by their provisions for securing fundamental personal, property and political rights. One of the primary precepts embodied in a constitution is the provision for authorized modification of the document. Experience in human and governmental relations

---

1. Kern Alexander, Ray Corns, Walter McCann, *Public School Law*, West Publishing Company, 1969, pp. 2-3.

teaches that to be effective a constitution must be flexible and provide for systematic change processes. The Constitution of the United States expressly provides in Article V a process for proposing amendments by a two-thirds vote of each house of Congress or by a convention which shall be called by Congress upon application by two-thirds of the state legislatures. Amendments must be ratified by the legislatures of three-fourths of the states or by conventions in three-fourths of the states.

Another precept reflected in the state and federal constitutions of this country is the importance of a government of separated powers. While all state constitutions do not expressly provide for a separation of the legislative, executive and judicial departments, in actual practice all states have governments of separated powers. There is no requirement in the federal constitution that the constitutions of states possess provisions for separation of powers. Theoretically, if a state so desired, it could clothe an officer or an agency with not only executive but plenary judicial and legislative powers. However, as indicated previously this is not the case and all states have governments with separate branches, each exercising checks and balances on the powers of other branches.

STATUTES

A statute is an act of the legislative branch of government expressing its will and constituting a law of the state. Statute is a word derived from the Latin term *stratutum*, which means "it is decided." A statute, in our American form of government, is the most effective means of making new law and it may either react to custom or forge ahead and establish law which shapes the future of the citizenry.

Statutes in this country are subject to review by the judiciary to determine constitutionality. This procedure is different from England where the legislative branch of government has ultimate authority and there are no means by which the courts can hold legislation unconstitutional. This is true primarily because in England the constitution for the most part is unwritten and the legislative branch, Parliament, may amend the constitution when it so desires.

Rules and regulations of public educational institutions fall within the category of statutory sources of law. As a general rule, the legislature cannot delegate away its legislative power to a subordinate agency or official. Public agencies must, in devising rules and regulations for the administration of education, do so within the limits defined by the legislature and cannot exercise legislative authority. However, the legislature may through statute expressly or impliedly confer administrative duties upon an agency or official. These administrative powers must be well defined and "canalized" within definitely circumscribed channels.

COURT OR CASE LAW

The third source of law is court or case law, also sometimes called common law. The term case law is used to distinguish rules of law which have originated in the courts from law originating in legislative bodies. The term common law originated in England where the word "common" was derived as customs of parts of the country became common to the entire country. The legal customs of various parts of the country became crystallized into principles of law which were applied and used as precedent throughout England.

JUDICIAL DECISIONS

(Reprinted with permission, Erwin H. Pollack, *Fundamentals of Legal Research*, The Foundation Press, 1962, pp. 6-9.)

The reasons for judicial *precedent* have been clearly stated by Professor Llewellyn. "Toward its [precedent] operation drive all those phases of human make-up which build habit in the individual and institutions in the group: laziness as to the re-working of a problem once solved; the time and energy saved by routine, especially under pressure of business; the values of routine as a curb on arbitrariness and as a prop of weakness, inexperience and instability; the social values of predictability; the power of whatever exists to produce expectations and the power of expectations to become normative. The force of precedent in the law is heightened by an additional factor: That curious, almost universal sense of justice which urges that all men are properly to be treated alike in like circumstances." [2]

Additional reasons have been suggested for the responsiveness to and acceptance of case law in America. Precedent preserves and utilizes the techniques and the knowledge of the past; and the application of case law to the facts in the dispute gives it specificity and meaning and imparts the dramatic, a characteristic which is missing from the code. [3]

Case law appears in administrative as well as judicial ad-

---

2. Llewellyn, "Case Law," 3 *Ency. Soc. Sci.* 249 (1930).
3. Patterson, *op. cit.* note 5, at 206.

judication; however, the application of precedent by administrative boards appears to be dependent upon their powers, practices and functions. While many federal administrative boards cite and appear to follow their earlier decisions, others are less given to support the rule of *stare decisis*.

How and to what extent is case law binding on the courts? In England, where the judicial system is unified, precedent has a very strong hold on the courts. The House of Lords and the Court of Appeal are bound absolutely by their earlier rulings which they cannot overrule. The decisions of superior courts are binding on lower courts and those of inferior courts of long standing generally are controlling over superior courts. The holdings of coordinate courts are conditionally binding. However, by restricting the scope of the precedent to those cases which duplicate a substantial number of the facts, the courts in effect can make the rule of precedent inoperative. This practice explains the quip of Mr. Justice Holmes, ". . . I will admit any general proposition that anyone wants to lay down and decide the case either way." [4]

In America, the practice generally prevails that the decisions of the highest court are deemed to be binding on all lower courts which is descriptive of the rule of *stare decisis*. However, all American courts of last resort may depart from previous decisions when a change in a rule appears to be compelling. It seems that lower courts consider themselves bound to follow, in their interpretations of the rulings of the highest court, the decisions of the next higher court in the hierarchy of authority. * * *

There is extensive literature on the nature and the function of judicial precedent. The declaratory theory of precedent, developed by Blackstone from the writings of Coke and Hale, holds that judicial decisions are not the ultimate sources of the law but are only evidences of the law, the evidence being rebuttable.[5] It is assumed that the actual rule of law is already in existence and is never encountered. At best the nearest approach to the legal principle is evidence of the rule. Thus, the overruling of a precedent and the endorsement of a conflicting legal principle, under this theory, is not a change in the law but the declaration of the true law upon its discovery.

The *declaratory theory* complements the rule of *stare de-*

---

4. 1 *Holmes-Laski Letters* 390 (Howe ed. 1953).
5. Blackstone, *Commentaries* 122 (Jones ed. 1916).

cisis, reaching its greatest popularity when the obligation to follow precedents is strongest. Although the declaratory theory gives rise to uncertainties in the law, its advantage rests in its flexibility, for the doctrine has enabled the law to grow in accordance with social and economic exigencies.

In the nineteenth century, vigorous attacks on the declaratory theory were made by Jeremy Bentham and John Chipman Gray.[6] They challenged the idea that a court merely "declares" the law as discovered by it. In their opinion, the appellate courts frequently "make" law, and the "existence" of law is to be found in the principles enunciated by the courts. Gray, by his famous inquiry: "What was the law in the reign of Richard I on the liability of a telegraph company to the addressee of a message?"[7] demonstrated judicial law-making and planted the seeds for the jurisprudential decline of the declaratory theory. However, the theory continues to have supporters among members of the judiciary and the bar.

But Gray, in his enthusiasm, exaggerated the law-making power of the courts. The extremeness of his views is reflected in the idea that statutes, apart from judicial interpretation, are not the law but merely "sources" of it.

Some judges, including Cardozo and Holmes, while acknowledging the law-creating function of the courts, subscribe to a more moderate view. They believe that the law is changed infrequently by the courts and then, in Holmes' words, only interstitially or microscopically. Yet, Holmes acknowledged that the body of the law is generally restated for each generation in the judicial reports of a jurisdiction.[8] Cardozo described the change as evolutionary, evolving a series of decisions over a long period of time. Their approach attempts to reconcile the pragmatic function with the accepted philosophy of Alexander Hamilton that the American judiciary has neither force nor will, but merely judgment.[9]

An awareness of the creative function of judicial law still leaves undisclosed the material sources from which courts make new law. Although reliance upon "the principles of natural justice, practical expediency, and common sense" is descriptive of the declaratory theory, the source of doctrinal

---

6. Bentham, *A Comment on the Commentaries* 190 (Everett ed. 1928); Gray, *op. cit.* note 9, at 94.

7. Gray, *op. cit.* note 9, at 100.

8. Holmes, "The Path of the Law," 10 *Harv. L. Rev.* 457, 458 (1897); Collected Legal Papers 167, 169 (1920).

9. Hamilton, in *The Federalist*, No. LXXVIII, 484 (Lodge ed. 1888).

novelties is generally found in originative precedents.[10] The originative process is a projection beyond standard precedents, utilizing persuasive authorities and analogous argument from pre-existing legal sources.[11] In their inception, the new policies are usually tentative and "Advance in firmness as they advance in acceptance. They do not, at a particular moment of time, spring full perfect in extent or means" from the judicial brain. "Time may be necessary to fashion them to precedent . . . and as they justify themselves . . . they pass from militancy to triumph." [12]

UNDERSTANDING JUDICIAL DECISIONS

In order to determine the rule of a case, it is necessary to find the *ratio decidendi* or the point on which the judgment balances. This is done primarily by carefully analyzing the facts of the case which are treated by the judge as being material. Judges will usually specify what are material and what are immaterial facts. Only the material facts are relevant to the identification of the *ratio decidendi* of a case. Conclusions of a judge based on hypothetical situations are *dicta* and are not binding as precedent.

Karl N. Llewellyn, late Professor of Law, University of Chicago, in his work *The Bramble Bush* (Oceana Publications, New York, 1960, pp. 41-43) probably offers the best and most concise explanation of what to look for when reading case law.

> * * * The first thing to do with an opinion, then, is read it. The next thing is to get clear the actual decision, the judgment rendered. Who won, the plaintiff or defendant? And watch your step here. You are after in first instance the plaintiff and defendant below, in the trial court. In order to follow through what happened you must therefore first know the outcome below; else you do not see what was appealed from, nor by whom. You now follow through in order to see exactly what further judgment has been rendered on appeal. The stage is then cleared of form—although of course you do not yet know all that these forms mean, that they imply. You can turn now to what you peculiarly do know. Given the actual judgments below and above as your indispensable frame-

10. Salmond recognized this problem by distinguishing between declarative and originative precedents, each of which is descriptive of a source of the law. Salmond, *Jurisprudence* § 61, p. 202 (7th ed. 1924).
11. *Id.* at § 61, p. 203.
12. Von Ihering, as quoted by Hutchinson, "The Principle and Price of Living Law," 10 *Wash. & Lee L. Rev.* 147, 158 (1953).

work—what has the case decided, and what can you derive from it as to what will be decided later?

You will be looking, in the opinion, or in the preliminary matter plus the opinion, for the following: A statement of the facts the court assumes; a statement of the precise way the question has come before the court—which includes what the plaintiff wanted below, and what the defendant did about it, the judgment below, and what the trial court did that is complained of; then the outcome on appeal, the judgment; and finally the reasons this court gives for doing what it did. This does not look so bad. But it is much worse than it looks. For all our cases are decided, all our opinions are written, all our predictions, all our arguments are made, on certain four assumptions. * * * (1) *The court must decide the dispute that is before it.* It cannot refuse because the job is hard, or dubious, or dangerous. (2) *The court can decide only the particular dispute which is before it.* When it speaks to that question it speaks *ex cathedra*, with authority, with finality, with an almost magic power. When it speaks to the question before it, it announces law, and if what it announces is new, it legislates, it makes the law. But when it speaks to any other question at all, it says mere words, which no man needs to follow. Are such words worthless? They are not. We know them as judicial *dicta*; when they are wholly off the point at issue we call them *obiter dicta*—words dropped along the road, wayside remarks. Yet even wayside remarks shed light on the remarker. They may be very useful in the future to him, or to us. But he will not feel bound to them, as to his *ex cathedra* utterance. They came not hallowed by a Delphic frenzy. He may be slow to change them; but not so slow as in the other case. (3) *The court can decide the particular dispute only according to a general rule which covers a whole class of like disputes.* Our legal theory does not admit of single decisions standing on their own. If judges are free, are indeed forced, to decide new cases for which there is no rule, they must at least make a new rule as they decide. So far, good. But how wide or how narrow, is the general rule in this particular case? That is a troublesome matter. The practice of our case-law, however, is I think, fairly stated thus: It pays to be suspicious of general rules which look too wide; it pays to go slow in feeling certain that a wide rule has been laid down at all, or that, if seemingly laid down, it will be followed. For there is a fourth accepted canon: (4) *Everything, everything, everything, big or small, a judge may say in an opinion, is to be read with primary reference to the particular dispute, the particular question before him.* You are not to think that the words mean what they might if they stood alone. You are to have your eye on the case in hand, and to learn how to interpret all that has been said merely as a reason for deciding that case that way. * * *

FUNCTION OF THE COURTS [13]

The courts in the United States, in dealing with problems involving colleges and universities, perform three essential functions. These are to:

(a) Settle controversies by applying appropriate laws or principles of law to a specific set of facts.

(b) Construe or interpret enactments of the legislature.

(c) Determine the constitutionality of enactments of the legislature.

APPLICATION OF APPROPRIATE LAWS

In applying appropriate laws or principles of law to a specific legal question, the court must first attempt to apply statutory or constitutional provisions and in the absence of such provisions rely on case law precedent for direction.

There is merely a very technical difference between functions (a) and (b) above when the court is dealing only with statutes. In the application of appropriate statutes, the court not only interprets the statutes in question but also relates the factual situation to the appropriate statute in handing down a decision.

Concerning the application of statutes, a New Jersey court has stated the principle as follows:

> Where the application of a statute is involved it is the duty of the court to determine the legislative intention from the plain meaning of the statute and to apply it to the facts * * *. Ordinarily, such intention is to be gleaned from the words used, and they are to be given their ordinary and well understood meaning in the absence of an explicit indication to the contrary * * *. Only if an ambiguity exists is it necessary to go beyond the words to the statute itself. * * * It is assumed that each word therein was incorporated by design of the Legislature * * *. [14]

In determining the rule of law by applying the appropriate statute, the court must exercise interpretative techniques. However, in the absence of statutory or constitutional law, the role of the judiciary becomes much more legislative in nature and thereby probably more significant. Cardozo related the situation in this manner:

> Where does the judge find the law he embodies in his

---

13. Alexander, *supra*, pp. 6-9.

14. Ruehl Co. v. Board of Trustees, 85 N.J. Super. 4, 203 A.2d 410 (1964).

judgment? There are times when the source is obvious. The rule that fits the case may be supplied by the constitution or by statute. If that is so, the judge looks no further. The correspondence ascertained, his duty is to obey. The constitution overrides a statute, but a statute, if consistent with the constitution, overrides the law of judges. In this sense, judge-made law is secondary and subordinate to the law that is made by legislators * * *. We reach the land of mystery when constitution and statute are silent, and the judge must look to the common law for the rule that fits the case. He is the "living oracle of the law" in Blackstone's vivid phrase.[15]

INTERPRETATION OF LEGISLATIVE ENACTMENTS

The second function of the courts, the task of construing and interpreting statutes, is probably the most common type of case involving colleges and universities. Of course, statutes are merely words to which many definitions may be applied, thus leaving to the courts the task of deciding the intent of the legislature. Pound conceives of four ways with which legislative enactments may be dealt by the courts once litigation arises.[16]

(1) They might receive it fully into the body of the law as affording not only a rule to be applied but a principle from which to reason, and hold it, as a later and more direct expression of the general will, of superior authority to judge-made rules on the same general subject; and so reason from it by analogy in preference to them.

(2) They might receive it fully into the body of the law to be reasoned from by analogy the same as any other rule of law, regarding it, however, as of equal or coordinate authority in this respect with judge-made rules upon the same general subject.

(3) They might refuse to receive it fully into the body of the law and give effect to it directly only; refusing to reason from it by analogy but giving it, nevertheless, a liberal interpretation to cover the whole field it was intended to cover.

(4) They might not only refuse to reason from it by analogy and apply it directly only, but also give to it a strict and narrow interpretation, holding it down rigidly to those cases which it covers expressly.

The fourth position is probably the orthodox, traditional common law approach; however, the courts today, in inter-

---

15. Benjamin N. Cardozo, *The Nature of the Judicial Process*, Yale University Press, New Haven and London, 1962, pp. 18-19.

16. Roscoe Pound, "Common Law and Legislation," 21 *Harvard Law Review*, pp. 383, 385 (1908).

preting statutes, are tending to adhere more and more to the second and third theses.

The philosophy of the courts toward statutory interpretation varies not only among judges and courts but also in the content of the legislation being interpreted. Courts are generally more willing to grant implied authority to educational functions where large sums of public monies are not involved. In cases where taxing authority is in question or where large capital outlay programs are at stake, the courts tend to require very specific and express statutory authority.[17]

CONSTITUTIONALITY OF LEGISLATION

The functions and responsibility of the judiciary were described as early as 1803 in *Marbury v. Madison*,[18] as it applied to the United States Supreme Court, but this general statement by Chief Justice Marshall may be applied to state courts as well. He explained:

> It is emphatically, the province and duty of the judicial department, to say what the law is. Those who apply the rule to particular cases, must of necessity expound and interpret that rule. If two laws conflict with each other, the courts must decide on the operation of each. So, if a law be in opposition to the constitution; if both the law and the constitution apply to a particular case, so that the court must either decide that case, conformable to the law, disregarding the constitution; or conformable to the constitution, disregarding the law; the court must determine which of these conflicting rules governs the case; this is of the very essence of judicial duty. If then, the courts are to regard the constitution, and the constitution is superior to any ordinary act of the legislature, the constitution, and not such ordinary act, must govern the case to which they both apply.

In determining the constitutionality of statutes the courts first presume the act to be constitutional and anyone maintaining the contrary must bear the burden of proof. The Florida Supreme Court has stated the principle in this manner: "* * * We have held that acts of the legislature carry such a strong presumption of validity that they should be held constitutional if there is any reasonable theory to that end * * *. Moreover, unconstitutionality must appear beyond all reasonable doubt before an Act is condemned * * *."[19] If a

---

17. Marion & M. Ry. Co. v. Alexander, 63 Kan. 72, 64 P. 978 (1901).
18. Marbury v. Madison, 5 U.S. (1 Cranch) 137 (1803).
19. Bonvento v. Board of Public Instruction of Palm Beach County, Fla., 194 So. 2d 605 (Fla. 1967).

statute can be interpreted in two different ways, one by which it will be constitutional, the courts will adopt the constitutional interpretation.[20]

STRUCTURE OF THE COURTS [21]

The court system in the United States, as one of the three branches of government, is provided for in the constitutions of both state and federal governments.

STATE COURTS

State constitutions provide for the separation of powers within the state and lay the framework for the court system of the state. State constitutions will generally prescribe the powers and the jurisdiction of the primary or main state courts. The legislature, through power granted in the same constitution, provides for the specific operation of the constitutional courts, and it may create new and additional courts if so authorized in the constitution.

The types of state courts may be classified into four categories: [22]

(1) Courts of general jurisdiction
(2) Courts of special jurisdiction
(3) Small claims courts
(4) Appellate courts

Courts of General Jurisdiction are usually called district or circuit courts. The jurisdiction of these courts cover all cases except those reserved for special courts. The subject matter of cases of general jurisdiction sometimes overlap with courts of special jurisdiction.

Courts of Special Jurisdiction are set up to handle cases involving litigation in special subject matter areas which generally involve large numbers of cases. Probate courts, domestic relations courts and juvenile courts are common types of courts of special jurisdiction.

Small Claims Courts are established to handle lawsuits involving small amounts of money. Justice of the peace courts are usually classified as small claims courts. However, some states may classify small claims courts and justice of the peace

---

20. Hobbs v. County of Moore, 267 N.C. 665, 149 S.E.2d 1 (1966).
21. Alexander, *supra*, pp. 9-11.
22. Auerbach, Carl A., Garrison, Lloyd K., Hurst, Willard, Mermin, Samuel, *The Legal Process*, Chandler Publishing Company, San Francisco, 1961, pp. 3-4.

courts as having separate jurisdictions; for example, in Florida small claims courts have civil jurisdiction in cases at law in which the demand or value of the property does not exceed two hundred and fifty dollars [23] while the justice of the peace courts have jurisdiction over disputes involving actions for not more than one hundred dollars.[24]

Appellate Courts are found in all states and in most are the only courts to which appeals may be made involving decisions of trial courts of general jurisdiction. These courts are usually called Supreme Courts or Courts of Appeals. Some states, because of the sheer volume of cases, have established intermediate appellate courts. New York and California have intermediate appellate courts, and Indiana has both a Court of Appeals and a Supreme Court. In states with intermediate courts of appeals, certain cases on appeal may terminate at the intermediate appellate court while other cases can be appealed to the state's highest court.

FEDERAL COURTS

Article III of the Constitution of the United States provides in part: "The judicial power of the United States, shall be vested in one Supreme Court, and in such inferior courts as the Congress may from time to time ordain and establish." [25] Pursuant to this provision Congress has established a network of "inferior" courts.

Today the federal court system in the United States includes District Courts, Courts of Appeals, Special Federal Courts and the Supreme Court.

There is at least one District Court in each state and usually more than two. Cases litigated before federal district courts may largely be classified into two types: (1) cases between citizens of different states and (2) cases involving litigation of federal statutes or the federal Constitution. Cases before district courts are usually presided over by one judge; however, in cases of injunction against the enforcement of a state or federal statute a three-judge court is required. A three-judge court is made up of the district judge, to whom the injunction is presented, and two other federal judges, one of which must be a circuit judge. Decisions of district courts may be appealed to the federal Courts of Appeals, and in some instances directly to the Supreme Court of the United States.

---

23. F.S.A. (Fla.) § 42.03.
24. F.S.A. (Fla.) § 37.01 (1).
25. U.S.C.A. Const. Art. III, § 1.

There are eleven Courts of Appeals in the eleven federal judicial circuits. (See map on page 14 *infra.*)

In addition, federal courts have been established by the Congress to handle special problems or to cover special jurisdiction. These courts are the courts of the District of Columbia, the Court of Claims, the Tax Court, the Customs Court, the Courts of Customs and Patent Appeals, the Emergency Court of Appeals, and the territorial courts.

The Supreme Court of the United States is the highest court in the land beyond which there is no redress. Cases may be brought before the Supreme Court by appeal, *writ of certiorari* or through the original jurisdiction of the Court.

Most education cases which go to the Supreme Court are taken on *writs of certiorari*, which certiorari is an original action whereby a case is removed from an inferior to a superior court for trial. A case may be taken to the Supreme Court from a state court by *writ of certiorari* where a state statute or federal statute is questioned as to its validity under the federal Constitution or where any title, right, privilege or immunity is claimed under the Constitution.

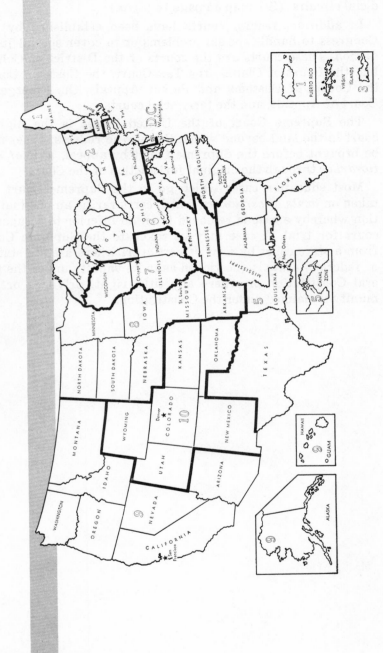

The Eleven Federal Judicial Circuits

PROCEDURE OF THE COURTS [26]

(Reprinted with permission, Carl A. Auerbach, Willard Hurst, Lloyd K. Garrison, Samuel Mermin, *The Legal Process*, Chandler Publishing Company, 1961, pp. 5-9.)

THE PARTIES TO A LAWSUIT

The party who starts the lawsuit is known as the plaintiff, the person who complains; the party against whom the action is brought is known as the defendant. The party appealing is known as the appellant; the other party as the respondent or appellee (in some cases, "petitioner" and "respondent" respectively). Generally, in the published report of a case decided by an appellate court, the name of the plaintiff appears first and the name of the defendant next, regardless of which party becomes the appellant and which the respondent. Thus "Smith v. Brown, 60 Mo. 126" means that in volume 60 of the Reports of the Missouri Supreme Court, at page 126, appears the report of a case decided by that court on appeal, which was started in the trial court by one Smith as plaintiff against one Brown as defendant. But whether it was Smith who appealed, or Brown, you couldn't tell from the title; you would have to get out the volume and look at the case.

THE COMMENCEMENT OF AN ACTION

The job of courts is to settle the controversies which persons bring to them. Courts do not start lawsuits. They have no investigating staff and do not conduct investigations. They do not arrest criminals nor prosecute them. Their sole job is to decide the cases that are brought before them. To get the proceedings going, the plaintiff will have to do three things: he will have to pick the proper court, he will have to see that the defendant or his property is brought before it, and he will have to state his complaint and what he wants the court to do about it.

Picking the Court. This is a technical matter. The point is, as we have seen, that there are various courts with different powers and it is essential to get started in the one whose jurisdiction fits the case.

Catching the Defendant. Courts do not hear lawsuits for the fun of it. It must be clear before they start that if they finally do render a decision it can be enforced. And since the

---

26. Reference here is generally to civil cases as opposed to cases involving criminal prosecutions.

power of every court has territorial limits prescribed by the
constitution or the legislature (such as the boundaries of a
municipality, a county, a state, or a federal district), it is
necessary to demonstrate at the outset that either the defendant or the property involved can be found within those limits, so that the judgment (that is, the court's ultimate decision) can be carried out. In criminal cases, if the defendant
is an individual, he is caught quite literally, by being arrested
within the territorial jurisdiction of the court, or by being
extradited from some other territory. In civil cases the catching is normally symbolic. A *summons* is served on the defendant within the jurisdiction. This demonstrates that he could
be arrested if necessary, and also gives him notice that a
lawsuit has been started against him, and in what court and
by whom. The summons does not, however, compel him to
attend court. If it were a *subpoena,* he would have to obey
it or be arrested. But the only result of disregarding a summons is that judgment is likely to be entered against him
by default. If the summons cannot be served personally, because the defendant is not there, it may commonly be served
by leaving it at his house, if he has one, in the jurisdiction.
If he is a non-resident, and does not come into the state, the
suit may be started if some property of the defendant can be
found and seized, by a proceeding usually called attachment.
* * *

Stating the Claim. The plaintiff must also tell the court and
the defendant what it is that he complains of and what he
wants the court to do about it. Conceivably this could be done
by having the judge orally question the plaintiff in the presence of the defendant. But we have deemed it more expeditious
to have the parties, in advance of the trial, attempt to narrow
down the issues of fact and law on which they differ by ex-
changing written statements of their respective claims. * * *
The written statements that are exchanged by the parties are
called pleadings. Thus the plaintiff is the first to state his
claim and request for relief, in a written document now commonly called the *complaint* (formerly sometimes called declaration, bill, or petition).

PLEADINGS AND OTHER PROCEDURES PRIOR TO TRIAL

Once the plaintiff has picked his court, caught the defendant or his property, and filed his complaint, the lawsuit is
on its way and the next move is up to the defendant. The defendant will no doubt see his lawyer, who will find out from
him what the row is all about. The claim may be admitted and

paid up, or compromised. If so, the suit will be dismissed by the lawyers, and the court will hear no more about it. Or the claim may be allowed to go by default, in which case, after a certain time lapse, the court will enter judgment for the plaintiff. But if the claim is really in dispute, and is not compromised, the defendant's lawyer will have to file an "Answer."

The answer, too, is a formal document. It states the defendant's position in the controversy, and its first job is to state his position on the things which the plaintiff says in his complaint. * * * Whatever the answer says about the plaintiff's claim, it may assert some counterclaim which the defendant has against the plaintiff. Formerly, such additional pleadings could be filed by plaintiff and defendant as were necessary to raise at least one disputed issue of fact or law determinative of the result in the case. But in most states today the pleadings terminate with the answer or with the plaintiff's reply to the defendant's answer.

If the defendant thinks that the complaint fails to state a claim for relief, even though all the statements therein may be true, he may file *a motion to dismiss* the complaint. In many states today, the same objective is achieved by filing a *demurrer*. The demurrer or motion to dismiss may, if appropriate, be used by a plaintiff to attack the answer. This procedural device challenges the *legal* sufficiency of a pleading (*i.e.*, on the temporary assumption that the *facts* alleged in the pleading are true) and the issues it raises will be decided by the judge, not the jury. The defendant need not necessarily choose between the two kinds of responses we have mentioned; he may combine them in one pleading, making his claims in the alternative. He could say: such and such facts alleged in the complaint are not true, but even if they are, the plaintiff's claim for relief is not legally valid.

In addition to the pleadings, other proceedings prior to trial are worth noting. To shorten the trial and reduce the element of surprise, various "discovery" devices are available, including the taking of "depositions" from expected opposing witnesses and asking the court to order production of certain documents by the opposing party. "Pre-trial conferences" of the judge with the opposing attorneys often narrow the issues of fact and law in real dispute, or lead to settlement of the case without trial.

THE TRIAL

If the only issue on which the parties are in dispute is one of law, the dispute is submitted to the court by the process known as argument. The lawyers appear before the judge, argue the disputed point or points, and perhaps also submit written arguments called briefs. Witnesses and jury are not necessary because there are no disputed facts to pass on. The judge decides the matter himself, on the basis of the arguments and of his own knowledge and study. In most lawsuits, the main dispute disclosed by the proceedings before trial is on the facts. To resolve such a dispute there has to be a trial. This is the familiar courtroom process and consists chiefly of the presentation by the two competing sides of their views of the facts, through documents, physical exhibits, and the oral testimony of witnesses. The decision is based on what is thus offered. Neither the judge nor the jury is supposed to make any independent investigations. * * *

THE JUDGMENT

If the case is tried by a jury, the issues of fact are settled, within limits determined by the judge, by the jury's *verdict*. If it is tried without a jury, they are settled by the judge's findings. The verdict or findings will be followed by a judgment or order of the court. If the defendant has won, the judgment will read substantially as follows: "Adjudged: that the plaintiff recover nothing by this action." If the plaintiff has won, let us say, a judgment for money, it might read: "Adjudged: that the plaintiff recover from the defendant one thousand dollars ($1000.00) with interest thereon at 6% per annum from this date until paid."

APPELLATE REVIEW

The judgment or order of the court is subject to appeal, or to be set aside or corrected by the court that entered it. The time within which either of these steps may be taken is strictly limited. When that time has passed and neither of these steps has been taken or the appellate court of last resort has upheld the judgment or order, it becomes final. The court will generally not hear applications to correct it. Even if the court became convinced, as a result of subsequent disclosures, that the case was wrongly decided, either in fact or law, while that might affect later similar cases between other people, it would not affect the judgment or order previously entered. For that controversy has been settled. "Nothing is settled until it is settled right" is not a maxim of judicial conduct, and for obvious, practical reasons.

When appeal is taken from the judgment or order of the trial court, the appellate court is given a condensed record of the proceedings in the trial court. It will usually contain the pleadings, verdict and judgment and so much of the proceedings at the trial as the attorneys for the parties regard as important. No testimony is heard by the appellate court; just argument by the lawyers as to the pros and cons of what the trial court decided. In addition, the lawyers are permitted to file *briefs* for the parties—printed documents containing legal arguments in much more detailed form than can be presented orally.

ENFORCEMENT OF THE JUDGMENT OR ORDER * * *

The simplest judgment to enforce is one for the defendant. No private or public person need do anything to enforce it, unless the plaintiff continues to assert the same claim or brings another lawsuit on it. If he does that, the defendant will simply plead the prior judgment in defense, and if it is really the same claim and between the same parties he will automatically prevail again. A judgment for the plaintiff for money is more difficult to enforce. You should notice that the court's judgment that the plaintiff recover money is not an order or command by the court to the defendant to pay the money; it is simply a declaration by the court that the law applicable to the facts obligates the defendant to pay the plaintiff a certain sum. The judge does not concern himself personally with seeing to it that the defendant satisfies his legal obligation to the plaintiff; he merely states what the obligation is.

How, then, does the plaintiff collect from the defendant if the defendant refuses to honor the judgment by paying up? He will get from the clerk of the court a writ (order) of "execution" which is a document directing the sheriff to satisfy the judgment out of the defendant's property. (Note: The *sheriff* is a county official, generally elected; he is an officer of the court, that is to say, he is subject to judicial supervision in the performance of his duties, which also include various police functions.) When the sheriff (or the United States Marshal in the federal system) receives the "execution" from the plaintiff he will proceed to take into his custody the property of the defendant which has not been exempted by statute from execution; to sell it at public auction; to pay the plaintiff's judgment out of the proceeds; and to remit the balance, if any, to the defendant. All the details of this process are regulated by statute. Judgments for the possession of specific property are enforced in much the same way. The sheriff takes away from the defendant the cow or the car which the defendant has improperly appropriated, and turns it over to the plaintiff. If the defendant has no property out of which the judgment can be satisfied, the plaintiff can do nothing unless and until the defendant acquires property; imprisonment for debt, which used to exist in England and to some extent in this country, has long since been abolished.

CHAPTER 2
LEGAL STRUCTURE OF HIGHER EDUCATION

Colleges and universities in the United States perform many and varied functions, coming in an array of shapes and sizes, and founded on a variety of legal structures. To define the role and functions the modern college or university is consonant with grasping the wind with perceived functions varying from the microcosm of teaching one freshman student to the macrocosm of tending to and changing society as a whole. Similarly, the legal structures under which higher education in the United States operates is quite complex, ranging from private to public with varying hues and shades in between. Contributing to this diversity is the intricate constitutional, statutory, and common law system of law which is the method of governance in this country.

STATE AND FEDERAL CONSTITUTIONS

Laws establishing and controlling higher education emanate fundamentally from two sources—constitutional or legislative law; however, common law exerts a profound influence in its interpretative capacity. Constitutions form the basic law under which the governments of all states and the federal government operate. These constitutions provide the framework for orderly governmental process. The Constitution of the United States delegates certain powers to the federal government and reserves other powers to the states or to the people.[1] It is through this residual power that most of higher education now operates, the public institutions under state control and the private institutions under the people as individuals or as corporations. Although the Constitution does not expressly delegate education as a function to the federal government, the legal presumption is that the general welfare clause [2] gives the federal government the power to expend public tax funds for the support of education.[3] The Su-

---

1. The Tenth Amendment of the Constitution provides: "The powers not delegated to the United States by the Constitution, nor prohibited by it to the States, are reserved to the States respectively or to the people."

2. Article I, § cl. 1. ". . . to lay and collect Taxes, Duties, Imports and Excises, to pay the Debts and provide for the common Defense and general welfare of the United States."

3. United States v. Butler, 297 U.S. 1 (1936).

preme Court of the United States has assigned a flexible meaning to the general welfare clause saying that the needs that were "narrow and parochial" a century ago may be interwoven in our day with the well-being of the nation.[4] Using these interpretations, there is little question that the Constitution gives the central government a vital role in the financing of education in the United States. The states, however, have assumed the primary responsibility for education, and it is generally within this context that we find the greatest amount of legal precedent regarding colleges and universities.

COLLEGE AND UNIVERSITY CORPORATIONS

Although this book is mainly concerned with public colleges and universities, it is necessary to discuss the *corporate* structure under which not only public but private institutions of higher education are established and operate.

CORPORATION

A "corporation" is a creature of law, an artificial person without natural rights, with powers defined by its certificate of incorporation. Chief Justice Marshall, in the famous *Dartmouth College* case,[5] provided a lasting definition of a corporation:

> A corporation is an artificial being, invisible, intangible, and existing only in contemplation of law. Being a mere creature of law, it possesses only those properties which the charter of its creation confers upon it, either expressly or as incidental to its very existence. These are such as are supposed best calculated to effect the object for which it was created. Among the most important are immortality, and, if that expression may be allowed, individuality; properties, by which a perpetual succession of many persons are considered as the same, and may act as a single individual. * * * By these means a perpetual succession of individuals are capable of acting for the promotion of a particular object like one mortal being.

Incorporated institutions of higher education are divided into two classes—private and public corporations.[6] Educational institutions which are unincorporated are usually es-

---

4. Helvering v. Davis, 301 U.S. 619 (1937).
5. Trustees of Dartmouth College v. Woodward, 4 Wheat. (U.S.) 518 (Marshall's Opinion) (1819).
6. 65 A.L.R. 1394.

tablished by the state and are considered public institutions serving merely as agents or an arm of the state.[7]

Distinguishing features between public and private corporations are not always readily apparent. The chief factor legally separating public corporations from private ones seems to depend on how the institution was founded. If its origins indicate it was founded by private individuals, then it is a private corporation, while if it were founded by the state through constitution or legislative act, it is a public corporation.

A corporation founded by private individuals or supported by private funds or endowment is considered to be a private corporation.[8] The fact that a private institution of higher education receives funds from the state or federal government does not in and of itself make the institution a public corporation.[9] The Supreme Court of the United States held in 1852 that Vincennes University, established by the territorial legislature of Indiana in 1806 and endowed by it with a grant of public lands received from the federal government, was not a public corporation, but was private in character.[10]

Also, the fact that a public educational corporation, founded by the state, is given or accepts gifts from private persons, does not alter the nature of its foundation or corporate character.[11] Thus, Blackwell has said that: "The corporate status of an institution of higher education in this country can only be determined by an analysis of its character and the method of its establishment, support, and control, as interpreted by the courts." [12]

The benefits, incidents, and results of incorporation of an educational institution are too numerous to list; however, some of the more notable should be pointed out. The *Dartmouth College* [13] case established that the charter of a private

7. Henn v. State University of Iowa, 22 Iowa 185 (1867); Weary v. State University, 42 Iowa 335 (1876); Neil v. Ohio A & M College, 31 Ohio St. 15 (1876).

8. Boehm v. Hertz, 182 Ill. 154, 54 N.E. 973 (1899).

9. Cleaveland v. Stewart, 3 Ga. 283 (1847); Board of Education v. Greenebaum, 39 Ill. 610 (1864).

10. Trustees of Vincennes University v. State of Indiana, 55 U.S. 269 (1852).

11. Head v. University of Missouri, 47 Mo. 220 (1871), *aff'd*, 19 Wall (U.S.) 526, 22 L. Ed. 160 (1874); University of North Carolina v. Maultsby, 43 N.C. (8 Ired. Eq.) 257 (1852).

12. Thomas E. Blackwell, *College Law*, American Council on Education, p. 24, 1961.

13. 4 Wheat (U.S.) 518 (1819).

corporation is a contract and any attempt by the state to unilaterally alter or rescind the contract violates the obligation of contract provision (Art. I, § 10) of the Constitution of the United States. On the other hand, the courts have held that the state can alter the charter of a public corporation without offending the same constitutional provision.[14] Another result which has different bearing on public and private corporations is that a public corporation is not subject to taxation,[15] while a private corporation, unless specifically exempted, is subject to taxation. One quite important difference between the two types of corporations is that a public corporation can exercise the power of eminent domain while a private corporation cannot.[16]

INTERPRETING CORPORATE CHARTERS

Corporate charters may be regarded in three different ways. First, a charter may be thought of as simply a license terminable at will by the state, but affording the incorporators, so long as it remains in force, the privileges and advantages of doing business in the form of a corporation. Second, a corporate charter may be looked upon as a franchise constituting a vested or property interest in the hands of the holders and, therefore, not forfeitable except for abuse or in accordance with its own decision. The third view was formulated by Chief Justice Marshall in the *Dartmouth College* case. The charter here was between the donors of a purely private institution and the British Crown, the outcome of which was a contract continuing in force between the State of New Hampshire, as the successor to the Crown, and the trustees, as successors to the donors. In other words, the Dartmouth charter was not simply a grant, but was the documentary record of a still existent agreement between existing parties.[17]

In the years following the *Dartmouth College* case, however, the Supreme Court set about lessening the impact of the case in favor of greater state legislative power. By virtue of the logic of the Dartmouth decision, the state could already reserve in a corporate charter the right to "amend, alter, and

---

14. State *ex rel.* Attorney General v. Knowles, 16 Fla. 577 (1878).

15. Academy of Richmond County v. Augusta, 90 Ga. 634, 17 S.E. 61 (1892).

16. Connecticut College v. Calvert, 87 Conn. 421, 88 A. 633 (1913).

17. *The Constitution of the United States of America*, U.S. Government Printing Office, Washington 1964, Document No. 39, 88th Congress, 1st Session, p. 390.

repeal" the same, with such reservation, thus becoming a part of the contract. The state could exercise its rights under this reservation at any time without impairment of the obligation of the contract.[18] Later cases carried the concept one step further by acknowledging that a state legislature could pass a general statute which incorporates the "amend, alter and repeal" provisions in all charters of subsequent date.[19] When the "amend" or "alter" provisions are included in a charter, the state is still bound to act reasonably and in good faith and any alteration must be made consistent with the scope and intent of the grant.[20] The general rule, with some limited exceptions,[21] is that all charter privileges and immunities are to be strictly construed as against changes by the state. As has been frequently said, "nothing passes by implication in a public grant." [22] This strict construction policy by the courts has served to protect the powers of the state as well as the privileges of corporations.[23] The power of the state cannot be pared away by implying conditions of a charter which do not expressly exist. A good explanation of the Supreme Court's position with regard to interpretation of charters is given in *Blair v. Chicago*: [24]

> Legislative grants of this character should be in such unequivocal form of expression that the legislative mind may be distinctly impressed with their character and import, in order that the privileges may be intelligently granted or purposely withheld. It is a matter of common knowledge that grants of this character are usually prepared by those interested in them, and submitted to the legislature with a view to obtain from such bodies the most liberal grant of privileges which they are willing to give. This is one among many reasons why they are to be strictly construed. * * * "The principle is this, that all rights which are asserted against the State must be clearly defined, and not raised by inference or presumption; and if the charter is silent about a power, it does

---

18. Dartmouth College v. Woodward, 4 Wheat (U.S.) 518 (Story's opinion) (1819).

19. Home of the Friendless v. Rouse, 8 Wall. (U.S.) 430 (1869); Pennsylvania College Cases, 13 Wall. (U.S.) 190 (1872); Miller v. New York, 15 Wall. (U.S.) 478 (1873).

20. Holyoke Company v. Lyman, 15 Wall. (U.S.) 500 (1873); Berea College v. Kentucky, 211 U.S. 45 (1908).

21. Thorpe v. R. & B.R. Company, 27 Vt. 140 (1854); Beer Co. v. Massachusetts, 97 U.S. 25 (1878).

22. *The Constitution of the United States of America, op. cit.*, p. 394.

23. Charles River Bridge v. Warren Bridge, 11 Pet. (U.S.) 420 (1837).

24. 201 U.S. 400 (1906).

not exist. If, on a fair reading of the instrument, reasonable doubts arise as to the proper interpretation to be given to it, those doubts are to be solved in favor of the State; and where it is susceptible of two meanings, the one restricting and the other extending the powers of the corporation, that construction is to be adopted which works the least harm to the State." [25]

THE CONSTITUTIONALLY AUTONOMOUS STATE UNIVERSITY

The several states have all exercised their residual powers to establish public institutions of higher education. Twenty-seven of the states make explicit reference to higher education in their constitutions.[26] The remainder of the states, through exercise of police powers, have legislatively provided for higher education.

Of the states with constitutional provisions for higher education, at least nine guarantee constitutional autonomy for universities.[27] In these states the constitution elevates the university above the condition of a mere agency of the legislature and places it in a position of pre-eminence in the state's legal structure. These autonomous constitutional university corporations are insulated to a large degree from the political entanglements of both the legislative and executive branches of state government. The most notable and pervasive of the constitutional provisions establishing autonomous universities are found in Michigan, Minnesota and California. The legal development of this constitutional university "triad" is important to student's understanding of the legal structure within which universities function.

Michigan. Michigan was the first state to place the state university in a constitutionally autonomous position. This special status which, at least theoretically, placed the University of Michigan, like Caesar's wife, above reproach, grew out of a popular dissatisfaction with the functioning of the university. The legislature of Michigan had made a habit of intervening in the internal affairs of the university by exercising its law-making powers rather capriciously and through manipulation of the university's board of trustees.[28] In 1840

---

25. *Ibid.*

26. Malcolm Moss and Francis E. Rourke, *The Campus and The State*, Johns Hopkins Press, 1959, p. 22.

27. Michigan, Minnesota, California, Colorado, Georgia, Idaho, Oklahoma, Nevada and Arizona.

28. Moss and Rourke, *op. cit.*, p. 24.

a study committee inquiring into the conditions at the University of Michigan observed:

> When legislatures have legislated directly for colleges, their measures have been fluctuating as the changing material of which the legislatures are composed. . . .
> [Legislatures] . . . have not been willing to appoint trustees . . . for a length of time sufficient for them to become acquainted with their duties . . . . A new board of trustees, like a legislature of new members not knowing well what to do, generally begins by undoing and disorganizing all that has been done before. At first they dig up the seed a few times to see what is going to come up and after it appears above the surface they must pull it up again to see if there is sufficient root to support so vigorous branches; then pull it up again to see why it is so sickly and puny and finally to see if they can discover what made it die. And, as these several operations are performed by successive hands, no one can be charged with the guilt of destroying the valuable tree.[29]

Such reactions to legislative control led to the adoption of provisions in the 1850 Michigan constitution which established the university in a position of inviolate constitutional independence. The key provision in the constitution provided that: "The board of regents shall have the general supervision of the university, and the direction and control of all expenditures from the university interest fund."[30] Later in 1909, the constitution was amended to remove the word "interest," and the word "fund" was replaced by the word "funds" in order to give the board of regents complete control of all university income regardless of source.[31]

Throughout the years the Michigan courts have rendered several decisions interpreting the constitutional status of the University of Michigan. Most of these cases involved controversies created by the legislature in attempting to establish a chair of homeopathy at the university. In the first of these cases in 1856,[32] a private citizen brought action in mandamus to compel the board of regents to appoint a homeopathic professor in the medical department of the university as re-

---

29. Michigan, House of Representatives, Report of the Select Committee to Inquire into the Conditions of the University, *House of Representatives Documents*, 1840, p. 470.

30. Michigan, Constitution (1850), Art. 13, § 8; other provisions appear in §§ 6 and 7.

31. Michigan, Constitution (1850), as amended (1909); Art. 11, § 5.

32. People *ex rel.* Drake v. The Regents of the University of Michigan, 4 Mich. 98 (1856).

quired by law.[33] Even though the regents believed the law to be unconstitutional as violating Article 13, Section 8 of the state constitution, they employed the quite common stalling tactic of appointing a committee to study the matter. Rather than attack the constitutional question head-on, the court denied the mandamus on the ground that the board of regents had not, in fact, violated the law but had only "acted tardily" in establishing the professorship. The court, however, did not say that the board of regents had the prerogative of disobeying the law; on the contrary, it said "The board of regents have a sound discretion to exercise, and until it is made apparent that they seek to evade the law, by unnecessary and willful delays, the exercise of our [the court's] discretionary power cannot be called into action." The implication was that if the board of regents did finally fail to act under the law that the court could compel such board action. As to the constitutional confrontation, the case was indecisive.

Later, in 1868, the board of regents sought to compel the auditor-general to pay the university a sum of $3,000 which had been appropriated by the legislature to establish a "school of homeopathy." [34] The board of regents had appointed a professor of homeopathic medicine, in the "Michigan school of homeopathy." The site of the school had not been selected but the board made it very clear that the location would not be Ann Arbor. Because the school was not located at Ann Arbor, or anywhere else for that matter, the auditor-general claimed the intent of the legislature had not been fulfilled and would not release the appropriated $3,000 to the regents. The court agreed with the auditor-general and denied the *writ of mandamus*, saying that the board of regents was premature in its application for the funds and should have waited until the professorship was "established as a practical entity, capable of vital action." On the question of the board's constitutional powers, the court commented:

> The mere power of "supervision" given by the constitution, whether subject to, or independent of, legislative

33. Sess. L. 1856, p. 234. The law provided: "that the regents shall have power to enact ordinances, by-laws, and regulations for the government of the university, to elect a president, to fix, increase and reduce the regular number of professors, and tutors, and to appoint the same, and to determine the amount of their salaries; provided there shall always be at least one professor of homeopathy in the department of medicine."

34. People *ex rel.* the Regents of the University v. Auditor-General, 17 Mich. 161 (1868).

control, should not, I think, be confounded with the power to create or establish a university, or to exchange its location, in whole or in part, as previously fixed by the legislature and recognized by the constitution.

Here, again, the court had not determined the regents' constitutional relationship to the legislature but had decided the case on the more narrow grounds that performance under the legislative act had not been consummated; therefore, the regents were not entitled to the appropriated funds.

In the year of 1868, the regents took no steps to establish the professorship in homeopathy in the department of medicine, and as a result another *writ of mandamus* was sought.[35] The board of regents responded by pointing out that: (1) the general supervision of the university, including direction and control of expenditures as well as appointment of professors was a power vested in the regents by the constitution, (2) the regents after careful consideration had decided that the appointment of a professor of homeopathy in the medical department at Ann Arbor would be detrimental to the university, (3) the regents wished to establish a medical department for homeopathy at some place other than Ann Arbor as soon as they were given the power to do so, and (4) they had no funds at the present time in the treasury of the university out of which to pay the salary of such a professor. Here the *writ of mandamus* to compel the board of regents to set up the professorship in the medical department at Ann Arbor presented the judges with the direct question of whether the legislature, or the courts, would substitute their judgment for that of the regents with regard to the location of the professorship and whether the legislative act was repugnant to Article 13 of the Michigan Constitution. The court was once again indecisive on this primary issue, this time because of an equal split among the members of the court on the issue.

This scenario was reenacted in 1874 in another attempt by the attorney general to compel the regents to appoint two professors of homeopathy in the department of medicine in accordance with a new legislative act of 1873.[36] Once again the application for *mandamus* was denied. In essence these cases resulted in a standoff between the legislature and the board of regents, which was, in itself, something of a victory for the regents. However, the denial of *mandamus* by the court in

35. People v. Regents of the University, 18 Mich. 469 (1868).
36. Sess. L., 1873, p. 73.

the last two cases did not directly confront nor settle the issue of constitutional autonomy for the University of Michigan.

Later in 1893, an affirmative step toward autonomy was taken when the Supreme Court of Michigan held that a statute requiring that the "boards, officers or agents of the state, entering into construction contracts to acquire security bonds did not apply to the board of regents of the university." [37] It was significant here that the court felt that the board of regents was not just another administrative agency of the state.

While the above cases, with the possible exception of the *Regents v. Auditor-General* in 1868, appeared to be moving gradually toward judicial acknowledgment of university independence from the legislature, it was not until 1896 that the *coup de grace* was administered. In this year the landmark rationale was enunciated which firmly implanted public university autonomy on the American scene.[38] The issue of the university's discretion in regard to location and establishment of a homeopathic medical college was again the issue in dispute, only this time the legislature had in 1895 enacted a statute requiring the board of regents to discontinue the existing homeopathic school in Ann Arbor and establish a new school in Detroit. The court, apparently, having no desire to continue the forty-year-old homeopathic struggle, settled the issue. The court spelled out the legislature-university relationship in an unmistakable fashion:

> The board of regents and the legislature derive their power from the same supreme authority, namely the constitution. . . . They are separate and distinct constitutional bodies, with the power of the regents defined. By no rule of construction can it be held that either can encroach upon or exercise the powers conferred upon the other.

In 1911, the position of the Board of Regents of the University of Michigan was reinforced when the Supreme Court of Michigan said: ". . . the Board of Regents is made the highest form of juristic person known to the law, a constitutional corporation of independent authority, which, within the scope of its functions, is co-ordinate with and equal to that of the Legislature." [39]

37. Weinberg v. Regents of University of Michigan, 97 Mich. 246, 56 N.W. 605 (1893).

38. Sterling v. Regents of the University of Michigan, 110 Mich. 369, 68 N.W. 253 (1896).

39. Board of Regents of University of Michigan v. Auditor-General, 167 Mich. 444, 132 N.W. 1037 (1911).

Minnesota. Two early decisions in Minnesota [40] concerning constitutional autonomy relegated the University of Minnesota's board of regents to a position somewhat less than a constitutional co-equal to the legislature; however, later decisions bestowed such equality. In 1862, a dispute over the use of a "perpetual fund" of the university led the Minnesota Supreme Court to conclude that "all property acquired by the regents, real or personal, with the fund placed at their disposal, is the property of the state, the corporation (university) being merely a trustee or agent, with specified and limited powers, to use it in a particular manner for a given end." In a later case,[41] the court held that the University of Minnesota was a public institution maintained and conducted by the state and, therefore, the taking of private property by the state for use by the university was for a public purpose. This case accepted and reinforced the precedent which established that the University of Minnesota was merely an agency of the state with ability to exercise certain limited and specified powers as prescribed by law.

A case directly testing the constitutional powers of the University of Minnesota was not litigated until 1928.[42] In 1925, the legislature had passed a new law entitled "An act in relation to the organization of the state government," which centralized the state administrative functions under the governor. Pursuant to this act, a commission on administration and finance operating under the governor's office claimed the authority to supervise and control the expenditure of moneys for the University of Minnesota. The court found that the university, from the standpoint of governmental purposes and functions, was an agency of the state subject to the administrative organization act.[43] However, the court went further and denied that the administration and finance commission of the governor could regulate or control the finances of the university. The court, citing the original territorial charter [44] and the Constitution of 1858, drew a distinction between legislative power and that of the board of regents, the essence of which was the difference between legislative and executive au-

---

40. Regents v. Hart, 7 Gil. 45, 7 Minn. 61 (1862).

41. State *ex rel.* Smith v. Van Reed, 125 Minn. 194, 145 N.W. 967 (1914).

42. State *ex rel.* University of Minnesota v. Chase, 175 Minn. 259, 220 N.W. 951 (1928).

43. Minnesota, Laws of 1925, Ch. 426.

44. Chapter 3, Laws of the Territory, 1851; Art. 8, § 4, Constitution of 1858.

thority. The board of regents is granted executive power with regard to university government and the legislature cannot in contravention of the constitution remove these powers to another state agency. Subsequent cases have reinforced the constitutional position of the University of Minnesota. In a 1931 decision,[45] the Supreme Court of Minnesota was asked to decide whether the university had the power to construct a dormitory upon the campus without legislative authority. The court held it did and commented that the Constitution vests the government of the University of Minnesota in the board of regents:

> . . . and in the exercise of its granted power of government, so long as it keeps within the limits of its grant, it is not subject to legislative or executive interference or judicial control at the suit of a taxpayer.

The court went on to observe that the property belongs to the state, not the university, but the people of the state have chosen to give charge of the university property to the board of regents. The "university is the people's university," the board of regents "does not rule; it serves." [46]

The Minnesota legislature struck to the very heart of the constitutional status of the University of Minnesota when it passed a law to allow the governor to appoint regents from congressional districts and enlarge the board of regents by designating that three state officers, *ex officio*, would serve on the board.[47] The court held the statute violated the constitutional provision granting the university "rights, immunities, franchises, and endowments." [48]

> The method of electing regents and so assuring corporate succession being of the very essence of the corporation, it is equally so of the franchises which gave it being. * * * Where sovereign power has first granted and then perpetuated a corporate franchise, selecting the original grantees and carefully designating how their successors shall be selected, the original grantees and the method of choosing their successors are "integral" with the franchise itself.[49]

---

45. Fanning v. University of Minnesota, 183 Minn. 222, 236 N.W. 217 (1931).

46. *Ibid.*

47. Laws 1923, Ch. 429, § 1 (Mason's Minn. Stat. 1927, § 3110).

48. Chapter 3, Laws of the Territory, 1851; Art. 8, § 4, Constitution of 1858.

49. State *ex rel.* Peterson v. Quinlivan, 198 Minn. 65, 268 N.W. 858 (1936). See also State *ex rel.* Sholes v. University of Minnesota, 54 N.W.2d 122 (1952).

The court in describing the university's relationship to the executive, legislative and judicial branches of government commented:

> The people by their Constitution chose to perpetuate the government of the University which had been created by their territorial Legislature in a board of regents, and the powers they gave are not subject to legislative or executive control; nor can the courts at the suit of a taxpayer interfere with the board while governing the university in the exercise of its granted powers. This does not mean that the people created a corporation or institution which is above the law. The board must keep within the limits of its grant.

California. The makers of the California Constitution of 1879, adopting the philosophy of the Michigan Constitution of 1850 and the Minnesota Constitution of 1858, provided for independence of the Board of Regents as follows:

> The University of California shall constitute a public trust, and its organization and government shall be perpetually continued in the form and character prescribed by the organic act creating the same passed March 23, 1868 (and the several acts amendatory thereof), subject only to such legislative control as may be necessary to ensure compliance with the terms of its endowments and the proper investment and security of its funds.[50]

In 1886, the Supreme Court of California held that Hastings College of the Law was an integral part of the University of California and as such had immunity from a legislative act changing the form of government of the college.[51]

A clearer statement of the University of California's independence was expounded by the California high court in a case involving a conflict between vaccination requirements of the legislature and those of the University of California.[52] The board of regents required *all* enrolling students to be vaccinated while the legislature required vaccinations for students in public and private schools *except* for those conscientiously opposed or for those whom vaccination would be harmful to their health. A student not having been vaccinated and conscientiously opposed to vaccination was denied entrance to the university and sued for admission. He had complied with the statutory requirements by submitting a statement in writing by his parents to the effect they too were conscientiously

---

50. California, Constitution of 1879, Art. 9, § 9.
51. People *ex rel.* Hastings v. Kewen, 69 Cal. 215, 10 P. 393 (1886).
52. Williams v. Wheeler, 23 Cal. App. 619, 138 P. 937 (1913).

opposed to vaccination. The question of legislative versus university predominance in making of admission and health policies was placed squarely before the court. The court held that the exceptions provided for in the vaccination law were not founded upon considerations of general health and did not constitute an exercise of the general police protection of the legislature. The university's vaccination policy cannot be nullified on this ground. More specifically with regard to the constitutional powers of the university, the court said:

> . . . it was the intention of the framers of the Constitution to invest the board of regents with a larger degree of independence and discretion in respect to these matters than is usually held to exist in such inferior boards and commissions as are solely subjects of legislative creation and control. This would seem to be a necessary conclusion from the fact of the evaluation of the university to the place and dignity of a constitutional department of the body politic. . . .

Since, on one hand, the exception from vaccination provision of the statute was not in the nature of a general health regulation and was not an exercise of the general police powers of the state, and, on the other hand, the university was not an ordinary administrative agency, these things combined to afford the university autonomy sufficient to overcome the statute.[53]

Some eight years after this vaccination case, the legislature of California amended the vaccination law to read: "The control of smallpox shall be under the direction of the state board of health, and no rule or regulation on the subject of vaccination shall be adopted by school or local health authorities."

Pursuant to this change in the law, a student again contested the legality of the university's regulation requiring *all* students to be vaccinated.[54] The court observed that there is no question that the legislature may under its police power enact laws for the general welfare of the public and such acts may be applicable to the university; however, here the law is not a regulation of health but merely a prohibition against the regulation of health by any agency other than the state board of health. With the prohibitory nature of the act in mind, the court held that the legislature could not take away or impair the regulatory power granted to the university by the constitution.

---

53. *Ibid.*
54. Wallace v. Regents of University of California, 75 Cal. App. 274, 242 P. 892 (1926).

A general law which does not itself regulate, but which merely provides, as here, that there shall be no local regulation, can have no proper application to local bodies deriving their powers under a constitutional grant, as such laws amount to no more than a legislative attempt to nullify such constitutional grant, and it is to that extent invalid.

The above cases are primarily concerned with legislative intervention into university affairs, but other questions can be raised regarding judicial intervention in university affairs by the courts. In California, the constitutional corporate status of the University of California prevents the courts from interfering with internal government of the university unless there is evidence of fraudulent conduct on the part of the university. "It is an elementary principle of law that a court has no power or right to intermeddle with internal affairs of a corporation, in the absence of fraudulent conduct on the part of those who have been lawfully entrusted with management and conduct of its affairs." [55]

Other States. Like the constitutional "triad" discussed above, six other states, Colorado, Georgia, Idaho, Oklahoma, Nevada, and Arizona have constitutional provisions which provide for independence of the state university. In Colorado the regents of the University of Colorado are given the general supervision of the university and exclusive control of the university funds and appropriations.[56] Another provision in the Colorado constitution mandating that the state university be located at Boulder led to two court decisions denying the university the right to establish new degree granting colleges and departments at other locations in the state without amending the constitution.[57] Because of these decisions it was necessary to amend the constitution in 1922 to permit the University of Colorado to have medical and dental schools at Denver. Until the creation of the new Metropolitan State College at Denver in 1966, the constitutional restrictions on location of degree programs prevented much needed programs from being offered in Denver by the University of Colorado.[58]

In Georgia the constitutional autonomy of the Board of Re-

---

55. Wall v. Board of Regents of University of California, 102 P.2d 533 (1940).

56. Constitution of Colorado, Art. 9, §§ 12 and 14.

57. *In re* State Institutions, 9 Colo. 626 (1886); People *ex rel.* Jerome v. Regents of the State University, 24 Colo. 175, 49 P. 286 (1897).

58. M.M. Chambers, *Higher Education in the Fifty States*, The Interstate Printers and Publishers, 1970, pp. 69-70.

gents of the State University System was established by a 1943 amendment to the Georgia constitution and saved in the comprehensive constitutional revision in 1945. Article VIII, Section 4, states:

> The said Board of Regents of the University System of Georgia shall have the powers and duties as provided by law existing at the time of the adoption of this Constitution, together with such further powers and duties as may be hereafter provided by law.

In 1921, the Supreme Court of Idaho officially placed the University of Idaho in the magic circle of autonomous universities. The decision was made with reference to Article 9, Section 10, of the Idaho Constitution: "The general supervision of the University, and the control and direction of all the funds of, and appropriations to, the university, under such regulations as may be prescribed by law." The Supreme Court interpreted this phrase to mean that while functioning within the scope of its authority, the board of regents is "not subject to the control or supervision of any other branch, board or department of the state government." [59] The portion of the constitution limiting the board of regent's authority, ("under such regulations as may be prescribed by law") refers to methods and rules for the conduct of business and accounting functions and does not interfere with the constitutional discretion of the board. The court went on to say that when an appropriation of public funds is made to the university and the university board of regents accepts the funds, the legislature may impose such conditions and limitations on the use of the funds as it deems necessary. However, where the board sells university property there is no obligation on the part of the regents to pay the proceeds from the sale of the property into the state treasury. In a later case, the Supreme Court of Idaho re-emphasized the independence of the board of regents from legislative regulation with regard to matters of employment of professors, officers, agents or employees.[60]

The authority of the board of regents of the state agricultural and mechanical college of Oklahoma was questioned when the state auditor refused to draw a warrant for payment of certain sums of money upon the submission of a voucher which had been approved by the regents.[61] The direct

59. State *ex rel.* Black v. State Board of Education and the Board of Regents of the University of Idaho, 33 Idaho 415, 196 P. 201 (1921).
60. Dreps v. Board of Regents of the University of Idaho, 139 P.2d 467 (1943).
61. Trapp v. Cook Const. Co., 24 Okla. 850, 105 P. 667 (1909).

question was whether the statutory power of the auditor was such as to divest the regents of their control over the funds. The board of regents rested its claim of discretion on implied powers given them by a general constitutional provision saying that the board: "shall discharge such *other* duties * * * as may be provided by law." The specific powers of the board of regents were not explicitly enumerated. Pursuant to this general constitutional provision, subsequent statutes had given the board of regents specific authority with regard to control of funds.

> In this case the specific duties of the board of regents were in no wise set out or enumerated by the constitution; but they were defined by the statutes of the territory, which are and were constitutional, and which in our judgment were the duties referred to by the convention and the people when they provided that the board of agriculture should be such board of regents, and made mention of the "other" duties which we have noticed.

With a conflict of statute, as well as the question of general constitutional authority in mind, the court said, "As we view it, additional duties may be required, but none vested by the Constitution may be taken away by the Legislature." In other words, under the constitution, the powers of the board of regents could be expanded by the legislature but could not be diminished.

One will notice, with reference to this case, that the constitutional authority for university autonomy in Oklahoma is the weakest provision of any of the provisions observed above. Without the benefit of an "understanding" court this case could easily have been decided against the board of regents.

The court's reasoning in this case was, however, reinforced a half century later in 1959 in an opinion by the Attorney General of Oklahoma. The legislature in 1959 had enacted a statute entitled the "Oklahoma Central Purchasing Act" which required all state departments and institutions to procure all contractual services, supplies, materials, and equipment through the purchasing division of the State Board of Public Affairs. The Attorney General, giving an opinion on request of the board of regents, declared that the act was unconstitutional insofar as it applied to the board of regents. The act was in conflict with Sections 31 and 31a of Article 6 of the Oklahoma Constitution, which gave independence to the Oklahoma Agricultural and Mechanical Colleges.[62]

---

62. Chambers, *op. cit.*, pp. 302-303.

The Oklahoma story of autonomy does not end here, however, for in this particular state, constitutional independence is granted to two boards of regents. In 1941, the Oklahoma constitution was amended to establish a Board of Regents for Higher Education which is separate from the previously mentioned agricultural and mechanical board.[63] The Board of Regents for Higher Education was given constitutional powers of coordination but not of governance; yet, the board was granted exclusive power to allocate legislatively appropriated funds to all institutions. When the legislature, four years later, made direct appropriations to Southern Oklahoma Hospital at Ardmore, bypassing the board of regents, the act was held to be unconstitutional.[64]

This exclusive power of the board of regents to allocate funds among institutions has led Chambers to comment that this board:[65] "is the most power-laden of all 'coordinating boards' of higher education."

In Nevada, Article XI, Section 4, of the 1864 Constitution states:

> The Legislature shall provide for the establishment of a state university, which shall embrace departments for agriculture, mechanic arts and mining, to be controlled by a board of regents, whose duties shall be prescribed by law.

It was not until 1948 that the Supreme Court of Nevada interpreted the meaning of this provision, concluding that:

> It was the intention of the framers of the constitution to vest exclusive executive and administrative control of the university in a board of regents to be elected by the people . . . .[66]

In a controversy in 1963 between the board of regents and a state planning board, the question arose as to which had final authority of approval of "architecture . . . supervision or inspection of construction or major repairs," of university buildings. The attorney general rendered an opinion in favor of the regents saying: "The Board of Regents of the University of Nevada is not within the purview of (the act establishing the state planning board); even if the money is appro-

63. *Ibid.*
64. Board of Regents of University of Oklahoma v. Childress, State Auditor, 170 P.2d 1018 (1946).
65. Chambers, *op. cit.*, p. 303.
66. King v. Board of Regents of University of Nevada, 200 P.2d 221 (1948).

priated by the legislature, the delegation of powers to the State Planning Board being in derogation of powers conferred on the Board of Regents by the Constitution." [67]

A series of court decisions in Arizona has established university independence. In two of these cases, conflict arose between the state auditor, one Frohmiller, and the Board of Regents of the University and State Colleges.[68] In both of these incidents the state auditor was ordered by *mandamus* to issue warrants to pay claims approved by the board of regents. The courts found that with regard to the payment of claims for the regents, the state auditor serves in a ministerial capacity and exercises no discretionary powers. Prior to these cases, two court decisions had held, likewise, that claims approved by the board of regents were conclusive and the state auditor could not interpose discretion in the audit, allowance, and payment of the claims.

The issue of constitutional autonomy of the Arizona Board of Regents was treated directly in another *Frohmiller* case which tested the jurisdiction and authority of a newly created civil service system.[69] The legislative act provided that the state civil service shall apply to all positions in the state service "except * * * members of teaching staffs of all educational institutions maintained or supported by the State * * *." The plain meaning of this provision was that all personnel of the universities except those in teaching positions were to be under the civil service system. The court held that this legislation ran counter to the Arizona constitutional provision, Article II, Section 2, which provided:

> [Supervision of school system.]—The general conduct and supervision of the public school system shall be vested in a state board of education, a state superintendent of public instruction, county school superintendents and *such governing boards for the state institutions as may be provided by law*. (Emphasis added.)

According to the court, this last phrase is critical to the question of university control and governance. Although the board of regents is not mentioned specifically in the constitution, the

---

67. Frank C. Newman, *The Legal Position of the University of Nevada as an Agency of the State of Nevada*, University of Nevada Press, 1963.

68. Frohmiller v. Board of Regents of University and State Colleges, 171 P.2d 356 (1946); Board of Regents of University and State Colleges v. Frohmiller, 69 Ariz. 50, 208 P.2d 833 (1949).

69. Hernandez v. Frohmiller, 68 Ariz. 242, 204 P.2d 854 (1949).

constitution does grant independence to whatever "governing board" is designated by law. The court said:

> Our governing board for the university and state colleges is the board of regents. To permit legislation to throw the employment and supervision of all personnel under the civil service law, except the teaching staff, would necessarily deprive the board of regents of a large portion of its constitutional supervisory power.

Although all the constitutional provisions establishing university autonomy in the foregoing states are not uniform and some are obviously weaker than others, all can be classified as constituting the legal and structural rationale for autonomous universities.

One may also observe that to establish constitutional autonomy, a great deal depends on the attitude of the court and how it, within the context of either implied or explicit constitutional provisions, is willing to view the relationship between the state and the university.

The lack of autonomy of some state universities may be attributed to attitudes of the courts or even to inaction on the part of university officials. The University of Utah, even though possessing a strong constitutional provision, allowed its authority to atrophy and ultimately was denied autonomy by the courts.[70]

STATE UNIVERSITY AS A CREATURE OF THE LEGISLATURE

The foregoing states, through their constitutions, place the university on a governmental pedestal above regular state agencies. These universities operating within the scope of their created powers are not subordinate to the legislature. On the contrary, they are placed on a governmental level equal in status to the legislature. This situation, however, is not typical among the colleges and universities in America today. Normally, state legislatures through their law-making powers reign supreme over the conduct and control of universities. Operating at the behest of the legislature, the boards controlling colleges and universities may be primary agencies responsible directly to the legislature or secondary agencies responsible to the legislature only through another intermediate agency. Trends toward centralization of governmental func-

---

70. University of Utah v. Board of Examiners of State of Utah, 4 Utah 2d 408, 295 P.2d 348 (1956).

tions during the past several years have led, in many instances, to the university board becoming functionally subordinate to departments of finance, administration, personnel, *et cetera*. Much case law has been created by disputes between higher education boards and administrators and central state administrative agencies. The line between auditing and accounting functions is many times confused with the discretionary prerogatives of higher education administration. Overzealousness by central state agency officials many times impinges on and restricts administrative and program discretion of college administrators. Actions of agencies or officials going beyond the powers delegated to them by the legislature are said to be beyond the law or *ultra vires*. Institutions of higher education created and governed by the legislature, rather than by constitutional provision, must like other state agencies have *explicit* or *implied* statutory powers to perform their functions. Therefore, rules, regulations, or administrative judgments in higher education as in other agencies, not made pursuant to explicit or implied statutory law are *ultra vires*. Colleges and universities as creatures of the legislature must operate within the legal framework circumscribed by the legislature, and no appeal, seeking independence or inviolability of control, to a higher law will succeed.

Implied Powers. Legislatively created universities are limited in their operation to powers expressly or impliedly given them. The term *implied* is quite important and represents the nexus between flexible and inflexible university government. In Arkansas, the question arose as to whether the Board of Trustees of Arkansas had the power to accept a site for a hospital from the state hospital board and to construct a building thereon.[71] The court relied on the law of trusts to conclude that such exercise of discretion was within the implied powers vested in the board of trustees by the legislature. The court relied on Section 186 of the *Restatement of Trusts* which says in part: "In addition to the powers conferred in specific words by the terms of the trust, the trustee has such powers as are necessary or appropriate to carry out the purposes of the trust . . . ." The court cited the situation at the university as being analogous to the public school and said:

> The law is well settled that school districts are not only authorized to exercise the powers that are expressly granted by statute, but also such powers as may be fairly implied therefrom, and from the duties which were ex-

---

71. Lindsay v. White, 206 S.W.2d 762 (1947).

pressly imposed upon them, and such powers are implied when the exercise thereof is clearly necessary to
enable them to carry out and perform the duties legally
imposed upon them.

Therefore, even universities operating directly under the
legislature instead of the constitution may have substantial
leeway in performing their functions so long as a legislative
implication of power is present.

In some states where universities are not constitutional
agencies, the legislatures have voluntarily allowed a great
degree of discretionary freedom. The courts, for example, after a somewhat restrictive decision in 1916, which held that
the University of Missouri was not constitutionally immune
from certain legislative enactments,[72] tended later to allow
for maximum decision making freedom for the university.
This judicial flexibility was first demonstrated in Missouri
when a mandamus was sought by the state treasurer to compel the board of regents of Northeast Missouri Teacher's College to deposit moneys received from payment for loss under an insurance policy into the state treasury.[73] The court
held that the control and expenditure of such funds was within the implied power given to the college by statute and the
college could not be forced to deposit the funds in the state
treasury without mandatory statutory directive.

In a similar decision, the Supreme Court of Missouri held
that the curators of the state university had the implied power
to issue revenue bonds to build dormitory and dining facilities,
even though municipal corporations must have express statutory powers to issue such bonds.[74] The court said it was not
obliged to treat the curators of the university as any other
subordinate state agency.

In areas where a gap in the law allows universities to assume prerogatives which are not expressly given by statute,
the courts will sometimes be swayed by what has been commonly accepted practice of the institution. In another bonding
dispute in which the power of the Board of Curators of the
University of Missouri to issue revenue bonds and construct
parking facilities was challenged, the court was influenced
by the board's historical assumption of power in the absence

---

72. State *ex rel.* Heimberger v. Board of Curators of University of
Missouri, 268 Mo. 598, 188 S.W. 128 (1916).
73. State *ex rel.* Thompson v. Board of Regents for Northeast Missouri State Teacher's College, 305 Mo. 57, 264 S.W. 698 (1924).
74. State *ex rel.* Curators of University of Missouri v. McReynolds,
193 S.W.2d 611 (1946).

of express legislative authorization.[75] In this case, evidence was presented to show that for over twenty-five years the Curators had been providing parking facilities on the university campuses. The court felt that since the Curators had been providing parking facilities on the university campuses for such a long time they were entitled to special consideration, even though no express legislative authority to provide such facilities was found. The court held the Curators had implied authority to construct the parking facilities. Historical assumption of a prerogative by a university board, and the general acceptance of such assumption, weighs for the university when the court is called upon to ascertain legislative intent and implied powers of institutions.

STATE UNIVERSITY AS A SUBORDINATE AGENCY

Where colleges and universities are not given regulatory autonomy by either the state constitution or the legislature, they become subordinate to other state agencies. In other words, the legislature may, if it so desires, relegate the university to a position of a secondary state agency in functional areas of operation or in most areas of discretion and control. The legislature has plenary power to make the college or university board responsible directly to the legislature or make it answerable to another state agency. Most legal conflicts over university control have occurred between university boards and state officials in charge of state agencies exercising some element of fiscal control.

The most notable example of such discord transpired in West Virginia over a period of some eighteen years involving university officials and a state auditor. The rub first came prior to 1939 when Edgar B. Sims, the long-time state auditor of West Virginia, refused to issue a warrant as requested by the University of West Virginia Board of Control.[76] The funds were requisitioned by the university for payment of a printer's claim against the school's athletic department. The athletic department had incurred a deficit because it had diverted some of its funds to pay principal and interest on a new stadium which was built by the University Stadium Corporation. The state legislature, by statute, had acknowledged these payments to the corporation as valid expenditures and had

---

75. State *ex rel.* Curators of the University of Missouri v. Neill, 397 S.W.2d 666 (1966).

76. Glover v. Sims, 121 W. Va. 407, 3 S.E.2d 612 (1939).

appropriated additional funds to cover the deficit. The state auditor denied the university's request for issuance of the warrant on the grounds that the payment to the stadium corporation violated Section 6 of Article X of the state constitution which prohibited the state to assume debts of "any county, city, township, *corporation* or person." Also, the auditor maintained that the legislature was without authority to authorize payment of the account, such an act violating Section 38 of Article VI of the state constitution which provides that any agreement made without prior express authority of law is null and void. The auditor, therefore, was not just challenging university authority but was questioning whether the legislature's act was constitutional. The court ruled against the state auditor, and with regard to the first constitutional issue, held that the printer's claim was not an obligation of the stadium corporation, but one of the university athletic department. The court relied on an equity argument to allow the legislature to subsequently assume a debt which had not been authorized by law. Commenting on this, the court said that the constitutional prohibition does not apply to claims predicated upon "simple justice and right" and was never intended to prevent the legislature from voluntarily righting a wrong. In justification, the court evidently being made up of justices who were supporters of athletics, then extolled the virtues of a university athletic program which was enhanced by the construction of the stadium:

> The state is the beneficiary of the whole project. No one can successfully assert that a proper athletic program is not appropriate to a great educational institution. The physical welfare of young men and women cannot with propriety be ignored. * * * The thousands of West Virginia boys and girls who, through the years, become students at the West Virginia University have better opportunity for well-rounded education by reason of the stadium's being on the campus. The outstanding fact is that the stadium was built and is now a valuable asset of the state of West Virginia.

Eleven years later the same state auditor challenged the expenditure of funds by the University of West Virginia, questioning the power of the legislature and the authority of the university. This case, like the previous one, involved the university athletic program.[77] The auditor refused to issue

---

77. State *ex rel.* Board of Governors of West Virginia University v. Sims, 134 W. Va. 428, 59 S.E.2d 705 (1950).

a warrant to pay for medical and hospital services rendered to a student football player injured in an intercollegiate athletic contest. The state auditor claimed once again that under Section 6 of Article X of the state constitution that the legislature could not grant state credit or assume debts to aid "any county, city, township, corporation, or *person.*" In other words, the auditor maintained that the state could not assume the debt for services rendered to an injured football player as a private person. In addition, the auditor maintained that even if the act were constitutional there was no implied legislative authority for the university to pay such costs. Responding to these issues, the court held that first the act of the legislature was not unconstitutional because the payment for services rendered to the injured athlete was a public claim of the university and not a private one; athletic activities of the university are a part of the system of public education, therefore, money expended in furtherance thereof is for a public purpose. Regarding the implied statutory power of the university to expend moneys for such purposes, the court found that the expenses incurred were incidental and necessary to the conduct of the athletic program which is an educational function.

These decisions must have incurred the wrath of the state auditor, because the next seven years were filled with almost constant litigation between the West Virginia state auditor and the University of West Virginia. In these cases respectively, the Supreme Court of Appeals of West Virginia held that: the Board of Governors of West Virginia University had the statutory authority to reemploy a person who has been granted a prior service allowance under the teachers' retirement system, and to pay for such service from the personal services appropriation of the university; [78] a statute authorizing the West Virginia Board of Education to grant sabbatical leaves to faculty members of educational institutions did not violate the state constitution which prohibits the payment of state moneys for a private purpose; [79] and the expenditure of public money for payment of dues for university membership in a regional educational accrediting association violates no state constitutional provision and is within the dis-

---

78. State *ex rel.* Board of Governors of West Virginia University v. Sims, 136 W. Va. 789, 68 S.E.2d 489 (1952).

79. State *ex rel.* West Virginia Board of Education v. Sims, 139 W. Va. 802, 81 S.E.2d 665 (1954).

cretion of university officials and a state auditor cannot substitute his judgment in such matters.[80]

After losing all of these decisions, State Auditor Sims made it unanimous by dropping a final verdict to Bluefield State College and the West Virginia Board of Education.[81] Here the court held that a gift, by will or otherwise, to a specified state institution is not within the class of grants, devises or bequests, which according to the West Virginia Constitution must be placed in the general school fund. On the contrary, the gift may be placed in a special fund and expended for the sole benefit of the institution for whose benefit it was given. So finding, the court, through a *writ* of *mandamus*, compelled the state auditor to honor the claims made by Bluefield State College on the special fund for payment for library shelving at the college.

Even though the West Virginia situation may represent the maximum in antagonism between a state finance official and a college or university and is, therefore, not typical, the cases, nevertheless, demonstrate the difficulties which an overzealous state agency official can cause college or university officials.

Conflicts over the power to govern institutions of higher education may manifest themselves in a variety of ways but usually reduce themselves to a question of fiscal autonomy. Fiscal problems, along with personnel problems, were present in a dispute between the Attorney General of Illinois and the Board of Trustees of the University of Illinois. In this case, the Attorney General purported to accept the resignation of the person acting as Assistant Attorney General and University Counsel for the University of Illinois.[82] The university maintained the resignation had never been submitted and that the Attorney General had no power to appoint or dismiss the University Counsel. Primarily, the question before the court was whether the Attorney General by virtue of his office is the sole legal advisor to the university and its Board of Trustees. Holding for the university, the court held that the Attorney General was in error in assuming he was the sole legal representative of the University of Illinois, and issued a *writ* of *mandamus* directing the Attorney General to

80. State *ex rel.* Board of Governors of West Virginia v. Sims, 140 W. Va. 64, 82 S.E.2d 321 (1954).

81. State *ex rel.* West Virginia Board of Education v. Sims, 143 W. Va. 269, 101 S.E.2d 190 (1957).

82. People *ex rel.* Board of Trustees of University of Illinois v. Barrett, 382 Ill. 321, 46 N.E.2d 951 (1943).

withdraw himself from appearing on behalf of the university in an action of law. However, the court did hold that the state auditor was justified in not issuing warrants for payment of the salaries of the University Counsel and Assistant University Counsel because the university was unable to show that the legislature had appropriated funds for such purposes.

Later in a 1957 case the Supreme Court of Illinois liberalized its attitude toward requiring the University of Illinois to adhere to line item appropriations of the legislature.[83] Here the court ruled that the Board of Trustees had the power to construct and maintain a television station for research and educational purposes, even in the absence of specific legislative line item appropriation for such purposes. The court said: "* * * the General Assembly cannot be expected to allocate funds to each of the myriad activities of the University and thereby practically substitute itself for the Board of Trustees in the management thereof."

Delegation of Legislative Power. Theoretically. the legislative branch of government does not have to create agencies subordinate to the legislative and executive branches of government to carry out law and policy. However, the creation of administrative agencies has become an integral part of the American system of government at both federal and state levels. The legislature may, if it wishes, confer upon these administrative agencies discretionary authority to enact rules and regulations made pursuant to statute for internal management functions; however, the legislature cannot constitutionally delegate away its own legislative powers.[84]

A Washington court [85] has explained the type of legislative authority which may be delegated to an administrative agency:

> The legislature may delegate these legislative controls to an administrative agency of the state, provided, in so doing, it defines what is to be done; the instrumentality which is to accomplish it; and the scope of the instrumentality's authority in so doing, by prescribing reasonable administrative standards.

Such an unconstitutional delegation was the issue in a North Dakota case in 1966. Here Chapter 155 of the 1965 Session Laws authorized the sale of bonds and directed that

83. Turkovich v. Board of Trustees of the University of Illinois, 11 Ill. 2d 460, 143 N.E.2d 229 (1957).

84. Kern Alexander, Ray Corns, Walter McCann, *Public School Law*, West Publishing Company, 1969, p. 125.

85. State v. Kinnear, 70 Wash. 2d 482, 423 P.2d 937 (1967).

"The proceeds . . . are hereby appropriated to the State Board of Higher Education for use in the construction and equipping of facilities authorized by this Act at state institutions of higher education *as determined by the Board in accordance with such schedule of priorities as may be prescribed by such Board.*" (Emphasis added.) The state supreme court [86] found this statute unconstitutionally delegated away the authority of legislature and said:

> In this case the Legislature has not determined the question of the necessity of any particular type of building, at any particular institution, nor laid down any rule to guide the Board in determining these questions. It has authorized the construction of facilities at some or all of the institutions. It has attempted to delegate to the Board the power to determine what facilities shall be constructed at the different institutions, and the amount, if any, to be expended at each. This, we find, is an unconstitutional delegation of legislative authority. . . .

Terms "college" and "university" defined

YALE UNIVERSITY v. TOWN OF NEW HAVEN

Supreme Court of Errors of Connecticut, 1899.
71 Conn. 316, 42 A. 87.

HAMERSLEY, J. In 1887 the corporation of the President and Fellows of Yale College in New Haven was authorized to use the title "Yale University," and gifts received and contracts made under either of said names were declared to be valid. The powers of the corporation were not otherwise changed. 10 Sp. Laws, p. 467. In October, 1895, the university filed with the assessors of the town of New Haven a list of the property owned by it subject to taxation for the year 1896. The list contained seven pieces of land, valued at $57,680. To this list the assessors added certain buildings used for dormitories and dining hall, with the land on which they stood, valued at $214,990, and also added certain vacant building lots, dwelling houses, and factories, valued at $167,112. The plaintiff appealed to the board of relief, which confirmed the action of the assessors. This appeal is an application to the superior court, alleging that the board of relief acted illegally in confirming the action of the assessors, and praying for appropriate relief. The alleged illegality depends on the meaning

---

86. Nord v. Grey, 141 N.W.2d 395 (N.D. 1966).

given to two statutes, viz. section 3820 of the General Statutes, and the act of 1834, amending the charter of the college, which appears also in section 3822 of the General Statutes.

1. Section 3820 of the General Statutes provides that "buildings or portions of buildings exclusively occupied as colleges, academies, churches or public school houses, or infirmaries" shall be exempt from taxation. If buildings used by the college exclusively as dormitories and dining halls for its students are buildings exclusively occupied as a college, then the action complained of, in adding to the list dormitories and dining hall, was illegal; if such use is not a college occupation, then said action was legal. The word "college," used to denote a constituent of or the equivalent of "university," has acquired a definite meaning. As first used, "college" indicated a place of residence for students, and occasionally a "universitas," or "studium generale." The expressions "universitas studii" and "universitatis collegium" occur in early official documents. A suggestion of the modern university appears in the College and Library of Alexandria, founded and endowed by Ptolemy Soter. Here the Museum provided from [for] the first lodgings and refectory for the professors, and later similar provisions were made for the students. A writer of the twelfth century speaks of the "handsome pile of buildings, which has twenty colleges, whither students betake themselves from all parts of the world." The university in Europe developed about the year 1200. It was a community organized for the study of all branches of knowledge, and authorized by pope, king, or emperor to confer degrees upon those found competent to instruct others. At Bologna—perhaps the earliest organized university—we find colleges almost from the beginning. Such college was a separate house, with a fund for the maintenance of a specified number of poor students. Similar colleges existed in Paris, Oxford, and other universities. At first little more than lodging rooms and refectory, they grew, especially in England, to be the home of the students for all purposes. The instruction and discipline of the university were through the colleges. The conditions of the early universities were peculiar. Vast throngs of students were gathered at one place. They were divided into "nations," each—as at Paris—with its own proctor or procurator. They were further divided among faculties, each with its dean. The divisions into nations and faculties were cross divisions; and another cross division was that into colleges and halls (hall sometimes meaning an unorganized college, and sometimes used as synonymous with

college). With changes in conditions, the college was largely eliminated from the continental universities, while in England the university became practically the associated colleges. Merton College, Oxford, founded in 1264, was the prototype of the English college. That college consisted of the chapel, refectory, and dormitories. Here the scholars, called "fellows," in token of the spirit of equality and companionship, lived under one government, educational and moral, and prepared to take the degree granted by the university. As the colleges increased, all noncollegiate students were driven away. The vagabonds or chamber-dekyns,—i. e. camera degens,—living in lodgings, as opposed to those who lived in a college, disappeared. Each student in a college must belong to the university, and each student of the university must be attached to a college; and the heads of the colleges administered the university. Thus was developed the English theory of the university, where the honors and influence of the studium generale are gained and enjoyed by students living and working under the government of their respective colleges. As Newman says, the university, to enforce discipline, developed itself into colleges, and so the term "college" "was taken to mean a place of residence for the university student, who would there find himself under the guidance and instructions of superiors and tutors, bound to attend to his personal interest, moral and intellectual." See, passim, 3 Newman, Hist. Sketches; Lyte's History of University of Oxford; 1 and 2 Huber's English Universities; Enc. Brit. "Universities." The college and university, however, were sometimes united in one corporation. Newman says, "The University of Toulouse was founded in a college; so was Orleans." Trinity College, Dublin, styled in its charter (1591) "The College of the Holy Undivided Trinity of Queen Elizabeth, near Dublin," is both university and college. It was founded by the queen as a "mater universitatis"; but the hope was not realized, and the university and college have ever since remained one, called in common speech indiscriminately "Trinity College, Dublin," "Dublin University," "The University of Trinity College, Dublin." Marischal College, Aberdeen, was founded in 1593 as a college and a university, with power of conferring degrees. And so at the beginning of the seventeenth century the students of an English university lived in colleges; were instructed and governed through colleges, whether the university included a number of colleges or a single college; and among the buildings indispensable for every college were the great hall, or dining room, and the living rooms, or dormitories.

In establishing universities in the new world the limitations of the people compelled the founders to follow the example of Trinity College, Dublin, and Marischal College, Aberdeen, and not that of Oxford and Cambridge. Upon the same corporation was conferred the power of the university in granting degrees and of the college in government, and such community and the buildings required for its use were known as "the college." The first appropriation to endow a university in Virginia was made in 1607. In 1660 an act of the colonial legislature endowed "The College," and in 1693 William III. established the university, described in the charter as "a certain place of universal study, or perpetual college of divinity, philosophy, languages, and other good arts and sciences," and named it "The College of William and Mary in Virginia." The settlers of New England early felt the need of a local university, and the first step was the erection of a college; i. e. a building where the students were to be lodged, fed, and instructed while pursuing the university studies and qualifying for its degrees. In 1630 the general court at Boston advanced £400 for this purpose, and subsequently appointed Newtown as the seat of the university, and for this reason changed the name of the town to Cambridge. 2 Mather's Magnalia, pp. 7-9, 19, 20; Quincy's History of Harvard. In 1642, the court established overseers of "a college founded in Cambridge," and in 1650 the charter was granted. The statutes immediately adopted provided that all students admitted to the college "must board at the commons," and also provided for conferring the first and second degrees in arts. While the college exercised some of the privileges of a university, doubt was felt as to the power of the general court to confer such privileges. The colonial charter of 1692 was construed as authorizing the court to erect a university, and immediately, as Mather says, the general assembly granted "a charter to this university," authorizing it to grant degrees "as in the universities in England." This charter expired within three years, from failure to receive the royal approval, and the college was subsequently reorganized under the charter of 1650. The degree of D. D. was conferred by the college in 1693 on Increase Mather, its president, who, in conferring the degrees at the first commencement after the new charter, maintained that "the right of establishing universities (academias) is reserved to all those, and to those only, who hold the sovereignty in the state," and that the general court, under the charter of 1692, possessed such sovereignty. No other degree of doctorate was conferred until

1771, when Nathaniel Appleton was made doctor of divinity; and a few years later George Washington was made doctor of laws. The Massachusetts constitution of 1779 recognized "the University at Cambridge," and ratified and confirmed all the rights and privileges it had been accustomed to exercise.

The colonies of Connecticut and New Haven were at first unable to erect a college by themselves, and for some years contributed to that of Cambridge. The plan of a college at New Haven was early mooted, and in 1654 steps were taken towards its consummation. Davenport wished to direct the benefaction of Gov. Hopkins to the founding of a college, and the court of that colony acceded to that plan. The difficulties attending the union of the colonies of New Haven and Connecticut obstructed the execution of the plan, and eventually the funds were appropriated to the Hopkins Grammar School. In 1698 the plan was revived, and ten of the principal ministers agreed to stand as trustees to found, erect, and govern a college. They formed themselves into a society at New Haven in 1700, and the same year, at a meeting at Branford, they (in the language of Trumbull) "founded the University of Yale College." 1 Trum. Hist. Conn. 402. In 1701 the general court of Connecticut granted to said trustees the privilege of founding, endowing, and ordering a "collegiate school," and authorized them to acquire and hold real estate, not exceeding the value of £500 per annum, and personal property to any amount, for the use of said school, and for erecting and endowing the same. 4 Col. Rec. 363. The act did not purport to establish a college and university, unless by indirection; but the trustees, following the example of Harvard, proceeded at once to grant degrees in arts. Until 1716 the school was migratory. The trustees then decided that it should be established at New Haven, and this decision was confirmed by the legislature the following year. 6 Col. Rec. 30. In pursuance of this authority, aided by appropriations by the colonial government, as well as by gifts from Gov. Yale and other benefactors, a college house "for the entertainment of the scholars" was so far finished in 1718 as "to be fit for the reception and accommodation of all the students." It contained nearly 50 studies, and was furnished with a convenient hall, library, and kitchen. At the commencement for that year, in the presence of the authorities of the colony, the trustees did, "with one consent, agree, determine, and ordain that our college house shall be called by the name of its munificent patron, and shall be named Yale College." * * * The "college" and the buildings for entertaining the students under college government were inseparable. In 1818, Yale College consisted of three college buildings for housing the officers and students, a lyceum, a chapel, a kitchen, and large dining room; and it was this college whose charter was confirmed by our constitution of 1818.

The settled meaning of "college" as a building or group of buildings in which scholars are housed, fed, instructed, and governed under college discipline, while qualifying for their university degree, whether the university includes a number of colleges or a single college, is now attacked. We have deemed it proper to trace this meaning with sufficient detail to demonstrate the utter unreason of the attack. This peculiar function of a college is inherent in the best conception of the university. This meaning has been attached to the English word for 800 years; it was the only meaning known at the time our first American colleges were founded; it was recognized and distinctly affirmed in the charter of Yale College; it has since been affirmed by repeated acts of legislation, and has received the sanction of constitutional confirmation. It was impossible for the legislature to express its meaning more clearly than in the language of section 3820, "buildings occupied as colleges." If it had said, "dormitories, dining halls, and other buildings occupied as colleges," the meaning would have been the same, and the amplification would have added nothing to the precise certainty of the language used. * * *

The fact that certain sums are paid for use of the rooms occupied does not alter the character of the occupation. A church is none the less a church because the worshipers contribute to the support of services by way of pew rent. A hospital is none the less a hospital because the beneficiaries contribute something towards its maintenance. And a college is none the less a college because its beneficiaries share the cost of maintenance; and it is immaterial whether such contribution is lumped in one sum, or apportioned to sources of expense, as tuition, room rent, lecture fee, dining hall, etc.

The defendant further claims that, even if some dormitories may be occupied as a college, yet section 3820 must be construed strictly, because it is a statute exempting property from taxation; and that, so construed, the finding of the committee requires the court to hold that the dormitories assessed are not in fact buildings erected for the use of students, but in substance constitute an investment in the business of furnishing apartments for rich men at highly remunerative rates; and that the student, as student, is in fact, and by the very necessity of the case, excluded from any occupation of the buildings; * * *

This clause of section 3820 does not exempt any individuals from the burden of taxation that is common to all. It does not grant to one particular privileges denied to all others. It declares that lands and buildings sequestered to certain public uses—i. e. taken out of the body of private property, and devoted exclusively to the common good, from which no individual can derive any profit—are not taxable property. And this has been, not the exception, but the rule, from the foundation of our government. The seats of government, state or municipal, highways, parks, churches, public school houses, colleges, have never been within the range of taxation. They cannot be exceptions from a rule in which they were never included. * * * When the legislature, in 1822, saw fit to formally declare that property of the United States, of the state, and of municipal governments, and "the buildings occupied as colleges," etc., should be exempt from taxation (Pub. Acts 1822, p. 25), it did not alter the character of the property, or the reason of its not being taxed. The declaration was not an exemption, in the strict sense of the word, as to buildings occupied as colleges and schools, any more than as to property of the United States. They were untaxed, as they had been for nearly 200 years without any legislative declaration, because they are not "ratable estate," because they had been placed in that class of property which ought not to be taxed by virtue of a public policy too clear to be questioned, and which had been followed without any specific legislation by our government from its very beginning. * * *

2. The act of 1834 amending the charter of Yale College is as follows: "That the funds which have been or may hereafter be granted, provided by the state of Connecticut, or given by any person or persons to the corporation of the President and Fellows of Yale College in New Haven, and by them invested and held for the use of that institution, shall, with the interest thereof, be and remain exempt from taxation: provided, however, that the said corporation shall never hold in this state real estate free from taxation affording an annual income of more than six thousand dollars: and provided also that the private property of the officers of the institution shall not be exempt from taxation, and that the said corporation shall on or before the first day of September, A. D.

1834, give its assent to this act, and transmit the evidence thereof to the secretary of the state, to be by him recorded." 1 Priv. Laws, p. 481. * * *

The contention of the defendant is that, whenever the income from real estate exceeds the sum of $6,000, not only the real estate producing such excess of income, but also all the unproductive real estate the college may hold, becomes at once liable to taxation. We think this requires us to interpolate into the charter a limitation it does not contain. * * * The act of 1834 plainly exempts all the property of the college from taxation, and the proviso qualifies this exemption only for the purpose of imposing a limited restraint on the mode of investment. It is not an absolute limitation to the holding of real estate, but it is a provision which makes it the interest of the college to itself limit its holding. It is not presumed that the college will, to any considerable extent, invest its funds in unproductive property, so there is no direct limit to its holding of such land; but the college might well be tempted to put all its funds into productive real estate, and the proviso directly restrains this tendency by limiting its right to hold real estate producing more than $6,000 a year, unless it pays taxes on the excess. If the college finds in any year that its revenues from land exceed $6,000, it must choose between its unlimited exemption from taxation and its unlimited right to hold real estate. If it chooses the former, it must sell so much of its productive land as will reduce its income within the limit; if it chooses the latter, it must pay taxes on the land, instead of selling it. In this way the state sought to exempt all the funds of the college from taxation, and, through the potent operation of self-interest, to keep the investment of those funds in real estate within reasonable bounds. * * *

For reasons before given, we think that students' fees, whether apportioned to room rent or tuition, cannot be treated as income of real estate, and that land occupied and reasonably necessary for the plant of the college is not productive real estate, within the meaning of the proviso in the act of 1834. The vacant lots added by the assessors are exempt from taxation. The dwelling houses and factories added by the assessors are also exempt, unless some one or more of these must be added to the list returned by the plaintiff in order to reduce its net income from all its other real estate within the prescribed limit.

Certain questions as to a few items of property were submitted without argument. The nature of these questions is not quite clear. It appears that a lot on Cannon street was sold to one Robert Brown, a professor in the university, by parol, and the money needed to build a dwelling house advanced to him; that he has built and occupied the house, and has repaid a portion of the loan, but has paid nothing on the purchase price. This presents a case of property substantially owned and enjoyed by a private person, while the title remains in the college. The lot and house should be added to the plaintiff's list. Its charter does not exempt from taxation property held for private use. It appears also that a number of lots have been leased to private parties on long leases, the tenants agreeing to pay the taxes. So far as the town is concerned, such agreements by the tenants are inoperative. If the revenue from these leases is in excess of the $6,000 derived from the other real estate, the lots should be added to the plaintiff's list. It will be necessary for the superior court to proceed to a further hearing for the purpose of ascertaining these facts, unless the parties shall agree.

The record does not show any impropriety on the part of the plaintiff in dealing with its exemption, unless, possibly, in the case of the Brown house; but, in order to exclude any false implication, we deem it proper to add that the charter does not authorize the college to hold any property exempt from taxation for any private use, and does not authorize any commercial dealings with its exemptions, whether by way of mere speculation in vacant land, of selling land on long leases at nominal rents, or otherwise. This statute was intended to serve a great public use in pursuance of a most beneficial public policy, and the construction to be given such a statute requires that the intent shall not be defeated either by clear evasion or undue restriction. The superior court is advised to render judgment ordering the board of relief to strike from the plaintiff's tax list all the items added by the assessors except the Brown house, and except such items, if any, of productive real estate, as it may find to be necessary to retain in order to bring the net income from all other real estate within the sum of $6,000; and to take further proceedings for the purpose of ascertaining this fact, unless it shall be settled by agreement of the parties. The other judges concurred.

NOTES

Definition of University

"It is an institution in which the education imparted is

universal, embracing many branches, such as the arts, sciences, and all manner of learning, and possessing power to confer degrees which indicate proficiency in the branches taught. In the collegiate department, or 'department of arts,' as it has been called, the ordinary scholastic education is imparted, upon which the degree of bachelor of arts and master of arts is conferred, in the medical department the degree of doctor of medicine is conferred, and in the law department the degree of bachelor of laws. * * * The words 'school,' 'academy,' and 'college,' are applied to institutions which are confined to some special course of instruction." Commonwealth v. Banks, 198 P. 397, 48 A. 277 (1901).

Generally junior colleges, normal schools or teachers colleges, colleges and universities have been held not to be "common" or "public" schools. Pollitt v. Lewis, 269 Ky. 680, 108 S.W.2d 671, 113 A.L.R. 691 (1937); State Teachers' College v. Morris, 165 Miss. 758, 144 So. 374 (1932); Normal School Dist. v. Painter, 102 Mo. 464, 14 S.W. 938 (1890); Agricultural and Mechanical College v. Hager, 121 Ky. 1, 87 S.W. 1125 (1905); Regents of University v. Board of Education, 20 Okla. 809, 95 P. 429 (1908). See 15 Am. Jur. 2d 588.

In *Pollitt*, referred to above, the court held that a junior college, the principal work of which is the maintenance of courses of instruction in advance of the instruction maintained in high schools, is not a part of the common-school system, within a constitutional provision stating that no sum shall be raised or collected for education other than in common schools without the approval of a majority of those voting at an election held for the purpose.

A corporation is not per se a public corporation and a legislative act altering its charter violates the obligation of contract provision of the Constitution

THE TRUSTEES OF DARTMOUTH COLLEGE v. WOODWARD

Supreme Court of the United States, 1819.
4 Wheat (U.S.) 518.

MARSHALL, C. J., delivered the opinion of the court, as follows:—

This is an action of trover, brought by the Trustees of

Dartmouth College, against William H. Woodward, in the state court of New Hampshire, for the book of records, corporate seal, and other corporate property, to which the plaintiffs allege themselves to be entitled.

A special verdict, after setting out the rights of the parties, finds for the defendant, if certain acts of the legislature of New Hampshire, passed on the 27th of June, and on the 18th of December, 1816, be valid, and binding on the trustees without their assent, and not repugnant to the constitution of the United States; otherwise it finds for the plaintiffs.

The superior court of judicature of New Hampshire rendered a judgment upon this verdict for the defendant, which judgment has been brought before this court by writ of error. The single question now to be considered is, do the acts to which the verdict refers violate the constitution of the United States?

This court can be insensible neither to the magnitude nor delicacy of this question. The validity of a legislative act is to be examined; and the opinion of the highest law tribunal of a State is to be revised; an opinion which carries with it intrinsic evidence of the diligence, of the ability, and the integrity with which it was formed. On more than one occasion this court has expressed the cautious circumspection with which it approaches the consideration of such questions; and has declared that, in no doubtful case, would it pronounce a legislative act to be contrary to the constitution. But the American people have said, in the constitution of the United States, that "no State shall pass any bill of attainder, *ex post facto* law, or law impairing the obligation of contracts." In the same instrument they have also said, "that the judicial power shall extend to all cases in law and equity arising under the constitution." On the judges of this court, then, is imposed the high and solemn duty of protecting, from even legislative violation, those contracts which the constitution of our country has placed beyond legislative control; and, however irksome the task may be, this is a duty from which we dare not shrink.

The title of the plaintiffs originates in a charter, dated the 13th day of December, in the year 1769, incorporating twelve persons therein mentioned, by the name of "The Trustees of Dartmouth College," granting to them and their successors the usual corporate privileges and powers, and authorizing the trustees, who are to govern the college, to fill up all vacancies which may be created in their own body.

The defendant claims under three acts of the legislature of

New Hampshire, the most material of which was passed on the 27th of June, 1816, and is entitled, "An act to amend the charter, and enlarge and improve the corporation of Dartmouth College." Among other alterations in the charter, this act increases the number of trustees to twenty-one, gives the appointment of the additional members to the executive of the State, and creates a board of overseers, with power to inspect and control the most important acts of the trustees. This board consists of twenty-five persons. The president of the senate, the speaker of the house of representatives of New Hampshire, and the governor and lieutenant governor of Vermont, for the time being, are to be members *ex officio*. The board is to be completed by the governor and council of New Hampshire, who are also empowered to fill all vacancies which may occur. The acts of the 18th and 26th of December are supplemental to that of the 27th of June, and are principally intended to carry that act into effect.

The majority of the trustees of the college have refused to accept this amended charter, and have brought this suit for the corporate property, which is in possession of a person holding by virtue of the acts which have been stated.

It can require no argument to prove, that the circumstances of this case constitute a contract. An application is made to the crown for a charter to incorporate a religious and literary institution. In the application it is stated, that large contributions have been made for the object, which will be conferred on the corporation, as soon as it shall be created. The charter is granted, and on its faith the property is conveyed. Surely, in this transaction, every ingredient of a complete and legitimate contract is to be found.

The points for consideration are,

1. Is this contract protected by the constitution of the United States?

2. Is it impaired by the acts under which the defendant holds? * * *

It becomes then the duty of the court most seriously to examine this charter, and to ascertain its true character.

From the instrument itself, it appears, that about the year 1754, the Rev. Eleazer Wheelock established, at his own expense, and on his own estate, a charity school for the instruction of Indians in the Christian religion. The success of this institution inspired him with the design of soliciting contributions in England, for carrying on and extending his undertaking. In this pious work, he employed the Rev. Nathaniel

Whitaker, who, by virtue of a power of attorney from Dr. Wheelock, appointed the Earl of Dartmouth and others, trustees of the money which had been and should be contributed; which appointment Dr. Wheelock confirmed by a deed of trust authorizing the trustees to fix on a site for the college. They determined to establish the school on Connecticut River, in the western part of New Hampshire; that situation being supposed favorable for carrying on the original design among the Indians, and also for promoting learning among the English; and the proprietors in the neighborhood having made large offers of land, on condition that the college should there be placed. Dr. Wheelock then applied to the crown for an act of incorporation; and represented the expediency of appointing those whom he had, by his last will, named as trustees in America, to be members of the proposed corporation. "In consideration of the premises," "for the education and instruction of the youth of the Indian tribes," &c., "and also of English youth, and any others," the charter was granted, and the Trustees of Dartmouth College were by that name created a body corporate, with power, for the use of the said college, to acquire real and personal property, and to pay the president, tutors, and other officers of the college, such salaries as they shall allow. * * *

This charter was accepted, and the property, both real and personal, which had been contributed for the benefit of the college, was conveyed to, and vested in, the corporate body.

From this brief review of the most essential parts of the charter, it is apparent, that the funds of the college consisted entirely of private donations. It is, perhaps, not very important, who were the donors. The probability is, that the Earl of Dartmouth, and the other trustees in England, were, in fact, the largest contributors. Yet the legal conclusion, from the facts recited in the charter, would probably be, that Dr. Wheelock was the founder of the college.

The origin of the institution was, undoubtedly, the Indian charity school, established by Dr. Wheelock, at his own expense. It was at his instance, and to enlarge this school, that contributions were solicited in England. The person soliciting these contributions was his agent; and the trustees, who received the money, were appointed by, and act under, his authority. It is not too much to say, that the funds were obtained by him, in trust, to be applied by him to the purposes of his enlarged school. The charter of incorporation was granted at his instance. The persons named by him in his last will, as the trustees of his charity school, compose a part of the corporation, and he is declared to be the founder of the college, and its president for life. Were the inquiry material, we should feel some hesitation in saying, that Dr. Wheelock was not, in law, to be considered as the founder (1 Bl. Com. 481) of this institution, and as possessing all the rights appertaining to that character. But be this as it may, Dartmouth College is really endowed by private individuals, who have bestowed their funds for the propagation of the Christian religion among the Indians, and for the promotion of piety and learning generally. From these funds the salaries of the tutors are drawn; and these salaries lessen the expense of education to the students. It is then an eleemosynary, (1 Bl. Com. 471) and, as far as respects its funds, a private corporation.

Do its objects stamp on it a different character? Are the trustees and professors public officers, invested with any portion of political power, partaking in any degree in the administration of civil government, and performing duties which flow from the sovereign authority?

That education is an object of national concern, and a proper subject of legislation, all admit. That there may be an institution founded by government, and placed entirely under its immediate control, the officers of which would be public officers, amenable exclusively to government, none will deny. But is Dartmouth College such an institution? Is education altogether in the hands of government? Does every teacher of youth become a public officer, and do donations for the purpose of education necessarily become public property, so far that the will of the legislature, not the will of the donor, becomes the law of the donation? These questions are of serious moment to society, and deserve to be well considered.

Doctor Wheelock, as the keeper of his charity school, instructing the Indians in the art of reading, and in our holy religion; sustaining them at his own expense, and on the voluntary contributions of the charitable, could scarcely be considered as a public officer, exercising any portion of those duties which belong to government; nor could the legislature have supposed, that his private funds, or those given by others, were subject to legislative management, because they were applied to the purposes of education. When afterwards, his school was enlarged, and the liberal contributions made in England and in America, enabled him to extend his cares to the education of the youth of his own country, no change was wrought in his own character, or in the nature of his duties. Had he employed assistant tutors with the funds contributed by others, or had the trustees in England established a school, with Dr. Wheelock at its head, and paid salaries to him and his assistants, they would still have been private tutors; and the fact that they were employed in the education of youth, could not have converted them into public officers, concerned in the administration of public duties, or have given the legislature a right to interfere in the management of the fund. The trustees, in whose care that fund was placed by the contributors, would have been permitted to execute their trust, uncontrolled by legislative authority.

Whence, then, can be derived the idea, that Dartmouth College has become a public institution, and its trustees public officers, exercising powers conferred by the public, for public objects? Not from the source whence its funds were drawn; for its foundation is purely private and eleemosynary. Not from the application of those funds; for money may be given for education, and the persons receiving it do not, by being employed in the education of youth, become members of the civil government. Is it from the act of incorporation? Let this subject be considered.

A corporation is an artificial being, invisible, intangible, and existing only in contemplation of law. Being the mere creature of law, it possesses only those properties which the charter of its creation confers upon it, either expressly, or as incidental to its very existence. These are such as are supposed best calculated to effect the object for which it was created. Among the most important are immortality, and, if the expression may be allowed, individuality; properties by which a perpetual succession of many persons are considered as the same, and may act as a single individual. They enable a corporation to manage its own affairs, and to hold property without the perplexing intricacies, the hazardous and endless necessity of perpetual conveyances, for the purpose of transmitting it from hand to hand. It is chiefly for the purpose of clothing bodies of men, in succession, with these qualities and capacities, that corporations were invented, and are in use. By these means a perpetual succession of individuals are capable of acting for the promotion of the particular object, like one immortal being. But this being does not share in the civil government of the country, unless that be the purpose for which it was created. Its immortality no more confers on it political power, or a political character, than immortality would confer such power or character on a natural person. It is no more a State instrument, than a natural person exercising the same powers would be. If, then, a natural person, employed by individuals in the education of youth, or for the government of a seminary in which youth is educated, would not become a public officer, or be considered as a member of the civil government, how is it that this artificial being, created by law, for the purpose of being employed by the same individuals for the same purposes, should become a part of the civil government of the country? Is it because its existence, its capacities, its powers, are given by law? Because the government has given it the power to take and to hold property in a particular form, and for particular purposes, has the government a consequent right substantially to change that form, or to vary the purposes to which the property is to be applied? This principle has never been asserted or recognized, and is supported by no authority. Can it derive aid from reason?

The objects for which a corporation is created are universally such as the government wishes to promote. They are deemed beneficial to the country; and this benefit constitutes the consideration, and, in most cases, the sole consideration, of the grant. In most eleemosynary institutions, the object would be difficult, perhaps unattainable, without the aid of a charter of incorporation. Charitable, or public spirited individuals, desirous of making permanent appropriations for charitable or other useful purposes, find it impossible to effect their design, securely and certainly, without an incorporating act. They apply to the government, state their beneficent object, and offer to advance the money necessary for its accomplishment, provided the government will confer on the instrument, which is to execute their designs, the capacity to execute them. The proposition is considered and approved. The benefit to the public is considered as an ample compensation for the faculty it confers, and the corporation is created. If the advantages to the public constitute a full compensation for the faculty it gives, there can be no reason for exacting a further compensation, by claiming a right to exercise over this artificial being a power which changes its nature, and touches the fund, for the security and application of which it was created. There can be no reason for implying in a charter, given for a valuable consideration, a power which is not only not expressed, but is in direct contradiction to its express stipulations.

From the fact, then, that a charter of incorporation has been granted, nothing can be inferred which changes the character of the institution, or transfers to the government any new power over it. The character of civil institutions does not grow out of their incorporation, but out of the manner in which they are formed, and the objects for which they are created. The right to change them is not founded on their being incorporated, but on their being the instruments of government, created for its purposes. The same institutions, created for the same objects, though not incorporated, would be public institutions, and, of course, be controllable by the legislature. The incorporating act neither gives nor prevents this control. Neither, in reason, can the incorporating act change the character of a private eleemosynary institution.

We are next led to the inquiry, for whose benefit the property given to Dartmouth College was secured? The counsel for the defendant have insisted, that the beneficial interest is in the people of New Hampshire. The charter, after reciting the preliminary measures which had been taken, and the application for an act of incorporation, proceeds thus: "Know ye, therefore, that we, considering the premises, and being willing to encourage the laudable and charitable design of spreading Christian knowledge among the savages of our American wilderness, and, also, that the best means of education be established, in our province of New Hampshire, for the benefit of said province, do, of our special grace," &c. Do these expressions bestow on New Hampshire any exclusive right to the property of the college, any exclusive interest in the labors of the professors? Or do they merely indicate a willingness that New Hampshire should enjoy those advantages which result to all from the establishment of a seminary of learning in the neighborhood? On this point we think it impossible to entertain a serious doubt. The words themselves, unexplained by the context, indicate, that the "benefit intended for the province" is that which is derived from "establishing the best means of education therein;" that is, from establishing in the province Dartmouth College, as constituted by the charter. But if these words, considered alone, could admit of doubt, that doubt is completely removed by an inspection of the entire instrument.

The particular interests of New Hampshire never entered into the mind of the donors, never constituted a motive for their donation. The propagation of the Christian religion among the savages, and the dissemination of useful knowledge among the youth of the country, were the avowed and the sole objects of their contributions. * * * The clause which constitutes the incorporation, and expresses the objects for which it was made, declares those objects to be the instruction of the Indians, "and also of English youth, and any others." So that the objects of the contributors, and the incorporating act, were the same; the promotion of Christianity, and of education generally, not the interests of New Hampshire particularly.

From this review of the charter, it appears, that Dartmouth College is an eleemosynary institution, incorporated for the purpose of perpetuating the application of the bounty of the donors, to the specified objects of that bounty; that its trustees or governors were originally named by the founder, and invested with the power of perpetuating themselves; that they are not public officers, nor is it a civil institution, participating in the administration of government; but a charity school, or a seminary of education, incorporated for the preservation of its property, and the perpetual application of that property to the objects of its creation. * * *

This is plainly a contract to which the donors, the trustees, and the crown, (to whose rights and obligations New Hampshire succeeds,) were the original parties. It is a contract made on a valuable consideration. It is a contract for the security and disposition of property. It is a contract, on the faith of which, real and personal estate has been conveyed to the corporation. It is then a contract within the letter of the constitution, and within its spirit also, unless the fact that the property is invested by the donors in trustees, for the promotion of religion and education, for the benefit of persons who are perpetually changing, though the objects remain the same, shall create a particular exception, taking this case out of the prohibition contained in the constitution. * * *

The opinion of the court, after mature deliberation, is, that this is a contract, the obligation of which cannot be impaired, without violating the constitution of the United States. This opinion appears to us to be equally supported by reason, and by the former decisions of this court.

2. We next proceed to the inquiry, whether its obligation has been impaired by those acts of the legislature of New Hampshire, to which the special verdict refers.

From the review of this charter, which has been taken, it appears that the whole power of governing the college, of appointing and removing tutors, of fixing their salaries, of directing the course of study to be pursued by the students, and of filling up vacancies created in their own body, was vested in the trustees. On the part of the crown, it was expressly stipulated that this corporation, thus constituted, should continue forever; and that the number of trustees should forever consist of twelve, and no more. By this contract, the crown was bound, and could have made no violent alteration in its essential terms, without impairing its obligation.

By the Revolution, the duties as well as the powers of government devolved on the people of New Hampshire. It is admitted, that among the latter was comprehended the transcendent power of parliament, as well as that of the executive department. It is too clear to require the support of argument, that all contracts and rights, respecting property, remained unchanged by the Revolution. The obligations, then, which were created by the charter to Dartmouth College, were the same in the new that they had been in the old government. The power of the government was also the same. A repeal of this charter at any time prior to the adoption of the present constitution of the United States, would have been an extraordinary and unprecedented act of power, but one which could have been contested only by the restrictions upon the legislature, to be found in the constitution of the State. But the constitution of the United States has imposed this additional limitation, that the legislature of a State shall pass no act "impairing the obligation of contracts."

It has been already stated, that the act "to amend the charter, and enlarge and improve the corporation of Dartmouth College," increases the number of trustees to twenty-one, gives the appointment of the additional members to the executive of the State, and creates a board of overseers, to consist of twenty-five persons, of whom twenty-one are also appointed by the executive of New Hampshire, who have power to inspect and control the most important acts of the trustees.

On the effect of this law, two opinions cannot be entertained. Between acting directly, and acting through the agency of trustees and overseers, no essential difference is perceived. The whole power of governing the college is transferred from trustees, appointed according to the will of the founder, expressed in the charter, to the executive of New Hampshire. The management and application of the funds of this eleemosynary institution, which are placed by the donors in the hands of trustees named in the charter, and empowered to perpetuate themselves, are placed by this act under the control of the government of the State. The will of the State is

substituted for the will of the donors, in every essential operation of the college. This is not an immaterial change. The founders of the college contracted, not merely for the perpetual application of the funds which they gave, to the objects for which those funds were given; they contracted also, to secure that application by the constitution of the corporation. They contracted for a system, which should, as far as human foresight can provide, retain forever the government of the literary institution they had formed, in the hands of persons approved by themselves. This system is totally changed. The charter of 1769 exists no longer. It is reorganized; and reorganized in such a manner, as to convert a literary institution, moulded according to the will of its founders, and placed under the control of private literary men, into a machine entirely subservient to the will of government. This may be for the advantage of this college in particular, and may be for the advantage of literature in general; but it is not according to the will of the donors, and is subversive of that contract, on the faith of which their property was given.
* * *

It results from this opinion, that the acts of the legislature of New Hampshire, which are stated in the special verdict found in this cause, are repugnant to the constitution of the United States, and that the judgment on this special verdict ought to have been for the plaintiffs. The judgment of the state court must, therefore, be reversed.

College as a public corporation

LEWIS v. WHITTLE

Supreme Court of Appeals of Virginia, 1883.
77 Va. 415.

It is earnestly contended by respondents that this college is a private corporation and not under the control of the governor, or any other public authority, * * *.

In 1854 the Medical College was incorporated, with a board of visitors—nineteen in number, and the said visitors were named in the charter.

By the seventh section it was provided, that "whenever any vacancy shall *occur* in the said board by reason of death, resignation or otherwise, *then* the governor shall fill the same, selecting the visitors so appointed from each of the grand divisions of the state."

The board of visitors were required to make an annual report to the second auditor, such as is required by the twelfth section of the eighty-third chapter of the Code.

In the charter, the legislature reserved the right at its pleasure to modify, alter, or repeal the charter, provided for an acceptance by the then existing faculty, and disclaimed any intention by the legislature to reflect on the trustees of Hampden-Sidney College, or the faculty of the medical school in Richmond.

Before the passage of this act there was a medical school in Richmond, which was under the patronage of Hampden-Sidney College. Dissensions between the faculty of the medical school and the trustees of Hampden-Sidney College led to the act of incorporation seen above. In 1860 the legislature appropriated $30,000 to this college upon the condition that the college authorities should execute and record a deed conveying all the property of the college to the literary fund of the state; this deed to be drawn by the attorney-general and approved by the governor. This deed was executed, and by another act of February 26, 1866, the legislature of the state appropriated $1,500 to the said college, which has been annually appropriated by the legislature ever since. This brief history of this college shows that once in its history it was a private school; that upon its solicitation, and by the consent of its authorities it was incorporated, and the succession of its board of visitors placed under public control; that by subsequent solicitation and consent it parted with all its property to the state, and executed and delivered a deed to the state for the same, and received from the state $30,000. That subsequently it has solicited and received $1,500 annually from the state, and has undertaken to submit an annual report, on the part, both of its board of visitors and of its faculty, to a public officer of the state; so that it now appears, by its own consent, to have become a public corporation, holding its life and chartered existence, and the possession of all its property, at the pleasure of the legislature of the state.

Strictly speaking, public corporations are such only as are founded by the government for public purposes—where the whole interest belong also to the government.

The *Trustees of Dartmouth College v. Woodward*, 4 Wheaton, 669. See opinion of Story, judge.

This medical college is in every sense a public corporation, made so in the manner already stated. The visitors of this college are then holding under an act of the legislature a public office or employment, subject to the control and direction of the state—to be appointed and to be removed by competent public authority. The visitorial power of this college is therefore in the state of Virginia, and to be exercised under the laws of the state. What is the competent public authority vested by law with the power to remove the visitors of the said college? This is the last and only question in this controversy about which there can be any real dispute.

To this question, in fact, has been mainly directed the efforts of the counsel who have argued this case here. Many authorities have been cited, and illustrations drawn from the common law offices, and the rules and principles by which they are governed, have no application to such offices as these. The tenure in those cases depends upon ancient usage in a great measure. But here we have no ancient usage which can apply to and govern the tenure of offices created by our constitution and laws. They are of recent origin, and must depend entirely on a just construction of the law by which they are created. In such case, the tenure of the office must be determined by the meaning and intention of the statute by which they are created.

What are the terms of the charter of this college concerning the visitors appointed thereunder?

The legislature not only incorporates the college, but appoints the board of visitors; it *reserves* the right to *modify, alter* or *amend* the charter at its pleasure. It grants to the governor of this state certain powers, and so far as these powers are granted and no further, can they be exercised by the governor. Under our system of government, the governor has and can rightly exercise no power except such as may be bestowed upon him by the constitution and the laws. The charter of this college confers on him the power to fill by executive appointment such vacancies as may *occur* in the office of visitor of this college by *death*, resignation or otherwise. The power to fill vacancies as they have occurred for the last twenty-nine years, comprising the existence of the college has been exercised by many successive governors of this state, and has never been questioned or denied.

But, as is disclosed by the proceedings here, on the 22nd day of September, 1882, the governor *removed* the entire board of visitors of the college. The said board of visitors deny the power or authority of the governor to so remove them, and refuse to give possession of the college to petitioners here, who have been designated by the governor as their successors, and this court is now asked by *mandamus* to compel the said respondents to surrender possession of the said college. * * * Petitioners claim that the governor is the appointing power, and that without any express authority in the law the power to remove is incident to the power to appoint. Into this wide and much contested field it cannot be necessary to go until we settle the question whether the governor is the appointing power. By the charter of the college, as we have seen, the legislature appointed the visitors, and reserved to itself only the power to *alter* or *modify* or *amend* the said charter. The appointing power in *general* terms is not conferred on the governor in the charter, but a limited power of appointment —to wit, the power to fill vacancies—and when we look to see what vacancies we find that the power is granted to fill vacancies that may occur (that is, may happen—an occurrence is an accidental event) by death, resignation, or otherwise. A death may occur, a resignation may occur, and the attorney-general insists earnestly in the argument in this case that the word otherwise, coupled with the word occur—that is, *"occur otherwise"*—is broad enough to cover a wholesale removal of the nineteen members of the board by a single order to that end. If the legislature had so desired or intended, it was as easy to use the word removal as any actually used, and we think it is safer to consider that such words as are used are those intended to be used, and such words as are not used were not intended to be used.

If we consider this charter in the light of the circumstances which surrounded its enactment, we are strengthened in our views. When it was enacted, the state was not the owner, as now, of all its property, and was not, as now, maintaining the college, in part, by annual appropriations. The power to repeal was reserved, and it may be inferred that as long as the college was used for the purposes for which it was incorporated, that there could be no desire to repeal the charter, or to remove the visitors, and no such desire existing, it would be a strained construction to discern an authority to remove, ingeniously disguised in an authority to fill occurring vacancies. If we remember that the state had at the time the charter was granted no greater interest in the college than such as might desire its greatest usefulness and prosperity, independent of any right of property therein, it is not difficult to discover why removals were not provided for, and indeed why no term was limited in the office of visitor. And when we remember that in twenty-eight years, this act has received only this construction at the hands of successive governors, who, during many successive terms of office, and many years, have filled only such vacancies as have occurred under the terms and within the exact limit of the language itself, we are sustained by the contemporaneous construction which this charter has thus received. If the present governor of the state is authorized to make these removals, then each governor who has filled the gubernatorial office since 1854, has had the same authority, and yet it has never been exercised. If the governor of the state had, under this charter, enacted in 1854, removed all the visitors of this college in 1855, it would have doubtless been received with surprise, but it cannot be denied that *he* would have had all the authority which exists now to that end.

This much for the executive contemporaneous construction of this charter. What has been the legislative construction of the same? The attorney-general, in the argument of this case here, exhibited two bills introduced into the legislature of the state at its last session, having for their object the removal of the board of visitors of this college. If the legislative construction of this charter was that the governor already had the power to remove all the visitors and appoint others, where was the necessity of passing a law to that effect? * * *

But no case has been cited, and no case, we believe, can be cited, where an officer appointed by the legislature is held to be removable by the governor without *express authority to that end*, and where the power to fill a casual and occurring vacancy, a power to appoint expressly limited, has been ever held to carry with it, either a general power of appointment or the authority *to remove*, and so create *a vacancy* in order to fill it.

To conclude, we are of opinion that the power of visitation as to this college, is in the state, and by the charter expressly reserved in the legislature, and not granted to the governor. We hazard nothing in saying that there is no such thing in this state as a visitor holding, as in England, by life tenure. These visitors in this case hold simply at the will of the legislature, subject to be removed whenever the legislature shall so provide—the legislature has not so provided; and so the writ in this case must be denied.

MANDAMUS DENIED.

NOTES

1. The power of the legislature to create public corporations is practically unlimited. It may create any conceivable

kind of corporation it deems necessary for the more efficient
administration of public affairs and endow the corporation
with such powers and functions as it deems necessary and
proper. In creating corporations, the legislature provides for
officers through whom corporate powers are exercised and
corporate functions performed. When the legislature creates
an office, either public or corporate, such office is wholly
within the power of the legislature and as such the legislature can prescribe and limit the powers and duties of the
incumbent holding office. People *ex rel.* Board of Trustees of
University of Illinois v. Barrett, 382 Ill. 321, 46 N.E.2d
951 (1943).

2. Incorporated universities which are founded and supported by the state are generally treated by the courts as
being public, rather than private, corporations. Russell v.
Trustees of Purdue University, 168 N.E. 529 (1929).

3. When universities are founded and supported by the
state they are generally treated by the courts as *public* rather
than *private* corporations. State *ex rel.* Little v. University of
Kansas, 55 Kan. 389, 40 P. 656.

4. The Florida Agricultural College, having been founded
by the state with public money derived in trust from the
government of the United States, is a *public* corporation, and
the legislature has the power to change the school's trustees.
State v. Knowles, 16 Fla. 577.

5. The Supreme Court of Alabama in a very old, 1833, case
decided that the University of Alabama was a public corporation and as such, its incorporation charter could be altered by
the legislature. The plaintiffs in the case had contended that
the University was a private corporation, that it was first
created by contract, and that any material alteration in the
contract by the Alabama legislature would constitute a violation of the "obligation of contracts" provision of the federal
constitution. The court's discussion of issue was as follows:

> It probably would be sufficient reply to this objection,
> to say, that the corporators have assented to, by acting
> under every statute amendatory of the original act consti-
> tuting them a corporation, which has been passed. * * *
> We will, however, examine the position apart from this
> consideration.
>
> Probably a fuller investigation of the distinctive char-
> acteristics of public and private corporations, can no
> where be found, than in the celebrated case of the "Dart-
> mouth College vs. Woodward," decided by the Supreme
> Court of the United States, and reported in 4 Wheat. 518
> [4 L. Ed. 629]. It is admitted throughout the argument

and in the opinion of the Court, in that case, that if the property possessed by a corporation is altogether the property of the State, if the corporators have paid and done nothing, amounting to a valuable consideration for the act of incorporation; in fine, if there is no contract upon valuable consideration between the State and the corporators, it is a public, not a private corporation. If it be public, it is certainly within the complete control of the General Assembly.

The counsel for the Dartmouth College, in the argument, asked, "if the property of this corporation be public, when did it become so?"

The opinion of the Court is rested entirely upon that clause in the Constitution of the United States which declares that "no State shall pass any law impairing the obligation of contracts." This language is used in the opinion, (page 627 [4 Wheat., page 656 4 L. Ed.]) —"It can require no argument to prove that the circumstances of this case constitute a contract. An application is made to the Crown for a charter to incorporate a religious and literary institution. In the application, it is stated that large contributions have been made for the object, which will be conferred on the corporation, as soon as it shall be created. The charter is granted, and on its faith the property is conveyed. Surely in this transaction, every ingredient of a complete and legitimate contract, is to be found."

Again, on pages 629, 630 [4 Wheat., page 657, 4 L. Ed.] —"If the act of incorporation be a grant of political power, if it create a civil institution to be employed in the administration of the government, or if the funds of the College be public property, or if the State of New Hampshire, as a government, be alone interested in its transactions, the subject is one in which the Legislature of the State may act according to its own judgment, unrestrained by any limitation of its power, imposed by the Constitution of the United States."

Does the act of incorporation, in the case at bar, form a contract upon valuable consideration?

If it does, what is the consideration from which the members of the corporation or any other person, has parted, or what risk do they run, or labor have they undertaken, to form that consideration? It is true they have many services and duties imposed upon them by the charter; but for all these, they have compensation allowed them out of the funds of the institution. But whence are these funds derived? They are altogether public property. The lands from which they accrue, have been granted to the State by the United States, for the purpose of endowing a University, it is true, yet the property in these lands is not the less in the State because the purpose to which they are to be appropriated is restricted in the grant.

Chief Justice Marshall, in the same opinion from which

the foregoing extracts are made, also says—"the character of civil institutions does not grow out of their incorporation, but out of the manner in which they are formed, and the objects for which they are created. The right to change them is not founded on their being incorporated, but on their being the instruments of government, created for its purposes."

What is the corporation, consisting of the President and Trustees of the University of Alabama, but an "instrument of government, created for its purposes?" It is true this instrumentality is confined to the disposition of a particular part of the public domain, the collection and appropriation of the proceeds in a particular way, the erection of College buildings, and other duties attendant upon the establishment and support of an institution of learning. Yet this institution is, in every respect, a public one, originated and prosecuted by legislative enactment, towards which no citizen has contributed one cent, either in money, other property, labor, or services, even as a trustee, without pecuniary remuneration.

It is useless to refer to other books, to prove that this is a public corporation. Authorities might easily be multiplied, but it would be a work of supererogation.

While we would unhesitatingly maintain the doctrine that an act establishing a private corporation, forms a contract by which the state is bound, we have no doubt but the President and Trustees of the University of Alabama, constitute a public corporation, and that their charter may be altered, amended, or repealed, by the General Assembly, at pleasure.

Trustees of the University of Alabama v. Winston, 5 Stew. & P. 17, 5 Ala. Rep. 1 (1833).

Consolidation of college and university continues property rights in new corporation

CENTRAL UNIVERSITY OF KENTUCKY v. WALTERS' EXECUTORS

Court of Appeals of Kentucky, 1906.
122 Ky. 65, 90 S.W. 1066.

O'REAR, J. A schism in the Presbyterian Church of the United States of America resulted in about 1865 in the withdrawal of a considerable number of its members, who subsequently organized themselves into a separate body known as the Presbyterian Church of the United States. Historically their difference grew out of political questions and the deep

feeling wrought by the distractions of the Civil War, then just ended. There seems to have been no difference in doctrinal faith or teaching. The original church had in 1819 founded an institution of liberal education at Danville, Ky., Centre College. It had been maintained as an institution of the church, and had been added to all along until 1901. After the division of the church in 1865, the Presbyterian Church of the United States, usually called the "Southern Presbyterian Church," found itself, as the result of unsuccessful litigation with the other branch, generally called the "Northern Presbyterian Church," without an educational institution; it having been decided by the courts that the school property belonged exclusively to the latter body. Thus excluded from participation in the control of the college, in which hitherto they had been interested in common with their fellows, they set about establishing one of their own, where their youth could be instructed in the liberal arts and sciences under tutorship and conditions believed to be most consistent with their spiritual faith and temporal well-being. So, in 1872, at a gathering at Lexington, Ky., of the alumni of Centre College and the alumni of other institutions of learning who held allegiance to Southern Presbyterianism, a memorial was addressed to the Synod of Kentucky (Southern Presbyterian), submitting that it was the sense of that convention "that steps be taken to at once establish, on a broad and liberal basis, an institution of the highest order, under the auspices of the Synod of Kentucky, and thus carry out the earnest wishes of the fathers, as demonstrated by the establishment of Centre College, now lost to this church." As a result of the representations and efforts then made and undertaken, a university was established under the auspices of the Southern Presbyterian Church in Kentucky, acting officially and formally through its synod. A charter was procured from the Kentucky Legislature March 3, 1873. The institution thus formed was named the "Central University of Kentucky." An endowment was provided by donations subscribed by members and friends of that church.
* * *

In the provision for securing an endowment, as an inducement to subscribers it was stipulated that they had the right severally to designate the chair or purpose to which the subscription should be applied. The articles expressly prohibited a diversion of money or other thing subscribed specially for a particular purpose to a different one. In casting about for a location for the school, Richmond was finally selected. The citizens of that town and the county of Madison were liberal in their donations, which doubtless controlled the selection. Among them Mr. S. P. Walters, husband of Ann W. Walters, was conspicuous as one of the most generous. * * * He subscribed first and last $26,000 toward the endowment of the university. * * * After the death of his son, Henry Bell Walters, he gave $8,000 more; the whole of his subscription to be dedicated to founding and maintaining a chair in the university, to be called the "Henry Bell Walters Professorship of Mathematics." He contemplated adding $4,000 more to this endowment, but died before it was done. After his death his widow, Ann W. Walters, who was also a member of that church residing at Richmond, to carry out her late husband's wishes (which were in accord with her own), to raise the endowment of the Henry Bell Walters Chair of Mathematics to $30,000, executed her note to the university for $4,000. The note is as follows: "Richmond, Ky., March 29th, 1886. Feeling a deep interest in Christian education, and especially in the education of young men for the gospel ministry, I promise to pay to the order of the board of curators of the Central University of Kentucky the sum of four thousand dollars ($4,000), to be paid at my death; the said curators binding themselves to add this amount ($4,000) to the sum of $26,000, contributed by my late husband, S. P. Walters, for the endowment of the Henry Bell Walters Professorship of Mathematics in said university. Ann W. Walters."

In 1901 the financial condition of the Central University was far from promising. Indeed, in the opinion of its managers and most interested friends, it was believed to be unable to accomplish, with the income it was receiving and with the constituency back of it, the purpose for which it was established. Its failure was contemplated as a probability, unless new ways and means of support could be supplied. Negotiations between Central University and Centre College were opened, resulting in an agreement for their consolidation. The agreement was submitted to the synods of the respective churches, and approved, and was finally executed in form by the official boards of the two institutions, so as to comply with the requirements of Kentucky Statutes concerning consolidation of corporations. The title of the new corporation is "Central University of Kentucky." The articles of consolidation provide: "Said Central University of Kentucky shall be vested with and own all property, business, credits, assets, and effects of said constituent corporations without further deed of transfer, and shall be bound for all the contracts and liabilities of each of the constituent corporations. * * * This trans-

fer and conveyance are made subject to the trust herein declared respecting particular property. * * * (7) All property
and funds which have been donated or contributed to either of
said constituent corporations for the support or maintenance
of special chairs or schools, or for any specific purpose, shall be
held by said Central University of Kentucky, and dedicated
to and used for such specific purpose, in accordance with the
terms of the gift or contract under which the same shall have
been received." * * *

This consolidation having been effected, it is conceded that
the school formerly taught at Richmond under the auspices of
old Central University has been discontinued, but that the
new institution has conducted and is conducting the school at
Danville upon the lines indicated in the new charter, at which
is maintained a chair of mathematics known as the "Henry
Bell Walters Professorship of Mathematics." After the consolidation had been consummated in 1901, Mrs. Ann W.
Walters brought this suit against Central University of Kentucky to cancel the $4,000 note set out above. She alleged that
the consideration for which it had been executed had failed;
that the payee thereof, the Central University of Kentucky,
had voluntarily surrendered its charter, abandoned its purpose
of conducting the school therein required, and was therefore
unable to maintain the chair for which the subscription had
been made. It is also claimed that the note was voluntary, and
that the maker had revoked it as an executory promise to give
money. * * *

When the state, by the general law enacted in 1893, provided for the consolidation of corporations in this state, the
statute became as it were a part of the charter of the Central
University, as if written therein originally. We do not mean to
go further here than to decide the precise question presented,
which is the power of the corporation to consolidate with
another corporation having the same end to accomplish and
using substantially the same means to accomplish it. So long
as the consolidated corporation undertook to do the thing
originally undertaken by its constituents, we hold that the
purpose of the original incorporators and of those whose
means set the thing on foot was not being diverted. The only
matter altered was the means by which it was to be accomplished. The statute (Carroll's Ky. St. 1903, § 555) provides:
"Any two or more corporations organized under this chapter
or under the law of this state, may consolidate into a single
corporation." This power of consolidation is conferred in

amplest terms. It is not confined to any class of corporations.
* * *

While the statute provides that the old corporations shall
cease to exist upon such consolidation, it was never intended
to destroy anything except the separate identity, the shell, as
it were, preserving, however, all that was vital or valuable.
The object was, not to destroy, but to preserve and enlarge.
The result is amalgamation, not annihilation.

Some courts, construing somewhat similar statutes, have
noticed a distinction between consolidation and merger; the
former term being used to describe the result of two corporations being combined into a new one, and the latter to describe
the result where one corporation absorbs another. As corporate franchises are generally deemed unassignable without
permission of the state, a merger is, after all, under our statute at least, a consolidation; for, although the old name of one
may be retained and the other dropped, still the course to be
pursued under the statute for one corporation to acquire the
property and franchises of another is precisely the same as if
an entirely new name were adopted. The result is a merging
of corporate property and constituents, as where two streams
flow together. At the junction they may be said to constitute a
new stream, but essentially the latter takes in and is made
up of all that formerly flowed in and now flows out of the two
from which it gets its being. To use another figure, it is a
marriage of two, in which neither is lost, but in which the two
are blended into one in contemplation of law. The original
corporate existence is merely a legal status. It is not a thing
at all. The power that gave it its so-called existence is competent to change it into a new being, with all the rights and
attributes of the old. No physical phenomenon is involved. The
legislative purpose, and the practical application of it, will not
stagger in execution at an imaginary difficulty in harmonizing
a thing dead with a thing which is alive. We are of opinion,
and hold, that the effect of the consolidation was to continue
in the new corporation, Central University of Kentucky, all
the franchises, and vest in it all the property rights, subject to
the terms upon which it was acquired, of the two constituent
corporations, the Central University of Kentucky and Centre
College of Kentucky. This carried over to appellant all notes
and other property owned by those two corporations, which
included the note forming the subject of this suit. * * *

As there is nothing in the note, or in the contemporaneous
transaction, binding the payee to apply the money otherwise
than in the maintenance of a chair of mathematics in its uni-

versity, being conducted for Christian education, there was no limitation upon the power of the payee to change the location of its school or schools, or to change the manner of their government, or the adoption of particular means of effectuating the general purpose for which the institution was founded. The very nature of the enterprise, on the contrary, looked to improvement. It contemplated, by every reasonable implication, that new methods, new people, even new ideas, would be employed, when approved by the governing body of the institution. A college means, or ought to mean, growth; the elimination of the false; the fostering of the true. As it is expected to be perpetual in its service, it must conform to the changed condition of each new generation, possessing an elasticity of scope and work commensurate with the changing requirements of the times which it serves. For the past to bind it to unchangeableness would be to prevent growth, applying the treatment to the head that the Chinese do to the feet. Presbyterians as a body have always been noted as patrons of education. This characteristic, shared signally by the Walterses, will not, upon mere conjecture, be restrictive into the unnatural, self-destructive channel now contended for by appellees. Their subscriptions to this college, in the absence of some limitation in the agreement, must be conclusively deemed to have been in accord with the general purpose of the educational movement then undertaken by the body of the church, and necessarily subject to the power of the governing constituency of the institution to conform its course and adopt such means to the accomplishment of its great purpose, as are not inconsistent with its object or with the charter granted by the state. So, when the governing body and all the constituents of the corporation have decided to change the location of the university, to include a broader field of work, to add new forces and bring to its aid additional endowment, all tending to the same end contemplated in its establishment, the enterprise is not abandoned, but is continued; and subscriptions made to it are enforceable, whether their consideration is the maintenance of the original institution or particular chairs therein, if such chairs are in fact maintained by the new institution. This is in no sense an application of the cy-pres doctrine; the substitution by the court of an equivalent for the charitable use selected by the donor. The finding is, on the contrary, that the original object still exists and is being conducted to all intents and purposes as contemplated by the donor and the trustees. Therefore, there is not a failure of the consideration of the note sued on.

Wherefore the judgment of the circuit court is reversed, and cause remanded, with directions to overrule the demurrer to the answer, and for further proceedings not inconsistent herewith.

University is not under control of Legislature

STERLING v. REGENTS OF THE UNIVERSITY OF MICHIGAN

Supreme Court of Michigan, 1896.
110 Mich. 369, 68 N.W. 253.

In 1895 the legislature passed Act No. 257, Laws 1895, the material part of which reads as follows: "That the board of regents of the University of Michigan are hereby authorized and directed to establish a homeopathic medical college as a branch or department of said university, which shall be located in the city of Detroit, and the said board of regents are hereby authorized and directed to discontinue the existing homeopathic college now maintained in the city of Ann Arbor as a branch of said university and to transfer the same to the city of Detroit." The title of the act is "An act to amend sec. one of an act entitled, 'An act for the establishment of a homeopathic medical department of the University of Michigan,' approved April 27, 1875, being sec. 4932 of How. Ann. St." The regents of the university declined to comply with said act. The relator thereupon presented this petition for the writ of mandamus to compel the regents to comply with the act. The ground for such refusal is (1) that it was not, in their judgment, for the best interests of the university; (2) that the legislature has no constitutional right to interfere with or dictate the management of the university. * * * The claim which is made under the application of the relator, that the provisions of Act No. 257 command the discontinuance and removal of the homeopathic medical department of the university by the regents, without any reference to their power of supervision of the university, suggests to the regents the question whether such provisions do not curtail and impair the power of supervision and control of the university which has been vested in the regents by the constitution of the state. It is the purpose, as well as the plain duty, of the regents, to exercise, according to their best judgment, the supervision and control of the university, which has been vested in them by the state constitution, to promote both the interests of the university and the interests of the people of the state, which are involved in the welfare of the university. * * *

The University of Michigan was founded under an act of congress making an appropriation of lands for the support of a university in this state, approved May 20, 1826. * * *

Under the constitution of 1835, the legislature had the entire control and management of the university and the university fund. They could appoint regents and professors and establish departments. The university was not a success under this supervision by the legislature, and, as some of the members of the constitutional convention of 1850 said in their debates, "some of the denominational colleges had more students than did the university." Such was the condition of affairs when that convention met. It is apparent to any reader of the debates in this convention in regard to the constitutional provision for the university that they had in mind the idea of permanency of location, to place it beyond mere political influence, and to intrust it to those who should be directly responsible and amenable to the people. * * * The public men of those times were greatly interested in the university. Methods for its management were discussed by governors in their messages, by reports of the board of regents to the legislature, and by committees of the legislature. The general consensus of opinion was that it should be under the control and management of a permanent board, who should be responsible for its management. The regents, in March, 1840, in obedience to a joint resolution of the legislature, reported that "the first change in the organic law deemed essential is the proper restriction of responsibility to the board of regents. At present the responsibility is divided, and the board would be greatly facilitated in their action were such amendments made as would throw entire responsibility on them." In the same report they also urged that the trust and management of the funds of the university should be placed in the regents. A select committee was appointed by the legislature in 1840 to inquire into the condition of the university. No more forcible argument could well be made than is found in that report for placing the entire control of the university in the hands of a permanent board, and taking it away from the legislature. House Documents 1840, p. 470. I quote from that report as follows: "* * * The argument by which legislatures have hitherto convinced themselves that it was their duty to legislate universities to death is this: 'It is a state institution, and we are the direct representatives of the people, and therefore it is expected of us; it is our right. The people have an interest in this thing, and we must attend to it.' As if, because a university belongs to the people, that were reason why it should be dosed to death for fear it would be sick, if left to be nursed, like other institutions, by its immediate guardians. Thus has state after state, in this American Union, endowed universities, and then, by repeated contradictory and over legislation, torn them to pieces with the same facility as they do the statute book, and for the same reason, because they have the right." All these reports and discussions were undoubtedly known to the members of the convention, and their action should be construed in the light of such knowledge. I am unable to find a single utterance by any member of that convention from which it could be inferred that the members believed or supposed that they were leaving the control of that institution to the legislature. The result has proved their wisdom, for the university, which was before practically a failure, under the guidance of this constitutional body, known as the "Board of Regents," has grown to be one of the most successful, the most complete, and the best-known institutions of learning in the world. * * *

The provisions of the constitution of 1850 in regard to the university are these (article 13):

"Sec. 2. The proceeds from the sales of all lands that have been or hereafter may be granted by the United States to this state, for educational purposes, and the proceeds of all lands or other property given by individuals, or appropriated by the state for like purposes, shall be and remain a perpetual fund, the interest and income of which, together with the rents of all such lands as may remain unsold, shall be inviolably appropriated and annually applied to the specific objects of the original gift, grant or appropriation."

"Sec. 6. There shall be elected in the year 1863, at the time of the election of a justice of the supreme court, eight regents of the university, two of whom shall hold their office for two years, two for four years, two for six years and two for eight years. They shall enter upon the duties of their office on the first of January next succeeding their election. At every regular election of a justice of the supreme court thereafter, there shall be elected two regents, whose term of office shall be eight years. When a vacancy shall occur in the office of regent, it shall be filled by appointment of the governor. The regents thus elected shall constitute the board of regents of the University of Michigan.

"Sec. 7. The regents of the university, and their successors in office, shall continue to constitute the body corporate, known by the name and title of the 'Regents of the University of Michigan.'

"Sec. 8. The regents of the university shall, at their first annual meeting, or so soon thereafter as may be, elect a president of the university, who shall be ex officio a member of their board, with the privilege of speaking but not of voting. He shall preside at the meetings of the regents, and be the principal executive officer of the university. The board of regents shall have the general supervision of the university, and the direction and control of all expenditures from the university interest fund."

The board of regents, elected under the new constitution, immediately took control of the university, interpreted the constitution in accordance with its plain provisions, denied the power of the legislature to interfere with its management or control, and for 46 years have declined obedience to any and every act of the legislature which they, upon mature reflection and consideration, have deemed against the best interests of the institution. * * * It is obvious to every intelligent and reflecting mind that such an institution would be safer and more certain of permanent success in the control of such a body than in that of the legislature, composed of 132 members, elected every two years, many of whom would, of necessity, know but little of its needs, and would have little or no time to intelligently investigate and determine the policy essential for the success of a great university.

Now, in the face of the facts that the regents have for 46 years exercised such control, and openly asserted its exclusive right to do so; that the courts have refused to compel them to comply with the acts of the legislature; that this court held in Weinberg v. Regents, 97 Mich. 246, 56 N. W. 608, that they were a constitutional body, upon whom was conferred this exclusive control; and in the face of this plain constitutional provision,—this court is now asked to hold that the regents are mere ministerial officers, endowed with the sole power to register the will of the legislature, and to supervise such branches and departments as any legislature may see fit to provide for. By the power claimed, the legislature may completely dismember the university, and remove every vestige of it from the city of Ann Arbor. It is no argument to say that there is no danger of such a result. The question is one of power, and who shall say that such a result may not follow? The legislature did once enact that there should be a branch of the university in every judicial circuit. If the regents comply with the present act, the next legislature may repeal it, and restore that department to the university at Ann Arbor, or place it elsewhere. Some legislatures have attached conditions, and they have the undoubted right to do so, to appropriations for the support of the university, and a subsequent legislature has removed the conditions. Some legislatures have attached to appropriations the condition for the establishment of a homeopathic professorship in the old medical department. Other legislatures have refused to attach any such condition. What permanency would there be in an institution thus subject to the caprice and will of every legislature? Under this power, the legislature could remove the law department from the university at Ann Arbor to Detroit, and provide that the law library, to which one citizen of Michigan has donated $20,000, could also be removed. * * * It appears to us impossible that such a power was contemplated. Furthermore, it renders nugatory the express provision of the constitution that "the regents shall have the direction and control of all expenditures from the university interest fund." It is significant that, at the time of the adoption of the constitution, this fund constituted the sole support of the university, aside from fees which might be received from students. The state had made no appropriations for its support, and there is nothing to indicate that any such appropriations were contemplated. It is unnecessary to argue that the above provision means what it says, and that it takes away from the legislature all control over the income from that fund. The power therein conferred would be without force or effect if the legislature could control these expenditures by dictating what departments of learning the regents shall establish, and in what places they shall be located. Neither does it need any argument to show that the power contended for would take away from the regents the control and direction of the expenditures from the fund. The power to control these expenditures cannot be exercised directly or indirectly by the legislature. It is vested in the board of regents in absolute and unqualified terms. This act, in express terms, prohibits the regents from using any of this fund to support a homeopathic department at the university at Ann Arbor, since it prohibits them from maintaining such a department there. This power cannot be sustained without overruling the case of Weinberg v. Regents. The basis of the majority opinion in that case is

that the board of regents is a constitutional body, charged by
the constitution with the entire control of that institution.
The result could not have been reached upon any other basis.
It was held not to be a state institution under the control
and management of the legislature, as were the other corporations enumerated in the statute then under discussion. We
there said: "Under the constitution, the state cannot control
the regents. It cannot add to or take away from its property
without the consent of the regents." We might with propriety
rest our decision upon that case, and should be disposed to do
so were it not for the urgent contention of the counsel on the
part of the relator that that case does not apply. We are therefore constrained to state some further reasons to show that the
legislature has no control over the university or the board
of regents.

(1) The board of regents and the legislature derive their
power from the same supreme authority, namely, the constitution. In so far as the powers of each are defined by that instrument, limitations are imposed, and a direct power conferred upon one necessarily excludes its existence in the other,
in the absence of language showing the contrary intent.
Neither the university nor the board of regents is mentioned
in article 4, which defines the powers and duties of the legislature; nor in the article relating to the university and the
board of regents is there any language which can be construed into conferring upon or reserving any control over
that institution in the legislature. They are separate and distinct constitutional bodies, with the powers of the regents defined. By no rule of construction can it be held that either can
encroach upon or exercise the powers conferred upon the
other.

(2) The board of regents is the only corporation provided
for in the constitution whose powers are defined therein. In
every other corporation provided for in the constitution it is
expressly provided that its powers shall be such as the legislature shall give.* * *

Thus, in every case except that of the regents the constitution carefully and expressly reposes in the legislature the
power to legislate and to control and define the duties of
those corporations and officers. Can it be held that the framers of the constitution, and the people, in adopting it, had no
purpose in conferring this power, viz. the "general supervision," upon the regents in the one instance, and in restricting it in the others? No other conclusion, in my judgment, is

possible than that the intention was to place this institution in the direct and exclusive control of the people themselves, through a constitutional body elected by them. As already shown, the maintenance of this power in the legislature would give to it the sole control and general supervision of the institution, and make the regents merely ministerial officers, with no other power than to carry into effect the general supervision which the legislature may see fit to exercise, or, in other words, to register its will. We do not think the constitution can bear that construction. The writ is denied.

University is not a constitutional corporation completely free from legislative control

UNIVERSITY OF UTAH v. BOARD OF EXAMINERS OF STATE OF UTAH

Supreme Court of Utah, 1956.
4 Utah 2d 408, 295 P.2d 348.

WORTHEN, Justice.

This is an appeal from a declaratory judgment holding that Article X, Section 4 of the Utah Constitution establishes the University as a constitutional corporation free from the control of the Legislature, administrative bodies, commissions and agencies and officers of the State.

The action was instituted by the University of Utah, acting through its Board of Regents, against the named defendants alleging that said defendants, pursuant to claimed legislative and constitutional mandate, asserted the legal right to exercise control over and management of the University in derogation of the claimed rights of the University and its Board of Regents granted by Article X, Section 4 of the Constitution of Utah. * * * The questions raised as to control and supervision of certain funds and as to the claimed curtailment of powers of the University will be resolved by our construction of Article X, Section 4 of the Constitution of Utah which provides:

> "The location and establishment by existing laws of the University of Utah, and the Agricultural College are hereby confirmed, and all the rights, immunities, franchises and endowments heretofore granted or conferred, are hereby perpetuated unto said University and Agricultural College respectively."

* * * The defendants pray that a declaratory judgment be entered declaring that the University is a state institution subject to and bound by the laws of Utah from time to time enacted.

The issues were submitted to the court upon stipulations of fact, and the trial court decreed that the University is a constitutionally confirmed body corporate, perpetually vested with all the rights, immunities, franchises and endowments of the territorial institution, beyond the power of the Legislature, all administrative bodies, commissions, agencies, and officers of the State of Utah to infringe upon, curtail, abrogate, interfere with or obstruct the enjoyment of the same, or otherwise, or at all, assume, or exercise any jurisdiction over the affairs of the University of Utah, and the powers of its Board of Regents, except for the general control and supervision conceded by the University to the State Board of Education.

The trial court declared unconstitutional certain statutes which treated the University as other state institutions, requiring preaudit of bills, submission of work programs and deposit of funds into the State Treasury, including University funds from appropriations and dedicated credits.

What is the effect of the quoted section on the power of the Legislature to act respecting the University?

We must determine what rights, immunities, franchises and endowments are perpetuated unto the University by Article X, Section 4 of the Constitution. In order to answer this question, resort must be made to territorial laws fixing the rights and status of the University at the time the Constitution was adopted.

That the issues and questions presented may be understood, it is deemed advisable to set out the history of the plaintiff University in full detail.

1. The University of the State of Deseret was instituted and incorporated by an ordinance of the State of Deseret approved February 28, 1850, reading as follows:

"Sec. 1. Be it ordained by the General Assembly of the State of Deseret: That a University is hereby instituted and incorporated, located at Great Salt Lake City, by the name and title of the University of the State of Deseret. * * *

The University was constituted a corporation de jure by the joint resolution legalizing the laws of the Provisional Government of the State of Deseret approved October 4, 1851, by the Legislative Assembly of the Territory of Utah as follows:

"Resolved, by the Legislative Assembly of the Territory of Utah, That the laws heretofore passed by the provisional government of the State of Deseret, and which do not *conflict with the 'Organic Act,'* of said Territory, be, and the same are hereby declared to be legal, and in full force and virtue, and shall so remain until *superseded by the action of the Legislative Assembly of the Territory of Utah.*

"Approved October 4, 1851." (Emphasis added.)

3. Its name was changed to the University of Utah by Ch. IX, Laws of Utah 1892, an act of the territorial legislature, approved February 17, 1892, as follows: * * *

"Section 1. The name of the University organized under an act approved February 28th 1850, and laws amendatory of and supplementary to said act, shall hereafter be 'University of Utah,' and with and by said name it is constituted and continued a body corporate, with perpetual succession, and it may have and use a corporate seal, and by said name sue and be sued, and contract and be contracted with. It is vested with all the *property,* credits, effects and franchises, and is subject to all the contracts, obligations and liabilities of the existing corporation.

"It may take and hold to its use by purchase, gift, devise or bequest, real and personal property and moneys, credits and effects, and by sale or exchange receive and use the proceeds of property not applicable to its uses in specie. It shall *be deemed a public corporation and be subject to the laws of Utah, from time to time enacted,* relating to its purposes and government, and its property, credits and effects shall be exempt from all taxes and assessments. * * *

Respondent contends that the language constituting the University a body corporate with perpetual succession, and declaring that it should be deemed a public corporation, were rights perpetuated by the Constitution, but that the words: *"and be subject to the laws of Utah, from time to time enacted, relating to its purposes and' government"* were not a part of any right, immunity, franchise or endowment and were not perpetuated by the Constitution.

Appellants contend that the language: *"and be subject to the laws of Utah,* from time to time enacted, relating to its purposes and government," conditions every right, immunity, franchise and endowment mentioned in Chapter IX, Laws of 1892, and that the words are part and parcel of the rights.

Respondent urges that the words: "and be subject to the laws of Utah, from time to time enacted, relating to its purposes and government," are of no significance since the Legislative Assembly had the right to amend or repeal the *corporate* privileges and other rights granted without an express reservation of that right. The question then arises, why did the 1892 Legislative Assembly use the quoted language if it was unnecessary? We must assume that the Assembly knew that it was empowered to amend or repeal the act upon which respondent relies for its rights. We believe that the language declaring that the University should be subject to the laws of Utah from time to time enacted was used in Section 1 for the purpose of doing what appears to have been intended, to-wit: To make the University subject to the laws of Utah from time to time enacted. * * *

The following statement appears in respondent's brief: "The following institutions are constitutional corporations: University of Michigan; Michigan State College of Agriculture and Applied Science; University of Minnesota; University of Colorado; University of Idaho; Oklahoma Agricultural and Mechanical College; University of California; University of Georgia; and University of Utah."

The constitutions of the states wherein said institutions are located, respecting said universities and colleges, are different in form and substance from Article X, Section 4, Utah Constitution, and each carries specific provisions granting control and management of the university to the regents or vesting the lands granted by Congress or the proceeds thereof and other donations in the university.

Michigan Constitution 1850, Article 13, Section 8, provides: "The board of regents shall have the general supervision of the university, and the direction and control of all expenditures from the university interest fund."

Michigan Constitution of 1908, Article 11, Section 8—"The board shall have the general supervision of the college, and the direction and control of all agricultural college funds; and shall perform such other duties as may be prescribed by law."

Minnesota Constitution, Article VIII, Section 4, provides: "and all lands which may be granted hereafter by Congress, or other donations for said university purposes, shall vest in the institution referred to in this section."

Colorado Constitution, Article IX, Section 14, provides: "The board of regents shall have the general supervision of the university, and the exclusive control and direction of all funds of, and appropriations to, the university."

Idaho Constitution, Article IX, Section 10—(Regents were

given "custody of the books, records, buildings and other property" and control over tax funds "subject to the orders of the Board of Regents.")

Oklahoma Constitution 1907, Article 6, Section 31—"A Board of Agriculture is hereby created to be composed of eleven members, all of whom shall be farmers * * *. Said Board shall be maintained as a part of the State government, and shall have jurisdiction over all matters affecting animal industry and animal quarantine regulations, and shall be the Board of Regents of all State Agricultural and Mechanical Colleges, and shall discharge such other duties and receive such compensation as may be provided by law."

California Constitution 1879, Article IX, Section 9—"The University of California shall constitute a public trust, to be administered by the existing corporation known as 'the Regents of the University of California,' *with full powers of organization and government*, subject only to such legislative control as may be necessary to insure compliance with the terms of the endowments of the university and the security of its funds. * * * *Said corporation shall be vested with the legal title and the management and disposition of the property* of the university and of property held for its benefit * * *." (As amended November 5, 1918.) (Emphasis added.)

Georgia Constitution, Article VIII, Section 4, Par. 1— "There shall be a Board of Regents of the University System of Georgia, and the government, control, and management of the University System of Georgia and all of its institutions in said system shall be vested in said Board of Regents of the University System of Georgia. * * *"

It should be further observed that the Michigan Constitution of 1850, Article 13, Section 6, provided for the election of the Regents of the University of Michigan; and that the Michigan Constitution of 1908, Article 11, Section 7, provided for the election of the State Board of Agriculture; and the Constitution of Colorado, Article IX, Section 12, provides for the election of the Regents of the University of Colorado, thus further distinguishing those institutions from the University of Utah, whose Regents are appointed by the Governor.

We are constrained to the view that the University of Utah is not brought into the group of constitutional corporations mentioned by respondent when there exists such differences between the Utah Constitution and the constitutional provisions affecting the other universities mentioned.

If the framers of the Utah Constitution had intended to create the University of Utah a constitutional corporation, completely autonomous and free from legislative control, it is difficult to understand why language such as was used in the constitutions of Michigan, Minnesota and the other constitutions referred to was not used.

Had the framers of the Utah Constitution added after "respectively" in Article X, Section 4: The Board of Regents of the University of Utah shall have general supervision of the University and the direction and control of all expenditures from the University Interest Fund, or All lands which may be granted hereafter by Congress, or other donations for said University purposes, shall vest in the University of Utah, we would be presented with language supporting respondent's argument.

That the framers of the Utah Constitution did not adopt language similar to the constitutions of Minnesota and Idaho, even though the Convention had before it the constitutions of those states is evidence that a different result was intended. Respondent relies heavily on the University of Michigan as supporting the argument for like result in the instant case. The framers of the Utah Constitution did not adopt language similar to that found in the Michigan Constitution, even though that language had been held by the Michigan court in 1893 to constitute the University of Michigan a constitutional corporation free from legislative control.[3]

We are, therefore, of the opinion that the language used in Article X, Section 4, Constitution of Utah, is not so clear that it can be said that it created the University a constitutional corporation completely freed from legislative control. Rather, we are inclined to the view that the language failed to create the University a constitutional corporation free from legislative control. But if we accept the view that there is present some ambiguity and some justification for diverse opinions, we may look to other sources of interpretation to clarify the instrument.

We must bear in mind that our Constitution is not one of grant, but one of limitation. Consequently, in order that the legislative body be restricted in educational as well as all other matters, it is imperative that the Legislature be restricted expressly or by necessary implication by the Consti-

---

3. Weinberg v. Regents of University of Michigan, 97 Mich. 246, 56 N.W. 605.

tution itself. This court in the case of Kimball v. Grantsville City [4] said:

> "* * * The state having thus committed its whole lawmaking power to the legislature, excepting such as is expressly or impliedly withheld by the state or federal constitution, it has plenary power for all purposes of civil government. Therefore, in the absence of any constitutional restraint, express or implied, the legislature may act upon any subject within the sphere of the government * * * and, whenever an inquiry is directed questioning the constitutionality of a legislative enactment, it is for him who asserts its invalidity to show that it is forbidden." * * *

If there is no ambiguity as to the status of the University and its powers; if there is no uncertainty as to the controls (if any) on the University; if all the provisions of the Constitution are crystal clear as to those powers and controls, then extraneous or contemporaneous construction may not be resorted to. But if the words are ambiguous or their meaning not clear, or if the several provisions of the basic instrument are susceptible to two or more possible meanings or constructions, then it is proper to look outside the instrument itself to ascertain what the framers meant by the language used.

In 16 C.J.S., Title Constitutional Law, § 32, page 70, it is said:

> "In determining the meaning of an ambiguous constitutional provision the courts may properly seek extrinsic aid by ascertaining the construction given such provision at the time of its adoption and since by those whose duty it has been to construe, execute, and apply it in practice. * * *"

In 16 C.J.S., Title Constitutional Law, § 33, page 72, it is said:

> "Subject to the limitations discussed in the preceding section, a contemporaneous legislative or executive construction is entitled to, and will be given, serious consideration by the courts in determining the meaning of an ambiguous constitutional provision, both as a matter of policy, and also because it may be presumed to represent the true intent of the instrument. In doubtful cases such a construction should, and ordinarily will, be followed, unless it is manifestly erroneous. Reasonable, and it has been said, wide latitude should be allowed the legislative department in interpreting a constitutional pro-

---

4. 19 Utah 368, 57 P. 1, 4, 45 L.R.A. 628. See, also, Parkinson v. Watson, 4 Utah 2d 191, 291 P.2d 400.

vision. So, where a state constitutional provision is susceptible of two reasonable constructions, the action of the legislature in adopting one of those constructions is sometimes deemed conclusive."

In 16 C.J.S., Title Constitutional Law, § 34, page 74, it is said:

"Long acquiescence by the people in legislative or judicial construction of constitutional provisions is entitled to great weight with the courts.
"A contemporaneous uniform legislative or executive construction of constitutional provisions, adopted and acted on with the acquiescence of the people for many years, is entitled to great weight with the courts, * * *. Such construction, however, is not necessarily controlling, and plain, direct, and unambiguous provisions of a constitution cannot be modified or amended by practice or custom, no matter how long continued. * * *"

There is abundant contemporaneous construction of Article X, Section 4, inconsistent with or in direct contradiction of the position of the University. In fact, as heretofore observed, action was brought to have the court declare that substantial legislation enacted since statehood and to which there has been no objection by the University, be declared beyond the power of the Legislature to enact, notwithstanding the University has acquiesced for over 50 years with certain legislation now most criticized and objected to. * * *

For over 50 years the University has never raised the point of independent control, but during the period has accepted the declaration contained in Section 1, Chapter 83, Laws of 1896, that it "should be subject to the laws of this State" and has acquiesced in and complied with the legislative enactments relating to its purposes and government. * * *

Many statutes have been passed since statehood restricting the giving of certain courses of study and mandating the giving of others. By Chapter 133, Laws of 1905, the University was prohibited from including in its courses agriculture, horticulture, animal industry, veterinary science, domestic science and art (except in connection with the normal course). In 1921 c. 116, the University was prohibited from awarding degrees in domestic science or art. In 1923, c. 4, the University was required to give instruction in the Constitution of the United States. * * *

Chapter 65, Laws of Utah 1897 at page 248 provides for appropriations for University as follows:

"Appropriations

"To the University of Utah:

"For general maintenance for the two academic years ending June 30, 1899, or so much thereof as may be necessary $73,000.00

"*Provided*, that no officer or member of the faculty of said University, for all service *rendered to the State* during the term herein named shall be paid any salary in excess of $2,500.00 per annum." * * *

The Regents accepted the appropriation and, we may assume, expended it without protest. No objection was made that the Legislature *was powerless* to tell the Regents what salaries might be paid. * * *

The Regents, officials and personnel of the University in the early years after statehood were indeed grateful for the beneficence of those early legislatures, during which time appropriations for buildings, new schools and enlarged teaching staffs were made, without which the University would have failed to attain the eminence it now enjoys. The University enjoyed and thrived on its dependence on the Legislature, but lately it seeks a change. It chooses to declare that independence, which the institution never has had, and which has never, prior to the bringing of this action, been asserted. After these 50 years of acquiescence it is difficult to understand this sudden quest for independent control.

The people of Utah are proud of the great progress made by the University; its history and attainment are a glowing tribute to the Regents, the Presidents and the Faculties that have guided it along its glorious course as well as to its donors and the 30 legislatures that have furnished the funds to assure its growth. Nor is there anything made to appear which should cause alarm or concern to any. It must be conceded that had its Regents in those early years asserted its independence from the Legislature, it is doubtful that it would have attained a stature which would induce it to declare its independence. * * *

Let us consider the result were we to accept respondent's contention. The University contends and the trial court held that the State of Utah, including the Legislature, Board of Examiners, Finance Department and the other named defendants have no control, check or audit of the money used by the University, whether appropriated funds or dedicated funds; that the University is entitled to keep the same in its own bank and expend it free from any review or control, except post audit (but post audits are valuable only as a matter of history) ; that the Regents of the University may authorize out of state travel for University employees and pay the same without previous approval therefor by the Board of Examiners (yet the Governor, Secretary of State, Attorney General and all other state officers must obtain such previous approval) ; that the University is not subject to laws enacted by the Legislature, and the statutes so declaring are unconstitutional; that the University is authorized to draw from the Treasurer of the State of Utah quarter yearly in advance its biennial legislative appropriations for maintenance, whereas, all other legislative appropriations may be procured only after pre-audit and approval of some or all of the defendants; that the University may retain all unexpended surpluses from all funds, and that the Legislature has no power to order such surpluses closed out, and that any condition attached to appropriations to the University restricting the powers of the Board of Regents are unconstitutional and void; that the University is empowered to carry out its own building and expansion program without any control or supervision on the part of the State Building Board. In short, the University and its Board of Regents contend that they have been given a blank check enabling them to expend all funds without any semblance of supervision or control.

Article X, Section 1 of our Constitution provides:

> "The Legislature shall provide for the establishment and *maintenance* of a uniform system of public schools, which shall be open to all children of the State, and be free from sectarian control." (Emphasis added.)

Article X, Section 2 of our Constitution declares:

> "The public school system shall include kindergarten schools; common schools, consisting of primary and grammar grades; high schools, an agricultural college; a university, and such other schools as the Legislature may establish. The common schools shall be free. The other departments of the system shall be supported as provided by law. * * *"

Would it be contended by the University that under Article X, Section 1 it might compel the Legislature to appropriate money the University considers essential? Is it contended that the demands of the University are not subject to constitutional debt limits? If so, respondent would have the power to destroy the solvency of the State and all other institutions by demands beyond the power of the State to meet.

Article X, Section 5 provides:

> "The proceeds of the sale of lands reserved by an Act of Congress, approved February 21st, 1855, for the establishment of the University of Utah, and of all the lands granted by an Act of Congress, approved July 16th, 1894, shall constitute permanent funds, to be safely invested and held by the State; and the income thereof shall be used exclusively for the support and maintenance of the different institutions and colleges, respectively, in accordance with the requirements and conditions of said acts of Congress."

Article X, Section 7 of our Constitution declares:

> "All public School Funds shall be guaranteed by the State against loss or diversion."

It is inconceivable that the framers of the Constitution in light of the provisions of Sections 1, 5 and 7 of Article X, and the provision as to debt limitations, intended to place the University above the only controls available for the people of this State as to the property, management and government of the University. We are unable to reconcile respondent's position that the University has a blank check as to all its funds with no pre-audit and no restraint under the provisions of the Constitution requiring the State to safely invest and hold the dedicated funds and making the State guarantor of the public school funds against loss or diversion. To hold that respondent has free and uncontrolled custody and use of its property and funds, while making the State guarantee said funds against loss or diversion is inconceivable. We believe that the framers of the Constitution intended no such result.

Appellants and respondent agree that the interpretation which we put on Article X, Section 4 will determine the other questions presented. It has not been urged by respondent that if the University is subject to legislative control that any of the enactments complained of are invalid. Respondent's objection is that the Legislature had no power to confer on the Boards, Commissions and Officers the authority to supervise and control the University. Since no complaint is made against the defendants named, except that the duties being performed by them are in violation of respondent's constitutional rights because the Legislature could not legally invest said defendant with authority to infringe upon the rights secured by the Constitution, it must follow that the objections of respondent as to the acts complained of must fall by reason of the conclusion reached herein; that the University is a public corporation not above the power of the Legislature to control, and is subject to the laws of this State from time to time enacted relating to its purposes and government.

The judgment is reversed and remanded with directions to set aside the judgment entered and to enter a declaratory judgment in favor of the defendants in accordance with the opinions herein expressed, the respective parties to bear their own costs.

NOTES

The University of Minnesota was chartered by the territorial legislature in 1851 and granted powers and authority almost identical with the territorial act which created the University of Idaho. On coming into statehood in 1858, the constitution (Art. 8, § 4) confirmed the establishment and location of the university as follows:

" 'And said institution is hereby declared to be the "University of the State of Minnesota." All the rights, immunities, franchises and endowments heretofore granted or conferred are hereby *perpetuated* unto the said university; and all lands which may be granted hereafter by Congress, or other donations for said university purposes, shall vest in the institution referred to in this section.' " State *ex rel.* University of Minnesota v. Chase, 175 Minn. 259, 220 N.W. 951, 953 (1928).

In commenting on this constitutional provision, the supreme court of Minnesota said:

> That a corporation was created by the act of 1851 and "perpetuated" by the constitution with all the rights, immunities, franchises, and endowments which it then possessed is plain. Of that corporation the regents were both the sole members and the governing board. They were the corporation in which were perpetuated the things covered by the constitutional confirmation. The language has a definite legal import; the terms are those of confirmation in perpetuity of a prior grant of corporate rights. So the University, in respect to its corporate status and government, was put beyond the power of the Legislature by paramount law, the right to amend or repeal which exists only in the people themselves.

Curators have authority under constitution and statutes
to issue revenue bonds and construct
parking facilities

STATE EX REL. CURATORS OF THE UNIVERSITY OF MISSOURI v. NEILL

Supreme Court of Missouri, 1966.
397 S.W.2d 666.

STORCKMAN, Chief Justice.

This is an original proceedings for a writ of mandamus brought by the Curators of the University of Missouri to require Robert Neill, the president of the Board of Curators, to execute revenue bonds which the Board proposes to issue for the construction of parking facilities for motor vehicles on the campus of the University of Missouri at Columbia, which bonds are to be paid, both principal and interest, solely from revenues derived from the operation of the parking facilities. The return of the respondent admits all facts alleged in the petition for the writ. The parties have also filed a stipulation of agreed facts. From these sources the essential facts will be stated. * * *

The primary questions involved are whether the Curators have authority under the Constitution and statutes to construct the parking facility in question and, if such power exists, whether the Curators can borrow money and issue revenue bonds for that purpose. The Curators contend that they have constitutional power supplemented by statutes to perform both of these functions. The constitutional provision, § 9(a) of Art. IX of the 1945 Constitution, V.A.M.S., provides that: "The government of the state university shall be vested in a board of curators consisting of nine members appointed by the governor, * * *." The following section, 9(b), provides that: "The general assembly shall adequately maintain the state university and such other educational institutions as it may deem necessary."

The general assembly, in recognition of the broad grant of constitutional power, has also provided in § 172.010, RSMo 1959, V.A.M.S., that "the government" of the University shall be vested in the Board of Curators. Section 172.020 incorporates and creates the University as "a body politic" under the name, "The Curators of the University of Missouri", and, among other things, grants this public corporation the power to purchase and sell lands and chattels, and to condemn property for its public purposes.

Section 172.260 provides that: "It shall be the duty of the curators to provide for the protection and improvement of the site of the university of the state of Missouri, as selected and established by law; to erect and continue thereon all edifices designed for the use and accommodation of the officers and students of the university, and to furnish and adapt the same to the uses of the several departments of instruction." Thus, "the government" of the University is committed to the Curators both by the Constitution and the statutes and it is the Curators' duty "to provide for the protection and improvement of the site of the university" and "to erect and continue thereon all edifices" for the use of the officers and students of the University. * * *

The term "government" has been defined as the act or process of governing, authoritative direction or control, and the office, authority or function of governing. To govern is to control the workings or operation of, and to determine, guide and regulate. * * *

The word "improvement" has for one of its specific definitions: A permanent addition to or betterment of real property that enhances its capital value and that involves the expenditure of labor or money and is designed to make the property more useful or valuable as distinguished from ordinary repairs. * * *

The Curators are more than a mere regulatory agency. It is the clear intent of the Constitution and statutes to confer on the Curators the authority to select sites on which to carry out the functions of the University and to acquire real estate for such purposes by purchase or condemnation. It is also clear that the Curators are authorized to construct improvements on the real estate constituting the site of a University function. In fact such authority is spelled out as a *duty* of the Curators by § 172.260. For the possible origin of this grant of power and imposition of duty, see Constitution of Missouri 1820, Art. VI, § 2, V.A.M.S., Vol. 1, p. 91, Laws 1889, p. 265, and Laws 1909, p. 889.

It is too late in the motor age to contend successfully that parking facilities are not a necessary adjunct of the proper use of improved real estate. One does not have to travel far to see their inevitable presence at modern shopping centers, factories, schools, churches, apartments and even private residences. A place to park an automobile is indispensable to its use. The larger businesses and institutions find it necessary to provide parking facilities for the persons with whom they deal since streets are no longer adequate or available for that purpose.

It is an admitted fact that for more than twenty-five years the Curators have been providing parking facilities on its campuses in Columbia and at Rolla and more recently on the campuses established at St. Louis and Kansas City. The administrative interpretation given a constitutional or statutory provision by public officers charged with its execution, while not controlling, is entitled to consideration, especially in case of doubt or ambiguity. * * * The parking facility in question is a structure or improvement which the Curators are authorized to construct on University property. * * *

Our next inquiry concerns the power of the Curators to issue revenue bonds for the money necessary to defray the cost of constructing the parking facility. The respondent contends that the Curators have no express or implied power to issue revenue bonds for this purpose. This contention must be denied on the authority of State ex rel. Curators of University of Missouri v. McReynolds, 354 Mo. 1199, 193 S.W.2d 611, a decision of this court en banc, which held that the Curators had implied power to issue revenue bonds for money borrowed to build dormitories and dining room facilities to take care of increased enrollment at the University. Regarding this aspect of the case, the McReynolds opinion states:

"* * * while the curators may have no general implied power to borrow money and issue securities, still it may be fairly implied from their express powers that under the particular circumstances they have the power presently to capitalize such future accumulation of fees even though they must borrow to do so. By borrowing by the method contemplated the curators do not create a general obligation, only a limited one. The only funds pledged are those to be realized from the operation of the particular properties to be built out of the proceeds of the bonds. There is no pledge of funds to be ultimately realized from tax revenues.

"* * * The broad powers historically exercised by the curators without specific legislative authority or appropriations present a different situation from an ordinary municipal corporation depending entirely upon taxation for its support and with powers rigidly limited by statute or charter.

"* * * By issuing the Dormitory Revenue Bonds the curators are merely adopting a modern device to implement the powers they have long and properly exercised." 193 S.W.2d at 613. * * *

We have considered all questions presented and decided them adversely to the respondent. Accordingly it is ordered that the peremptory writ of mandamus be issued.

University has implied power to construct and maintain a television station

TURKOVICH v. BOARD OF TRUSTEES OF THE UNIVERSITY OF ILLINOIS

Supreme Court of Illinois, 1957.
11 Ill. 2d 460, 43 N.E.2d 229.

Mr. JUSTICE HOUSE delivered the opinion of the court:

This is a taxpayers' suit by Stephen and Betty Turkovich and Dahlen's Drug Stores, Inc., to enjoin the Board of Trustees of the University of Illinois from spending State funds for the construction, equipment and operation of a television station. The Auditor of Public Accounts and State Treasurer are joined as defendants, and plaintiffs seek to restrain them from paying out funds from the State Treasury for such purposes. Plaintiffs appeal from the decree of the circuit court of Sangamon County dismissing the complaint for want of equity. This court has jurisdiction since the constitutionality of a statute is involved and the case relates to the public revenue.

Plaintiffs contend that there is no valid appropriation for the purpose of constructing and operating a television station and that disbursement of funds under the appropriation acts involved is in violation of section 17, article IV, of the Illinois constitution. They further assert that if such acts be construed to permit such expenditure, then their failure to specify the purposes for which the appropriations were made violates section 16, article V, and section 1, article IV, of said constitution. * * *

In the trial court plaintiffs contended that, wholly apart from the reach and validity of the appropriation acts in question, the University is without legal power and authority to maintain and operate an educational television station. * * *

The Board of Trustees was empowered to administer the University of Illinois by an act of the General Assembly passed in 1867. (Ill. Rev. Stat. 1953, chap. 144, pars. 22 *et seq.*) By section 7 thereof it was authorized to provide requisite buildings, apparatus and conveniences, to appoint professors and instructors and to teach in the most thorough manner such branches of learning as are related to agriculture and the mechanical arts, without excluding other scientific studies.

The Board of Trustees has, within such authorization, greatly expanded the facilities of the University. It has constructed and maintains the requisite buildings, apparatus and conveniences for and gives instruction in more than 2600 courses taught in 15 colleges, 5 schools, 2 divisions, 3 institutes and 2 Reserve Officers Training Corps, on three campuses. In addition, it maintains libraries, museums, hospitals, clinics, institutes, research programs, extension services, recreational facilities and a radio station.

A School of Journalism and Communications was established in 1927, pursuant to an act of the General Assembly. Three major curricula are offered by this school: journalism, advertising, and radio-television. Approximately one third of the student body in that school is enrolled in the latter curriculum.

The Board of Trustees in 1953 obtained a permit from the Federal Communications Commission to construct and operate a noncommercial television station. With the aid of gifts, including a transmitter, a television station was constructed which consisted of the erection of an antenna, the partitioning into rooms of space in the west hall of Memorial Stadium and the installation therein of the transmitting equipment. The station went on the air August 1, 1955, and has continually operated since. The Trustees allocated $24,000 for original construction and maintenance.

Professor Schooley, who is director and in charge of radio and television broadcasting for the University, testified that the station was an experiment to see what could be done in program operations for a year or two. He indicated the desirability of expansion and relocation after the experimentation is completed.

According to the record the purposes of the University's television station are to train students to enter the field of communication and broadcasting; to give instruction for University credit; to carry on research in mass communication; to disseminate the results of research in all fields of learning at the University; to experiment in program planning and technique and to employ the medium for the education of the public at all levels.

There is nothing unusual in the University's power, in the objectives to be obtained, or the cost thereof, in the construction and operation of a television station. We take judicial notice of the fact that our great universities, through experimentation and research in many scientific fields totally beyond the comprehension of normal man, are the prime source of discoveries for the betterment of mankind. How then can we say that the University of Illinois should be restricted to specific authorizations in its proposed research and experimentation such as this?

The Board of Trustees has, by the statute creating the University, the power and authority to do everything necessary in the management, operating and administration of the University, including any necessary or incidental powers in the furtherance of the corporate purposes. *People ex rel. Board of Trustees v. Barrett,* 382 Ill. 321.

We are of the opinion that, aside from the question of the proper appropriation and use of State funds for the purpose, the construction and maintenance of a television station is well within the powers of the University without any additional statutory enactment upon the subject.

We now turn to the contention that there was no valid appropriation of State funds for the construction and operation of a television station. It is argued that the act making appropriations to the Board of Trustees to meet the ordinary and contingent expenses of the University of Illinois is not broad enough to permit the expenditure complained of. Apparently, it is plaintiffs' theory that activities of the University such as this must be particularized in the appropriation act or by separate enabling legislation. * * *

Similar appropriation acts for the University and many other branches and agencies of the State have been used continuously since the enactment of the Civil Administrative Code of 1917, (Ill. Rev. Stat. 1955, chap. 127, pars. 1 *et seq.,*) and the State Finance Act of 1919 (Ill. Rev. Stat. 1955, chap. 127, pars. 137 *et seq.*) It cannot reasonably be said that expenditures for purposes such as those complained of here would not have come to the attention of, and been curbed by, the legislature over the years if the funds appropriated were used for purposes not contemplated by that body. The General Assembly cannot be expected to allocate funds to each of the myriad activities of the University and thereby practically substitute itself for the Board of Trustees in the management thereof.

We have heretofore held that the construction and operation of a television station is within the powers delegated to the Board of Trustees. It follows that the several appropriation acts included funds for the construction, maintenance and operation of the television station as a part of the ordinary and contingent expenses of the University, and the Trustees had the authority to pay the cost thereof from such appropriations.

The final question is whether the Appropriation Act is violative of section 16 of article V of the constitution by failing to specify the object or purpose for which the appropriations were made, and an unlawful delegation of legislative power in violation of section 1 of article IV of the constitution.

Plaintiff makes the point that the Board of Trustees in its internal budget makes a separate allocation for television, but that it is not carried over into the appropriation Act. A review of budgeting and appropriating procedure, under the Civil Administrative Code and State Finance Act, indicates that such a statement is misleading.

The various departments, divisions and colleges submit their estimated needs to the University Budget Committee. The estimates are then correlated and a report made to the President of the University who, in turn, makes his budget recommendation to the Board of Trustees. The Board then submits the University's budget, as approved by it, to the State Director of Finance, accompanied by a written statement explaining each item of appropriation requested. The University's internal budget is published as "The University Bulletin" and for the year 1954-1955, consisted of 272 pages. After hearings and revisions the Governor submits the budget to the General Assembly as a division of his biennial executive budget recommendations. An appropriation act, in the form outlined above, is then passed.

The several line items in the Appropriation Act are the totals of the needs in each category of the various departments, divisions and colleges. For example, the salaries of the professors in the College of Law and those in the College of Engineering are paid out of the line item for "Personal Services," and the equipment needed by both colleges is purchased out of the line item for "Equipment." This practice has been followed by the General Assembly for many years.

The impracticability of detailing funds for the many activities and functions of the University in the Appropriation Act is readily apparent. If, as plaintiffs' counsel argues, a $24,000 annual expenditure out of a biennial appropriation in excess of $82,000,000 is required, then practically every proposed expenditure would have to be itemized. Television cannot be singled out for special treatment merely because it is relatively new. It is one of the many activities incident to the management and operation of the University included in the single objective of maintaining an institution of higher learning.

We have been called upon to test various appropriation statutes with regard to the itemization requirements of section 16 of article V of the constitution. * * * The rationale of the foregoing cases is that the statutes appropriating funds in a lump sum for a single general purpose and without further itemization do not contravene the itemization provisions of said section 16 merely because the single general purpose may be subdivided into various details of the object and purpose, where it appears the various details are embraced within and reasonably related to the general purpose. * * *

We have carefully considered *People ex rel. State Board of Agriculture v. Brady*, 277 Ill. 124, and other cases referred to by plaintiffs' counsel and find them distinguishable from the present case.

Plaintiffs do not pursue the charge of unlawful delegation of power other than in connection with their other charge of unconstitutionality. If the appropriation act meets constitutional requirements with respect to itemization, and in our opinion it does, then there is no unconstitutional delegation of legislative power to the Board of Trustees in their expenditure of funds for the purposes for which such funds were appropriated. The discretion granted to the Board of Trustees is but a ministerial discretion rather than a legislative discretion. * * *

In our opinion no constitutional provisions have been violated in the construction and operation of the University television station, nor is the appropriation and expenditure of funds therefor. The decree of the circuit court of Sangamon County is correct, and it is hereby affirmed.

Decree affirmed.

NOTES

Delegation of Legislative Power

The legislature may not abdicate its power to make laws nor delegate its supreme legislative power to any other coordinate branch or to any agency which it may create. State Education Assistance Authority v. Bank of Statesville, 174 S.W.2d 551 (N.C. 1970).

A statute which gives unlimited regulatory power to a commission, board, or agency with no prescribed restraint offends the state constitution as an illegal delegation of legislative power. Southern Pacific Co. v. Cochise County, 377 P.2d 770 (Ariz. 1963).

The legislature is not permitted to relieve itself of lawmaking power by delegation of it to any person, instrumentality or board, but the legislature may authorize designated administrative officers to promulgate rules and regulations within the scope of legislation to administer it fully and give effect to it. Crawley v. Seignious, 102 S.W.2d 38 (Ga. 1962).

The legislature may not delegate power to enact law, or to declare what law shall be, or to exercise unrestricted discretion in applying law, but may enact law complete in itself and designed to accomplish public purposes and may expressly authorize designated officials within definite valid limitations to provide rules for complete operation and enforcement of law. Stewart v. Stone, 130 So. 2d 577 (Fla. 1965).

Administrative rule-making power is predicated on the theory that in certain fields and in some respects public interest is better served by delegating a large part of detailed lawmaking to expert administrators controlled by policies, objects and standards laid down by the legislature, but an expressed will and legislative imposition of limitations on the administrative agencies' power to adopt rules and regulations are prerequisites to valid delegation of such power. Affiliated Distillers Brands Corp. v. Gillis, 130 N.W.2d 597 (S.D. 1964).

A statute permitting the state board of regents to charge and collect fees from university students for construction and use of self-liquidating buildings did not unconstitutionally delegate legislative power to administrative agency. Iowa Hotel Association v. State Board of Regents, 114 N.W.2d 539 (Iowa, 1965) ; see also, Association of New Jersey State College Faculties v. Board of Higher Education, 112 N.J. Super. 237, 270 A.2d 744 (1970).

Assignment by the legislature to the state university the task of implementing a certification statute—by recognizing acceptable courses, by determining scope of the qualifying examination, by deciding on "equivalent" experience and degrees—did not constitute an invalid delegation of legislative power. National Psychological Association for Psychoanalysis, Inc. v. University of State of New York, 203 N.Y.S.2d 821, 168 N.E.2d 649 (1966).

CHAPTER 3

RELIGION AND HIGHER EDUCATION

The history of religion and religious conflict is the history of civilization. Religious strife has been well known to men of every century from Babylon to the Crusades, to the Spanish Inquisition, to Ireland, Vietnam, and Israel today. A peculiar aspect of religion is man's desire to make his fellow man believe as he does. This tendency of man to force his religion on others has been attributed by some historians to the monotheism of Moses which is possessed of the "spirit of proselytism." Northcott observed that:

> Historically it was the Hebrew and Christian concept of a single and universal God that introduced a religious exclusivism leading to compulsion and persecution in the realm of religion. Ancient religions were regarded as confined to each separate people believing in them, and the question of change from one religious belief to another did not arise. It was not until an exclusive dogma appeared, as in Christianity, with its belief in an exclusive fellowship, that the questions of proselytism, change of belief and liberty of religion arose.[1]

CHURCH AND STATE

The quest for religious supremacy, unfortunately, was not confined to individuals and individual persuasion, but spilled over into the affairs of state. Emperors and rulers historically either attempted to suppress religion or used it for political advantage. Few instances are recorded where tolerance was the rule rather than the exception.

Under the Romans, as Christianity moved from being the victim of persecution to a new role of oppressor, state favors were bestowed on the church. Non-Christian temples were closed by Rome and the church worked in consort with the state. Deviation from the accepted orthodox religion of Christianity was made a crime against the state; bishops and emperors merged forces to purge the earth of heretics.

It was soon evident, however, that church and state could not be mutually cooperative partners without one seeking control over the other. As early as 496 A.D., Pope Gelasius I informed the emperor of Rome that: "There are two things, most august emperor, by which this world is chiefly ruled:

---

1. Cecil Northcott, *Religious Liberty*, The Macmillan Co., 1949, p. 24.

The sacred authority of the priesthood and the royal power. Of these two the priests carry the greater weight, because they will have to render account in the divine judgment even for the kings of men." [2] The power of the church increased steadily down through the years until, in the thirteenth century, Pope Innocent III held supreme temporal dominion over the Italian State, the Spanish peninsula, the Scandinavian states, Hungary, Bohemia, Poland, Servia, Bosnia, Bulgaria, the Christian State of Syria, and England.

The position of the church was unmistakable. The church's view of the relationship between church and state is represented in the classic statement of Thomas Aquinas:

> The highest aim of mankind is eternal happiness. To this chief aim of mankind all earthly aims must be subordinated. This chief aim cannot be realized through human direction alone but must obtain divine assistance which is only to be obtained through the church. Therefore the State, through which earthly aims are obtained, must be subordinate to the Church. Church and State are as two swords which God has given to Christendom for protection; both of these however, are given by him to the Pope and the temporal sword by him handed to rulers of the State.[3]

Religious oppression accompanied the establishment of the church in each country. Throughout this period nonbelievers and believers in other faiths alike were branded and punished as heretics with punishment ranging from penances and fasting to life imprisonment or death by fire. The more serious punishments were always accompanied by confiscation of the accused's property.[4]

The outburst of Protestantism on the continent added fuel to the flame of intolerance and set in motion a waive of religious oppression and persecution which has affected church and state to the present day. One observable tendency though, regardless of whether the religion was Protestant or Catholic, was that the pleader for religious tolerance was always the religion in the minority.[5] As a religion gained the majority and obtained the status of orthodoxy, it became intolerant of opposing religious views. As John Robinson, a Pilgrim pastor, observed:

---

2. Searle M. Bates, *Religious Liberty: An Inquiry*, International Missionary Council, 1945, p. 134.

3. *Ibid.*, p. 140.

4. Leo Pfeffer, *Church State and Freedom*, Beacon Press, 1967, p. 22.

5. *Ibid.*, p. 23.

> Protestants living in the countries of papists commonly plead for toleration of religions: so do papists that live where Protestants bear sway: though few of either especially of the clergy . . . would have the other tolerated, where the world goes on their side.[6]

CHURCH CONTROL OF UNIVERSITIES

Nor were the universities immune from religious control. During the early development period of universities on the continent of Europe, the church generally was dominant in all university matters. At this time, impingement on academic freedom was a phenomenon of the church and not of the state. In the well known case of Abelard at Paris in the twelfth century, the Church condemned and ostracized him for questioning the contradictory views and works of the church fathers.[7] The impact of the church on academic society is illustrated by the statement of a doctor of law in Bologna upon completion of his course of lectures:

> Now gentlemen, we have begun and finished and gone through this book, as you know who have been in the class, for which we thank God and His Virgin Mother and all His Saints. It is an ancient custom in this city that when a book is finished mass should be sung to the Holy Ghost, and it is a good custom and hence should be observed.[8]

One should bear in mind that the university of the twelfth century was not necessarily public, private or parochial as we view it today. Most universities of that period constituted a mobile society of scholars holding classes and lectures without centralized power or authority. Later, at the University of Paris a trend of centralized organized university control developed. The teachers or masters appointed a Rector and the Bishop of the church appointed a Chancellor. In today's parlance the Rector was a general administrator while the Chancellor exercised ecclesiastical jurisdiction over the entire university society. This arrangement, of course, bred conflict which resulted in many cases of church denial of academic freedom. The Twelfth Century Renaissance was characterized by such free speculation on the theories of Aristotle and other scholars, that the church became fearful of the independence

---

6. Bates, *op. cit.*, p. 155.

7. William Boyd, *The History of Western Education*, A & C Black, Limited, 1928, p. 143.

8. Frederick Ely and Charles F. Arrowood, *The History and Philosophy of Education Ancient and Medieval*, Prentice-Hall, Inc., 1940, p. 758.

and energy of the universities. In 1215 the papal legate forbade Paris Masters to study Aristotle's physics and metaphysics "until they had been examined and purged from all heresy." [9] The fear of the independent thinking in the university community led Francis Bernadone of Assisi (1182-1226) to exclaim: "Doctors will be the destruction of my vineyard." [10]

In the fourteenth century, England was a devout Catholic nation which absolutely supported the infallible judgments of the church. As Levy says, "The state was responsible, as a partner of the church, for the souls of its subjects and was obliged to protect them against heresy . . . . Moreover, any sovereign who did not bid the command of the church on matters of faith might himself be condemned as a heretic . . ." [11] In 1401 the English Parliament took the ultimate step in intermingling the ecclesiastical and temporal when it enacted the statute *De Haeretico Comburendo*. The statute placed the full coercive power of the state behind the Catholic Church and for the first time in England gave statutory foundation for the arrest, trial and burning of heretics. The statute was directed at the Lollard sect which opposed Catholicism, "subverted the faith and seduced people into sedition." Bishops were given the power to arrest and imprison anyone "defamed or evidently suspected" of heresy.

With the death of Henry VIII in 1547, the crown passed to his young son, Edward VI, a Protestant. Edward's short and mild reign saw few religious executions. Edward, however, did remove Catholic priests, enforced the Anglican Book of Common Prayer, and established religious uniformity. With Edward's death came a Catholic restoration under Queen Mary which was marked by its brutality. Religious intolerance prevailed in England under both Protestant and Catholics, the difference being only a matter of quantity of executions. However, if the number of burnings is the test of intolerance Mary was the supreme champion. The cliché "Bloody Mary" of English history is testimony to the cruelty of this period.

Under Elizabeth, Protestantism came back into power and all Catholic legislation against heresy was repealed. Government policy was decided on a secular basis rather than a spi-

9. Albert Mansbridge, *The Older Universities of England*, Longmans, Green and Co., 1923, p. 19.

10. *Ibid.*, p. 20.

11. Leonard Levy, *Origins of the Fifth Amendment*, Oxford University Press, 1968, p. 54.

ritual one. A complete reversal had taken place in England, by statute Elizabeth was made the Supreme Governor of the church and all members of the clergy, all ministers of state, judges and mayors were compelled to swear an oath acknowledging Elizabeth's supremacy in "all spiritual or ecclesiastical things or causes."

UNIVERSITIES IN ENGLAND

The religious upheavals in England were reflected in the universities. The church had a strong hand in early university development, and its influence was maintained until the Reformation. Mansbridge has commented that:

> There is, as we have seen, too little evidence to justify the confident assertion that the religious orders originated University life in England, but that they were concerned in it from the beginning is almost certain, and that they sought to dominate it until they were destroyed or swept from the country by the Reformation is well proven.[12]

John Wyclif, the protestant, was a popular teacher at Oxford but his denunciations of the Church and the Crown led to his expulsion from the university. He, it was said, "proposed strange views of the Holy Eucharist" and "the poisons of his heresy," a church spokesman commented later, "had so widely spread that the university found it necessary in 1412 to compel all masters to formally abjure Wyclifism." [13]

Dominion over the university by the Catholic Church gradually gave way to state control over the university by the protestant crown in England. The climax of the change in power came during the 1500's. Under Elizabeth England severed its ties with Rome and the position of government was assumed by the university. Religious ornaments and "evidences of papery" were destroyed and "Edwardism statutes" were strictly adhered to. But, then, Mary succeeded Edward and the university like a volleyball bounced back to the Catholic Church side of the net. The manner of the university and the entire expression of the university changed. Martyrs were burned at Oxford and "religious trials usurped academic disputations." The conflict between church and state and its influence on the academic freedom of the university is vividly portrayed as follows:

> It must have been a discomforting thing to have been

12. *Mansbridge, op. cit.,* p. 15.
13. *Ibid.,* p. 42.

a University teacher with any convictions, "much troubled and hurried up and down by the changes in religion," each of which brought with it a Commission and a purgation of the Universities by the removal of the prominent supporters of whichever party was for the moment declared to be heretical. At one moment we find a teacher, skilled in the dialectic of the Schoolmen, enjoying quiet and unchallenged communion with Holy Church. Suddenly his subject or his treatment of it is discredited. He is ordered to abandon it, or at least to support the introduction of the New Learning. Hardly has he adapted himself, if at all, when he is hurried into a repudiation of his old religious loyalties, by a royal will that brooks no delay. Perchance he manages to keep his old faith, and blossoms forth again in Mary's reign, finally to suffer, or again disguise it, when Elizabeth throws her lot of England once and for all with the Protestants.[14]

By the 1600's, the Protestants, somewhat less concerned about the dangers of Catholicism, began to struggle among themselves for the control of the state. Presbyterianism had become powerful, controlled the House of Commons, and sought to replace Anglicanism as the state church. The Puritan opponents of the Presbyterians eventually gathered around Oliver Cromwell. The exploits of Cromwell, and his military enforcement of morality in England, was a peculiar amalgam of religious devotion and healthy distrust for the clergy. Under Cromwell, the state was supreme and Cromwell's conscience was the religion of the state.

After Cromwell, the church and state conflicts in England mellowed under Charles II, with the Declaration of Indulgence in 1672 which benefited Protestant dissenters and to some extent even Catholics. Following this, the Act of Toleration was issued by William III in 1689 which established "a de facto toleration for all except Catholics." [15] In England, religious freedom was not obtained for Catholics until the nineteenth century with the repeal of the Tests Acts, and Jews did not gain their religious freedom until 1858 when they were finally allowed to sit in Parliament.

It is with this history of continuing religious conflict that the founders of America were familiar. The religious wars of sixteenth and seventeenth century Europe were history, but were still recent enough to be vivid in the minds of the participants in the Constitutional Convention in Philadelphia in

14. *Ibid.*, p. 52.
15. Leo Pfeffer, *op. cit.*, p. 28.

the summer of 1787. The United States Supreme Court has summarized the religious turbulence in this way:

> The centuries immediately before and contemporaneous with the colonization of America had been filled with turmoil, civil strife, and persecution, generated in large part by established sects determined to maintain their absolute political and religious supremacy. With the power of government supporting them, at various times and places, Catholics had persecuted Protestants, Protestants had persecuted Catholics, Protestant sects had persecuted other Protestant sects, Catholics of one shade of belief had persecuted Catholics of another shade of belief, and all of these had from time to time persecuted Jews. In efforts to force loyalty to whatever religious group happened to be on top and in league with the government of a particular time and place, men and women had been fined, cast in jail, cruelly tortured, and killed. Among the offenses for which these punishments had been inflicted were such things as speaking disrespectfully of the views of ministers of government-established churches, non-attendance at those churches, expressions of non-belief in their doctrines, and failure to pay taxes and tithes to support them.

At the time the First Amendment was promulgated, the affairs of state had always been inextricably mingled with those of faith and in no meaningful instance had church and state been successfully separated. On the contrary, where church was dominant, state machinery had been used to further the imposition of the orthodox religion on minorities. Where the power of the state held sway over religion, the church was used to support and reinforce the power of the ruling party. The separation of church and state was yet an untried theory.

ANTECEDENTS OF THE FIRST AMENDMENT

The familiar pattern of governmental establishment of religion accompanied the founders of colonies in America. The Church of England was established in the Virginia and Carolina colonies and were strengthened by subsequent legislative enactments. The New England colonies, with the exception of Rhode Island, established the Congregational Church. In this group were New Hampshire, which included Vermont at that time, and Massachusetts, which encompassed Maine and Connecticut.

The colonies of New Jersey, Maryland, New York and Georgia did not establish and maintain one church. The history of each indicates a changing establishment. New York and New Jersey were originally settled by the Dutch and established Dutch Reform Churches but were shortly thereafter conquered by England, which brought about the governmental sanction of the Church of England. Maryland, though originally organized as a refuge for persecuted Catholics, later granted religious freedom to both Catholics and Protestants, but denied such freedom to non-Christians. The original Charter of Georgia did not provide for a state religion; however, shortly thereafter this instrument was nullified and the Anglican Church was established, by both royal decree and by act of the colony's legislature.

Nessel has summarized the colonial religious experience as falling into four categories: "(1) Initial Establishment of the Church of England, (2) Puritan Establishment, (3) Changing Establishments, and (4) Non-Establishment." [16] Of all the colonies, Rhode Island stood out as the only profound example of separation of church and state. Disestablishment prevailed in Rhode Island from its birth and remained a haven for those who fled religious persecution in the establishment colonies. Progress toward religious freedom in the colonies was very gradual and establishment features remained in the state constitutions until well into the nineteenth century.

The weariness with religious struggles was quite evident when the new republic was created in the summer of 1787. Implicit in the Constitution was the separation of church and state. John Adams expressed the sentiments of most of the Continental Congress when he expressed the hope that "Congress will never meddle with religion further than to say their own prayers, and to fast and to give thanks once a year." [17] The Constitution, as it was finally enacted, did not expressly separate church and state, but simply ignored the question. Since the Constitution is a document which expressly delegates power to the federal government, the absence of a delegation of some religious function must be assumed to imply separation of church and state. While the Constitution contained no express general statement of separation, it did contain a clause which left little doubt as to

16. William Nessel, *First Amendment Freedoms, Papal Pronouncements and Concordat Practice*, The Catholic University of America Press, 1961, p. 1.

17. Evarts B. Green, *Religion and the State*, New York University Press, 1941, p. 83.

the Convention's feeling on the subject. For fear that the federal government might incorporate the customary religious test for office, the Convention expressly prohibited such tests through the last clause of Article VI of the Constitution which states ". . . no religious test shall ever be required as a qualification to any office or public trust under the United States." Justice Joseph Story, an outstanding opponent of the principle of separation,[18] admitted that: "This clause is not introduced merely for the purpose of satisfying the scruples of many respectable persons who feel an invincible repugnance to any religious test or affirmation. It had a higher object: to cut off forever every pretense of any alliance between church and state in national government." [19]

After and during the ratification of the Constitution, a nagging doubt prevailed that the civil rights of the individual had not been clearly assured in the document. Indeed, the ratification was strongly opposed in some states because of the lack of a general statement guaranteeing religious freedom and other basic natural rights of man. Several states ratified but proposed religious liberty amendments to the Constitution, and two states, Rhode Island and North Carolina, insisted on a bill of rights including a disestablishment provision.[20] Defense of the Constitution was made on the ground that a bill of rights was not necessary because powers to include the natural rights were not delegated to Congress. Alexander Hamilton maintained that a bill of rights was not necessary and would be potentially dangerous to the delegated powers of the central government. In the *Federalist,* he said:

> I go further and affirm that bills of rights in the sense and to the extent in which they are contended for, are not only unnecessary in the proposed Constitution, but would even be dangerous. They would contain various exceptions to powers not granted; and, on this very account, would afford a colorable pretext to claim more than was granted. For why declare that things shall not be done which there is no power to do? [21]

Jefferson, however, held the pulse of the people when he wrote concerning the new Constitution to Madison:

18. Leo Pfeffer, "No Law Respecting an Establishment of Religion," *Buffalo Law Review,* Spring, 1953.

19. Joseph Story, *Commentaries on the Constitution of the United States,* Hillard, Gray and Co., 1833, III, p. 705.

20. Freeman R. Butts, *The American Tradition in Religion and Education,* Beacon Press, Boston, 1950, p. 27.

21. *Federalist Papers,* Modern Library ed., 1937, p. 559.

I will now add what I do not like. First, the omission of a bill of rights providing clearly and without the aid of sophisms for freedom of religion, freedom of the press, protection against standing armies, restriction against monopolies, the eternal and unremitting force of the habeas corpus laws, and trials by juries . . . . [A] bill of rights is what the people are entitled to against every government on earth, general or particular, and what no just government should refuse or rest on inference.[22]

Shortly after the Constitution was ratified in 1789, Madison introduced a series of proposals before the Congress to be considered as amendments to the Constitution. Madison's bill of rights were argued and in substance agreed to by the House of Representatives. On September 25, 1789, the Senate and the House agreed on a Bill of Rights, of which the First Amendment provided:

> Congress shall make no law respecting an establishment of religion, or prohibiting the free exercise thereof; or abridging the freedom of speech, or of the press; or the right of the people peaceably to assemble and to petition the Government for a redress of grievances.

The Bill of Rights was approved by the requisite number of states in 1791.

What precisely the First Amendment's religious clauses mean is still an unsettled question in the field of education and religion. To say that the Amendment creates a "wall of separation between church and state," Jefferson's famous words, is to leave much unanswered. Proponents of religious education reflect one concept of religious freedom while advocates of public education generally project a different and more civil libertarian point of view.

STATE CONSTITUTIONAL PROVISIONS FOR RELIGIOUS FREEDOM

After the adoption of the First Amendment, only four of the original thirteen states maintained basic laws which established a particular religion. One of these basic constitutional provisions [23] in Massachusetts provided for the use of the public taxing power to support religious education. This constitutional provision read:

> And all moneys paid by the subject to the support of public worship, and of the public teachers aforesaid, shall,

22. *Jefferson's Writings*, ed. Ford, V, pp. 371-372.
23. Massachusetts Constitution of 1780, Art. 3.

if he requires it, be uniformly applied to the support of the public teacher or teachers of his own religious sect or denomination, provided there be any on whose instruction he attends; otherwise, it may be paid towards the support of the teacher or teachers of the parish or precinct in which the said moneys are raised.

As the principle of separation of church and state became more entrenched in America, prohibitions against public aid for religious functions became more common. By 1833, Massachusetts, the last state maintaining an establishment, abandoned it.

The fervor of American people to provide for religious freedom reached its pinnacle shortly after the Civil War. At this time, in 1876, President Grant recommended a constitutional amendment which would forbid states to teach religious tenets in public schools or to provide public tax funds for aid of religion. Since the First Amendment, at this time,[24] only applied to the federal government, Grant was fearful that states would not strictly adhere to the separation doctrine. James G. Blaine did introduce a federal constitutional amendment which would have mandated that ". . . no money raised by taxation in any state for the support of public schools . . . shall ever be under the control of any religious sect or denomination nor shall any money so raised on lands so devoted be divided between religious sects or denominations." [25]

Even though Blaine's constitutional restriction on states did not succeed, the principle of separation had become such an integral part of our governmental system that each state admitted to the Union subsequent to 1876 was required to have in its constitution a provision guaranteeing the maintenance of a school system "free from sectarian control." [26]

Today, all states have at least some provision guaranteeing the free exercise of religion and all states except Vermont [27] have constitutional provisions prohibiting the expenditure of public funds for sectarian purposes.[28] Phraseology varies greatly among these state constitutional provisions, making generalizations difficult; however, one study [29] suggests seven

---

24. Cantwell v. Connecticut, 310 U.S. 296 (1940).
25. Congressional Record (44th Congress), p. 5580 (1876).
26. McCollum v. Board of Education, 333 U.S. 203 (1948).
27. Vermont Constitution, C.I., Art. 3.
28. Donald E. Boles, *The Bible, Religion and The Public Schools*, Iowa State Press, 1966, p. 43.
29. "Catholic Schools and Public Money," 50 *Yale Law Journal* 917 (1940). See also Boles, *op. cit.*, p. 44.

generic types, varying both as to content and to restrictive-
ness. They are: "(1) public school funds may not be used
for any purpose other than for the support of common schools;
(2) no public grants or appropriation of money, property,
or credit can be made to any institution not under the state's
exclusive control; (3) no public appropriation may be made
for any sectarian purpose, institution, or society; (4) no state
aid may be granted to educational institutions controlled by
a sectarian denomination; (5) no state aid may be extended
to sectarian schools; (6) no state aid may be granted to
private schools; (7) no public appropriation may be made
for any school in which sectarian doctrines are taught."

PUBLIC AID TO RELIGIOUS EDUCATION

Few decisions have been rendered by state and federal
courts regarding public aid to religious institutions of higher
education. Most cases deal with situations arising in elementary and secondary schools, but from these lower education
decisions, one can gain much insight into judicial interpretations of the principles of religious freedom.

THE EVERSON PRECEDENT

Until 1971 the two most important decisions regarding state
aid to parochial education were rendered by the Supreme
Court of the United States in *Everson v. Board of Education* [30]
and *Board of Education v. Allen*.[31] In *Everson*, Justice Black
laid down the rule that "No tax in any amount, large or
small, can be levied to support any religious activities or
institutions, whatever they may be called, or whatever form
they may adopt to teach or practice religion." [32] However,
Justice Black, writing for the majority, did not feel that this
strong disestablishment interpretation prevented a state from
providing payment for school transportation of parochial
school pupils. On the contrary, in this five to four decision,
the Supreme Court suggested that the peripheral aid of transportation was for the benefit of the child and did not constitute state aid to a religious institution. Black said:

> Its [the state of New Jersey] legislation, as applied,
> does no more than provide a general program to help
> parents get their children, regardless of the religion,
> safely and expeditiously to and from accredited schools.[33]

30. 330 U.S. 1 (1947).
31. 392 U.S. 236 (1968).
32. 330 U.S. 1 (1947).
33. *Ibid.*

This theme was carried through in *Allen* in 1968 when the Supreme Court upheld a New York statute which loaned textbooks free of charge to students regardless of whether they were enrolled in public or private religious schools. Here the court again emphasized that the benefit was to the child and not necessarily to the religious institution. Justice White, writing for the majority, gave great weight to the "public purpose" theory, that is, the private school serves a secular purpose and state aid for these purposes is not violative of the First Amendment.

Ironically, Justice Black, the author of the majority opinion in *Everson,* vociferously dissented in this case. Black said that he believed, "The New York law held valid is a flat, flagrant, open violation of the First and Fourteenth Amendments which together forbid Congress or state legislatures to enact any law 'respecting an establishment of religion.'" While White in *Allen* cited Black in *Everson* as prevailing precedent, Justice Black denied that White had properly interpreted him. Black said:

> I know of no prior opinion of this court upon which the majority here can rightfully rely to support its holding this New York law constitutional. In saying this, I am not unmindful of the fact that the New York Court of Appeals purported to follow *Everson v. Board of Education, supra,* in which this court, in an opinion written by me, upheld a New Jersey law authorizing reimbursement to parents for the transportation of children attending sectarian schools. That law did not attempt to deny benefit of its general terms to children of any faith going to any legally authorized school. Thus, it was treated in the same way as a general law paying the streetcar fare of *all school children,* or a law providing midday lunches for all children or all school children, or a law to provide police protection for children going to and from school, or general laws to provide police and fire protection for buildings, including, of course, churches and church school buildings as well as others. * * *
>
> Books are the most essential tool of education since they contain the resources of knowledge which the educational process is designed to exploit. In this sense, it is not difficult to distinguish books, which are the heart of any school, from bus fares, which provide a convenient and helpful general public transportation service.

Black supported state neutrality to the extent of providing "general welfare benefits" to individual pupils, regardless of their school, but would invalidate state support which assisted the religious institution. White, on the other hand, suggested that so long as religious schools play "a significant and valuable role in raising national levels of knowledge, competence, and experience," then it is permissible for the state to compensate the pupils or the schools for these services. White left the question open and defined no particular parameters limiting public aid, so long as the religious institution is in some way meeting a secular educational need.

STATE AID TO SECTARIAN COLLEGES

Religious freedom provisions in state constitutions generally make it more difficult for religious schools to obtain state aid than does the United States Constitution. With such strong standards, few states have attempted to directly appropriate funds for assistance to religiously controlled colleges or universities. Indirect assistance to private and parochial institutions, such as tuition payments for students, has occasionally been litigated.

In one early case in South Dakota, the court found that tuition payments for students to attend Pierre University violated the South Dakota Constitution.[34] Here the board of education of the territory of Dakota, in 1877, had contracted with private Presbyterian Pierre University to provide tuition for students instructed in the methods and practice of teaching in the common schools. Section 3, Article 6 of the South Dakota Constitution stated, ". . . no money or property of the state shall be given or appropriated for the benefit of any sectarian or religious society or institution." The court queried, "Is not the tuition received from every student for the benefit of or to aid the school, to support, to strengthen it?" The court answered this question by saying:

> The paying of the tuition of pupils in the Pierre University to the plaintiff [Synod of Dakota] in this case will, in our opinion, be for the benefit of or to aid such school institution, and is clearly within the prohibition of the Constitution.[35]

The court further pointed out that such tuition contracts could lead to one sect controlling the schools, institutions and funds of the state.

Much later in another case, the Virginia Supreme Court of Appeals struck down a state appropriation act providing tuition for orphans of soldiers, sailors, and marines to attend any

---

34. Synod of Dakota v. State, 2 S.D. 366, 50 N.W. 632 (1891).
35. *Ibid.*

educational or training institution approved by the state school superintendent. The tuition recipients could attend public, private or parochial schools.[36] Defenders of the statute claimed the schools themselves were not the beneficiaries of the funds, instead ". . . school children and the state alone are the beneficiaries." The court, after examining this logic and the precedents, concluded that:

> Tuition and institutional fees go directly to the institution and are its very life blood. Such items are the main support of private schools which are not sufficiently endowed to insure their maintenance. Surely a payment by the state of the tuition and fees of the pupils of a private school begun on the strength of a contract by the state to do so would be an appropriation to that school.[37]

A contrary opinion was reached in the same year, 1955, in New Hampshire in a case involving aid to hospitals even though sectarian hospitals would receive substantial benefits.[38] Grants were made available to all hospitals in the case offering approved training for professional nursing as well as annual nursing scholarships. The court held the grants did not violate a state constitutional prohibition against the granting or applying of money raised by taxation for use of schools or institutions of any religious sect. The court emphasized that the aid did not assist any particular sect but furthered the teaching of nurses; if incidental benefits were derived by some religious denomination, this was immaterial.

In a Massachusetts case which involved no actual case or controversy, the Justices of the Supreme Judicial Court of Massachusetts provided an opinion to the Massachusetts Senate relating to the constitutionality of a bill establishing a building authority to assist both public and private institutions of higher education.[39] The authority would issue revenue bonds for construction projects at individual participating colleges, and the institutions would in turn make payments to the authority sufficient to retire the bonds, principal and interest plus administrative costs of the authority. The revenue bonds do not constitute a debt of the Commonwealth of Massachusetts. The primary question before the Justices was whether the legislation violated freedom of religious guarantees of both the Massachusetts and United States Constitution

---

36. Almond v. Day, 197 Va. 419, 89 S.E.2d 851 (1955).
37. *Ibid.*
38. Opinion of Justices, 99 N.H. 519, 113 A.2d 114 (1955).
39. Opinion of the Justices, 236 N.E.2d 523 (1968).

since private denominational colleges and universities could participate and derive benefit from the authority. The court held that the legislation would not violate the Massachusetts constitutional provision which states: ". . . no grant, appropriation or use of public money or property or loan of public credit shall be made or authorized by the commonwealth." The court held that the creation of the authority in no way appropriated public tax funds for religious purposes and that the prohibition against the loan of public credit was not violated since the individual institution was obligated to pay the principal and interest sufficient to retire bonds for which the bonds were issued. The court did not discuss the possible interest savings to the private institutions by having large authority bond issues rather than small individual college issues. Whether lower interest rates obtained through a public authority constituted state assistance was not considered in the decision.

Regarding the prohibitions of the Federal Constitution, the court said the assistance in financing and construction of facilities did not violate either the "free exercise" or the "establishment" clauses. The court, while recognizing the uncertainty of the United States Supreme Court's attitude in this area, decided that by allowing all colleges and universities to benefit from use of the authority the state was not aiding any particular denomination; therefore, the legislation had a secular purpose.

The building authority technique for assisting private college construction projects was, likewise, upheld in Vermont in 1968.[40] The statute was contested when the state building agency issued revenue bonds, constructed buildings and leased the buildings to denominational colleges. The Supreme Court of Vermont, here, simply said that the Vermont Constitution (Chapter I, Article 3rd, Vt. Con.) was less restrictive than the First Amendment of the United States Constitution. No provision exists in the ". . . explicit injunction precluding assistance to sectarian education." Further efforts were made by the court to support the contention that although the College of St. Joseph, one of the colleges receiving benefits of the authority, was church related and was controlled by a Mother Superior and trustees of the Catholic faith, the ". . . relationship between the college to the Church is one of affinity, rather than direct dominion."

---

40. Vermont Educational Buildings Financing Agency v. Mann, 127 Vt. 262, 247 A.2d 68 (1968).

In dissent, Justice Smith maintained, "There can be no doubt that the agency [authority] is authorized to use the power and prestige of the state to aid the educational institutions with which it contracts, which is sufficient to raise the question" (of religious freedom). "The proposed aid to be furnished to St. Joseph by the Vermont Educational Building Financing Corporation, created by legislative enactment, would inevitably result in the advancement of the particular religious culture which is its stated educational purpose." [41]

Of all the state court decisions involving state aid to religious colleges and universities, the most pervasive is the *Horace Mann League* case in Maryland.[42] Here the issue was precisely whether the State of Maryland could constitutionally provide outright matching grants for construction of buildings at four private colleges. This case is unique for two reasons: (1) Here the state was attempting to provide direct financial assistance to religious institutions, and (2) the issue of what constitutes a church-related college as opposed to a strictly private college was examined and decided on by the court. Under four separate statutes the legislature of Maryland had provided for a total of $2.5 million in matching grants for four private colleges. In order to render a decision, the court was forced to first decide on a definition describing a church-related college. The factors identified by the court which are significant for determining whether an educational institution is religious are: (1) stated purposes of the college, (2) religious affiliation on personnel or college, including governing board, administrative officers, faculty and student body, (3) the college's relationship with religious organizations and groups, (4) the place of religion in the college's program, (5) the result or outcome of the college's program, accreditation and activities of alumni, and (6) the work and image of the college in the community. Upon applying these criteria to the four colleges in question the court held that aid to three of the colleges (one Methodist and two Roman Catholic) transgressed the First Amendment of the Constitution of the United States.

FEDERAL AID TO SECTARIAN COLLEGES

Federal legislation currently provides substantial financial

---

41. *Ibid.*
42. Horace Mann League of U.S. v. Board of Public Works, 242 Md. 645, 220 A.2d 51, (1966), *cert. denied in part, dismissed in part*, 87 S. Ct. 317, 385 U.S. 97 (1966).

assistance to religious or sectarian colleges. In fact, so many federal acts provide such assistance that no realistic assessment of the benefits has ever been made. For example, federal statutes such as the Atomic Energy Act of 1946, as amended, makes grants to institutions of higher education for such things as nuclear laboratory equipment and research reactors.[43] Such federal assistance is provided on contract grant basis for research activities and fall within a different category than other types of federal grants which are made directly to private and sectarian colleges and universities for the stated purpose of directly strengthening the institution or aiding students.

Famous among acts for student assistance and a boon to private colleges was the G. I. Bill of Rights, 1944, which provided for tuition for veterans who wished to attend colleges and universities, including theological seminaries.[44] Other programs benefiting veterans have been enacted but in none of these acts is there any distinction drawn between secular and sectarian institutions. Later the National Defense Education Act of 1958 allocated funds directly to both students and institutions. Subchapter II authorized funds for low-interest loans to students to attend either public or private colleges.[45] Subchapter IV established National Defense Fellowships primarily for graduate students being trained to teach in higher education, stipends from these grants going to both students and institutions they attend. In 1964 a restriction was placed on the use of these funds to prohibit training of ministers or preparation for teaching theology.[46] This amendment, however, does not affect other phases of sectarian college training. In addition, the NDEA provided for grants to improve guidance and counseling [47] and grants to set up institutes for advanced study.[48] Both of these grant programs are available to sectarian universities without limitation.[49]

The Higher Education Facilities Act of 1963 [50] represented

---

43. 42 U.S.C. § 2051 (1964). See also Sutherland, "Establishment of Religion—1968," *Case Western Reserve*, Vol. 19, pp. 479-482 (1968).

44. Walter Gellhorn and R. Kent Greenwalt, "Public Support and The Sectarian University," *Fordham Law Review*, March 1970.

45. 20 U.S.C. § 421-26 (Supp. IV 1969).

46. 20 U.S.C. § 463 (d) (1964).

47. *Ibid.* § 491.

48. 20 U.S.C. § 591 (Supp. IV, 1969), amending 20 U.S.C. § 591 (1964).

49. *Gellhorn, op. cit.*, p. 427.

50. 20 U.S.C. § 701-57 (1964), as amended, 20 U.S.C. § 711-19, 731-33, 743-46, 751, 758 (Supp. IV, 1969).

a major breakthrough for federal financing of higher education, and church-related colleges and universities gained substantial benefits. The only limitation on sectarian colleges was
that the facilities constructed with these funds could not be
used for "sectarian instruction or as a place of religious worship" or for a "school or department of divinity" [51] In the Senate debates before the passage of the Higher Education Facilities Act, Senator Sam Ervin proposed amendments which
would have barred aid to church-related colleges, contending
that as the act stood it was unconstitutional. Senator Ervin's
amendment failed, primarily on the pragmatic ground that if
the bill were amended the private and parochial school contingent in the Congress would kill the bill completely.[52] It is
interesting to note that in his dissent in the *Allen* case, Justice
Black cited the Higher Education Facilities Act of 1963 as an
example of unconstitutional use of government funds.

> And that there are already efforts to have government
> supply the money to erect buildings for sectarian re-
> ligious schools is shown by a recent Act of Congress
> which apparently allows for precisely that. See Higher
> Education Facilities Act of 1963 * * *.[53]

Two years later another substantial federal subvention for
higher education was authorized by the passage of the Higher
Education Act of 1965.[54] Subchapters I and II provide funds
for community service and continuing education programs
and grants for acquisition of library materials.[55] Under both
of these provisions the funds may not be used for "sectarian
instruction" or "religious worship." Subchapter III authorizes
funds for cooperative arrangements allowing "developing institutions" to draw on the talent and resources of other established institutions.[56] The term "developing institutions" is defined to exclude institutions and branches of institutions preparing students for the ministry, a religious vocation, or to
teach religion.[57] However, sectarian institutions controlled by
religious groups can receive funds for portions of the school's
program which train students for something other than the
enumerated religious pursuits. No such restrictions are en-

---

51. 20 U.S.C. § 751 (2) (Supp. IV, 1969).
52. Gellhorn, *op. cit.*
53. Board of Education v. Allen, *supra* at p. 253.
54. 20 U.S.C. § 1001-150 (Supp. IV, 1969).
55. *Ibid.* § 1001-11.
56. *Ibid.* § 1027.
57. *Ibid.* § 1052 (h).

compassed in subchapter IV (A) and (B) which provide for grants to high school graduates of exceptional need and which strengthen programs of low interest insured loans. Under subchapter IV (C) there is a limitation on work study grants which prohibits students from helping construct, operate, or maintain facilities used for sectarian instruction or religious worship.[58] Fellowships to teachers, under subchapter V (C), are available through church-related colleges and universities, for all programs, except those devoted to departments or schools of divinity.[59] Amendments to the Higher Education Act in 1968 expand these programs but do not alter the treatment of church-related institutions.[60]

In retrospect, one can observe that the federal government has been much more permissive regarding grants to church-related colleges and universities than have individual states. One factor contributing to this was that a taxpayer did not have capacity to sue the federal government to question a federal aid program until 1968. Prior to that year the United States Supreme Court had maintained that the individual taxpayer's interest in the federal treasury was so infinitesimal that no actual case or controversy existed on which a Congressional grant program could be constitutionally tested.[61] In 1968 the Supreme Court re-examined the taxpayer "standing" issue and held that henceforth a taxpayer did have standing to sue to contest a federal appropriation.[62] Now a taxpayer can contest the constitutionality of a federal higher education grant program solely on the basis that he is a citizen and a taxpayer, and an unconstitutional appropriation of public funds violates the First Amendment which guarantees religious freedom.

Prior to the enactment of the major higher education legislation in the 1960's the only precedent concerning a direct attack on federal expenditure of funds was handed down by the Supreme Court in 1908. This case, *Quick Bear v. Leupp*, [63] has limited utility since the issue of church and state was clouded by a distinction between public appropriations from general taxation and permanent trust funds provided to Indians by

---

58. 42 U.S.C. § 2751-57 (Supp. IV, 1969) and 20 U.S.C. § 1111-18 (Supp. IV, 1969).
59. *Ibid.*
60. Gellhorn, *op. cit.*, p. 428.
61. Frothingham v. Mellon, 262 U.S. 447 (1923).
62. Flast v. Cohen, 392 U.S. 83 (1968).
63. 210 U.S. 50 (1908).

treaty. The court held that the provisions of the Indian Appropriation Acts, 1895 through 1899, prohibiting contracts for education of Indians in sectarian schools related only to appropriations of public moneys raised by general taxation and did not relate to the disposition of tribal and trust funds which belonged to the Indians. The court further held that the religion clauses of the Federal Constitution did not restrict the Indians' use of the tribal permanent trust funds.

Before the enactment of the Higher Education Facilities Act of 1963, the Senate requested [64] an opinion by the Secretary of Health, Education and Welfare regarding the constitutionality of providing loans for construction purposes to private and parochial schools. The resulting opinion readily identified several conditions under which aid to sectarian schools would be unconstitutional: [65] (1) "Across-the-board grants to church schools may not be made;" (2) "Across-the-board grants to church schools are equally invalid;" (3) "Tuition payments for all church school pupils are invalid since they accomplish by indirection what grants do directly." From this beginning, which referred to elementary and secondary education, the opinion then branched into higher education. The opinion reasoned that the constitutional prohibitions against aid to elementary and secondary schools were not applicable to higher education. After looking at the historical development of elementary and secondary schools as a public phenomenon, as opposed to the evolution of higher education as an essentially private one, the opinion concluded that two different constitutional standards exist. Expanding on the differences between lower education and higher education, the memorandum pointed out that attendance of college students is wholly voluntary and these older students, being more mature, can understand the significance of sectarian teaching. While on the other hand, the pupils in lower grades are subject to compulsory attendance, are less mature, and do not have the freedom to choose among institutions as do the college students. Weighing these factors, the opinion held that federal aid, either grants or loans, to sectarian colleges and universities are within constitutional limits.[66] Pfeffer in disagreeing with the logic of the legal memorandum commented:

(1) The distinction between lower and higher educa-

---

64. Senate Resolution 126, May 1, 1961.
65. *Constitutionality of Federal Aid to Education in Its Various Aspects*, Documents No. 29, 87th Congress, 1st Session, G.P.O., 1961, p. 6.
66. *Ibid.*, p. 26.

tion in respect to the church-state issue appears to be a novel one. Nothing in the language of any Supreme Court decision supports it; nor does it appear to have been made in any state court decision. (2) The factors listed in the memorandum may well be relevant to a decision on the wisdom or desirability of according governmental aid at the higher level, but hardly to the question of constitutionality. (3) It is particularly difficult to comprehend the relevancy of the argument—often made—that aid at the college level is constitutionally permissible because "collegiate enrollment does not have the power of state compulsion supporting it." If relevant at all, it would seem to point to a directly contrary conclusion. One of the arguments most often asserted by Catholic spokesmen in support of their claim to governmental funds for parochial schools is that unless the government makes it financially feasible for Catholic children to attend parochial schools their religious liberty is violated by being forced against their consciences to attend secular public schools pursuant to compulsory attendance laws. This argument is obviously absent where, as at the college level, there is no compulsion by law to attend.[67]

Ultimately, the memorandum served its purpose in supporting passage of the Higher Education Facilities Act of 1963, but became an anathema to the Johnson administration in 1964 when hearings were held concerning federal aid to elementary and secondary education. The memorandum was finally regarded very lightly as the federal government enacted the Elementary and Secondary Education Act of 1965 providing in several ways for assistance to sectarian elementary and secondary schools.

However, the two-level constitutional standard propounded in the H.E.W. memorandum was in essence adopted by the United States Supreme Court in 1971 when the Court held that salary supplements paid to teachers of secular subjects in elementary and secondary parochial schools were unconstitutional.[68] The Court then on the same day, June 28, 1971, handed down another decision holding that Higher Education Facilities Act of 1963 grants to church-related colleges were not unconstitutional.[69] While justifying the dichotomy to some extent by explaining that religion does not necessarily "permeate" or "seep into" the use of facilities, the Court further distinguished the elementary and secondary situation from that of higher education by pointing out that college stu-

67. Pfeffer, *op. cit.*, p. 598.
68. Lemon v. Kurtzman, 91 S. Ct. 2105 (1971).
69. Tilton v. Richardson, 91 S. Ct. 2091 (1971).

dents are "less susceptible to religious indoctrination." The Court said:

> There are generally significant differences between the religious aspects of church-related institutions of higher learning and parochial elementary and secondary schools. The "affirmative, if not dominant policy" of the instruction in pre-college church-schools is "to assure future adherents to a particular faith by having control of their total education at an early age." * * * There is substance to the contention that college students are less susceptible to religious indoctrination.[70]

TEACHING RELIGION IN STATE UNIVERSITIES

Close relationship between university and religious groups has been a hallmark of American higher education. The desire to train young men for the ministry was a primary motivation of early colleges and universities. As state universities began to increase in number and size the role of higher education became more diverse. State institutions tended to concentrate their efforts in areas of secular professional training and were influenced greatly by the new scientific and technological advances. Even with these tendencies many state schools continued to hold scheduled religious services for the student body, and more often than not such activities were compulsory.

No definitive statement was made by the Supreme Court regarding religious services and exercises in public institutions until *McCollum*,[71] in 1948, and even then the case involved elementary and secondary schools and not higher education. In *McCollum* the Supreme Court held unconstitutional a program whereby students were released from class to attend religious instructional classes in another part of the school building. The religious instruction was carried out by Jewish, Roman Catholic and Protestant faiths, and children not wishing to attend these religious activities were allowed to study separately in another room. The Court held that the arrangment was unconstitutional, reasoning that the use of tax-supported property for religious instruction and the close cooperation between school authorities and the religious groups violated the First Amendment. The point is made rather strongly that the compulsory attendance laws of the state tend to support religion in a school sanctioned religious program of this nature.

---

70. *Ibid.*
71. McCollum v. Board of Education, 333 U.S. 203 (1948).

This emphasis might tend to lead one to believe that a similar program at the college level, where attendance is voluntary, may be constitutional. However, the prevailing point made by the Court seemed to be that the use of tax-supported school property and the *too* close cooperation between school and church personnel was the dominate reason for holding the practice unconstitutional.

In a later case, originating in New York, the Court held another type of released time program constitutional.[72] Here, legislators in New York had, with *McCollum* in mind, carefully circumscribed procedures by which children could be released from school to attend religious services off school grounds, with a minimum of school personnel involvement. The chief differences between the two programs were:

(1) In the *McCollum* case the pupils who did not want to participate had to move to a different room: in the *Zorach* case the pupils who *did* want to participate had to move.

(2) In the *McCollum* case the religious instruction took place in a regular public school classroom: in *Zorach* the religious instruction took place off school grounds.

(3) In the *McCollum* case the teacher and other school personnel cooperated closely with the religious instructional program: in *Zorach* the office of the teacher was not used to persuade, force, or coerce students to take religious instruction.

Since the property of the state was not involved and the influence and cooperation of the public school was remote, the Court found no violation of religious freedom existed.

Curiously, the facts of the *Zorach* case are not too far removed from the situation which existed at the University of Virginia in 1822 when Thomas Jefferson was Rector. Thomas Jefferson, the chief proponent of separation of church and state, had allowed no professorship of divinity[73] at the university, but within four years sectarian demands had become

---

72. Zorach v. Clauson, 343 U.S. 306 (1952).

73. Jefferson's report to the commissioners for the University of Virginia in 1818 stated: "In conformity with the principles of our Constitution, which places all sects of religion on an equal footing . . . we have proposed no professor of divinity. . . . Proceeding this far without offence to the Constitution, we have thought it proper at this point to leave every sect to provide, as they think fittest, the means of further instruction in their own peculiar tenets." Leonard W. Levy, *Jefferson and Civil Liberties*, Harvard University Press, 1963, pp. 11-12.

so great that Jefferson was forced to compromise his position and reluctantly accepted the suggestion "by some pious individuals . . . to establish their religious schools on the confines of the university, so as to give their students ready and convenient access and attendance to the scientific lectures of the university." Jefferson also observed that these religious schools would offer places where regular students at the university could worship as they pleased, "But always understanding that these schools shall be independent of the university and of each other."[74]

So the released time concept is not new and is familiar at both elementary and secondary levels as well as university levels. Of course, the voluntary nature of attendance at modern colleges and universities coupled with the student's freedom on campus to come and go as he pleases, probably makes the entire released time question moot as it applies to institutions of higher education. However, the Supreme Court cases involving released time do provide valuable dictum for analyzing the application of the *principle* of separation to colleges and universities.

In the early sixties the Supreme Court once again was faced with the question of religion in public education. Three cases, all involving prayer and/or Bible reading, updated the Court's views regarding the teaching of religion in the public schools. The first of these cases, decided in 1962, held that the State Board of Regents of New York could not compose an official state prayer and require it to be recited in the public schools.[75] The prayer was denominationally neutral and pupils wishing to remain silent or be excused from class could do so. The prayer to be said aloud stated: "Almighty God, we acknowledge our dependence upon Thee and we beg Thy blessings upon us, our parents, our teachers and our Country."

The Court pointed out that the governmentally composed and required prayer was one of the most obnoxious practices of establishment governments, and with respect to the nondenominational noncompulsory aspects of the prayer, the Court commented:

> Neither the fact that the prayer may be denominationally neutral nor the fact that its observance on the part of the students is voluntary can serve to free it from the limitations of the Establishment Clause * * *. The Establishment Clause, unlike the Free Exercise Clause, does

---

74. *Ibid.*, pp. 12-13.
75. Engel v. Vitale, 370 U.S. 421 (1962).

not depend upon any showing of direct governmental compulsion and is violated by the enactment of laws which establish an official religion whether those laws operate directly to coerce nonobserving individuals or not. * * * When the power, prestige and financial support of government is placed behind a particular religious belief, the indirect coercive pressure upon religious minorities to conform to the prevailing officially approved religion is plain."

The other two cases, companion cases before the Court, followed a year later and brought forth the question of both prayer and Bible reading in the public schools.[76] Prior to this decision several states had statutes or school board regulations requiring prayer and Bible reading as opening exercises at the beginning of each school day. In the *Schempp* case, as in *Engel*, individual students could be excused from attending or participating in such exercises upon written request of their parents. The primary difference, with regard to prayers, between *Engel* and *Schempp* was that in the former the state composed the prayer and in the latter the Lord's Prayer was used. With respect to Bible reading, although state courts had dealt with this issue on numerous occasions, this was the first Bible reading decision for the Supreme Court. The Court found that Bible reading did inculcate religion and denied that the Bible in this case was being used either as "an instrument for nonreligious moral inspiration or as a reference for the teaching of secular subjects." In defense of the prayer and Bible reading requirements, it was insisted that unless religious exercises are permitted "a religion of secularism" is established by the state. In response, the Court said that a "religion of secularism" would not be permitted where the state affirmatively opposed or was hostile to religion; however, this was not the case here.

> Finally, we cannot accept that the concept of neutrality, which does not permit a state to require religious exercise with the consent of the majority of those affected, collides with the majority's right to free exercise of religion. While the Free Exercise Clause clearly prohibits the use of state action to deny the rights of free exercise to anyone, it has never meant that a majority could use the machinery of the state to practice its beliefs.

Significantly, the Court did not deny the right or necessity of public schools to teach religion for its literary and historic values.

---

76. School District of Abington Township v. Schempp, 374 U.S. 203 (1963).

In addition, it might well be said that one's education is not complete without a study of comparative religion or the history of religion and its relationship to advancement of civilization. It certainly may be said that the Bible is worthy of study for its literary and historic qualities. Nothing we have said here indicates that such study of the Bible or of religion, when presented objectively as a part of a secular program of education, may not be effected consistently with the First Amendment.

The religion courses taught by public colleges and universities generally fall within the realm of this qualification. Such courses are taught not to inculcate religion but to examine the literary, historic, and philosophic values as well as comparisons of religions in the development and evolvement of man. Situations, on the other hand, where state institutions hold required religious worship exercises or teach religion for purposes of proselytism are clearly unconstitutional.

In summarizing the position of religion in the state university, Pfeffer has set forth the following propositions: [77]

    (1) Courses in comparative religion, the philosophy of religions, and similar studies are constitutionally permissible if the end sought is understanding rather than belief—although of course belief may well result from understanding.

    (2) Compulsory religious chapel attendance, whether sectarian or nonsectarian, and whether on or off the campus, is unconstitutional. Even if it is not compulsory, college credit may not be accorded such attendance.

    (3) Whether college credit may be granted for courses attended at a theological or denominational institution would depend on whether the courses attended could constitutionally have been given at the state university.

    (4) College administrators may not take the responsibility for religious initiative and action; religious organizations should assume this responsibility, and should maintain privately owned chapels and religious centers adjacent to the campus. The religious activities of these organizations may be publicized, as a public service, within the college, but the college administration and faculty should refrain from encouraging or discouraging attendance.

---

77. Pfeffer, *op. cit.*, p. 508.

State aid for transportation of children to sectarian schools is not unconstitutional

EVERSON v. BOARD OF EDUCATION

Supreme Court of the United States, 1947.
330 U.S. 1, 67 S. Ct. 504.

MR. JUSTICE BLACK delivered the opinion of the Court.

A New Jersey statute authorizes its local school districts to make rules and contracts for the transportation of children to and from schools. The appellee, a township board of education, acting pursuant to this statute authorized reimbursement to parents of money expended by them for the bus transportation of their children on regular busses operated by the public transportation system. Part of this money was for the payment of transportation of some children in the community to Catholic parochial schools. These church schools give their students, in addition to secular education, regular religious instruction conforming to the religious tenets and modes of worship of the Catholic Faith. The superintendent of these schools is a Catholic priest.

The appellant, in his capacity as a district taxpayer, filed suit in a State court challenging the right of the Board to reimburse parents of parochial school students. He contended that the statute and the resolution passed pursuant to it violated both the State and the Federal Constitutions. That court held that the legislature was without power to authorize such payment under the State constitution. 132 N.J.L. 98, 39 A.2d 75. The New Jersey Court of Errors and Appeals reversed, holding that neither the statute nor the resolution passed pursuant to it was in conflict with the State constitution or the provisions of the Federal Constitution in issue. 44 A.2d 333, 133 N.J.L. 350. The case is here on appeal under 28 U.S.C. § 344(a), 28 U.S.C.A. § 344(a). * * *

The only contention here is that the State statute and the resolution, in so far as they authorized reimbursement to parents of children attending parochial schools, violate the Federal Constitution in these two respects, which to some extent, overlap. First. They authorize the State to take by taxation the private property of some and bestow it upon others, to be used for their own private purposes. This, it is alleged violates the due process clause of the Fourteenth Amendment. Second. The statute and the resolution forced inhabitants to

pay taxes to help support and maintain schools which are dedicated to, and which regularly teach, the Catholic Faith. This is
alleged to be a use of State power to support church schools
contrary to the prohibition of the First Amendment which
the Fourteenth Amendment made applicable to the states.

First. The due process argument that the State law taxes
some people to help others carry out their private purposes is
framed in two phases. The first phase is that a state cannot
tax A to reimburse B for the cost of transporting his children
to church schools. This is said to violate the due process clause
because the children are sent to these church schools to satisfy the personal desires of their parents, rather than the
public's interest in the general education of all children. This
argument, if valid, would apply equally to prohibit state payment for the transportation of children to any non-public
school, whether operated by a church, or any other non-gov-
ernment individual or group. But, the New Jersey legislature has decided that a public purpose will be served by using tax-raised funds to pay the bus fares of all school children, including those who attend parochial schools. The New
Jersey Court of Errors and Appeals has reached the same
conclusion. The fact that a state law, passed to satisfy a
public need, coincides with the personal desires of the individuals most directly affected is certainly an inadequate reason for us to say that a legislature has erroneously appraised
the public need. * * *

It is much too late to argue that legislation intended to facilitate the opportunity of children to get a secular education
serves no public purpose. Cochran v. Louisiana State Board
of Education, 281 U.S. 370, 50 S.Ct. 335, 74 L.Ed. 913; * * *
The same thing is no less true of legislation to reimburse
needy parents, or all parents, for payment of the fares of their
children so that they can ride in public busses to and from
schools rather than run the risk of traffic and other hazards
incident to walking or "hitchhiking." * * * Nor does it follow that a law has a private rather than a public purpose
because it provides that tax-raised funds will be paid to reimburse individuals on account of money spent by them in a
way which furthers a public program. * * * Subsidies and
loans to individuals such as farmers and home owners, and
to privately owned transportation systems, as well as many
other kinds of businesses, have been commonplace practices
in our state and national history.

Insofar as the second phase of the due process argument

may differ from the first, it is by suggesting that taxation for transportation of children to church schools constitutes support of a religion by the State. But if the law is invalid for this reason, it is because it violates the First Amendment's prohibition against the establishment of religion by law. This is the exact question raised by appellant's second contention, to consideration of which we now turn.

Second. The New Jersey statute is challenged as a "law respecting an establishment of religion." The First Amendment, as made applicable to the states by the Fourteenth * * * commands that a state "shall make no law respecting an establishment of religion, or prohibiting the free exercise thereof." These words of the First Amendment reflected in the minds of early Americans a vivid mental picture of conditions and practices which they fervently wished to stamp out in order to preserve liberty for themselves and for their posterity. Doubtless their goal has not been entirely reached; but so far has the Nation moved toward it that the expression "law respecting an establishment of religion," probably does not so vividly remind present-day Americans of the evils, fears, and political problems that caused that expression to be written into our Bill of Rights. * * *

The "establishment of religion" clause of the First Amendment means at least this: Neither a state nor the Federal Government can set up a church. Neither can pass laws which aid one religion, aid all religions, or prefer one religion over another. Neither can force nor influence a person to go to or remain away from church against his will or force him to profess a belief or disbelief in any religion. No person can be punished for entertaining or professing religious beliefs or disbeliefs, for church attendance or non-attendance. No tax in any amount, large or small, can be levied to support any religious activities or institutions, whatever they may be called, or whatever form they may adopt to teach or practice religion. Neither a state nor the Federal Government can, openly or secretly, participate in the affairs of any religious organizations or groups and vice versa. In the words of Jefferson, the clause against establishment of religion by law was intended to erect "a wall of separation between Church and State." Reynolds v. United States, supra, 98 U.S. at page 164, 25 L.Ed. 244.

We must consider the New Jersey statute in accordance with the foregoing limitations imposed by the First Amendment. But we must not strike that state statute down if it is within the state's constitutional power even though it approaches the verge of that power. * * * New Jersey cannot consistently with the "establishment of religion" clause of the First Amendment contribute tax-raised funds to the support of an institution which teaches the tenets and faith of any church. On the other hand, other language of the amendment commands that New Jersey cannot hamper its citizens in the free exercise of their own religion. Consequently, it cannot exclude individual Catholics, Lutherans, Mohammedans, Baptists, Jews, Methodists, Non-believers, Presbyterians, or the members of any other faith, *because of their faith, or lack of it,* from receiving the benefits of public welfare legislation. While we do not mean to intimate that a state could not provide transportation only to children attending public schools, we must be careful, in protecting the citizens of New Jersey against state-established churches, to be sure that we do not inadvertently prohibit New Jersey from extending its general State law benefits to all its citizens without regard to their religious belief.

Measured by these standards, we cannot say that the First Amendment prohibits New Jersey from spending tax-raised funds to pay the bus fares of parochial school pupils as a part of a general program under which it pays the fares of pupils attending public and other schools. It is undoubtedly true that children are helped to get to church schools. There is even a possibility that some of the children might not be sent to the church schools if the parents were compelled to pay their children's bus fares out of their own pockets when transportation to a public school would have been paid for by the State. The same possibility exists where the state requires a local transit company to provide reduced fares to school children including those attending parochial schools, or where a municipally owned transportation system undertakes to carry all school children free of charge. Moreover, state-paid policemen, detailed to protect children going to and from church schools from the very real hazards of traffic, would serve much the same purpose and accomplish much the same result as state provisions intended to guarantee free transportation of a kind which the state deems to be best for the school children's welfare. And parents might refuse to risk their children to the serious danger of traffic accidents going to and from parochial schools, the approaches to which were not protected by policemen. Similarly, parents might be reluctant to permit their children to attend schools which the state had cut off from such general government services as ordinary police and fire protection, connections for sewage disposal, public highways and sidewalks. Of course, cutting off church schools from these services, so separate and so indisputably marked off from the religious function, would make it far more difficult for the schools to operate. But such is obviously not the purpose of the First Amendment. That Amendment requires the state to be a neutral in its relations with groups of religious believers and non-believers; it does not require the state to be their adversary. State power is no more to be used so as to handicap religions, than it is to favor them. * * *

The First Amendment has erected a wall between church and state. That wall must be kept high and impregnable. We could not approve the slightest breach. New Jersey has not breached it here.

Affirmed.

MR. JUSTICE RUTLEDGE, with whom MR. JUSTICE FRANKFURTER, MR. JUSTICE JACKSON and MR. JUSTICE BURTON agree, dissenting.

"Congress shall make no law respecting an establishment of religion, or prohibiting the free exercise thereof. * * *." U.S. Const.Am. Art. I.

* * *

"Well aware that Almighty God hath created the mind free; * * * that to compel a man to furnish contributions of money for the propagation of opinions which he disbelieves, is sinful and tyrannical; * * *

"We, the General Assembly, do enact, That no man shall be compelled to frequent or support any religious worship, place, or ministry whatsoever, nor shall be enforced, restrained, molested, or burthened in his body or goods, nor shall otherwise suffer on account of his religious opinions or belief. * * *" 7

I cannot believe that the great author of those words, or the men who made them law, could have joined in this decision. Neither so high nor so impregnable today as yesterday is the wall raised between church and state by Virginia's great statute of religious freedom and the First Amendment, now made applicable to all the states by the Fourteenth. New Jersey's statute sustained is the first, if indeed it is not the

---

7. "A Bill for Establishing Religious Freedom," enacted by the General Assembly of Virginia, January 19, 1786. See 1 Randall, The Life of Thomas Jefferson (1858) 219-220; XII Hening's Statutes of Virginia (1823) 84.

second breach to be made by this Court's action. That a third, and a fourth, and still others will be attempted, we may be sure. For just as Cochran v. Louisiana State Board of Education, 281 U.S. 370, 50 S.Ct. 335, has opened the way by oblique ruling for this decision, so will the two make wider the breach for a third. Thus with time the most solid freedom steadily gives way before continuing corrosive decision.

This case forces us to determine squarely for the first time what was "an establishment of religion" in the First Amendment's conception; and by that measure to decide whether New Jersey's action violates its command. * * *

Not simply an established church, but any law respecting an establishment of religion is forbidden. The Amendment was broadly but not loosely phrased. It is the compact and exact summation of its author's views formed during his long struggle for religious freedom. In Madison's own words characterizing Jefferson's Bill for Establishing Religious Freedom, the guaranty he put in our national charter, like the bill he piloted through the Virgina Assembly, was "a Model of technical precision, and perspicuous brevity." Madison could not have confused "church" and "religion," or "an established church" and "an establishment of religion."

The Amendment's purpose was not to strike merely at the official establishment of a single sect, creed or religion, outlawing only a formal relation such as had prevailed in England and some of the colonies. Necessarily it was to uproot all such relationships. But the object was broader than separating church and state in this narrow sense. It was to create a complete and permanent separation of the spheres of religious activity and civil authority by comprehensively forbidding every form of public aid or support for religion. In proof the Amendment's wording and history unite with this Court's consistent utterances whenever attention has been fixed directly upon the question. * * *

No provision of the Constitution is more closely tied to or given content by its generating history than the religious clause of the First Amendment. It is at once the refined product and the terse summation of that history. The history includes not only Madison's authorship and the proceedings before the First Congress, but also the long and intensive struggle for religious freedom in America, more especially in Virginia, of which the Amendment was the direct culmination. In the documents of the times, particularly of Madison, who was leader in the Virginia struggle before he became the

Amendment's sponsor, but also in the writings of Jefferson and others and in the issues which engendered them is to be found irrefutable confirmation of the Amendment's sweeping content.

For Madison, as also for Jefferson, religious freedom was the crux of the struggle for freedom in general. * * * Madison was coauthor with George Mason of the religious clause in Virginia's great Declaration of Rights of 1776. He is credited with changing it from a mere statement of the principle of tolerance to the first official legislative pronouncement that freedom of conscience and religion are inherent rights of the individual. He sought also to have the Declaration expressly condemn the existing Virginia establishment. But the forces supporting it were then too strong.

Accordingly Madison yielded on this phase but not for long. At once he resumed the fight, continuing it before succeeding legislative sessions. As a member of the General Assembly in 1779 he threw his full weight behind Jefferson's historic Bill for Establishing Religious Freedom. That bill was a prime phase of Jefferson's broad program of democratic reform undertaken on his return from the Continental Congress in 1776 and submitted for the General Assembly's consideration in 1779 as his proposed revised Virginia code. With Jefferson's departure for Europe in 1784, Madison became the Bill's prime sponsor. Enactment failed in successive legislatures from its introduction in June 1779, until its adoption in January, 1786. But during all this time the fight for religious freedom moved forward in Virginia on various fronts with growing intensity. Madison led throughout, against Patrick Henry's powerful opposing leadership until Henry was elected governor in November, 1784.

The climax came in the legislative struggle of 1784-1785 over the Assessment Bill. * * * This was nothing more nor less than a taxing measure for the support of religion, designed to revive the payment of tithes suspended since 1777. So long as it singled out a particular sect for preference it incurred the active and general hostility of dissentient groups. It was broadened to include them, with the result that some subsided temporarily in their opposition. As altered, the bill gave to each taxpayer the privilege of designating which church should receive his share of the tax. In default of designation the legislature applied it to pious uses. But what is of the utmost significance here, "in its final form the bill left the taxpayer the option of giving his tax to education."

Madison was unyielding at all times, opposing with all his vigor the general and nondiscriminatory as he had the earlier particular and discriminatory assessments proposed. The modified Assessment Bill passed second reading in December, 1784, and was all but enacted. Madison and his followers, however, maneuvered deferment of final consideration until November, 1785. And before the Assembly reconvened in the fall he issued his historic Memorial and Remonstrance. * * *

The Remonstrance, stirring up a storm of popular protest, killed the Assessment Bill. It collapsed in committee shortly before Christmas, 1785. With this, the way was cleared at last for enactment of Jefferson's Bill for Establishing Religious Freedom. Madison promptly drove it through in January of 1786, seven years from the time it was first introduced. This dual victory substantially ended the fight over establishments, settling the issue against them. * * *

The next year Madison became a member of the Constitutional Convention. Its work done, he fought valiantly to secure the ratification of its great product in Virginia as elsewhere, and nowhere else more effectively. Madison was certain in his own mind that under the Constitution "there is not a shadow of right in the general government to intermeddle with religion" and that "this subject is, for the honor of America, perfectly free and unshackled. The Government has no jurisdiction over it. * * *" Nevertheless he pledged that he would work for a Bill of Rights, including a specific guaranty of religious freedom, and Virginia, with other states, ratified the Constitution on this assurance.

Ratification thus accomplished, Madison was sent to the first Congress. There he went at once about performing his pledge to establish freedom for the nation as he had done in Virginia. Within a little more than three years from his legislative victory at home he had proposed and secured the submission and ratification of the First Amendment as the first article of our Bill of Rights.[8]

All the great instruments of the Virginia struggle for religious liberty thus became warp and woof of our constitu-

---

8. The amendment with respect to religious liberties read, as Madison introduced it: "The civil rights of none shall be abridged on account of religious belief or worship, nor shall any national religion be established, nor shall the full and equal rights of conscience be in any manner, or on any pretext, infringed." 1 Annals of Congress 434. In the process of debate this was modified to its present form. See especially 1 Annals of Congress 729-731, 765; also note 34.

tional tradition, not simply by the course of history, but by the common unifying force of Madison's life, thought and sponsorship. He epitomized the whole of that tradition in the Amendment's compact, but nonetheless comprehensive, phrasing.

As the Remonstrance discloses throughout, Madison opposed every form and degree of official relation between religion and civil authority. For him religion was a wholly private matter beyond the scope of civil power either to restrain or to support. Denial or abridgment of religious freedom was a violation of rights both of conscience and of natural equality. State aid was no less obnoxious or destructive to freedom and to religion itself than other forms of state interference. "Establishment" and "free exercise" were correlative and coextensive ideas, representing only different facets of the single great and fundamental freedom. The Remonstrance, following the Virginia statute's example, referred to the history of religious conflicts and the effects of all sorts of establishments, current and historical, to suppress religion's free exercise. With Jefferson, Madison believed that to tolerate any fragment of establishment would be by so much to perpetuate restraint upon that freedom. Hence he sought to tear out the institution not partially but root and branch, and to bar its return forever.

In no phase was he more unrelentingly absolute than in opposing state support or aid by taxation. Not even "three pence" contribution was thus to be exacted from any citizen for such a purpose. * * * Tithes had been the life blood of establishment before and after other compulsions disappeared. Madison and his coworkers made no exceptions or abridgments to the complete separation they created. Their objection was not to small tithes. It was to any tithes whatsoever. "If it were lawful to impose a small tax for religion the admission would pave the way for oppressive levies." Not the amount but "the principle of assessment was wrong." And the principle was as much to prevent "the interference of law in religion" as to restrain religious intervention in political matters. In this field the authors of our freedom would not tolerate "the first experiment on our liberties" or "wait till usurped power had strengthened itself by exercise, and entangled the question in precedents." * * * Nor should we.

In view of this history no further proof is needed that the Amendment forbids any appropriation, large or small, from public funds to aid or support any and all religious exercises. But if more were called for, the debates in the First Congress and this Court's consistent expressions, whenever it has touched on the matter directly, supply it. * * *

Compulsory attendance upon religious exercises went out early in the process of separating church and state, together with forced observance of religious forms and ceremonies. Test oaths and religious qualification for office followed later. These things none devoted to our great tradition of religious liberty would think of bringing back. Hence today, apart from efforts to inject religious training or exercises and sectarian issues into the public schools, the only serious surviving threat to maintaining that complete and permanent separation of religion and civil power which the First Amendment commands is through use of the taxing power to support religion, religious establishments, or establishments having a religious foundation whatever their form or special religious function.

Does New Jersey's action furnish support for religion by use of taxing power? Certainly it does, if the test remains undiluted as Jefferson and Madison made it, that money taken by taxation from one is not to be used or given to support another's religious training or belief, or indeed one's own. Today as then the furnishing of "contributions of money for the propagation of opinions which he disbelieves" is the forbidden exaction; and the prohibition is absolute for whatever measure brings that consequence and whatever amount may be sought or given to that end.

The funds used here were raised by taxation. The Court does not dispute nor could it that their use does in fact give aid and encouragement to religious instruction. It only concludes that this aid is not "support" in law. But Madison and Jefferson were concerned with aid and support in fact not as a legal conclusion "entangled in precedents." * * * Here parents pay money to send their children to parochial schools and funds raised by taxation are used to reimburse them. This not only helps the children to get to school and the parents to send them. It aids them in a substantial way to get the very thing which they are sent to the particular school to secure, namely, religious training and teaching. * * *

New Jersey's action therefore exactly fits the type of exaction and the kind of evil at which Madison and Jefferson struck. Under the test they framed it cannot be said that the cost of transportation is no part of the cost of education or of the religious instruction given. * * *

The reasons underlying the Amendment's policy have not vanished with time or diminished in force. Now as when it was adopted the price of religious freedom is double. It is that the church and religion shall live both within and upon that freedom. There cannot be freedom of religion, safeguarded by the state, and intervention by the church or its agencies in the state's domain or dependency on its largesse. * * * The great condition of religious liberty is that it be maintained free from sustenance, as also from other interferences, by the state. For when it comes to rest upon that secular foundation it vanishes with the resting. * * * Public money devoted to payment of religious costs, educational or other, brings the quest for more. It brings too the struggle of sect against sect for the larger share or for any. Here one by numbers alone will benefit most, there another. That is precisely the history of societies which have had an established religion and dissident groups. * * * It is the very thing Jefferson and Madison experienced and sought to guard against, whether in its blunt or in its more screened forms. * * * The end of such strife cannot be other than to destroy the cherished liberty. The dominating group will achieve the dominant benefit; or all will embroil the state in their dissensions. * * *

Two great drives are constantly in motion to abridge, in the name of education, the complete division of religion and civil authority which our forefathers made. One is to introduce religious education and observances into the public schools. The other, to obtain public funds for the aid and support of various private religious schools. * * * In my opinion both avenues were closed by the Constitution. Neither should be opened by this Court. The matter is not one of quantity, to be measured by the amount of money expended. Now as in Madison's day it is one of principle, to keep separate the separate spheres as the First Amendment drew them; to prevent the first experiment upon our liberties; and to keep the question from becoming entangled in corrosive precedents. We should not be less strict to keep strong and untarnished the one side of the shield of religious freedom than we have been of the other.

The judgment should be reversed.

NOTES

The opinions, both majority and minority, in the *Everson* case relied to a great extent on the historical development of religious liberty in the United States. Thomas Jefferson's "An Act for Establishing Religious Freedom" was referred to on several occasions and the text of James Madison's "Memorial and Remonstrance Against Religious Assessments" was attached as an appendix to the *Everson* case. The following notes present the complete text of Jefferson's act and selected passages from Madison's work.

AN ACT FOR ESTABLISHING RELIGIOUS FREEDOM

by Thomas Jefferson (1786)

Well aware that Almighty God hath created the mind free; that all attempts to influence it by temporal punishments or burdens, or by civil incapacitations, tend only to beget habits of hypocrisy and meanness, and are a departure from the plan of the Holy Author of our religion, who being Lord both of body and mind, yet chose not to propagate it by coercions on either, as was in his Almighty power to do;

That the impious presumption of legislators and rulers, civil as well as ecclesiastical, who, being themselves but fallible and uninspired men, have assumed dominion over the faith of others, setting up their own opinions and modes of thinking as the only true and infallible, and as such endeavoring to impose them on others, hath established and maintained false religions over the greatest part of the world, and through all time;

That to compel a man to furnish contributions of money for the propagation of opinions which he disbelieves, is sinful and tyrannical; that even the forcing him to support this or that teacher of his own religious persuasion, is depriving him of the comfortable liberty of giving his contributions to the particular pastor whose morals he would make his pattern, and whose power he feels most persuasive to righteousness, and is withdrawing from the ministry those temporal rewards, which proceeding from an approbation of their personal conduct, are an additional incitement to earnest and unremitting labors for the instruction of mankind;

That our civil rights have no dependence on our religious opinions, more than our opinions in physics or geometry; that, therefore, the proscribing any citizen as unworthy the public confidence by laying upon him an incapacity of being called to the offices of trust and emolument, unless he profess or renounce this or that religious opinion, is depriving him injuriously of those privileges and advantages to which in common with his fellow citizens he has a natural right;

That it tends also to corrupt the principles of that very religion it is meant to encourage, by bribing, with a monopoly of worldly honors and emoluments, those who will externally profess and conform to it; that though indeed these are criminal who do not withstand such temptation, yet neither are those innocent who lay the bait in their way;

That to suffer the civil magistrate to intrude his powers into the field of opinion and to restrain the profession or propagation of principles, on the supposition of their ill tendency, is a dangerous fallacy, which at once destroys all religious liberty, because he being of course judge of that tendency, will make his opinions the rule of judgment, and approve or condemn the sentiments of others only as they shall square with or differ from his own;

That it is time enough for the rightful purposes of civil government, for its officers to interfere when principles break out into overt acts against peace and good order;

And finally, that truth is great and will prevail if left to herself, that she is the proper and sufficient antagonist to error, and has nothing to fear from the conflict, unless by human interposition disarmed of her natural weapons, free argument and debate, errors ceasing to be dangerous when it is permitted freely to contradict them.

Be it therefore enacted by the General Assembly, that no man shall be compelled to frequent or support any religious worship, place or ministry whatsoever, nor shall be enforced, restrained, molested, or burthened in his body or goods, nor shall otherwise suffer on account of his religious opinions or belief; but that all men shall be free to profess, and by argument to maintain, their opinions in matters of religion, and that the same shall in nowise diminish, enlarge, or affect their civil capacities.

And though we well know this Assembly, elected by the people for the ordinary purposes of legislation only, have no power to restrain the acts of succeeding assemblies, constituted with the powers equal to our own, and that therefore to declare this act irrevocable, would be of no effect in law, yet we are free to declare, and do declare, that the rights hereby asserted are of the natural rights of mankind, and that if any act shall be hereafter passed to repeal the present or to narrow its operation, such act will be an infringement of natural right.

MEMORIAL AND REMONSTRANCE AGAINST RELIGIOUS ASSESSMENTS

To the Honorable General Assembly of the Commonwealth of Virginia. A Memorial and Remonstrance.

We, the subscribers, citizens of the said Commonwealth, having taken into serious consideration, a Bill printed by order of the last Session of General Assembly, entitled "A Bill establishing a provision for teachers of the Christian Religion," and conceiving that the same, if finally armed with the sanctions of a law, will be a dangerous abuse of power, are bound as faithful members of a free State, to remonstrate against it, and to declare the reasons by which we are determined. We remonstrate against the said Bill,

Because we hold it for a fundamental and undeniable truth, "that religion, or the duty which we owe to our Creator, and the manner of discharging it, can be directed only by reason and conviction, not by force or violence." [9] The Religion then of every man must be left to the conviction and conscience of every man; and it is the right of every man to exercise it as these may dictate. This right is in its nature an unalienable right. * * *

Because, it is proper to take alarm at the first experiment on our liberties. We hold this prudent jealousy to be the first duty of citizens, and one of [the] noblest characteristics of the late Revolution. The freemen of America did not wait till usurped power had strengthened itself by exercise, and entangled the question in precedents. They saw all the consequences in the principle, and they avoided the consequences by denying the principle. We reverse this lesson too much, soon to forget it. Who does not see that the same authority which can establish Christianity, in exclusion of all other Religions, may establish with the same ease any particular sect of Christians, in exclusion of all other Sects? That the same authority which can force a citizen to contribute three pence only of his property for the support of any one establishment, may force him to conform to any other establishment in all cases whatsoever?

Because, the bill violates that equality which ought to be the basis of every law, and which is more indispensable, in proportion as the validity or expediency of any law is more liable to be impeached. If "all men are by nature equally free and independent," [10] all men are to be considered as entering

---

9. Decl. Rights, Art. 16. [Note in the original.]
10. Decl. Rights, Art. 1. [Note in the original.]

into Society on equal conditions; as relinquishing no more, and therefore retaining no less, one than another, of their natural rights. Above all are they to be considered as retaining an "equal title to the free exercise of Religion according to the dictates of conscience." [11] Whilst we assert for ourselves a freedom to embrace, to profess and to observe the Religion which we believe to be of divine origin, we cannot deny an equal freedom to those whose minds have not yet yielded to the evidence which has convinced us. If this freedom be abused, it is an offense against God, not against man: To God, therefore, not to men, must an account of it be rendered. As the Bill violates equality by subjecting some to peculiar burdens; so it violates the same principle, by granting to others peculiar exemptions. Are the Quakers and Menonists the only sects who think a compulsive support of their religions unnecessary and unwarrantable? Can their piety alone be entrusted with the care of public worship? Ought their Religions to be endowed above all others, with extraordinary privileges, by which proselytes may be enticed from all others? We think too favorably of the justice and good sense of these denominations, to believe that they either covet preeminencies over their fellow citizens, or that they will be seduced by them, from the common opposition to the measure.
* * *

What influence in fact have ecclesiastical establishments had on Civil Society? In some instances they have been seen to erect a spiritual tyranny on the ruins of Civil authority; in many instances they have been seen upholding the thrones of political tyranny; in no instance have they been seen the guardians of the liberties of the people. Rulers who wished to subvert the public liberties, may have found an established clergy convenient auxiliaries. A just government, instituted to secure and perpetuate it, needs them not. Such a government will be best supported by protecting every citizen in the enjoyment of his Religion with the same equal hand which protects his person and his property; by neither invading the equal rights by any Sect, nor suffering any Sect to invade those of another.

Because the proposed establishment is a departure from that generous policy, which offering an asylum to the persecuted and oppressed of every Nation and Religion, promised a lustre to our country, an accession to the number of its citi-

---

11. Art. 16. [Note in the original.]

zens. What a melancholy mark is the Bill of sudden degeneracy? Instead of holding forth an asylum to the persecuted, it is itself a signal of persecution. It degrades from the equal rank of citizens all those whose opinions in Religion do not bend to those of the Legislative authority. Distant as it may be, in its present form, from the Inquisition it differs from it only in degree. The one is the first step, the other the last in the career of intolerance. * * *

Because, it will destroy that moderation and harmony which the forbearance of our laws to intermeddle with Religion, has produced amongst its several sects. Torrents of blood have been spilt in the old world, by vain attempts of the secular arum to extinguish Religious discord, by proscribing all difference in Religious opinions. Time has at length revealed the true remedy. Every relaxation of narrow and rigorous policy, wherever it has been tried, has been found to assuage the disease. The American Theatre has exhibited proofs, that equal and complete liberty, if it does not wholly eradicate it, sufficiently destroys its malignant influence on the health and prosperity of the State. If with the salutary effects of this system under our own eyes, we begin to contract the bonds of Religious freedom, we know no name that will too severely reproach our folly. At least let warning be taken at the first fruit of the threatened innovation. The very appearance of the Bill has transformed that "Christian forbearance,[12] love and charity," which of late mutually prevailed, into animosities and jealousies, which may not soon be appeased. What mischiefs may not be dreaded should this enemy to the public quiet be armed with the force of a law? * * *

Because, finally, "the equal right of every citizen to the free exercise of his Religion according to the dictates of conscience" is held by the same tenure with all our other rights. If we recur to its origin, it is equally the gift of nature; if we weigh its importance, it cannot be less dear to us; if we consult the Declaration of those rights which pertain to the good people of Virginia, as the "basis and foundation of Government," [13] it is enumerated with equal solemnity, or rather studied emphasis. Either then, we must say, that the will of the Legislature is the only measure of their authority; and that in the plentitude of this authority, they may sweep away all our fundamental rights; or, that they are bound to leave this particular right untouched and sacred: Either we

12. Art. 16. [Note in the original.]
13. Dec. Rights-title. [Note in the original.]

must say, that they may control the freedom of the press, may abolish the trial by jury, may swallow up the Executive and Judiciary powers of the State; nay that they may despoil us of our very right of suffrage, and erect themselves into an independent and hereditary assembly: or we must say, that they have no authority to enact into law the Bill under consideration. We, the subscribers, say, that the General Assembly of this Commonwealth have no such authority: And that no effort may be omitted on our part against so dangerous an usurpation, we oppose to it, this remonstrance; earnestly praying, as we are in duty bound, that the Supreme Lawgiver of the Universe, by illuminating those to whom it is addressed, may on the one hand turn their councils from every act which would affront his holy prerogative, or violate the trust committed to them: and on the other, guide them into every measure which may be worthy of his [blessing, may re]dound to their own praise, and may establish more firmly the liberties, the prosperity, and the happiness of the Commonwealth. II Madison, 183-191.

Tuition payments for war orphans to attend sectarian schools is unconstitutional

ALMOND v. DAY

Supreme Court of Appeals of Virginia, 1955.
197 Va. 419, 89 S.E.2d 851.

EGGLESTON, Justice.

This is a petition for a writ of mandamus filed by the Attorney General of Virginia to determine the validity of Item 210 of the Appropriation Act of 1954, Acts of Assembly 1954, ch. 708, p. 970, which appropriates funds for the "education of orphans of soldiers, sailors and marines" who were citizens of Virginia and were "killed in action or died, or who are totally and permanently disabled as a result of service during the World War." * * *

Pursuant to the provisions of Code, § 8-714, the Attorney General filed in this court a petition for a writ of mandamus directing the State Comptroller to issue warrants upon the State Treasurer for the payment of such amounts as are authorized by vouchers approved by the Superintendent of Public Instruction. The petition alleged that the proposed payments were not prohibited by Section 141 of the State Constitution.

The respondent State Comptroller filed an answer admitting the allegations of fact in the petition, but expressing the view that he should not make such payments until it had been adjudicated whether the appropriation contravened Section 141 of the State Constitution, and also Sections 16, 58 and 67 of that Constitution, and the Fourteenth Amendment to the Federal Constitution.

The text of Item 210 of the Appropriation Act of 1954 is copied in the margin.[1]

Section 141 of the Constitution of Virgina, as amended in 1952, reads thus:

"State appropriations prohibited to schools or institutions of learning not owned or exclusively controlled by the State or some subdivision thereof; exceptions to rule.—No appropriation of public funds shall be made to any school or institution of learning not owned or exclusively controlled by the State or some political subdivision thereof; provided, first, that the General Assembly may appropriate funds to an agency, or to a school or institution of learning owned or controlled by an agency, created and established by two or more states under a joint agreement to which this State is a party for the purpose of providing educational facilities for the citizens of the several states joining in such agreement; second, that counties, cities, towns and districts may make appropriations to nonsectarian schools of manual, industrial, or technical training, and also to any school or institution of learning owned or exclusively controlled by such county, city, town, or school district."

The first question presented is whether the provisions of

---

1. "Item 210

"For the education of orphans of soldiers, sailors and marines who were killed in action or died, or who are totally and permanently disabled as a result of service during the World War $12,000

"It is provided that the sum hereby appropriated shall be expended for the sole purpose of providing for tuition, institutional fees, board, room rent, books and supplies, at any educational or training institution of collegiate or secondary grade in the State of Virginia, * * *

"Such children, upon recommendation of the Superintendent of Public Instruction, shall be admitted to State institutions of secondary or college grade, free of tuition. * * *

"Not exceeding four hundred dollars shall be paid hereunder for any one child for any one school year; and no child may receive benefits of this or similar appropriations for a total of more than four school years. * * *

this section of the Constitution prohibit the payments authorized by Item 210 of the Appropriation Act for tuition, institutional fees and other designated expenses of eligible children attending private schools.

The argument of the petitioner Attorney General runs thus: Section 141, being a restraint on the plenary power of the General Assembly, must be strictly construed; the express language of the section merely prohibits a *direct* "appropriation of public funds" *to* "any school or institution of learning not owned or exclusively controlled by the State or some political subdivision thereof;" Item 210 is not an appropriation *directly to* the institutions which the eligible children may attend, but is an appropriation to the parents or guardians of such children, is primarily for the benefit of such children, and only incidentally for the benefit of the selected private schools. Hence, it is said, the appropriation is "not antagonistic either to the letter or spirit of Section 141."

The position of the respondent State Comptroller is that the constitutionality of a statute is to be tested by its normal effect and the practical consequences to which it leads; that the provision for the payment of tuition, institutional fees and other designated expenses at a private school, to be attended by children eligible under the Act, is a direct and substantial aid to such institution, and falls within the inhibition of Section 141 which was designed to prohibit such diversion of public funds from the public school system to the aid or benefit of private schools.

A glance at the 1954 Appropriation Act will show that appropriations are not usually made directly "to" the various beneficiaries, whether they be State educational institutions or State departments. They are stated to be "for" a specific purpose; for example, "For maintenance and operation of" the particular educational institution, or "for" some specific purpose at the institution, or "For expenses of administration" of a department of the State. But no one would question that these appropriations are in effect "to" these institutions and departments in the sense that they are "set apart" for their use.

Similarly the appropriation in Item 210, now before us, for the purpose of "providing for tuition, institutional fees," etc., at private schools to be approved by the Superintendent of Public Instruction, is an appropriation for the benefit of such schools. The fact that in the administration of the Act the funds may be paid to the parents or guardians of the children and not directly to the institutions does not alter their underlying purpose and effect. As a matter of fact the record shows that from July, 1950, through June, 1954, payments of these appropriations have usually been made directly to the institutions.

It is urged that we should apply the reasoning of certain recent cases which have validated appropriations for transportation of children to private schools, and the furnishing of textbooks for the use of children at such schools, upon the theory that such aid is primarily for the benefit of the children and only incidentally for the benefit of the institutions involved. Typical of these is Everson v. Board of Education, 330 U.S. 1, 67 S.Ct. 504, 91 L.Ed. 711, in which the Supreme Court in a 5 to 4 decision held that a New Jersey statute, N.J. S.A. 18:14-8, authorizing school district boards to provide for the transportation of pupils to and from parochial schools was not violative of the "establishment of religion" clause of the Federal Constitution, Amendment 1.

Upon the same theory Borden v. Louisiana State Board of Education, 168 La. 1005, 123 So. 655, 67 A.L.R. 1183, relied upon by the petitioner, validated the expenditure of public funds to provide free school books to pupils at private schools against a constitutional provision similar to Section 141 in the Virginia Constitution. The crux of that case, as stated in the court's opinion, is that "The schools, however, are not the beneficiaries of these appropriations. They *obtain nothing from them*, nor are they relieved of a single obligation, because of them. The school children and the state alone are the beneficiaries." (Italics supplied). 123 So. at pages 660, 661.

Clearly such reasoning does not apply to the appropriation here under consideration. Assuming, but not deciding, the soundness of the view that the private institutions involved receive no direct benefit from the transportation of pupils or the furnishing of textbooks to them, the same cannot be said of provisions for the payment of tuition and institutional fees at such schools. Tuition and institutional fees go directly to the institution and are its very life blood. Such items are the main support of private schools which are not sufficiently endowed to insure their maintenance. Surely a payment by the State of the tuition and fees of the pupils of a private school begun on the strength of a contract by the State to do so would be an appropriation to that school. * * *

The basis of this concession is that the payment of such

tuition would directly benefit and support a *sectarian* school contrary to the purpose and spirit of these constitutional provisions. The same principle would, of course, apply to the payment of tuition at a private *nonsectarian* school. In both cases the parent or guardian to whom the tuition fees are paid is merely the conduit or channel through whom the aid from the State to the school is transmitted. Such natural and reasonable effect of the appropriation is proof of its invalidity. * * *

"The general rule is that in whatever language a statute may be framed, its purpose and its constitutional validity must be determined by its natural and reasonable effect. * * *" 11 Am.Jur. Constitutional Law, § 101, p. 735, and cases there cited.

When we consider the natural, reasonable and realistic effect of the provision in Item 210 for the payment of tuition, institutional fees and other designated expenses of eligible children who attend private schools approved by the Superintendent of Public Instruction, we are forced to the conclusion that it constitutes a direct and substantial aid to such institutions and falls within the prohibition of Section 141 of our Constitution.

We further agree with the position of counsel for the respondent State Comptroller that in so far as Item 210 purports to authorize payments for tuition, institutional fees and other designated expenses of eligible children who attend *sectarian* schools, it falls within the prohibitions of Sections 16, 58 and 67 of the Constitution of Virginia and the First and Fourteenth Amendments to the Federal Constitution. * * *

These provisions in our basic law guarantee freedom of religion and complete separation of Church and State in civil affairs.

The First Amendment to the Federal Constitution provides that, "Congress shall make no law respecting an establishment of religion, * * *."

It has been settled by the decisions of the Supreme Court that the Due Process Clause of the Fourteenth Amendment "has rendered the legislatures of the states as incompetent as Congress to enact such laws." Cantwell v. State of Connecticut, 310 U.S. 296, 303, 60 S.Ct. 900, 903, 84 L.Ed. 1213, 128 A.L.R. 1352. * * *

The payment of such items to sectarian schools as directed or authorized by the terms of Item 210 is unconstitutional because, (1) It utilizes public funds to support religious institutions contrary to the principles laid down in Everson v. Board of Education, supra, 330 U.S. at page 16, 67 S.Ct. at page 511; (2) It "affords sectarian groups an invaluable aid in that it helps to provide pupils for their religious classes through use of the state's compulsory public school machinery", condemned in People of State of Illinois ex rel. McCollum v. Board of Education, 333 U.S. 203, 212, 68 S.Ct. 461, 466, 92 L.Ed. 649; (3) It compels taxpayers to contribute money for the propagation of religious opinions which they may not believe. See Protestant Episcopal Education Society v. Churchman's Representatives, 80 Va. 718, 775; Jones v. Commonwealth, 185 Va. 335, 344, 345, 38 S.E.2d 444, 448. * * *

Since, in our opinion, Item 210 is unconstitutional and void to the extent that it purports to authorize payments for tuition, institutional fees and other designated expenses of eligible children who attend approved or designated private schools, the writ prayed for is denied.

Writ denied.

Public funds for facility construction at sectarian colleges is unconstitutional

HORACE MANN LEAGUE ET AL. v. BOARD OF PUBLIC WORKS OF MARYLAND

Court of Appeals of Maryland, 1966.
242 Md. 645, 220 A.2d 51.

PRESCOTT, Chief Judge.

After dismissal of their bill of complaint, which challenged the validity, as violating the Federal and Maryland Constitutions, of four separate statutes, providing outright, matching grants, totaling $2,500,000, for the construction of buildings, to four private colleges, the plaintiffs appealed. The four colleges and appropriate public officials were named as defendants; injunctive relief and a declaration to the effect that the grants were unlawful were prayed.

The questions involved have been briefed and argued with signal care, skill, and ability by counsel for the respective parties.

The appellees contend that appellants lack standing to invoke the jurisdiction of the courts. The principal issue, of course, is whether any one (or more) of the statutes violates the First and Fourteenth Amendments to the Federal Constitution, or Articles XV, XXIII, or XXXVI of our Declaration of Rights. Appellants concede that some degree of relationship to church or religion may exist in an educational institution without rendering it "sectarian"; they contend, however, that when such a relationship is "substantial," it renders the institution sectarian and grants of public funds may not constitutionally be made to it. * * * We think the orderly and efficacious sequence in which to consider these issues is first to determine the question of standing, for if the appellees prevail thereon, it will control the entire appeal; next to decide the test to be applied to the statutes in determining whether they are constitutionally permissible or impermissible under the First Amendment; then to apply that test to the facts in the record pertaining to the individual colleges; and finally to consider whether the grants violate the named sections of the Maryland Constitution.

THE STANDING OF THE PARTIES PLAINTIFF

The Chancellor held that the Horace Mann League of the United States of America, Inc., lacked standing. We agree. It is a non-profit educational and charitable Maryland corporation organized, as claimed by it, for the purpose of fostering and strengthening the American public school system. * * *

Most of the appellees, rightly we think, concede that the recently decided case of Murray v. Comptroller of the Treasury, 241 Md. 383, 216 A.2d 897, fatally undermines their argument here. Having so recently considered and enunciated our conclusions on the question, it would be a useless gesture to elaborate further thereon. We hold that *Murray* is controlling on this point, and the individual appellants do not lack standing for the reasons there assigned. * * *

We hold that the Chancellor was correct in ruling that the individual appellants had standing.

THE TEST TO BE APPLIED

It should be noted at the outset that nothing in this opinion is intended as a criticism of, or a boost to, any religion, sect, or schism, or lack of religion. Our task is to decide a constitutional issue. We proceed to do just that, and that alone. * * *

We shall not discuss in detail the complexities that arose

concerning Church and State in each of the Colonies. It seems obvious that our revered Pilgrim Fathers, who had come here to seek religious freedom, were not in a mood to grant complete religious freedom of thought to all others. We all know of the banishment of Roger Williams. It also is apparent that Maryland's vaunted Toleration Act of 1649 granted religious tolerance only to Christians, and it is entirely possible that it was prompted, at least in part, by expediency. The Puritans had taken over the government in the Mother Country in the early part of that year, and the Lord Proprietor, in order to strengthen his position with the Home Government had issued invitations to settle here to the New England Puritans and those of Virginia, where Governor Berkeley, in spite of the Puritan successes in England, remained a Royalist and an adherent of the Anglican Church. * * *

Thus it is seen that the Framers knew man's difficult-to-suppress (and still unextinct) desire to persuade, and failing in persuasion, to compel others to adopt and believe his religious views, and man's unswerving determination to select the religious views most appealing to him individually and his quest to believe those views and to worship without fear or favor had been potently divisive forces ever since the deeds of mankind had been recorded. So great had been the impact of the latter determinants that neither dungeons, mortally bleak winters in far-distant colonies, plain executions, wholesale burnings at the stake, nor the prolonged and "exquisite" agonies produced by the tortures of machinations developed by the most ingenious minds of the ages (i. e., "persecution in perfection") had dissuaded man in his pursuit of religious freedom and religious equality.

Even though the above is but a sketchy outline of the subject involved (as we stated above), we have set the same forth at some length to demonstrate that the problem to be considered and solved when the First Amendment was proposed was not one of hazy or comparative insignificance, but was one of blunt and stark reality, which had perplexed and plagued the nations of Western Civilization for some 14 centuries, and during that long period, the union of Church and State in the government of man had produced neither peace on earth, nor good will to man.

In an attempt to prevent recurrences of many of the unfortunate evils mentioned above (and those mentioned in the opinions named in footnote 1) our forebears decided it was best for Government, best for Religion and best for mankind that the two be kept separate and apart. In order to effectuate this goal, the First Amendment was adopted which provides that "Congress shall make no law respecting an establishment of religion, or prohibiting the free exercise thereof * * *." [13]

This brings us to a consideration of the Supreme Court decisions bearing on the questions here involved. The parties on both sides of the controversy have carefully analyzed the same in their briefs. Justice Clark did likewise in his opinion in *Schempp, supra,* as to the decisions preceding it. However, we do not deem it necessary or desirable to take up each of these decisions and analyse them in detail, for this Court has very recently stated their rationale in Murray, supra. (241 Md. at pp. 398 and 401, 216 A.2d at pp. 905, 906 and 907, involving church exemptions from taxation), where Judge Oppenheimer, for the Court without dissent, said:

> "In our reading of the opinions, however, we find broad guide lines which form the frame within which the case before us is to be considered. We are a religious people and recognize the effect religious institutions have on human activity. The First Amendment was designed to erect 'a wall of separation between church and State.' Mutual Independence, under our Constitution, is deemed best for the State and best for religion. *The State cannot forbid nor can it perform or aid in performing the religious function. Like other broad constitutional concepts, the meaning of 'separation' is to be ascertained in the application of the principle to specific cases.* A state cannot pass a law to aid one religion or all religions, but state action to promote the general welfare of society, apart from any religious considerations, is valid, even though religious interests may be indirectly benefited. If the primary purpose of the state action is to promote religion, that action is in violation of the Amendment, *but if a statute furthers both secular and religious ends, an examination of the means used is necessary to determine whether the state could reasonably have attained the secular end by means which do not further the promotion of religion.*" (Emphasis added.) * * *

After a consideration of all of the Supreme Court decisions and our statement of their rationale, quoted above, we have reached the conclusion that, insofar as the issue of the First Amendment is concerned, we should apply the following standards in measuring the statutes under consideration.

---

13. At this late date, it requires no citation of authority to assert that the same proscription applies to the states through the Fourteenth Amendment.

As it is claimed that First Amendment liberties have been infringed upon, we must closely scrutinize and carefully consider the issues presented. *McGowan*, supra, 366 U.S. at p. 449, 81 S.Ct. 1101. Each case must be determined on its particular facts. *Murray*, supra, 341 Md. at p. 398, 216 A.2d 897. We must examine each of the statutes and decide whether it can be demonstrated that its purpose—as evidenced either on its face, in conjunction with its legislative history, or in its operative effect—is to use the State's coercive power to aid religion. *Schempp*, supra, 374 U.S. 203, 83 S.Ct. 1560, and Justice Frankfurter's opinion in *McGowan*, 366 U.S. at pp. 466, 467, 81 S.Ct. 1101. "If the primary purpose [as contradistinguished from an incidental one] of the state action is to promote religion, that action is in violation of the Amendment, but if [the operative effect of] a statute furthers both secular and religious ends, an examination of the means used is necessary to determine whether the state could reasonably have attained the secular end by means which do not further the promotion of religion." *Murray*, supra. Cf. *McGowan*, supra. No tax, in any amount, large or small, can be levied to support any religious activities or institutions, whatever they may be called or whatever form they may adopt to teach or practice religions. *Everson*, supra, 330 U.S. at p. 16, 67 S.Ct. at p. 512. Although a state cannot "contribute tax-raised funds to the support of an institution which teaches the tenets and faith of any church," it cannot exclude individuals, because of their faith or lack of it, from receiving the benefits of valid public welfare legislation. *Everson*, supra, (a case wherein the Court stated the factual situation "verged" upon the impermissible). When the power, prestige and financial support of government is placed behind a particular religious belief, the indirect coercive pressure upon religious minorities to conform to the prevailing offically approved religion is plain. *Engel*, supra, 370 U.S., at p. 431, 82 S.Ct. 1261. We are unable to accept appellees' contention that every religious observance by an institution sectarianizes the same, but feel that the question of sectarianization depends upon a consideration of the observances, themselves, and the mode, zeal, and frequency with which they are made. These principles are sufficient, we think, to determine our present issues, and we shall apply them in considering the four statutes involved.

* * * As we have stated above, it is a question of degree as to how far all religions or a specific religion may be bene-

fited by State action without the State stepping out of its role of complete "neutrality," and such action losing its character as being incidental to lawful general welfare legislation.

APPLYING THE STANDARDS TO THE INDIVIDUAL COLLEGES

There is little controversy over the facts in any of the cases; rather the dispute is as to the legal effects of the facts.

The experts on both sides are in general accord that the following factors are significant in determining whether an educational institution is religious or sectarian: (1) the stated purposes of the college; (2) the college personnel, which includes the governing board, the administrative officers, the faculty, and the student body (with considerable stress being laid on the substantiality of religious control over the governing board as a criterion of whether a college is sectarian); (3) the college's relationship with religious organizations and groups, which relationship includes the extent of ownership, financial assistance, the college's memberships and affiliations, religious purposes, and miscellaneous aspects of the college's relationship with its sponsoring church; (4) the place of religion in the college's program, which includes the extent of religious manifestation in the physical surroundings, the character and extent of religious observance sponsored or encouraged by the college, the required participation for any or all students, the extent to which the college sponsors or encourages religious activity of sects different from that of the college's own church and the place of religion in the curriculum and in extra-curricular programs; (5) the result or "outcome" of the college program, such as accreditation and the nature and character of the activities of the alumni; and (6) the work and image of the college in the community.

With these criteria and the standards we named above in mind, we consider the schools, individually. In setting forth the facts relevant to each, we have followed, in considerable measure, appellants' brief with reference to some of the schools, after carefully checking the same with the evidence.

HOOD COLLEGE

Chapter 88 of the Acts of the General Assembly of 1962 grants to Hood College $500,000 to help erect a dormitory and a classroom building.

According to the College Bulletin issued in 1963, Hood is

"an independent liberal arts college for women," and it "is church related through its affiliation with the United Church of Christ [U.C.C.], but welcomes students of all religious faiths." It is listed in a Tabulation of the Danforth Foundation of Institutions Associated with Religious Bodies as "reflecting religious orientation." It is a small college, limited to an enrollment of about 650 students, and is governed by a Board of Trustees consisting of 35 members. Seven of these are elected by agencies of the U.C.C.; 22 by the Board itself; and 6 by the Alumnae Association from its membership. * * * There are no sectarian requirements for members of the faculty; the President thought that Hood had "virtually all shades of religious affiliations represented [thereon] and non-religious affiliation." In the year 1963-1964, there were 7 Episcopalians, 2 of the Jewish faith, 3 Lutherans, 6 Methodists, 1 with no affiliation indicated, 13 Presbyterians, 2 listed as Protestant but non-denominational, 5 Roman Catholics, 3 members of the Society of Friends, 3 Unitarians, and 10 members of the U.C.C., a rather heterogeneous faculty for a sectarian school.

There is no requirement that any member of the officers of administration be of any particular religious denomination, and, in fact, the officers of administration do not represent any particular church or religious body. Included among these are Baptists, Lutherans, Methodists, Presbyterians, one Roman Catholic and one Unitarian, and 7 members of the U.C.C.

There is no requirement that the Chaplain, who supervises, generally, the religious lives of the student body be of any particular denomination, although the present one is a member of the U.C.C.

The student body is primarily selected according to educational records supplied by the students and by the schools from whence they come; there is absolutely no requirement based on race, creed, color, or sectarian affiliation in the student body. An examination of their religious affiliation for the year 1963-1964 shows such a diversification that it would unduly prolong this opinion to include them all. Among a student body of some 675 students, were included 146 Episcopalians, 29 Jewish students, 83 Methodists, 72 Roman Catholics, 108 Presbyterians, and 89 members of the U.C.C.

The college confers only two earned degrees; the A.B. degree, which is, of course, a liberal arts degree; and the B.S. degree in Home Economics. It has a department of religion and philosophy; the courses taught therein are conducted in the same manner as the courses in other departments. These courses are not geared to aiding the Protestant religions or any other; they are primarily historical studies in religion and "there is absolutely no attempt at indoctrination in any way." The President was emphatic in stating that he believed proselytizing had no place in higher education. * * * The requirements for attendance at chapel (indeed, if they may be termed requirements from the evidence) do not call for frequent services, with the student being allowed generous "cuts" without excuse. On the Wednesday evening services, of which there are approximately 15 per semester, clergymen of various denominations come in and talk to the students. * * *

In the year mentioned above, the U.C.C. contributed 2.2% of the college's total operating budget; but contributed nothing in the way of capital gifts, with the exception of one gift in the amount of $10,000 for endowed scholarships. * * *

The above summarization, we think, discloses that Hood, although it is a church-related school, may constitutionally receive the money mentioned in the Bill. * * *

Applying the criteria we named above, we are unable to say that the College is sectarian in a legal sense under the First Amendment, or to a degree that renders the grant invalid thereunder. * * *

We hold, therefore, that the primary purpose of the grant here involved was not to aid or support religion; that there is nothing on the face of the Bill or its legislative history to demonstrate that its purpose was to use the State's coercive power to aid religion; and that its operative effect is not to aid religion (as we read the record, we see no aid to religion here; if there be any it assuredly is incidental and very remote in nature), but to promote the educational facilities for women. Consequently, the Bill does not violate the First Amendment.

WESTERN MARYLAND

Chapter 546 of the Acts of the General Assembly of 1963 grants $500,000 to Western Maryland College for the purpose of aiding in the construction of a science wing and dining hall.

The stated purposes include religious objectives to a considerable extent. The college characterizes itself as a "religiously oriented institution" and "make[s] no bones about the fact that our philosophy at Western Maryland is a Christian philosophy."

One more than one-third of the members of the governing

board are required by its Charter to be Methodist Ministers, so as to give the clergy the veto power over any change inimical to the interests of the church. The required percentage "binds the college very closely to the Church." The board is heavily Methodist, and nearly all Protestant, although quite a number of denominations are represented thereon. All the presidents have been Methodist Ministers. The administration is almost entirely Protestant, although, again, quite a number of denominations are represented.

Care is taken to obtain a faculty committed to the Christian philosophy of life, and an atheist would not be employed. Almost half of the faculty is Methodist, and almost all Protestant. Approximately 40% of the student body is Methodist, and almost all Protestant. The large number of Methodists is due to greater likelihood of acceptance of Methodist "borderline cases * * * because they seem part of the constituency of the college," and to the large number of Methodist students who become familiar with the college during church conferences on the campus. The college has a significant number of Methodist pre-ministerial students. Some of these are given scholarships ranging from ½ to full tuition. And the children of Methodist Ministers are charged only half tuition.

The church provides "financial support of considerable value," both operational and capital, the operational contribution being between 2 and 3% of the budget. The college is affiliated with, and supports, denominational educational associations.

The college campus is very heavily used by Protestant religious groups (some at actual cost), and "logically and naturally, there have been of course more of the Methodist program here than any of the other denominations."

The college fosters a religious program, under the direction of a Methodist Minister. Participation in Protestant religious services is required of all students. The requirement is publicized so that if anyone has conscientious scruples about attending such services "he should know that before he comes."

The college makes a conscious effort to integrate religion, and specifically Christianity, with the curriculum and extracurricular life. Because Methodism does not have the wide range of dogma that one, or more, religions have, there is less specific religious restriction in regard to curriculum, but the school endeavors to provide a religious motivation. * * *

The college is accredited by the Middle States Association

of Schools and Colleges and the University Senate of the Methodist Church. It is proud of the number of its alumni who enter the Christian, and particularly the Methodist ministry. The image of the college in the community is strongly Methodist.

Applying the criteria and principles of law we named above to this College, we reach the conclusion that it is sectarian in a legal sense under the First Amendment, and may not constitutionally receive the grant named in the Bill. * * *

We shall not repeat all of what we said above concerning the College's activities. We find nothing on the face of the bill or its legislative history to demonstrate a purpose to use the State's coercive power to aid religion, but a careful consideration of all the facts impels us to the conclusion that the operative effect will be such, if the grant be effectuated. * * * "The most effective way to establish any institution is to finance it * * *. Financing a church either in its strictly religious activities or in its other activities is equally unconstitutional * * *."

Without laboring the question further, we hold that Chapter 546 transgresses the proscriptions of the Establishment Clause, consequently, it is unconstitutional and invalid.

NOTRE DAME

Chapter 66 of the Acts of the General Assembly of 1962 grants $750,000 to this College to aid in the construction of a science building.

Notre Dame's stated purposes are deeply and intensely religious. The theory of Catholic education is that Prayer, Holy Mass and the Sacraments represent "the Unifying forces," and "the instructional program interlocks with the non-instructional program; objectives with methods and means, and all to an essential, interwoven unity." "All of [the College's] objectives are implemented in some degree in every department." The institution's "whole life is lived in the Catholic atmosphere, which assumes that earthly life is to be lived * * * in terms of a preparation for the future life with God," and to that end, it "harmonizes" its entire "program with the philosophy and theology of the Catholic Church." The entire program of the College is so ordered "that [the student's] life and study and the atmosphere of the college are *permeated, motivated, enlarged and integrated by the Catholic way of life* as developed and expressed in the daily prayer, liturgy, Sacraments and Holy Mass of the Church." (Emphasis ours.) "And Outward Grace * * *. Since the Christ-thought, the Christ-word and the Christ-deed are the norms of community living in a Catholic college for women, intimations of this presence should be found everywhere: In the Chapel—[and] in the Class Room * * *." "This expresses our aim to have the spiritual support and vivify the whole college atmosphere." Extracts taken from Exhibits in evidence. "God bless you and your apostolate in the home, class-room, laboratory, business office, etc. Gratefully in Our Lady." (Sentence from a letter of Sister Miriam to the Girls of 1961.) "Make your payment a Christmas Gift this year. Help meet the $750,000 Matching Grant for the Science Building [the building involved in the grant under Chapter 66]. * * * And you know that your gift to the College is a gift to God for the furtherance of his work. May the Christ Child bless you for your generosity * * *." (Letter from Sister Miriam dated December, 1962.)

If erected, each class in the new science building will open with a prayer.

The governing body is controlled by a Catholic religious order whose members are completely committed to Catholic discipline and educational philosophy. The administration is almost entirely religious. The faculty are predominantly nuns who are appointed by the Provincial Superior of the religious order (who is Chairman of the governing board), in consultation with the President, who is also a member of the order. Administration and faculty are chosen on the basis of commitment to the college objectives and ideals, and are overwhelmingly Catholic. Ten per cent of the students are candidates for a religious order and more than 97% of the whole student body are Catholic. This percentage cannot be deemed coincidental.

The college is owned and has been given heavy financial assistance by the religious order. It is officially a member of, and supports, a number of distinctly Catholic associations and institutions. It makes its campus available for use by the Catholic Church and related groups, but not to non-Catholic organizations. It has close ties with the Archdiocese of Baltimore.

Catholicity permeates the college program: the physical surroundings; the rich variety of college-sponsored, exclusively Catholic observances, many of which are compulsory for Catholic students, if not for the entire student body; the curriculum; extracurricular activities; and the student advisory and counseling program. * * *

As the situation presented by the facts relating to St. Joseph College are so analogous to those regarding Notre Dame, we set forth St. Joseph's fact picture before stating our holdings with reference to Notre Dame.

ST. JOSEPH COLLEGE

Chapter 545 of the Acts of the General Assembly of 1963 grants to St. Joseph College $750,000 to assist in erecting a science building.

Since the evidence relating to this institution is so similar to that regarding Notre Dame, we curtail, somewhat, our analysis thereof.

The stated purposes of St. Joseph College seem to be even more strongly religious than Notre Dame's. The religious order of dedicated nuns has complete control of the government and administration. The nuns have taken and abide by vows of strict obedience. The faculty is chosen with a view to achieving the religious ideals of the college, both by precept and example, and preference is given to Catholics; it, as a whole, is sympathetic to the Catholic philosophy of education. The majority of the faculty are Catholic priests or nuns, and there are but a small number of non-Catholic members. The student body includes candidates for the religious order, and has consistently been virtually 100% Catholic; approximately 90% of the students are graduates of Catholic parochial high schools. The Catholic character of the student body is achieved by design.

The religious order owns the college through the corporate form and has provided virtually 100% of the financial assistance needed over and above operating income.

The college is affiliated with, and supports, distinctly Catholic associations and institutions, and, like Notre Dame, is a certified affiliate of the Catholic University of America. The supplementary uses of the campus have been exclusively by Catholic religious groups.

The physical surroundings are strongly religious. Religious observance is strongly Catholic, richly textured, and extensively participated in: "In general, the Theocentric orientation of a Christian student's life is encouraged."

The accrediting agencies have specifically found St. Joseph to be accomplishing its religious objectives. The alumnae, individually and as an organization, are distinguished by the number of members of religious orders, the high percentage of active Catholic workers, and the devotion to the alumnae association's objectives: "to promulgate the principles and ideals of Catholicism * * * defending and promoting the interest of the Church, in promulgating Catholic education and in supporting the Church and its activities." * * *

If erected, the new science building will house crucifixes, "maybe" statues, and "very likely" waterfonts.

Again, we find nothing on the faces of the above two Bills or in their legislative histories to demonstrate a purpose to use the State's coercive power to aid religion, but a consideration of the totality of attendant circumstances impels a conclusion that their operative effect (if the grants be effectuated) demonstrates such a purpose. It must be remembered that here involved are direct grants of tax-raised funds to the educational *institutions*, themselves, which will become the sole owners of the buildings if erected. If appellees' contention that there is nothing in the Establishment Clause which proscribes direct grants to aid and support sectarian educational institutions were correct, it seems that *Everson,* supra, would have been decided quite easily and without dissent, even though no direct grant was there involved. * * *

In basing its holding in *Everson* on public welfare legislation, the Supreme Court was careful to say:

> "New Jersey cannot consistently with the 'establishment of religion' clause of the First Amendment contribute tax-raised funds to the support of an institution [directly involved therein were students in parochial educational schools—no church, or institution set aside especially for religious worship, was involved] which teaches the tenets and faith of any church."
>
> And "no tax in any amount, large or small, can be levied to support any religious activities or institutions, whatever they may be called, or whatever form they may adopt to preach or practice religion."

We do not deem it desirable to add materially to what we have already said with reference to Western Maryland. The facts relating to Notre Dame and St. Joseph speak for themselves. We think they clearly show that the operative effect of the Bills (if the grants are permitted to be made) demonstrates, in a legal and constitutional sense, a purpose to use the State's coercive power to aid religion; that the grants, if made, would constitute a contribution by the State of tax-raised funds to support institutions which teach the tenets and faith of a particular church; and that the taxes levied to raise the funds for the grants would be levied to help support religious activities and religious institutions. * * *

We, therefore, hold that both Notre Dame and St. Joseph are sectarian in a legal sense under the First Amendment, and neither can constitutionally receive the grant made to it; hence Chapter 66 of the Acts of 1962 and Chapter 545 of the Acts of 1963 are unconstitutional and invalid.† * * *

Decree affirmed in part, and reversed in part; and cause remanded for the entry of a decree in accordance with this opinion. The costs to be paid ¼ by the appellants, ¼ by Western Maryland College, ¼ by St. Joseph College, and ¼ by Notre Dame College.

NOTES

A denominational institution cannot receive a state appropriation by creating a local board which was stated to have power to conduct the institution where the local board had no authority over internal management, and another denominational board still had the authority to demand resignations of local board members.

The fact that appropriations had been made for nearly forty years to denominational or sectarian institutions, contrary to constitutional provisions, and had been generally acquiesced in by legislators and governors, does not make such appropriations legal.

A college, whose name was selected in recognition of its relation between itself and a distinctly religious organization, whose faculty was obtained largely from the religious organization, which conducted religious services in accordance with that church, which, however, did not require students to attend religious services, and maintained elective courses of instruction, is, nevertheless, a sectarian or denominational institution.

A hospital whose charter indicated no sectarian purpose and claimed to be nonsectarian, but which occupied property owned by a denominational society and was under contract to giving the denominational society full management and control of the institution, is a denominational institution which cannot receive state appropriations. Collins v. Kephart, 117 A. 440 (Pa. 1921).

---

† The Court further held that unlike the First Amendment, the act did not violate the Maryland Constitution. ED.

Federal aid for construction of facilities at sectarian colleges is not unconstitutional

TILTON v. RICHARDSON

Supreme Court of the United States, 1971.
—— U.S. ——, 91 S. Ct. 2091.

Mr. Chief Justice BURGER announced the judgment of the Court and an opinion in which Mr. Justice HARLAN, Mr. Justice STEWART and Mr. Justice BLACKMUN join.

This appeal presents important constitutional questions as to federal aid for church-related colleges and universities under Title I of the Higher Education Facilities Act of 1963, 20 U.S.C. §§ 701-758, which provides construction grants for buildings and facilities used exclusively for secular educational purposes. We must determine first whether the Act authorizes aid to such church-related institutions, and if so, whether the Act violates either the Establishment or Free Exercise Clauses of the First Amendment.

I

The Higher Education Facilities Act was passed in 1963 in response to a strong nationwide demand for the expansion of college and university facilities to meet the sharply rising number of young people demanding higher education. The Act authorizes federal grants and loans to "institutions of higher education" for the construction of a wide variety of "academic facilities." But § 751 (a) (2) expressly excludes

> "any facility used or to be used for sectarian instruction or as a place for religious worship, or * * * any facility which * * * is used or to be used primarily in connection with any part of the program of a school or department of divinity * * *."

The Act is administered by the United States Commissioner of Education. He advises colleges and universities applying for funds that under the Act no part of the project may be used for sectarian instruction, religious worship, or the programs of a divinity school. The Commissioner requires applicants to provide assurances that these restrictions will be respected. The United States retains a 20-year interest in any facility constructed with Title I funds. If, during this period, the recipient violates the statutory conditions, the United States is entitled to recover an amount equal to the proportion of its present value which the federal grant bore to the original cost of the facility. During the 20-year period, the statutory restrictions are enforced by the Office of Education primarily by way of on-site inspections.

Appellants are citizens and taxpayers of the United States and residents of Connecticut. They brought this suit for injunctive relief against the officials who administer the Act. Four church-related colleges and universities in Connecticut receiving federal construction grants under Title I were also named as defendants. Federal funds were used for five projects at these four institutions: (1) a library building at Sacred Heart University; (2) a music, drama, and arts building at Annhurst College; (3) a science building at Fairfield University; (4) a library building at Fairfield; and (5) a language laboratory at Albertus Magnus College. * * *

II

We are satisfied that Congress intended the Act to include all colleges and universities regardless of any affiliation with or sponsorship by a religious body. Congress defined "institutions of higher education," which are eligible to receive aid under the Act, in broad and inclusive terms. Certain institutions, for example, institutions which are neither public nor nonprofit, are expressly excluded, and the Act expressly prohibits use of the facilities for religious purposes. But the Act makes no reference to religious affiliation or nonaffiliation. Under these circumstances "institutions of higher education" must be taken to include church-related colleges and universities. * * *

III

Numerous cases considered by the Court have noted the internal tension in the First Amendment between the Establishment Clause and the Free Exercise Clause. Walz v. Tax Commission, 397 U.S. 664, 90 S.Ct. 1409, 25 L.Ed.2d 697 (1970), is the most recent decision seeking to define the boundaries of the neutral area between these two provisions within which the legislature may legitimately act. There, as in other decisions, the Court treated the three main concerns against which the Establishment Clause sought to protect: "sponsorship, financial support, and active involvement of the sovereign in religious activity." *Id.*, at 668, 90 S.Ct., at 1411.

Every analysis must begin with the candid acknowledgment that there is no single constitutional caliper which can be used to measure the precise degree to which these three factors are present or absent. Instead, our analysis in this area must begin with a consideration of the cumulative criteria developed over many years and applying to a wide range of governmental action challenged as violative of the Establishment Clause.

There are always risks in treating criteria discussed by the Court from time to time as "tests" in any limiting sense of that term. Constitutional adjudication does not lend itself to the absolutes of the physical sciences or mathematics. The standards should rather be viewed as guidelines with which to identify instances in which the objectives of the Religion Clauses have been impaired. And, as we have noted in Lemon v. Kurtzman and Earley v. DiCenso, 401 U.S. ——, 91 S.Ct. 2105, 28 L.Ed.2d —— decided today, candor compels the acknowledgment that we can only dimly perceive the boundaries of permissible government activity in this sensitive area of constitutional adjudication.

Against this background we consider four questions: First, does the Act reflect a secular legislative purpose? Second, is the primary effect of the Act to advance or inhibit religion? Third, does the administration of the Act foster an excessive government entanglement with religion? Fourth, does the implementation of the Act inhibit the free exercise of religion?

(a)

The stated legislative purpose appears in the preamble where Congress found and declared that

> "the security and welfare of the United States require that this and future generations of American youth be assured ample opportunity for the fullest development of their intellectual capacities, and that this opportunity will be jeopardized unless the Nation's colleges and universities are encouraged and assisted in their efforts to accommodate rapidly growing numbers of youth who aspire to a higher education." 20 U.S.C. § 701.

This expresses a legitimate secular objective entirely appropriate for governmental action.

* * * The crucial question is not whether some benefit accrues to a religious institution as a consequence of the legislative program, but whether its principal or primary effect advances religion.

A possibility always exists, of course, that the legitimate objectives of any law or legislative program may be subverted by conscious design or lax enforcement. There is nothing new in this argument. But judicial concern about these possibilities cannot, standing alone, warrant striking down a statute as unconstitutional.

The Act itself was carefully drafted to ensure that the federally subsidized facilities would be devoted to the secular and not the religious function of the recipient institutions. It authorizes grants and loans only for academic facilities that will be used for defined secular purposes and expressly prohibits their use for religious instruction, training, or worship. These restrictions have been enforced in the Act's actual administration, and the record shows that some church-related institutions have been required to disgorge benefits for failure to obey them.

Finally, this record fully supports the findings of the District Court that none of the four church-related institutions in this case has violated the statutory restrictions. The institutions presented evidence that there had been no religious services or worship in the federally financed facilities, that there are no religious symbols or plaques in or on them, and that they had been used solely for nonreligious purposes. On this record, therefore, these buildings are indistinguishable from a typical state university facility. Appellants presented no evidence to the contrary.

Appellants instead rely on the argument that government may not subsidize any activities of an institution of higher learning which in some of its programs teaches religious doctrines. * * *

Under this concept appellants' position depends on the validity of the proposition that religion so permeates the secular-education provided by church-related colleges and universities that their religious and secular educational functions are in fact inseparable. The argument that government grants would thus inevitably advance religion did not escape the notice of Congress. It was carefully and thoughtfully debated, 109 Cong.Rec. 19474-19475 (1963), but was found unpersuasive. It was also considered by this Court in *Allen*. There the Court refused to assume that religiosity in parochial elementary and secondary schools necessarily permeates the secular education that they provide.

This record, similarly, provides no basis for any such assumption here. Two of the five federally financed buildings involved in this case are libraries. The District Court found that no classes had been conducted in either of these facilities and that no restrictions were imposed by the institutions on the books that they acquired. There is no evidence to the contrary. The third building was a language laboratory at Albertus Magnus College. The evidence showed that this facility was used solely to assist students with their pronunciation in modern foreign languages—a use which would seem peculiarly unrelated and unadaptable to religious indoctrination. Federal grants were also used to build a science building at Fairfield University and a music, drama, and arts building at Annhurst College.

There is no evidence that religion seeps into the use of any of these facilities. Indeed, the parties stipulated in the District Court that courses at these institutions are taught according to the academic requirements intrinsic to the subject matter and the individual teacher's concept of professional standards. Although appellants introduced several institutional documents which stated certain religious restrictions on what could be taught, other evidence showed that these restrictions were not in fact enforced and that the schools were characterized by an atmosphere of academic freedom rather than religious indoctrination. All four institutions, for example, subscribe to the 1940 Statement of Principles on Academic Freedom and Tenure endorsed by the American Association of University Professors and the Association of American Colleges.

Rather than focus on the four defendant colleges and universities involved in this case, however, appellants seek to shift our attention to a "composite profile" that they have constructed of the "typical sectarian" institution of higher education. We are told that such a "composite" institution imposes religious restrictions on admissions, requires attendance at religious activities, compels obedience to the doctrines and dogmas of the faith, requires instruction in theology and doctrine, and does everything it can to propagate a particular religion. Perhaps some church-related schools fit the pattern that appellants describe. Indeed, some colleges have been declared ineligible for aid by the authorities that administer the Act. But appellants do not contend that these four institutions fall within this category. Individual projects can be properly evaluated if and when challenges arise with respect to particular recipients and some evidence is then presented to show that the institution does in fact possess these characteristics. We cannot, however, strike down an Act of Congress on the basis of a hypothetical "profile."

(b)

Although we reject appellants' board constitutional arguments we do perceive an aspect in which the statute's enforcement provisions are inadequate to ensure that the impact of the federal aid will not advance religion. If a recipient institution violates any of the statutory restrictions on the use of a federally financed facility, § 754(b) (2) permits the Government to recover an amount equal to the proportion of the facility's present value which the federal grant bore to its original cost.

This remedy, however, is available to the Government only if the statutory conditions are violated "within twenty years after completion of construction." This 20-year period is termed by the statute as "the period of Federal interest" and reflects Congress' finding that after 20 years "the public benefit accruing to the United States" from the use of the federally financed facility "will equal or exceed in value" the amount of the federal grant. 20 U.S.C. § 754(a).

Under § 754(b) (2), therefore, a recipient institution's obligation not to use the facility for sectarian instruction or religious worship would appear to expire at the end of 20 years. We note, for example, that under § 718(b) (7) (C), an institution applying for a federal grant is only required to provide assurances that the facility will not be used for sectarian instruction or religious worship "during at least the period of the Federal interest therein (as defined in section 754 of this title)."

Limiting the prohibition for religious use of the structure to 20 years obviously opens the facility to use for any purpose at the end of that period. It cannot be assumed that a substantial structure has no value after that period and hence the unrestricted use of a valuable property is in effect a contribution of some value to a religious body. Congress did not base the 20-year provision on any contrary conclusion. If, at the end of 20 years the building is, for example, converted into a chapel or otherwise used to promote religious interests, the original federal grant will in part have the effect of advancing religion.

To this extent the Act therefore trespasses on the Religion Clauses. The restrictive obligations of a recipient institution under § 751(a) (2) cannot, compatible with the Religion Clause, expire while the building has substantial value. This circumstance does not require us to invalidate the entire Act, however. "The cardinal principle of statutory construction is to save and not to destroy." * * *

We have found nothing in the statute or its objectives intimating that Congress considered the 20-year provision essential to the statutory program as a whole. In view of the broad and important goals which Congress intended this legislation to serve, there is no basis for assuming that the Act would have failed of passage without this provision; nor will its excision impair either the operation or administration of the Act in any significant respect.

IV

We next turn to the question of whether excessive entanglements characterize the relationship between government and church under the Act. * * * Our decisions today in Lemon v. Kurtzman and Robinson v. DiCenso have discussed and applied this independent measure of constitutionality under the Religion Clauses. There we concluded that excessive entanglements between government and religion were fostered by Pennsylvania and Rhode Island statutory programs under which state aid was provided to parochial elementary and secondary schools. Here, however, three factors substantially diminish the extent and the potential danger of the entanglement.

In *DiCenso* the District Court found that the parochial schools in Rhode Island were "an integral part of the religious mission of the Catholic Church." There, the record fully supported the conclusion that the inculcation of religious values was a substantial if not the dominant purpose of the institutions. The Pennsylvania case was decided on the pleadings, and hence we accepted as true the allegations that the parochial schools in that State shared the same characteristics.

Appellants' complaint here contains similar allegations. But they were denied by the answers, and there was extensive evidence introduced on the subject. Although the District Court made no findings with respect to the religious character of the four institutions of higher learning, we are not required to accept the allegations as true under these circumstances, particularly where, as here, appellants themselves do not contend that these four institutions are "sectarian."

There are generally significant differences between the religious aspects of church-related institutions of higher learning and parochial elementary and secondary schools. The "affirmative, if not dominant, policy" of the instruction in pre-college church-schools is "to assure future adherents to a particular faith by having control of their total education at an early age." Walz v. Tax Commission, *supra,* at 671, 90 S. Ct., at 1412. There is substance to the contention that college students are less impressionable and less susceptible to religious indoctrination. Common observation would seem to support that view, and Congress may well have entertained it. The skepticism of the college student is not an inconsiderable barrier to any attempt or tendency to subvert the congressional objectives and limitations. Furthermore, by their very nature, college and postgraduate courses tend to limit the opportunities for sectarian influence by virtue of their own internal disciplines. Finally, many church-related colleges and universities seek to evoke free and critical responses from their students and are characterized by a high degree of academic freedom.

The record here would not support a conclusion that any of these four institutions departed from this general pattern. All four schools are governed by Catholic religious organizations, and the faculties and student bodies at each are predominantly Catholic. Nevertheless, the evidence shows that non-Catholics were admitted as students and given faculty appointments. Not one of these four institutions requires its students to attend religious services. Although all four schools require their students to take theology courses, the parties stipulated that these courses are taught according to the academic requirements of the subject matter and the teacher's concept of professional standards. The parties also stipulated that the courses covered a range of human religious experiences and are not limited to courses about the Roman Catholic religion. The schools introduced evidence that they made no attempt to indoctrinate students or to proselytize. Indeed, some of the required theology courses at Albertus Magnus and Sacred Heart are taught by rabbis. Finally, as we have noted, these four schools subscribe to a well-established set of principles of academic freedom, and nothing in this record shows that these principles are not in fact followed. In short, the evidence shows institutions with admittedly religious functions but whose predominant higher education mission is to provide their students with a secular education.

Since religious indoctrination is not a substantial purpose or activity of these church-related colleges and universities, there is less likelihood than in primary and secondary schools that religion will permeate the area of secular education. This reduces the risk that government aid will in fact serve to support religious activities. Correspondingly the necessity for intensive government surveillance is diminished and the resulting entanglements between government and religion lessened. Such inspection as may be necessary to ascertain that the facilities are devoted to secular education is minimal and indeed hardly more than the inspections that States impose over all private schools within the reach of compulsory education laws.

The entanglement between church and state is also lessened here by the nonideological character of the aid which the government provides. Our cases from *Everson* to *Allen* have permitted church-related schools to receive government aid in the form of secular, neutral, or nonideological services, facilities, or materials that are supplied to all students regardless of the affiliation of the school which they attend. In *Lemon* and *DiCenso*, however, the state programs subsidized teachers, either directly or indirectly. Since teachers are not necessarily religiously neutral, greater governmental surveillance would be required to guarantee that state salary aid would not in fact subsidize religious instruction. There we found the resulting entanglement excessive. Here, on the other hand, the government provides facilities that are themselves religiously neutral. The risks of government aid to religion and the corresponding need for surveillance are therefore reduced.

Finally, government entanglements with religion are reduced by the circumstance that, unlike the direct and continuing payments under the Pennsylvania program, and all the incidents of regulation and surveillance, the government aid here is a one-time, single-purpose construction grant. There are no continuing financial relationships or dependencies, no annual audits, and no government analysis of an institution's expenditures on secular as distinguished from religious activities. Inspection as to use is a minimal contact.

No one of these three factors standing alone is necessarily controlling; cumulatively all of them shape a narrow and limited relationship with government which involves fewer and less significant contacts than the two state schemes before us in *Lemon* and *DiCenso*. The relationship therefore has less potential for realizing the substantive evils against which the Religion Clauses were intended to protect.

We think that cumulatively these three factors also substantially lessen the potential for divisive religious fragmentation in the political arena. This conclusion is admittedly difficult to document, but neither have appellants pointed to any continuing religious aggravation on this matter in the political processes. Possibly this can be explained by the character and diversity of the recipient colleges and universities and the absence of any intimate continuing relationship or dependency between government and religiously affiliated institutions. The potential for divisiveness inherent in the essentially local problems of primary and secondary schools is significantly less with respect to a college or university whose student constituency is not local but diverse and widely dispersed.

V

Finally, we must consider whether the implementation of the Act inhibits the free exercise of religion in violation of the First Amendment. Appellants claim that the Free Exercise Clause is violated because they are compelled to pay taxes, the proceeds of which in part finance grants under the Act. Appellants, however, are unable to identify any coercion directed at the practice or exercise of their religious beliefs. Board of Education of Central School District No. 1 v. Allen, *supra,* 392 U.S., at 248-249, 88 S.Ct., at 1929, 20 L.Ed.2d 1060. Their share of the cost of the grants under the Act is not fundamentally distinguishable from the impact of the tax exemption sustained in *Walz* or the provision of textbooks upheld in *Allen.*

We conclude that the Act does not violate the Religion Clauses of the First Amendment except that part of § 754(b) (2) providing a 20-year limitation on the religious use restrictions contained in § 751(a) (2). We remand to the District Court with directions to enter a judgment consistent with this opinion.

Vacated and remanded.

Mr. Justice DOUGLAS, with whom Mr. Justice BLACK and Mr. Justice MARSHALL concur, dissenting.

The correct constitutional principle for this case was stated by President Kennedy in 1961 when questioned as to his policy respecting aid to private and parochial schools: [1]

"* * * the Constitution clearly prohibits aid to the school, to parochial schools. I don't think there is any doubt of that.

"The Everson case, which is probably the most celebrated case, provided only by a 5 to 4 decision was it possible for a local community to provide bus rides to nonpublic school children. But all through the majority and minority statements on that particular question there was

1. Public Papers of the Presidents 1961, pp. 142-143, Press Conference March 4, 1961.

a very clear prohibition against aid to the school direct.
The Supreme Court made its decision in the Everson case
by determining that the aid was to the child, not to the
school. Aid to the school is—there isn't any room for debate on that subject. It is prohibited by the Constitution,
and the Supreme Court has made that very clear. And
therefore there would be no possibility of our recommending it." * * *

Title I of the Higher Education Facilities Act of 1963 authorizes grants and loans up to 50% of the cost for the construction of undergraduate academic facilities in both public
and private colleges and universities. A project is eligible if
construction will result "in creating urgently needed enrollment capacity, capacity to provide needed health care to students or personnel of the institution, or capacity to carry out
extension and continuing education programs on the campus
of such institution." 20 U.S.C. § 716. The Commissioner of
Education is authorized to prescribe basic criteria and is instructed to "give special consideration to expansion of undergraduate enrollment capacity." 20 U.S. C. § 717.

Academic facilities are "structures suitable for use as classrooms, laboratories, libraries, and related facilities necessary
or appropriate for instruction of students, or for research
* * * programs * * *." Specifically excluded are facilities
"used or to be used for sectarian instruction or as a place of
religious worship" or any facilities used "primarily in connection with any part of the program of a school or department
of divinity." 20 U.S.C. § 751(a). The United States retains a
20-year interest in the facilities and should a facility be used
other than as an academic facility then the United States is
entitled to recover an amount equal to the proportion of present value which the federal grant bore to the original cost of
the facility. 20 U.S.C. § 754(b). According to a stipulation
entered below, during the 20 years the Office of Education attempts to insure that facilities are used in the manner required by the Act primarily by on-site inspections. At the end
of the 20-year period the Federal interest in the facility ceases
and the college may use it as it pleases. See 20 U.S.C. § 754(a).

The public purpose in secular education is, to be sure,
furthered by the program. Yet the sectarian purpose is aided
by making the parochial school system viable. The purpose is
to increase "student enrollment" and the students obviously
aimed at are those of the particular faith now financed by taxpayers' money. Parochial schools are not beamed at agnostics,
atheists, or those of a competing sect. The more sophisticated

institutions may admit minorities; but the dominant religious character is not changed.

The reversion of the facility to the parochial school [2] at the end of 20 years is an outright grant, measurable by the present discounted worth of the facility. A gift of taxpayers' funds in that amount would plainly be unconstitutional. The Court properly bars it even though disguised in the form of a reversionary interest. See Lane v. Wilson, 307 U.S. 268, 275, 59 S.Ct. 872, 876, 83 L.Ed. 1281.

But the invalidation of this one clause cannot cure the constitutional infirmities of the statute as a whole. The Federal Government is giving religious schools a block grant to build certain facilities. The fact that money is given once at the beginning of a program rather than apportioned annually as in *Lemon* and *DiCenso* is without constitutional significance. The First Amendment bars establishment of a religion. And as I noted today in *Lemon* and *DiCenso*, this bar has been consistently interpreted from Everson v. Board of Education, 330 U.S. 1, 16, 67 S.Ct. 504, 511, 91 L.Ed. 711, through Torcaso v. Watkins, 367 U.S. 488, 493, 81 S.Ct. 1680, 1682, 6 L.Ed.2d 982, as meaning: "No tax in any amount, large or small, can be levied to support any religious activities or institutions, whatever they may be called, or whatever form they may adopt to teach or practice religion." Thus it is hardly impressive that rather than giving a smaller amount of money annually over a large period of years, Congress instead gives a large amount all at once. The majority's distinction is in effect that small violations of the First Amendment over a period of years are unconstitutional (see *Lemon* and *DiCenso*) while a huge violation occurring only once is *de minimus*. I cannot agree within such sophistry.

What I have said in *Lemon* and in the *DiCenso* cases decided

---

2. "It should be clear to all that a Roman Catholic parochial school is an integral part of that church, as definitely so as is the service of worship. A parochial school is usually developed in connection with a church. In many cases the church and school monies are not even separated. Such a school is in no sense a public school, even though some children from other groups may be admitted to it. The buildings are not owned and controlled by a community of American people, not even by a community of American Roman Catholic people. The title of ownership in a public school is vested in the local community, in the elected officers of the school board or the city council. But the title of ownership in a parochial school is vested in the bishop as an individual, who is appointed by, who is under the direct control of, and who reports to the pope in Rome." Boettner, Roman Catholicism, p. 375 (1970).

today is relevant here. The facilities financed by taxpayers' funds are not to be used "for sectarian" purposes. Religious teaching and secular teaching are so enmeshed in parochial schools that only the strictest supervision and surveillance would insure compliance with the condition. Parochial schools may require religious exercises, even in the classroom. A parochial school operates on one budget. Money not spent for one purpose becomes available for other purposes. Thus the fact that there are no religious-observances in federally financed facilities is not controlling because required religious observances will take place in other buildings. Our decision in Engel v. Vitale, 370 U.S. 421, 82 S.Ct. 1261, 8 L.Ed.2d 601, held that a requirement of a prayer in public schools violated the Establishment Clause. Once these schools become federally funded they become bound by federal standards (Ivanhoe Irrig. Dist. v. McCracken, 357 U.S. 275, 296, 78 S.Ct. 1174, 1186, 2 L.Ed.2d 1313; Rosado v. Wyman, 397 U.S. 397, 427, 90 S.Ct. 1207, 1225, 25 L.Ed.2d 442 (concurring opinion); Simkins v. Moses H. Cone Memorial Hosp., 4 Cir., 323 F.2d 959) and accordingly adherence to *Engel* would require an end to required religious exercises. That kind of surveillance and control will certainly be obnoxious to the church authorities and if done will radically change the character of the parochial school. Yet if that surveillance is not searching and continuous, this federal financing is obnoxious under the Establishment and Free Exercise Clauses all for the reasons stated in the companion cases.

In other words, surveillance creates an entanglement of government and religion which the First Amendment was designed to avoid. Yet after today's decision there will be a requirement of surveillance which will last for the useful life of the building and as we have previously noted, "[it] is hardly lack of due process for the Government to regulate that which it subsidizes." Wickard v. Filburn, 317 U.S. 111, 131, 63 S.Ct. 82, 92, 87 L.Ed. 122. The price of the subsidy under the Act is violation of the Free Exercise Clause. Could a course in the History of Methodism be taught in a federally financed building? Would a religiously slanted version of the Reformation or Quebec politics under Duplessis be permissible? How can the Government know what is taught in the federally financed building without a continuous auditing of classroom instruction? Yet both the Free Exercise Clause and academic freedom are violated when the Government agent must be present to determine whether the course content is satisfactory.

As I said in the *Lemon* and *DiCenso* cases, a parochial school is a unitary institution with subtle blending of sectarian and secular instruction. Thus the practices of religious schools are in no way affected by the minimal requirement that the government financed facility may not "be used for sectarian instruction or as a place of worship." Money saved from one item in the budget is free to be used elsewhere. By conducting religious services in another building, the school has—rent free—a building for nonsectarian use. This is not called Establishment simply because the government retains a continuing interest in the building for its useful life, even though the religious schools need never pay a cent for the use of the building.

Much is made of the need for public aid to church schools in light of their pressing fiscal problems. Dr. Eugene C. Blake of the Presbyterian Church, however, wrote in 1959: [3]

> "When one remembers that churches pay no inheritance tax (churches do not die), that churches may own and operate business and be exempt from the 52 percent corporate income tax, and that real property used for church purposes (which in some states are most generously construed) is tax exempt, it is not unreasonable to prophesy that with reasonably prudent management, the churches ought to be able to control the whole economy of the nation within the predictable future. That the growing wealth and property of the churches was partially responsible for revolutionary expropriations of church property in England in the sixteenth century, in France in the eighteenth century, in Italy in the nineteenth century, and in Mexico, Russia, Czechoslovakia and Hungary (to name a few examples) in the twentieth century, seems self-evident. A government with mounting tax problems cannot be expected to keep its hands off the wealth of a rich church forever. That such a revolution is always accompanied by anticlericalism and atheism should not be surprising."

The mounting wealth of the churches makes ironic their incessant demands on the public treasury. I said in my dissent in Walz v. Tax Commission, 397 U.S. 664, 714, 90 S.Ct. 1409, 1434, 25 L.Ed.2d 697.

> "The religiously used real estate of the churches today constitutes a vast domain. See M. Larson & C. Lowell, The Churches: Their Riches, Revenues, and Immunities (1969). Their assets total over $141 billion and their an-

3. Tax Exemption and the Churches, 3 Christianity Today No. 22, Aug. 3, 1959, p. 7.

nual income at least $22 billion. *Id.*, at 232. And the extent to which they are feeding from the public trough in a variety of forms is alarming. *Id.*, c. 10." Walz v. Tax Commission, 397 U.S. 664, 714, 90 S.Ct. 1409, 1434; Balk, The Religion Business (1968) ; 20 Church and State 8 (1967).

It is almost unbelievable that we have made the radical departure from Madison's Remonstrance memorialized in today's decision.

I dissent not because of any lack of respect for parochial schools but out of a feeling of despair that the respect which through history has been accorded the First Amendment is this day lost.

It should be remembered that in this case we deal with federal grants and with the command that "Congress shall make no law respecting an establishment of religion or prohibiting the free exercise thereof." The million-dollar grants sustained today put Madison's miserable "three pence" to shame. But he even thought, as I do, that even a small amount coming out of the pocket of taxpayers and going into the coffers of a church was not in keeping with our constitutional ideal.

I would reverse the judgment below.

NOTES

In a 1970 decision, the Supreme Court of South Carolina held that a statute establishing a state school facility authority and permitting issuance of revenue bonds for the benefit of church-related colleges did not violate the religious freedom provisions of the South Carolina constitution. Hunt v. McNair, 177 S.E.2d 362 (1970).

Holding of religious exercises, prayer and Bible reading in public schools is unconstitutional

SCHOOL DISTRICT OF ABINGTON TOWNSHIP
v.
SCHEMPP

Supreme Court of the United States, 1963.
374 U.S. 203, 83 S. Ct. 1560.

Mr. Justice Clark delivered the opinion of the Court.

Once again we are called upon to consider the scope of the provision of the First Amendment to the United States Constitution which declares that "Congress shall make no law respecting an establishment of religion, or prohibiting the free exercise thereof * * *." These companion cases present the issues in the context of state action requiring that schools begin each day with readings from the Bible. While raising the basic questions under slightly different factual situations, the cases permit of joint treatment. In light of the history of the First Amendment and of our cases interpreting and applying its requirements, we hold that the practices at issue and the laws requiring them are unconstitutional under the Establishment Clause, as applied to the States through the Fourteenth Amendment.

The Facts in Each Case: No. 142. The Commonwealth of Pennsylvania by law, 24 Pa.Stat. § 15-1516, as amended, Pub.Law 1928 (Supp. 1960) Dec. 17, 1959, requires that "At least ten verses from the Holy Bible shall be read, without comment, at the opening of each public school on each school day. Any child shall be excused from such Bible reading, or attending such Bible reading, upon the written request of his parent or guardian." The Schempp family, husband and wife and two of their three children, brought suit to enjoin enforcement of the statute, contending that their rights under the Fourteenth Amendment to the Constitution of the United States are, have been, and will continue to be violated unless this statute be declared unconstitutional as violative of these provisions of the First Amendment. They sought to enjoin the appellant school district, wherein the Schempp children attend school, and its officers and the Superintendent of Public Instruction of the Commonwealth from continuing to conduct such readings and recitation of the Lord's Prayer in the public schools of the district pursuant to the statute. * * *

No. 119. In 1905 the Board of School Commissioners of Baltimore City adopted a rule pursuant to Art. 77, § 202 of the Annotated Code of Maryland. The rule provided for the holding of opening exercises in the schools of the city, consisting primarily of the "reading, without comment, of a chapter in the Holy Bible and/or the use of the Lord's Prayer." The petitioners, Mrs. Madalyn Murray and her son, William J. Murray III, are both professed atheists. Following unsuccessful attempts to have the respondent school board rescind the rule, this suit was filed for mandamus to compel its rescission and cancellation. It was alleged that William was a student in a public school of the city and Mrs. Murray, his mother, was a taxpayer therein; that it was the practice under the rule to have a reading on each school morning from the King James version of the Bible; that at petitioners' insistence the rule was amended [32] to permit children to be excused from the exercise on request of the parent and that William had been excused pursuant thereto; that nevertheless the rule as amended was in violation of the petitioners' rights "to freedom of religion under the First and Fourteenth Amendments" and in violation of "the principle of separation between church and state, contained therein. * * *" * * *

Applying the Establishment Clause principles to the cases at bar we find that the States are requiring the selection and reading at the opening of the school day of verses from the Holy Bible and the recitation of the Lord's Prayer by the students in unison. These exercises are prescribed as part of the curricular activities of students who are required by law to attend school. They are held in the school buildings under the supervision and with the participation of teachers employed in those schools. None of these factors, other than compulsory school attendance, was present in the program upheld in Zorach v. Clauson. The trial court in No. 142 has found that such an opening exercise is a religious ceremony and was intended by the State to be so. We agree with the trial court's finding as to the religious character of the exercises. Given that finding, the exercises and the law requiring them are in violation of the Establishment Clause.

There is no such specific finding as to the religious character of the exercises in No. 119, and the State contends (as does the State in No. 142) that the program is an effort to extend its benefits to all public school children without regard to their religious belief. Included within its secular purposes, it says, are the promotion of moral values, the contradiction to the materialistic trends of our times, the perpetuation of our institutions and the teaching of literature. The case came up on demurrer, of course, to a petition which alleged that the uniform practice under the rule had been to read from the King James

---

32. The rule as amended provides as follows "Opening Exercises. Each school, either collectively or in classes, shall be opened by the reading, without comment, of a chapter in the Holy Bible and/or the use of the Lord's Prayer. The Douay version may be used by those pupils who prefer it. Appropriate patriotic exercises should be held as a part of the general opening exercise of the school or class. Any child shall be excused from participating in the opening exercises or from attending the opening exercises upon the written request of his parent or guardian."

version of the Bible and that the exercise was sectarian. The short answer, therefore, is that the religious character of the exercise was admitted by the State. But even if its purpose is not strictly religious, it is sought to be accomplished through readings, without comment, from the Bible. Surely the place of the Bible as an instrument of religion cannot be gainsaid, and the State's recognition of the pervading religious character of the ceremony is evident from the rule's specific permission of the alternative use of the Catholic Douay version as well as the recent amendment permitting nonattendance at the exercises. None of these factors is consistent with the contention that the Bible is here used either as an instrument for nonreligious moral inspiration or as a reference for the teaching of secular subjects.

The conclusion follows that in both cases the laws require religious exercises and such exercises are being conducted in direct violation of the rights of the appellees and petitioners. Nor are these required exercises mitigated by the fact that individual students may absent themselves upon parental request, for that fact furnishes no defense to a claim of unconstitutionality under the Establishment Clause. See Engel v. Vitale, supra, 370 U.S., at 430, 82 S.Ct., at 1266-1267, 8 L.Ed.2d 601. Further, it is no defense to urge that the religious practices here may be relatively minor encroachments on the First Amendment. The breach of neutrality that is today a trickling stream may all too soon become a raging torrent and, in the words of Madison, "it is proper to take alarm at the first experiment on our liberties." Memorial and Remonstrance Against Religious Assessments * * *.

It is insisted that unless these religious exercises are permitted a "religion of secularism" is established in the schools. We agree of course that the State may not establish a "religion of secularism" in the sense of affirmatively opposing or showing hostility to religion, thus "preferring those who believe in no religion over those who do believe." Zorach v. Clauson, supra, 343 U.S., at 314, 72 S.Ct., at 684, 96 L.Ed. 954. We do not agree, however, that this decision in any sense has that effect. In addition, it might well be said that one's education is not complete without a study of comparative religion or the history of religion and its relationship to the advancement of civilization. It certainly may be said that the Bible is worthy of study for its literary and historic qualities. Nothing we have said here indicates that such study of the Bible or of religion, when presented objectively as part of a secular program of education, may not be effected consistently with the First Amendment. But the exercises here do not fall into those categories. They are religious exercises, required by the States in violation of the command of the First Amendment that the Government maintain strict neutrality, neither aiding or opposing religion.

Finally, we cannot accept that the concept of neutrality, which does not permit a State to require a religious exercise even with the consent of the majority of those affected, collides with the majority's right to free exercise of religion. While the Free Exercise Clause clearly prohibits the use of state action to deny the rights of free exercise to *anyone*, it has never meant that a majority could use the machinery of the State to practice its beliefs. Such a contention was effectively answered by Mr. Justice Jackson for the Court in West Virginia Board of Education v. Barnette, 319 U.S. 624, 638, 63 S.Ct. 1178, 1185, 87 L.Ed. 1628 (1943) :

"The very purpose of a Bill of Rights was to withdraw certain subjects from the vicissitudes of political controversy, to place them beyond the reach of majorities and officials and to establish them as legal principles to be applied by the courts. One's right * * * freedom of worship * * * and other fundamental rights may not be submitted to vote; they depend on the outcome of no elections."

The place of religion in our society is an exalted one, achieved through a long tradition of reliance on the home, the church and the inviolable citadel of the individual heart and mind. We have come to recognize through bitter experience that it is not within the power of government to invade that citadel, whether its purpose or effect be to aid or oppose, to advance or retard. In the relationship between man and religion, the State is firmly committed to a position of neutrality. Though the application of that rule requires interpretation of a delicate sort, the rule itself is clearly and concisely stated in the words of the First Amendment. Applying that rule to the facts of these cases, we affirm the judgment in No. 142. In No. 119, the judgment is reversed and the cause remanded to the Maryland Court of Appeals for further proceedings consistent with this opinion.

It is so ordered.

Judgment in No. 142 affirmed; judgment in No. 119 reversed and cause remanded with directions.

College course dealing with literary features of the Bible does not violate Constitution

CALVARY BIBLE PRESBYTERIAN CHURCH OF SEATTLE

v.

BOARD OF REGENTS OF THE UNIVERSITY OF WASHINGTON

Supreme Court of Washington, 1967.
72 Wash. 2d 912, 436 P.2d 189.

WEAVER, Judge.

Since 1919, the Department of English of the University of Washington, a state tax-supported university, has offered an elective course of study presently designated "English 390: The Bible as Literature."

Two churches, incorporated organizations, and their respective ministers commenced this action against the Board of Regents of the University of Washington praying (1) for an injunction pendente lite directing the defendants to discontinue "the prescribed course [1] until such time as the matter may be fully considered by the Court;" and (2) for a "permanent injunction * * * restraining the Board of Regents from authorizing any course of instruction dealing with the historical, biographical, narrative or literary features of the Bible."

Plaintiffs contend that the teaching of English 390 is violative of Art. 1, § 11 and Art. 9, § 4 of the Washington State Constitution, which provide:

> No public money or property shall be appropriated for, or applied to any religious worship, exercise or instruction, * * *. [Art. 1, § 11].
> All schools maintained or supported wholly or in part by the public funds shall be forever free from sectarian control or influence. [Art. 9, § 4].

Plaintiffs also contend that the teaching of English 390 violates the First Amendment of the United States Constitution ("Congress shall make no law respecting an establishment of religion, or prohibiting the free exercise thereof; * * *.") as applied to the states through the Fourteenth Amendment.

Although the constitutional violations are urged, the major premise of plaintiffs' argument, as alleged in their amended complaint, is:

---

1. The course is not prescribed; it is an elective.

> That the manner in which said presentation is made [of English 390] is contrary to the religious beliefs of Plaintiffs, both individually and as church organizations and congregations. That said manner of presentation is in itself the presentation of a religious point of view, being one of several theological positions within the Protestant faith. * * *

The trial court dismissed plaintiffs' complaint with prejudice. * * *

The sole question remaining is whether the conclusions of law, based upon the findings, are violative of the constitutional provisions quoted supra.

The touchstone of the problem is the meaning attributed to "religious * * * instruction," as used in Art. 1, § 11 of our constitution. It must be kept in mind that the words appear after two more specific terms: "worship" and "exercise." This, we believe, is an indication that the framers of our constitution did not intend the word "instruction" to be construed without limit, but that the proscribed field be confined to that category of instruction that resembles worship and manifests a devotion to religion and religious principles in thought, feeling, belief, and conduct, i. e., instruction that is devotional in nature and designed to induce faith and belief in the student.

There can be no doubt that our constitutional bars are absolute against *religious* instruction and indoctrination in specific religious beliefs or dogma; but they do not proscribe open, free, critical, and scholarly examination of the literature, experiences, and knowledge of mankind. If they did, many fields of scholarship—anthropology, zoology, the theory of evolution, astronomy, the germ theory of disease and medical cure, to mention only a few—would have to be removed from our university. It might be said that the objective examination of these theories conflicts with the religious beliefs of certain persons entertaining contrary beliefs based upon the religious convictions. This would, indeed, be true "sectarian control or influence," which is prohibited by Art. 9, § 4 of our constitution. It would, as Mr. Justice Brennan said so recently,

> cast a pall of orthodoxy over the classroom. Keyishian v. Board of Regents, 385 U.S. 589, 87 S.Ct. 675, 17 L.Ed.2d 629 (1967).

The result advocated by plaintiffs would be catastrophic in the field of higher education. Would plaintiffs have us strike the words of Milton, Dante, and the other ancient authors whose writings have survived the ages, because they wrote of religious theories with which plaintiffs quarrel? Our constitution does not guarantee sectarian control of our educational system.

In People of State of Illinois ex rel. McCollum v. Board of Education of School Dist. No. 71, 333 U.S. 203, 68 S.Ct. 461, 92 L.Ed. 649 (1948), Mr. Justice Jackson, in a concurring opinion, pointed out that:

> Music without sacred music, architecture minus the cathedral, or painting without the scriptural themes would be eccentric and incomplete, even from a secular point of view. * * * Even such a "science" as biology raises the issue between evolution and creation as an explanation of our presence on this planet. Certainly a course in English literature that omitted the Bible and other powerful uses of our mother tongue for religious ends would be pretty barren.

In the final analysis, plaintiffs contend: (1) That the Bible *cannot* be taught objectively as a course in literature, for the attempt to do so violates their personal beliefs (sectarian); hence, the teaching is unconstitutional; (2) That the course is *not* taught objectively, but is slanted against plaintiffs' beliefs.

It is apparent that the two contentions overlap factually. The case was well presented to the court, although the evidence of the parties splashes over the guidelines set by the trial court, established both by pretrial order and at the commencement of the trial.

The testimony is fascinating reading for one interested in the subject. Competent scholars, educators, professors, ministers, theologians, and students who had taken the course testified. It would unduly extend this opinion to analyze the testimony of any group of witnesses, except, perhaps, to mention the testimony of the students.

There is competent testimony to support the trial court's conclusion that "English 390—The Bible as Literature" *can* be taught objectively in a course in literature, without religious implications, for the court found that the course does not promote a particular theology for purposes of religious indoctrination; that it is not slanted in a religious direction; that it does not induce any particular religious belief; and that it does not advance any particular religious interest or theology. * * *

Experts may talk in the abstract, but the "proof of the pudding is in the eating." Besides the experts, the following students who had taken English 390 testified: one who had no personal religious beliefs; a Catholic with a parochial school education; one who described herself as "a rather devout Methodist"; one a Christian Scientist; one a member of a Jewish synagogue (an outstanding student and the University's nominee as a Rhodes scholar).

Telescoping their testimony, we find that English 390 was taught in a completely objective manner; had no effect on religious beliefs; was not slanted toward any particular theological or religious point of view; did not indoctrinate anyone; did not enter into the realm of belief or faith; and was not taught from a religious point of view.

This, we believe, is sufficient to support the trial court's findings and to justify its conclusion that "English 390—The Bible as Literature," as taught at the University of Washington, is not violative of the constitutional provisions we have identified. * * *

Recently, the Supreme Court in Whitehill v. Elkins, 389 U.S. 54, 88 S.Ct. 184, 19 L.Ed.2d 228 (1967), quoted with approval from Sweezy v. State of New Hampshire, by Wyman, 354 U.S. 234, 250, 77 S.Ct. 1203, 1 L.Ed.2d 1311 (1957). Although the facts are different, the language has a bearing upon the problem before us. The court said:

> "The essentiality of freedom in the community of American universities is almost self-evident. No one should underestimate the vital role in a democracy that is played by those who guide and train our youth. To impose any straitjacket upon the intellectual leaders in our colleges and universities would imperil the future of our Nation. No field of education is so thoroughly comprehended by man that new discoveries cannot yet be made. *Particularly is that true in the social sciences, where few, if any, principles are accepted as absolutes.* Scholarship cannot flourish in an atmosphere of suspicion and distrust. Teachers and students must always remain free to inquire, to study and to evaluate, to gain new maturity and understanding; otherwise our civilization will stagnate and die." (Italics ours.)

The judgment is affirmed.

**Law requiring college military training of all able-bodied
males does not violate students'
constitutional rights**

HAMILTON v. REGENTS OF THE UNIVERSITY
OF CALIFORNIA

Supreme Court of the United States, 1934.
293 U.S. 245, 55 S. Ct. 197, 79 L. Ed. 343.

Mr. Justice BUTLER delivered the opinion of the Court:

This is an appeal under § 237 (a), Judicial Code, 28 U. S. C.,
§ 344 (a), from a judgment of the highest court of California
sustaining a state law that requires students at its university
to take a course in military science and tactics, the validity of
which was by the appellants challenged as repugnant to the
Constitution and laws of the United States.

. . . So far as they are material to the questions presented
here, the allegations of the petition are:

In October, 1933, each of these minors registered, became
a student in the university and fully conformed to all its requirements other than that compelling him to take the course
in military science and tactics in the Reserve Officers Training
Corps, which they assert to be an integral part of the military
establishment of the United States and not connected in any
way with the militia or military establishment of the State.
The primary object of there establishing units of the training corps is to qualify students for appointment in the Officers
Reserve Corps. The courses in military training are those
prescribed by the War Department. The regents require enrollment and participation of the able-bodied male students
who are citizens of the United States. These courses include
instruction in rifle marksmanship, scouting and patrolling,
drill command, musketry, combat principles, and use of automatic rifles. Arms, equipment and uniforms for use of students in such courses are furnished by the War Department
of the United States government.

These minors are members of the Methodist Episcopal
Church and of the Epworth League and connected religious
societies and organizations. For many years their fathers have
been ordained ministers of that church.

* * *

And in 1932 the General Conference of that Church adopted
as a part of its tenets and discipline:

We hold that our country is benefited by having as

citizens those who unswervingly follow the dictates of their consciences. . . . Furthermore, we believe it to be the duty of the churches to give moral support to those individuals who hold conscientious scruples against participation in military training or military service. We petition the government of the United States to grant to members of the Methodist Episcopal Church who may be conscientious objectors to war the same exemption from military service as has long been granted to members of the Society of Friends and other similar religious organizations. Similarly we petition all educational institutions which require military training to excuse from such training any student belonging to the Methodist Episcopal Church who has conscientious scruples against it. We earnestly petition the government of the United States to cease to support financially all military training in civil educational institutions.

* * *

Appellants, as members of that church, accept and feel themselves morally, religiously and conscientiously bound by its tenets and discipline as expressed in the quoted conference resolutions; each is a follower of the teachings of Jesus Christ; each accepts as a guide His teachings and those of the Bible and holds as a part of his religious and conscientious belief that war, training for war, and military training are immoral, wrong and contrary to the letter and spirit of His teaching and the precepts of the Christian religion.

Therefore these students, at the beginning of the fall term in 1933, petitioned the university for exemption from military training and participation in the activities of the training corps, upon the ground of their religious and conscientious objection to war and to military training. Their petition was denied. Thereupon, through that church's bishop in California, they and their fathers petitioned the regents that military training be made optional in order that conscientious and religious objectors to war, training for war and military training might not be confronted with the necessity of violating and foreswearing their beliefs or being denied the right of education in the state university to which these minors are entitled under the constitution and laws of the State of California and of the United States.

The regents refused to make military training optional or to exempt these students. Then, because of their religious and conscientious objections, they declined to take the prescribed course, and solely upon that ground the regents by formal notification suspended them from the university, but with leave to apply for readmission at any time, conditioned upon their ability and willingness to comply with all applicable regulations of the university governing the matriculation and attendance of students. The university affords opportunity for education such as may not be had at any other institution in California, except at a greater cost which these minors are not able to pay. And they, as appellees at the time of their suspension well knew, are willing to take as a substitute for military training such other courses as may be prescribed by the university.

* * *

The university is a land grant college. An act of Congress (Morrill Act approved July 2, 1862, 12 Stat. 503; 7 U.S.C., §§301-308) donated public lands to the several States in order that upon the conditions specified all moneys derived from the sale of such lands or from the sale of land script issued under the act should be invested and constitute a perpetual fund the interest of which should be inviolably appropriated by each State accepting the benefits of the act "to the endowment, support, and maintenance of at least one college where the leading object shall be, without excluding other scientific and classical studies, and including military tactics, to teach such branches of learning as are related to agriculture and the mechanic arts, in such manner as the legislatures of the States may respectively prescribe, in order to promote the liberal and practical education of the industrial classes in the several pursuits and professions in life."

March 23, 1868, the legislature of California passed an act creating the university "in order to devote to the largest purposes of education the benefaction made to the State" by the Morrill Act. Stats. 1867-8, p. 248. This law of the State, called the organic act, provides that "any resident of California, of the age of fourteen years or upwards, of approved moral character, shall have the right to enter himself in the University as a student at large, and receive tuition in any branch or branches of instruction at the time when the same are given in their regular course, on such terms as the Board of Regents may prescribe. . . ."

"[A]nd in order to fulfill the requirements of the said Act of Congress, all able-bodied male students of the University, whether pursuing full or partial courses in any college, or as students at large, shall receive instruction and discipline in military tactics in such manner and to such extent as the Regents shall prescribe, the requisite arms for which shall be furnished by the state."

. . .

[T]he state constitution as amended November 5, 1918, declares:

> The University of California shall constitute a public
> trust, to be administered by the existing corporation
> known as "The Regents of the University of California"
> with full powers of organization and government, sub-
> ject only to such legislative control as may be necessary
> to insure compliance with the terms of the endowments
> of the university and the security of its funds . . . *pro-*
> *vided,* that all moneys derived from the sale of public
> lands donated to this State by act of Congress approved
> July 2, 1862 (and the several acts amendatory thereof),
> shall be invested as provided by said acts of Congress
> and the income from said moneys shall be inviolably ap-
> propriated to the endowment, support and maintenance
> of at least one college of agriculture, where the leading
> objects shall be (without excluding other scientific and
> classical studies, and including military tactics) to teach
> such branches of learning as are related to scientific and
> practical agriculture and mechanic arts, in accordance
> with the requirements and conditions of said acts of Con-
> gress.

September 15, 1931, pursuant to the provisions of the organic act and constitution, the regents promulgated the following order:

> "Every able-bodied student of the University of Cali-
> fornia who, at the time of his matriculation at the Uni-
> versity, is under the age of twenty-four years and a citi-
> zen of the United States and who has not attained full
> academic standing as a junior student in the University
> and has not completed the course in military science and
> tactics offered to freshmen and sophomore students at
> the University shall be and is hereby required as a condi-
> tion to his attendance as a student to enroll in and com-
> plete a course of not less than one and one-half units
> of instruction in military science and tactics each semes-
> ter of his attendance until such time as he shall have
> received a total of six units of such instruction or shall
> have attained full academic standing as a junior student."

In the court below appellants assailed the laws and order
above referred to as repugnant to specified provisions of the
California constitution, and political code. And they adequately
challenged the validity of the state constitution, organic act
and regents' order, in so far as they were by the regents construed to require these students to take the prescribed course
in military science and tactics, as repugnant to the Constitution and laws of the United States.

The state court, without announcing an opinion, denied the

petition for a writ of mandate. Appellants applied for a re-hearing. The court, denying the application handed down an opinion in which it held that Art. IX, § 9, reposes in the regents full powers of organization and government of the university subject to legislative control in respect of its endowments and funds; that by § 6 of the organic act and Art. IX, § 9, military tactics is expressly required to be included among the subjects which shall be taught at the university and that it is the duty of the regents to prescribe the nature and extent of the courses to be given and to determine what students shall be required to pursue them, and that the suspension of the petitioning students because of their refusal to pursue the compulsory courses in military training involved no violation of their rights under the Constitution of the United States.

By their assignment of errors, appellants call upon this court to decide whether the challenged provisions of the state constitution, organic act and regents' order, in so far as they impose compulsory military training, are repugnant to the privileges and immunities clause of the Fourteenth Amendment, the due process clause of the amendment or the treaty that is generally called the Briand-Kellogg Peace Pact. . . .

. . . The allegations of the petition do not mean that California has divested itself of any part of its power solely to determine what military training shall be offered or required at the university. While, by acceptance of the benefits of the Morrill Act of 1862 and the creation of the university in order appropriately to comply with the terms of the grant, the State became bound to offer students in that university instruction in military tactics, it remains untrammeled by federal enactment and is entirely free to determine for itself the branches of military training to be provided, the content of the instruction to be given and the objectives to be attained. That State —as did each of the other States of the Union—for the proper discharge of its obligations as beneficiary of the grant made the course in military instruction compulsory upon students. Recently Wisconsin and Minnesota have made it elective. The question whether the State has bound itself to require students to take the training is not here involved. The validity of the challenged orders does not depend upon the terms of the land grant.

The petition is not to be understood as showing that students required by the regents' order to take the prescribed course thereby serve in the army or in any sense become a part of the military establishment of the United States. Nor is the allegation that the courses are prescribed by the War Department to be taken literally. We take judicial notice of the long-established voluntary cooperation between federal and state authorities in respect of the military instruction given in the land grant colleges. The War Department has not been empowered to determine or in any manner to prescribe the military instruction in these institutions. The furnishing of officers, men and equipment conditioned upon the giving of courses and the imposing of discipline deemed appropriate, recommended or approved by the Department does not support the suggestion that the training is not exclusively prescribed and given under the authority of the State. . . . And, when made possible by the national government, the State in order more effectively to teach and train its citizens for these and like purposes, may avail itself of the services of officers and equipment belonging to the military establishment of the United States. So long as its action is within retained powers and not inconsistent with any exertion of the authority of the national government, and transgresses no right safeguarded to the citizen by the Federal Constitution, the State is the sole judge of the means to be employed and the amount of training to be exacted for the effective accomplishment of these ends. . . .

The clauses of the Fourteenth Amendment invoked by appellants declare: "No State shall make or enforce any law which shall abridge the privileges or immunities of citizens of the United States; nor shall any State deprive any person of life, liberty or property, without due process of law." Appellants' contentions are that the enforcement of the order prescribing instruction in military science and tactics abridges some privilege or immunity covered by the first clause and deprives of liberty safeguarded by the second. The "privileges and immunities" protected are only those that belong to citizens of the United States as distinguished from citizens of the States—those that arise from the Constitution and laws of the United States as contrasted with those that spring from other sources. . . . The "privilege" of attending the university as a student comes not from federal sources but is given by the State. It is not within the asserted protection. The only "immunity" claimed by these students is freedom from obligation to comply with the rule prescribing military training. But that "immunity" cannot be regarded as not within, or as distinguishable from, the "liberty" of which they claim to have been deprived by the enforcement of the regents' order. If the regents' order is not repugnant to the due process clause, then it does not violate the privileges and immunities clause. Therefore, we need only decide whether by state action the "liberty" of these students has been infringed.

There need be no attempt to enumerate or comprehensively to define what is included in the "liberty" protected by the due process clause. Undoubtedly it does include the right to entertain the beliefs, to adhere to the principles and to teach the doctrines on which these students base their objections to the order prescribing military training. . . . The fact that they are able to pay their way in this university but not in any other institution in California is without significance upon any constitutional or other question here involved. California has not drafted or called them to attend the university. They are seeking education offered by the State and at the same time insisting that they be excluded from the prescribed course solely upon grounds of their religious beliefs and conscientious objections to war, preparation for war and military education. Taken on the basis of the facts alleged in the petition, appellants' contentions amount to no more than an assertion that the due process clause of the Fourteenth Amendment as a safeguard of "liberty" confers the right to be students in the state university free from obligation to take military training as one of the conditions of attendance.

Viewed in light of our decisions that proposition must at once be put aside as untenable.

Government, federal and state, each in its own sphere owes a duty to the people within its jurisdiction to preserve itself in adequate strength to maintain peace and order and to assure the just enforcement of law. And every citizen owes the reciprocal duty, according to his capacity, to support and defend government against all enemies. . . .

* * *

Plainly there is no ground for the contention that the regents' order, requiring able-bodied male students under the age of twenty-four as a condition of their enrollment to take the prescribed instruction in military science and tactics, transgresses any constitutional right asserted by these appellants.

. . . Affirmed.

Mr. Justice CARDOZO, joined by Justices BRANDEIS and STONE, concurring:

I assume for present purposes that the religious liberty

protected by the First Amendment against invasion by the nation is protected by the Fourteenth Amendment against invasion by the states.

Accepting that premise, I cannot find in the respondents' ordinance an obstruction by the state to "the free exercise" of religion as the phrase was understood by the founders of the nation, and by the generations that have followed. . . .

There is no occasion at this time to mark the limits of governmental power in the exaction of military service when the nation is at peace. The petitioners have not been required to bear arms for any hostile purpose, offensive or defensive, either now or in the future. They have not even been required in any absolute or peremptory way to join in courses of instruction that will fit them to bear arms. If they elect to resort to an institution for higher education maintained with the state's moneys, then and only then they are commanded to follow courses of instruction believed by the state to be vital to its welfare. This may be condemned by some as unwise or illiberal or unfair when there is violence to conscientious scruples, either religious or merely ethical. More must be shown to set the ordinance at naught. In controversies of this order courts do not concern themselves with matters of legislative policy, unrelated to privileges or liberties secured by the organic law. The First Amendment, if it be read into the Fourteenth, makes invalid any state law "respecting an establishment of religion or prohibiting the free exercise thereof." Instruction in military science is not instruction in the practice or tenets of a religion. Neither directly nor indirectly is government establishing a state religion when it insists upon such training. Instruction in military science, unaccompanied here by any pledge of military service, is not an interference by the state with the free exercise of religion when the liberties of the constitution are read in the light of a century and a half of history during days of peace and war.

The meaning of those liberties has striking illustration in statutes that were enacted in colonial times and later. . . . From the beginnings of our history Quakers and other conscientious objectors have been exempted as an act of grace from military service, but the exemption, when granted, has been coupled with a condition, at least in many instances, that they supply the army with a substitute or with the money necessary to hire one. . . . For one opposed to force, the affront to conscience must be greater in furnishing men and money wherewith to wage a pending contest than in studying military science without the duty or the pledge of service. Never in our history has the notion been accepted, or even, it is believed, advanced, that acts thus indirectly related to service in the camp or field are so tied to the practice of religion as to be exempt, in law or in morals, from regulation by the state. On the contrary, the very lawmakers who were willing to give release from warlike acts had no thought that they were doing anything inconsistent with the moral claims of an objector, still less with his constitutional immunities, in coupling the exemption with these collateral conditions.

Manifestly a different doctrine would carry us to lengths that have never yet been dreamed of. The conscientious objector, if his liberties were to be thus extended, might refuse to contribute taxes in furtherance of a war, whether for attack or for defense, or in furtherance of any other end condemned by his conscience as irreligious or immoral. The right of private judgment has never yet been so exalted above the powers and the compulsion of the agencies of government. One who is a martyr to a principle—which may turn out in the end to be a delusion or an error—does not prove by his martyrdom that he has kept within the law.

NOTES

Conscientious Objectors

1. The Supreme Court of the United States has held that exemption from combatant military training and service must be granted if the beliefs professed by the registrant are sincerely held and whether they are, in his own scheme of things, religious.

Language defining "religious training and belief" as used in statute exempting conscientious objectors (U.S.C.A. Const. Amends. 1, 5; Universal Military Training and Service Act, § 6 (j), as amended 50 U.S.C.A. App. § 456 (j)) from military service as "belief in relation to a Supreme Being" excludes those persons who, disavowing religious belief, decide on political, social, or economic bases that war is wrong and they will have no part of it. Also, excluded are those whose opposition to war stems from a merely personal moral code.

Test of belief "in a relation to a Supreme Being," within statute (cited above), is whether a given belief that is sincere and meaningful occupies a place in the life of its possessor parallel to that filled by orthodox belief in God of one who clearly qualifies for the exemption. United States v. Seeger,

380 U.S. 163, 85 S. Ct. 850 (1965) ; see also Clay v. United States, 91 S. Ct. 2068 (1971).

2. The Court of Appeals of Maryland in 1958 followed the *Hamilton* case and held that a mandatory requirement of the University of Maryland that physically able students take basic military training did not violate the religious liberties of conscientious objectors under either the Maryland or United States Constitution. The Maryland Court said: "We need not speculate as to where the line may ultimately be drawn or redrawn. Unless and until the Hamilton case is overruled, we think it is controlling, so far as the interpretation of the federal Constitution is concerned, in its application to the facts of the instant case." Hanover v. Elkins, 217 Md. 213, 141 A.2d 903 (1958).

3. The Supreme Court has held that there is no violation of the establishment clause by the Military Service Act which exempts persons from participation in war of any form but does not exempt a person for a particular war. Neither does the act violate the free exercise clause by conscripting persons who oppose a particular war on the grounds of conscience and religion. The incidental burdens felt by a person denied exemption from military service because they object to participation in a particular war is justified by substantial government interests. Gillette v. United States, 91 S. Ct. 828 (1971).

4. A conscientious objector is entitled to exemption if he holds beliefs which impose upon him a duty of conscience to refrain from participating in any war at any time. Welsh v. United States, 90 S. Ct. 1792 (1970).

CHAPTER 4
TAXES AND TAX EXEMPTION
SOURCES OF REVENUE

Funds for financing higher education emanate primarily from three sources: governmental taxation, private gifts and student fees and tuition. A body of law has evolved around each of these revenue sources describing the legal fiscal boundaries within which colleges operate. This chapter dis-, cusses taxation and its impact on higher education with primary reference to the tax exempt nature of institutions of higher education and their ancillary functions. The discussion extends to a brief analysis of the exempt status of gifts and grants under selected state and federal tax laws.

TAXATION GENERALLY

Each state has an inherent power to tax, limited only by the constraints of its own and the federal constitution. The sovereign qualities of state taxation have produced many and varied legal bases which reflect the governmental philosophies of the citizens of each of the fifty states. Even with these variations, commonalities can be found which reflect the historical concern of the body politic for justifiable use of public resources and fairness of taxation.

STATE CONSTITUTIONAL REQUIREMENTS

These concerns are manifested in state constitutional tax provisions which mandate first that tax funds be used for only public purposes and second that taxes be levied uniformly and taxpayers be treated equally. A "public purpose" has been defined to be synonymous with "governmental purpose." [1] Whether a tax is levied for a public or private purpose balances on the fulcrum of usage. If the purpose for which the tax money is used is for the general good and the benefits satisfy the needs of the citizenry in general, then such tax is usually held to be constitutional.[2]

All states, except Connecticut, Iowa, and New York have constitutional requirements of "uniformity" and "equality"

---

1. Stanley v. Jeffries, 86 Mont. 114, 284 P. 134, 70 A.L.R. 166 (1929).
2. City of Tombstone v. Macia, 30 Ariz. 218, 245 P. 677, 46 A.L.R. 828 (1926). (See also the Chapter in this book dealing with Church and State.)

of taxation.[3] These provisions are by no means consonant and, in fact, present substantial diversification of interpretation. Newhouse categorized the "uniform" and "equal" provisions in no less than nine basic types.[4] The uniformity and equality taxation provisions of several states apply only to property taxes, however, courts in other states have ruled that constitutional uniformity provisions govern all taxes.[5] For example, the Georgia constitution requires uniformity of both property and nonproperty taxes,[6] as does the Missouri constitution which requires that "Taxes . . . shall be uniform upon the same class of subjects within the territorial limits of the authority levying the tax. . . ."

It is interesting to note that some state courts have held that an income tax is a tax upon property itself,[7] thus, falling under uniform property tax provisions. Contrarily, however, the more modern view is espoused by an Arkansas court[8] and the previously cited 1930 Georgia case of *Featherstone v. Norman.*[9] Newhouse credits the Georgia decision with tipping the scales away from the idea that an income tax was in fact a property tax.[10] In keeping with this precedent, the prevailing view of the courts today is that an income tax is not subject to the uniformity requirements in states having only property tax uniformity provisions.

The comparisons of the state constitutional requirements in this area are truly voluminous; suffice it to say that such provisions are extremely important in interpreting the tax exempt status of college and university funds as demonstrated, for example, in a Tennessee case involving Cumberland University.[11] Plaintiffs insisted that two constitutional provisions, one to cherish educational institutions and the other authorizing the exemption of literary institutions, worked in concert to exempt taxation on bonds as tax exempt property. Article

---

3. Conn. Const. 1818, Art. I, § 1; Iowa Const. 1857, Art. I, § 6; New York Const. 1938 (1894), Art. I, § 11. (These states do have equal protection clauses similar to that of the Fourteenth Amendment which effectively requires uniformity.)

4. Wade J. Newhouse, Jr., *Constitutional Uniformity and Equality in State Taxation,* University of Michigan Law School, 1959.

5. *Ibid.,* p. 648.

6. Featherstone v. Norman, 170 Ga. 370, 153 S.E. 58 (1930).

7. *In re* Opinion of the Justices, 220 Mass. 613 (1915).

8. Stanley v. Gates, 179 Ark. 886, 19 S.W.2d 1000 (1929).

9. 170 Ga. 370, 153 S.E. 58 (1930).

10. Newhouse, *op. cit.,* 707.

11. Cumberland University v. Golladay, 274 S.W. 536 (Tenn. 1925).

2, Section 28, of the Tennessee constitution gave the legislature power to exempt property from taxation which was used for charitable, educational and literary purposes. The court held the legislature could exempt the specified properties from taxation, as provided for in the constitution, however, bonds, when sold, were not tax exempt as property.

FEDERAL LIMITATIONS

Federal constitutional limitations on state taxing power springs principally from the commerce clause and the Fourteenth Amendment. Under the commerce clause, a state tax is unconstitutional if it restricts trade or impedes access to the market. In other words, if a state levies a tax the impact of which effectively denies or limits commerce, then it is unconstitutional. Although taxation is an inherent power of the state, the Supreme Court recognized very early that this power could not go completely unbridled. In the landmark case of *Brown v. Maryland* [12] in 1827, the Court said ". . . The taxing power of the states must have some limits. It cannot reach and restrain the action of the national government within its proper sphere. . . . It cannot interfere with the regulation of commerce."

The other federal constitutional provision which is commonly invoked as a constraint on state taxation is the Fourteenth Amendment. The Fourteenth Amendment protects the citizen against state taxation which is discriminatory, confiscatory, or disproportionate. Tax classifications must be reasonable and without arbitrariness in order to be constitutional. Similar restrictions are imposed on federal taxation by the Fifth Amendment.

TAX EXEMPTION IN GENERAL

When discussing taxation of higher education, the conversation usually reduces itself to tax exemption. Institutions, like individuals, continually demonstrate adversity to taxation. This is quite understandable since a court's determination involving tax exempt status of a college can be crucial to the college's very existence. Mr. Justice Marshall in discussing the limits of state taxing powers observed in the well known case of *McCulloch v. Maryland* [13] that "the power to tax involves the power to destroy." Logically, then, "not to tax involves the power to create." It is no wonder, therefore, that so many

---

12. 12 Wheat. 419, 6 L. Ed. 678 (1827).
13. 4 Wheat. 316, 4 L. Ed. 579 (1819).

legal actions are brought and judicial opinions rendered concerning tax exemption.

Charitable, religious and educational organizations are usually exempt from taxation when they are in direct performance of their functions. The justifications usually given for tax exemption are: [14]

1. If these particular functions were not provided by some private institution or organization the ultimate burden of rendering them would fall on the state.
2. The performance of their functions by these private agencies actually increases the capacity of other property to pay taxes, and, thus, exemption is no burden upon taxed property.
3. Being non-profit organizations, they possess no net income and, therefore, no capacity to pay taxes.
4. The organizations or institutions are engaged in a service which is beneficial to the public in general or to some class thereof and for purely humanitarian reasons the tax exemption should be allowed.

DEFINITION OF A COLLEGE

Where statutes do provide for tax exemptions for educational institutions, the first question which usually arises is the meaning of the terms "college, educational institution, school, academy," etc. A Connecticut court held that a tax exemption provision applying exclusively to colleges, academies, churches, public schoolhouses, or infirmaries "did not apply to a private school whose patronage was those people having the means and disposition to separate their children from public schools since the school lacked the attributes indicative of devotion to such public use as the statute contemplated." [15]

A Kansas court held that the narrowness of the field of instruction of a business college did not prevent it from being regarded as an "educational institution" within the meaning of a state constitutional provision exempting from taxation property used solely for educational purposes.[16] A similar decision was arrived at in Nebraska, where the court ruled that a commercial college teaching the subjects common to such schools came within the statutory meaning of the term "school" in a tax exemption statute.[17]

---

14. P. Taylor, *The Economics of Public Finance*, 3d ed. 1961, p. 336.
15. Female Academy of Sacred Heart v. Darien, 108 Conn. 136, 142 A. 678 (1928).
16. Lawrence Business College v. Bussing, 117 Kan. 436, 231 P. 1039 (1925).
17. Rohebough v. Douglas County, 76 Neb. 679, 107 N.W. 1000 (1906).

The general pattern over the years by the courts has been to allow exempt status to business colleges and to consider them as *bona fide* colleges. In keeping with this precedent, the Alabama Supreme Court allowed tax exemption to a nonprofit business college for a site and building used for housing students.[18] A Florida court reached a similar decision when it considered the nature of the "business college."

> A nonprofit corporation which operated an educational institution developing learning and skill in the fields of business law, accounting, and secretarial capacities, offering courses that substantially paralleled those offered in public educational institutions, some of which were accepted by the state department of education for the education of teachers, was an educational institution qualified for tax exemption under the Florida constitution and statutes.[19]

The Florida court also pointed out that the business college was listed as accredited by an accrediting agency relied upon by the United States Commissioner of Education.

The Florida court implied that if courses offered by the private business college are roughly commensurate in quality with those offered in public institutions then the school falls within the meaning of an "educational institution." This determination by the court tends to raise as many questions as it solves, the most pressing of which are: What criteria are used to ascertain whether programs are commensurate or parallel and who applies the decision and makes the accrediting judgment? The Florida court was apparently content to accept the evaluations of the Florida state department of education supported by a regional accrediting organization which was relied upon by the U. S. Commissioner of Education. However, some other courts have established their own methods of comparison. The Minnesota Supreme Court for instance has gone to considerable lengths to prescribe the institutional qualifications for that which was described by Minnesota statute and constitution [20] as a "seminary of learning." This court made it clear that a private school could not

18. Birmingham Business College v. Whetstone, 263 Ala. 369, 82 So. 2d 539 (1955).

19. Simpson v. Jones Business College, 118 So. 2d 779 (Fla. 1960). See also National College of Business v. Pennington County, 146 N.W.2d 731 (1966).

20. Minnesota Constitution, Art. 9, § 1, and its statutory counterpart use identical language in exempting from taxation all ". . . academies, colleges, universities, and all seminaries of learning. . . ."

gain tax exemption simply by adopting the name of institute, college, seminary of learning or whatever the case might be. The court held that exemption was not justified unless the courses offered could be readily assimilated into subject areas of publicly supported elementary schools, high schools, colleges, seminaries of learning, or universities. In the first of two relevant cases, in Minnesota, the court relied on testimony of professional educators to show that the Northwestern Vocational Institute was in fact a trade school and could not be classified within the statutory meaning of a seminary of learning.[21]

The same court reinforced this standard two years later when it found that the course offerings of the Graphic Arts Educational Foundation was not comprehensive enough to justify being called a seminary of learning.[22] The court reasoned that to accomplish the intended public purpose to qualify as a seminary of learning the school must show that a "substantial part" of the educational training is equivalent to that furnished by publicly supported schools and colleges. To the court a "substantial part" meant that to have a seminary of learning some kind of "general educational program" must be offered. In giving a rule of thumb the court said:

> Such program need not be as broad as that offered by the public educational system. It may feature particular subjects or be directed toward preparing its students for certain vocations, but it cannot solely train these students in the mechanical aptitude of a single trade and thereby qualify as a "seminary of learning." It must offer enough of a variety of general academic subjects to qualify as a reasonable substitute for a usual program of courses pursued by a student at the comparative level of the public system.[23]

"Educational" is a comprehensive term embracing mental, moral and physical education. In relating to this definition, a New York court ruled that property devoted to teaching courses in continuing education dealing with race relations and social problems was used for an "educational" purpose. The nature of the courses, the method of financing (Peace Corps, Vista, Headstart, and Manpower Training Program funds were used), method of selecting students and credit re-

---

21. State v. Northwestern Vocational Institute, Inc., 232 Minn. 377, 45 N.W.2d 653 (1951).

22. Graphic Arts Educational Foundation, Inc. v. State, 240 Minn. 143, 59 N.W.2d 841 (1953).

23. *Ibid.*

ceived for completion of the courses, while unique, did not make the university-owned property nonexempt.[24] In this case, much was made of the fact that the continuing education courses were not open to all students and that some of the students were unqualified for admission to the university's regular undergraduate program. The court responded that "The purpose of continuing education courses was to fill a need in the adult's life or career, not to build on his or her prior education necessarily. That is the program's virtue, not its defect."

Whether or not a college is nonprofit is crucial to tax exempt status in some states, depending on statutory requirements. A business college owned and operated by a private corporation which provided shorthand courses, bookkeeping, penmanship, typewriting, business law, and grammar was not held to be tax exempt because the court found the school was incorporated chiefly to avoid taxation. In justifying its decision, the court said that the statute in question had reference only to institutions of general education.[25]

When a statute makes no mention of the nature of the school exempted, the courts may not impose restrictions themselves. Where a statute excluded from taxation all property of schools and colleges, the court said:

> They make no mention as to whether they are private or public schools. Neither is there any mention made as to whether or not they shall or shall not be run for profits. The requirement is that they shall be used exclusively for schools and colleges. Under these provisions, as we view it, it is immaterial as to whether or not the institution produces a profit or loss. If it had been the intention of the framers of the Constitution to exempt a private school, then there would have been no necessity for including the word "schools" in the constitutional provision, because all property of the public schools is public property and exempt from taxation.[26]

When nonprofit status is required for tax exemption, the burden of proof is on the college to show that it is not conducted for the purpose of making a profit. The courts will ex-

---

24. Application of Syracuse University, 59 Misc. 2d 684, 300 N.Y.S.2d 129 (1969).

25. Parsons Business College v. Kalamazoo, 166 Mich. 305, 131 N.W. 553 (1911). See also Lichtontag v. Tax Collector, 46 La. Ann. 572, 15 So. 176 (1894).

26. Tulsa County v. Tulsa Business College, 150 Okla. 197, 1 P.2d 351 (1931).

amine each institution's past and present scheme of operation to determine its eligibility. A New Jersey court has held that the nonprofit requirement does not mean that a college's revenues cannot exceed its expenditures or that it must operate at a loss. It need not gear its tuition rates and other receipts to avoid an excess of revenue. The key to whether a college is organized for profit is its intended use of surplus funds, if the funds are used for the educational program then the school will be tax exempt.

> The dominant motive to foster education and to make a college readily available to those of the public seeking higher education may coexist with an intention to have the books balance in the black rather than in the red.[27]

If, however, the operating fund surplus of a school is traced to "someone's personal pocket, as the *raison d'être* of the school," then even though it claims to be nonprofit, it is not entitled to tax exemption.

Tax Exemption of Public Colleges

The general rule of law covering taxation of public property succinctly stated is: "When public property is involved, exemption is the rule and taxation is the exception." [28] It is obvious, that to tax state property simply creates a need for intergovernmental transfers of funds. For example, if a local property tax is levied on a state college, the state must from other sources channel more funds to the college to pay the taxes.

More than one-third of the land area of the United States is owned by state and federal governments.[29] It is easy to see how large amounts of tax exempt property can place a financial strain on local government, especially since most of the resources for local government are derived from property taxes. Some states provide state subventions to local taxing units which have a severely diminished property tax base as a result of property tax exemptions. Such aid to local districts, whether it be state or federal, is usually accomplished by one of four means: (1) per acre payment, (2) revenue sharing, percentage of the revenue generated on the public land being

27. City of Trenton v. State, Department of Treasury, and Rider College, 65 J.J. Super. 1, 166 A.2d 777 (1960).

28. State *ex rel.* Wisconsin University Bldg. Corp. *et al.* v. Bareis, 257 Wis. 497, 44 N.W.2d 259 (1950). See 50 Am. Jur., p. 550, § 557; 2 *Cooley on Taxation*, 4th ed., pp. 1414-15, § 673.

29. Bureau of the Census, U.S. Department of Commerce, *Statistical Abstract of the United States*, p. 191 (1970).

returned to the local government, (3) percentage of value method, requires payment to local government measured by a percentage of the public land value, and (4) negotiated payment, administrator determines amount to be paid to local government.[30] Where these payments are made it is logically assumed that all the people of the state, regardless of where they live, should pay for the state operation and the burden should not rest on one locale. Usually, however, most local communities are very happy to have large universities or other major installations for their economic spillover to the community probably will outweigh the detriments of tax exemption. Many thriving university towns would be ghost towns except for the economic benefits derived from the employment, large payrolls and student expenditures.

Tax assessors, though, with an eye out for the public dollar, look yearningly at multi-million dollar university complexes and occasionally succumb to the temptation to tax them. The tax assessor's action is almost always sharply contested by college administrators, with money problems of their own, and the entire matter quickly finds its way to the courts. One such case occurred in Wisconsin where a building corporation was organized under the direction of the board of regents of the state university.[31] The corporation was established to acquire real property for exclusive uses, purposes, and benefits of the university with the entire net income being turned over to the board of regents. Such building corporations are usually established in order to bypass debt limitations imposed by state constitutions. These corporations issue revenue bonds, build buildings and pay the principal and interest on the bonds from rental of the facility. In this case the city tax assessor included the property of the corporation on his tax rolls claiming that the deed simply conveyed the property to the Wisconsin University Building Corporation, the state was not involved and, therefore, the property was subject to taxation. The court said that the city tax assessor must look behind the deed to determine the true ownership of the property, which, in fact, was the board of regents. The court concluded that the corporation was organized solely for state purposes, in the interest of the state and, therefore, was tax exempt.

---

30. "Public Land in Minnesota: Should It Pay Its Fair Share of Compensation in Lieu of Taxation?" *Minnesota Law Review*, Vol. 54, pp. 182-185 (Nov. 1969).

31. State *ex rel.* Wisconsin University Bldg. Corp. *et al.* v. Bareis, *supra.*

When the state's relationship to property is ambiguous or there is no clear cut state ownership and benefit, the question of tax assessment quickly surfaces, as it did in Nashville, Tennessee, in 1962.[32] Here, the State of Tennessee held land, as trustee, for Watkins Institute in Nashville. In 1880, the state was made trustee of money and property of Samuel Watkins, the money and land to be used for the establishment and maintenance of an educational institution to be known as Watkins Institute. The General Assembly of Tennessee passed an act accepting the trust, commissioners were appointed to manage the property and a building was constructed to house the Institute. From the beginning the lower floors of the building were leased to private businesses, and the rental income was used to maintain the educational program of the Institute. The rub came when the city decided to assess rental property for taxation. The court, citing an earlier decision [33] concerning the same property, decided that the trustee status of the state was sufficient to maintain the tax exemption of the property. The court reasoned that the educational program of the Institute was for a public purpose and if the state had wanted to it could have levied a local tax for the school's support just as it has created and supported local school districts.

EXEMPTION OF RELIGIOUS AND CHARITABLE INSTITUTIONS

Private colleges may obtain tax exemption by virtue of either their educational, religious or charitable nature. The preceding pages generally describe the requirements for tax exemption as an educational institution, but the requirements for religious and charitable institutions are another issue. Usually little attention is given by the courts to distinguishing religious from charitable, the courts assuming in most instances that religious institutions are actually charitable.[34] Some courts, however, have narrowly distinguished charities as institutions founded for public use such as hospitals, schools, and museums,[35] while other courts have given chari-

32. City of Nashville v. State Board of Equalization (Tenn. App.), 363 S.W.2d 520 (1962).

33. State *ex rel.* Beeler v. Nashville, 178 Tenn. 344, 157 S.W.2d 839 (1941); Quinn v. Hester, 135 Tenn. 373, 186 S.W. 459.

34. Trustees of Griswold College v. State, 46 Iowa 275 (1877). See also Fred A. Hurvich, "Religion and the Taxing Power," *University of Cincinnati Law Review*, Vol. 35, No. 4, pp. 541-542 (Fall 1966).

35. Southern Methodist Hospital and Sanitorium v. Wilson, 51 Ariz. 424, 77 P.2d 458 (1938).

ties a broader definition including "all activity which aids man and seeks to improve his condition, without remuneration." [36] Regulations of the Internal Revenue Service of the United States do not define religion, but describe a charity as including "advancement of religion." [37]

Governments throughout history of western civilization have exempted churches and religious activities from taxation. With the early influence of Christianity in all the colonies, except one,[38] establishing state religions, it was only natural that religion gain tax exempt status in the United States. Today tax advantages are given religion by all fifty states and the federal government. Hurvich [39] lists a sampling of federal tax benefits given to religion among which are: (a) income tax exemption, (b) testamentary gifts to religious organizations are deducted from gross estate without limitation, and (c) gifts to religious organizations are not taxable. These federal tax advantages coupled with tax exemptions amount to millions of dollars each year in benefits to religious organizations, schools, and colleges. Stimson provides the commonly accepted rationale for religious exemption: [40]

> It should be recognized . . . that exemptions should not be granted merely because of custom or tradition. Their justification today clearly must rest upon the basis of the best interest of society as it now exists. This fact is recognized by the courts when they attempt to justify the exemption of church property, for instance, on the basis of moral influence rather than on tradition and custom. The influence of churches upon the character of the various members of society is said to be sufficiently desirable to warrant the removal of church property from the tax roll. Religious societies devote their efforts and their property to the moral uplifting of society, in most cases seeking no pecuniary profit for themselves. Should not the government assist, to the extent of relieving them from the burden of taxation?

This view, however, has recently come under criticism as various church groups have compiled vast fortunes by entering into commercial enterprises unhampered by tax obliga-

---

36. Hurvich, *op. cit.*

37. *Ibid.* See also Treas. Reg. § 1.501 (c) (3)—1(d) (2) (1959), as amended, T.D. 6525, 1969—1 Cum. Bull. 186.

38. Rhode Island did not establish a state religion.

39. Hurvich, *op. cit.*, pp. 532-533.

40. Stimson, "The Exemption of Property From Taxation in the United States," 18 *Minnesota Law Review* 411, 416 (1934).

tions. The opposition to religious tax exemption is ably stated by Hurvich: [41]

> Is it in the best interest of the state to promote good morals by supporting religion? The state should promote good morals in the schools, and government leaders should set examples by maintaining the highest moral character but in so doing, the wall of separation of church and state should be kept high and impregnable. To give a subsidy to religion, whether directly or by tax exemption, is to say that religion is a public affair. This ceased to be in the nineteenth century. By eliminating all subsidy to religion, it shall be put in its proper place—a very private place.

The argument over tax exemption of religion resulted in the Supreme Court of the United States in 1970 establishing a benchmark in the field of church and state tax relationships. The case was brought by a realty owner in New York City seeking to prevent the New York City Tax Commission from granting exemptions to religious organizations for properties used solely for religious worship.[42] The Supreme Court decided that tax exemption of church property was not excessive governmental involvement with religion. The Court decided that there was no genuine nexus between tax exemption and the establishment of religion and interestingly observed that such tax exemption was too remote and minimal an involvement of the state in religion to be a violation of the "establishment clause" of the First Amendment.

With this decision reinforcing religious tax exemptions, it seems that colleges and universities with religious affiliations have little to fear in constitutionally maintaining either religious or educational exemption from taxation.

Leo Pfeffer has summarized the constitutional aspects of religion and taxation in seven propositions.[42a]

> (1) The exemption of religious groups from the taxation of property is a fairly universal practice throughout the United States. Although its constitutionality under the principle of the separation of church and state is arguable, the practice is so well established that it is unlikely that the courts—including the United States Supreme Court—would disturb it if the issue were pre-

---

41. Hurvich, *op. cit.*, p. 547.

42. Walz v. Tax Commission of the City of New York, 90 S. Ct. 1409 (1970).

42a. Leo Pfeffer, *Church State and Freedom*, Beacon Press, Boston, rev. ed. 1967, pp. 725-726.

sented for judicial determination. (See Walz v. Tax Commission of the City of New York, 90 S. Ct. 1409 (1970).)

(2) The exemption is a matter of grace, not of constitutional right. A state is free to withdraw the exemption at any time; and as long as a property tax is not discriminatory against religious groups its constitutionality is hardly open to question. Church buildings—no less than office buildings—receive police and fire protection, and may be required, through real property taxation, to pay their share of the cost of these services. There can therefore be no doubt as to the right of the state to limit (as they generally do) tax exemption to property used exclusively for religious purposes, and to exclude from that exemption property used for commercial purposes—even though its income be used exclusively for religious purposes.

(3) Exclusively religious practices, such as preaching or performing mass, may not be taxed, even under a nondiscriminatory tax law.

(4) Practices that are primarily religious, such as the evangelical sale of religious tracts, are likewise immune from taxation, even though they are income-producing, and the income inures to the benefit of an individual who earns his livelihood by engaging in the practice.

(5) Religious practices that are constitutionally subject to nondiscriminatory regulation in the interest of public order or safety, such as the requirement of obtaining a license to conduct a (religious) parade on the public streets, may be taxed a "nominal" amount to help defray the cost of such regulation.

(6) Purely commercial transactions engaged in by churches and religious groups, such as operating an ordinary business, are subject to nondiscriminatory license taxes even if the profits are used exclusively for religious purposes.

(7) The income of clergymen or others who earn their livelihood solely through the practice of religion is subject to general nondiscriminatory income tax laws.

STATE AND LOCAL EXEMPTIONS

Since tax exemption is dependent on the precise wording of the governing statute, little uniformity exists among court decisions of the various states.

PROPERTY TAXES

However, the exemption usually extends to all property used as adjuncts of the college, including college buildings, the land on which the buildings are located, land and buildings used for ancillary activities of the college although not used directly for teaching and educational equipment. Specifically, exemptions have been granted for dormitories, sleeping rooms, stables, armories, library buildings, recreation halls, dining halls,[43] athletic fields, university presses, farm property, faculty and president residences. While it is not necessary to examine each of the cases granting these exemptions individually, it is beneficial to review the relevant decisions describing certain college properties.

House for the President. By long established custom, most colleges furnish houses for their presidents. Many of these houses are quite sumptuous and tend to attract the attention of the ubiquitous tax assessor. The courts have generally held these houses to be exempt from taxation so long as their use is necessary [44] and relates to the performance of the duties of the president. A court in Nebraska held that necessary use of the property was established by showing that the house was used for student and college activities.[45] Similarly a District of Columbia court held that the house owned by the Brookings Institution, where the Brookings president resides, is not subject to taxation.[46]

One of the leading cases in this area involved the residence of the chancellor of the University of Pittsburgh.[47] The court in this case made it very clear that a primary principle of law, covering exemption cases, is that where a constitution does not itself exempt property, the matter is presumed to be exempt unless the legislature so provides. In the Pittsburgh case, the state statute provided for exemption of the property of universities, seminaries, academies, associations and institutions of learning, not mentioning specific properties such as university-owned houses. The primary issue in the dispute seemed to be whether the chancellor's house at the University of Pittsburgh, located approximately 2½ miles from the campus, was exempt. The court in deciding this issue laid down three principles of law: (1) A claimant for tax exemption has the burden of bringing himself within the exemption statute. The burden of proof is on the university to show that the chancellor's house falls within the

43. Thomas M. Cooley, *The Law of Taxation*, Vol. II, Callaghan and Company, 1924, pp. 1613-1614.

44. Doane College v. County of Saline, 173 Neb. 8, 112 N.W.2d 248 (1961).

45. *Ibid.*

46. District of Columbia v. Brookings Institution, 254 F.2d 955 (D.C. Cir. 1958).

47. Appeal of University of Pittsburgh, 407 Pa. 416, 180 A.2d 760 (1962).

intent of the statute. (2) Statutory provisions exempting property from taxation are subject to a strict, not a liberal construction. (3) The fact that the "residence of the president, chancellor or head of a university or college is not located on the campus is not controlling."

In expanding on the discussion, the court said the "real nub" of the controversy is the use to which the residence is put. In this regard the court found that using the residence to receive and entertain students, faculty, alumni, administrative staff, donors, visiting presidents, etc., was sufficient to establish that the dominant use was an integral part of the larger educational functions and objectives of the University. In a bit of *obiter dictum* the court further commented:

> The university or college of today is a far cry from "Mark Hopkins" at one end of a log and a student on the other [48] of another not too distant day and age. The universities and colleges of today are mammoth in the size of their student bodies, faculties and physical equipment compared to the universities and colleges of just several decades ago . . . . The functions of a modern university are and must be almost unbelievably broad in scope and its influence is evident in many and varied fields.
>
> The head of such an institution, whether he be called president or chancellor, represents to the public eye the "image" of the institution . . . . The usage and customs of the college impose upon the president certain social obligations . . . noncompliance with them unquestionably would subject him to unfavorable comment from the trustees and others, or, at least be regarded as a failure on his part to discharge the obligations and hospitality associated with his official position . . . .[49]

Houses for the Faculty. A few colleges hold charters granted by special legislative acts granting broad tax exemptions. Chambers [50] points out that these acts may not contain provisions by which the legislative can amend and repeal, thus, in some cases, authorizing almost unlimited exemption from taxation.[51]

Such a charter provision, as Chambers says, an "antique

48. Misquoted from a speech given by James A. Garfield at Williams College (1872), "A pine bench with Mark Hopkins at one end of it and me at the other is a good enough College for me."

49. Appeal of University of Pittsburgh, *supra.*

50. M.M. Chambers, *The Colleges and The Courts Since 1950*, Interstate, 1964, p. 199.

51. State *ex rel.* Bannister v. Trustees of William Jewell College, 364 Mo. 199, 260 S.W.2d 479 (1953).

example," [52] is found in the Brown University charter granted in 1764 by the "general assembly of the Governor and Company of the Colony of Rhode Island and Providence Plantations." [53] This old charter exempted from taxation "the estates, persons, and families of the President and Professors." Apparently in the early days Brown had only full "professors" and no associate or assistant professors. Later for tax exemption purposes the term "professor" was administratively interpreted to include both associate and assistant professors. This administrative determination was challenged by the assessor, and the real and personal property of an assistant professor was assessed. The Rhode Island Supreme Court, in following the general rule that tax exemption provisions should be strictly interpreted, held that the charter meant precisely what it said, only property of "professors" was tax exempt and this did not include associate or assistant professors.[54]

The normal pattern for exempting faculty housing from taxation, however, does not emanate from charters but from legislative statute granting exemption for educational or charitable purposes. Courts in interpreting legislative intent have not been as lenient toward granting exemptions for faculty housing as they have been for presidents' houses. A case in point is the *Doane College* case in Nebraska [55] where, as shown above, the president's house was held to be exempt from taxation while college-owned housing units for faculty was held to be subject to taxation.

As in the case of presidents' houses, the general rule prevails that the houses must be used by or in some way related to the purposes of the college in order to be exempt. While not controlling, the fact that a college rents housing to a faculty member seems to be an important criterion in determining whether the house is used exclusively as a private residence by the faculty member or is occupied for college purposes. In the *Doane College* case, the college charged monthly rent. In a Williams College case the court held that houses owned by the college and rented to professors were not occupied by the college for college purposes. This court said that "the occupants were each in the sole occupation of the premises . . . for strictly private purposes with control in them, not the col-

52. Chambers, *op. cit.*, p. 200.
53. *Ibid.*
54. Weimar *et ux.* v. Newman *et al.*, 78 R.I. 221, 80 A.2d 887 (1951).
55. Doane College v. County of Saline, *supra*.

lege." [56] Distinguishable is another Massachusetts case where a cottage was occupied in part by the principal as his office and dwelling, rent free, except for a deduction from the principal's salary which "did not more than pay for heating and lighting." [57] The occupation was held to be essential to the orderly and efficient management of the school. Following this reasoning, it has more recently been held that apartments owned by a charitable preparatory school, and occupied by both faculty and students in conducting a "school family plan" type of instructional program, is exempt from property taxation.[58] The court found that such use of the apartment house assisted directly and immediately in promotion of the school's purposes and was not merely "consequential."

A statute providing for tax exemption for all "buildings actually used for colleges, school, academics or seminaries; . . . the land whereon any of the buildings hereinbefore mentioned are erected, and which may be necessary for the fair enjoyment thereof . . ." was interpreted to exempt property for the school business manager and treasurer.[59] It was substantiated by the school that the school official was required to live on the school grounds and be available 24 hours a day, in addition to other financial duties, to maintain the school property and buildings.

As these cases indicate, if a college shows that the educational use is primary and other uses are incidental, then, exemption will probably be granted. On the other hand, the court will not be swayed by isolated instances of use for activities. There must be regular use by students, faculty, college administration, or other related college-connected groups.[60]

Student Housing. Dormitories have usually been held exempt from taxation when devoted to student use.[61] The ex-

56. President and Trustees of Williams College v. Assessors of Williamstown, 167 Mass. 505, 46 N.E. 394 (1897).
57. South Lancaster Academy v. Inhabitants of Town of Lancaster, 242 Mass. 553, 136 N.E. 626 (1922).
58. Board of Assessors of New Braintree v. Pioneer Valley Academy, Inc., 246 N.E.2d 792 (1969).
59. Blair Academy v. Township of Blairstown, 95 N.J. Super. 583, 232 A.2d 178 (1967).
60. MacMurray College v. Wright, 38 Ill. 2d 272, 230 N.E.2d 846 (1967).
61. Yale University v. Town of New Haven, 71 Conn. 316, 42 A. 87 (1899); Harvard College v. Assessors of Cambridge, 175 Mass. 145, 55 N.E. 8449 (1900).

emption has been upheld even though a certain sum was charged students for use of the facility.[62] However, where a building was used in part for a dormitory and the remainder used for commercial purposes, at least one court has denied property tax exemption.[63]

In a case where faculty and students incorporated and purchased property, the court held that the certificate stating the intended use of the property, which said that the nonprofit corporation was formed to promote social relations among students and faculty and to aid students and faculty by assisting them in every way possible in their study, work, living and extracurricular activities, was sufficient to show that the property was organized exclusively for educational purposes within the tax exemption statute of New York.[64]

Housing facilities owned by the college and on college property, for married students and their families, have been held to be an integral part of the college and university education process.[65] The Supreme Court of Tennessee distinguished this case from an earlier ruling where it held that a cafeteria, snack bar and parking lots were only coincidental to the primary purpose of an institution.[66]

Sororities and Fraternities. With only few exceptions the courts have held that sororities and fraternities are not exempt from taxation. The courts reason that the facilities exist primarily for the convenience of members and are mainly concerned with room, board, recreation and other social activities. Educational, charitable and benevolent activities are not primary purposes.[67]

---

62. Yale University v. Town of New Haven, *supra.*

63. Phillips Exeter Academy v. Exeter, 58 N.H. 306 (1878), 42 Am. Rep. 589.

64. Faculty-Student Association of Harpur College v. Dawson, 57 Misc. 2d 112, 292 N.Y.S.2d 216 (1967).

65. George Peabody College for Teachers v. State Board of Equalization, 407 S.W.2d 443 (Tenn. 1966).

66. City of Nashville v. State Board of Equalization, 210 Tenn. 587, 360 S.W.2d 458 (1962).

67. Mu Beta Chapter Chi Omega House Corp. v. Davidson, 192 Ga. 124, 14 S.E.2d 744 (1941); Knox College v. Board of Review, 308 Ill. 160, 139 N.E.56 (1923); Theta Xi Bldg. Assoc. v. Board of Review, 217 Iowa 1181, 251 N.W. 76 (1933); Alpha Tau Omega Fraternity v. Board of County Comrs., 136 Kan. 675, 18 P.2d 573 (1933); Powers v. Harvey, 81 R.I. 378, 103 A.2d 551 (1954); *Re* South Dakota Sigma Chapter House Assoc., 65 S.D. 559, 276 N.W. 258 (1937). See also 66 A.L.R.2d 904; Metropolitan Government v. Nashville Pi Beta Phi H. Corp., 407 S.W.2d 179 (1966).

One fraternity attempted to obtain tax exempt status on "educational, scientific and literary" grounds because it was furnished with a library which was sometimes used by members.[68] The court said that the statute was not met unless the house was used exclusively for one of the three purposes. The court held that for all intents and purposes the fraternity was a clubhouse for rest and recreation of members and its literary purposes were clearly secondary and incidental.

Courts have not been overly impressed by some fraternity appeals for charitable exemption. A fraternity in New Orleans, obviously finding it difficult to recall anything it had done that was charitable, based its claim of tax exemption primarily on the fact that it furnished Christmas baskets to needy families and on occasion extended credit to its own members.[69] The plea fell significantly short of its mark and the court denied exemption.

Professional fraternities have had relatively more success at gaining property tax exemption than have social fraternities. A Tennessee court dismissed garnishment proceedings against a medical fraternity for failure to pay property taxes, reasoning that the fraternity property was used exclusively for educational purposes within the meanings of the constitution and Tennessee statutes.[70] The court was swayed by evidence that the fraternity house was acquired for the purpose of housing students together for instructional purposes. Eminent doctors and upper classmen tutored lower classmen, gave lectures and generally performed educational functions.

On the other hand, a Nebraska court denied a refund of property taxes paid under a protest by a national medical fraternity, because it concluded that educational purposes of the fraternity were incidental to the other purposes and benefits. This court did, however, acknowledge that a professional fraternity probably provided greater educational benefits than does a social fraternity.[71]

When exemptions have been upheld, there has generally

---

68. People *ex rel.* Delta Kappa Epsilon Soc. v. Lawler, 74 App. Div. 553, 77 N.Y.S. 840, *aff'd*, 179 N.Y. 535, 71 N.E. 1136 (1902).

69. Beta Xi Chapter of Beta Theta Pi v. New Orleans, 18 La. App. 130, 137 So. 204 (1931).

70. Memphis v. Alpha Beta Welfare Assoc., 174 Tenn. 440, 126 S.W.2d 323 (1939).

71. Iota Ben. Assoc. v. County of Douglas, 165 Neb. 330, 85 N.W.2d 726 (1957).

been a statute specifying fraternity or sorority tax exemption. Where a statute exempted property of "any college or university society . . . if not leased or otherwise used with a view of profit," the court interpreted the meaning as providing exemption to a social sorority. The sorority was built by voluntary subscriptions, never leased, and never paid any rent to the national association which held title to the real estate.[72]

In a case with a different twist, a statute in New Jersey provided tax exemption to all fraternal organizations. A subsequent statute in 1937 was passed seeking to remove from exempt status only college fraternities. As might be expected the college fraternities brought a successful action claiming the act was unconstitutional as violative of the constitutional requirement that all tax laws shall be general.[73]

A subsequent New Jersey case in effect changed the impact of the above case when it was decided that the amendatory statute in 1937 in fact had superseded the previous statute, and when the portion of the act dealing with denial of exemption to college fraternities was held to be unconstitutional, the entire statute exempting all other fraternities was likewise unconstitutional.[74] The net effect was that tax exemption was denied to both college and other fraternities. The court wove its way through a morass of legal logic most of which seemed to be designed to disguise the court's feeling that tax exemption for fraternities is not in the best public interest. Some of the court's more lucid comments are worth repeating:

> The existence of grounds for exemption is a mixed question of law and fact. For obvious reasons, exemptions from taxation are not favored, and so are strictly construed. Such renunciation of sovereignty is sustainable only on grounds of public policy, i.e., the service of an interest fundamentally public and not private. Exemptions not so grounded place an unequal and unjustifiable burden upon property taxed for the operation of government in the common interest. Apart from the criteria laid down in the statute, unless the exemption is founded on a "quid pro quo for the performance of a service essentially public, and which the state thereby is relieved

72. Kappa Kappa Gamma House Assoc. v. Pearcy, 92 Kan. 1020, 142 P. 294 (1914).

73. Alpha Rho Alumni Assoc. v. New Brunswick, 126 N.J.L. 233, 18 A.2d 68, aff'd, 127 N.J.L. 232, 21 A.2d 737 (1941).

74. Rutgers Chapter of Delta Upsilon Fraternity v. City of New Brunswick, 129 N.J.L. 238, 28 A.2d 759, aff'd, 32 A.2d 364 (1942).

pro tanto from the necessity of performing," it constitutes a "gift of public funds, at the expense of the taxpayer," and is "indefensible both under our public policy of equal taxation and constitutional safeguard against illegal taxation." [75]

Property Used for Social and Recreation Purposes. Almost without exception, courts have held that tax exemption for educational purposes extends to athletic fields or property used for social or recreation purposes. A vacant lot used by students to play games has been held tax exempt.[76] A park or recreation area has been recognized as a part of the educational institution qualifying for tax exemption,[77] as has a lake used by students for swimming, boating, and winter sports.[78] Lots used for baseball and football and a thinly wooded area used by pupils for open-air recreation and amusement were held exempt.[79]

The list goes on, with other courts saying that the cultivation of athletics is an educational purpose and, therefore, college fields where both intramural and interscholastic sports are played are exempt.[80]

Cafeterias and Dining Halls. Portions of buildings of educational institutions used for feeding students have in most cases been held to be within exemption provisions, "used exclusively for educational or school purposes." [81] The fact that a college charges students for dining does not defeat exempt status, so long as the charges are not fixed with a view to profit.[82]

Some colleges have found that it is more economical to turn the meal serving functions over to catering services, commercially organized for that purpose. This type of ar-

---

75. *Ibid.*

76. Elder v. Atlanta University, 22 S.E.2d 515 (1942).

77. People *ex rel.* Thompson v. St. Francis Xavier Female Academy, 233 Ill. 26, 84 N.E. 55 (1908).

78. People *ex rel.* Pearsall v. Catholic Bishop, 311 Ill. 11, 142 N.E. 520 (1924).

79. Emerson v. Milton Academy, 185 Mass. 414, 70 N.E. 442 (1904). See also People *ex rel.* Goodman v. University of Illinois Foundation, 388 Ill. 363, 58 N.E.2d 33 (1944).

80. People *ex rel.* Adelphi College v. Wells, 97 App. Div. 312, 89 N.Y.S. 957 (1904), *aff'd,* 180 N.Y. 534, 72 N.E. 1147 (1905); *Re* Syracuse University, 214 App. Div. 375, 212 N.Y.S. 253 (1925). See also 143 A.L.R. 274.

81. 72 A.L.R.2d 529.

82. People *ex rel.* Hesterman v. North Cent. College, 336 Ill. 263, 168 N.E. 269 (1929).

rangement was the issue in a New York case. The court held that the college cafeteria was tax exempt, regardless of whether the school operated the cafeteria itself or through others.[83] It made no difference whether the operation was carried out by servants employed directly by the college or by independent contractors since the college retained general supervision which was directed exclusively to accomplish its educational purpose.

STATE NONPROPERTY TAXES

State legislatures levy or authorize the levy of many different types of taxes on both the local and state level. These include income taxes, sales taxes, succession taxes on the transfer of estates and gifts. Local government has no inherent power to levy taxes;[84] such power can only be derived from the state.

License Tax on Admissions. The State of South Carolina levied an admission tax on tickets sold for university football games. Furman University paid the tax under protest and then sued to recover in an action against the South Carolina Tax Commission.[85] The trial judge held the state license tax exempted eleemosynary institutions and nonprofit corporations or organizations and, therefore, Furman University football tickets were exempt from the tax. The Supreme Court of South Carolina reversed the lower court on the grounds that Furman University did not pay the taxes; the ticket holder paid the tax, and the university merely served as a collection agency for the state.

State Succession Taxes. The Supreme Court of Ohio has held that a society organized for missionary work was not entitled to exemption from a succession tax as an institution of learning. In the will of Helen S. Osborn, the National Holiness Missionary Society obtained a bequest on which a succession tax was assessed in an amount of $8,417.31.[86] The Society filed exceptions claiming exemption because the society was an institution of learning under Section 5334, Gen-

83. Pace College v. Boyland, 4 N.Y.2d 528, 176 N.Y.S.2d 356, 151 N.E.2d 900 (1958).
84. Marion and McPherson Railway Co. v. Alexander, 63 Kan. 72, 64 P. 978 (1901).
85. Furman University v. Livingston, 136 S.E.2d 254 (S.C. 1964).
86. *In re* Osborn's Estate, 159 Ohio St. 63, 110 N.E.2d 791 (1953). See also Board of National Missions of Presbyterian Church v. Neeld, 9 N.J. 349, 88 A.2d 500; Salisbury's Estate v. Department of Taxation, 101 N.E.2d 304 (1951).

eral Code of Ohio. The society gave evidence that it operated 53 elementary schools and five Bible training institutions. The court in denying tax exemption said that:

> . . . even though the society does conduct many schools and uses a large part of its income for that purpose, the carrying out of this educational work is merely subsidiary to its main objective of religious and missionary endeavors.

A Maryland statute exempted from the Maryland inheritance tax bequests made to charitable organizations "a substantial part or all of the activities and work of which are carried on in the state of Maryland." The Linguistic Society of America received a bequest amounting to about $40,000 and sought inheritance tax exemption under the statute claiming, a substantial part of its activities were carried on in Maryland. The Linguistic Society had only 17 of its 748 members and four of its 294 subscribing libraries in Maryland, but it published several journals and monographs all of which were printed and mailed at Waverly Press in Baltimore. The court found that this constituted a "substantial part" of the society's activities and granted exemption to the bequest which consisted of a house in Baltimore and philological library.[87]

FEDERAL TAXATION

As mentioned previously in this Chapter, public and private institutions of higher education derive benefits from federal tax laws not only through subventions for research, facilities, training and general operation, but also by virtue of federal tax exemption policies. Federal tax exemption benefits to colleges may derive from direct tax exemption to the college itself and/or from exemptions which encourage individuals to aid educational institutions through personal gifts and grants.

INCOME TAX

Organizations such as colleges and universities are usually classed as corporations and as such are governed by the provisions of federal corporate income tax. The federal corporate income tax exempts religious, scientific and charitable or-

87. Shaughnessy v. Linguistic Society of America, 198 Md. 446, 84 A.2d 68 (1951). See also M.M. Chambers, *The Colleges and the Courts Since 1950, op. cit.*, pp. 235-236.

ganizations from taxation. In commenting on these exemptions, Pechman [88] observes that:

> Favorable tax treatment for those organizations dates from a time when the federal government assumed little responsibility for relief and welfare activities and the value of the tax exemption was relatively small. Today, the federal government has substantial responsibilities for public assistance and welfare activities, while the revenue loss from the exemptions has become significant.

This statement, of course, raises questions regarding federal taxation, the arguments of which are not within the scope of this book. However, it takes no astute analysis to see that such exemptions today shift the decision making authority, relative to expenditure of such tax funds, from the realm of the elected public official to that of the executives of private organizations. In recent years, the exempt status of private and religious organizations has come under close governmental scrutiny because of their competition with small businesses. By utilizing federal tax exemption, a religious, charitable or educational organization holds a significant fiscal advantage over a non-tax exempt competition in the marketplace. This economic edge has historically been used to gain breaks on unrelated business income and lease-back arrangements. Unrelated business income and lease-back arrangements are created by exempt organizations purchasing property from private business firms with borrowed funds and then leasing the property back to the same firms. Such devices which trade on the tax exempt status of organizations have caused concern and have resulted in some adjustments being made in the *Internal Revenue Code*.

In regard to interpretation of the meaning of charitable, scientific and educational, The United States Court of Claims has given little leeway for commercial undertakings. This court held that a corporation which had a stated aim of teaching and disseminating economic knowledge did not qualify as having charitable, scientific, or educational purposes, because it sold two semimonthly periodicals and its investment advice services were available for a fee.[89]

Generally, to maintain tax exempt status under federal

---

88. Joseph A. Pechman, *Federal Tax Policy*, (rev. ed.), The Brookings Institution, Wash. D.C., 1971, p. 136.

89. American Institute for Economic Research v. United States, 302 F.2d 934 (1962).

income tax laws, a corporation (1) must be organized for religious, charitable, scientific, literary, or educational purposes, (2) no part of its earnings can inure to the benefit of any private shareholder or individual, and (3) it cannot carry on propaganda to influence legislation. Where the *destination*[90] of expenditures of a foundation included private gain rather than being exclusively for public benefit, the federal courts have declared the funds to be nonexempt.[91] In similar cases the courts have held that trusts for one's own children are not charitable and cannot be so classified for federal income tax purposes.[92] Where a donor contributes money to a college for scholarships, he destroys the deductibility of the gift if he specifies its use for that of only one pupil.[93] The courts tend to view such a gift as lacking in public purpose since the benefit of the funds can only accrue to a private individual. The granting of funds to an acquaintance or to a relative is a private benevolence and is not deductible.

An unreasonably large accumulation of income may be sufficient rationale for the court to deny income tax exemption. Federal income tax law[94] states that:

> Exemption * * * is to be denied to charitable organizations which accumulate sums "out of income during the taxable year or any prior taxable year and not actually paid out by the end of the taxable year—[which] (1) are unreasonable in amount or duration" * * *.

The critical question is whether the organization can justify the total accumulation of income based on the charity's intent and actual program.[95] If the excess in income is reasonable in view of the organization's charitable purposes, exemption will be allowed. In defining reasonableness one court said:[96]

> "Reasonableness" that hobgoblin of judicial minds, can only be defined on the basis of relevant facts. The standard to be applied is whether the taxpayer can justify the total accumulation of income at the end of

90. People's Educational Camp Society v. Commissioner of Internal Revenue, 331 F.2d 923 (1964).

91. Horace Heidt Foundation v. United States, 170 F. Supp. 634 (1959). See also Texas Trade School v. Commissioner of Internal Revenue, 272 F.2d 168 (1959).

92. Morrill v. United States, 228 F. Supp. 734 (1964); Hall v. United States, 208 F. Supp. 584 (1962).

93. Tripp v. Commissioner of Internal Revenue, 337 F.2d 432 (1964).

94. 26 U.S.C. § 504 (a).

95. Erie Endowment v. United States, 316 F.2d 151 (1963).

96. *Ibid.*

the taxable year, in terms of both time and amount, on the basis of a rational total program of charitable intent.

With this measure of reasonableness, one court held that an eight-year plan to accumulate $500,000 for a university medical center was reasonable,[97] as was an accumulation of funds to construct a civic building where the charitable organization was organized for that specific purpose.[98] Likewise, a plan was upheld to build up sufficient funds over a ten-year period for employee retirement benefits, where this was the sole purpose of the foundation.[99] However, where a justifiable program of accumulation is not shown, tax exemption will be denied.

In 1950 the Congress amended the Internal Revenue Act and among other things said that the *source* rather than the *destination* [100] was the critical factor in determining whether a corporation is tax exempt.[101] Section 301 (b) said:

> An organization operated for the primary purpose of carrying on a trade of business for profit shall not be exempt under any paragraph of this section on the ground that all of its profits are payable to one or more organizations exempt under this section from taxation.

This amendment took away the tax exempt status previously enjoyed by "feeder corporations." A "feeder corporation" is one which operates a business and feeds its income to a charitable or educational organization. The "feeder" organization gained exemption by providing net profits to charity; this permitted it to prosper on the residue between its gross income and the net income it actually turned over to charity. In a 1962 case, the Sico Foundation was held not to be exempt from taxation for income which it channeled to a state teachers college,[102] while before the 1950 amendment, the courts had upheld the "feeder" foundation's tax exemption.[103]

---

97. Samuel Friedland Foundation v. United States, 144 F. Supp. 74 (D.N.J. 1956).

98. Hulman Foundation v. United States, 217 F. Supp. 423 (S.D. Ind. 1962).

99. Truscott v. United States, 1 Am. Fed. Tax R. 2d 1743 (E.D. Pa. 1958). See also Danforth Foundation v. United States, 222 F. Supp. 761, aff'd, 347 F.2d 763 (1965), *cert. denied*, 382 U.S. 955.

100. Trinidad v. Sagrada Orden de Predicadores, 263 U.S. 578 (1924).

101. 26 U.S.C.A. § 101 and § 301 (b) (Internal Revenue Act of 1950).

102. Sico Foundation v. United States, 295 F.2d 924 (1961), *rehearing denied*, 297 F.2d 557 (1962).

103. Sico Company v. United States, 121 Ct. Cl. 373, 102 F. Supp. 197 (1952).

The 1950 amendment came about because of problems attendant to the sweeping exemptions which Congress had bestowed on certain organizations, feeders being only one type. These problems, relating to income-producing activities of foundations, were:

(1) Corporations operating as businesses but distributing their net income to charitable organizations, these "feeder corporations" claimed exemption under the "destination of income" concept;

(2) Foundations which were engaged in charitable activities but at the same time undertook income activities producing support for charitable programs, and

(3) Organizations, controlled by private interests, established for charitable purposes used exempt status to business advantages.[104]

In dealing with these situations, Congress enacted legislation disallowing exemption where there was "unreasonable accumulations" of income, unfair competition with nonexempt organizations, as well as "feeder corporations" which operate for profit. It is easy to see the rationale for the 1950 amendments even though in some instances it may have curtailed some substantial income sources of certain colleges. Congress could obviously not allow such loopholes to create and maintain a thriving business while other similar corporations were penalized by taxation.

FEDERAL ESTATE AND GIFT TAXES

One's estate consists of all property owned at the time of death including real estate, mortgages, stocks, bonds and other types of property belonging to the decedent.[105] The taxable estate, however, is somewhat less than the gross estate since various deductions are made before taxation. The estate tax charitable deduction is not subject to limitations such as are required in income tax deductions.[106] Deductible bequests cannot be made to individuals. Qualified recipients include political subdivisions, such as cities, towns, and counties, and extends to private corporations "organized and operated exclusively for religious, charitable, scientific, literary or educational purposes." As in the case of exemptions of

104. Norman A. Sugarman and Haslan Pomeroy, "Business Income of Exempt Organizations," *Virginia Law Review*, Vol. 46, p. 424 (1960). See also Notes in this book, pages 262-264, on status of "leasebacks."

105. Pechman, *op. cit.*, p. 181.

106. Richard B. Stephens and Guy B. Maxfield, *The Federal Estate and Gift Taxes*, Federal Tax Press, Inc., 1967, p. 179.

other taxes previously discussed, corporations, to qualify, must
not be set up in such a way that any part of their net earnings
inure to the benefit of a private person. The other qualification
is that the corporation cannot engage in propaganda or lob-
bying activities.[107] With regard to the charitable character
of gift recipients, a New York court looked at the purpose
for which the organization was organized, the manner in
which it operated, and its activities in attempting to influence
legislation and concluded that the city, county, and state bar
associations in New York did not qualify as charitable lega-
tees.[108] The court acknowledged that the bar associations did
much for public good, such as legal aid for poor and lectures
for the public; however, it found that public service was not
the "exclusive" purpose of the associations. On the contrary,
bar associations exist primarily for the benefit of their own
membership and, therefore, cannot be classified as charitable.
On the other hand, in the same case, a bequest to the "William Nelson Cromwell Foundation for Research of the Law
and Legal History of the Colonial Period of the United States
of America" was held to be deductible, since this organization
could be classified as having charitable, scientific, literary
and educational purpose.[109]

In determining deductibility of charitable bequests from
estate taxes, it is, of course, necessary for the court to be
able to ascertain how much will pass on to charity. If the
conditions of a testamentary trust are so vague that the
trust can be invaded and used at the discretion of the trustees, or vagueness makes the charitable remainder unascertainable, then tax deduction will not be allowed. In a case
where a will gave trustees "uncontrolled discretion" in distributing principal of the trust to the testator's widow, the
court held the remainder was unascertainable and, therefore, nondeductible.[110] The court commented:

> In a sense in every instance where invasion of prin-
> cipal is authorized, but the value of the remainder is
> claimed as a deduction, the testator has been attempting
> to eat his cake and have it, too. * * * we believe the risk
> of uncertainty should be his and not the governments.

---

107. *Ibid.*, pp. 180-181.

108. Dulles v. Johnson, 155 F. Supp. 275 (S.D.N.Y. 1957).

109. *Ibid.*

110. State Street Bank and Trust Co. v. United States, 313 F.2d 29
(1963). See also Merchants National Bank v. Commissioner, 320 U.S.
256, 64 S. Ct. 108 (1943).

If the possibility of invasion of the trust principal is so remote to be negligible, then the courts have allowed deduction.[111] A professor at Johns Hopkins University died in 1954 and bequeathed his residual estate of $315,000 to his aged, senile sister for life and then to the Johns Hopkins University for endowment of a library.[112] He authorized the trustee to spend, in its discretion, such amount from the net income as might be necessary to maintain and comfort his sister. His sister had an income of $10,000 per year and assets of $135,-000. The executor bank claimed the entire residual estate was deductible for purposes of federal estate taxation. The local director of Internal Revenue ruled the amount of the deduction should be reduced, claiming that Johns Hopkins University would not ultimately receive the bequest in its entirety. The court held for the executor and found that "The possibility that any of the income from the trust under the will * * * will be used for the benefit of his sister is so remote as to be negligible; it is highly probable that the Johns Hopkins University will ultimately receive the entire trust property, income as well as principal." [113]

Even though the federal gift tax bears close relationship to income tax, it should be considered as a companion to the estate tax. The gift tax is sometimes referred to as a "backstop" for both the federal income and the estate tax.[114] It represents an attempt by the government to extract taxes from gifts which reduce the property of the estate. The federal Congress first enacted the gift tax in 1924 [115] and subsequently did away with it in 1926.[116] The reason for abandoning the tax emanated from the adoption of a federal estate tax provision which conclusively presumed that gratuitous transfers within two years of death were made in contemplation of death and was, therefore, subject to the federal estate tax.[117] This conclusive presumption provision, however, was held unconstitutional by the Supreme Court in 1932 [118] and, thus, prevented taxation of gifts made within two years

111. Ithaca Trust Co. v. United States, 279 U.S. 151, 49 S. Ct. 291 (1929).

112. Mercantile Safe Deposit and Trust Company v. United States, 172 F. Supp. 72 (D. Md. 1959).

113. *Ibid.*

114. Stephens and Maxfield, *op. cit.,* p. 276.

115. Rev. Act of 1924, § 319 et seq., 43 Stat. 253, 313.

116. Rev. Act of 1926, § 1200, 44 Stat. 125.

117. Rev. Act of 1926, § 302 (c), 44 Stat. 70.

118. Heiner v. Donnan, 285 U.S. 312 (1932).

of death. Congress responded by reenacting the gift tax and filling the loophole.[119] The federal gift tax has been in continuing effect since 1932, but was held not to be retroactive prior to 1932.[120]

Provisions for deductions of gifts are similar to those of other taxes discussed above and provide for deduction of gifts for certain types of recipients:

> Any corporation, trust, community chest, fund, or foundation that is organized and operated exclusively for religious, charitable, scientific, literary or educational purposes. But such organizations qualify only if their net earnings do not inure at all to private individuals and only if their activities do not substantially involve propaganda or lobbying.[121]

Internal Revenue rulings have held that gifts to colleges to be used for construction or renovation of designated fraternity houses may qualify as deductions,[122] however, gifts to fraternities themselves not used for construction or renovation have been held subject to taxation.[123] Such gift deductions can have substantial influence on the amount of funds provided for charitable and educational institutions since such bequests and gifts are deductible without limit (under the personal or individual income tax, contributions are deductible up to 30 percent of income and up to 5 percent in the case of corporation income tax).[124]

State income taxes do not violate constitutional uniformity provisions

FEATHERSTONE v. NORMAN

Supreme Court of Georgia, 1930.
170 Ga. 370, 153 S.E. 58, 70 A.L.R. 449.

HINES, J., delivered the opinion of the court:

1. Can the Legislature levy an income tax? It is clear that it can, unless the levy offends some provision of the Constitu-

---

119. § 501 et. seq., 47 Stat. 169, 245.

120. Untermyer v. Anderson, 276 U.S. 440 (1928).

121. See Regs. § 25.2522 (a)-1(a).

122. Rev. Rul. 60-367, 1960-2 C.B. 73.

123. Rev. Rul. 56-329, 1956-2 C.B. 125. See Stephens and Maxfield, *op. cit.*, pp. 361-379.

124. Pechman, *op. cit.*, p. 195.

tion of this state. This instrument declares that "the right of taxation is a sovereign right, inalienable, indestructible, is the life of the State, and rightfully belongs to the people in all republican governments." Constitution, art. 4, § 1, ¶ 1 (Civil Code of 1910, § 6462). "The right of taxation, in the Legislature, is without limit, except as provided in the Constitution. It is not a power specially granted; it is assumed to exist, and is limited by special clauses." * * *

2. Does the 1929 Income Tax Act of this state violate article 7, § 2, ¶ 1, of the Constitution of this state, which provides that "all taxation shall be uniform upon the same class of subjects, and ad valorem on all property subject to be taxed within the territorial limits of the authority levying the tax?" * * *

The question again came before that court [the Missouri Supreme Court] in Ludlow-Saylor Wire Co. v. Wollbrinck, 275 Mo. 339, 205 S.W. 196, 198. That court * * * said: "The court held in effect that in directing, as the Constitution does, that taxes on property should be levied according to value, reference was intended to be made to other species of property than that which a person has in his income; that the Constitution did not abridge the power of the Legislature to provide revenue by a taxation of income, that its command was directed to other and distinct classes of property, which on account of their peculiar nature could be measured in value, become the object of taxation independent of the owner, and were susceptible, by proper procedure, to lien or seizure for the enforcement of the tax. The court held that it was property having such a nature and characteristics, and not the mere usufruct of such property, nor the earnings of physical or mental labor, which was referred to in the clause under review, and intended thereby to be subjected to taxation according to its value." Income does not constitute property in its proper sense.

* * *

"Income is something derived from property, labor, skill, ingenuity or sound judgment, or from two or more in combination. It is not commonly thought of as property but as gain derived from property, or some other productive source." * * * Income in common parlance and in the law is used in contradistinction to property. 31 C.J. 397 (§ 2), B.

"The term 'property,' as used in reference to taxation, means the corpus of an estate or investment, as distinguished from the annual gain or revenue from it. Hence a man's income is not 'property' within the meaning of a constitutional requirement that taxes shall be laid equally and uniformly upon all property within the State." Black on Income and Other Federal Taxes (3d Ed.), § 44. "Constitutional prohibitions and limitations applicable to property taxes are generally held not applicable to an income tax, unless the income tax is held to be a property tax. And even where an income tax is held to be a tax on property, the courts sometimes have failed to apply such constitutional limitations to them. The better rule seems to be that an income tax is not a tax on property within a constitutional requirement that taxation on property shall be in proportion to its value." Cooley on Taxation (4th Ed.), § 1751.

* * * So we have reached the conclusion that a tax on income is not a tax upon property under our Constitution, and that this conclusion is supported by the number and weight of the outside authorities.

Does this act infringe the uniformity clause of this provision of the Constitution? The uniformity required is one "upon the same class of subjects," and not uniformity with the tax upon property. By this provision the makers of the Constitution put property in one class and clothed the Legislature with ample and full power to classify the subjects of taxation other than property. The Legislature cannot classify property and impose upon one species thereof a different tax from that imposed on other species. Property subject to be taxed is treated as one single class, and there can be levied but one rate on all species of it. Verdery v. Summerville. * * * But such uniformity does not require that a tax upon all classes of subjects shall be the same or be uniform with the tax imposed upon property. In any class the uniformity required is that a tax upon each member shall be the same. * * *

So in Joseph v. Milledgeville, 97 Ga. 513, 25 S.E. 323, this court decided that a municipal ordinance imposing a business tax of one per cent upon "all gross sales of goods, wares, and merchandise of every kind" was not obnoxious to the uniform clause of the provision of the Constitution of 1877 which we now have under consideration. The gross sales of the merchant are the gross income from his mercantile business. A tax upon the proceeds arising from the gross sales of merchandise comes much closer to being a tax on property than a tax on income comes to being a tax on property. This is so for the reason that the proceeds of the sale of merchandise stand in the place of the merchandise itself, being the merchandise in a converted form, while income from property is not in any sense the property from which the income is derived.

* * *

If, then, an occupation or excise tax can be levied upon the gross earnings of a business, and not violate this provision of the Constitution, we see no reason why an income tax cannot be imposed upon the net income of one receiving it, without violating the same, especially as a tax upon net income is more favorable to the taxpayer than one on gross income. * * *

This act is not lacking in uniformity because it provides for a graduated tax and makes certain exemptions from such tax. As we have seen, the Legislature can classify the subjects of taxation other than property. It can likewise subclassify them. * * * A tax may be levied according to the number of drays, carriages, or wagons used in a business. * * * An occupation tax may be graduated according to population. * * * An occupation tax of 1 per cent. of the gross sales of a merchant can be levied. * * * Barber shops may be classified for taxation according to the number of chairs. * * * If an occupation tax can, under this provision, be graded according to the number of drays used in a business, or according to population, or according to gross sales, or according to the number of chairs in a barber shop, we can see no valid reason why an income tax cannot be graded according to the amount of income received. Ordinarily, the only uniformity required of a state income tax is uniformity within the class. An income tax statute is not unconstitutional because it exempts incomes under a certain amount, or because it increases the rate as the income increases. To be uniform under this provision, taxation need not be universal. Certain objects may be made its subjects, and others may be exempted from its operation. Certain occupations may be taxed, and others not; but as between the subjects of taxation in the same class there must be equality. All that the law requires is that classification of persons who are to be exempt shall not be arbitrary and unreasonable. * * * A statute is not unconstitutional because it exempts salaries of state officers, rentals of real estate, profits derived from agriculture, and incomes under a thousand dollars. * * * There may be a separate classification, with different rates, of individuals and corporations.

* * *

Counsel for complainant rely upon certain other decisions of the Supreme Court of the United States, to which we shall now refer. In Pollock v. Farmers' Loan & Trust Co., 157 U.S. 429, 15 S.Ct. 673, 39 L.Ed. 759; id., 158 U.S. 601, 15 S.Ct. 912, 39 L.Ed. 1108, the Supreme Court of the United States was dealing with the question whether the incomes from real estate and from personal property were direct taxes within the meaning of that provision of the Federal Constitution which requires that direct taxes must be laid in proportion to the population of the several states; and by a decision of five justices to four that court held that taxes upon the income from both of these sources were direct taxes within the meaning of the provision of the Constitution of the United States, which requires direct taxes to be laid in proportion to population. In that case the court was dealing with the meaning of direct taxes in the above provision of the Federal Constitution. This decision is not authority for the proposition that income is property within the meaning of the provision of our state Constitution which requires taxation to be ad valorem and uniform upon each class of subjects upon which taxes are laid.*

* * *

Judgment affirmed.

NOTES

1. Typical state constitutional provisions requiring taxes to be uniform and legal.

"[Taxes] shall be uniform on the same class of subjects within the territorial limits of the authority levying the tax." [Missouri Const., Art. X, § 3.]

"All taxes upon real or personal estate assessed by authority of this state, shall be apportioned and assessed equally, according to the just value thereof." [Maine Const., Art. IX, § 8.]

2. Some state constitutions require the rate of taxation or assessment to be uniform and equal.

"The General Assembly shall provide, by law, for a uniform and equal rate of assessment and taxation; and shall prescribe such regulations as shall secure a just valuation for taxation of all property, both real and personal, excepting such only, for municipal, educational, literary, scientific, re-

---

* [The Georgia statute provided that the tax was to be levied on net income as determined for federal income tax purposes, except that income from federal instrumentalities was to be excluded from the state levy and income from state instrumentalities was to be added to the amount reported to the Federal Government. The Court upheld this feature of the levy.]

ligious, or charitable purposes, as may be specially exempted by law." [Indiana Const., Art. X, § 1.]

3. Equal Protection of the Fourteenth Amendment.

The Supreme Court of the United States has said:

"The States have a very wide discretion in the laying of their taxes. When dealing with their proper domestic concerns, and not trenching upon the prerogatives of the National Government or violating the guarantees of the Federal Constitution, the States have the attribute of sovereign powers in devising their fiscal systems to ensure revenue and foster their local interests. Of course, the States, in the exercise of their taxing power, are subject to the requirements of the Equal Protection Clause of the Fourteenth Amendment. But that clause imposes no iron rule of equality, prohibiting the flexibility and variety that are appropriate to reasonable schemes of taxation. * * * It [State] is not required to resort to close distinctions or to maintain a precise, scientific uniformity with reference to composition, use of value. * * * To hold otherwise would be to subject the essential taxing power of the State to an intolerable supervision, hostile to the basic principles of our government and wholly beyond the protection which the general clause of the Fourteenth Amendment was intended to assure. * * * But there is a point beyond which the State cannot go without violating the Equal Protection Clause. The State must proceed upon a rational basis and may not resort to a classification that is palpably arbitrary. The rule often has been stated to be that the classification 'must rest upon some ground of difference having a fair and substantial relation to the object of the legislation.' * * * If the selection or classification is neither capricious nor arbitrary, and rests upon some reasonable consideration of difference or policy, there is no denial of the equal protection of the law." Allied States of Ohio, Inc. v. Bowers, Tax Commissioner of Ohio, 358 U.S. 522, 79 Sup. Ct. 437 (1959).

State university system involved in business enterprise must pay federal admissions tax

ALLEN v. REGENTS OF THE UNIVERSITY SYSTEM OF GEORGIA

Supreme Court of the United States, 1938.
304 U.S. 439.

MR. JUSTICE ROBERTS delivered the opinion of the Court.

The question on the merits is whether the exaction of the

federal admissions tax, in respect of athletic contests in which teams representing colleges conducted by the respondent participate, unconstitutionally burdens a governmental function of the State of Georgia. * * * The court below decided * * * the questions involved against the petitioner. Because of their importance we granted certiorari.

Section 500 (a) (1) of the Revenue Act of 1926, as amended by § 711 of the Revenue Act of 1932 imposes "a tax of 1 cent for each 10 cents or fraction thereof of the amount paid for admission to any place . . . to be paid by the person paying for such admission; . . ." Subsection (d) commands that the price (exclusive of the tax to be paid by the person paying for admission) at which every admission ticket is sold shall be conspicuously printed, stamped, or written on the face or back of that portion of the ticket which is to be taken up by the management and imposes a penalty for failure to comply with its terms. * * *

The respondent is a public corporation, created by Georgia as an instrumentality of the State, having control and management of The University of Georgia and the Georgia School of Technology. Athletics at these institutions are conducted under the respondent's authority by two corporations, the University of Georgia Athletic Association and the Georgia Tech. Athletic Association. The expense of physical education and athletic programs at each school is defrayed almost entirely from the admission charges to athletic contests and students' athletic fees collected for the purpose. During September and October 1934 football games were played at the institutions, for which admissions were charged and collected by the associations. Each ticket showed on its face the admission price, the amount of the tax, and the total of the two, and also carried the following printed notice:

"The University of Georgia [or Georgia School of Technology] being an instrumentality of the government of the State of Georgia, contends that it is not liable for any admission tax. The amount stated as a tax is so stated because the University is required to do so by Treasury regulations pending a decision as to its liability in this respect. This amount is collected by the University as a part of the admission and will be retained as such unless it is finally determined that the University is itself liable for the tax."

* * * For present purposes we assume the truth of the following propositions put forward by the respondent: That it is a public instrumentality of the state government carrying

out a part of the State's program of public education; that public education is a governmental function; that the holding of athletic contests is an integral part of the program of public education conducted by Georgia; that the means by which the State carries out that program are for determination by the state authorities, and their determination is not subject to review by any branch of the federal Government; that a state activity does not cease to be governmental because it produces some income; that the tax is imposed directly on the state activity and directly burdens that activity; that the burden of collecting the tax is placed immediately on a state agency. The petitioner stoutly combats many of these propositions. We have no occasion to pass upon their validity since, even if all are accepted, we think the tax was lawfully imposed and the respondent was obligated to collect, return and pay it to the United States.

The record discloses these undisputed facts: The stadium of the University of Georgia has a seating capacity of 30,000, cost $180,000, and was paid for by borrowed money which is being repaid by the Athletic Association, whose chief source of revenue is admissions to the contests in the stadium. $158,000 of the amount borrowed has been repaid since the stadium was completed in 1929. The student enrollment is about 2,400. Each student pays an annual athletic fee of $10.00 which confers the privilege of free admission to all the school's athletic events. All admissions collected, and the tax paid on them, are paid by the general public, none by the students.[17] The total receipts of the Athletic Association from all sources for the year ending August 31, 1935, were $91,620.25 of which $71,323.27 came from admissions to football games.

The stadium of the Georgia School of Technology has a seating capacity of 29,000. It cost $275,000 and was paid for by a gift of $50,000 and from admissions charged and student fees. The enrollment is about 2,000 students, each of whom pays an annual athletic fee of $7.50 which gives the privilege of free admission to all games. All admissions collected, and the tax paid on them, are paid by the general public, none by the students.[17] The total receipts of the Athletic Association for the six months ended December 31, 1934, were $119,436.75 of which $74,168.51 came from admissions to football games.

It is evident that these exhibition enterprises are comparatively large and are the means of procuring substantial aid

---

[17] Student athletic fees are not treated as admissions subject to the tax. See Cumulative Bulletin XI-2 (July-December 1932), p. 522.

for the schools' programs of athletics and physical education. In final analysis the question we must decide is whether, by electing to support a governmental activity through the conduct of a business comparable in all essentials to those usually conducted by private owners, a State may withdraw the business from the field of federal taxation.

When a State embarks in a business which would normally be taxable, the fact that in so doing it is exercising a governmental power does not render the activity immune from federal taxation. In *South Carolina* v. *United States*, 199 U. S. 437, it appeared that South Carolina had established dispensaries for the sale of liquor and prohibited sale by other than official dispensers. It was held that the United States could require the dispensers to take licenses and to pay license taxes under the Internal Revenue laws applicable to dealers in intoxicating liquors, and this notwithstanding the State had established the dispensary system in the valid exercise of her police power. * * *

The legislation considered in *South Carolina* v. *United States, supra,* provided for a division of the profits of the dispensary system between the state treasury and cities and counties. Thus the enterprise contributed directly to the sustenance of every governmental activity of the State. In the present instance, instead of covering the proceeds or profits of the exhibitions into the state treasury, the plan in actual operation appropriates these monies in ease of what the State deems its governmental obligation to support a system of public education. The difference in method is not significant. The important fact is that the State, in order to raise funds for public purposes, has embarked in a business having the incidents of similar enterprises usually prosecuted for private gain. If it be conceded that the education of its prospective citizens is an essential governmental function of Georgia, as necessary to the preservation of the State as is the maintenance of its executive, legislative, and judicial branches, it does not follow that if the State elects to provide the funds for any of these purposes by conducting a business, the application of the avails in aid of necessary governmental functions withdraws the business from the field of federal taxation.

Under the test laid down in *Helvering* v. *Gerhardt, ante,* p. 405, however essential a system of public education to the existence of the State, the conduct of exhibitions for admissions paid by the public is not such a function of state government as to be free from the burden of a non-discriminatory tax laid on all admissions to public exhibitions for which an admission fee is charged. * * *

Moreover, the immunity implied from the dual sovereignty recognized by the Constitution does not extend to business enterprises conducted by the States for gain. As was said in *South Carolina* v. *United States, supra,* at p. 457: "Looking, therefore, at the Constitution in the light of the conditions surrounding at the time of its adoption, it is obvious that the framers in granting full power over license taxes to the National Government meant that that power should be complete, and never thought that the States by extending their functions could practically destroy it." * * * The decree is

Reversed.

Term "college" used for purposes of taxation takes on varying aspects in different times and places

TOWNSHIP OF PRINCETON v. INSTITUTE FOR ADVANCED STUDY

Superior Court of New Jersey, Appellate Division, 1960.
59 N.J. Super. 46, 157 A.2d 136.

Princeton Township appeals from a judgment of the Division of Tax Appeals exempting from local property taxation Olden Manor, the official residence of the Director of the Institute for Advanced Study ("Institute").

The township had assessed the residence, the land on which it was erected, and personal property located therein, at $105,900 for the year 1957, without granting the exemption claimed by the Institute under N.J.S.A. 54:4-3.6, which reads in part as follows:

> "The following property shall be exempt from taxation under this chapter: All buildings actually used for colleges, schools, academies or seminaries; * * * all buildings actually and exclusively used in the work of associations and corporations organized exclusively for the moral and mental improvement of men, women and children, or for religious, charitable or hospital purposes, or for one or more such purposes; * * *."

On appeal, the Mercer County Board of Taxation affirmed the assessment. On further appeal, the State Division of Tax Appeals concluded that the Legislature did not intend to limit the application of the words "colleges, schools, academies or seminaries" only to institutions offering "the more orthodox or traditional methods of instruction." It held that the Institute is a college within the meaning of N.J.S.A. 54:4-3.6 and that Olden Manor is actually used for college purposes. The Division thereupon cancelled the assessment with respect to Olden Manor and the land surrounding it not in excess of five acres. This appeal followed. * * *

The Institute has 22 permanent faculty members and a transient student body, designated as members (these might in other institutions be called graduate or post-doctoral student), of about 125. * * *

The Institute has three disciplines—mathematics, physics and historical studies. They meet as schools, and they conduct the business of the Institute as a body under the chairmanship of the Director. There is no formal instruction. However, seminars are scheduled weekly, or even more frequently. Student members are furnished office space and secretarial help, and are free to pursue their own research, with no commitment whatsoever that it be along a given line or that the results accrue to the institution. Although the Institute has the corporate power to grant diplomas and award degrees, there are no degrees because the members are all at the post-doctorate level when they arrive, and already have their highest degree.

Olden Manor is a substantial dwelling owned and maintained by the Institute and located on its main campus on Olden Lane in Princeton Township. It is the principal residence of the Director and his family, to whom it is furnished rent-free and as a term of his employment. It is also used by the Director, on behalf of the Institute, for official entertainment and for numerous faculty and trustees' meetings and conferences.

We are concerned here with only the first clause of N.J.S.A. 54:4-3.6, exempting from taxation all buildings actually used for colleges, schools, academies or seminaries. The subsequent portion of the statute quoted above is not involved on this appeal; the Institute concedes that although Olden Manor is actually used in connection with its activities and programs, it is not "exclusively" so used.

The Township contends that the Institute is not entitled to tax exemption under the statute because it lacks the usual indicia of a college, school, academy or seminary; "it has neither teachers nor pupils, in the ordinary sense, since it offers no curricula or instruction; it does not prepare its students for undergraduate or postgraduate academic degrees, since its members are on the post-doctoral level and no degrees are awarded; it imposes no discipline, since its keynote is unlimited individual freedom, unencumbered by institutional requirements." However, it readily concedes that the Institute is a unique development in American education; counsel describes it as "a constellation of brilliant men whose sole occupation is thinking and whose frontier is 'the growing tip of civilization.' * * * It is the epitome of the contemplative method and pure research." Nonetheless—so runs the argument—it does not fairly fall within the statutory intendment of a college or school.

We are not persuaded that "college," as used in the statute, is to be confined to the kind of institution that has become so familiar to us, where there are teachers and pupils, courses of instruction, a conferring of degrees, and an extended discipline. The concept of a college is an organic one, taking on a varying aspect in different times and places. * * *

In its earliest and most fundamental sense it meant a collection of persons united by the same office, interest or occupation—the Roman *collegium*. Among the many definitions of "college" given in the New Oxford English Dictionary on Historical Principles (1893), we find

> "1. An organized society of persons performing certain common functions and possessing special rights and privileges; a body of colleagues * * *.
> "4. A society of scholars incorporated within, or in connexion with, a university, or otherwise formed for purposes of study or instruction. * * *"

We do not understand "college" to be a word of art which, by universal understanding, has acquired a definite, unchanging significance in the field of education, fixed forever in its meaning like a bug in amber. * * *

Is the Institute to be barred from exemption from taxation of a component building because the members, already possessing doctorate degrees, cannot receive further academic honors? Or because the illustrious few scholars who are chosen to study there are deemed to profit most by introspective and individual research, rather than by instruction in the more usual teacher-pupil relationship? Is exemption to be denied merely because discipline, in the strict sense of the word, is kept at a minimum because of the very quality of those constituting the Institute and their particular and individualized pursuit of knowledge and ideas? To do so is to impose an arbitrary limitation on the legislative intent, to

ignore the clearly discernible evolution in modern-day higher
education toward less formal instruction, with greater emphasis on individual study and creative research—a development
which has arrived at its greatest refinement in the activities
of the Institute.

A college, in whatever mold it be cast, is expected to be
perpetual in its service and undeviating in its ultimate purpose, which is the elimination of the false and the fostering
of the true. There must of necessity be a flexibility of form
and approach if this goal is even to be approximated. * * *

As we have observed, the powers of the Institute include
the power to make rules and regulations for its government
and with respect to the appointment and duties of its members,
admission with or without payment of dues or charges, discipline, and the granting of such diplomas and the awarding of
such degrees, including honorary degrees, as the corporation
might decide upon. If instruction be a determinant, we must
consider instruction in its broadest sense and as inclusive of
self-instruction and the benefits scholars derive, one from the
other, in daily association at a place like the Institute and in
their frequent seminars.

While the Institute is unique, occupying as it does an unex-
ampled position on the farthest frontier of American education, it surely possesses every attribute of an institution of
learning. It fits well within the frame of those institutions
which, for over a century * * *, have been the particular concern of the Legislature in extending tax benefits to colleges,
schools, academies and seminaries, thereby encouraging the
cause of education and research. It is reasonable, if not indeed
compelling, that this court give effect to the obvious purpose
of the Legislature. To that end the word "college" may be
given an expanded interpretation comporting with the manifest reason and obvious purpose of the law. The spirit of the
legislative direction must prevail over any literal or conventional sense of the term. * * *

We conclude that to deny exemption in this case to an institution which stands at the very apex of American higher education, one which has attracted to Princeton some of the
finest minds of our generation, would be a perversion of the
legislative intention expressed in the first clause of N.J.S.A.
54:4-3.6.

The township does not contend that Olden Manor is not
actually used (as was fully established in the record) in the
work of the Institute and therefore not entitled to tax exemp-

tion—once it is decided that the Institute falls within the category of "colleges, schools, academies or seminaries." We have so concluded. * * *

Affirmed.

NOTES

KILLOUGH, "EXEMPTIONS TO EDUCATIONAL, PHILANTHROPIC AND RELIGIOUS ORGANIZATIONS"

Tax Exemptions 23 (Tax Policy League, 1939).*

* * * Let us consider first the reasons for exempting from taxation private organizations which are supplying services which the State would be called upon to supply if it were not for the private organizations. If private schools, colleges, and charitable institutions were taxed, their services and benefactions would be cut down by the amount of their taxes. Then if the State were to take over some of the functions which these institutions have had to give up because of taxation, there would be no net gain to the community. Money would simply have been put into one pocket and taken out of another. There would even be a net loss to the community if it is true, as tax exemption proponents frequently argue, that private institutions are more efficiently managed than public ones.

So far the argument has assumed that taxation would cut down the amount of service rendered by educational and charitable institutions and that, if taxed, they would continue to function but on a somewhat lesser scale. It is frequently implied, however, that private benefactions would cease if it were not for tax exemptions of contributions to and of the property of these private organizations. Tax exemption is cited as a necessary incentive to private giving, and taxation called a menace to philanthropy. For those who believe that taxation would mark the beginning of the end of privately supported education and charity the justification of exemption is complete. If taxation were to make it necessary for government to supply not only those services formerly rendered with funds not collected in taxes, but also to supply many services formerly rendered through private gifts, governmental costs would increase by an amount materially greater than the new tax collections. It follows from this line of reasoning that the

---

* [This material is reprinted with the consent of the Tax Institute of America, which was formerly known as the Tax Policy League.] Some footnotes have been deleted to conserve space.

community receives a net profit from tax exemption which is the difference between the total value of the services of the tax-exempt organizations and the cost, in foregone taxes, of the exemption.

The second category of exemptions includes those to religious and other organizations which perform services not likely to be thought of as state functions, although commonly held to be socially desirable. The reasons usually given for these exemptions are more general in nature and somewhat less concerned with dollars and cents. Tax exemption of church property is defended on the ground that religious organizations promote morality and thus further the welfare of the state. It is said that without the influence of religion "the whole framework of our civilization would be severely threatened," and that "religion and morality are essential * * * to the very existence of the organic state."

The aspect of the present method which is most in need of modification concerns the problem of control. If an institution falls within a category generally accepted as educational, benevolent, literary, charitable, or whatever fits into a particular legally accepted vocabulary, it is automatically exempted from taxation by constitutional or legislative requirement. There is no way of effectively considering the question as to whether the community or the tax-exempt organization would make best use of the money not paid in taxes at a particular time. The mildest reform would provide for periodic evaluations of the status of even the most deserving recipients of exemption. Similarly no addition should be made to the tax-exempt list without careful evaluation, if, in fact, they should be made at all. These minor changes would require constitutional amendment in many states and the repealing of existing and enactment of new legislation by others and by the federal government. Educational institutions can scarcely uphold their status as bulwarks of democracy if they are unwilling to subject their efforts to this small measure of democratic control.

* * *

This is probably too half-hearted a measure. It might be better if all individuals and institutions paid taxes without exemptions for any contribution to, or expenditure for, however charitable or educational a purpose. When the indirect subsidies had been disposed of in this way the question of direct grants should be considered. In response to a plea for exemptions from a group of hospitals the special California Tax Commission of 1929 stated:

It is the feeling of the Commission that the exemptions should be curtailed, rather than extended, but it also realizes the extreme difficulty of bringing about such a contraction. With respect to the plea of the hospitals, to which it has given sympathetic study, it has concluded that, while it cannot recommend any expansion of the exemption list, it does desire to record its conviction that recognition should be given to the public importance of the work of certain of these institutions through more liberal public grants and payments where activities of these institutions clearly have the effect of caring for cases which otherwise would be a charge on the public funds.[26]

This recommendation might well be heeded by other States and applied not only to hospitals but also to other organizations.

There are a number of advantages in direct grants. They provide for continuous evaluation of the merits of particular projects. They might be made by more appropriate jurisdictions than frequently happens at present with many communities granting enormous indirect subsidies to institutions largely used by people from other regions. Direct grants would make evident the real financial relationship between the institutions and the community. Direct grants might be a simpler way of distinguishing between functions entitled to public support and those not so entitled than an attempt partially to tax and partially to exempt institutions performing such mixed functions. It seems to the writer that these advantages outweigh the disadvantages many of which have been suggested in the foregoing pages.

There is little reason to believe that any such great change in present practice is probable in the near future. The difficulties involved are emotional as well as legal and financial. The first step should be the prevention of increases in the exemptions, to be followed as far as possible by their gradual elimination.

---

[26] Final Report of the California Tax Commission, Sacramento, 1929, p. 90.

Court identifies factors necessary to obtain tax exemption for college residential property

CONCORDIA COLLEGE CORPORATION v. STATE

Supreme Court of Minnesota, 1963.
120 N.W.2d 601.

SHERAN, Justice.

The appeal is from a judgment of the district court determining that certain real estate in the city of Moorhead, Minnesota, owned by Concordia College Corporation and designated as 507 South 10th Street is not presently entitled to tax-exempt status.

Statutory proceedings for judicial determination of tax exemption (Minn.St. 278.01) with respect to the realty here involved were instituted in behalf of Concordia College Corporation by a petition, the essential averments of which are as follows: Petitioner is a seminary of learning incorporated under the laws of the State of Minnesota and engaged in conducting and operating Concordia College at Moorhead. It is a coeducational, liberal arts college operated wholly as a seminary of learning and not for any profit. The real estate involved (and other tracts not now relevant) is located in the city of Moorhead and consists of a dwelling house located several blocks from the college campus. It is devoted to and reasonably necessary for the accomplishment of the purposes of the college as a seminary of learning, being used by the institution to provide temporary housing for faculty members who have not been able to find suitable housing immediately after accepting positions at the college. * * *

Real estate owned by a college is entitled to the tax exemption if, but only if, the real estate is devoted to and reasonably necessary for the accomplishment of its educational purposes. State v. Carleton College, 154 Minn. 280, 191 N.W. 400. Although the petition alleges that the real estate here involved was devoted to and reasonably necessary for the accomplishment of the purposes of Concordia College, no finding on this particular point was made by the trial court. While conceivably the finding that President Knutson had testified that the house was not necessary to the operation of the college might, in a proper case, be construed as a finding that the house was not devoted to and reasonably necessary for the accomplishment of the educational purposes of the college, such a construction is not permissible here where the testimony of Dr. Knutson previously set out demonstrates his views to be otherwise. In similar situations the supreme court has remanded the case to the trial court for vacation of the judgment and for additional findings relating to the matters involved, and for further evidence thereon, if deemed advisable by the trial court. * * *

2. Petitioner, in its brief, states the legal issue involved on this appeal to be:

> "Is a residence three blocks from the main campus and which is owned by a College which is a Seminar of learning and rented to a professor of that College, exempt from real estate taxation?"

The state, in its brief, has, in substance, accepted this statement. * * *

Where it has been determined that the institution involved is an academy, college, university, or seminary of learning, the constitutional and statutory provisions are construed less strictly than other tax-exemption provisions since the policy of the state has consistently been to encourage the establishment of private educational institutions. * * * But the mere fact that the rental received from real estate owned by a tax-exempt institution is used exclusively for the needs of such institution does not give the rent-producing property tax-exempt status. * * * The physical separation of a residence from the principal situs of a tax-exempt institution does not, of itself, preclude exemption. * * *

From a review of the decisions of the Minnesota Supreme Court and of the courts of other jurisdictions [1] it can be seen that the question of reasonable relationship between the purposes of the institution and the use of the property and the necessity thereof is generally a question of fact to be determined initially by the trial court. * * * Numerous factors are relevant for consideration in arriving at such a decision including the following:

(a) *Expressed intent.* While the motivation of the educational institution as expressed by its administrative leaders is not conclusive, such expressions are entitled to careful consideration and will not be rejected without good reason. * * *

(b) *History of acquisition and use.* If a residence is built by an educational institution in order to provide housing for a

---

1. A more restricted exemption has been noted in states where it is required that the property be used "exclusively" for the tax-exempt purpose. People ex rel. Kelly v. Avery Coonley School, 12 Ill. 2d 113, 145 N.E.2d 80.

faculty member, * * * or if the dwelling is purchased in order to fulfill a need of this kind, the necessity of such a dwelling in relation to the objects of the educational institution appears more clearly than in cases where the realty is obtained by gift or devise not prompted by such need. If during the ownership of a house by the educational institution involved it has been used continuously and exclusively by a member of the faculty, the need of such ownership appears more clearly than is the case if the house in question is used sometimes by a faculty member and sometimes for other and unrelated purposes.

(c) *Necessity*. If the employment market is such that provision for housing is needed to secure faculty members, the college's need for such accommodation becomes clear. If adequate teaching staff can be obtained without such inducement, ownership of the home by the college for this purpose would not be essential.

(d) *Rental arrangement*. If the tenancy of the faculty member is at will or from month to month or during his service as a member of the faculty, the lease is consistent with the theory that faculty housing is needed. Where the tenancy is wholly unrelated to the function of the tax-exempt institution, the realty is taxable. * * * While the mode by which rent is paid, that is, whether it is deducted from the salary of the faculty member or paid directly to the educational institution, is not determinative, it is important to consider whether the rent received, if any, is comparable to rentals charged for like property in the community. If a lesser amount is charged than the realty would ordinarily bring on the open market, the likelihood is suggested that the maintenance of such a house for faculty members is reasonably required by the institution to accomplish its educational objectives. On the other hand, if the rent charged for the housing facilities is equal to or greater than that charged in the community for like housing, the inference may be that the educational institution has ownership of such real estate for purposes of raising revenue rather than for purposes of accommodating faculty members. * * *

(e) *Use of the real estate*. If the housing accommodations are used only to provide a place of residence for a faculty member and his family, the inference of a relationship between the educational objectives of the institution and the ownership of the realty is more obscure than is the case if the realty is used also as a place where functions of the educational institution are carried out, as for example, receptions and meetings. If students have access at certain times to the house for consultation with the faculty member occupying it, an inference of reasonable necessity is more apparent than is the case if such access is not available.

(f) *Location.* While the location of the house is not necessarily determinative of the issue of tax exemption, it is evident that housing on the campus or near the campus to the extent that it brings the faculty member closer to the students being educated is a fact more persuasive of tax-exempt status than is the case where the house is so far removed from the campus as to make these points of contact difficult or impossible.

(g) *Housing availability.* If faculty housing is wholly unavailable in the area of the institution where the teaching is to be conducted, the procurement of faculty housing either on or near the campus by the administration of the institution seems essential. * * * On the other hand, if there is, or over a reasonable period of time has been, other housing of a suitable nature adequately located which can be obtained by the faculty member at rent permitted by the salary which the educational institution is able to afford, the necessity from the standpoint of the college for the maintenance of such housing accommodations is more tenuous.

(h) *Occupant's duties.* If under the employment arrangement between the faculty member and the educational institution his presence on or near the campus is required or preferred, the need of such housing by the school is more clear than if duties of this nature are not involved.

The evidence as disclosed by the record gives some information on the relevant factors. Dr. Knutson, president of the college, expressed the view that the ownership of the housing is reasonably necessary in order to secure and obtain faculty members. Although the realty was obtained by devise, it has been used exclusively by the faculty members since its acquisition approximately nine years ago. The ownership of other houses for faculty members is consistent with the stated purpose of providing new additions to the faculty each year with a temporary place of abode. However, there is no evidence in the record as to the term of the tenancy. The occupant of the house pays $75 per month to the college, but there is nothing to indicate whether the amount so paid is more or less than the reasonable rental value of this housing on the Moorhead rental market. While the evidence is clear that the housing is used exclusively for residential purposes and is located some three blocks distant from the campus, and while the testimony indicates that the duties of the present occupant of the house are not such as to require his presence proximate to the campus, there is no testimony in the record as to the availability of other housing accommodations in the vicinity of the campus. Additional information on this point would have made unnecessary the judicial notice of housing conditions which was embodied by the trial court in his findings.

The judgment from which the appeal is taken is reversed and the case is remanded to the district court for further proceedings consistent with this opinion.

Reversed and remanded.

Residence of president emeritus of college not exempt from property tax

ALBRIGHT COLLEGE v. COUNTY OF BERKS

Superior Court of Pennsylvania, 1968.
213 Pa. Super. 478, 249 A.2d 833.

HANNUM, Judge.

Is the residence of the president emeritus of Albright College wherein he resided during his tenure as president, owned by the College and directly across the street from the eastern boundary of the main campus, exempt from local taxation?

The property in 1964, then the president's residence, was exempt and taken from exempt to taxable for the year 1965. Albright College paid taxes during 1965 and 1966.

The Vice-Chairman of the County of Berks Assessment Board testified that the reason the property was removed from the exempt list in 1965 was because it was no longer occupied by the president of the College.

In 1967 Albright College appealed the assessment as excessive and as wholly or partially exempt. Later the parties stipulated that the assessment was fair and reasonable. Following the appeal by Albright College from the refusal of the Board for the Assessment and Revision of Taxes of Berks County to exempt the residence from taxation, the court below held that the residence was exempt.

The propriety of that ruling is now before us. The critical issue of this dispute is the use to which the residence of the president emeritus is put.

Applicable legal principles were stated by Mr. Justice Jones in University of Pittsburgh Tax Exemption Case, 407 Pa. 416, 418, 180 A.2d 760 (1962) : "The Constitution exempts nothing from taxation but simply permits the General Assembly to exempt within a limited and restricted area: City of New Castle v. Lawrence County, 353 Pa. 175, 44 A.2d 589. Section 1 of Article IX of the Constitution authorized the General Assembly to exempt from taxation 'public property used for public purposes, actual places of religious worship, places of burial not used or held for private or corporate profit, institutions of purely public charity and real and personal property owned, occupied, and used by any branch, post or camp of honorably discharged soldiers, sailors and marines.' Section 2 of the same Article provides: 'All laws exempting property from taxation, other than the property above enumerated shall be void.'

"Pursuant to this constitutional authority, the General Assembly under The General County Assessment Law, Section 204 provided: 'The following property shall be exempt from all county, city, borough, town, township, road, poor and school tax, to wit: * * * (c) All hospitals, universities, colleges, seminaries, academies, associations and institutions of learning, benevolence, or charity, [including fire and rescue stations] with the grounds thereto annexed and necessary for the occupancy and enjoyment of the same, founded, endowed, and maintained by public or private charity: Provided, That the entire revenue derived by the same shall be applied to the support and to increase the efficiency and facilities thereof, the repair and the necessary increase of grounds and buildings thereof, and for no other purpose; (1) * * * Except as otherwise provided * * * all property, real or personal, other than that which is in actual use and occupation for the purposes specified in this section, and all such property from which any income or revenue is derived, other than from recipients of the bounty of the institution or charity, shall be subject to taxation, * * *.'

"In the disposition of this appeal we are bound not only by the provisions of the Constitution and the Act of 1933, supra, but also by certain principles well settled in this area of the law. In the first place, a claimant for a tax exemption has the burden of bringing himself within the exemption statute: * * * In the second place statutory provisions exempting property from taxation are subject to a strict, not a liberal, construction * * * and to this rule of construction there is no exception in the case of property owned by nonprofit educational institutions devoted to educational purposes and objectives."

University of Pittsburgh Tax Exemption Case, 407 Pa. 416, 180 A.2d 760 (1962) held that a president's or chancellor's residence could enjoy tax exemption, where the record showed that the majority of the events for which the residence was utilized bore a direct relationship to the proper functioning of the University of Pittsburgh and served its aims and objectives. In this appeal the record does not support the test laid down in the *University of Pittsburgh Tax Exemption Case*. This record reflects that the president emeritus is retained on a consultative basis in development and public relations. The residence provided the president emeritus by the Trustees appears to properly afford him an appropriate dwelling house commensurate with his past worthy service to Albright College. The record does not support, as in the case of the chancellor's residence of the University of Pittsburgh, that the residence in fact was used for the general purposes of Albright College. Although we are guided by the Constitution and the laws thereunder at this date, it is current and significant to note that the declared intent of the citizens of the Commonwealth of Pennsylvania in the area of tax exemption was to support Constitutional Proposal No. 5, where the limitations imposed on tax exemption are even more strictly defined and prohibit the exemption of property that has only a peripheral relationship to charitable purposes. Constitutional Proposal No. 5 limits exemption from taxation to "Institutions of purely public charity, but in the case of any real property tax exemptions only that portion of real property of such institution which is actually and regularly used for the purposes of the institution." Under the Constitution and the Act of May 22, 1933, P.L. 853, as amended, 72 P.S. § 5020-101 et seq., the residence of the president emeritus of Albright College fails to qualify for tax exempt status.

Order reversed.

Corporation organized to provide lodging for needy students is exempt from property tax

M.I.T. STUDENT HOUSE, INC. v. BOARD OF ASSESSORS OF BOSTON

Supreme Judicial Court of Massachusetts, 1966.
215 N.E.2d 788.

SPIEGEL, Justice.

This is an appeal by the M.I.T. Student House, Inc. (hereinafter called the corporation) from a decision of the Appellate Tax Board sustaining an assessment on the real estate of the corporation at 111 Bay State Road for the year 1959. The corporation asserts that it is a charitable corporation and therefore entitled to an exemption by reason of G.L. c. 59, § 5. The Appellate Tax Board made "Findings of Fact and Report."

The facts do not appear to be in dispute. The corporation was established under G.L. c. 180 for the following purposes: "To help needy students, including those who otherwise could not afford to attend, secure an education at the Massachusetts Institute of Technology by providing the facilities for and maintaining an M.I.T. Student House, or M.I.T. Student Houses, which shall offer room and board in clean healthful surroundings to said students at a cost which is less than that otherwise available to them at said Institute; to rent, lease, purchase, acquire, own, mortgage, operate, and maintain a house or houses for the dormitory and dining facilities and meetings of said Student House, or Student Houses; and to foster support by the alumni of said Institute to said Student House or Houses."

The premises are occupied in strict conformity with the aims and purposes as set out in the corporation's charter and by-laws. Any person may become a member by payment of $50, but no part of the corporation's funds inures to the benefit of any member or officer of the corporation. The annual budget figure is set by the board of directors of the corporation, and is submitted to the students who live at the student house and who as a group are obligated to pay this figure to the corporation. The students have their own management system and "do all of their own work except that they do hire a cook." Students who are to live at the student house are selected by an admission committee from a list of needy students supplied by the dean of student aid at M.I.T. The cost to the student is approximately $200 less than if he were to live in an M.I.T. dormitory. The Appellate Tax Board found "that the dominant purpose and activity of the corporation is affording needy and deserving students a dormitory and boarding house."

The sole issue before us is whether the corporation is exempt from taxation of its property under G.L. c. 59, § 5, Third, the pertinent portion of which provides and exempts "Personal property of a charitable organization, which term, as used in this clause, shall mean * * *, a literary, benevolent, charitable or scientific institution * * * incorporated in the commonwealth, * * * and real estate owned by or held in trust for a charitable organization and occupied by it or its officers for the purposes which it is organized * * *."

The board of assessors contends that the corporation is not a "literary, benevolent, charitable or scientific institution" as those words are used in G.L. c. 59, § 5, Third, and relies on the case of Phi Beta Epsilon Corp. v. Boston, 182 Mass. 457, 65 N.E. 824, to support its position. In that case, the students were the active members of the corporation and received in return for their dues the use of a building for meetings, study, and living. Membership was not based on or limited to the needy students. We think the instant case is easily distinguishable. Here the corporation's members derive no material advantages from their membership. The corporation benefits only needy students and they are not members of the corporation. We have no doubt that to provide living quarters for needy persons is a charitable purpose. * * *

The board of assessors also contends that the finding of the Appellate Tax Board that the "premises are occupied and utilized" by the corporation is "unsupported by substantial evidence" and that "this general finding is qualified and controlled by other findings of specific or subsidiary facts." We do not agree.

Because the individual students participate in the management of the house and pay for the use of the house as a group does not rebut the finding of the Appellate Tax Board that "[t]he premises are occupied and utilized by * * * [the corporation] only in strict conformity with the aims and purposes as set out in its charter and by laws." Quite obviously, this "cooperative living arrangement" resulted in a reduced cost to the students and was in furtherance of the general charitable purpose. Although the students have a "cooperative living arrangement" the character of the premises is that of a "dormitory and boarding house." As was said in Franklin Square House v. City of Boston, 188 Mass. 409, 411, 74 N.E. 675, 676, "[t]he occupation of the property is that of the corporation itself, and not of those to whom it affords a home, just as the occupation of a college dormitory or refectory is that of the institution of learning, rather than that of its students." * * *

The decision of the Appellate Tax Board is reversed, and an abatement of the 1959 tax must be granted in the amount of $1,771 with interest and costs.

So ordered.

NOTES

Tax Exemption of Fraternities and Sororities

Greek Letter Fraternity chapter houses, constructed on university-owned land in which only university students reside, are exempt from property taxation. Alford v. Emory University, 216 Ga. 391, 116 S.E.2d 596 (1960).

University press not entitled to tax exemption under "exclusively used" provision

PRINCETON UNIVERSITY PRESS v. BOROUGH OF PRINCETON

Supreme Court of New Jersey, 1961.
35 N.J. 209, 172 A.2d 420.

SCHETTINO, J.

The issue before us is whether the property of Princeton University Press (hereafter referred to as the Press) is tax exempt within the meaning of N.J.S.A. 54:4-3.6.

The Borough of Princeton assessed a tax for land, improvements and personalty for 1957. The Mercer County Board of Taxation denied petitioner's claim of exemption. This action was affirmed by the Division of Tax Appeals on the ground that the property of the Press was not used exclusively for the moral and mental improvement of men, women and children as required by the statute. The Press appealed and, while the matter was pending in the Appellate Division, we certified it.

An examination of the purposes, structure and activities of the Press is necessary for a disposition of the question. The Press was incorporated in 1910. The certificate specifically states that the Press is not incorporated for pecuniary profit and the corporation was formed under the laws applicable to non-profit organizations. * * *

The structure, activities and financial situation of the Press reveal the extent to which the association adheres to these purposes. The membership consists essentially of past, present and *ex officio* members of its Board of Trustees and the various committees of the Press. The main function of its membership is to elect the Board of Trustees, a policy-setting body. The Board itself consists of not more than fifteen individuals, nine of whom are trustees, alumni, or faculty members of Princeton University. * * *

The reason for this close relationship between the Press and the University is clear. As noted, the Press must act "in the interests of" the University and must "serve the University". Additionally, the deed which granted the Press its original land and building specifically provides for a reversion to the University if the Press ceases to act in or serve the University's interests.

The activities of the Press are diversified. A portion of its output consists of scholarly works selected, printed, and distributed by the Press. The research for these works is not necessarily done at Princeton, nor need the author be affiliated with Princeton. The Press also publishes the "Princeton Alumni Weekly," which reports the activities of University alumni and plays a part in University fund-raising endeavors. The "Weekly" also contains informative articles on subjects of interest to alumni.

In contrast to its publishing endeavors, the Press engages in activity which can be classified as purely printing work. The Press engages in this printing operation to offset the losses incurred publishing scholarly works. The profit realized from the printing represents a form of subsidy to scholarly publishing. The printing includes work for Princeton University such as examinations, letterheads, billheads, football programs, pamphlets and catalogs.

The remaining printing is done for a variety of educational institutions, not affiliated with Princeton, and for other non-profit organizations. * * *

Profit and loss figures are available for the period, 1947-1957. * * *

* * * The overall financial picture shows that the Press began with a balance of $101,515.51 in 1947 and climbed to

$641,231.83 in 1957, resulting in an earned surplus of $539,-716.32 for the eleven-year period.

Petitioner claims that under the language of N.J.S.A. 54:4-3.6 it is entitled to a tax exemption. The pertinent portions of the statute are as follows:

"The following property shall be exempt from taxation under this chapter: * * * all buildings actually and exclusively used in the work of associations and corporations organized exclusively for the moral and mental improvement of men, women and children, or for religious, charitable or hospital purposes * * *.

The fundamental approach of our statutes is that ordinarily all property shall bear its just and equal share of the public burden of taxation. As the existence of government is a necessity, taxes are demanded and received in order for government to function. 51 Am. Jur., Taxation, § 9, p. 42. Statutes granting exemption from taxation represent a departure and consequently they are most strongly construed against those claiming exemption. * * * The burden of proving a tax-exempt status is upon the claimant. * * *

Under the statute, exemption from taxation is tested by exclusiveness both of purpose of the organization and of use of the property for the moral and mental improvement of men, women and children. * * *

There is no question that the petitioner has been organized exclusively for the mental and moral improvement of men, women and children. The Press's publication of outstanding scholarly works, which the trade houses would not be apt to publish because of insufficient financial returns, carries out not only the purposes for which it was organized but also performs a valuable public service. It cannot be likewise concluded, however, that the property is *exclusively used* for the mental and moral improvement of men, women and children as required by the statute. A substantial portion of the Press's activity consists of printing work taken in for the purpose of offsetting the losses incurred in the publication of scholarly books. Such printing, which includes work done for educational and non-profit organizations other than Princeton University, is undertaken for the purpose of making a profit. Hence, in this sense the printing takes on the nature of a commercial enterprise and, therefore, it cannot be said that the property is *exclusively used* for the statutory purpose.

Petitioner contends that the printing business conducted by the Press and the profit derived therefrom are for the purpose of supporting the publication of scholarly books. This fact cannot alter the requirement that the property be exclusively used for the purposes mentioned in the statute. At best, it indicates that the property for which the tax exemption is claimed is being used only indirectly, and not exclusively, for the purpose for which exemption is granted. * * *

The outside printing business is not an occasional or incidental activity, or, if engaged in regularly, one which is of an inconsequential or *de minimis* character. It is a substantial, independent and permanent endeavor specifically designed to make a profit. The fact that the Press has realized an earned surplus of $540,000 and has made an annual profit of more than $90,000 per year for the last three recorded years reinforces this conclusion. It cannot be said that the Press has satisfied, as it must, the statutory prerequisite that its property be "actually and exclusively used" in the work of a corporation organized exclusively for the mental improvement of men, women and children.

Affirmed.

NOTES

1. *Property tax exemption in New York*. Curtiss has interpreted the New York state law in regard to tax exemption of educational property as follows:

"To qualify for exemption, the property must:

(1) be owned by a corporation or association organized exclusively for educational purposes, and (2) be used exclusively for carrying out such purposes. In addition, property which yields 'pecuniary profit,' as contrasted with 'reasonable compensation' for services rendered, to any member or employee of the corporate owner is precluded from exemption." W. David Curtiss, "Tax Exemption of Educational Property in New York," *Cornell Law Quarterly*, Vol. 52, 1967, pp. 551-552.

2. *Federal taxes*.

a. For organization to qualify for income tax exemption as a religious organization it must be organized and operated exclusively for religious purposes, no part of the net earnings may inure to the benefit of any private shareholder or individual and no substantial part of the activities may be used to attempt to influence legislation, and all three of these elements are prerequisite to exemption. 26 U.S.C.A. (I.R.C. 1954) § 501; Parker v. Commissioner of Internal Revenue, 365 F.2d 792 (1966).

b. The presence of a single substantial non-exempt purpose of a corporation will defeat its claim for exemption. An economic institute was held not to have charitable, scientific, or educational purposes because it published two semi-monthly periodicals available by subscription and its investment advice services were available for a fee. The activities indicated a commercial purpose. American Institute for Economic Research v. United States, 302 F.2d 934 (1962).

c. Schools and novitiate operated by a nonprofit corporation composed of nonclerical members of religious order are not "churches" within the meaning of the United States Internal Revenue Code. 26 U.S.C.A. (I.R.C. 1939) §§ 101 (6), 421 and subd. (b) (1) (A); 26 U.S.C.A. (I.R.C. 1954) § 170, 501(c) (2,3,), 502, 511(a) (2) (A).

In this case the plaintiff, the De La Salle Institute, claimed that income from its winery and distillery, Christian Brothers, the largest winery in the United States, was entitled to tax exemption since it also operated a novitiate for training of postulates and novices of the Christian Brothers Order, Catholic schools, and homes for retired Brothers. The court disagreed and said that: "One can conceive of a winery, in which religiously habited monks would be among the workers. These monks might pray frequently, retire to an attached chapel for prayers and meditation according to a regular schedule * * * and live by their religious creed at all times. The winery would nonetheless be a winery, and this would be true regardless of the conduct of certain of its employees. By the same token, a school which has teachers similar to the monks * * * remains a school." De La Salle Institute v. United States, 195 F. Supp. 891 (1961).

3. *Charitable organizations and "leaseback" arrangements.* (Quoted with permission from John C. Chommie, *The Law of Federal Income Taxation,* West Publishing Company, St. Paul, Minn., pp. 393-395; see also pp. 70-71, 1970 Cumulative Pocket Part.)

The activities of charitable organizations have received considerable attention in recent years, and restrictive legislation, particularly with respect to private charitable foundations, can be anticipated. However, their exempt status has long been subject to substantial regulation. For example, a section 501(c) (3) charitable organization not only must be non-profit but "no substantial part" of its activities may consist in "carrying on propaganda, or otherwise attempting to influence legislation." The terms "exclusively for * * * educational purposes" in conjunction with the propaganda prohibition has generated a substantial body of case law. Broadly, the courts have construed the statutory terms liberally in favor of exempt status. Unless the organization itself engages in direct political activity in favor of candidates or legislative measures, unless it has a "legislative program hovering over its activities," it is not likely to lose its exempt status notwithstanding its ultimate propaganda purpose may be that of spreading particular beliefs or opinions. * * *

The Code, pursuant to amendments enacted in 1950, also imposes other restrictions on charitable organizations. Thus, under section 502, a profit making "feeder" organization to a charity is subject to tax,[6] and under section 511 "unrelated business" income [7] of a charity is also taxable, though without working a loss of exempt status. However, exempt status may be lost if a charity engages in certain "prohibited" transactions, or unreasonably accumulates or diverts income. These latter provisions are designed to control abuse of private charitable trusts and foundations and do not apply to religious organizations, to educational institutions with a campus, curriculum, faculty and student body, or to certain medical institutions and governmental entities. On the other hand, the corrective legislation enacted in 1950 did not end trading by charitable organizations on their tax exemptions; in fact, in one area, the legislation simply provided the tax planner with a blueprint for tax avoidance plans of various types, the most notorious of which is the so-called "three-cornered bootstrap transaction." This transaction depends for its success upon the receipt of rental income from a leaseback of land

---

6. For example, X University owns the stock of Y corporation which conducts a trade or business for profit; Y is subject to corporate tax even though all its profits are distributed to X, a tax exempt entity. However, if Y's primary activity was the rental of real property section 502 does not apply.

7. Broadly, "unrelated business" income is income from a trade or business other than investment income and other than income from business activities normally performed by the organization such as a university press or a college bookstore; it does include, as discussed in the text, rental income from certain "lease-backs," long-term leases (more than five years) of property acquired with borrowed funds. 26 U.S.C.A. §§ 511-514.

(including machinery and equipment) which falls outside the category of taxable unrelated business income of a charity. Under the terms of sections 512 and 514 this will be the result if the lease is for five years or less. The "bootstrap" aspect comes into play when future profits of a business sold to a charity are used by the charity to pay the purchase price of the shares. A three-cornered bootstrap transaction was involved in Commissioner v. Brown,[9] in which the Supreme Court validated the device.

In the Brown case, under a transaction concluded in 1953, the taxpayers, shareholders of a closely held corporation engaged in the manufacture of lumber, sold their shares to a charitable organization for some $1.3 million. The parties valued the assets at some $1 million and the balance of $300,-000 as the equivalent of 6% interest. The consideration for the shares was payable only out of the future earnings of the business over a ten year period. The sales agreement called for the charity to liquidate the corporation and lease its operating assets for five years to a new corporation formed and owned by the attorney for the seller. The new corporation was to pay 80% of its operating profits as deductible rent to the charity which, in turn, was to pay 90% of such nontaxable rent income to the taxpayer as payments on the mortgage and note securing the sale of the shares. In this manner, the seller would be able to convert future business income, generally taxable at ordinary rates, into a capital gain. This, all the courts agreed, was what was accomplished notwithstanding a frank admission by Mr. Justice Harlan in a concurring opinion that "obviously" the charity "traded on its tax exemption."

The Commissioner chose to attack the transaction by proceeding against the sellers—rather than the charity or the operating company—who claimed capital gain treatment on the sale of the shares reportable on a deferred basis. In the Tax Court, the Commissioner asserted that the sale was a sham and that the proceeds were ordinary income. A divided Court upheld the transaction. It found good faith bargaining at arm's length, a sales price within a "reasonable range" in light of earnings and assets, and concluded that the sale was bona fide. The Court of Appeals affirmed. On appeal, the Commissioner abandoned the sham argument but contended that the sale lacked substance for tax purposes because the charity

9. 380 U.S. 563, 85 S.Ct. 1162, 14 L.Ed.2d 75 (1965).

neither invested any of its own funds or bore any of the risk since the seller could look only to future profits from the business for the purchase price.

The Supreme Court, with three justices dissenting, affirmed. The Court stated that the treatment of the transaction as a sale was consistent with the statutory purpose of according capital treatment to appreciated property held over a long period of time, as there was no showing that the parties had used inflated values. It rejected the Commissioner's risk theory on grounds that such argument denied the finding that the price was not excessive, and because it was "at odds with commercial practice and common understanding of what constitutes a sale." The Court also distinguished the mineral interest cases relied upon by the Commissioner, and found further reason not to disturb the ruling of the lower courts in the legislative history of both the 1950 legislation and the Revenue Act of 1964. In the latter instance, the Treasury had requested and been denied a change in the law which would have taxed as ordinary income the payments on the sale of a capital asset which were deferred over more than five years and which were contingent on future income. Consequently, the Court deemed it wise to leave corrective measures to Congress.

(Clay-Brown Rule: Unrelated Debt-Financed Income — 1969 Act). The 1969 Act restructured and retitled § 514 ("Unrelated Debt-Financed Income") in an attempt to meet the Clay-Brown bootstrap purchase device. For post-1969 years (pre-June 28, 1966 acquisitions are not taxable until June 1972) § 514 treats the rent income (and gain on resale) of an exempt organization's "debt-financed property" as taxable unrelated business income.

CHAPTER 5

PRIVATE SUPPORT FOR HIGHER EDUCATION

Even though the relative importance of private support has declined in recent years, nevertheless, it still serves as a major source of income for higher education in the United States. This chapter discusses the legal issues involved in obtaining private support with primary attention being given to charitable trusts as a major source of private support.

GIFTS AND CHARITABLE TRUSTS

Gifts and charitable trusts have historically been and remain today a basic source of revenue for institutions of higher education. Many private colleges still rely upon gifts and charitable trusts as a primary source of revenue, while most public institutions seek and obtain such financial assistance for the purpose of enriching existing programs or creating new programs over and above public tax support of universities. Moos has commented:

> If you look in each of our 50 states, you will not find any truly great public university which has been financed entirely by state appropriations. Rather you will find that all public universities that we associate with excellence receive generous private support. There can be no doubt. This is where the margin between a good and a great institution lies. Legislators build basically sound public universities, but great public universities are built by private bequests, gifts and grants.[1]

Legislatures and courts have long recognized the benefits of private revenues for charitable organizations, and laws have been shaped to not only accommodate such support but to encourage and cultivate it. The preceding chapter in this book evidences governments' attempts through the power of taxation to promote private charitable giving.

Although the terms gift and charitable trust are sometimes used interchangeably, a more technical legal differentiation exists. An absolute gift is the total transfer of the "entire

---

1. *Margin for Excellence and Opportunity, The Impact of Private Investment on Public Colleges and Universities*, National Association of State Universities and Land-Grant Colleges, quote by Malcolm Moos, p. 15.

interest, beneficial as well as legal." [2] In other words, the person conveying a gift retains no legal interest in its disposition. With the trust, on the other hand, the legal title pertaining to regulation and dispensation is withheld from the beneficial owner. The trust is a legal device invented by man to preserve interest in his property and to "project his personality into the future." [3] Newman's statement that "Man's rebellion against mortality is largely responsible for his desire to control his property after death" [4] is confirmed by a New Jersey judge commenting on the rational basis of trusts where he said: "I am not unaware of that human instinctive propensity to reach beyond death in the control of property interest by means of a testamentary declaration." [5] Regardless of the human frailties of mortality and possessiveness, colleges and universities, with few exceptions, are glad to accept charitable trust support even with trust strings attached.

The *trust* first came into common acceptance in England following the signing of the Magna Charta in 1215 and the Statute of Mortmain in 1279.[6] The Magna Charta and subsequently the Statute of Mortmain forbade the conveyance of land to churches or religious orders, which had gained control of such enormous quantities of land that the land market was drastically reduced.[7] Persons on their death beds had for centuries made it a practice to give their property to the church in penance for their sins. The *trust*, or the *use* as it was called at that time, was a device to evade the law by conveying property to a close friend who allowed the church or religious order to use the property as if it were its own. The employment of uses continued to lead to abuses of the law until 1535 when the Statute of Uses was passed. This act by Parliament, at the instigation of Henry VIII, converted the equitable interest of the *cestui que use* into a legal estate. Under the prevailing common use practices to that time, the beneficiary of the trust, *cestui que use*, had been placed in a position to reap the benefits of use and enjoyment of the land without having legal possession and liabilities attendant thereto. In 1601, another statute, the Statute of 43 Elizabeth,

---

2. Ralph A. Newman, *Newman on Trusts*, The Foundation Press, Inc., 2d ed. 1955, p. 10.

3. *Ibid.*, p. 1.

4. *Ibid.*

5. Septh v. Septh, 8 N.J. Super. 587, 74 A.2d 344 (1950).

6. 2 Pollock and Maitland, *History of English Law*, p. 326.

7. Newman, *op. cit.* p. 19.

also called the Statute of Charitable Uses, was enacted. This statute provided a legal definition for charitable trusts and set up a supervisory system of official inspectors to guard against abuses. In England it is still the law that a purpose is not charitable if it does not fall within the preamble of the Statute of Charitable Uses which was continued in effect through Section 13(2) of the Mortmain and Charitable Uses Act of 1888.[8] Some states in this country today have Mortmain [9] or charitable use statutes which prescribe minimal intervals for execution of a will before death and also limit the percentage of an estate which a testator may leave to charity in the event that relatives survive. Such restrictions protect the family of the testator and are a direct outgrowth of another Mortmain statute which was enacted during the reign of George II in 1736.[10] Several states in this country today have similar Mortmain statutes; among these are New York, Idaho, Ohio, Missouri, Pennsylvania, Florida, Montana, Iowa, Georgia, Maryland, Louisiana and California.[11]

Gifts and trusts to aid education have always been classified as charitable. Private support resulting in the spread and dissemination of knowledge, training and discipline of the mind, the discovery of truth, and the accomplishment of ends which increase culture and extend civilization are of the highest value to mankind and are, therefore, charitable.[12] Statutes in many states declare that all gifts made for educational purposes are to be looked upon by the law as charitable.[13] California statute provides for charitable classification for gifts in trust to found, endow and maintain universities, colleges, schools, seminaries, and mechanical institutes.[14] In the absence of statute, common law brings educational institutions within the definition of a charitable trust.[15]

---

8. *Ibid.*, p. 169.

9. Mortmain means, literally, "dead hand" and is used to describe statutes which prevent property from being held in perpetuity by religious or charitable organizations.

10. 9 Geo. 2, c. 36 (1736).

11. Thomas E. Blackwell, *College Law*, American Council on Education, 1961, p. 215.

12. *Re* Astor's Settlement Trusts, 1 All Eng. R. 1067; 51 *Michigan Law Review* 1104; 68 *Law Quarterly Review* 449.

13. George G. Bogert and George T. Bogert, *The Law of Trusts and Trustees*, Vernon Law Book Co. and West Publishing Co., § 375, p. 116 (1964).

14. Cal. L., c. 71, p. 767 (1943).

15. Russell v. Allen, 107 U.S. 163, 2 S. Ct. 327, 27 L. Ed. 397 (1883).

Trusts usually take one of three forms: (1) *A* declares himself trustee of property for *C*; (2) *A* conveys property to *B* in trust for *A*; and (3) *A* conveys property to *B* in trust for *C*. The law governing the charitable trust differs in two essentials from the private trust; the charitable trust may be perpetual and the *cestui que use* need not be definite. Theoretically, the public should ultimately benefit from a charitable trust, therefore, the identification of a beneficiary and restrictions on duration of the trust are not critical to the charitable trust's validity.[16] In *Jackson v. Phillips* the court expanded on the differentiation between charitable trusts and other types of trusts saying:

> The most important distinction between charities and other trusts is in the time of duration allowed and the degree of definiteness required. The law does not allow property to be inalienable, by means of private trust, beyond the period prescribed by the rule against perpetuities, being a life or lives in being and twenty-one years afterwards; and if the persons to be benefited are uncertain and cannot be ascertained within that period, the gift will be adjudged void, and a resulting trust declared for the heirs at law or distributees. But a public or charitable trust may be perpetual in its duration, and may leave the mode of application and the selection of particular objects to the discretion of the trustees." [17]

Where a charitable corporation, such as a university, is named as the immediate *cestui* to a trust, the corporation is the proper party to enforce the trust.[18] This seemingly simple observation raises some interesting legal questions which should be touched upon here. The primary question is, if the university holds the trust property as its own under trust law, does a trust actually exist where the university is at once both the trustee and the beneficiary and the trust arrangement bestows maximum discretion as to the disposition of the trust on the trustee? This question is not well settled by the courts. A Wisconsin court held that a trust, providing for funds to go to a university for student loans and to a foundation for such charitable purposes as the foundation might from time to time determine, was not technically a trust but constituted an "outright gift." The distinction between a trust and a gift becomes rather obscure where charities are concerned. This may be attributed in part to the

---

16. Jackson v. Phillips, 14 Allen 539 (Mass. 1867).
17. *Ibid.*
18. Clark *op. cit.*, p. 271.

courts' tendency to favor charitable purposes, and in so doing they have allowed more liberal interpretation of charitable trust arrangements, giving the charity more latitude in enforcement of the trust. Whether a college obtains a gift in trust or simply a gift, is a question of flexibility in use of resources. A gift made in trust requires that the college hold the property not as its own, but as a trustee, and in this capacity the college can only carry out the directions of the settlor of the trust. On the other hand, if the property constitutes a mere gift, then the college can use the property in the manner it chooses, providing, of course, that the use is within the corporate purpose of the institution.[19] The *Restatement of the Law of Trusts* distinguishes gifts from trusts as follows:

> Where property is given to a charitable corporation, a charitable trust is not created, even though by the terms of the gift the corporation is directed . . . to use the property only for a particular one of its purposes.[20]

A North Dakota court reached a similar conclusion when it stated that the corporation "does not hold the property in trust in the true sense of the term. It holds the property as its own to be devoted to the purpose for which it was formed." [21]

Chambers, on the other hand, assumes an eclectic position saying that "it seems simpler and more accurate to say that any gift to a charitable corporation carries with it a species of trust obligation." [22]

Though resolution of the trust versus gift question is not easy, it is safe to conclude that the answer rests basically on the *intention of the settlor*. A trust is not created unless the settlor properly manifests an intention to create a trust.[23] If the settlor indicates either impliedly or expressly that he intended to create a trust, then the courts will acknowledge the trust.

Educational trusts may be either general or specific. A general trust for education may simply provide for the cre-

---

19. Stockton v. Northwestern Branch of Women's Foreign Missionaries Society, 127 Ind. App. 193, 133 N.E.2d 875 (1956).

20. *Restatement of Trusts*, Vol. 2, p. 1093.

21. *In re* Myra Foundation, 112 N.W.2d 552 (N.D. 1961).

22. M.M. Chambers, *The Colleges and The Courts*, 1962-1966, The Interstate Printers and Publishers, Inc., 1967, p. 70.

23. Thomas P. Guszkowski, "Gifts to Charitable Corporations—In Trust or Not in Trust," Law Note, *Marquette Law Review*, Vol. 50, p. 671 (1967).

ation of some educational activity, leaving the particulars to the discretion of the trustee. Some general trusts have, in fact, great breadth and have been known to include such broad purposes as education of poor children,[24] education among Indian and African youth of the United States and elsewhere,[25] education of working classes in the United States,[26] education of colored children,[27] and education of the freedmen of this nation.[28] Such broad trusts are designed for flexibility of administration and exemplify the testator's confidence in the judgment of the trustee. Some of these trusts do not even attempt to describe the methods to be used to accomplish the stated purpose.

Many instances exist where the settlor prescribes no method of administration but does limit the trust for the education of a certain class of people.[29] Such trusts are valid provided they do not contravene state or federal constitutions.[30] Other than constitutional restrictions, the courts impose no limitations except that the class of people included must be sufficiently large to insure substantial social and public benefits. Such benefits, however, have been imputed to a scholarship for "one worthy, poor, literary man."[31] Classifications may be based on geography, age, economic status or other considerations. Some particularly notable instances of such trusts are for the education of poor children of a particular county,[32] for education within a parish,[33] for educating boys of Illinois of

---

24. Hitchcock v. Board of Home Missions of Presbyterian Church, 259 Ill. 288, 102 N.E. 741 (1913).

25. Treat's Appeal, 30 Conn. 113 (1861).

26. Sweeney v. Sampson, 5 Ind. 465 (1854).

27. Hunt v. Edgerton, 19 Ohio C. Dec. 377, 9 Ohio Cir. Ct. R. (n.s.) 353, aff'd, 75 Ohio St. 549, 80 N.E. 1126 (1906).

28. McAllister v. McAllister's Heirs, 46 Vt. 272 (1873).

29. Bogert, op. cit., § 375, pp. 117-118.

30. Commonwealth of Pennsylvania v. Board of Directors of City of Philadelphia, 353 U.S. 230, 77 S. Ct. 806 (1957), rehearing denied, 353 U.S. 989, 77 S. Ct. 1281; Girard College Trusteeship, 391 Pa. 434, 138 A.2d 844 (1958), appeal dismissed and certiorari denied, 357 U.S. 570, 78 S. Ct. 1383, rehearing denied, 358 U.S. 858, 79 S. Ct. 14. (The Girard College case is treated more extensively in the chapter on racial segregation of this book.)

31. Thompson v. Thompson, 1 Coll. 381. See also King v. Newman, 1 Lev. 284, Champlin v. Powers, 80 R.I. 30, 90 A.2d 787, 33 A.L.R.2d 1176 (1952).

32. Newson v. Starke, 46 Ga. 88 (1872).

33. Attorney General v. President, etc., of Commons of Kaskaskia, 243 Ill. 239, 90 N.E. 654 (1910).

certain ages,[34] and for education of poor orphans of Harrison County.[35]

The types and means by which a settlor can specify educational objectives of a trust are almost unlimited. He may specify use of thé trust for one field of education, such as music, arts or religion, or he may establish a school or provide for support and maintenance of an existing institution.[36] Even more specifically, a trust may be established to create a lectureship or a professorship [37] in a college or university or to establish a course [38] or endow a department.[39]

CHARITABLE TRUSTS FOR STUDENTS

Since students are essential to the educational process, the law encourages charitable support which seeks to stimulate and enhance the student's pursuit of educational attainment. Various types of student aid trusts include tuition scholarships, student loans, housing, clothing and awards for literary and scientific pursuits.

As mentioned briefly above, whether or not a charitable trust exists rests primarily on the court's determination of what constitutes a public or social benefit. Courts are generally very protective of trusts which project a public benefit, a position which is generally supportable by the philosophy of education of the masses. It is commonly accepted today that education benefits not only the individual but also the community, state and nation. Extralegal support of this thesis is easily obtained from studies of economists confirming not only the private individual benefits of education but also the effects of education on the nation's economy as a whole. Economists have attributed specific percentages of the unexplained increase in the Gross National Product to education.

The empirical studies of economics are corroborated by judicial philosophy which is succinctly described by Justice Graves

---

34. Grand Prairie Seminary v. Morgan, 171 Ill. 444, 49 N.E. 516 (1898).

35. Moore's Heirs v. Moore's Devisees, 4 Dana (Ky.) 354 (1836).

36. Bogert, *op. cit.*, pp. 119-120.

37. *In re* Estate of Royer, 123 Cal. 614, 56 P. 461 (1899); American Academy of Arts and Sciences v. President of Harvard College, 12 Gray (Mass.) 582 (1832); Attorney General v. Margaret, 1 Vern. 55.

38. *In re* Mear's Estate, 299 Pa. 217, 149 A. 157 (1930).

39. Massachusetts Inst. of Technology v. Attorney General, 235 Mass. 288, 126 N.E. 521 (1920).

of the Supreme Court of Kansas: "The advantages direct and indirect which a highly educated citizen imparts to the general public cannot be estimated . . . . As higher education increases, civilization advances." It is on this basis that trusts for students as well as for institutions are justified. In one case where plaintiffs charged that a trust to provide for the education of young men for the ministry was invalid because it lacked a valid public purpose, the court said that it was not necessary to show that any benefits accrued to the institution of higher education.[40] The requirement of a public benefit may be accomplished even though the trust is designated for use by only individual students. The United States Supreme Court has said that "Charity, in a legal sense, is rather a matter of description than of definition," [41] which is the Court's way of saying that with charities, flexibility is the rule and not the exception. In this respect the concept of charity has broadened just as our concepts of benefits of education have expanded.[42] This rationale has led courts to consistently uphold grants as charitable when they are to aid students who are partially or wholly self-supporting [43] and to establish scholarships for needy, worthy and ambitious students.[44]

Wills providing for the establishment of trusts for the purpose of loaning funds to students have also been upheld by the courts. Such loans have been considered charitable trusts even though the conditions of the loan benefit only a very small number of persons.[45] Even where the loan requirements are quite onerous on the student, the courts have maintained a valid charity exists. For example, where a trust was established to loan money to needy college students and required that the recipients work in their spare time and on vacation and could not keep a car or marry during their college careers, the court held that regardless of these restrictions the trust was a valid public charity. The court reasoned that the requirements were entirely consistent with the testator's intent to aid a class of needy students who were willing to work.[46]

The courts have likewise generally held that trusts for student loans are charitable even when the student is charged

---

40. Field v. Drew Theological Seminary (C.C.), 41 Fed. 371.
41. Perin v. Carey, 24 How. 465, 65 U.S. 465 (1860).
42. Harold v. First Nat. Bank of Forth Worth, 93 F. Supp. 882 (1950).
43. *In re* Yule's Estate, 57 Cal. App. 2d 652, 135 P.2d 386 (1943).
44. *In re* McNair's Estate, 74 S.D. 369, 53 N.W.2d 210 (1952).
45. 33 A.L.R.2d 1176.
46. Champlin v. Powers, 90 A.2d 787 (1952).

with interest on the loan. The intent of the trust, however, must require that the interest earned on the loans be added to the trust fund and used on future student loans and no part of the interest can be used for commercial or personal gain.[47] For example, loans for law and medical students for senior year tuition, with four per cent interest to be paid back in four years, have been held charitable trusts.[48]

In spite of the apparent ease by which gifts for educational purposes are classified as charitable trusts, the courts have on occasion struck down trusts as being for private purposes and hence by definition not charitable. Courts will not regard a trust as charitable if it is designed to benefit the members of one's family or his descendants. The courts are especially cognizant of attempts to gain tax deductions for charitable purposes while yet retaining the trust in the family.[49] A "family foundation" established for the purpose of receiving gifts and lending money to the founder's descendants and their husbands and wives for educational purposes was held not to be a charitable corporation by a Utah court.[50] The court said that the purpose of insuring family educational advantages was lacking in the public interest.

All charitable corporations must have a public purpose, but educational charities must also have a definitive educational purpose. In other words, if no educational intent is found to be present where the trust is ostensively for educational purposes, the trust cannot be classified as charitable. The lack of an educational purpose was found in a Virginia case where a trust was created to make gifts to students on Christmas and Easter "to be used by such child in the furtherance of his or her obtainment of education." [51] The court determined that a charitable trust of the educational type was not created since the spending of the money indicated no intent to advance the schooling of the children. The gift was merely one of generosity, which could be spent at the whim of the recipients.

---

47. Waterbury Trust Co. v. Porter, 131 Conn. 206, 38 A.2d 598 (1944).

48. Summers v. Chicago Title and Trust Co., 335 Ill. 564, 167 N.E. 777 (1929). See also Re Davidge's Will, 200 App. Div. 437, 193 N.Y.S. 245 (1922).

49. See the previous chapter of this book on taxation.

50. Marriner W. Merrill Family Foundation, Inc. v. State Tax Commission, 3 Utah 2d 244, 282 P.2d 333 (1955).

51. Shenandoah Valley Nat. Bank of Winchester v. Taylor, 192 Va. 135, 63 S.E.2d 786 (1951).

CY PRES

The doctrine of *cy pres* meaning "as near as" has been employed since Roman times [52] as an alternative to legacies which were impossible to perform. By invoking *cy pres* the court liberalizes the trust specifications and determines the disposition of the charitable trust based on the general intent of the settlor or "as near as" the court can ascertain general intent. The doctrine is defined by the *Restatement of Trusts* as:

> If property is given in trust to be applied to a particular charitable purpose, it is or becomes impossible or impracticable or illegal to carry out the particular purpose, and if the settlor manifested a more general intention to devote the property to charitable purposes, the trust will not fail but the court will direct the application of the property to some charitable purpose which falls within the general charitable intention of the settlor.[53]

Three prerequisites are necessary for the use of *cy pres*. They are: (1) the existence of a charitable trust, (2) the impossibility or impracticality of abiding by the settlor's specified intent, and (3) the existence of a general intent rather than or in addition to a specific intent on the part of the settlor.[54] *Cy pres* will not be applied where the trust is not for charitable purposes; however, the terms "charity" and "trust" do not need to be mentioned in order for a charitable trust to exist.[55]

In a Michigan case demonstrating the application of *cy pres*, a philanthropic organization deeded a parcel of land to the University of Detroit in 1924; [56] as partial consideration for the transfer the university agreed to accept 24 students, tuition free, nominated by the philanthropic organization. Originally, the rent on the property covered the tuition costs; however, with the inflationary spiral of recent years the university discovered it was losing large sums of money under the agreement. The university asked the court to grant

---

52. *Digest of Justinian*, 33: 2:16, cited in Late Corporation of the Church of Jesus Christ of the Latter-Day Saints v. U.S., 136 U.S. 1, 10 S. Ct. 792 (1889).

53. *Restatement (Second) of Trusts* § 399 (1959).

54. John Thompson Peters, Jr., "A Decade of Cy Pres: 1955-1965," *Temple Law Quarterly*, Vol. 39, p. 256 (1966).

55. *Ibid.*, p. 260.

56. Knights of Equity Memorial Scholarships Commission v. University of Detroit, 395 Mich. 235, 102 N.W.2d 463 (1960).

cy pres whereby the rental income would be only partial payment of the student's tuition. The granting organization claimed the agreement was a contract and not a trust. In keeping with the traditionally favorable treatment of charities, the Supreme Court of Michigan found that a charitable trust did exist and granted *cy pres* to the University of Detroit. While the words of trust were not present in the agreement, the court, nevertheless, found that a reading of the entire instrument indicated an intent to create a trust.

Existence of a charitable trust as a condition precedent to granting *cy pres* may be more difficult to establish in some jurisdictions than in others. In a 1961 case, the Court of Appeals of Kentucky declined to apply *cy pres* because of failure to establish the prerequisite charitable trust arrangement.[57] Here, an 1849 deed devised a forty-acre tract of land to the Presbyterian Church for use as grounds for a parsonage. The deed contained the words, fee simple; however, it further said that if the property ceased to be used by the church it was to be used for the benefit of the local common school. The Presbytery dissolved the church in 1957 and sought to sell the property and apply the proceeds to the church's general fund. The Garrard County Board of Education contested and asked the court to invoke *cy pres* and grant the proceeds from the land to the school board. The Kentucky court found that because of the "fee simple" clause no charitable trust existed, the church owned the land, therefore, *cy pres* could not be granted.

The second prerequisite given above for granting *cy pres* is the impossibility or the impracticality of fulfilling the specific intent of the grantor. This provision is older than Anglo-American law and harkens back to the *Digest of Justinian,* where in the third century a Roman's legacy was left to a city for the purpose of preserving the name of the donor by conducting yearly games. The games that were to be held were illegal at the time and the question of what to do with the legacy arose.[58] The jurist Modestinus solved the problem by proclaiming: [59]

Since the testator wished games to be celebrated which

57. Trustees of Transylvania Presbytery United States of America v. Garrard County Board of Education, 348 S.W.2d 846 (Ky. 1961).

58. Edith L. Fisch, *The Cy Pres Doctrine in the United States,* Matthew Bender and Company, Inc., 1950, pp. 3-4.

59. Late Corporation of the Church of Jesus Christ of the Latter-Day Saints v. U. S., *supra* note 52.

are not permitted, it would be unjust that the amount which he has destined to that end should go back to the heirs. Therefore, let the heirs and magnates of the city be cited, and let an examination be made to ascertain how the trust may be employed so that the memory of the deceased may be preserved in some other and lawful manner.

The same logic has carried throughout the ages [60] with recent cases demonstrating essentially the same basic philosophy used by Modestinus.[61]

A case in Louisiana illustrates the complexity with which the court is sometimes faced in ascertaining whether a trust is impossible or impractical to administer.[62] In 1836 the settlor left certain lands to be used for destitute boys, a female asylum, and to two nonexistent asylums, one for destitute girls and one for boys of the same description. The latter two asylums were to be established at Milnebury and be called Milne Asylums incorporated. In 1934 the trustees leased six squares of the land to the City of New Orleans for ninety-nine years in consideration for the city's promise to build a Milne Municipal Boys Home on the land. The home was built at an expense of $80,000 to the trustees and $100,000 to the city. The trustees, subsequently, without court sanction, sold portions of the remaining land for $1,000,000. The trustees then petitioned the court to divide the proceeds of the land sale among Tulane University the Young Men's Christian Association, the Boy Scouts, and the New Orleans Catholic Charities. The trustees sought application of *cy pres* urging that it was impossible and impractical to fulfill the settlor's desire since adequate facilities already existed as a result of the home construction in 1934 and because there was a declining need for destitute orphan boys homes.

The Supreme Court of Louisiana granted *cy pres* but not for the purposes sought by the trustees. The court found that while the establishment of the Milne Municipal Boys Home in 1934 met the primary intent of the settlor, to "establish" a destitute orphan boys home, there was no specific provision for maintaining the home. Instead of granting the funds to the four charities, the court interpreted the settlor's intent, under the *cy pres* doctrine, as providing the funds for the

---

60. See Fisch, *op. cit.*, pp. 9-91.

61. *In re* Lee's Will, 3 Misc. 2d 1072, 156 N.Y.S.2d 813 (1956); *In re* Scott's Will, 8 N.Y.2d 419, 208 N.Y.S.2d 984 (1960); Grace Episcopal Church v. Nicholas, 341 Mass. 736, 171 N.E.2d 285 (1961).

62. *In re* Milne's Succession, 230 La. 729, 89 So. 2d 281 (1956).

maintenance of the boys home. The court further denied the trustees' claim that it was impossible to fulfill the trust because of the declining need for orphan boys homes. On the contrary, the court pointed out that the very fact that the Milne Municipal Boys Home was *now* used by orphans established the need for a use.

The third prerequisite to the application of *cy pres* is the existence of a broad and general charitable intent. *Cy pres* will not be applied where it is evident that the settlor had only narrow and specific purposes to which no broader intent is attributable. For example, to assist higher education is an expression of general intent, while specific intent could be assistance to students attending college from one's own home town. Under the latter provision alone *cy pres* would not be granted; however, if the two are coupled, the specific with the general, the court then may grant *cy pres*. The court is not free to decide the question at its own whim or fancy, the charitable objective is not what the court thinks but what the actual intent of the donor desired it to be. This is the common law rule and may be varied by statute. Some states make no mention of the general intent provision; [63] on the other hand, other states such as Pennsylvania provide that *cy pres* shall be applied whether the charitable intent was general or specific.[64]

As one might imagine, determining the actual intent can be extremely difficult, especially since in most cases the donor expected fulfillment of the original conditions and probably had no other alternatives in mind. In some of these cases, the courts tend to deal in the area of speculation in determining the intent of the donor. The intent of the donor is, however, paramount, and the court must justify its decision in terms of such intent.

The complex question of interpretation was demonstrated in a New York case involving Syracuse University.[65] The testator, a physician and a life long benefactor of Syracuse University Medical School, left the school certain funds in trust. Shortly before the benefactor's death, the control of Syracuse was transferred to the State University of New York. The will was not changed when the transfer transpired and the words of condition in the will remained, which pro-

---

63. Bogert, *op cit.*, p. 423.
64. 20 P.S. § 301.10.
65. Application of Syracuse University, 3 N.Y.2d 665, 171 N.Y.S.2d 545 (1958).

vided that the medical school would receive the funds only if:

> Within one year after my death the Medical College thereof shall be assured of permanency and of support adequate to keep the same forever in the rank of "Class A" medical schools . . . and expressed by a written statement . . . signed [by the] President and Secretary of the Board of Trustees.

In interpreting the donor's words the court found two possible intentions: (1) to benefit humanity generally in the field of medicine, or (2) to benefit humanity only through the means of Syracuse University. The court found that the latter was the true intent and the settlor's estate vested in the heirs rather than in the State University. The court apparently felt that the settlor's close association with Syracuse University as it was formerly constituted and his specific reference to the school's permanency were sufficient to deny the more general interpretation necessary for *cy pres.*

In disagreeing with this court's ruling, Peters commented in the *Temple Law Quarterly* that: [66]

> The condition, however, should not have been construed as an express denial of the possibility of utilizing *cy pres,* for its words are directed at the quality of the school, not its ownership.

These comments only highlight the dilemma faced by the courts in trying to equitably reestablish the thoughts, purposes, and intent of the dead.[67]

Will bequeathing funds to train young men for Christian ministry creates an educational trust

TRUSTEES OF WASHBURN COLLEGE v. O'HARA

Supreme Court of Kansas, 1907.
90 P. 234.

In the matter of the accounting in the estate of Samuel Dilley, deceased, D. L. O'Hara and others claim money in the hands of the executor. From an order distributing the same among them, the trustees of Washburn College appeal to the

---

66. Peters, *op. cit.,* p. 271.

67. See also Snow v. President and Trustees of Bowdoin College, 133 Me. 195, 175 A. 268 (1934); Harvard College President and Fellows v. Jewett, 11 F.2d 119 (1926).

district court and from an order affirming the order of distribution they bring error. Reversed.

On June 5, 1898, Samuel Dilley died in Reno county, Kan., leaving a will, which, after making various bequests to children and grandchildren, provides as follows:

"After paying the above legacies, I give and bequeath to the Trustees of Washburn College, located at Topeka, Kansas, the balance of my estate, be it more or less, to be held by them as a permanent fund and invested and secured as such. The annual interest to be used for the higher education (mainly) of young men for the Christian ministry, on the following conditions:

"1st. They must be members in good standing in some Christian church, denominated evangelical, Congregational preferred.

"2d. They must present to said trustees testimonials of such standing, and that they possess piety and natural talent that will qualify them for usefulness in Christian work, if the necessary education can be secured.

"3d. They must not use alcoholic beverages except for medicine, nor tobacco in any form. * * *

GRAVES, J. (after stating the facts). The residuary clause of this will is assailed upon the ground that it creates a trust which is not a public charity. The case of Troutman v. De Boissiere, 66 Kan. 1, 71 Pac. 286, is cited as being directly in point and controlling upon this question. The argument of the defendant in error is founded chiefly upon a statement in that opinion, which reads: "A public charity is a gift to a public object which the state itself, with public resources, should, or lawfully might, foster." This proposition does not appear in the syllabus, and is not the question upon which the court divided. It cannot be said therefore that the court intended to decide that every public charity must be such as the state may lawfully maintain by public taxation. The real point decided was that in the trust there being considered the beneficiaries were limited to such an extent that the gift could not be regarded as a public charity. This statement was used in the opinion by way of an argument to illustrate the general scope and extent of a trust which may be properly classed as a public charity. In that case the fund provided could only be used for the benefit of the orphans of deceased Odd Fellows of the state of Kansas. This limitation excluded it from the category of public charities. The line of distinction which determines where a private charity ends and a public one begins is at times difficult to locate, and this difficulty has caused much of the apparent want of harmony which prevails among the decisions upon this subject. In this case, however, there is no uncertainty. The object of the trust provided for by the will of Samuel Dilley is the higher education of young men and women. Bequests for educational purposes have been regarded by the courts of this country with special favor, and donations made for the founding and maintenance of institutions of learning, or for increasing educational facilities, have very generally been upheld as public charities. The numerous and varied educational purposes in support of which trusts have been created, and sustained as public charities, are partially collected in 2 Perry on Trusts, § 700, which reads: "Almost all gifts for educational purposes are held to be charitable; as gifts for the advancement of learning in every part of the world, so far as circumstances will permit; or for the diffusion (a part in Pennsylvania, the residue in the United States) of useful knowledge and instruction among the institutes, clubs, or meetings of the working classes, or manual laborers by the sweat of their brow; to build or erect a school or free grammar school, or a school for the sons of gentlemen, for the education of the scholars of poor people in a particular county; or to maintain a schoolmaster; or for the masters and fellows of a college; or for the foundation of a scholarship, fellowship, or lectureship in a college or university; or for the perpetual endowment of two schools; or to establish a college for orphans, although all ministers are forever excluded from its walls; or for the education of young men at Oxford for the Church of England, to be selected; or to maintain a library and reading room; or for paying premiums for the most important discoveries or useful improvements made public upon light and heat; or for the civilization of Indians; or to assist literary persons in their pursuits; or to publish an essay on science; or to publish and distribute the works of Joanna Southcote; or to promote the moral, intellectual, and physical instruction and education of a city; or to create a 'change of sentiment,' which means to educate; or a fund to increase the salaries of teachers. Money in trust to support a school for the use of poor children cannot be applied to a public school where rich and poor are educated together; but it may be used in purchasing food and clothing and books for poor children, to enable them to attend such school."

The advantages direct and indirect which the highly educated citizen imparts to the general public cannot be estimated. Every advancement made in the scientific, mechanical, moral, literary, or other pursuits of life adds to the general sum of human knowledge, comfort, and happiness. As higher education increases, civilization advances. The elevating and beneficent influences which the general public receives from educational sources make every citizen a beneficiary thereof, and furnish complete justification for placing every educational trust, not strictly private, having increased learning for its object, in the category of public charities. It has been suggested that the rule stated applies to ordinary education such as may be acquired at public institutions of learning, but has no application here, for the reason that the education provided for these beneficiaries is to be such as will fit them for the Christian ministry, in which the public, as such, can have no interest. We are unable to see how the future vocation of the student can be material in this inquiry. It is not important to the general public whether highly educated men engage in the law, medicine, mechanics, the ministry, or some other pursuit in which specialized learning is useful. The public is concerned, however, in having the greatest possible number of persons receive an educational training which will prepare them for successful work in whatever field of human knowledge they may desire to enter. Persons educated for the ministry do not always persist in preaching the Gospel. Many instances might be given of men who drifted away from this their chosen profession, and by the application of their early educational training became public benefactors in other pursuits. There is nothing in the will of Samuel Dilley which amounts to a requirement or even a request that those who receive the education provided by him shall enter or continue in the ministry. If any of them shall feel that their lives will be more useful if devoted to other pursuits, no restraint has been imposed to prevent the exercise of a free choice therein. This bequest may be construed as having been designed either for the promotion of religion or for educational purposes, but, judging from its practical effects, the educational feature seems to be its principal and paramount purpose. * * *

Whether the testator in this case intended by his donation to promote the interests of religion, or to increase the opportunities for higher education, or both, is of little moment. In either case it is a matter in which the general public will be sufficiently benefited to make the bequest a public charity, and it should be upheld and administered as such.

The judgment of the district court is reversed, with direction to enter judgment in favor of the plaintiffs in error, and

order the executor of the last will and testament of Samuel
Dilley, deceased, to pay to the plaintiffs in error the amount
due them under the residuary clause of said will, and otherwise carry out the views herein expressed. All the Justices
concurring.

NOTES

1. *Endowment* is a term often heard when higher education financing is being discussed. An endowment is merely
one type of charitable trust with the distinguishing feature
that the principal of the fund is permanent and inviolate;
only the income or interest on the fund can be used in the
administration of the proposed work. St. Joseph's Hospital v.
Bennett, 281 N.Y. 115, 22 N.E.2d 305 (1939).

2. *Endowment.* "The endowment of a college, unless the
term is qualified by other words or phrases, is commonly understood as including all property, real or personal, given to
the college for its permanent support." Millsaps College v.
City of Jackson, 136 Miss. 795, 101 So. 574 (1924).

"The bestowment of money as a permanent fund, the income of which is to be used in administration of a proposed
work." *In re* Pelton's Will, 190 Misc. 624, 74 N.Y.S.2d 743
(1947).

Funds bequeathed to college for education of ministers' sons held to be a valid trust

SPARKS v. WOOLVERTON

Supreme Court of Alabama, 1924.
210 Ala. 669, 99 So. 102.

The bill of complaint is filed by Cora Sparks and Veattriss
Johnson for a construction of the will of their aunt, Margaret
T. Johnson, who was a resident of Birmingham. Complainants
are among the next of kin of the testator, and the respondent,
W. H. Woolverton, is the executor of the will. The will in
question leaves a small legacy to each of the testator's
nephews and nieces, and item 3 then provides:

"I hereby give, devise and bequeath all the rest and residue
of my estate to the trustees of Birmingham College, of Birmingham, Alabama, to be held by them as a fund for the edu-

cation of the sons of Methodist ministers of Alabama and to be known as 'the Margaret T. Johnson endowment fund.' "
* * *

SOMERVILLE, J. There can be no question as to the validity of the testator's gift to the trustees of Birmingham College as a public charity, if under the terms of the trust its beneficiaries can be ascertained with reasonable certainty. * * *

Complainants' theory of invalidity may be briefly stated as follows: (1) If the gift was intended to be distributed among *all* the members of the designated class of beneficiaries, "the sons of Methodist ministers of Alabama," the income from the fund is too small, and the number of the beneficiaries is too great, to permit of any beneficial or even practicable administration of the trust, and hence, administration as intended by the donor being practically impossible, the trust must of necessity fail. (2) If the gift was intended to be applied to the education of only a limited and practical number of the sons of Methodist ministers, no authority was given to the trustees, nor to any one else, to select individuals from the designated class for the enjoyment of the benefits provided.

If the first alternative presented the only rational construction of the terms of the gift, we would be disposed to agree with the view of counsel that the trust must fail because its administration would be practically impossible, or, if possible, barren of benefit to any one. Such a trust the courts would not sustain. But we cannot adopt the theory of an irrational intention, impossible of fulfillment, and barren of good, when a rational intention, easy of fulfillment, and beneficial in results, can be gathered from the words of the donor. Unquestionably, we think, the donor of this fund intended that it should be used for the education of selected members of the general class to whom its benefits were limited.

The donor did not expressly authorize the trustees to select any particular subjects for charitable favor, and the decisive question—the only question—presented is whether such an authority is clearly implied by the nature of the gift, the purpose the donor had in view, and the character and station of the trustees who are intrusted with the custody and administration of the fund.

The gift here under consideration is for a clearly defined purpose—the education of the sons of Methodist ministers of Alabama. It is given to the "trustees of Birmingham College," an institution which, as we judicially know, is devoted to the higher education of men, and is owned and controlled by the

Methodist Church of Alabama. A gift to the trustees of an institution is in law and in fact a gift to the institution itself. * * * And when a gift is made to an educational institution, such as the Birmingham College, to be held as an "endowment fund," and to be used for the education of a specified class of men, the implication is clear, and indeed unavoidable, that the fund is to be used for the endowment of scholarships in the college itself, and thus, in that customary and methodical way, applied to the use declared by the donor. * * * Necessarily, the administration of the fund for scholarship endowments must be, as to its details, subject to the regulation and control of the college authorities, and this would include the selection of the individuals to whom the scholarships should be given.

But, apart from the considerations above stated, it is a well-settled principle that charitable trusts are especially favored by courts of equity, and hence all reasonable intendments, consistent with the terms and purpose of the gift, will be made in support of their validity. Hence the rule, which is supported by reason as well as authority, that where the fund is limited, and the scope of the charity is broader than the fund, and the donor or founder does not provide a rule or order of selection, there is "in every public charity a necessary power of selection of beneficiaries in the trustees." * * *

> "Even where neither the trustee nor any other person or corporation is expressly given the power of selection, the courts are very liberal, in construing the instrument creating the trust, in giving the trustee an implied power of selection."

Our opinion is that, even though the education provided for were not limited by implication to education at Birmingham College, the implied power of selection by the trustees would save the trust from the invalidating vice of uncertainty as to its beneficiaries. It results that the charitable trust in question is valid and must be sustained. * * *

Affirmed.

University directors have discretionary power to use trust funds to pay portion of salaries.

CARREL, AUDITOR, ET AL. v. THE STATE EX REL. BROWN ET AL., DIRECTORS OF THE UNIVERSITY OF CINCINNATI

Court of Appeals of Ohio, 1919.
11 Ohio App. 281.

SHOHL, P. J. On April 30, 1917, shortly after the declaration by the United States of a state of war against the imperial German government, the directors of the University of Cincinnati adopted the following resolution, which was communicated to all the professors, instructors, officers and other employees of the university:

"Resolved, That all professors, instructors, officers and other employees of the University who enlist or are drafted in the army, navy, medical or hospital service of the United States or in recognized training camps of the United States who are now permanently employed for next year be assured that their positions will be held for them, and that they will receive compensation out of trust funds under our control at regular times in such amount as will make up the difference between the army, navy, hospital or other service pay and their regular salaries in this institution."

At that time a substantial number of professors and instructors had already entered the military service and others were about to do so. A list of the names, with the amount of compensation due each of the members of the teaching force under the resolution, was certified in 1918 by the directors of the university to the Civil Service Commission and by it transmitted to the auditor of Cincinnati. Under the direction of an examiner in the office of the auditor of state, the city auditor refused to draw his warrant on the treasurer to make the payments called for by the list unless ordered to do so by the courts. The directors of the university thereupon brought this action in mandamus against the auditor and treasurer of Cincinnati, and the court of common pleas, after a trial, rendered judgment against the defendants and ordered a peremptory writ of mandamus to issue, directing the drawing and the payment of the warrant. The city auditor and city treasurer prosecute error to this court.

The refusal of the city officials to pay the professors and instructors is based upon the contention that it constitutes a payment of public money as a gratuity or donation, and that the board of directors is exceeding its powers in attempting to use funds for such purpose. * * * In the case at bar, however, the resolution does not call for the payment out of money received from taxation. The disbursements are to be from trust funds. The record establishes that in addition to the funds raised by taxation, the board has an income from certain trust funds, among which are the McMicken fund and the Thoms fund.

Under the will of Charles McMicken a large amount of property was left for the purpose of establishing a college or university. Items 21 and 37 provide:

"Item XXI: I therefore devise, and bequeath to the City of Cincinnati and its successors for the purpose of building, establishing and maintaining, as soon as practicable after my decease, two colleges for the education of white boys and girls, all the following real and personal estate in trust forever."

"Item XXXVII: The establishment of the regulations necessary to carry out the objects of my endowment, I leave to the wisdom and discretion of the corporate authorities of the City of Cincinnati, who shall have power to appoint directors of said institution." * * *

All the powers granted by these bequests are vested in the board of directors, under Sections 7902 and 7915 of the General Code. Under the wills the disbursement of the money is left to the wisdom and discretion of the board, in the one case; and, in the other, it is to be applied to such uses as the directors may provide. The directors justify the expenditure in accordance with the resolution on the ground that in a proper aspect and under a broad view it promotes the purposes and objects of the donors and tends to further the success of the University of Cincinnati. If so, it comes within the discretionary powers granted to them.

The vital force of a university is its teaching body. No matter how fine the buildings, equipment and appointments devoted to the university purposes may be, the ultimate achievement of the university is accomplished by its staff of teachers. The establishment of a staff of professors in a university and the welding of all into a unit is a slow growth. The number of teachers who are the most competent and desirable is necessarily limited. In securing professors and instructors, and in retaining them, the University of Cincinnati comes into competition with the other institutions of learning throughout the country.

The uncontradicted evidence shows that the policy of paying the professors and instructors of universities, who entered the war service of the United States, the difference between the amount paid them at the university and the amount received from the government has been so generally followed in the universities and other institutions of learning that it may fairly be said to be the generally accepted policy in the country. While the professors and instructors had no contractual obligation to resume their positions after the war, it was hoped that they would do so, and the directors knew that the continuing payments would operate in fact to bind them to the university. * * * Had the university declined to follow the accepted and prevailing policy, there might well have been a feeling among the members of the teaching body that the university was lacking in appreciation of its members, as well as in patriotism for the country, and it might have impaired the standing and reputation of the university with the teachers whom it sought to attract.

The trusts under the will mentioned, being given for the purpose of education, are within the rules governing charitable trusts. * * *

Courts are liberal in the construction of powers of trustees of charitable trusts. * * *

While courts in proper proceedings will restrain trustees from dealing with trust funds in a manner not authorized by law, they will not interfere with the discretion of the trustees in a charitable trust and will not control their discretionary application of the funds except to prevent abuse or misuse. * * *

Just what expenditures are suitable and necessary to carry on a university must be determined in view of the facts and conditions that exist at the time. * * * Under the circumstances it can not be said that the money in question was not devoted to the uses and purposes of the university. The resolution was designed to promote the objects of the donors of the trust funds, and the payments therein provided for should be made.

Judgment affirmed.

**Trust remains valid even though recipient two-year Junior
College becomes a four-year College**

THE LITTLE ROCK JUNIOR COLLEGE v. GEORGE W.
DONAGHEY FOUNDATION

Supreme Court of Arkansas, 1955.
224 Ark. 895, 277 S.W.2d 79.

ROBINSON, J. This is a suit for a declaratory judgment whereby the beneficiary of a trust asks that a deed in trust be construed. George W. Donaghey and his wife, Louvenia Donaghey, conveyed by a deed in trust to named trustees, "for the exclusive use and benefit of the present Little Rock Junior College," certain real estate in the City of Little Rock. The deed provides, *inter alia*:

"It is the object and purpose of this deed to convey the property herein described to said Trustees, their successors and assigns for the purpose of creating a fund or foundation to be used for the sole and exclusive benefit of the present Little Rock Junior College, an institution of learning in said city, at the present time operated under the management of the Board of School Directors of the Special School District of Little Rock, Arkansas, investing said Trustees with full discretion to select some other public school or schools in said city, operated by or under the management or supervision of the Board of School Directors of the said Special School District of Little Rock, and their successors in charge of the public schools in the said City of Little Rock, in the event the present Little Rock Junior College or its successors, should at any time cease to be operated by or under the supervision of the public school authorities in said City." * * *

At the time the trust was set up the Little Rock Junior College was a two year school. During the first years of the trust, due to a mortgage indebtedness on the property conveyed to the trust, only a comparatively small amount was paid to the college; but subsequent to 1939 payments increased. In 1950 the payment by the trust to the college was in the sum of $45,037.50, and in 1953 it was $75,050.00. In May, 1954, the trustees of the college decided to expand it to a four year college and wrote to the Donaghey trustees as follows:

"It is recommended that the Little Rock Junior College be expanded to a four year senior college, the third year to be added in September, 1954, and the fourth year in September, 1955."

As a result of this letter from the college, the Donaghey trustees adopted the following resolution:

"It is the sense of the trustees of the George W. Donaghey Foundation that it is their duty to exercise their discretion within the scope of Governor Donaghey's deed in trust to determine a proper worthy beneficiary of the Foundation: That, because of their knowledge of the vastly greater requirements of an adequate four year college over those of a Junior College, the present program of the Board of Trustees of Junior College for its expansion into a four year college has created grave doubts in the minds of the Donaghey Foundation Trustees and that they are therefore not in a position at this time to obligate Foundation Funds to Junior College for the ensuing year, as requested by President Granville Davis."

The effect of this resolution was to deprive the college of any funds from the Donaghey trust, and it appears that the school could not survive without such aid. Hence the college rescinded its action in expanding to a four year school, and following this step the Donaghey trust again allotted $75,-000.00 to the school for the year 1954-1955. There is no contention that the trustees of the Donaghey trust adopted the resolution stopping payment of trust funds to the school for any reason other than that the college intended to expand.

The college then filed this suit asking that the deed in trust be construed to mean that it is the duty of the trustees of the Donaghey Foundation to pay the profits of the trust to the school, and that the trustees do not have authority to withhold such profits from the college merely because it expands to a four year school. The Chancellor held that the trustees were acting within the authority vested in them by the deed in trust in stopping payment to the school when it was expanded.

On appeal the college contends that a four year school would have the same rights, powers, duties and obligations as a two year school; that the Donaghey trustees acted arbitrarily in withholding the profits of the trust from the college upon its being expanded to a four year institution; and that the college may compel a distribution of the profits from the trust.

Appellees contend a four year college would not be the same school as or a successor to the present Little Rock Junior College; and further that since the founding of the trust the school has become a corporation, is not supervised by the Board of Directors of the Little Rock school district, and hence is no longer entitled to receive anything from the trust.

Considerable argument is devoted to the question of whether a four year college would be a successor to the present school; however, in our opinion the proposition of a successor does not enter into the picture, for the mere fact that the school authorities decided to expand into a four year college in no way changes the identity of the school and does not make of it a school other than the one that the trust was set up to help. *Little Rock Junior College* is merely the name of the school; it is inconceivable that the settlors of the trust used the words in any other way. Loving the college as they did, it is unthinkable that they wanted to help it only if it remained limited in the educational advantages it had to offer, and did not want to give it any further aid if through their generosity the school was able to grow and become a great institution of learning. It is true the deed uses the words "the present Little Rock Junior College." The deed provides: "It is the object and purpose of this deed to convey the property herein described to said trustees, their successors and assigns, for the purpose of creating a fund or foundation to be used for the sole and exclusive benefit of the present Little Rock Junior College." But "the present Little Rock Junior College" is the very same school that wants to expand into a four year college, and by so expanding it does not become another school. When John Doe, a boy 15 years of age, grows up and becomes a man 21 years of age, he is still the same John Doe. It is suggested that the name of the school has now been changed to Donaghey College; in the future another school may adopt the name Little Rock Junior College. That is when the wording in the deed in trust "the present Little Rock Junior College: would come into play; the new school adopting that name would not be the *present* Little Rock Junior College.

It is argued that Governor Donaghey was interested only in a junior college because he knew of the trials and tribulations of those unable to obtain a higher education, and he wanted to make a junior college available to those unable to bear the expense of a full four year course and that he endowed a "junior college" as such and gave the trustees of the Donaghey Foundation the discretion of selecting some other school as a beneficiary of the trust in the event the Little Rock Junior College ceased to be a junior college. But it is shown conclusively by the writings of both the Governor and Mrs. Donaghey that it was their fondest hope that the Little Rock Junior College would grow into a four year school. * * * [T]he Governor wrote in his volume *Home Spun Philosophy:* "Then, whoever aids in the development of this human power, for any of the vocations of life, renders his community and State a forward service. That is the object of the establishment of the Donaghey Foundation. Today it is sponsoring the fortunes of Little Rock Junior College. This college is affording the young people of Greater Little Rock and the contiguous territory the opportunity of a two-year course in college work with the object of eventually making it four years." It is shown that Mrs. Donaghey stated "that her greatest wish was to see the aim of her husband fulfilled—a four year college in Little Rock." * * *

Here the principal issue in dispute is the meaning in which the settlor of the trust used the words "the present Little Rock Junior College." Were the words used as meaning a Junior College only, or were they used in the sense of meaning the name of the school endowed? Governor Donaghey's feeling toward the school, and his hopes and ambitions for it, are of paramount importance in arriving at the true meaning of the words used. * * *

Here, if we had to construe the deed in trust by staying within its four corners, it would appear that the words "the present Little Rock Junior College" refer to the name of the school. However, since the appellants contend that the words have a different meaning and are used as pertaining only to a Junior College as such, we may go beyond the deed in trust for aid in its construction. It would be hard to find any evidence more satisfactory than the writings of the settlor. * * *

Likewise the declarations of Governor Donaghey were admissible for the purpose of showing his interpretation of what he had done. Such declarations show, beyond any shadow of a doubt, that he had endowed a school which he hoped would some day grow into a four-year college.

It appears that in attempting to develop a four-year college the school authorities were doing exactly what Governor Donaghey hoped would be done. The trustees of the Donaghey Foundation cannot arbitrarily withhold profits of the trust from the college; and on the other hand, of course, the school authorities cannot expend such money in a manner that would amount to waste. Undoubtedly under the terms of the deed in trust, the trustees have full management and supervision of the trust property, and have full authority to exercise good business practices in connection therewith; but the profits must be paid to the beneficiary of the trust, Little Rock Junior

College, and the trustees of that institution are the ones who are charged with the responsibility of conducting a school that will use the funds received from the trust to the very best advantage. * * *

Reversed with directions to enter a decree not inconsistent herewith. * * *

Application of cy pres was warranted in order to eliminate a Protestant-Gentile restriction in a trust

HOWARD SAVINGS INSTITUTION OF NEWARK v. PEEP

Supreme Court of New Jersey, 1961.
34 N.J. 494, 170 A.2d 39.

PROCTOR, J.

This appeal and cross appeal from a judgment of the Chancery Division primarily involve the question of whether that court properly applied the doctrine of *cy pres* to the terms of a trust established by the will of C. Edward McKinney, Jr. Mr. McKinney, a resident of the City of East Orange, died on October 21, 1957. His will, admitted to probate by the Surrogate of Essex County on November 6, 1957, designates the plaintiff, the Howard Savings Institution, as executor and provides in part as follows:

> "Thirtieth: I give and bequeath the sum of Fifty Thousand Dollars ($50,000) to Amherst College, an institution of learning, situate at Amherst, Massachusetts, to be held in trust to be used as a scholarship loan fund for deserving American born, Protestant, Gentile boys of good moral repute, not given to gambling, smoking, drinking or similar acts. (It being my thought that if a young man has enough funds to allow the waste of smoking, he certainly does not need help.) The money loaned from said fund is to be repaid to the fund at the earliest moment so that others may benefit from its use.
>
> * * * * * *
>
> "Thirty-third: All the rest, residue and remainder of my estate, real, personal and mixed, of whatsoever kind and wheresoever situate, of which I shall die seized or possessed, I give, devise and bequeath unto Amherst College aforesaid to be held on the same trusts as mentioned in paragraph Thirtieth aforesaid."

The charter of Amherst College provides that "no student shall be refused admission to, or denied any of the privileges, honors, or degrees of said College, on account of the religious opinions he may entertain." On June 7, 1958 the Board of Trustees of Amherst College adopted a resolution stating that it believed acceptance of a trust discriminating among students on religious grounds would contravene the letter and spirit of the charter and the policy of the college. Accordingly, the Board declined to accept the trust funds unless the Protestant-Gentile restriction was eliminated from the terms of the trust. Plaintiff-executor thereupon instituted this action to obtain judicial construction of paragraphs Thirty and Thirty-three of Mr. McKinney's will and conformable instructions. It joined as defendants the Board of Trustees of Amherst, the Attorney General of New Jersey, and the next-of-kin of the testator.

The Chancery Division, applying the doctrine of *cy pres*, entered a judgment excluding the words "Protestant" and "Gentile" from paragraph Thirty of the will and ordering the executor to turn the trust funds over to Amherst to be administered in accordance with the remaining terms and conditions of the will. * * *

This brings us to the merits of the case. No one urges on this appeal that the Protestant-Gentile restriction or its enforcement by the court offends public policy or the Fourteenth Amendment to the Federal Constitution. Hence, we have no occasion to express a view as to those issues. * * *

We first consider whether the Chancery Division should have applied the doctrine of *cy pres* to the terms of the trust. The doctrine of *cy pres* is a judicial mechanism for the preservation of a charitable trust when accomplishment of the particular purpose of the trust becomes impossible, impracticable or illegal. In such a situation if the settlor manifested an intent to devote the trust to a charitable purpose more general than the frustrated purpose, a court, instead of allowing the trust to fail, will apply the trust funds to a charitable purpose as nearly as possible to the particular purpose of the settlor. * * * Three observations about the doctrine may aid analysis of its applicability to the facts of the present case. First, the term "general charitable intent" ordinarily used by courts articulating the doctrine does not require an intention to benefit charity generally. It requires only a charitable purpose which is broader than the particular purpose the effectuation of which is impossible, impracticable or illegal. * * * Second, the inquiry "did the settlor manifest a general charitable intent" is just another way of asking "would he have wanted the trust funds devoted to a like charitable purpose, or would he have wanted them withdrawn from charitable channels." * * * So stated, it can be seen that *cy pres* is an intent-enforcing doctrine. But it is well to keep in mind that it is a surmise rather than an actual intent which the courts enforce through application of the doctrine. Rarely does a settlor contemplate the possible nonfulfillment of his precise purpose. Therefore, the court must make an educated guess based on the trust instrument and relevant extrinsic evidence as to what he would have intended had be been aware of the contingency which has frustrated the exact effectuation of his expressed intent. * * * And third, recognizing the social benefit deriving from the devotion of property to charitable purposes, courts ascertaining a settlor's surmised intent are guided by the policy of preserving charitable trusts whenever possible and by the established presumption against partial intestacy. * * *

Similar to, but distinct from, *ey pres* is the doctrine of deviation from the terms of a trust. Applicable to private as well as charitable trusts, the doctrine of deviation comes into play when compliance with an administrative provision of the trust is impossible, illegal or in conflict with the essential purpose of the trust. * * * In such a situation, a court, pursuant to its general equity power, may allow modification of the provision. The doctrine is commonly applied, for example, to appoint a substituted trustee when the trustee designated by the settlor cannot or will not serve. * * * Essential to application of the doctrine of deviation is a finding that the term of the trust to be deviated from is an administrative one—that is, that it is not essential to fulfillment of the settlor's scheme. * * * This finding, in turn, depends on an intepretation of the settlor's intent. Ultimately, therefore, applicability of the doctrine of deviation, like the doctrine of *cy pres*, depends on what the court concludes the settlor would have wanted to happen if he were aware of the contingency which has made the exact effectuation of his expressed intent impossible.

With the above principles in mind, we return to the question of whether the Chancery Division should have disposed of the trust funds in the present case as it did.

We first consider the next-of-kin's contention that the doctrines of *cy pres* and deviation are inapplicable to the trust established by Mr. McKinney's will and that therefore the Chancery Division should have declared an intestacy. The next-of-kin's initial argument is that the bequest provided for in paragraphs Thirty and Thirty-three is not a charitable trust. They do not quarrel with the well-settled proposition that a trust for the advancement of learning is charitable. * * * Instead, they rely on the rule that to be characterized as charitable, a trust, regardless of its purpose, must encompass a sufficient number of beneficiaries to warrant a community interest. * * * In order to qualify for scholarship loan aid under Mr. McKinney's will, an Amherst student must be an American born Protestant-Gentile, not given to gambling, smoking, drinking or similar conduct. The next-of-kin assert, and ask us to take judicial notice of, the fact that in light of contemporary social conditions and *mores*, few if any Amherst students could comply with all of the trust requirements. Paragraph Thirty is not so worded that an isolated indulgence in the proscribed activities would result in disqualification. The testator said that the beneficiaries are to be boys "not given to" smoking, drinking, etc. "Given to" is ordinarily defined as meaning "disposed; inclined; addicted; * * * as, given to drink." Webster's New International Dictionary (2d ed. 1959). It implies at least some degree of regular indulgence. This construction is confirmed by the testator's parenthetical observation: "It being my thought that if a young man has enough funds to allow the waste of smoking, he certainly does not need help." It is obvious that the testator had in mind a person who is so committed to the act of smoking that it becomes a financial drain. Presumably, there are and will be at Amherst enough American born Protestant-Gentiles who do not regularly smoke, drink, gamble or engage in similar conduct, and who thus fall within the class of potential beneficiaries to justify categorizing the trust as charitable. We think that there is a sufficiently broad classification combined with Mr. McKinney's worthy purpose to warrant that appellation. See Clark, op. cit. supra, at p. 998. In any event, we have no information which would merit our taking judicial notice to the contrary. Accordingly, we hold that paragraphs Thirty and Thirty-three of Mr. McKinney's will establish a charitable trust.

The next-of-kin also argue that the Chancery Division erred in applying the doctrine of *cy pres* because the testator had no general charitable intention. He had, they say, a particular, unitary and inseparable purpose of benefiting Protestant students at Amherst; he was equally interested in Protestantism and the college. Therefore, they contend, since the testator's intent cannot be effectuated exactly as expressed, the funds must pass by intestate succession.

As mentioned above, in ascertaining the existence of a general charitable intent the court must determine whether the testator would have wanted the trust funds to remain devoted to a charitable purpose similar to, but not the same as, he provided, or to go to his next-of-kin. For the answer, we must first look to the will. * * *

The will in the present case strongly indicates that Mr. McKinney would not have wanted his next-of-kin to receive the trust funds. There is no provision in paragraphs Thirty and Thirty-three for reverter or a gift over if the trust bequest cannot be carried out in its exact terms. * * * Indeed, the residuary legatee is Amherst College under paragraph Thirty-three of the will. Moreover, the testator made specific legacies in varying amounts to twenty different persons, and did not include his next-of-kin. It is apparent from these detailed provisions that he executed his will after careful consideration and did not want his next-of-kin to share in his estate.

Evidence extrinsic to the will confirms the foregoing conclusion. The testator had no close relatives. * * * In a memorandum of instructions for the use of his scrivener in the preparation of the will the testator states in four separate places: "I have no immediate relatives, and any others omitted are either well-fixed financially or deliberately omitted for reasons very well known to themselves."

The aforementioned facts in and out of the will compel the conclusion that the Chancery Division properly found that the testator had a general charitable intent in the sense that he would have preferred to retain the charitable bequest—though in modified form—rather than leave the money to his cousins.

This brings us to the question of whether the Chancery Division correctly applied the doctrine of *cy pres*. First, we consider the executor's argument that the testator's intent can be fully effectuated by turning the funds over to another educational institution willing to honor the Protestant-Gentile restriction. This argument is based on the premise that the testator's intent was to benefit needy Protestant students, and that Amherst was designated trustee merely for administrative purposes. We think that the executor's argument is based on a faulty premise.

The very nature of the bequest indicates that the testator

was interested in benefiting Amherst as well as the recipients of scholarship loans. A donor interested in benefiting only students presumedly would make funds available to them regardless of what institution they wished to attend. * * * It is reasonable to conclude, therefore, that the creator of such a program intended to benefit the college identified therewith. That Mr. McKinney also intended to benefit the unknown student recipients of loans does not diminish at all his purpose of advancing the interests of Amherst. The foregoing shows, we think, that Amherst was designated trustee for more than mere administrative reasons. But this conclusion does not alone answer the executor's argument. Amherst will not accept the trust if it must enforce the Protestant-Gentile restriction. The question therefore is, would Mr. McKinney rather have the trust remain at Amherst with the restriction eliminated, or would he have preferred that the funds be turned over to another institution with the restriction? The facts indicate that Mr. McKinney was more interested in benefiting Amherst and its needy students than he was in Protestantism.

Mr. McKinney was a graduate of Amherst who continuously manifested an interest in the college. According to the records of contributions to the Alumni Fund which begin with the year 1932, the testator contributed to such fund in 1932 and every succeeding year until his death. In addition, he attended the 50th, 55th and 60th reunions of his graduating class in 1946, 1951 and 1956 respectively. (Amherst College has no record of the attendance of members of his class at previous reunions.) On the other hand, there is no evidence in the record that testator was a church-goer or actively interested in any church activities. In his will he made a bequest of $2,000 to the Board of Congregational Missions in memory of his father, who was born in Natal, and gave the Board the books in his home to be used in their Natal Mission. This modest bequest to the mission in memory of his father contrasts markedly with the sum left to Amherst ($50,000) and the designation of Amherst as legatee of the residuary estate (about $150,000). Additionally, the will contains no bequest to any church. Finally, the trust bequest is so worded that the Protestant-Gentile restriction is merely one of a series of qualifications to be met by recipients of scholarship loan aid. Accordingly, we conclude that Mr. McKinney's primary purpose was to advance the interests of Amherst by making available to it funds for needy students as well as to aid such students, and that to award the funds to another educational institution—if one could be found to enforce the Protestant-Gentile restriction—would contravene that purpose.

The executor further argues that Mr. McKinney's intent can be best effectuated by appointing a substituted trustee to administer the scholarship loan fund for Amherst students. We disagree because we find that it would be impracticable in the circumstances of this case to have a substituted trustee administer the trust for Amherst. In response to an inquiry from this court as to whether the college could cooperate with a substituted trustee, the Board of Trustees of Amherst adopted and forwarded to us, without objection from any party to this appeal, a resolution which states in pertinent part:

> "the policy of Amherst College would be to avoid any involvement whatsoever in the administration of the trust in question. Specifically, the College would in no way participate in identifying, evaluating, or selecting persons who might be beneficiaries of the trust; the College would not use its facilities to publicize the trust or otherwise bring its existence to the attention of present or future students; the College would neither solicit nor serve as a depository of scholarship applications; the College would not refer its students or other persons to the trust administrator; the College would decline to serve as an intermediary between the trust administrator and potential or actual candidates for benefits under the trust; the College would not at the behest of the trust administrator provide information concerning the scholastic achievement, character, or financial status of any student or applicant for admission. Upon a student's direct request, the College would provide information concerning that student, so far as that information may be readily available in the College's records and so far as its disclosure is consistent with general policies bearing upon confidentiality of the records. A person to whom financial aid has been granted by an outside organization, individual, or trustee would be neither advantaged nor disadvantaged in respect of his becoming or remaining a student at Amherst College."

It is clear from the above-cited resolution that Amherst believes it cannot under its charter cooperate in the administration of the trust if its benefits are confined to Protestant-Gentile students.

Without Amherst's cooperation the administration of this trust would be so impracticable as to defeat the general purpose of the testator. The substituted trustee would have to be a qualified educator with experience in the allocation of scholarship funds. Even if such a willing trustee could be found, the practical disadvantages are numerous. There would be no feasible way in which the scholarship fund could be used to aid students who are seeking to enter Amherst. Often, the availability of scholarship aid will affect the decision of a needy student to attend a particular college. It would be most difficult for a substituted trustee to know who was applying or considering applying for entrance to Amherst without the cooperation of the college. Thus a class of students and the college would be denied the benefit of what must have been one of the purposes of the trust. If the funds are made available only to matriculated students, the trustee would still face well-nigh insuperable obstacles. He would have to obtain detailed information about a scholarship applicant. Whether an applicant was being considered for other aid by the college, for example, would obviously be relevant to a decision to award him aid from the McKinney trust. Then, the award of a scholarship loan involves a delicate weighing of the financial needs of the applicant, his scholastic standing, and his development potential. Moreover, in providing a fund to aid "deserving" boys at Amherst, the testator manifested an essential reliance on the personal discretion of Amherst as trustee. For an applicant is "deserving" in a meaningful sense only in relation to the competency and worth of others who seek to enter or remain at the college. Surely Amherst would not violate the trust if it denied aid to a specific applicant or admitted student if it determined another applicant was more "deserving." Mr. McKinney, therefore, must have contemplated that the merits of loan applications be judged according to those relative standards which Amherst itself may establish to further its conception of what individuals are worthy of membership in its student body. We are unable to understand how any trustee without Amherst's cooperation can possibly make the comparative value judgment which Mr. McKinney had in mind. Finally, once an award is made, the trustee must have some policing mechanism to assure that the recipient continues to meet the trust qualifications. Determination of whether he deserved a loan renewal would realistically require access to college records and consultations with college instructors and administrators. The above factors clearly show that without the college's cooperation it would be impracticable, if not impossible, for a substituted trustee to administer the scholarship loan fund for Amherst students.

The executor argues that to apply *cy pres* because Amherst will not cooperate with a substituted trustee would be to allow the college by its own action to vary the testator's intent. It cites the rule that a trustee cannot by his own act produce changed conditions which frustrate the donor's intention and still claim the gift. * * * In the present case, the refusal of Amherst to accept and administer the trust with the Protestant-Gentile restriction was not merely to serve trustee convenience. The refusal was prompted by the college charter which expressly prohibits the college from denying any privileges of the school to a student because of the religious opinion he may entertain. Clearly, scholarship loan aid is one of those privileges. It seems to us therefore that in the sense required for the application of *cy pres*, it is impossible for Amherst to accept and administer the trust exactly as desired by the testator. It is as equally clear that college cooperation in the administration of the trust by a substituted trustee would be an indirect violation of the college's charter.

In view of the fact that Mr. McKinney had a general charitable intent, we hold that the bequest does not fail and the funds do not pass to the next-of-kin. And, in view of the additional facts that Amherst conceives it to be inconsistent with its charter to administer or assist in the administration of the trust so long as its funds are available only to Protestants, and that it would be impracticable for a substituted trustee properly to administer the trust, we hold that the testator's intent can be effectuated as nearly as possible by striking the Protestant-Gentile restriction and turning the funds over to Amherst to be administered in accordance with the remaining terms and conditions of the trust. Of course, striking the Protestant-Gentile restriction does not mean that Protestant-Gentile students will be excluded as beneficiaries of the trust. Any Amherst students who meet the other qualifications set forth in the will will be eligible for scholarship loan aid. Accordingly, the judgment of the Chancery Division is affirmed.

NOTES

1. "Very briefly stated, when a charitable purpose cannot be fulfilled according to its terms, equity will attempt to do the next best similar charitable thing. This is the *cy pres* doctrine. Saletri v. Clark, 13 Wis. 2d 325, 108 N.W.2d 548 (1961).

2. A gift to a charitable or eleemosynary corporation does not create a trust in a technical sense. Where a will provided that a loan fund be "turned over" to a college, the court held that a gift not a trust was intended. "The expression 'turned over' is clearly indicative of the relinquishment of any control

by the executor." *In re* Berry's Estate, 29 Wis. 2d 506, 139 N.W.2d 72 (1966).

3. Under trust doctrine of deviation, no rights of college donors were invaded when Fenn College transferred its facilities to the newly created Cleveland State University and transformed itself into an educational foundation which would support worthy educational, literary, charitable and scientific endeavors. Fenn College v. Nance, 4 Ohio Misc. 183, 210 N.E.2d 418 (1965).

4. "Where a literal compliance with the condition [of a trust] has become impossible *by reason of circumstances over which the devisee or legatee had no control, and through no fault on his part,* he is held to be entitled to take the gift,— the condition imposed by the testator being deemed to be satisfied by performance as nearly as possible, or *cy pres.*" *In re* Costalo's Will, 167 Misc. 755, 4 N.Y.S.2d 665 (1938).

5. *Cy pres* will not be applied by the courts where the trustee simply chooses to vary the intent of a bequest. In a case involving the United States Military Academy at West Point, a sum of $300,000 was left to the Academy to construct a memorial building to cost not less than $300,000 for use as a meeting place and lodging for graduates of West Point. The Military Academy sought the application of *cy pres* to use the money to construct a wing on a building since it was claimed the funds were insufficient for a separate building and the designated grounds were to be used for other purposes. The United States Court of Appeals for the District of Columbia denied *cy pres*. "The probable insufficiency of the bequest for the construction of a separate building does not, in the circumstances here, justify the authorization of its use for constructing an attachment or wing to a different building; for Mrs. Crozier did not require, or even anticipate, that the total cost of the separate building provided for by her would be covered by her bequest. She stipulated that the building cost not less than $300,000, but by no means did she restrict its cost to that sum. Plainly she expected the United States to supplement her bequest should it be too small to construct the separate building she specified. This shows, we think, that she did not contemplate or anticipate that her money would be used for an attachment or wing to another building, should it be insufficient to defray the cost of a separate memorial.

In view of the clear intention on the part of the testatrix, the performance of her plan for a separate building has not

become impossible or impracticable merely because the bequest
may not be large enough to cover the cost of the sort of building the Government would be willing to construct. Either impossibility or impracticability of literal compliance with the
donor's plan is indispensably necessary if *cy pres* is to be applied." Connecticut College v. United States, 276 F.2d 491
(1960).

CHAPTER 6

STUDENT FEES AND TUITION

BASIS FOR FEES AND TUITION

The importance of student fees as a source of revenue for colleges varies greatly among institutions. Considerable variation exists among public colleges both within and among states, while private colleges, generally operating without comparable public tax support, find it necessary to charge a vast range of student tuition and other fees [1] in order to operate. These fees are usually accepted by students and parents as a part of getting a college education, thus little legal controversy has arisen contesting fee assessment practices. Of course, where private colleges are involved and *laissez faire* education is based on supply and demand, the student has little legal redress unless substantial "state participation" can be imputed to the school.

On the other hand, the levy of tuition fees and charges at public colleges and universities has for years been a source of contention among educators and legislators. The notion that "every man will appreciate his education more if he contributes monetarily to it" has been popular with legislatures for years. With tax revenue always at a premium, the ethic of "paying for one's education" is usually exposed as a facade for remedying revenue needs without additional taxation. In this regard, tuition charges to attend public institutions have at times been regarded as taxes, and quite loathsome and regressive taxes at that. Where tuition rates are flat levies, assessed against all students uniformly, the poor student is required to pay as much as the wealthy student; then the burden of acquiring a higher education is much more onerous to the poor student. Does the state have the responsibility to equalize the opportunity of all students in providing public higher education? At what level do tuition and other fees become a deterrent to education of the total public and result in only the middle and upper class obtaining the educational advantages? Can a state deny a public service such as an education on the sole basis of the economic condition of the recipient? These are legal questions which may be answered in the years to come. However, to date, the courts have not at-

---

1. Colleges often charge student "activity fees" and other rates which are levied uniformly across the student body. While these fees may not be *de jure* tuition, they are *de facto* tuition.

tuned themselves to such problems and have been content to let legislatures and administrative agencies make the decisions bearing on these areas. While these complex issues have not been directly attacked, the courts have handed down several decisions describing the power of universities to levy fees and to charge both resident and nonresident tuition.

INCIDENTAL FEES

Whether incidental fees can be charged and collected as a condition precedent to entrance to a state university, depends to a large degree on individual state laws.[2] In a state where tuition to a state university is free, the board of regents cannot charge a fee and require its payment as a condition precedent to entering the university.[3] A court in Kansas held that the Board of Regents of the University of Kansas had no power to collect a fee of five dollars from each student for the use of the library.[4] Kansas statute provided for free admission to the University for all Kansas residents. The court found the Regents had no power to raise a fund by charging fees for the use of the library unless expressly authorized by law. Such authorization was not given.

The courts, in some states, however, have held that where a university board is not prohibited by law to do so, it has the power to levy and collect incidental fees for the heating and lighting of public halls and rooms of the university where no provision is made for such to be done at the expense of the state.[5] This view is contrary to most precedents governing public agencies, whereby the courts have held that a public agency's actions are *ultra vires,* if it acts without either the express or implied consent of the legislature.

In some states with prohibitions against "tuition," courts have upheld special fees for the matriculation and use of the student union,[6] as well as for the hospital, laboratory, and athletic fees.[7]

---

2. 15 Am. Jur. 2d 605, 606.

3. Connell v. Gray, 33 Okla. 591, 127 P. 417 (1912).

4. Kansas *ex rel.* Attorney General v. Board of Regents of University of Kansas *et al.,* 55 Kan. 389, 40 P. 656 (1895).

5. State *ex rel.* Priest v. Regents of the University of Wisconsin, 54 Wis. 159, 11 N.W. 472 (1882).

6. State *ex rel.* Veeder v. State Board of Education, 97 Mont., 121, 33 P.2d 516 (1934).

7. State v. Regents of University System, 179 Ga. 210, 175 S.E. 567 (1934).

NONRESIDENT TUITION

What the courts have decided to date regarding tuition is rather peripheral and only outlines the broad area of education equality. The traditional position of the courts has been to require only that public institutions not unconstitutionally discriminate in the assessment and levy of tuition fees. As early as 1927, Spencer observed that:

> Most tax supported higher educational institutions in the United States discriminate among their students in the matter of tuition fees, basing this discrimination on residence of students; the purpose being to collect an additional fee from non-residents.[8]

Most states require a student to be domiciled in the state where he is attending college for from six to twelve months prior to enrollment in order to be classified as a "resident" and thereby avoid a higher nonresident tuition fee. These waiting periods have been justified on essentially two grounds: (1) restrains a heavy influx of nonresidents from entering the state to take advantage of a state benefit, thus providing greater access to residents where enrollments are limited; and (2) seeks to distinguish between residents and nonresidents on the basis of the contribution made to the state through payment of taxes.[9] Interwoven with these two purposes is the idea that the taxpayers of state *A* should not furnish benefits to a resident of state *B,* if state *A* receives no benefit from the expenditure. Such a situation transpires where the student of a particular states goes to another to obtain his education with no intention of ultimately living there. This is only one facet of the entire problem of educational and economic spillover which plagues all states, and is particularly acute for those states with static or decreasing populations. Recognizing this dilemma most states have erected tuition barriers to reduce the out-flow of state fiscal and human resources.

Precedents to date indicate that the classification of students into two classes, resident and nonresident, for tuition purposes does not violate the rights of the nonresident student. An early California case served as the only precedent in this area until recently.[10] In this case, the court held that

8. Carlton E. Spencer, "The Legal Aspects of the Non-resident Tuition Fee," *Oregon Law Review,* Vol. 6, p. 332 (1927).

9. See Deborah F. Masters, "Non-resident Tuition Charged by State Universities in Review," *University of Missouri at Kansas City Law Review,* Vol. 38, p. 341 (1970).

10. Bryan v. Regents of University of California, 188 Cal. 559, 205 P. 1071 (1922).

306   COLLEGE AND UNIVERSITY LAW

state classification of nonresident students for tuition and admission fee purposes was neither arbitrary nor unreasonable and did not violate the students' rights under the California constitution. Another court, the Idaho Supreme Court, ruled on a similar case in 1960 and decided three essential questions.[11] First, it held that the State Board of Education acting as the Board of Trustees for Idaho State College had the legislatively delegated power to make reasonable rules and regulations regarding tuition. Second, the board could set higher tuition rates for out-of-state students than for in-state students, and third, the board's rule which required that a student classified as nonresident on initial enrollment to remain so classified regardless of his residence or domicile during his entire career at the college, was arbitrary, capricious and unreasonable. In other words, in the last provision, the court found that a student was entitled to reclassification if he, in fact, changed his domicile during his career at the college. While this court did, to some extent, refine the issue it did not change the prevailing view that nonresidents can be classified separately and charged higher tuition rates.

The Supreme Court of Colorado reached the same conclusion in 1964.[12] Here the student sued the Regents of the University of Colorado claiming that statutes classifying students as "in-state" and "out-of-state" and charging higher tuition to the latter violated the federal constitution, to-wit: equal protection and due process clauses of the Fourteenth Amendment; the commerce clause, Article 1, section 8(3); the privileges and immunities of citizens clause, Article IV, section 2; along with Article V, section 25 and Article II, section 3 of the Colorado Constitution. The court said:

> It is our considered view that this classification is not arbitrary or unreasonable . . . . We find no basis whatever for the contention . . . that the statute violates the United States Constitution which delegates power to the Congress to regulate commerce.

Since this relatively recent decision, the Supreme Court of the United States has handed down several decisions which have opened the area of nonresident tuition to new consideration. One of the cases involved a nonresident voting restric-

11. Newman v. Graham *et al.*, 82 Idaho 90, 349 P.2d 716, 83 A.L.R.2d 492 (1960).
12. Landwehr v. Regents of University of Colorado, 156 Colo. 1, 396 P.2d 451 (1964).

tion on servicemen in Texas.[13] The Supreme Court held that a state could impose reasonable residence voting requirements; however, it could not deny servicemen the opportunity of ever converting from nonresidence to resident status. By such a continuing denial the Texas Constitution imposed an invidious discrimination. Along with this case, the Supreme Court held in *Shapiro v. Thompson* in 1969,[14] that a one-year waiting period provided for in-state welfare laws constituted an invidious discrimination denying equal protection of the law. Arguments by the state that welfare mothers receipt of welfare was a privilege, not a right, and that one-year residence requirement was reasonable since this is the length of time forming the cycle from payment of taxes to the receipt of services by the citizenry, were denied by the court. The court said:

> More fundamentally, a state may no more try to fence out those indigents who seek higher welfare benefits than it may try to fence out indigents generally. Implicit in any such distinction is the notion that indigents who enter a state with the hope of securing higher welfare did not take this consideration into account. But we do not perceive why a mother who is seeking to make a new life for herself and her children should be regarded as less deserving because she considers, among others [sic] factors, the level of a state's public assistance. *Surely such a mother is no less deserving than a mother who moves into a particular state in order to take advantage of its better educational facilities.*[15]

The Supreme Court has not yet sought to extend the welfare residence rule to education. Sometime after its determination in *Shapiro* the Supreme Court denied certiorari in the case of *Clarke v. Redeker*, a case dealing precisely with the question of the constitutionality of nonresident tuition.[16] If the court were going to declare dual classification of students unconstitutional, this would have been an excellent time to do it. In *Clarke*, a student in the law school of the State University of Iowa, claimed his being charged a nonresident

---

13. Carrington v. Rash, 380 U.S. 89, 85 S. Ct. 775, 13 L. Ed. 2d 675 (1965). A New York court held in 1947 that students could not be denied the right to vote if they had rejected their previous domicile and establish necessary residency requirements. Matter of Robbins v. Chamberlain, 297 N.Y. 108, 75 N.E.2d 617 (1947).

14. 393 U.S. 618 (1969).

15. *Ibid.*

16. 259 F. Supp. 117 (S.D. Iowa 1967), *aff'd*, 406 F.2d 883 (1969), *cert. denied*, 396 U.S. 862 (1969).

tuition fee violated the equal protection clause of the Fourteenth Amendment. Judge Stephenson of the federal district
court in Iowa found the regulation to be a reasonable one and
did not constitute an invidious class discrimination. The
judge's reasoning in this case was followed by United States
Court of Appeals, Eighth Circuit, held before Justices Ooster-
hout, Blackmun and Lay.[17] The court said:

> A substantial portion of the funds needed to operate
> the Regents' schools are provided by legislative appro-
> priation of funds raised by taxation of Iowa residents
> and property. Non-residents and their families generally
> make no similar contribution to the support of the schools.
> A reasonable additional tuition charge against non-resi-
> dent students which tends to make the tuition charge
> more nearly approximate the cost per pupil of the oper-
> ation of the schools does not constitute an unreasonable
> and arbitrary classification violative of equal protection.

STUDENT FEES FOR CAPITAL OUTLAY

One of the primary uses of student fees is for capital improvements, including acquisition of sites, buildings and equipment. Funds for capital outlay are usually acquired through
borrowing or from legislative appropriations. Since it is extremely difficult for a state to finance large capital projects
on a pay-as-you-go basis, borrowing is usually involved. When
long-term borrowing is used as the means of financing it takes
one of two forms, either general obligation or revenue bonds.
General obligation bonds are secured with the full faith and
credit of the state and constitute a debt of the state. Revenue
bonds are secured by pledging the revenues from the facility
for the payment of the principal and interest on the bonds.
Revenue bonds are used by the public to finance toll roads, toll
bridges, parking lots, college dormitories, golf courses and so
forth. Sometimes civic auditoriums or athletic facilities used
by public colleges, public schools, and municipalities are financed jointly by use of revenue bonds.[18]

Revenue bonds are attractive to college administrators for
several reasons:

---

17. Johns v. Redeker, 406 F.2d 878 (1969). See also Kirk v. Board of
Regents of University of California, 273 Cal. App. 2d 463, 78 Cal. Rptr.
260 (1969), *appeal dismissed for want of a substantial federal question,*
396 U.S. 554.

18. Dewey H. Stollar, *Managing School Indebtedness*, The Interstate
Printers and Publishers, Inc., 1967, p. 5.

(a) Revenue bonds are not included in state statutory debt limitations,

(b) Their use permits quick action by the college, since voter approval is not required to authorize them,

(c) Participants or users pay for the bonds, a good selling point to the public.[19]

On the other hand, many of the good points of revenue bonds are outweighed by certain fiscal and philosophical detriments. Fiscally, interest rates on revenue bonds are almost always higher than general obligation bonds, because they have a greater element of risk. Revenue bonds in many cases serve as a loophole to bypass constitutional debt limitations; whether such loopholes are desirable in view of contrary constitutional mandates is both a legal and moral question.[20] Philosophically, the logic which supports the issuance and payment of revenue bonds can strike to the heart of the entire nature of public education. In most cases, prinicpal and interest is paid through charging the user, the student, a fee. Dormitories, dining halls, student service buildings and parking lots are all examples of "self-liquidating" facilities, the cost of which can be passed on directly to the student. The fundamental question is, of course, how far can a public institution go in this direction before it assumes the vestiges of a private enterprise and, in fact, becomes fiscally quasi-public or private. The impact of these fees and others can be of such magnitude on a student's personal finances as to discourage the enrollment of students with less financial ability, the very students the public universities were originally designed to attract.

Generally, the governing boards of state universities do not have the power to issue revenue bonds and assess student fees without either express or implied authority from the legislature. This is not the case, however, in constitutionally independent universities such as the University of Minnesota.[21] The Supreme Court of Minnesota has held that the board of regents has the authority to construct dormitory facilities and to pay for them with revenue from net earnings on the dormitory, earnings from the university press, and other rentals. The court said that with revenue bonds:

---

19. *Ibid.*

20. See Thomas E. Blackwell, *College Law*, American Council on Education, 1961, pp. 259-261.

21. Fanning *et al.* v. University of Minnesota *et al.*, 183 Minn. 222, 236 N.W. 217 (1931).

310   COLLEGE AND UNIVERSITY LAW

. . . there is no attempt to pledge university or state property. There is no individual liability or state or board or university money obligation sought to be created. If the board finds this a convenient way of dealing with money coming to it and subject to its disposal, it may make use of it.[22]

With the great influx of students after World War II, the University of Missouri faced a student housing shortage typical of all state universities. The Supreme Court of Missouri viewed this situation and in a 1946 case held that the Curators of the University of Missouri had the implied power to issue Dormitory Revenue Bonds.[23] More recently, the Missouri Supreme Court upheld the authority of the Curators of the University of Missouri to issue revenue bonds to construct parking facilities.[24]

Even where universities are given authority through statute to construct buildings by means of revenue bonds, attack can and has been made on the grounds that the university is in fact using the credit of the state to issue bonds but is bypassing the state debt limitation. In one such instance, the Wisconsin legislature created the Wisconsin University Building Corporation in order to provide badly needed student housing and other facilities.[25] The corporation, a holding company, was to build the facilities through the use of revenue bonds and then rent the facilities to the university to retire the debt. The university gained the revenues for rental of the facilities primarily through student fees. The Supreme Court of Wisconsin held the state had not lent its credit since there was no legally enforceable obligation on the part of the state to pay the obligations of the building corporation. Theoretically, the building corporation could default on the revenue bonds without detriment to the state's bonding capacity.

The University of Washington was not so successful in a similar attempt to set up a building authority.[26] Although the authority was organized for much needed campus housing and improvements, the Supreme Court of Washington said:

22. *Ibid.*
23. State *ex rel.* Curators of University of Missouri v. McReynolds, 354 Mo. 1199, 193 S.W.2d 611 (1946).
24. State *ex rel.* Curators of University of Missouri v. Neill, 397 S.W.2d 666 (Mo. 1966).
25. State v. Giessel, 271 Wis. 15, 72 N.W.2d 577 (1955).
26. State v. Yelle, 46 Wash. 2d 166, 289 P.2d 355 (1955). A similar conclusion was reached in North Dakota, Wilder v. Murphy, 56 N.D. 436, 218 N.W. 156 (1928).

"When we strip the plan down to fundamentals, we find that it is not a leasing arrangement between landlord and tenant, but the installment purchase, by the state, of certain buildings and facilities . . . ." This case, however, had a different twist in that the rental payments were to be made "with state moneys raised by taxation . . ." all of which exceeded the state constitutional debt limitation.[27]

Where courts have denied the use of revenue bonds as violating constitutional debt limits they have generally concluded that revenues gained, such as student fees, from rental of state property are as much a part of the state funds as if the funds were derived from any other tax source. In following this position, the Oklahoma Supreme Court in taking a somewhat different position toward television authorities in 1954 than it did with regard to dormitories in 1933 said:

> When a dollar comes into the possession and ownership of the state, it is of no more or no less value to the state and to its citizens because it comes from the cigarette tax or the gasoline tax . . . or from the rental of lands owned by the state. We consider it beyond question that the state and the people of the state have the power, by constitutional provision, to protect all funds belonging to the state from future debt.[28]

The Oklahoma Supreme Court had previously in 1933, upheld the constitutionality of an act by the state legislature authorizing the Board of Regents of the Oklahoma Agricultural and Mechanical University to issue $450,000 in revenue bonds for dormitory construction.[29]

Required Residence of Students. Any time the state requires individuals to conduct their lives in a certain manner, constitutional protections of the individual are brought to the forefront. Required dormitory residence of students to gain revenues to amortize revenue bonds is no exception. Where a college requires students to live in college dormitories in order to gain additional revenues, a rub is sometimes created not only between the student and college but also between business interests in the community and the college. In the latter instance, persons in communities with public colleges, owning boarding houses, apartments and the like claim that the power of the state is being exerted in a man-

27. State v. Yelle, *supra.*
28. Application of Oklahoma Educational Television Authority, 272 P.2d 1027 (Okla. 1954).
29. Baker v. Carter, 165 Okla. 116, 25 P.2d 747 (1933).

ner which deprives them of their livelihood. The precedent to date indicates that colleges have little to fear from such constitutional actions by private property owners. The leading case [30] on this particular topic was decided in favor of a state university which had required undergraduate students to live in housing facilities provided by the university. In this case, a federal district court in Oklahoma held that the state, by virtue of its interest in education, well-being, morals, health, safety and convenience of its youth has the power to provide university housing facilities for students and has the attendant power to promulgate over-all rules providing for payment of the facilities.

The other question involves the constitutional rights of the individual student. Does the state impair his constitutional guarantees by requiring him to live in a state owned university dormitory? The courts have generally held for the university; [31] however, recently the issue has been redefined by one court.[32] In a 1969 Louisiana case, a federal district court held that a regulation which required girls 21 years of age and younger to live in dormitories for the sole purpose of amortizing revenue bonds, while other students were allowed to live off campus violated the girls' constitutional rights. The court reasoned that requiring only these girls to live in the dormitories and, thereby pay for the facility, was an unconstitutional classification amounting to denial of equal protection. The burden of the expense for the dormitory was not uniformly spread among all students but fell on the girls. The college did not attempt to show that the dormitory residence of the girls was required for their well-being but instead justified their residence solely on the basis of providing revenue for the college housing system.

30. Pyeatte v. Board of Regents of University of Oklahoma et al., 102 F. Supp. 407 (1951), aff'd, 72 S. Ct. 567 (1952).

31. See Chapter 8, Pratz v. Louisiana Polytechnic Institute, 316 F. Supp. 872, aff'd, 91 S. Ct. 1252 (1971).

32. Mollere v. Southeastern Louisiana College, 304 F. Supp. 826 (E.D. La. 1969). Compare this case with Pratz v. Louisiana Polytechnic Institute, in Chapter 8.

Board of Regents has no power to collect
student library fee

STATE EX REL. LITTLE v. REGENTS OF UNIVERSITY

Supreme Court of Kansas, 1895.
55 Kan. 389, 40 P. 656.

ALLEN, J. This action is prosecuted in the name of the state, on the relation of the attorney general, against the regents of the university, the chancellor, and the treasurer, to oust them from the exercise of the power, which it is alleged they have usurped, of charging the students who are residents of the state an annual library fee of five dollars, and a graduating fee of five dollars, and of excluding such students who fail to pay the library fee from the use of the books. It is alleged that the university is a corporation, and that enforcing the payment of such fees by residents of the state is an assumption of unwarranted corporate powers by the regents; that the statute makes admission to the university free to all residents of the state. It is admitted that the regents have been collecting such library fee, and claim the right to do so, and also the right to exclude students who refuse to pay from the use of the library. * * *

A further objection is made to the prosecution of this action in the name of the state, on the ground that the imposition of a library fee on students in the university is in the nature of levying a tax; that it affects not the state, but the individual students; that they have an adequate remedy, if the tax be unlawful, by injunction; and that the attorney general may not use the name of the state merely for the purpose of protecting their private interests. The fee imposed is not a tax, within the ordinary meaning of the term. It cannot be collected in the ordinary manner of collecting taxes. It is not expressly provided for by any law of the state. It is at least doubtful whether the students are so united in interest that they could join in an action to restrain the collection of the fee. Whether they could do so or not, however, we are clearly of the opinion that the conduct of the university is a matter of state concern; that the public maintains the institution, not for the special advantages conferred by it on particular individuals, but for the great advantage accruing to the state by reason of the maintenance of a great institution of learning within its borders, and the diffusion of knowledge and advancement of the people in literature and art. All its people gain through the instrumentality of this great institution. It is to attain these public ends that the state lavishes money, raised by taxation, on the institution. It is because of the interest of the state in the education of its youth that the university was created at all. Having created a university, the state is directly concerned in its being conducted in accordance with the provisions of law. It is directly concerned in the education of the students. It is directly concerned when the youth of the state are, for any unwarranted cause, excluded from it. The legislature has undertaken to open the way to a higher education to the poorest of the youth of the state. Whenever the board of regents places any unwarranted obstacle in the way of the accomplishment of that end, they affect and oppose the public interest.

This disposes of the objections to the form of the action. But little need be said on the merits of the case. Section 11, c. 258, Laws 1889, which was in force at the time the action was brought, reads: "Admission into the university shall be free to all the inhabitants of the state, but a sufficient fee shall be required from nonresident applicants, to be fixed by the board of regents, and no person shall be debarred on account of age, race or sex." Notwithstanding the apparently plain provisions of this section, it is contended that the board of regents may yet collect a reasonable fee for the wear and tear of the books; that the word "free" must be taken with qualifications; that in the nature of things there must be rules and regulations; that each and every student cannot be permitted to occupy the chancellor's seat at his desk, or any other place in the university he may choose, at his own sweet will, but that the regents and the chancellor have a right to make proper regulations; and that the fee imposed is no more than is reasonable to preserve and protect the library. We fully agree with so much of the claim of the learned counsel as asserts the right of the regents and the chancellor to make all necessary and proper rules and regulations for the orderly management of the school, the preservation of discipline therein, and the protection of its property, but that it may require the payment of money as a condition precedent to the use of the property of the state is another and a different claim, with which we do not agree. If the regents may collect five dollars for the use of the library, why may they not collect also for the use of the rooms of the building and of its furniture? Why may they not impose fees for walking in the campus, or for the payment of instructors? All these things have cost money. There are expenses incurred by the state on behalf of the students in connection with every department of the school. If they may collect for one thing, it is not apparent why they may not collect for another. It is suggested that supplies are furnished in the laboratories for the use of students, which are destroyed, that vessels and implements may be broken, and that the students should certainly be required to pay for these things. No question of that kind, however, is now presented, and express provision therefor is made by chapter 226, Laws 1895. The library is provided for permanent use. Each volume with proper care may be used by a great number of students, and for a long term of years. The library as a whole is subjected to wear and tear, but only in the same manner as furniture and other properties furnished by the state. The buildings, furniture, library, and apparatus, as well as the services of the faculty, are furnished and paid for by the state. These, we hold, under the provisions of the statute quoted, are free to all residents of the state who are entitled to admission into the university. The regents have no power to raise a fund to be managed and disposed of at their discretion by charging fees for the use of the library, or under any other claim for any other purpose, unless expressly authorized to do so by law. Judgment of ouster will be entered in accordance with the prayer of the petition. All the justices concurring.

NOTES

THE ROLE OF STUDENT FEES IN THE FINANCE OF HIGHER EDUCATION

A Statement of the State Board of Regents of Iowa
May 12, 1967

1. The state university is an instrument of the open democratic society. Its basic function is to open up opportunity to young men and women of all socio-economic classes, and in so doing to provide an abundant supply of educated people to serve our economy and our society.

One of the most significant American innovations and one of the most cherished American institutions has been free public education. The idea is well established that education at the elementary and secondary levels should be free to all regardless of socio-economic class. Since the founding of our public universities and especially since the land-grant movement starting in 1862, under Abraham Lincoln, it has been equally accepted that public higher education should be open to all at low cost. This tradition has been especially strong in the states west of the Alleghenies and is now spreading rapidly to the states of the Northeast.

The practice of charging tuition, even at the presently moderate rates, has emerged not from principle—educators have consistently opposed them—but simply because finance from tax sources has not been adequate to take care of university enrollments and to prevent deterioration of educational quality. Increased tuitions have been charged only as a last resort to protect the integrity of the education offered.

2. Even though tuitions at state universities are, on the whole, moderate, the present costs to students and their families are substantial. The costs include board and room, books and supplies, travel, clothing, and incidentals. These average $1,500 to $2,000 a year. Another cost is the loss of income because the student is not employed full time. This cost is as much as $4,000 to $6,000 a year. Any increase in tuition is on top of an already heavy cost, and would increase what is already a heavy burden to families and their student-children.

3. While a student loan system with liberal loans, long repayment periods, and low interest is surely an important part of any system for the finance of students, it is not socially desirable to load too much of the cost on students by means of loans—certainly not to substitute student loans for tax support of higher education. The students who need loans are those from families of modest income. It is neither equitable nor socially desirable to expect this group of young people to start out life with substantial indebtedness. The problem is compounded when two young people with indebtedness marry. The loan system is especially undesirable for women who are reluctant to go into debt knowing that the indebtedness may be a burden to a future husband.

The effort to shift costs from taxpayers to student borrowers is in reality only a shift from one kind of taxation to another. The new taxation in the form of repayment of loans places a special burden on those who have come from low-income backgrounds and need special help in starting out on their careers rather than the handicap of debt repayment.

Indebtedness at the end of a college career has the effect of undesirably restricting educational and vocational choices. A student with several thousand dollars of indebtedness tends to avoid low-paying vocations like teaching or the ministry, and he is often not in a position to enter the Peace Corps or the Job Corps or advanced study. To keep open the freedoms of occupational choice which is part of the American heritage, it would be best to use student loans with moderation and prudence.

4. It is often argued that those who benefit from education should pay a large part of the cost. In fact they do, because the burden of the cost of board and room, books, etc., as well as the loss of income while in college, falls largely on them. But society-at-large benefits from the nurses, engineers, scientists, teachers, physicians and the like who are the product of our universities. Society-at-large also benefits from the broad cultural advancement which derives from higher education, and it benefits from keeping the doors of opportunity wide open to its young people even if some do not or cannot take advantage of the opportunity. The broad social benefits are surely sufficient to justify public and philanthropic support of most of the cost of higher education. This has long been recognized not only by the traditionally low tuition in state universities but also by the practice of providing scholarships and other grants to help low-income students meet not only tuitions but other college costs as well.

5. Universities should clearly be responsive to the needs of the society they serve, and everyone recognizes the important role of legislatures in determining the amount of state funds to be invested in higher education. However, one of the fundamental principles of the governance of universities is that they should be free of direct political influence. That is why state universities are not part of state government but rather are governed by separate lay boards, and it is why universities are conducted as semi-autonomous organizations—sometimes as corporations. An important element in the freedom of the university is diverse sources of revenue of which one is state appropriation, and others are fees, federal grants, foundation gifts, and private donations.

Historically, the governing boards of state universities have controlled their own fees and their own fund-raising from non-state sources. These boards are close in touch with financial needs and are in a position to deal with a variety of donors. Any other arrangement has been found through experience to erode away the freedom of the University. Iowa has a superb record of maintaining the freedom of its Universities. This policy has resulted in three excellent institutions which have been consistently operated with concern for the interests of the people of the state. To encroach upon the freedom of the Universities at this time, by the Legislature's taking over in effect the function of fee assessment, would be a serious backward step.

6. It is sometimes argued that if private colleges can charge high tuitions, state universities should do the same. In reality there is no inconsistency between the two practices. It is only because open opportunity is provided in the state institutions that it is defensible for the private institutions to charge a large share of instructional costs to the students. Our dual system of education is highly desirable and the two parts are complementary. The job of the state university is to keep opportunity open to everyone who can benefit from higher education; the job of private education is to serve special constituencies, to assure diversity of control over higher education, to experiment, to set standards, and the like. Private education is free to do these things precisely because public education exists to keep the doors of opportunity open to all. This does not mean that the public institution must be an inferior institution—only that it must be an "opportunity institution."

7. The proposal to raise fees drastically for students at Iowa Universities would discriminate against Iowa students as compared with those of other states. The fees for Iowa students are already high relative to those of most comparable Midwestern state institutions. In view of the relatively high fees at the three state universities in Iowa, further increases should be established only as a last resort. However, increased fees would be preferable to deterioration in the effectiveness of the three universities.

The most practical argument against the proposal is that it would cut the tax support of higher education below realistic levels. Higher education at this time needs solid increases in financial support from state appropriations, not only because the money is needed but because adequate state appropriations will help to attract needed supplemental funds from the federal government and private foundations.

State constitution is not violated by classification of nonresident students for tuition and fee purposes

BRYAN v. REGENTS OF UNIVERSITY OF CALIFORNIA

Supreme Court of California, 1922.
188 Cal. 559, 205 P. 1071.

WILBUR, J. The petitioner seeks a writ of mandate to compel the respondent to admit her to the University of California. The respondent is willing to admit her as a student providing she will pay the fee fixed by the respondent for nonresidents, amounting to $75 a semester. This refusal of the respondent is in accordance with section 1394½ of the Political Code and rules of the state board of regents adopted in accordance therewith. This section, adopted in 1921, reads as follows:

"An admission fee and rate of tuition fixed by the board of regents must be required of each nonresident student. The board of regents shall cause to be computed the actual cost to the university of maintaining one student in each of the respective courses of the several colleges for the period of one year. Each nonresident student shall be required to pay as the rate of tuition the sum provided for by the above computation for the particular course such student is following: Provided, that the maximum sum to be paid shall not exceed five hundred dollars: And provided, further, that such sum may be remitted in whole or in part in the case of graduate students in other than professional colleges and schools. A nonresident student as used in this section shall mean any person who has not for more than one year immediately preceding his entrance into the university been a bona fide resident of the state of California." Stats. 1921, p. 541.

It is contended that this legislation and the rule of the board of regents adopted in pursuance thereof violates article 1, sections 11 and 21 of the Constitution of the state of California. These sections prohibit the granting of privileges or immunities to any citizen or class of citizens "which upon the same terms shall not be granted to all citizens." It is pointed out that all persons residing within the state of California, except the children of transient aliens and of alien public ministers and consuls, are citizens (Pol. Code, § 51) and that, therefore, the petitioner is a citizen within the meaning of article 1, section 21, of the state Constitution. It is conceded that the Legislature has power to enact laws classifying citizens, where the classification is not unreasonable and arbitrary, and that legislation with reference to such classification is constitutional, but it is contended that there is no reasonable basis for extending the rights of the university to all other citizens and denying such privileges to citizens who have not resided within the state for one year. It must be conceded that it is permissible to classify citizens who have resided within the state one year for certain purposes, notably, that of voting. Section 50 of the Political Code provides:

> "The people, as a political body, consist: (1) Of citizens who are electors; (2) of citizens not electors."

The Constitution itself makes this classification. Article 2, § 1. Now, one reason for denying a citizen of the state the right to vote in the state until he has been a resident of the state one year is that his residence for one year within the state is evidence of his bona fide intent to remain in the state permanently, and for the same reason the requirement that the voter shall reside 90 days in the county and 30 days in the election precinct in which he seeks to vote, is also considered necessary. Only such persons are eligible to become public officers. Pol. Code, § 58.

There seems to be no good reason for holding that the Legislature may not make a similar classification in fixing the privilege for attendance upon the state university. It would be impossible for the state university to provide educational opportunities for all the citizens of the state. These facilities are necessarily limited. It is stated by the respondent that the number of scholars at the university have increased from 1,783 in 1900 to 10,599 in 1920. The expenditures for the next current biennial period are estimated at $9,000,000, almost equal to the entire annual expenditures of the United States government during the first years of its existence ($10,-000,000). This expenditure is a heavy burden upon the taxpayers of the state. Taxes are payable annually and the requirement that a student shall maintain a residence in the state of California during one taxation period as an evidence of the bona fides of his intention to remain a permanent resident of the state and that he is not temporarily residing within the state for the mere purpose of securing the advantages of the university, cannot be held to be an unreasonable exercise of discretion by the Legislature or by the respondent. It follows that the exclusion of the petitioner does not violate her constitutional rights.

Petition denied.

Regulation classifying students as nonresidents for tuition purposes does not violate the Fourteenth Amendment

CLARKE v. REDEKER

United States District Court,
Southern District Iowa, Central Division, 1966.
259 F. Supp. 117.

THE CONTROVERSY

The principal question before the Court [2] involves a determination of whether the plaintiff, George Clarke,[3] is being deprived of certain constitutional rights because he is charged a nonresident rather than a resident tuition fee while attending the College of Law at the State University of Iowa. Plaintiff seeks to enjoin state officials from charging him nonresident tuition at the University.

The plaintiff entered the State University of Iowa (hereinafter referred to as SUI) in September, 1961. Prior to that time he had resided in Illinois. Since the plaintiff enrolled at SUI, he has been continuously attending the University and, at the age of 22, is presently a student in the College of Law. During August 1964, the plaintiff married Joan Weaver. Mrs. Clarke has lived in Iowa all of her life.

During his entire tenure as a student at SUI, the plaintiff has been charged the nonresident tuition fee, which is approximately twice as much as the tuition fee charged students who are classified as residents. The plaintiff is now contending that there is no basis for charging him a nonresident tuition fee and seeks to enjoin SUI from doing so. The plaintiff premises his contention upon the following allegations: (1) It is a violation of the equal protection and privileges and immunities clauses of the fourteenth amend-

---

2. Since the plaintiffs herein seek to enjoin the enforcement of a state policy promulgated by the Iowa State Board of Regents for State Educational Institutions, a three-judge federal court was designated to hear this case. See Phillips v. United States, 312 U.S. 246, 251, 61 S. Ct. 480, 85 L.Ed. 800 (1941).

3. Although the wife of George Clarke—Joan—also joins as a plaintiff in this lawsuit, she is not presently attending school and her claim is based on the allegation that she is being injured as a result of the tuition fee which her husband is being forced to pay. Since this lawsuit is thus focused on the contentions of George Clarke, all references hereinafter made to the plaintiff will pertain to that individual.

ment to the Constitution for a state operated university to charge a nonresident student a higher rate of tuition than that charged a resident student. (2) The tuition regulations applied by SUI unreasonably discriminate between a nonresident male whose wife is a resident of Iowa and a nonresident female whose husband is a resident of Iowa. (3) He is a resident and citizen of the State of Iowa.

The regulations concerning the classification of residents and nonresidents for admission and tuition fee purposes are attached to the application for admission which must be filled out by all individuals seeking admission to SUI. The regulations which resulted in the plaintiff being classified as a nonresident student are as follows.

> Students enrolling at The University of Iowa, Iowa City, shall be classified as Resident or Nonresident for admission, fee, and tuition purposes by the Registrar. The decision shall be based upon information furnished by the student and all other relevant information. The Registrar is authorized to require such written documents, affidavits, verifications, or other evidence as are deemed necessary to establish the domicile of a student, including proof of emancipation, adoption, award of custody, or appointment of a guardian. The burden of establishing that a student is exempt from paying the nonresident fee is upon the student.
>
> For purposes of resident and nonresident classifications, the word "parents" as herein used shall include legal guardians or others standing in *loco parentis* in all cases where lawful custody of any applicant for admission has been awarded to persons other than actual parents.
>
> Regulations regarding residence for admission, fee, and tuition payment are generally divided into two categories—those that apply to students who are minors and those that apply to students who are over 21 years of age. The requirements in these categories are different. Domicile within the state means adoption of the state as fixed permanent home and involves personal presence within the state. The two categories are discussed in more detail below.

* * * * * *

> A resident student 21 years of age or over is (1) one whose parents were residents of the state at the time he reached his majority and who has not acquired a domicile in another state or (2) who, while an adult, has established a bona fide residence in the state of Iowa by residing in the state for at least 12 consecutive months immediately preceding registration. Bona fide residence in Iowa means that the student is not in the state primarily to attend a college; that he is in the state for pur-

poses other than to attempt to qualify for residence status.

Any nonresident student who reaches the age of 21 years while a student at any school or college does not by virtue of such fact attain residence in this state for admission or tuition payment purposes.

The residence of a wife is that of her husband. A nonresident female student may attain residence through marriage, and correspondingly, a resident female student may lose residence by marrying a nonresident. Proof of marriage should be furnished to the Registrar at the time change of status is requested.

* * * * * *

Ownership of property in Iowa, or the payment of Iowa taxes, does not in itself establish residence.

A student from another state who has enrolled for a full program, or substantially a full program, in any type of educational institution will be presumed to be in Iowa primarily for educational purposes, and will be considered not to have established residence in Iowa. Continued residence in Iowa during vacation periods or occasional periods of interruption to the course of study does not of itself overcome the presumption.

All students not classified as resident students shall be classified as nonresidents for admission, fee, and tuition purposes. A student who willfully gives incorrect or misleading information to evade payment of the nonresident fees and tuition shall be subject to serious disciplinary action and must also pay the nonresident fee for each session attended.

* * * * * *

The decision of the Registrar on the residence of a student for admission, fee, and tuition purposes may be appealed to a Review Committee. The finding of the Review Committee shall be final.

The fourteenth amendment to the Constitution provides that a state cannot deny to any person within its jurisdiction the equal protection of the law. This constitutional provision, however, does not prohibit classifications by the states. Any classification by a state which is not palpably arbitrary and is reasonably based on a substantial difference or distinction is not a violation of the equal protection clause so long as the classification is rationally related to a legitimate state object or purpose. In this instance then, the Court must determine whether the classification of students as residents or nonresidents for the purpose of paying tuition is reasonable and whether that classification is rationally related to a legitimate object of the State of Iowa.

In contending that the classification involved herein is unconstitutional the plaintiff relies quite heavily upon the Supreme Court's decision in Carrington v. Rash, 380 U.S. 89, 85 S.Ct. 775, 13 L.Ed.2d 675 (1965). The *Carrington* case involved a provision of the Texas Constitution prohibiting any member of the Armed Services of the United States who first establishes his home in Texas while a member of the Armed Services from voting in any election in that State so long as he remained a member of the Armed Forces. The constitutional provision involved constituted an absolute denial to servicemen falling within its purview of the right to vote in Texas. The Supreme Court specifically recognized that Texas has unquestioned power to impose reasonable residence restrictions on the right to vote. In this instance, however, Texas transcended the scope of that power. The Supreme Court held that by denying a serviceman the opportunity of ever controverting the presumption of nonresidence, the Texas Constitution imposed an invidious discrimination in violation of the equal protection clause of the fourteenth amendment.

Although the *Carrington* case is helpful, it is by no means dispositive of the issue now before the Court. In deciding that case, the Supreme Court placed great emphasis on the absoluteness of the Texas rule. The regulations pertaining to the classification of students at SUI for the charging of tuition contains the following paragraph:

> A student from another state who has enrolled for a full program, or substantially a full program, in any type of educational institution will be presumed to be in Iowa primarily for educational purposes, and will be considered not to have established residence in Iowa. Continued residence in Iowa during vacation periods or occasional periods of interruption to the course of study does not of itself overcome the presumption.

The Iowa tuition regulations are thus not set up in terms of an absolute classification. A student from another state is classified as a nonresident because he is presumed to be in Iowa primarily for educational purposes. If appropriate facts and circumstances arise subsequent to a student's classification as a nonresident, there is nothing in the regulations which would prevent his reclassification as a resident. The student is merely required to present sufficient evidence to overcome the presumption of nonresidency. * * *

The students at SUI who are classified as nonresidents are charged a higher tuition than resident students. The defendants justify the discrimination primarily on the basis that resident students or their parents pay taxes to the State of Iowa which, in turn, supports and maintains SUI. The higher tuition charged nonresident students tends to distribute more evenly the cost of operating and supporting SUI between residents and nonresidents attending the University. Although there is no way for this Court to determine the degree to which the higher tuition charge equalizes the educational cost of residents and nonresidents, it appears to be a reasonable attempt to achieve a partial cost equalization. The regulation classifying students as residents or nonresidents for tuition payment purposes is not arbitrary or unreasonable and bears a rational relation to Iowa's object and purpose of financing, operating and maintaining its educational institutions.

The plaintiff further contends that SUI's tuition regulations constitute an unconstitutional discrimination against him on the basis of his sex. The regulation which gives rise to this contention is as follows:

> The residence of a wife is that of her husband. A nonresident female student may attain residence through marriage, and correspondingly, a resident female student may lose residence by marrying a nonresident. Proof of marriage should be furnished to the Registrar at the time change of status is requested.

Plaintiff contends that this regulation discriminates against him on the basis of his sex because it permits a nonresident female to acquire residence through marriage and does not give a nonresident male the same opportunity. This regulation is obviously an attempt to adhere to the well established legal concept that the domicile of a wife is the same as that of her husband. Classification under this regulation is not automatic. The regulation merely serves as a guideline for the classification of both nonresident females marrying Iowa residents and resident Iowa females marrying nonresidents.

This Court is convinced that, when a resident marries a nonresident, it is reasonable for SUI to classify both the husband and wife as residents of the same state. This does not mean, however, that it is required to do so. Such classifications should be left to the sound discretion of the appropriate University officials.

Although it is reasonable to classify a husband and wife as residents of the same state, it does not necessarily follow that they must be classified as residents of the state where the husband was a resident prior to the marriage. The marriage of a resident and a nonresident should merely be a factor in determining the residency classification. While it is by no means controlling, such a marriage is a relevant consideration in determining a student's residency for tuition purposes. The regulation of SUI on this point pertains only to female students. It is not expressed in absolute terms requiring reclassification of the female student if a resident marries a nonresident. The regulation serves only as a guideline for the possible reclassification of the female student. The fact that there is not a similar guideline for male students involved in such a marriage does not prevent the appropriate University officials from considering his marriage when he is attempting to overcome the rebuttable presumption of nonresidency. Although it is possible that the University regulations on this point could be clarified, they do not presently constitute a constitutional violation.

Plaintiff further contends that he is a resident of Iowa and has been improperly classified as a nonresident for tuition payment purposes. In reviewing a determination of an administrative body, a Court is normally limited to ascertaining whether the administrative action was arbitrary, unreasonable, or capricious or unlawful. This Court is thus somewhat limited in considering the plaintiff's contention that he should be classified as a resident.

While the administrative rules and regulations pertaining to classification of residents and nonresidents for tuition payment purposes are slightly confusing and could be improved in some aspects, they are not unlawful and any determination in conformity with them which is not unreasonable or arbitrary must be upheld by the courts. As previously discussed, a student from another state attending SUI is presumed to be a nonresident. The presumption is by no means conclusive. If a proper showing is made, a student originally from out of state should be reclassified as a resident. Although the Registrar at SUI does not appear to be applying the regulations as creating only a rebuttable presumption, the Review Committee, as final arbiter of residency classifications at SUI, correctly interprets those regulations in this regard. The Review Committee recognizes that a student originally classified as a nonresident may, under appropriate circumstances, be reclassified as a resident even though he has been enrolled in a full program at SUI or another Iowa educational institution since his arrival in the State.

While the Review Committee's interpretation of the regulations is correct, its application of them in this instance appears to be unduly rigid. It is the view of the Court that the plaintiff herein has established a substantial basis for being classified as a resident for tuition payment purposes. The Review Committee should be given an opportunity to reconsider the plaintiff's classification in light of this opinion. This cause is therefore remanded to the Review Committee for appropriate action.

Jurisdiction of this cause will be retained by the Court pending action by the Review Committee, and for such further relief as either party may request.

NOTES

1. The Board of Regents complied with the judgment and effective September 1966, the plaintiff, after that date, was no longer charged with nonresident tuition. Subsequently, Clarke, the plaintiff, sued to obtain damages for the excess nonresident tuition charged him between August of 1964 and September 1966. On appeal, the United States Court of Appeals, Eighth Circuit, *Clarke v. Redeker*, 406 F.2d 883 (1969), held that such issues might have and should have been decided in the first case and since they were not the appellant cannot raise the issue now. The doctrine of *res judicata* applies.

> The law of res judicata as it relates to claim preclusion is firmly established. In a subsequent action by the same parties, a judgment on the merits in a former action based upon the same cause of action precludes relief on the grounds of res judicata. The judgment is conclusive, not only as to matters which were decided, but also as to all matters which might have been decided.

2. The United States Supreme Court has affirmed a U. S. District Court decision which upheld the constitutionality of a one-year domicile for a student to acquire resident classification for tuition purposes at the University of Minnesota. Such a requirement does not violate the nonresident students equal protection rights. Starns v. Malkerson, 91 S. Ct. 123 (1971).

Curators have implied power to issue
dormitory revenue bonds

STATE EX REL. CURATORS OF UNIVERSITY OF
MISSOURI v. McREYNOLDS

Supreme Court of Missouri, 1946.
193 S.W.2d 611.

DOUGLAS, Judge.

The Curators of the University of Missouri, a public corporation, bring this original proceeding in mandamus to test its authority to issue $2,732,000 of Dormitory Revenue Bonds. The proceeds are to be used for building dormitories. * * *

The first constitutional provision for the government of the University is found in the Constitution of 1875 (Art. XI, Sec. 5) as follows: "The government of the State University shall be vested in a Board of Curators, to consist of nine members, to be appointed by the Governor, by and with the advice and consent of the Senate." The same provision was carried over into the Constitution of 1945, Art IX, Sec. 9.

The General Assembly has vested the University with the express powers, among others, to sue and be sued; to take, purchase, sell, and otherwise dispose of lands and chattels; to condemn and appropriate real estate and other property. Sec. 10783, R.S.1939, Mo.R.S.A. The statutory duty is placed on the curators "to erect and continue thereon [the site of the university] all edifices designed for the use and accommodation of the officers and students of the university." Sec. 10810, R.S.1939, Mo.R.S.A.

* * * Housing for students is overcrowded and inadequate. There are dormitory facilities now available for only 158 men and 158 women. Auto-trailers have been installed as an emergency measure to house married veterans. To remedy the situation and provide proper rooming and boarding facilities the curators propose to erect on the campus of the University at Columbia dormitories and dining rooms to accommodate 1850 men and 550 women and 250 married students, and on the campus of the School of Mines and Metallurgy at Rolla dormitories and dining rooms for 300 men, all at a total cost of $5,464,000. The curators are looking to the Legislature for an appropriation of one-half that sum and propose to issue Dormitory Revenue Bonds in the amount of $2,732,000 to raise the balance. The bonds will mature in 20 years unless called for redemption. They will bear 3% interest payable

semi-annually. They are declared to be fully negotiable. The bonds provide they are not an indebtedness or general obligation of the State of Missouri, or of the University of Missouri, or of the Curators of the University of Missouri. The principal and interest of the bonds "are payable solely and only from the net income revenues derived from the operation of said dormitories and dining room facilities" and a lien is imposed against such revenue.

The question for decision is whether the curators have the power to borrow money for building the dormitories and issue such revenue bonds as security. * * *

The curators state they have no express power to issue revenue bonds for money borrowed. Have they the implied power? We are convinced they have in this instance.

The curators have not only the express power but are directed by law to erect and maintain buildings for the use and accommodation of the students. They have determined additional dormitories and dining rooms are required for the health and welfare of the students. They have sole control and custody of the fees received from dormitories and dining rooms. * * * Such fees are expressly excepted by statute from those funds required to be placed in the State Treasury. Sec. 13051, R.S. 1939, Mo.R.S.A. The power of the curators to accumulate such fees and when sufficient to build dormitories could not be questioned. They built the original buildings and operated them with funds not received through legislative appropriations. Therefore, we believe that while the curators may have no general implied power to borrow money and issue securities, still it may be fairly implied from their express powers that under the particular circumstances they have the power presently to capitalize such future accumulation of fees even though they must borrow to do so. By borrowing by the method contemplated the curators do not create a general obligation, only a limited one. The only funds pledged are those to be realized from the operation of the particular properties to be built out of the proceeds of the bonds. There is no pledge of funds to be ultimately realized from tax revenues.

Although the Legislature has specifically authorized cities to issue revenue bonds, the fact it has not given the curators such express power does not prevent the implication of such power. The broad powers historically exercised by the curators without specific legislative authority or appropriations present a different situation from an ordinary municipal corporation depending entirely upon taxation for its support and with powers rigidly limited by statute or charter. * * *

The remaining question is whether the limitation imposed on the curators by Section 10791, R.S.1939, Mo.R.S.A., prevents their issuing the Dormitory Revenue Bonds. That section states: "* * * and in no instance shall the board of curators create any indebtedness in any one year above what they can pay out of the annual income of said year." That provision was adopted in 1877, Laws 1877, p. 271, after the General Assembly was expressly directed for the first time by the Constitution to aid and maintain the University. Constitution of 1875, Art. XI, Sec. 5. Prior to that time, as pointed out above, the University was supported by the income from the Seminary Fund, subscriptions and fees. By the limitation of Section 10791 the General Assembly evidently intended that the curators should not incur an indebtedness to be paid out of any future appropriation of State funds raised by taxation. Moreover, it is the established rule in this and other jurisdictions that the obligation created by revenue bonds payable out of the income to be realized from the particular property acquired with the proceeds of the bonds, does not constitute a debt or indebtedness as those terms are used in constitutional and statutory limitations. * * * Therefore, the limitation of Section 10791 does not prohibit the curators from issuing the Dormitory Revenue Bonds as they do not create an indebtedness in the sense which is prohibited.

It is our conclusion that the curators have full power and authority to issue the Dormitory Revenue Bonds. Accordingly, our peremptory writ of mandamus should issue.

It is so ordered.

All concur.

Boarding house operator's rights are not violated by rule requiring undergraduates to live in university owned housing.

PYEATTE v. BOARD OF REGENTS OF UNIVERSITY OF OKLAHOMA

District Court of the United States,
Western District, Oklahoma, 1951.
102 F. Supp. 407, *affirmed*, 72 S. Ct. 567 (1952).

WALLACE, District Judge.

This is a class action for an interlocutory injunction and a permanent injunction to restrain the enforcement of a ruling of an administrative board acting under and by authority of a State statute. * * *

The plaintiff in this class action seeks an injunction to prevent the enforcement of certain rules promulgated by the Board of Regents of the University of Oklahoma, contending that the enforcement of such rules denies the liberties of the plaintiff and others in a similar situation as guaranteed by the Fourteenth Amendment of the Constitution of the United States.

The facts are as follows: * * *

The defendant University of Oklahoma Housing Authority was created by Title 70 O.S.A. § 1306.1, designated as a body corporate, and given the power to erect dormitories, and create and furnish dining facilities. By Title 70 O.S.A. § 1306.3, the membership of the Board of Directors of the University Housing Authority was made identical with the Board of Regents of the University. Subsequent to the statutory provisions above, other statutes became effective which dealt in substance with the same subject matter, but were broader in scope and contained many new provisions. This later legislation is contained in Title 70 O.S.A. §§ 2071 to 2080, passed in 1945 and later amended in 1947. The provisions of the original Act of 1945 and the amendment in 1947 are for all practical purposes and for the purposes of this litigation, the same.

The 1945 Act, both before and after its amendment, authorizes both the Board of Regents of the University of Oklahoma and the Board of Regents of the Oklahoma Agricultural and Mechanical Colleges to set aside such portions of their respective campuses as may be necessary and suitable for the construction thereon of dormitories, kitchens, and other self liquidating projects, and other revenue producing buildings including additions to existing buildings used for such purposes and to construct such buildings or additions thereon and to equip, furnish, maintain and operate such buildings. The Act also provides for authorization by the Board of Regents to issue bonds for the purpose of paying the cost of the above projects and "to provide for the payment" thereof. Another provision of the Act provides that said bonds shall be paid "solely from the revenues to be derived from the operation of" said dormitories and other buildings, same to be pledged "to the payment of principal of and interest on the bonds."

In furtherance of the statutory provisions and in order to

meet the obligations of any bonds which were issuable under the authority delegated to the Board of Regents, Title 70 O.S.A. § 2073 provides as follows:

"* * * In order to secure the prompt payment of such principal and interest and the proper application of the revenues pledged thereto, the board is authorized by appropriate provisions in the resolution or resolutions authorizing the bonds:

*   *   *   *   *   *

"(f) To fix rents, charges and fees to be imposed in connection with and for the use of the building and the facilities supplied thereby, which rents, charges and fees shall be considered to be income and revenues derived from the operation of the building, and are hereby expressly required to be fully sufficient to assure the prompt payment of principal and interest on the bonds as each becomes due, and to make and enforce such rules and regulations with reference to the use of the building, and with reference to requiring any class or classes of students to use the building as it may deem desirable for the welfare of the institution and its students or for the accomplishment of the purposes of this act;

"(g) to covenant to maintain a maximum percentage of occupancy of the building;"

*   *   *   *   *   *

The Board of Regents of the University of Oklahoma adopted a Resolution Of Student Housing on September 10, 1947, amended February 14, 1948, which provides as follows:

*   *   *   *   *   *

"(1) That all undergraduate, unmarried students be required to live in University-operated dormitories to the extent that such dormitory rooms are available on the Main Campus of the University; provided that such requirement shall not apply to undergraduate, unmarried students who (a) live with parents or other relatives in Norman or (b) commute from a place of residence outside Norman or (c) work for room in lieu of paying rent; and provided further that such requirement shall not apply to students who live in a fraternity, sorority or approved student cooperative house, except that all freshman women students not in categories (a), (b) or (c) above shall live in University-operated dormitories to the extent such facilities are available.

"(2) That all undergraduate, married students living in Norman with husband or wife be required to live in University operated family dwelling units in Sooner City, Boyd House, and Niemann Apartments to the extent that such family dwelling units are available, provided that such requirements shall not apply to undergraduate, married students who (a) live with parents or other relatives in Norman (b) work for living quarters in lieu of paying rent or (c) own and occupy their homes in Norman."

* * * * * *

There are specific exemptions from housing regulations as to married students with children, all graduate students and in special cases of hardship exceptions are made for individuals.

It is a prerequisite that all persons who seek enrollment in the University of Oklahoma comply with the Housing Regulations before they are permitted to attend the University.

The plaintiff in this case is a resident of Norman, Oklahoma, a taxpayer of the State and is engaged in the rooming and boarding house business. Prior to 1947, students in attendance at the University were permitted to live in approved rooming and boarding houses, fraternity and sorority houses, private dormitories, and dormitories maintained and operated by the University of Oklahoma, all under the supervision and control of the University of Oklahoma. The home of the plaintiff was one of the private homes that was approved by the authorities for the keeping of male students in attendance at the University. In other words, her home met the specifications and requirements exacted by the Board of Regents for the housing of students. * * *

Under the Housing Regulations as they now exist, plaintiff finds herself in the position where facilities of the University and other approved dormitories such as fraternities and sororities are adequate to house all or a great majority of the university students. As a result, plaintiff has difficulty, if not finding it impossible, to fill her rooms with students. It is the contention of the plaintiff that the defendants are violating her constitutional rights in the following particulars:

(1) That the rules pertaining to housing of students which are or were allegedly promulgated under and by authority of the statutes set out above, insofar as they prevent contractual relations from being entered into between members of the student body of the University of Oklahoma and the plaintiff, deprive the plaintiff of her liberty to contract and her property without due process of law, contrary to the Fourteenth Amendment of the Constitution of the United States.

(2) That the rules, insofar as they permit fraternal organizations, and a dormitory known as Newman Hall run by a religious organization, to contract with students for their room and board, while denying a similar privilege to the plaintiff, are unreasonable, arbitrary, and discriminatory, and deny to the plaintiff the equal protection of the laws.

The Fourteenth Amendment of the federal Constitution provides in part: "* * * nor shall any State deprive any person of life, liberty, or property, without due process of law; nor deny to any person within its jurisdiction the equal protection of the laws." * * *

The enactment of statutes, or rules and regulations promulgated under authority of statute, invariably involve a modification of existing private rights and privileges of at least some persons. The due process clause does not prevent extensive governmental control of private interests for the protection and welfare of the public at large. It is quite impossible to draw a distinct line between the permissible and the prohibited forms of regulation to which the due process clause applies and in the final analysis of judicial construction of constitutional provisions, it becomes necessary to weigh the individual interests against the social desirability of governmental control or regulations which may or do affect those interests. A general rule has developed for reconciling the claims of government to regulate, and those of private interests to freedom from regulation, as pertaining to due process, and this is that due process is a guarantee only against unreasonable and arbitrary legislative or other governmental control. * * *

Many times legislation is upheld upon the theory that regulatory measures in a certain degree are permissible under the "police power" of the state. Not all legislation or administrative rulings need rely upon or be "justified" upon the theory of police power. As was said by Mr. Justice Holmes, dissenting in Tyson Bros. v. Banton, 273 U.S. 418, 445, 47 S.Ct. 426, 433, 71 L.Ed. 718: "* * * police power often is used in a wide sense to cover and, as I said, to apologize for the general power of the Legislature to make a part of the community uncomfortable by a change."

It is immaterial whether the terminology used is police power or the general power of the Legislature, since the issue as to whether or not due process has been denied to the plaintiff hinges upon whether or not the statutes and rules are arbitrary, unreasonable, or capricious. When inquiring into the reasonableness of an act, the court must evaluate the benefit to be derived from upholding the statute or regulation and the loss suffered or likely to be suffered by a resulting deprivation of some private interest. In analyzing reasonableness of an act, several elements should be considered:

* * * * * *

"* * * The conditions existing prior to the legislation, the effectiveness of the new rule to improve them, the deprivation resulting from the new rule, and the possibility of achieving the same benefits at a lower price." * * *

Title 70 O.S.A. § 1218 provides as follows: "The said board of regents shall make rules, regulations and by-laws for the good government and management of the university and of each department thereof; prescribe rules and regulations for the admission of students * * *."

Over and above the express power conferred upon the Board of Regents by the statutory provision, the Oklahoma Constitution also provides for government of the University by the Board of Regents. Article 13, § 8, Oklahoma Constitution. The term "government" is very broad and necessarily includes the power to pass all rules and regulations which the Board of Regents considers to be for the benefit of the health, welfare, morals and education of the students, so long as such rules are not expressly or impliedly prohibited. * * *

The plaintiff has not in any way had her rights to contract for roomers and boarders impaired. It is true and regrettable that a certain number of persons designated as students are not available for taking the rooms offered by the plaintiff. This state of affairs was brought about by the Housing Regulations and does affect the plaintiff adversely, but when a state acting in a proper sphere passes regulations which are valid and suitable to attain a desired end, the mere fact that such legislation or regulatory measures has an incidental effect upon a few individuals, does not make the regulation invalid or abridge the constitutional rights of the individual. Stating it another way, the effect of the Housing Resolution does not destroy the plaintiff's right to contract with respect to her property. It does not forbid her to contract with any student. It merely creates a condition of affairs which renders the making of a related contract, lawful in itself, ineffective, and this is not fatal to its constitutionality. * * *

The Constitution of the United States guarantees to all persons certain liberties, but many times these liberties must give way in part to co-existing or co-equal rights invested in others. It would appear that if any right has been violated, it would be the right of the student to contract for a place to live of his own choice and not a right of a person in the position of the plaintiff. Even so, as stated in Alaska Packers Ass'n v. Industrial Accident Commission of California, 294 U.S. 532, 543, 55 S.Ct. 518, 522, 79 L.Ed. 1044: "Legislation otherwise within the scope of acknowledged state power, not unreasonable or arbitrarily exercised, cannot be condemned because it curtails the power of the individual to contract."

The Housing Regulations in effect at the University of Oklahoma result in completely depriving a student of freely contracting with whom he pleases for a place to live. If this restriction upon the student is a valid exercise of the power conferred upon the Board of Regents to prescribe rules for admission of the University, it is absurd for the plaintiff to contend that the indirect effect deprives her of her liberty to contract, for the fact that regulatory law enacted under state power imposes hardship in individual cases, due to special circumstances or other factors, does not subject the law to constitutional objections.

There is a presumption of the validity of state statutes or regulations passed by an administrative agency acting by authority delegated to the agency. If there is any state of facts which tends to support the regulatory measures and such measures are not clearly unreasonable or arbitrary, then the statute or regulation will be upheld as being constitutional. This court cannot, in light of the evidence and in contravention of the good judgment of the Board of Regents of the University of Oklahoma, say that the action taken was unreasonable or arbitrary. The state has a decided interest in the education, well-being, morals, health, safety and convenience of its youth. When a situation arises where it becomes necessary to expend great sums for buildings to house students, it is within the power of the state acting through an administrative agency to provide such facilities, and when it is necessary for rules to be passed to provide payment for such buildings in furtherance of the object to be accomplished, such rules will be valid as a means accompanying the over all-policy of furnishing the needed facilities.

The question thus "do the statutes and rules involved here deprive the plaintiff of any property right without due process of law?" must be answered in the negative.

There is one further contention of the plaintiff which requires more consideration than the contention of a violation of her liberty to contract heretofore disposed of. This second contention is that plaintiff has been discriminated against without equal protection of the laws. Plaintiff bases this contention upon the ruling by the University that students may live in sorority or fraternity houses and Newman Hall, but cannot live in private homes approved by the University for the housing of students until university housing is filled.

It would appear here, as in the preceding discussion, that if any discrimination is involved, and we do not pass upon this point, it is against the students and not against the private home owners such as the plaintiff. Thus the plaintiff would not be in a position to challege the constitutionality of the statutes or regulations promulgated under and by force of the power conferred upon the Board of Regents by such statutes. However, the plaintiff has raised the issue of discrimination against herself as a private householder duly approved by the University to keep students and other private organizations such as fraternal organizations and Newman Hall owned by the Catholic Church. There is a substantial issue raised in this respect and the court must consider it with all due deference to the rights of plaintiff.

Substantive due process and equal protection of the laws are very similar in many respects. However, as stated in Rottschaefer on Constitutional Law, 1st Ed. (1939): "There is a marked difference between the protection accorded individual interests by the due process and equal protection clauses of the Fourteenth Amendment. The former limits the general character of regulation that may be imposed on conduct even when it is applied to every case in which the regulated conduct occurs; the latter is a limit merely on the power of making classifications in the enactment and enforcement of regulatory legislation. A regulation violates the former if it is arbitrary and unreasonable, but can violate the latter only if the group subjected to it has been arbitrarily selected and defined."

In the case of Lindsley v. Natural Carbonic Gas Co., 220 U.S. 61, 78-79, 31 S.Ct. 337, 340, 55 L.Ed. 369, certain rules were enumerated by which the equal protection contention is to be tested. These rules are as follows: "1. The equal-protection clause of the 14th Amendment does not take from the state the power to classify in the adoption of police laws, but admits of the exercise of a wide scope of discretion in that regard, and avoids what is done only when it is without any reasonable basis, and therefore is purely arbitrary. 2. *A classi-*

fication having some reasonable basis does not offend against that clause merely because it is not made with mathematical nicety, or because in practice it results in some inequality. 3. When the classification in such a law is called in question, if any state of facts reasonably can be conceived that would sustain it, the existence of that state of facts at the time the law was enacted must be assumed. 4. One who assails the classification in such a law must carry the burden of showing that it does not rest upon any reasonable basis, but is essentially arbitrary." (Emphasis added.)

The Fourteenth Amendment is thus not an absolutely inflexible and austere requirement of the impracticable. Equal protection of the law does not guarantee that every business or occupation that is similar must be treated in the precise manner as all others. As stated in Armour & Co. v. State of North Dakota, 240 U.S. 510, 517, 36 S.Ct. 440, 443, 60 L.Ed. 771, referring to the power of the State in making classifications: "The power may be determined by degrees of evil, or exercised in cases where detriment is especially experienced."

The court in its consideration or treatment of any particular basis of classification must ultimately refer to the problem in connection with which it was made. The record discloses that at the time the rules and regulations were promulgated there were between twelve and thirteen thousand students enrolled, with over a thousand students without proper or available accommodations, besides those commuting from other places. What brought about the condition, aside from the school out growing the community, is more or less speculative, but it can be fairly inferred it resulted by war activities that required housing units and living quarters in the community surrounding the University. The plaintiff would be an exception to the general run of landlords if she did not take advantage of such a situation.

The University in its over-all program for housing facilities has evidently come to rely in great measure upon the fraternal dormitories and Newman Hall as a complement to the housing owned and managed by the University itself. These dormitories are not available for any purpose other than housing students, and past experience indicates that they will be available to the University at all times. On the other hand, the private homes such as that owned by the plaintiff are not an integral part of the housing program but are furnished mainly for the purpose of earning for the benefit of the private owner. The private home owners may at any time use their homes for a variety of purposes and without any restrictions may deny their use to the University for the housing of students. It is true that many private homes were used in the past for the purpose of housing facilities for students and for this the private home owners are to be commended. However, it appears that in the light of the over-all picture the classification which has been made by the University Board of Regents is a reasonable one and not arbitrarily or capriciously exercised to deny to the plaintiff the equal protection of the laws.

The relief sought is denied and the action is dismissed.

Regulation requiring some girls to live in college dormitories constitutes unconstitutional classification

MOLLERE v. SOUTHEASTERN LOUISIANA COLLEGE

United States District Court, Eastern District
Louisiana, New Orleans Division, 1969.
304 F. Supp. 826.

CASSIBRY, District Judge:

This case poses the question whether state college girls under the age of 21 can constitutionally be required to pay more than other students to support the College's housing system.

The plaintiffs are upperclass women under 21 who have attended and who plan to continue to attend Southeastern Louisiana College located in Hammond, Louisiana. This is a four-year coeducational state college under the general direction and supervision of the Louisiana State Board of Education. Many on-campus dormitories have been constructed in recent years with federal financing. A portion of the rent paid by students is used to meet the dormitory debt obligation to the federal government. In recent years male students have used the dormitories in diminishing numbers so that the State Board of Education and College officials have become concerned about meeting the principal and interest obligations to the government. As a result the State Board of Education recently resolved that Southeastern Louisiana College require a sufficient number of students to live in the dormitories to meet the payments to the United States. In compliance with this resolution Southeastern Louisiana College promulgated a rule to be effective in the 1969-1970 academic year which, among other things, required unmarried women students under 21 not living with their parents or a close relative, to live in campus residence halls unless exception was granted by the Dean of Women. At the same time other rules required that any freshman male student, not living with his parents or a close relative, live on-campus unless exception was granted by the Dean of Men. Plaintiffs have not questioned the legality of requiring freshman boys and girls to live on-campus and both sides have agreed that that is not in issue in this case. As a matter of fact, no evidence was taken on that issue.

It is undisputed that the College's sole reason for requiring that women under 21 and freshman men live in college residence halls was to meet the financial obligations which arose out of the construction of those dormitories. When the Court specifically asked Mrs. Parker, the Dean of Women, the reason for the requirement, she testified that the sole and only reason was to increase the revenue of the housing system. Indeed, when she was asked why this particular category of students was chosen she replied that the girls in this group together with the freshman boys comprised the precise number needed to fill the dormitory vacancies.[1] This was confirmed by the Auditor of the University, and their testimony was not contradicted by any other College official.

For purposes of this case it might be conceded that a state university may require all or certain categories of students to live on-campus in order to promote the education of those students. It might reasonably be felt that on-campus living brings students together, promotes discussion and intellectual exchange, and so on. It might also be reasonable for a university to require on-campus living of students in order that the university may more closely supervise them and protect their welfare as *parens patriae* when they are away from home. The sole issue in this case, on the other hand, is whether the College may require a certain group of students to live on-campus, not for the welfare of the students themselves but simply to increase the revenue of the housing system. More specifically, can the College require girls under 21 to live on-campus while allowing others to live off-campus simply to meet expenses? Is this a valid classification under the Equal Protection Doctrine? I have decided that it is not; in effect, it is a

---

1. A hypothetical case may help to illustrate the arbitrariness of such a selection. Suppose there are 50 million adult male whites in the United States and 2 million adult male blacks. Supposing that the Army required precisely 2 million men, it could hardly draft all the blacks and none of the whites.

requirement that some students must pay while others need not. Why should the particular students who are the plaintiffs in this case bear any more of the financial obligation of the College housing system than any of their other fellow students? The burden of expense is falling on some but not on others. The sole reason offered by the College is that the plaintiffs comprised the precise number of students required to fill existing vacancies. If students with black eyes had filled the bill—i. e. comprised the desired number—they would have done equally well, so far as the evidence indicates, to satisfy the College's need. This is the type of irrational discrimination impermissible under the Fourteenth Amendment. Levy v. Louisiana, 391 U.S. 68, 88 S.Ct. 1509, 20 L.E.2d. 436 (1968); Griffin v. Tatum, 300 F.Supp. 60 (M.D. Ala. 1969); Breen v. Kahl, 296 F.Supp. 702 (W.D.Wis. 1969). Absent the special educational considerations previously mentioned the support of the housing system is an obligation which should fall on all students equally just as does, for example, tuition. Since the obligation is essentially *monetary*, then all must pay or none. To select a group less-than-all, to fulfill an obligation which should fall equally on all, is a violation of equal protection no matter how the group is selected.[2]

---

2. This case neither raises nor decides the issue of whether, apart from the equal protection issue, it is a valid exercise of a state university's power to dictate to a student where he shall live, not for reasons having anything to do with the student's welfare or the educational appropriateness of the place chosen, but simply for the purpose of increasing revenue to support the university housing system. This question has neither been briefed nor argued by the parties. The Court might simply note, however, that the question is not entirely obvious. Suppose, for example, that the State required poor people to live in public housing in order to finance that housing? Just as the State might claim that such a measure was designed ultimately to benefit poor people by providing housing for the future, so the state university might claim that requiring students to live in dormitories in order to finance them was ultimately for the benefit of students in the future. Do "students" lose the fundamental rights that adults normally possess simply because they are students? See Tinker v. Des Moines Independent Community School District et al., 393 U.S. 503, 89 S.Ct. 733, 21 L.Ed.2d 731 (1969). See also Goldstein, The Scope and Sources of School Board Authority to Regulate Student Conduct and Status: A Nonconstitutional Analysis, 117 U.Pa. L.Rev. 373 (1969).

CHAPTER 7

LAW AND THE FACULTY

The legal relationship between a college faculty member and the university has essentially three characteristics: (a) individual rights or freedoms which a teacher might possess in his capacity as teacher or person, (b) statutory requirements which must be followed by both institution and employee, and (c) contractual conditions of employment agreed upon between teacher and institution.

CONSTITUTIONAL AND ACADEMIC FREEDOM

The first of these, individual rights or freedoms of teachers, is probably the most complex because it involves the wide range of individual freedoms protected by both federal and state constitutions. Intermingled with these constitutional freedoms is the concept of academic freedom which presumably bestows upon a teacher the additional freedom of intellectual thought, learning, and teaching, a freedom which cannot be restricted or abrogated by institution or government. It is generally conceded that the idea of academic freedom as we now view it was formulated in Germany during the nineteenth century. This view is summed up by the words *Lernfreiheit* and *Lehrfreiheit,* the freedom to learn and the freedom to teach.[1]

Lehrfreiheit allowed the professor to do independent research and convey his findings to his students without fear of retribution from higher authority. In fact, where professors and students were concerned, there was no higher authority. The German university was predicated on the concept of academic freedom and without its presence there was no university. "Academic freedom . . . was not simply the right of professors to speak without fear or favor, but the atmosphere of consent that surrounded the whole process of research and institution."[2] In the German social setting, the university was an oasis in an otherwise autocratic and class conscious state. The professor by virtue of *Lehrfreiheit* was placed in a caste above that of the ordinary civil servant; the

---

1. Richard Hofstadter and Walter P. Metzger, *The Development of Academic Freedom in the United States,* Columbia University Press, New York, 1955, p. 275.
2. *Ibid.,* p. 387.

freedoms guaranteed and the dispensations granted to academia were not extended beyond the university.[3]

ACADEMIC FREEDOM IN THE AMERICAN UNIVERSITY

The United States inherited a somewhat diminished version of academic freedom. The cultural surrounding of the American university created something less than a mirror image of the German concept of academic freedom.

> The idea had changed its color, its arguments, and its qualifications in the process of domestication. All the peculiarities of the American university—its inclusion of a college, its eclectic purposes, its close ties to the community—and all the peculiarities of the American culture —its constitutional provision for free speech, its empiricist traditions, its abundant pragmatic spirit—contributed to a freedom that was characteristically American.[4]

The greatest difference between the academic freedom in the United States and its forerunner in Germany emanates from the fundamental differences in individual rights. In Germany, *Lehrfreiheit* and *Lernfreiheit* were extended to only faculty and students in the university, while in the United States the individual freedoms granted by the Constitution of the United States guaranteed all persons *Lehrfreiheit* and *Lernfreiheit* regardless of whether they are in universities or some other phase of American life.[5]

The general necessity and justification for academic freedom is, therefore, greatly reduced where all persons possess such fundamental liberties in the first place. "As a result of this constitutional 'incorporation,' the proposition that academic freedom should be considered a *right* with independent character as it was in Germany has not been generally accepted as a sound legal principle in the United States."[6]

In theory, academic freedom applies to both public and private universities; however, with the tendency in the United States to relate academic freedom only to constitutionally protected rights, there has developed no unified legal theory of academic rights applying to both public and private institutions. The constitutional guarantees of freedom of speech, liberty and property, and others, have been applied by the

---

3. *Ibid.*, p. 389.

4. *Ibid.*, p. 397.

5. Richard P. Tisdel, "Academic Freedom—Its Constitutional Context," *University of Colorado Law Review*, Vol. 40, p. 600, 1967-68.

6. *Ibid.*, p. 603.

country almost exclusively to situations involving state institutions, since it is the state and its agencies against which the individual is protected by the First and Fourteenth Amendments. The Fourteenth Amendment, designed to protect individual rights against the state, has not been applied to private institutions except in cases where a sufficiency of "state action" is shown.

This limitation on academic freedom has been accompanied by a traditional hesitancy on the part of the courts to intervene in matters involving substantiative due process. Courts seldom venture into substantiative questions involving curriculum, classroom activities, or other internal scholastic matters to protect intellectual liberty.[7] This hesitancy of the courts to intrude has many times lead to acquiescence to institutional restraint on the individual teacher's academic freedom.

The courts have in recent years tended to increase the constitutional protections afforded teachers in public institutions. The view that public employment is a privilege and the employee sheds his constitutional rights when he enters such employment has been discredited by modern courts. Restrictions placed on employees must be justified on the grounds of a "compelling state." This judicial logic covers all types of public employees and does not apply solely to situations involving academic freedom.[8] No court has, to date, squarely held that academic freedom is a distinct right which elevates the teacher's rights over and above those constitutional rights guaranteed to any public servant or citizen.[9]

LOYALTY OATHS

Loyalty oath requirements have precipitated many legal battles between teachers and the state. Disqualification of faculty under loyalty oath statutes is usually justified on the ground that teachers are in a sensitive area in the classroom,[10] and their extramural activities and associations may reflect on the teacher's competence or may predict a teacher's espousal of a potentially dangerous doctrine to receptive ears of students. Whether a teacher is a Marxist may bear relevance to his competency to teach economics, presenting an ever-present danger of proselytizing in the classroom.

7. "Developments in the Law—Academic Freedom," *Harvard Law Review*, Vol. 81, p. 1051, 1967-68.
8. Sweezy v. New Hampshire, 354 U.S. 234 (1957).
9. "Developments in the Law—Academic Freedom," *op. cit.*, p. 1065.
10. Adler v. Board of Education, 342 U.S. 485 (1952).

Although justification for loyalty oaths may seem quite simple, their constitutional application is so complex that the Supreme Court of the United States has in recent years gradually whittled away most of the content of such oaths.

The Supreme Court in 1971 held that a teacher could not be summarily dismissed from public employment for failure to sign a loyalty oath containing the following provision "that I do not believe in the overthrow of the government of the United States or of the State of Florida by force or violence." [11] Other provisions of the oath held to be unconstitutional by a three-judge U.S. District Court required the employee to swear: (a) "that I am not a member of the Communist Party"; (b) "that I have not and will not lend my support, advice, counsel or influence to the Communist Party," and (c) "that I am not a member of any organization or party which believes in or teaches, directly or indirectly, the overthrow of the Government of the United States or of Florida by force or violence."

The rationale of the Court was clouded by its statement that the "overthrow" portion of the oath "falls within the ambit of decisions of the court proscribing summary dismissals from public employment without hearing or inquiry required by due process." The invocation of the due process clause by the court appears to suggest that while the state cannot summarily dismiss a teacher for failure to sign the oath, it might dismiss the teacher if with due process it can be shown that she believes in overthrow of the government. A concurring opinion by Justice Marshall questioned this rationale by the majority saying:

> . . . the Court left the clear implication that its objection runs, not against Florida's determination to exclude those who "believe in the overthrow," but only against the State's decision to regard unwillingness to take the oath as conclusive, irrebuttable proof of the proscribed belief. Due process may rightly be invoked to condemn Florida's mechanistic approach to the question of proof. But in my view it simply does not matter what kind of evidence a State can muster to show that a job applicant "believes in overthrow." For state action injurious to an individual cannot be justified on account of the nature of the individual's beliefs, whether he "believes in the overthrow" or has any other sort of belief. "If there is any fixed star in our constitutional constellation, it is that no official, high or petty, can prescribe what shall be orthodox in politics, nationalism, religion, or other matters of opinion . . ."

---

11. Connell v. Higgenbotham, 91 S. Ct. 1772 (1971).

The Supreme Court let stand a clause of the oath requiring a teacher to swear: "I will support the Constitution of the United States and of the State of Florida. . . ."

In other loyalty oath decisions the Supreme Court had previously limited the power of the state to restrict a teacher's freedom of association. In *Keyishian v. Board of Regents of University of State of New York*,[12] the Court quite clearly pronounced the relationship between academic freedom and constitutional rights within the loyalty oath context. The opinion stated:

> Our nation is deeply committed to safeguarding academic freedom, which is of transcendent value to all of us and not merely to teachers concerned. That freedom is, therefore, a specific concern of the First Amendment, which does not tolerate laws that cast a pall of orthodoxy over the classroom.

Although the Court does not consider academic freedom to be an independent pedagogical right, it nevertheless makes it very clear that acts restricting academic freedom, such as loyalty oaths, will be carefully scrutinized with "specific concern" for the freedoms established by the First Amendment.

The Keyishian decision struck down a New York loyalty oath on the grounds that it was overly vague and excessively broad. The Court declared that mere knowing [13] membership in a "subversive" organization is an insufficient basis for disallowing public employment; the teacher must in addition have a specific and identifiable intent to accomplish the unlawful objectives of the association.

> The Keyishian formulation thus suggests that the state, in administering its loyalty program, must rely principally on overt acts or other direct evidence of specific illegal intent. Although evidence of an employee's associational affiliation may be relevant to the purpose of his acts, it seems unlikely after Keyishian that otherwise lawful general membership activities such as dues paying or voting could be made the basis for disqualification even when combined with "knowing" membership.[14]

In another key loyalty oath decision the Supreme Court in

---

12. Keyishian v. Board of Regents of University of State of New York, 385 U.S. 589 (1967).

13. In an earlier case, the Supreme Court had held that an oath could not be constitutionally exacted if it encompassed innocent or unknowing membership in a subversive organization. Wieman v. Updegraff, 344 U.S. 183 (1952).

14. "Developments in the Law—Academic Freedom," *op. cit.*, p. 1067.

1964 held two oath statutes in the State of Washington [15] unconstitutional. This case was brought by 64 professors contesting the statutes under the First and Fourteenth Amendments, claiming the statutory language was unduly broad and vague. In holding the oaths unconstitutional, Justice White laid down the following definition for unconstitutional vagueness: A law prohibiting or requiring conduct in terms so vague that men of common intelligence must necessarily guess at its meaning and differ as to its application violates due process of law." With similar application of the vagueness definition the Court has struck down disclaimer oaths intended for those who loaned their "aid, support, advice, or counsel" to the Communist Party; [16] and who committed "treasonable or seditious" acts or utterances.[17]

From this formulation of vagueness, the Court has moved to an apparently stricter vagueness interpretation. In *Whitehill v. Elkins*,[18] the Court held unconstitutional a loyalty oath which required teachers to swear that they were not "engaged in one way or another in the attempt to overthrow the Government . . . by force or violence." Here the oath had moved from the terminology with such sweeping application as words "aid," "advocate or abet," "treasonable" and "seditious" to the direct question of whether the teacher was engaged in the "overthrow" of the government.

This case and the previously discussed *Connell* decision [19] suggest that vagueness may not be an accurate measure for determining the constitutionality of loyalty oaths; on the contrary, the Court appears to say that any or all disclaimers regarding association are unconstitutional. The evolution of these cases suggests that the state cannot rely on loyalty oaths to prevent certain associations by teachers, but must instead show, after due process, that a teacher's acts are in fact intended to overthrow the government and/or that the teacher is actively attempting to subvert the minds of students. It is clear that the state does have a legitimate and justifiable concern for the prevention of overthrow of the government through subversion of the minds of students; however, the use of loyalty oaths is a particularly pernicious means by which to protect the state.

---

15. Baggett v. Bullitt, 377 U.S. 360 (1964).
16. Cramp v. Board of Public Instruction, 368 U.S. 278 (1961).
17. 385 U.S. 589 (1967).
18. 389 U.S. 54 (1967).
19. Connell v. Higgenbotham, *supra*.

POLITICAL ACTIVITY

Teachers in colleges and public schools are frequently restrained from participation in political activities. Such activities can, of course, range from a nonpartisan advocacy of a particular social or political view to the partisan participation in political campaign activities. Relatively few cases involving college faculty have reached the courts; however, a few cases give clues as to the teacher's constitutional right to participate in politics.

In *Pickering v. Board of Education* the Supreme Court held that "a teacher's exercise of his right to speak on issues of public importance may not furnish the basis for his dismissal from public employment." [20] In this particular case a teacher sent a letter to a local newspaper attacking a proposed tax increase by the Board of Education. The letter contained partially erroneous information and the teacher was dismissed by the board because the letter "impugned" the "motives," "honesty" and "integrity" of board and administration. The Court, acknowledging that a balance must be maintained regarding such political activity, gave the following guideline:

> . . . It cannot be gainsaid that the State has interests as an employer in regulating the speech of its employees that differ significantly from those it possesses in connection with regulation of the speech of the citizenry in general. The problem in any case is to arrive at a balance between the interests of the teacher, as a citizen, in commenting upon matters of public concern and the interest of the State, as employer, in promoting the efficiency of the public services it performs through its employees.

The Court pointed out that a board may be justified in dismissal of an employee if the statements or activities are of such a nature as to be detrimental to the actual operation of the schools. The Court, in *Pickering*, concluded that the activity was not inhibitive in any manner to the educational performance of the school. Also, it was not shown that the teacher's letter had any impact on the proposed tax increase nor was it shown that the false statements were made recklessly or knowingly. The Court said:

> On such a question free and open debate is vital to informed decision-making by the electorate. Teachers are, as a class, the members of a community most likely to have informed and definite opinions as to how funds al-

---

20. 391 U.S. 563, 88 S. Ct. 1731 (1968).

lotted to the operation of the schools should be spent. Accordingly, it is essential that they be able to speak out freely on such questions without fear of retaliatory dismissal.

The more extensive form of political activity—a teacher's participation in partisan political campaign activities—presents a somewhat different constitutional picture. Courts have acknowledged that the state has a legitimate interest in attempting to free public employees from the "spoils" of political involvement.[21] This governmental interest was upheld by the Supreme Court in *United Public Workers v. Mitchell*,[22] which upheld the Hatch Act [23] against a challenge under the First Amendment. The Hatch Act, prohibiting federal civil service employees from taking "any active part in political management or in political campaigns," was held to be a reasonable exercise of governmental power to preserve the efficiency, integrity and discipline of government employees.

Similar rationale has been used by other courts to prevent teachers from running for public office. The Florida Supreme Court held that a rule prohibiting university employees from seeking election to public office was not an unconstitutional abridgment of academic freedom or denial of substantive due process.[24] With regard to the plaintiff's (a university professor) claim that he was denied academic freedom, by the rule preventing him from running for public office, the court said to its knowledge there was no good definition of academic freedom and if the term is literally adopted to bestow unlimited privilege on academicians and teachers, then the court would be "compelled to concede that a license to teach in a public school system is subject to no regulations whatsoever"; this the court was not prepared to do. Quoting Justice Holmes dictum that "The petitioner [a policeman] may have a constitutionl right to talk politics, but he has no constitutional right to be a policeman," [25] the court held that a public employee's activities may be restricted by "reasonable rules and regulations promulgated by the government in the interest of the public and for the well-being of the public services." [26]

---

21. Such questions are many times disposed of by the courts on the basis of common law "incompatibility" of holding two public offices.

22. 330 U.S. 75 (1947).

23. 5 U.S.C. § 118 (i) (1964).

24. Jones v. Board of Control, 131 So. 2d 713 (Fla. 1961).

25. McAuliffe v. City of New Bedford, 155 Mass. 216, 29 N.E. 517 (1891).

26. 131 So. 2d 713.

Classroom Activities

It is generally assumed that the state can regulate minimum standards for accreditation purposes and generally control the overall curricular plan of a state institution. However, the actual restraint of classroom activity by the state and restrictions on the speech of the teacher may be constitutionally impermissible.

From cases testing state control of classroom activity some interesting judicial comments have emerged. In New Hampshire where the legislature gave the Attorney General the authority to investigate alleged "subversive persons," a professor refused to answer certain questions regarding a lecture and his knowledge of the Progressive Party of the State. Although the case was disposed of on the grounds that the Attorney General was not authorized to answer the questions involved, the Supreme Court made it quite clear that teachers have a privilege to be free from legislative scrutiny into their professorial activities. Chief Justice Warren in dictum said that:

> To impose any strait jacket upon the intellectual leaders in our colleges and universities would imperil the future of our nation. No field of education is so thoroughly comprehended by man that new discoveries cannot yet be made. Particularly is that true in the social sciences, where few, if any, principles are accepted as absolutes. Scholarship cannot flourish in an atmosphere of suspicion and distrust. Teachers and students must always remain free to inquire, to study, and to evaluate. . . .

Other examples of action by the Supreme Court in imposing *constitutional limitations* on the power of the state to restrict classroom activities are found in two elementary and secondary education cases. Even assuming that elementary and secondary children are more subject to danger of subversion than are students of college age, the Court nevertheless held that a criminal statute prohibiting the teaching of German in a parochial school denied the teacher liberty without due process of law.[27] In the other case, the Supreme Court held that Arkansas statutes forbidding the teaching of evolution in the public schools and in public colleges and universities, are contrary to the freedom of religion mandate of the First Amendment and in violation of the Fourteenth Amendment.[28]

In *Meyer v. Nebraska,* the Court recognized teaching as a

---

27. Meyer v. Nebraska, 262 U.S. 390, 43 S. Ct. 625 (1923).
28. Epperson v. Arkansas, 393 U.S. 97, 89 S. Ct. 266 (1968).

"liberty" protected by the Fourteenth Amendment. It is not clear, however, whether the Court in the various cases acknowledges that teaching is and of itself a "liberty" or merely notes that freedom of speech and due process are particularly important in academic settings.[29] It is clear, however, that teaching and academic freedom are not basic freedoms separate and apart from the established constitutional freedoms. In *Meyer* the Court indicates that teaching is a protected liberty, not absolute, but one which may be restrained only through the proper and reasonable exercise of police power of the state.

In this regard Justice McReynolds in *Meyer* stated in part:

> While this Court has not attempted to define with exactness the liberty thus guaranteed, the term has received much consideration and some of the included things have been definitely stated. Without doubt, it denotes not merely freedom from bodily restraint but also the right of the individual to contract, to engage in any of the common occupations of life, to acquire useful knowledge, to marry, establish a home, and bring up children, to worship God according to the dictates of his own conscience, and generally to enjoy those privileges long recognized at common law as essential to the orderly pursuit of happiness of free men. * * * Practically, education of the young is only possible in schools conducted by especially qualified persons who devote themselves thereto. * * * Mere knowledge of the German language cannot be regarded as harmful. * * * [The teacher] taught this language in school as part of his occupation. His right *thus to teach and the right of parents to engage him so to instruct their children, we think, are within the liberty of the Amendment.* (Emphasis added.) [30]

The Court acknowledged the State's power to prescribe the school curriculum, but held that the State's purposes were not sufficiently adequate to support the restriction upon the liberty of teacher and pupil.

One should bear in mind that the Court in *Meyer* was speaking of a situation where a teacher had been tried and convicted of teaching a foreign language in a parochial school. The combination of the private school setting coupled with the overzealousness of a criminal statutory proceeding undoubtedly weighed heavily on the final determination of the case. The teacher here had been tried and convicted under a criminal statute; therefore, a very clear denial of "liberty"

29. "Developments in the Law-Academic Freedom," *op. cit.*, p. 1080.
30. 262 U.S. 390, 43 S. Ct. 625 (1923).

by the state was imminent for the teacher. This denial was very much apparent to the Court and doubtlessly had substantial impact on the decision.

The situation was similar in *Epperson* except the case involved instruction in a public school instead of a private school. In holding anti-evolution statutes unconstitutional as violating the First Amendment, the Court said that the freedom of religion provision does not tolerate laws which cast a pall of orthodoxy over the classroom. But more directly with regard to state restriction of academic freedom, Justice Stewart in a concurring opinion noted:

> The states are most assuredly free "to choose their own curriculums for their own schools." A state is entirely free, for example, to decide that the only foreign language to be taught in its public school system shall be Spanish. But would a state be constitutionally free to punish a teacher for letting his students know that other languages are also spoken in the world? I think not.
>
> It is one thing for a state to determine that "the subject of higher mathematics, or astronomy, or biology" shall or shall not be included in its public school curriculum. It is quite another thing for a state to make it a criminal offense for a public school teacher so much as to mention the very existence of an entire system of respected human thought. That kind of criminal law, I think, would clearly impinge upon the guarantees of free communication contained in the First Amendment, and made applicable to the states by the Fourteenth.[31]

In another concurring opinion in *Epperson*, Justice Black made some comments which are quite relevant to any interpretation of the limits of "academic freedom."

> "I am also not ready to hold that a person hired to teach school children takes with him into the classroom a constitutional right to teach sociological, economic, political, or religious subjects that the school's managers do not want discussed. This Court has said that the rights of free speech "while fundamental in our democratic society, still do not mean that everyone with opinions or beliefs to express may address a group at any public place and at any time." * * * I question whether it is absolutely certain, as the Court's opinion indicates, that "academic freedom" permits a teacher to breach his contractual agreement to teach only the subjects designated by the school authorities who hired him.[32]

These comments identify a wide variation in perceptions of

---

31. 393 U.S. 97, 89 S. Ct. 266 (1968).
32. *Ibid.*

the meaning of "academic freedom" and the attendant suppositions regarding the extent of allowable state restriction and the limits to which a teacher, as a public employee, may extend her individual constitutional rights into the classroom. In all of these cases the Court appeared to be reacting in considerable degree to the teacher's conviction under a criminal statute, thereby casting some implications with regard to academic freedom which might not be consistently followed in a simple case of teacher dismissal or reprimand.

PRIVILEGE AGAINST SELF-INCRIMINATION

Even though the right *nemo tenetur seipsum prodere,* "no man is bound to accuse himself," as extended by the Fifth Amendment applies to teachers as individuals, it has not yet been applied in such a manner as to allow a person to avoid questions concerning his competency as a teacher. In *Beilan v. Board of Education,*[33] the dismissal of a teacher for failure to answer questions posed by his superintendent about alleged subversive activities was upheld by the Supreme Court. The teacher's refusal to answer pertinent questions regarding his employment was insubordination. In following *Beilan,* one can assume that teachers cannot refuse to answer questions relevant to their employment by "taking the Fifth."

A similar case by the Supreme Court upheld the dismissal of a New York transit employee who was dismissed on the ground that his failure to answer questions concerning Communist membership cast him in a light of doubtful trust and reliability.[34]

On the other hand, if a teacher is dismissed for invoking the privilege against self-incrimination where his capacity as a teacher is not in question, his dismissal is unconstitutional. In *Slochower v. Board of Education*[35] an associate professor at Brooklyn College was summarily discharged for his refusal to answer questions before a Congressional committee concerning membership in the Communist Party. His refusal was based on the Fifth Amendment—that his answers might tend to incriminate him. The Supreme Court held that *summary dismissal* for invoking the privilege violated the Due Process, Privileges and Immunities clauses of the Fourteenth Amendment and said that the privilege against self-incrimination would be a "hollow mockery" if its exercise could be taken as

33. 357 U.S. 399 (1958).
34. Lerner v. Casey, 357 U.S. 468 (1958).
35. 350 U.S. 551 (1956).

"equivalent either to a confession of guilt or a conclusive presumption of perjury." The Court further held that the board's
action could not be construed as a *bona fide* attempt to gain
needed and relevant information regarding his qualifications
as a teacher as had been the situation in *Beilan*.

Following the same reasoning the Supreme Court of
Pennsylvania held that teachers who were dismissed for asserting the plea against self-incrimination before a Congressional Committee, were deprived of liberty and property without due process of law, and such an act by the state worked an
abridgment of the same constitutional privilege in violation
of the Fourteenth Amendment. The Pennsylvania court distinguished this case from *Beilan* saying: [36]

> "What the Board of Education sought to accomplish in
> these cases goes far beyond anything that was either de-
> cided or implied by the opinion for this court in Beilan's
> case. His adjudged incompetency resided exclusively in
> the fact that he had refused to answer questions of his
> *administrative superior* concerning matters deemed to
> have bearing on his qualifications as a teacher in the pub-
> lic schools of Philadelphia, and not that he had refused to
> answer questions of a Congressional Committee. That
> such was the *ratio decidendi* in the Beilan case is not
> open to question. * * * The secretiveness (of Beilan)
> consisted of a deliberate and insubordinate refusal to
> answer questions of his *administrative superior* is a vi-
> tally important matter pertaining to his fitness. Such con-
> duct stamped him with *incompetence* as a professional
> employee in the public schools." (Emphasis added.)

In *Barenblatt v. United States* [37] the Court held that teachers could not take shelter behind the First Amendment and do
not solely, as teachers, have a special privilege against inter-
rogation before a Congressional Committee. Barenblatt, an instructor at the University of Michigan and later at Vassar objected generally to the right of a Congressional Committee to
inquire into his "political" and "religious" beliefs and any
"other personal and private affairs" or "associational activities." He claimed privilege and was convicted for contempt of
Congress. He, however, did not attempt to maintain privilege
against self-incrimination under the Fifth Amendment but instead based his refusal on tenets of the First Amendment
specifically and "academic freedom" in general. The Court

---

36. Board of Public Education School District of Philadelphia v. In-
tille, 401 Pa. 1, 163 A.2d 420 (1960).
37. 360 U.S. 109 (1959).

sustained the conviction and denied appellant's argument that "academic freedom" limited the investigatory power of Congress in the field of education. The Court distinguished this situation from that of *Sweezy v. New Hampshire* [38] where the Supreme Court held that teachers have a privilege to be free from legislative scrutiny into their conduct in the classroom as a part of a general loyalty investigation. This to the Court was very different from a direct inquiry into a person's activities before a Congressional Committee as was the situation in *Barenblatt*.

Barenblatt rested his case not on the inference of self-incrimination, but instead sought limitation on the power of Congress to question him regarding alleged subversive activities. The Supreme Court was not prepared to place such a constitutional limitation on the activities of Congress.

The cases involving self-incrimination are delicately balanced between the rights of the individual and the right of the public to protect itself against subversion of its government. Certainly, taking the privilege against self-incrimination under the Fifth Amendment does not indicate the guilt of a person. However, where a person refuses to answer questions directed by his administrative superior regarding his competence as a teacher, then the courts will apparently uphold dismissal for insubordination.

DISMISSAL OF TENURED FACULTY

As pointed out earlier, teachers possess not only constitutional protections, but also statutory and contractual protections against dismissal or other specified sanctions by a governing board or administrator. Tenure is not peculiar to education; federal judges have tenure for life and federal and state employees generally are protected by some type of tenure system after serving designated probationary periods. Tenure systems, now quite prevalent among the states, are essentially employment security devices under which teachers attain permanent status guaranteeing them against dismissal except for stated cause and through proper procedures. Tenure laws are calculated to increase teacher freedom of action both inside and outside the classroom. On the other hand, numerous disadvantages are also attached to tenure such as creating an inflexible staffing system which is difficult to upgrade, creating a problem of "deadwood" whereby tenured faculty

---

38. 354 U.S. 234 (1957).

becomes lazy and out-of-date and the entire institution deteriorates. Machlup, however, observes that the total benefit derived by society from the fruits of faculty tenure and freedom far outweigh the disadvantages.[39]

Tenure systems in public institutions are usually created by statute, while tenure in private institutions is created by the individual school itself. A minority of states utilize "continuing contracts," a partial tenure system or "spring notification" provision whereby employment is continued unless the contract is abrogated by either party. In such instances, a deadline date is usually specified in the spring of the year subsequent to which termination by one party is not valid.

When tenure laws are established by statute, governing subordinate institutions, an individual board or agency is powerless to change the conditions of tenure. Indeed, if a tenure law is established which creates a contractual relationship between the state and a teacher, then the state itself cannot unilaterally alter the obligations of the contract without violating the Federal Constitution.[40] However, the extent to which the teacher is protected against subsequent acts by the legislature is dependent on the precise wording of the statute. If the teacher has only a legislatively created status, noncontractual in nature, then the tenure provisions may be altered or eliminated by later legislative acts.[41] In order to avoid the inference of a contractual relationship between the teacher and the state, some legislatures have entered specific disclaimers in their tenure laws.

Tenured faculty can only be dismissed by following certain statutory procedural steps and any deviation from the procedures invalidates the dismissal. The procedures generally contain the following procedural requirements: (1) The faculty committee is to be given notice in writing of the proposed dismissal in sufficient time to ensure an opportunity to prepare for a hearing, (2) the teacher is to reply in writing within a given time whether he wishes to have a hearing, (3) a hearing is given the faculty member during which he should have an opportunity to testify and present evidence and witnesses and

39. Fritz Machlup, "In Defense of Academic Tenure," *Academic Freedom and Tenure; A Handbook of the AAUP*, edited by Louis Joughin, The University of Wisconsin Press, 1967, p. 326.

40. Indiana *ex rel.* Anderson v. Brand, 303 U.S. 95 (1938); U.S. Const. Art. 1, § 10.

41. Phelps v. Board of Education, 300 U.S. 319 (1937); Dodge v. Board of Education, 302 U.S. 74 (1937).

hear and question adverse witnesses, (4) the results of the hearing are made to the faculty member for possible appeal to the courts.[42]

A tenure teacher can only be dismissed for statutorily specified reasons including such causes as incompetency, insubordination, immorality, etc.

INCOMPETENCY

Incompetency is the most frequently stated cause for dismissal and is probably the most difficult to define. The complexity of the term is partially attributable to its overusage as a "catch-all" to describe numerous conditions which may not be covered by other statutorily stated causes for dismissal. For example, in the classic case where a teacher was dismissed for incompetency because of her afterhours activity in her husband's beer garden, where she served as a bartender and waitress, occasionally drinking beer, shaking dice, and playing the pinball machine with customers, the court maintained that "incompetency" was not confined to whether a teacher was competent to teach the 3R's but also the term included want of "physical, intellectual or moral ability."[43]

The Supreme Court of the United States has similarly broadly defined the teacher's standard of fitness: "We find no requirement in the Federal Constitution that a teacher's classroom conduct be the sole basis for determining his fitness. Fitness for teaching depends on a broad range of factors."[44]

The Court quoted a series of definitions broadly defining incompetency:

> The term "incompetency" has a "common and approved usage." The context does not limit the meaning of the word to lack of substantive knowledge of the subjects to be taught. Common and approved usage give a much wider meaning. * * * "A relative term without technical meaning. It may be employed as meaning disqualification; inability; incapacity; lack of ability, legal qualifications, or fitness to discharge the required duty." * * * "Lack of ability or fitness to discharge the required duty." * * * "Want of physical, intellectual, or moral ability; insufficiency; inadequacy; want of legal qualifications of

42. See Louis Joughin, *Academic Freedom and Tenure; A Handbook of the American Association of University Professors*, The University of Wisconsin Press, 1967, pp. 42-45.

43. Horosko v. School Dist. of Mount Pleasant, 335 Pa., 369, 6 A.2d 866 (1939).

44. Beilan v. Board of Public Education of Philadelphia, 357 U.S. 399, 78 S. Ct. 1317 (1958).

fitness." * * * "General lack of capacity of fitness, or lack of the special qualities required for a particular purpose." [45]

INSUBORDINATION

Insubordination is more specific than incompetency and is generally considered to constitute repeated refusal to abide by rules or regulations of the organization or to follow reasonable directions of a superior. The use of the term, warranting discharge of a university professor, "imports willful disregard of express or implied directions or such defiant attitude as to be equivalent thereto." [46] Another court defined insubordination as "disobedience of orders, infraction of rules, or generally synonymous with contumacious." [47] An employee cannot be dismissed for refusal to obey unreasonable rules or *ultra vires* acts of a governing board.

IMMORALITY

Immorality or immoral conduct is activity inconsistent with moral rectitude. Immorality is not necessarily confined to matters sexual in nature; "it may be that which is *contra bonos mores;* contrary to conscience or moral law; wicked, vicious or licentious." In a case where a teacher was engaged in the incompatible business of selling liquor under a fictitious name, the court held such misrepresentation was sufficient to support the teacher's dismissal for "immorality." [48] Proof that a teacher obtains his position by falsifying records also constituted proof of "immorality" within the meaning of tenure statute. [49]

A California court has said that the terms "immorality" and "evident unfitness for service" must be construed "according to their common and approved usage having regard for the context in which the legislature used them." The court sustained the findings for dismissal of a trial court from evidence produced showing that a teacher removed a school public address system from the classroom, used vulgar language,

45. *Ibid.*
46. State *ex rel.* Richardson v. Board of Regents of University of Nevada, 70 Nev. 347, 269 P.2d 265 (1954).
47. Muldrow v. Board of Public Instruction of Duval County, 189 So. 2d 414 (Fla. App. 1966).
48. Appeal of Batrus, 148 Pa. Super. 587, 26 A.2d 121 (1942).
49. Negrich v. Dade County Board of Public Instruction, 143 So. 2d 498 (Fla. App. 1962). See also Board of Education of San Francisco Unified School District v. Weiland, 179 Cal. App. 2d 808, 4 Cal. Rptr. 286 (1960).

warned several Mexican-American students, in the presence of the entire class, of the prevalence of syphillis in a nearby Mexican town, and made gestures including licking the wall with his tongue "to indicate that the superintendent of schools was a person who would rather curry favor with his supervisors than do his duty." These actions in addition to references to "whores" and "whorehouses" were not considered by the court as evidence of "immorality" but were considered as evidence of "unfitness" to serve as a teacher.[50]

"Immorality" or "immoral conduct" does not extend to actions which are merely considered to be in bad taste. For example, a junior college board of trustees sought to dismiss a teacher for "immoral conduct" and "evident unfitness for service." The proceedings stemmed from a teacher's assignment of an article entitled "Student as Nigger" and a poem containing vulgar language. The court held that while the use of the material was exceedingly ill-advised from a public relations standpoint, it fell short of "immoral conduct." The court maintained that it was "preposterous" to assume that junior college students could be "morally" harmed by exposure to such material.[51]

OTHER REASONS FOR DISMISSAL

Other commonly used reasons for dismissal include *neglect of duty* and *other good cause*. "Neglect of duty" is usually justification for dismissal of public officers, but is often given as reason for dismissal of public employees as well. "Neglect of duty" has been held by the courts to mean "nonfeasance",[52] "malfeasance"[53] as well as "misfeasance." Simple neglect may be committed through carelessness or an omission, where to satisfy a statute requiring "willful neglect of duty" it must be shown that a teacher's neglect was knowing, intentional, or deliberate. "Good cause" has been held to be any ground put forward in good faith by a board which is not "arbitrary, irrational, unreasonable, or irrelevant" to the board's task of maintaining an educational system.[54] The rule of *ejusdem generis* generally applies in such statutory construction, mean-

50. Palo Verde Unified School District of Riverside County v. Hensey, 88 Cal. Rptr. 570 (1970).

51. Board of Trustees of the Los Angeles Junior College District of Los Angeles County v. Hoag, No. 964,057 (Super. Ct. Los Angeles, Dec. 1970).

52. Holmes v. Osborn, 57 Ariz. 522, 115 P.2d 775 (1941).

53. State *ex rel.* Knabb v. Frater, 198 Wash. 675, 89 P.2d 1046 (1939).

54. Rinaldo v. Dreyer, 294 Mass. 167, 1 N.E.2d 37 (1936).

ing that the general words (good cause) following an enumeration of specific things are usually restricted to those things of the same class, kind or nature.

PROCEDURAL DUE PROCESS OF NONTENURE FACULTY

In the absence of tenure a teacher's employment rights are limited to the conditions embodied in his contract with the institution.[55]

CONTRACT RENEWAL

At the end of the contract period the teacher has no right of renewal. During the contract period the teacher can be dismissed only for statutory cause unless the contract calls for termination upon notice.[56] The view of the courts has historically been that teachers without tenure have no established right of employment subject to constitutional procedural termination.

More recently courts have tended to invoke constitutional protection for teachers if their rights have been infringed upon regardless of whether they are protected by tenure. The courts, though, have been rather selective in their invocation of constitutional protections because to apply procedural due process to all instances of employment termination would, in essence, negate the impact of tenure laws, allowing everyone the same protection whether it came from the tenure statute or the Constitution of the United States.

The dilemma of the courts in deciding these issues is reflected in a recent statement by a federal district court in Wyoming.

> . . . A teacher who has not had the privileges of tenure incorporated in his teaching contract simply cannot claim the benefit of tenure if such a system is to survive with any merit at all. The implementation of tenure is within the exclusive realm of the legislative process and it is not within the province of this court to establish tenure at community colleges in the State of Wyoming.[57]

In keeping with this philosophy, the Supreme Court of Illinois has commented in dictum, while affirming dismissal of

55. Keeney v. Ayers, 108 Mont. 547, 92 P.2d 306 (1939). See also "Developments in the Law-Academic Freedom," *op. cit.*, pp. 1100-1104.
56. Independent School District v. Samuelson, 222 Iowa 1063, 270 N.W. 434 (1936).
57. Schultz v. Palmberg, 317 F. Supp. 959 (1970).

two nontenure teachers from the faculty of Chicago State College, that:

> . . . However, even if the issue were before the court we would be inclined to find that a Board has a right, summarily, to terminate a probationary teacher's employment at the end of his employment term, and that he has no constitutional right to continued employment. . . . [And] if a probationary teacher has no constitutional right to continued employment under such circumstances, the Board would have no duty to provide him with specific reasons for his non-retention.[58]

The United States Supreme Court, in commenting on the right of a person to procedural due process before termination of welfare benefits said that whether and to what extent procedural due process is afforded the individual is influenced by (a) the extent to which he may be "condemned to suffer grievous loss," and (b) whether the recipient's interest in avoiding that loss outweighs the governmental interest which involves a determination of the "precise nature of the governmental function involved as well as of the private interest that has been affected by government action." [59]

EXPECTANCY OF REEMPLOYMENT

The relationship, however, can be such between a college and a nontenure teacher as to create an "expectation of reemployment" on the part of the teacher. If such an "expectation" is present, the courts have held that the college is obligated to provide the teacher with procedural due process upon termination of employment. In *Ferguson v. Thomas*,[60] the Court of Appeals for the Fifth Circuit said, that although plaintiff was not tenured:

> . . . [A] college can create an obligation as between itself and an instructor where none might otherwise exist under the legal standards for the interpretation of contract relationships regularly applied to transactions in the market place if it adopts regulations or standards of practice governing nontenured employees which create an expectation of reemployment.

In dismissing a nontenure teacher the college need only to indicate its intention to terminate the employment for cause.

---

58. Fooden v. Board of Governors of State Colleges and Universities of Illinois, Docket Nos. 42460 and 42461, Agenda 41, March 1970 (Ill. Sup. Ct., Jan. 25, 1970).

59. Goldberg v. Kelly, 397 U.S. 254, 90 S. Ct. 1011 (1970).

60. Ferguson v. Thomas, 430 F.2d 852 (5th Cir. 1970).

If the teacher accepts, so be it; if he challenges the termination, then the college should come forward with a statement of reasons and then the procedures for dismissal come into play. The court in *Ferguson*, commenting on this process for termination, said:

> The substance of due process requires that no instructor who has an expectancy of continued employment be deprived of that expectancy by mere ceremonial compliance with procedural due process. While he has no right to continued public employment, such a teacher may neither be dismissed or not be rehired for constitutionally impermissible reasons such as race, religion, or assertion of rights guaranteed by law or the Constitution. This rationale would even apply to a teacher without tenure or an expectancy of reemployment.[61]

PROCEDURAL DUE PROCESS REQUIRED

This court then outlined the steps necessary for minimum procedural due process: (a) notice of the cause or causes for termination in sufficient detail to enable the teacher to show any error which may exist; (b) be advised of the names and the nature of the testimony of witnesses against him; (c) at a reasonable time after such advice, he be accorded meaningful opportunity to be heard in his own defense, and (d) a hearing be held before a tribunal that both possesses the academic expertise and has apparent impartiality toward the charges. From these minimal steps a college possessing no established procedures may adopt any adequate method of due process; if, however, the college has published rules and regulations going beyond the above minimum standards, then they must be followed even though they are in more detail and exceed the constitutionally minimum requirement.

A teacher who is unable to show a constitutional deprivation or a valid "expectancy of employment" is not entitled to a hearing or a statement of causes for dismissal. Such a requirement by the courts:

> "* * * would have the legal effect of improperly denying to colleges freedom of contract to employ personnel on a probationary basis or under annual contracts which are unfettered by any reemployment obligation. Every teacher would thus be granted substantial tenure rights by court edict. Courts do not make contracts for colleges or teachers any more than for any other litigants." [62]

---

61. *Ibid.*
62. Sindermann v. Perry, 430 F.2d 939 (5th Cir. 1970).

A series of short-term contracts over a long period of time has been held to create an "expectancy of reemployment" by the teacher.[63] Similarly, a statement by a college saying, "The administration of the college wishes the faculty member to feel that he has permanent tenure as long as his teaching services are satisfactory * * *," may create a protectable interest as "expectancy of reemployment." [64]

The Court of Appeals for the Fifth Circuit disagreed with the contention by a teacher that a hearing must be held simply to prove to the teacher that the termination of his employment was not based on restraint of a constitutionally protected freedom.

> "Surely appellant would know whether he has been participating in constitutionally protected activities that might be irritating to school authorities. It is not too much to ask that appellant allege in his complaint a possible violation of constitutional rights if a basis for such an allegation exists. It would be too much to ask the school board to hold a hearing every time it determines not to renew the contract of a probationary teacher, or every time a terminated teacher requests a hearing without alleging unconstitutional action. . . . [T]he requirement proposed by the appellant would nullify the probationary system, whose purpose is to provide the school board a short term-test period during which the fledgling teacher may be examined, evaluated, and if found wanting for any constitutional reason, not rehired." [65]

No inference of guilt can be made from claiming privilege against self-incrimination before a federal committee

SLOCHOWER v. BOARD OF EDUCATION

Supreme Court of the United States, 1956.
350 U.S. 551, 76 S. Ct. 637.

MR. JUSTICE CLARK delivered the opinion of the Court.

This appeal brings into question the constitutionality of § 903 of the Charter of the City of New York. That section provides that whenever an employee of the City utilizes the privilege against self-incrimination to avoid answering a question

63. Lucas v. Chapman, 430 F.2d 945 (5th Cir. 1970).
64. Sindermann v. Perry, *supra*.
65. Thaw v. Board of Public Instruction of Dade County, Fla., 432 F.2d 98 (5th Cir. 1970).

relating to his official conduct, "his term or tenure of office or employment shall terminate and such office or employment shall be vacant, and he shall not be eligible to election or appointment to any office or employment under the city or any agency." Appellant Slochower invoked the privilege against self-incrimination under the Fifth Amendment before an investigating committee of the United States Senate, and was summarily discharged from his position as associate professor at Brooklyn College, an institution maintained by the City of New York. He now claims that the charter provision, as applied to him, violates both the Due Process and Privileges and Immunities Clauses of the Fourteenth Amendment.

On September 24, 1952, the Internal Security Subcommittee of the Committee on the Judiciary of the United States Senate held open hearings in New York City. The investigation, conducted on a national scale, related to subversive influences in the American educational system. At the beginning of the hearings the Chairman stated that education was primarily a state and local function, and therefore the inquiry would be limited to "considerations affecting national security, which are directly within the purview and authority of the subcommittee." Hearings Before the Subcommittee to Investigate the Administration of the Internal Security Act and Other Internal Security Laws of Senate Committee on the Judiciary, 82d Cong., 2d Sess., 1. Professor Slochower, when called to testify, stated that he was not a member of the Communist Party, and indicated complete willingness to answer all questions about his associations or political beliefs since 1941. But he refused to answer questions concerning his membership during 1940 and 1941 on the ground that his answers might tend to incriminate him. The Chairman of the Senate Subcommittee accepted Slochower's claim as a valid assertion of an admitted constitutional right. * * *

Shortly after testifying before the Internal Security Subcommittee, Slochower was notified that he was suspended from his position at the College; three days later his position was declared vacant "pursuant to the provisions of Section 903 of the New York City Charter."

Slochower had 27 years' experience as a college teacher and was entitled to tenure under state law. McKinney's New York Laws, Education Law, § 6206 (2). Under this statute, appellant may be discharged only for cause, and after notice, hearing, and appeal. § 6206 (10). The Court of Appeals of New York, however, has authoritatively interpreted § 903 to mean that "the assertion of the privilege against self incrimination is equivalent to a resignation." * * * Dismissal under this provision is therefore automatic and there is no right to charges, notice, hearing, or opportunity to explain. * * *

Slochower argues that § 903 abridges a privilege or immunity of a citizen of the United States since it in effect imposes a penalty on the exercise of a federally guaranteed right in a federal proceeding. It also violates due process, he argues, because the mere claim of privilege under the Fifth Amendment does not provide a reasonable basis for the State to terminate his employment. * * *

At the outset we must condemn the practice of imputing a sinister meaning to the exercise of a person's constitutional right under the Fifth Amendment. The right of an accused person to refuse to testify, which had been in England merely a rule of evidence, was so important to our forefathers that they raised it to the dignity of a constitutional enactment, and it has been recognized as "one of the most valuable prerogatives of the citizen." * * * The privilege against self-incrimination would be reduced to a hollow mockery if its exercise could be taken as equivalent either to a confession of guilt or a conclusive presumption of perjury. As we pointed out in *Ullmann*,* a witness may have a reasonable fear of prosecution and yet be innocent of any wrongdoing. The privilege serves to protect the innocent who otherwise might be ensnared by ambiguous circumstances. * * *

With this in mind, we consider the application of § 903. As interpreted and applied by the state courts, it operates to discharge every city employee who invokes the Fifth Amendment. In practical effect the questions asked are taken as confessed and made the basis of the discharge. No consideration is given to such factors as the subject matter of the questions, remoteness of the period to which they are directed, or justification for exercise of the privilege. It matters not whether the plea resulted from mistake, inadvertence or legal advice conscientiously given, whether wisely or unwisely. The heavy hand of the statute falls alike on all who exercise their constitutional privilege, the full enjoyment of which every person is entitled to receive. * * *

It is one thing for the city authorities themselves to inquire into Slochower's fitness, but quite another for his discharge to be based entirely on events occurring before a federal committee whose inquiry was announced as not directed at "the property, affairs, or government of the city, or . . . official

---

* Ullmann v. United States, 350 U.S. 422 (1956).

conduct of city employees." In this respect the present case differs materially from *Garner*, where the city was attempting to elicit information necessary to determine the qualifications of its employees. Here, the Board had possessed the pertinent information for 12 years, and the questions which Professor Slochower refused to answer were admittedly asked for a purpose wholly unrelated to his college functions. On such a record the Board cannot claim that its action was part of a bona fide attempt to gain needed and relevant information.

Without attacking Professor Slochower's qualification for his position in any manner, and apparently with full knowledge of the testimony he had given some 12 years before at the state committee hearing, the Board seized upon his claim of privilege before the federal committee and converted it through the use of § 903 into a conclusive presumption of guilt. Since no inference of guilt was possible from the claim before the federal committee, the discharge falls of its own weight as wholly without support. There has not been the "protection of the individual against arbitrary action" which Mr. Justice Cardozo characterized as the very essence of due process. * * *

This is not to say that Slochower has a constitutional right to be an associate professor of German at Brooklyn College. The State has broad powers in the selection and discharge of its employees, and it may be that proper inquiry would show Slochower's continued employment to be inconsistent with a real interest of the State. But there has been no such inquiry here. We hold that the summary dismissal of appellant violates due process of law.

The judgment is reversed and the cause is remanded for further proceedings not inconsistent with this opinion.

Reversed and remanded.

NOTES

In *Sweezy v. New Hampshire* * the Supreme Court of the United States struck down the dismissal of a university professor for declining to answer questions before a subversive activities committee of the New Hampshire legislature concerning: (1) the content of a lecture given at the University of New Hampshire, (2) activities of himself and others in the Progressive political organizations, and (3) "opinions and

---

* 354 U.S. 234 (1957).

beliefs," invoking the constitutional guarantees of free speech. In reversing the New Hampshire Supreme Court, the United States Supreme Court found that the legislative committee's activities did not constitute restraint supported by a reasonable governmental interest. The United States Supreme Court commenting on the desirability and necessity of free flow of ideas in a university said:

> Progress in the natural sciences is not remotely confined to findings made in the laboratory. Insights into the mysteries of nature are born of hypothesis and speculation. The more so is this true in the pursuit of understanding in the groping endeavors of what are called the social sciences, the concern of which is man and society. The problems that are the respective preoccupations of anthropology, economics, law, psychology, sociology and related areas of scholarship are merely departmentalized dealing, by way of manageable division of analysis, with interpenetrating aspects of holistic perplexities. For society's good—if understanding be an essential need of society—inquiries into these problems, speculations about them, stimulation in others of reflection upon them, must be left as unfettered as possible. Political power must abstain from intrusion into this activity of freedom, pursued in the interest of wise government and the people's well-being, except for reasons that are exigent and obviously compelling.
>
> These pages need not be burdened with proof, based on the testimony of a cloud of impressive witnesses, of the dependence of a free society on free universities. This means the exclusion of governmental intervention in the intellectual life of a university. It matters little whether such intervention occurs avowedly or through action that inevitably tends to check the ardor and fearlessness of scholars, qualities at once so fragile and so indispensable for fruitful academic labor. One need only refer to the address of T. H. Huxley at the opening of Johns Hopkins University, the Annual Reports of President A. Lawrence Lowell of Harvard, the Reports of the University Grants Committee in Great Britain, as illustrative items in a vast body of literature. Suffice it to quote the latest expression on this subject. It is also perhaps the most poignant because its plea on behalf of continuing the free spirit of the open universities of South Africa has gone unheeded.
>
> > "In a university knowledge is its own end, not merely a means to an end. A university ceases to be true to its own nature if it becomes the tool of Church or State or any sectional interest. A university is characterized by the spirit of free inquiry, its ideal being the ideal of Socrates—'to follow the argument where it leads.' This implies the right to examine, question, modify or reject traditional ideas

and beliefs. Dogma and hypothesis are incompatible, and the concept of an immutable doctrine is repugnant to the spirit of a university. The concern of its scholars is not merely to add and revise facts in relation to an accepted framework, but to be ever examining and modifying the framework itself."

"Freedom to reason and freedom for disputation on the basis of observation and experiment are the necessary conditions for the advancement of scientific knowledge. A sense of freedom is also necessary for creative work in the arts which, equally with scientific research, is the concern of the university."

". . . It is the business of a university to provide that atmosphere which is most conducive to speculation, experiment and creation. It is an atmosphere in which there prevail 'the four essential freedoms' of a university—to determine for itself on academic grounds who may teach, what may be taught, and who may be admitted to study." The Open Universities in South Africa 10-12. (A statement of a conference of senior scholars from the University of Cape Town and the University of the Witwatersrand, including A. v. d.S. Centlivres and Richard Feetham, as Chancellors of the respective universities.)

I do not suggest that what New Hampshire has here sanctioned bears any resemblance to the policy against which this South African remonstrance was directed. I do say that in these matters of the spirit inroads on legitimacy must be resisted at their incipiency. This kind of evil grows by what it is allowed to feed on. The admonition of this Court in another context is applicable here. "It may be that it is the obnoxious thing in its mildest and least repulsive form; but illegitimate and unconstitutional practices get their first footing in that way, namely, by silent approaches and slight deviations from legal modes of procedure. . . ."

A loyalty oath may be unconstitutionally vague

BAGGETT v. BULLITT

Supreme Court of the United States, 1964.
377 U.S. 360, 84 S. Ct. 1316.

Mr. Justice WHITE delivered the opinion of the Court.

Appellants, approximately 64 in number, are members of the faculty, staff and student body of the University of Washington who brought this class action asking for a judgment declaring unconstitutional two Washington statutes requiring the execution of two different oaths by state employees and for an injunction against the enforcement of these statutes by appellees, the President of the University, members of the Washington State Board of Regents and the State Attorney General.

The statutes under attack are Chapter 377, Laws of 1955, and Chapter 103, Laws of 1931, both of which require employees of the State of Washington to take the oaths prescribed in the statutes as a condition of their employment. The 1931 legislation applies only to teachers, who, upon applying for a license to teach or renewing an existing contract, are required to subscribe to the following:

> "I solemnly swear (or affirm) that I will support the constitution and laws of the United States of America and of the State of Washington, and will by precept and example promote respect for the flag and the institutions of the United States of America and the State of Washington, reverence for law and order and undivided allegiance to the government of the United States." Wash.Laws 1931, c. 103.

The oath requirements of the 1955 Act, Wash.Laws 1955, c. 377, applicable to all state employees, incorporate various provisions of the Washington Subversive Activities Act of 1951, which provides generally that "[n]o subversive person, as defined in this act, shall be eligible for employment in, or appointment to any office, or any position of trust or profit in the government, or in the administration of the business, of this state, or of any county, municipality, or other political subdivision of this state." Wash.Rev.Code § 9.81.060. The term "subversive person" is defined as follows:

> " 'Subversive person' means any person who commits, attempts to commit, or aids in the commission, or advocates, abets, advises or teaches by any means any person to commit, attempt to commit, or aid in the commission of any act intended to overthrow, destroy or alter, or to assist in the overthrow, destruction or alteration of, the constitutional form of the government of the United States, or of the state of Washington, or any political subdivision of either of them by revolution, force, or violence; or who with knowledge that the organization is an organization as described in subsections (2) and (3) hereof, becomes or remains a member of a subversive organization or a foreign subversive organization." Wash.Rev.Code § 9.81.010 (5).

The Act goes on to define at similar length and in similar terms "subversive organization" and "foreign subversive organization" and to declare the Communist Party a subversive organization and membership therein a subversive activity.

On May 28, 1962, some four months after this Court's dismissal of the appeal in Nostrand v. Little, 368 U.S. 436, 82 S.Ct. 464, 7 L.Ed.2d 426, also a challenge to the 1955 oath, the University President, acting pursuant to directions of the Board of Regents, issued a memorandum to all University employees notifying them that they would be required to take an oath. Oath Form A requires all teaching personnel to swear to the oath of allegiance set out above, to aver that they have read, are familiar with and understand the provisions defining "subversive person" in the Subversive Activities Act of 1951 and to disclaim being a subversive person and membership in the Communist Party or any other subversive or foreign subversive organization. Oath Form B requires other state employees to subscribe to all of the above provisions except the 1931 oath. Both forms provide that the oath and statements pertinent thereto are made subject to the penalties of perjury. * * *

Appellants contend in this Court that the oath requirements and the statutory provisions on which they are based are invalid on their face because their language is unduly vague, uncertain and broad. We agree with this contention and therefore, without reaching the numerous other contentions pressed upon us, confine our considerations to that particular question.

In Cramp v. Board of Public Instruction, 368 U.S. 278, 82 S.Ct. 275, 7 L.Ed.2d 285, the Court invalidated an oath requiring teachers and other employees of the State to swear that they had never lent their "aid, support, advice, counsel, or influence to the Communist Party" because the oath was lacking in "terms susceptible of objective measurement" and failed to inform as to what the State commanded or forbade. The statute therefore fell within the compass of those decisions of the Court holding that a law forbidding or requiring conduct in terms so vague that men of common intelligence must necessarily guess at its meaning and differ as to its application violates due process of law. * * *

The oath required by the 1955 statute suffers from similar infirmities. A teacher must swear that he is not a subversive person: that he is not one who commits an act or who advises, teaches, abets or advocates by any means another person to commit or aid in the commission of any act intended to overthrow or alter, or to assist the overthrow or alteration, of the constitutional form of government by revolution, force or violence. A subversive organization is defined as one which engages in or assists activities intended to alter or overthrow the Government by force or violence or which has as a purpose the commission of such acts. The Communist Party is declared in the statute to be a subversive organization, that is, it is presumed that the Party does and will engage in activities intended to overthrow the Government. Persons required to swear they understand this oath may quite reasonably conclude that any person who aids the Communist Party or teaches or advises known members of the Party is a subversive person because such teaching or advice may now or at some future date aid the activities of the Party. Teaching and advising are clearly acts, and one cannot confidently assert that his counsel, aid, influence or support which adds to the resources, rights and knowledge of the Communist Party or its members does not aid the Party in its activities, activities which the statute tells us are all in furtherance of the stated purpose of overthrowing the Government by revolution, force, or violence. The questions put by the Court in Cramp may with equal force be asked here. Does the statute reach endorsement or support for Communist candidates for office? Does it reach a lawyer who represents the Communist Party or its members or a journalist who defends constitutional rights of the Communist Party or its members or anyone who supports any cause which is likewise supported by Communists or the Communist Party? The susceptibility of the statutory language to require forswearing of an undefined variety of "guiltless knowing behavior" is what the Court condemned in Cramp. This statute like the one at issue in Cramp, is unconstitutionally vague.

The Washington statute suffers from additional difficulties on vagueness grounds. A person is subversive not only if he himself commits the specified acts but if he abets or advises another in aiding a third person to commit an act which will assist yet a fourth person in the overthrow or alteration of constitutional government. The Washington Supreme Court has said that knowledge is to be read into every provision and we accept this construction. * * * But what is it that the Washington professor must "know"? Must he know that his aid or teaching will be used by another and that the person aided has the requisite guilty intent or is it sufficient that he knows that his aid or teaching would or might be useful to others in the commission of acts intended to overthrow the Government? Is it subversive activity, for example, to attend and participate in international conventions of mathematicians and exchange views with scholars from Communist countries? What about the editor of a scholarly journal who analyzes and criticizes the manuscripts of Communist scholars submitted for publication? Is selecting outstanding scholars from Communist countries as visiting professors and advising, teaching, or consulting with them at the University of Washington a subversive activity if such scholars are known to be Communists, or regardless of their affiliations, regularly teach students who are members of the Communist Party, which by statutory definition is subversive and dedicated to the overthrow of the Government?

The Washington oath goes beyond overthrow or alteration by force or violence. It extends to alteration by "revolution" which, unless wholly redundant and its ordinary meaning distorted, includes any rapid or fundamental change. Would, therefore, any organization or any person supporting, advocating or teaching peaceful but far-reaching constitutional amendments be engaged in subversive activity? Could one support the repeal of the Twenty-second Amendment or participation by this country in a world government?

We also conclude that the 1931 oath offends due process because of vagueness. The oath exacts a promise that the affiant will, by precept and example, promote respect for the flag and the institutions of the United States and the State of Washington. The range of activities which are or might be deemed inconsistent with the required promise is very wide indeed. The teacher who refused to salute the flag or advocated refusal because of religious beliefs might well be accused of breaching his promise. Cf. West Virginia State Board of Education v. Barnette, 319 U.S. 624, 63 S. Ct. 1178, 87 L.Ed. 1628. Even criticism of the design or color scheme of the state flag or unfavorable comparison of it with that of a sister State or foreign country could be deemed disrespectful and therefore violative of the oath. And what are "institutions" for the purposes of this oath? Is it every "practice, law, custom, etc., which is a material and persistent element in the life or culture of an organized social group" or every "established society or corporation," every "establishment, esp[ecially] one of a public character"? The oath may prevent a professor from criticizing his state judicial system or the Supreme Court or the institution of judicial review. Or it might be deemed to proscribe advocating the abolition, for example, of the Civil Rights Commission, the House Committee on Un-American Activities, or foreign aid.

It is likewise difficult to ascertain what might be done without transgressing the promise to "promote * * * undivided allegiance to the government of the United States." It would not be unreasonable for the serious-minded oath-taker to conclude that he should dispense with lectures voicing far-reaching criticism of any old or new policy followed by the Government of the United States. He could find it questionable under this language to ally himself with any interest group dedicated to opposing any current public policy or law of the Federal Government, for if he did, he might well be accused of placing loyalty to the group above allegiance to the United States.

Indulging every presumption of a narrow construction of the provisions of the 1931 oath, consistent, however, with a proper respect for the English language, we cannot say that this oath provides an ascertainable standard of conduct or that it does not require more than a State may command under the guarantees of the First and Fourteenth Amendments.

As in Cramp v. Board of Public Instruction, "[t]he vice of unconstitutional vagueness is further aggravated where, as here, the statute in question operates to inhibit the exercise of individual freedoms affirmatively protected by the Constitution." 368 U.S. 278, 287, 82 S.Ct. 275, 281. We are dealing with indefinite statutes whose terms, even narrowly construed, abut upon sensitive areas of basic First Amendment freedoms. The uncertain meanings of the oaths require the oath-taker—teachers and public servants—to "steer far wider of the unlawful zone" Speiser v. Randall, 357 U.S. 513, 526, 78 S.Ct. 1332, 1342, 2 L.Ed.2d 1460, than if the boundaries of the forbidden areas were clearly marked. Those with a conscientious regard for what they solemnly swear or affirm, sensitive to the perils posed by the oath's indefinite language, avoid the risk of loss of employment, and perhaps profession, only by restricting their conduct to that which is unquestionably safe. Free speech may not be so inhibited. * * *

As in Cramp v. Board of Public Instruction, supra, we do not question the power of a State to take proper measures safeguarding the public service from disloyal conduct. But measures which purport to define disloyalty must allow public servants to know what is and is not disloyal. "The fact * * * that a person is not compelled to hold public office cannot possibly be an excuse for barring him from office by state-imposed criteria forbidden by the Constitution." Torcaso v. Watkins, 367 U.S. 488, 495-496, 81 S. Ct. 1680, 1684, 6 L.Ed.2d 982.

Reversed.

A loyalty oath is unconstitutional if it contains no exclusion for members who do not subscribe to organization's unlawful aims

ELFBRANDT v. RUSSELL

Supreme Court of the United States, 1966.
384 U.S. 11, 86 S. Ct. 1238.

Mr. Justice DOUGLAS delivered the opinion of the Court.

This case, which involves questions concerning the constitutionality of an Arizona Act requiring an oath from state employees, has been here before. We vacated the judgment of the Arizona Supreme Court which had sustained the oath (94 Ariz. 1, 381 P.2d 554) and remanded the cause for reconsideration in light of Baggett v. Bullitt, 377 U.S. 360, 84 S.Ct. 1316, 12 L.E.2d 377. See 378 U.S. 127, 84 S.Ct. 1658, 12 L.Ed.2d 744. On reconsideration the Supreme Court of Arizona reinstated the original judgment. 97 Ariz. 140, 397 P.2d 944. The case is here on certiorari. 382 U.S. 810, 86 S.Ct. 116, 15 L.Ed.2d 59.

The oath reads in conventional fashion as follows:[1]

"I, (type or print name) do solemnly swear (or affirm) that I will support the Constitution of the United States and the Constitution and laws of the state of Arizona; that I will bear true faith and allegiance to the same, and defend them against all enemies whatever, and that I will faithfully and impartially discharge the duties of the office of (name of office) according to the best of my ability, so help me God (or so I do affirm)."

The Legislature put a gloss on the oath by subjecting to a prosecution for perjury and for discharge from public office anyone who took the oath and who "knowingly and wilfully becomes or remains a member of the communist party of the United States or its successors or any of its subordinate organizations" or "any other organization" having for "one of its purposes" the overthrow of the government of Arizona or any of its political subdivisions where the employee had knowledge of the unlawful purpose. Petitioner, a teacher and a Quaker, decided she could not in good conscience take the oath, not knowing what it meant and not having any chance to get a hearing at which its precise scope and meaning could be determined. This suit for declaratory relief followed. On our remand the Arizona Supreme Court said that the gloss on the

---

1. Ariz.Rev.Stat. § 38-231 (1965 Supp.).

oath is "not afflicted" with the many uncertainties found potentially punishable in Baggett v. Bullitt, supra. * * *

The oath and accompanying statutory gloss challenged here suffer from an identical constitutional infirmity. One who subscribes to this Arizona oath and who is, or thereafter becomes, a knowing member of an organization which has as "one of its purposes" the violent overthrow of the government, is subject to immediate discharge and criminal penalties. Nothing in the oath, the statutory gloss, or the construction of the oath and statutes given by the Arizona Supreme Court, purports to exclude association by one who does not subscribe to the organization's unlawful ends. Here as in Baggett v. Bullitt, supra, the "hazard of being prosecuted for knowing but guiltless behavior" (id., 377 U.S. at 373, 84 S.Ct. at 1323) is a reality. People often label as "communist" ideas which they oppose; and they often make up our juries. "[P]rosecutors too are human." Cramp v. Board of Public Instruction, 368 U.S. 278, 287, 82 S.Ct. 275, 281, 7 L.Ed.2d 285. Would a teacher be safe and secure in going to a Pugwash Conference?[4] Would it be legal to join a seminar group predominantly Communist and therefore subject to control by those who are said to believe in the overthrow of the Government by force and violence? Juries might convict though the teacher did not subscribe to the wrongful aims of the organization. And there is apparently no machinery provided for getting clearance in advance.

Those who join an organization but do not share its unlawful purposes and who do not participate in its unlawful activities surely pose no threat, either as citizens or as public employees. Laws such as this which are not restricted in scope to those who join with the "specific intent" to further illegal action impose, in effect, a conclusive presumption that the member shares the unlawful aims of the organization. * * * The unconstitutionality of this Act follows a fortiori from Speiser v. Randall, 357 U.S. 513, 78 S.Ct. 1332, 2 L.Ed.2d 1460, where we held that a State may not even place on an applicant for a tax exemption the burden of proving that he has not engaged in criminal advocacy.

This Act threatens the cherished freedom of association protected by the First Amendment, made applicable to the States through the Fourteenth Amendment. * * * And, as a

---

4. The Pugwash Conferences, A Staff Analysis, Subcommittee to Investigate the Administration of the Internal Security Act, Senate Committee on the Judiciary, Committee Print, 87th Cong., 1st Sess. (1961); * * *

committee of the Arizona Legislature which urged adoption of this law itself recognized, public employees of character and integrity may well forgo their calling rather than risk prosecution for perjury or compromise their commitment to intellectual and political freedom:

> "The communist trained in fraud and perjury has no qualms in taking any oath; the loyal citizen, conscious of history's oppressions, may well wonder whether the medieval rack and torture wheel are next for the one who declines to take an involved negative oath as evidence that he is a True Believer." [6]

A statute touching those protected rights must be "narrowly drawn to define and punish specific conduct as constituting a clear and present danger to a substantial interest of the State." * * * Legitimate legislative goals "cannot be pursued by means that broadly stifle fundamental personal liberties when the end can be more narrowly achieved." * * * As we said in N.A.A.C.P. v. Button, 371 U.S. 415, 432-433, 83 S.Ct. 328, 338, 9 L.Ed.2d 405:

> "The objectionable quality of * * * overbreadth does not depend upon absence of fair notice to a criminally accused or upon unchanneled delegation of legislative powers, but upon the danger of tolerating, in the area of First Amendment freedoms, the existence of a penal statute susceptible of sweeping and improper application. * * * These freedoms are delicate and vulnerable, as well as supremely precious in our society. The threat of sanctions may deter their exercise almost as potently as the actual application of sanctions. * * *"

A law which applies to membership without the "specific intent" to further the illegal aims of the organization infringes unnecessarily on protected freedoms. It rests on the doctrine of "guilt by association" which has no place here. * * * Such a law cannot stand.

Reversed.

---

6. Report of the Judiciary Committee in Support of the Committee Amendment to H.B. 115, Journal of the Senate, 1st Reg.Sess., 25th Legislature of the State of Arizona, p. 424 (1961).

Merely knowing membership without specific intent to further unlawful aims of an organization is not a constitutionally adequate basis for imposing sanctions

KEYISHIAN v. BOARD OF REGENTS

Supreme Court of the United States, 1967.
385 U.S. 589, 87 S. Ct. 675.

MR. JUSTICE BRENNAN delivered the opinion of the Court.

Appellants were members of the faculty of the privately owned and operated University of Buffalo, and became state employees when the University was merged in 1962 into the State University of New York, an institution of higher education owned and operated by the State of New York. As faculty members of the State University their continued employment was conditioned upon their compliance with a New York plan, formulated partly in statutes and partly in administrative regulations, which the State utilizes to prevent the appointment or retention of "subversive" persons in state employment.

Appellants Hochfield and Maud were Assistant Professors of English, appellant Keyishian an instructor in English, and appellant Garver, a lecturer in philosophy. Each of them refused to sign, as regulations then in effect required, a certificate that he was not a Communist, and that if he had ever been a Communist, he had communicated that fact to the President of the State University of New York. Each was notified that his failure to sign the certificate would require his dismissal. Keyishian's one-year-term contract was not renewed because of his failure to sign the certificate. Hochfield and Garver, whose contracts still had time to run, continue to teach, but subject to proceedings for their dismissal if the constitutionality of the New York plan is sustained. Maud has voluntarily resigned and therefore no longer has standing in this suit.

Appellant Starbuck was a nonfaculty library employee and part-time lecturer in English. Personnel in that classification were not required to sign a certificate but were required to answer in writing under oath the question, "Have you ever advised or taught or were you ever a member of any society or group of persons which taught or advocated the doctrine that the Government of the United States or of any political subdivisions thereof should be overthrown or overturned by force, violence or any unlawful means?" Starbuck refused to answer the question and as a result was dismissed.

Appellants brought this action for declaratory and injunctive relief, alleging that the state program violated the Federal Constitution in various respects. A three-judge federal court held that the program was constitutional. 255 F. Supp. 981. We noted probable jurisdiction of appellants' appeal, 384 U.S. 998. We reverse.

We considered some aspects of the constitutionality of the New York plan 15 years ago in *Adler v. Board of Education*, 342 U.S. 485. That litigation arose after New York passed the Feinberg Law which added § 3022 to the Education Law. The Feinberg Law was enacted to implement and enforce two earlier statutes. The first was a 1917 law, now § 3021 of the Education Law, under which "the utterance of any treasonable or seditious word or words or the doing of any treasonable or seditious act" is a ground for dismissal from the public school system. The second was a 1939 law which was § 12-a of the Civil Service Law when *Adler* was decided and, as amended, is now § 105 of that law. This law disqualifies from the civil service and from employment in the educational system any person who advocates the overthrow of government by force, violence, or any unlawful means, or publishes material advocating such overthrow or organizes or joins any society or group of persons advocating such doctrine. * * *

Adler was a declaratory judgment suit in which the Court held, in effect, that there was no constitutional infirmity in former § 12-a or in the Feinberg Law on their faces and that they were capable of constitutional application. But the contention urged in this case that both § 3021 and § 105 are unconstitutionally vague was not heard or decided. Section 3021 of the Education Law was challenged in *Adler* as unconstitutionally vague, but because the challenge had not been made in the pleadings or in the proceedings in the lower courts, this Court refused to consider it. 342 U. S., at 496. Nor was any challenge on grounds of vagueness made in *Adler* as to subdivisions 1 (a) and (b) of § 105 of the Civil Service Law.[4] Subdivision 3 of § 105 was not added until 1958. Appellants in this case timely asserted below the unconstitutionality of all these sections on grounds of vagueness and that question is now properly before us for decision. Moreover, to the extent that

---

[4] The sole "vagueness" contention in *Adler* concerned the word "subversive," appearing in the preamble to and caption of § 3022. 342 U. S., at 496.

Adler sustained the provision of the Feinberg Law constituting membership in an organization advocating forceful overthrow of government a ground for disqualification, pertinent constitutional doctrines have since rejected the premises upon which that conclusion rested. *Adler* is therefore not dispositive of the constitutional issues we must decide in this case.

A 1953 amendment extended the application of the Feinberg Law to personnel of any college or other institution of higher education owned and operated by the State or its subdivisions. In the same year, the Board of Regents, after notice and hearing, listed the Communist Party of the United States and of the State of New York as "subversive organizations." In 1956 each applicant for an appointment or the renewal of an appointment was required to sign the so-called "Feinberg Certificate" declaring that he had read the Regents Rules and understood that the Rules and the statutes constituted terms of employment, and declaring further that he was not a member of the Communist Party, and that if he had ever been a member he had communicated that fact to the President of the State University. This was the certificate that appellants Hochfield, Maud, Keyishian, and Garver refused to sign. * * *

Section 3021 requires removal for "treasonable or seditious" utterances or acts. The 1958 amendment to § 105 of the Civil Service Law, now subdivision 3 of that section, added such utterances or acts as a ground for removal under that law also. The same wording is used in both statutes—that "the utterance of any treasonable or seditious word or words or the doing of any treasonable or seditious act or acts" shall be ground for removal. But there is a vital difference between the two laws. Section 3021 does not define the terms "treasonable or seditious" as used in that section; in contrast, subdivision 3 of § 105 of the Civil Service Law provides that the terms "treasonable word or act" shall mean "treason" as defined in the Penal Law and the terms "seditious word or act" shall mean "criminal anarchy" as defined in the Penal Law.

Our experience under the Sedition Act of 1798, 1 Stat. 596, taught us that dangers fatal to First Amendment freedoms inhere in the word "seditious." See *New York Times Co. v. Sullivan*, 376 U. S. 254, 273-276. And the word "Treasonable," if left undefined, is no less dangerously uncertain. Thus it becomes important whether, despite the omission of a similar reference to the Penal Law in § 3021, the words as used in that section are to be read as meaning only what they mean in subdivision 3 of § 105. Or are they to be read more broadly and to constitute utterances or acts "seditious" and "treasonable" which would not be so regarded for the purposes of § 105?

Even assuming that "treasonable" and "seditious" in § 3021 and § 105, subd. 3, have the same meaning, the uncertainty is hardly removed. The definition of "treasonable" in the Penal Law presents no particular problem. The difficulty centers upon the meaning of "seditious." Subdivision 3 equates the term "seditious" with "criminal anarchy" as defined in the Penal Law. Is the reference only to Penal Law § 160, defining criminal anarchy as "the doctrine that organized government should be overthrown by force or violence, or by assassination of the executive head or of any of the executive officials of government, or by any unlawful means"? But that section ends with the sentence "The advocacy of such doctrine either by word of mouth or writing is a felony." Does that sentence draw into § 105, Penal Law § 161, proscribing "advocacy of criminal anarchy"? If so, the possible scope of "seditious" utterances or acts has virtually no limit. For under Penal Law § 161, one commits the felony of advocating criminal anarchy if he ". . . publicly displays any book . . . containing or advocating, advising or teaching the doctrine that organized government should be overthrown by force, violence or any unlawful means." Does the teacher who carries a copy of the Communist Manifesto on a public street thereby advocate criminal anarchy? It is no answer to say that the statute would not be applied in such a case. We cannot gainsay the potential effect of this obscure wording on "those with a conscientious and scrupulous regard for such undertakings." *Baggett v. Bullitt*, 377 U.S. 360, 374. Even were it certain that the definition referred to in § 105 was solely Penal Law § 160, the scope of § 105 still remains indefinite. The teacher cannot know the extent, if any, to which a "seditious" utterance must transcend mere statement about abstract doctrine, the extent to which it must be intended to and tend to indoctrinate or incite to action in furtherance of the defined doctrine. The crucial consideration is that no teacher can know just where the line is drawn between "seditious" and nonseditious utterances and acts.

Other provisions of § 105 also have the same defect of vagueness. Subdivision 1 (a) of § 105 bars employment of any person who "by word of mouth or writing wilfully and deliberately advocates, advises or teaches the doctrine" of forceful overthrow of government. This provision is plainly susceptible of sweeping and improper application. It may well prohibit the employment of one who merely advocates the doctrine in the abstract without any attempt to indoctrinate others, or incite others to action in furtherance of unlawful aims. * * * And in prohibiting "advising" the "doctrine" of unlawful overthrow does the statute prohibit mere "advising" of the existence of the doctrine, or advising another to support the doctrine? Since "advocacy" of the doctrine of forceful overthrow is separately prohibited, need the person "teaching" or "advising" this doctrine himself "advocate" it? Does the teacher who informs his class about the precepts of Marxism or the Declaration of Independence violate this prohibition?

Similar uncertainty arises as to the application of subdivision 1 (b) of § 105. That subsection requires the disqualification of an employee involved with the distribution of written material "containing or advocating, advising or teaching the doctrine" of forceful overthrow, and who himself "advocates, advises, teaches, or embraces the duty, necessity or propriety of adopting the doctrine contained therein." Here again, mere advocacy of abstract doctrine is apparently included. And does the prohibition of distribution of matter "containing" the doctrine bar histories of the evolution of Marxist doctrine or tracing the background of the French, American or Russian revolutions? The additional requirement, that the person participating in distribution of the material be one who "advocates, advises, teaches, or embraces the duty, necessity or propriety of adopting the doctrine" of forceful overthrow, does not alleviate the uncertainty in the scope of the section, but exacerbates it. Like the language of § 105, subd. 1 (a), this language may reasonably be construed to cover mere expression of belief. For example, does the university librarian who recommends the reading of such materials thereby "advocate . . . the . . . propriety of adopting the doctrine contained therein"? * * *

There can be no doubt of the legitimacy of New York's interest in protecting its education system from subversion. But "even though the governmental purpose be legitimate and substantial, that purpose cannot be pursued by means that broadly stifle fundamental personal liberties when the end can be more narrowly achieved." *Shelton* v. *Tucker*, 364 U. S. 479, 488. The principle is not inapplicable because the legislation is aimed at keeping subversives out of the teaching ranks. In *De Jonge* v. *Oregon*, 299 U. S. 353, 365, the Court said:

"The greater the importance of safeguarding the community from incitements to the overthrow of our institutions by force and violence, the more imperative is the need to preserve inviolate the constitutional rights of free speech, free press and free assembly in order to maintain the opportunity for free political discussion, to the end that government may be responsive to the will of the people and that changes, if desired, may be obtained by peaceful means. Therein lies the security of the Republic, the very foundation of constitutional government."

Our Nation is deeply committed to safeguarding academic freedom, which is of transcendent value to all of us and not merely to the teachers concerned. That freedom is therefore a special concern of the First Amendment, which does not tolerate laws that cast a pall of orthodoxy over the classroom. "The vigilant protection of constitutional freedoms is nowhere more vital than in the community of American schools." *Shelton* v. *Tucker, supra,* at 487. The classroom is peculiarly the "marketplace of ideas." The Nation's future depends upon leaders trained through wide exposure to that robust exchange of ideas which discovers truth "out of a multitude of tongues, [rather] than through any kind of authoritative selection." *United States* v. *Associated Press,* 52 F. Supp. 362, 372. In *Sweezy* v. *New Hampshire,* 354 U. S. 234, 250, we said:

> "The essentiality of freedom in the community of American universities is almost self-evident. No one should underestimate the vital role in a democracy that is played by those who guide and train our youth. To impose any strait jacket upon the intellectual leaders in our colleges and universities would imperil the future of our Nation. No field of education is so thoroughly comprehended by man that new discoveries cannot yet be made. Particularly is that true in the social sciences, where few, if any, principles are accepted as absolutes. Scholarship cannot flourish in an atmosphere of suspicion and distrust. Teachers and students must always remain free to inquire, to study and to evaluate, to gain new maturity and understanding; otherwise our civilization will stagnate and die."

We emphasize once again that "[p]recision of regulation must be the touchstone in an area so closely touching our most precious freedoms," *N. A. A. C. P.* v. *Button,* 371 U. S. 415, 438; "[f]or standards of permissible statutory vagueness are strict in the area of free expression . . . . Because First Amendment freedoms need breathing space to survive, government may regulate in the area only with narrow specificity." * * *

The regulatory maze created by New York is wholly lacking in "terms susceptible of objective measurement." *Cramp v. Board of Public Instruction, supra,* at 286. It has the quality of "extraordinary ambiguity" found to be fatal to the oaths considered in *Cramp* and *Baggett* v. *Bullitt.* * * *

We therefore hold that § 3021 of the Education Law and subdivisions 1(a), 1(b) and 3 of § 105 of the Civil Service Law as implemented by the machinery created pursuant to § 3022 of the Education Law are unconstitutional.

Appellants have also challenged the constitutionality of the discrete provisions of subdivision 1(c) of § 105 and subdivision 2 of the Feinberg Law, which make Communist Party membership, as such, prima facie evidence of disqualification. The provision was added to subdivision 1 (c) of § 105 in 1958 after the Board of Regents, following notice and hearing, listed the Communist Party of the United States and the Communist Party of the State of New York as "subversive" organizations. Subdivision 2 of the Feinberg Law was, however, before the Court in *Adler* and its constitutionality was sustained. But constitutional doctrine which has emerged since that decision has rejected its major premise. That premise was that public employment, including academic employment, may be conditioned upon the surrender of constitutional rights which could not be abridged by direct government action. Teachers, the Court said in *Adler,* "may work for the school system upon the reasonable terms laid down by the proper authorities of New York. If they do not choose to work on such terms, they are at liberty to retain their beliefs and associations and go elsewhere." 342 U. S., at 492. The Court also stated that a teacher denied employment because of membership in a listed organization "is not thereby denied the right of free speech and assembly. His freedom of choice between membership in the organization and employment in the school system might be limited, but not his freedom of speech or assembly, except in the remote sense that limitation is inherent in every choice." *Id.,* at 493.

However, the Court of Appeals for the Second Circuit correctly said in an earlier stage of this case, ". . . the theory that public employment which may be denied altogether may be subjected to any conditions, regardless of how unreasonable, has been uniformly rejected." *Keyishian* v. *Board of Regents,* 345 F.2d 236, 239. Indeed, that theory was expressly rejected in a series of decisions following *Adler.* * * * In *Sherbert* v. *Verner,* 374 U. S. 398, 404, we said: "It is too late in the day to doubt that the liberties of religion and expression may be infringed by the denial of or placing of conditions upon a benefit or privilege."

We proceed then to the question of the validity of the provisions of subdivision 1(c) of § 105 and subdivision 2 of § 3022, barring employment to members of listed organizations. Here again constitutional doctrine has developed since *Adler*. Mere knowing membership without a specific intent to further the unlawful aims of an organization is not a constitutionally adequate basis for exclusion from such positions as those held by appellants.

In *Elfbrandt* v. *Russell*, 384 U. S. 11, we said, "Those who join an organization but do not share its unlawful purposes and who do not participate in its unlawful activities surely pose no threat, either as citizens or as public employees." *Id.*, at 17. We there struck down a statutorily required oath binding the state employee not to become a member of the Communist Party with knowledge of its unlawful purpose, on threat of discharge and perjury prosecution if the oath were violated. We found that "[a]ny lingering doubt that proscription of mere knowing membership, without any showing of 'specific intent,' would run afoul of the Constitution was set at rest by our decision in *Aptheker* v. *Secretary of State*, 378 U. S. 500." *Elfbrandt* v. *Russell*, *supra*, at 16. In *Aptheker* we held that Party membership, without knowledge of the Party's unlawful purposes *and* specific intent to further its unlawful aims, could not constitutionally warrant deprivation of the right to travel abroad. As we said in *Schneiderman* v. *United States*, 320 U. S. 118, 136, "[U]nder our traditions beliefs are personal and not a matter of mere association, and . . . men in adhering to a political party or other organization . . . do not subscribe unqualifiedly to all of its platforms or asserted principles." "A law which applies to membership without the 'specific intent' to further the illegal aims of the organization infringes unnecessarily on protected freedoms. It rests on the doctrine of 'guilt by association' which has no place here." *Elfbrandt*, *supra*, at 19. Thus mere Party membership, even with knowledge of the Party's unlawful goals, cannot suffice to justify criminal punishment, * * * nor may it warrant a finding of moral unfitness justifying disbarment. * * *

* * * *Elfbrandt* and *Aptheker* state the governing standard: legislation which sanctions membership unaccompanied by specific intent to further the unlawful goals of the organi-

zation or which is not active membership violates constitutional limitations.

Measured against this standard, both Civil Service Law § 105, subd. 1 (c), and Education Law § 3022, subd. 2, sweep overbroadly into association which may not be proscribed. The presumption of disqualification arising from proof of mere membership may be rebutted, but only by (a) a denial of membership, (b) a denial that the organization advocates the overthrow of government by force, or (c) a denial that the teacher has knowledge of such advocacy. * * * Thus proof of nonactive membership or a showing of the absence of intent to further unlawful aims will not rebut the presumption and defeat dismissal. * * *

Thus § 105, subd. 1 (c), and § 3022, subd. 2, suffer from impermissible "overbreadth." * * * They seek to bar employment both for association which legitimately may be proscribed and for association which may not be proscribed consistently with First Amendment rights. Where statutes have an overbroad sweep, just as where they are vague, "the hazard of loss or substantial impairment of those precious rights may be critical." * * *

We therefore hold that Civil Service Law § 105, subd. 1 (c), and Education Law § 3022, subd. 2, are invalid insofar as they proscribe mere knowing membership without any showing of specific intent to further the unlawful aims of the Communist Party of the United States or of the State of New York.

The judgment of the District Court is reversed and the case is remanded for further proceedings consistent with this opinion.

Reversed and remanded.

A court is powerless to interfere with board of trustees' judgment exercised with regard to welfare of school

RANEY v. BOARD OF TRUSTEES, COALINGA JUNIOR COLLEGE DISTRICT

District Court of Appeal, Fifth Circuit, California, 1966.
48 Cal. Rptr. 555.

CONLEY, Presiding Justice.

Joseph F. Raney, a former probationary school teacher of

the Coalinga Junior College District, was denied a writ of mandate directing respondent to reemploy him and to pay his back salary for the 1964-65 school term. The superior court found that Mr. Raney had been a probationary teacher of the Coalinga Junior College District for two previous years and was teaching for the third year when on or about May 11, 1964, the board of trustees of the college district caused written notice to be given him that his services would not be required for the 1964-65 school year; that upon request, the board gave him a written statement of the reasons for not hiring him and that on or about June 11, 1964, it served him with a formal accusation; that following the filing of his notice of defense and request for a hearing, such hearing was regularly held by the school board on July 9, 1964, and that thereafter the board made findings of fact and rendered a decision, copies of which are attached to the petition for the writ of mandate. The trial court found that the matters set forth in paragraphs 1, 2, and 3 of the board's findings of fact are supported by substantial evidence in the light of the whole record, as follows:

> "1. That the philosophy of the said Joseph F. Raney with respect to grading is unsuitable for the junior college level and is contrary to the accepted practices of the administration of the Coalinga College in that he has an extremely 'tough' attitude toward his students which causes excessive dropouts during the semester and between semesters; that his severity of grading as aforesaid, his tough philosophy, his sarcasm towards his students, particularly those who may disagree with his philosophy, results in many students either failing to take his course or failing to complete them, resulting in said students missing an important basic course.
> "2. That originally employed as a counselor, he proved ineffective as such with extremely poor rapport with his students, necessitating his reassignment to classroom work; that he would not ever be suitable for counseling.
> "3. That he has a general reputation among students, faculty and the community as a contentious person which lessens their respect for him, thereby reducing his effectiveness as a teacher."

The trial court determined that said reasons "relate solely to the welfare of the school and the pupils thereof." In his conclusions of law, the trial judge held that the respondent board duly and regularly acted within the authority granted by sections 13443 and 13444 of the Education Code, as they then existed.

The judgment is "* * * that the petitioner take nothing by

this action, and that each party shall bear his own costs of suit herein."

The decision is in accordance with the law. In the case of Griggs v. Board of Trustees, 61 Cal.2d 93, 96, 37 Cal.Rptr. 194, 197, 389 P.2d 722, 725, the Supreme Court succinctly states the statutory limitations upon the right of the courts to consider such discretionary decisions of a school board:

> "The inquiry [of judicial review] extends to the questions whether the board has proceeded without or in excess of jurisdiction, whether there was a fair trial, and whether there was any prejudicial abuse of discretion. An abuse of discretion is established if the board has not proceeded in the manner required by law, the order or decision is not supported by the findings, or, with regard to local boards like the one before us, the findings are not supported by substantial evidence in the light of the entire record. [Citations.] However, section 13444 of the Education Code specifically limits the scope of judicial review, stating, '[T]he determination of the board as to the sufficiency of the cause for dismissal shall not be subject to judicial review,' and '[T]he determination of the board as to the sufficiency of the cause for dismissal shall be conclusive, but the cause shall relate solely to the welfare of the schools and the pupils thereof.' "

The quotation from section 13444 of the Education Code contained in the opinion of the Griggs case referred to section 13444 of the Education Code as it existed, after amendment, in 1961. * * *

In 1965, section 13444 of the Education Code was repealed,* and the pertinent subject matter thereof is covered in section 13443, which provides:

> "The governing board's determination not to reemploy a probationary employee for the ensuing school year shall be for cause only. The determination of the governing board as to the sufficiency of the cause pursuant to this section shall be conclusive, but the cause shall relate solely to the welfare of the schools and the pupils thereof."

It will thus be seen that notwithstanding frequent amendments of the code sections involved, the same rule has at all times applied, namely, that the sufficiency of the cause adopted by the board of trustees for failing to reemploy a teacher for a fourth year, thus giving him permanent status, is conclusive within specified limits, and the courts cannot interfere with

---

* Stats. 1965, ch. 1110, § 3.

the judgment of the school board with respect to reemployment.

The trial judge correctly determined that there was substantial evidence before the board of trustees supporting the findings which they made. It is not within our power to substitute our own judgment of the character and ability of the petitioner or his worthiness as a teacher; we are powerless to pass judgment on the "sufficiency of the cause for dismissal."

It would be a useless consumption of time and space for us to discuss in detail the evidence at the hearing before the board of trustees. The board believed the evidence, which was countered by other testimony, that Mr. Raney was too strict in his insistence that his students should attain a high degree of efficiency approximating a university level of scholarship, and that the grades given by him were not in line with the customary relaxed attitude of certain other teachers. Some of his students found his comments disagreeable. As a counselor, during part of his three years of teaching, he did not meet with unanimous approval, and some of the students and faculty and the school community believed that he was a contentious person, and that such belief tended to reduce his effectiveness as a teacher.

If this court were at liberty to supervise the judgment of the members of the school board and to reverse their decision as to the retention of appellant on the basis of his ability and merits as a teacher, we might well reach an opposite conclusion. As remarked by the learned trial judge, who had been both a teacher and a school trustee prior to his elevation to the bench, Mr. Raney "* * * is a highly intelligent [and] courageous * * * individual," and the record evidences qualities of the petitioner which are desirable in the profession. If education is to achieve its asserted end of causing young people to think and to reach independent conclusions about the issues that agitate the world, there must be afforded to their teachers a sufficient independence to permit them to inculcate these virtues. Ideally, a teacher should be a little contentious, rather than stodgy and lethargic, but our theory of government gives to the school trustees, for better or for worse, an almost absolute choice either to "hire or fire" teachers who have not yet attained tenure. It might well be argued that the Legislature has created a mirage for probationary teachers by seeming to assure them that they may demand a hearing if they are not retained for a fourth year. In practice, such an official inquiry does not result in a reinstatement of the teacher but only produces a possibly expanded assignment of reasons why the board does not wish to give him permanent status by re-hiring him for a fourth year. This is how it is, and probationary teachers should clearly understand the way of the world insofar as their jobs are concerned.

The judgment is affirmed.

RALPH M. BROWN and STONE, JJ., concur.

NOTES

1. A tenured professor's verbal criticism of the public schools, colleges of education, teachers' colleges and professional educators according to the Supreme Court of Nevada, do not constitute causes for removal on grounds of insubordination, uncooperativeness and conduct not in accord with the university's welfare. State *ex rel.* Richardson v. Board of Regents of University of Nevada, 269 P.2d 265 (1954).

2. The Supreme Court of Florida has held that a university rule prohibiting employees from seeking public office is not an unconstitutional abridgment of academic freedom or a denial of substantive due process. The court in justifying the reasonableness of the rule commented:

> [Appellant's argument necessarily recognizes a truism to the effect that the right to teach or the right to seek public office is not a constitutional absolute. Each of the privileges is subject to reasonable restraint and reasonable conditions. The test of reasonableness in either situation involves a consideration of the nature of the right asserted by the individual and the extent that it is necessary to restrict the assertion of the right in the interest of the public.] * * *
> Here, the rule promulgated by the Board of Control had no relevancy whatever to the subjects which Professor Jones might teach. It dealt merely with his right to teach and simultaneously carry on a political campaign for an elective public office. The rule prohibits no one from teaching. Neither does it prohibit a teacher from running for public office. It merely provides that he cannot do both simultaneously. There is adequate justification for the rule in the public interest, as well as in the interest of the University student body which looks to its professors for instruction. As the circuit judge points out, there are many reasons why the appellee Board would be justified in placing restrictions on the University faculty in connection with political campaigns. The demands upon the time and energies incident to a warmly contested campaign for an important public office would necessar-

ily affect the efficiency of the candidate; the potential
effect upon the students, not only as the result of such
inefficiency, but also in the nature of the political influences that might be brought to bear upon them would
be further justification; the potential involvement of the
State University which is dependent upon public support
from all political elements would be another major consideration supporting the reasonableness of the rule. Although appellant suggests that he might as well have
conducted his campaign in the evening so as not to interfere with his professorial duties, the reasons which we
have epitomized above would still apply. Moreover, anyone who has ever been associated with a heated political
campaign well knows that it involves handshaking, speech
making, telephone calling, letter writing, and door to
door campaigning from morning well into the night. To
anyone familiar with the practical aspects of American
politics, it is asking too much to expect him to agree that
success in a strenuous political campaign can be achieved
merely by appearances at Saturday afternoon fish fries
or early evening precinct rallies. The result simply is
that it would be extremely difficult for a university professor to conduct his classroom courses with efficiency
over a period of eight to ten weeks while simultaneously
"beating the bushes" in search of votes to elevate him to
the position of a circuit judge.

Jones v. Board of Control, 131 So. 2d 713 (Fla. 1961).

**College did not have just cause for dismissal of research
associate prior to expiration of contract**

PAN AMERICAN COLLEGE v. ROJAS

Court of Civil Appeals of Texas, 1965.
392 S.W.2d 707.

GREEN, Chief Justice.

Appellee Dr. Hector R. Rojas, plaintiff below, secured judgment after jury verdict against appellant, Pan American College, defendant in the trial court, for damages for breach of
employment contract. Motion for new trial was overruled, and
defendant has perfected this appeal.

Appellee, a Doctor of Astronomy whose residence is in
France, was employed by appellant in September, 1962, by
contract to expire May 31, 1963, as Research Associate under
Professor Paul Engle in a program of astronomical and
astrophysical research. This program, which was conducted
by appellant college in Edinburg, Texas, and at its high al-

titude observatory on Mount Infiernillo, State of Nuevo Leon, Mexico, was sponsored and financed by a grant from the National Science Foundation. Professor Engle was Director of the grant, and controlled the expenditure of the funds.

In June, 1963, appellee's contract with appellant was renewed by the parties for one year, to be in effect until May 31, 1964. Although appellant questions the existence of sufficient pleadings and evidence of a contract, this matter was definitely settled by a stipulation, hereinafter copied in this opinion, entered into by the parties after the evidence was in and before the preparation of the charge to the jury, and we shall not deem it necessary to discuss at any length any issue as to the existence of such contract.

During the early months of their association, the relationship between Professor Engle and appellee seems to have been satisfactory. In a report by Engle to the National Science Foundation in March, 1963, he spoke most highly of Rojas, saying: "Dr. Hector R. Rojas is deeply involved in this work here and has proved to be a most highly satisfactory research associate." However, it appears from the testimony that after the renewal of appellee's contract, strong personal animosity developed between the two men. There is much conflicting testimony of the quality and value to appellant of appellee's services, as well as on the subject of whether appellee acted insubordinately toward his superior, Engle, and refused to accept instructions from him. The evidence conflicts sharply as to Engle being in fact an astronomer qualified to give directions concerning the technical details of the observation project, and it is clear that appellee did not consider him to be such. On September 21, 1963, in reply to a letter from Engle, appellee wrote him stating that he agreed that they should work together to insure the success of the research project, but that "Because you are not an astronomer at all and anymore, I will not accept from you any instruction regarding what to do or what not to do in the research project." Appellee on the stand explained that he did not write that he would not recognize Engle as his superior, or as the director of his department, but that since Engle was not an astronomer, he could not permit him to interfere with appellee's work as an astronomer. After receipt of this letter, the college authorities not only continued to allow him to go on with his work, but furnished him with a new and better office.

The event that evidently brought on the appellee's dismissal from employment happened on October 25, 1963. A fight occurred just outside of appellee's office between Rojas and Engle, in which blows were struck by both parties and both were knocked to the ground. There were no known eye witnesses to the fight other than the participants, and each gave an entirely different version as to the details of the beginning of the struggle, and as to which was the aggressor and which was merely acting in self-defense. The statement of facts contains testimony from an adult student that Engle's reputation for truth and veracity was bad.

Shortly after the fight, Engle insisted to the college president that appellee be dismissed, and this was done. The dismissal was confirmed by the Board of Regents. The law suit followed.

At the conclusion of the evidence, the parties to the case entered into a stipulation of facts as follows:

> "1. That Plaintiff and Defendant did enter into an employment contract for one year, beginning June 1, 1963, and ending May 31, 1964, and for which Plaintiff was to receive a salary of $8,000.00, for his professional services.
> "2. That a term of said contract was that Plaintiff receive from Defendant travelling expenses for himself in returning to France in the sum of $434.00.
> "3. That Plaintiff was dismissed from employment on October 31, 1963, and a balance of $4,666.64 would still be owing on Plaintiff's annual salary, unless Defendant had just cause to dismiss Plaintiff on said date."

The case was submitted to the jury on a single issue, as follows:

> "Do you find from a preponderance of the evidence that Pan American College had just cause for the dismissal of Dr. Hector R. Rojas on or about the 1st day of November, 1963?"

To which the jury answered: "IT DID *NOT HAVE* JUST CAUSE."

By agreement of counsel for both parties, and under the provisions of Rule 269, Texas Rules of Civil Procedure, since the burden of proving the affirmative of the special issue was assumed, without objection, by appellant, its counsel were given the right to open and close the jury argument.

Judgment was rendered favorable to appellee for $5,100.64, being the total of the unpaid salary and travelling expenses set forth in the agreed facts. Appellant's motion for new trial was overruled, and it has appealed. We affirm the judgment.
* * *

Much of the evidence has already been summarized. There is a distinct disagreement in the testimony on the subject of whether or not appellee was guilty of insubordinate actions toward his superior, Professor Engle, and a fact issue exists on this. Personal conflict existed between them even before the contract was renewed in June, 1963. According to appellee, he offered to resign and return to France on June 24, 1963, and was reluctant to accept an appointment for another year, but was persuaded to do so by officials of appellant. Whether the professional independence of an astronomer in his celestial observations and reports can be regarded as sufficiently insubordinate to justify cancellation of an admittedly valid contract became, in this instance, a question of fact on conflicting evidence.

Appellant on appeal seeks to justify its alleged breach of the contract on the proposition that the Board of Regents had authority by statute (Art. 2619a, Sec. 7, Vernon's Ann.Tex.-Civ.St.) to remove appellee as an employee *when in its judgment the interests of the College shall require it*. Appellant contends that appellee had the burden of pleading and proving that the Board of Regents abused their discretion in discharging plaintiff, or acted arbitrarily and capriciously in such discharge. We feel that the negative of this would constitute a defensive issue, required to be plead and proved by defendant in the trial court, and is not available when raised, as here, for the first time on appeal. We further are convinced that any such contention as is thus made by appellant was waived when it stipulated that a certain sum would be owing appellee "unless Defendant had just cause to dismiss Plaintiff on such date," and assumed the burden of proof on such issue.

Furthermore, there is no evidence that before discharging appellee the Board of Regents reached any judgment that the interests of the college required the removal of appellee. (Art. 2619a, Sec. 7) The testimony appears to reflect that appellee was discharged to satisfy the demands of Professor Engle who, as Director of the grant, controlled the expenditure of the funds. In this connection Dr. Schilling, President of the College, testified:

"Q Did you subsequently tell Dr. Rojas that he was relieved of his duties?
 A Yes, later, I don't know the exact day of the week, but not an immediate thing. Some thinking went into it, and of course, talking with Mr. Engle. I think something should be brought out here, that

Mr. Engle is the Director of the grant. We can not write a check at the college on this grant unless Mr. Engle approves it. He has to place a purchase order with us with his approval before we can write a check on the grant. Although, we have the book-keeper, and Mr. Sawyer is our comptroller, Mr. Engle informed me that he would not approve other checks for Mr. Rojas. He also informed me that he would not go to Infiernillo with Mr. Rojas, and Mr. Rojas could not operate the instruments there unless he had some instructions from Mr. Engle. *On the basis of this,* of course, we informed Mr. Rojas, in front of witnesses, we had witnesses present, that his position with the college was terminated. That we would make a recommendation to the Board, as such we did.

Q   And, the Board confirmed the recommendation?

A   Yes, sir."

From such testimony, we are unable to find *as a matter of law* that appellant had good cause to cancel out the contract between it and appellee, and discharge appellee, without incurring liability for appellee's lawful damages. * * *

In view of the stipulation of the parties, the existence of conflicting evidence raising issues of fact as to whether appellant had just cause to cancel the contract and dismiss appellee, and the absence of any objections to the charge and of any requested definitions or special instructions, we find no reversible error in the trial court's entry of the judgment appealed from.

The judgment of the trial court is affirmed.

Hearing must be provided for nontenured faculty whose employment was terminated after contractual deadline for notice of nonreappointment

GREENE v. HOWARD UNIVERSITY

United States Court of Appeals, District of Columbia Circuit, 1969.
412 F.2d 1128.

McGOWAN, Circuit Judge:

This appeal is from the denial by the District Court of motions for a preliminary injunction. 271 F.Supp. 609 (1967). One group of appellants consist of four persons who were students at Howard University in the spring of 1967 when serious disturbances occurred on the campus. The second is made up of five faculty members holding nontenured positions at that time. After making an investigation which purported to find both groups actively involved in the disorders, the University, without according them a hearing of any kind although one was requested, terminated the connection of both student and faculty appellants with the school as of the close of the academic year on June 30. Actions were brought by these student and faculty groups to restrain the University from interfering with the relationships between them and the University. We hold that (1) the litigation has become moot as to the student appellants, and (2) the faculty appellants have stated a cause of action which, upon proof of monetary damage, would entitle them to relief of that nature.

* * *

The teacher appellants had not achieved a tenure status and thus, in the familiar academic tradition, the renewal of their appointments was at the University's pleasure. They do not now challenge the general applicability of this principle. Instead, they assert that the University failed in its obligation, incident to their contracts, to give the appropriate advance notice of non-renewal. They point out that, far from having given such notice, the University explicitly refrained from doing so under circumstances which warranted appellants in entertaining and acting upon the clear expectations that their reappointments would be forthcoming. In these conditions, say appellants, irrespective of the generally unqualified nature of the University's power to determine whether non-tenure teachers shall continue beyond their appointed terms, the University was required, if it gave a last-minute notice of non-renewal because of alleged campus misconduct, to allow appellants to be heard on those charges before making them the occasion of non-renewal.

It is helpful in this regard to examine the relevant sections of the Faculty Handbook, a manual which governs the relationship between faculty members and the University.[3] Section VIII states the normal University practice with respect to dismissals:

> A. The Board of Trustees reserves the right of dismissal, regardless of tenure, in cases of moral delinquency, or other personal conduct incompatible with the welfare

---

3. The manual also summarizes the usual and customary practice which had built up in the University-faculty relationship. *See* A. Corbin, Contracts §§ 556, 558 (1960); Restatement of Contracts § 246 (1932); Uniform Commercial Code § 1-205.

of the University. In such cases, the President of the University reserves the right of immediate suspension, regardless of tenure. The person concerned, upon written request, shall be given a hearing before a committee of the Board of Trustees, prior to the meeting of the Board of Trustees at which final action on the case is taken under procedures to be established by the Board of Trustees.

B. The Board of Trustees reserves the right of dismissal, regardless of tenure, for professional conduct incompatible with the best interests of the University. The person will be given reasonable notice and an opportunity to be heard by a committee of his peers with the right to a hearing by a committee of the Board of Trustees, prior to the meeting of the Board of Trustees at which final action on the case is taken under procedures to be established by the Board of Trustees.

Section IX states its position as to notice of Non-reappointment and Reappointment:

Notice of Non-reappointment and Reappointment: It will be the practice of the University, without contractual obligation to do so, to give written notice at the following times to officers of instruction whose services are no longer required: A) Deans will give notice each year to those whose terms expire and whom they do not propose to recommend for reappointment, not later than December 15 of that year; B) The Board of Trustees will give notice to those teachers whose terms expire and whose services are no longer required, directly following its meeting in January of each year.

EXCEPTIONS: An exception to this practice will obtain in the case of teachers on one-year appointments to whom the Board of Trustees will give notice immediately following its meeting in April; the Dean will give notice to such persons not later than March 15. Teachers not to be continued as regular appointees at the conclusion of seven years of service will be notified one year prior to the expiration of the seventh year.

A member of the faculty who wishes to resign from an appointment at the end of a given year is expected to notify his dean or the proper administrative official in writing not later than April 15th of that year."

It is clear from a close examination of these sections, buttressed by affidavits and depositions admitted in the District Court, that the usual practice of the University was to inform non-tenured faculty members by January or April, depending on the length of their appointments, whether they would be reappointed for the next school year.[4] This gave them the

---

4. This usual practice, of course, can be raised to the level of a contractual obligation. *See* note 3, *supra*.

opportunity to seek employment elsewhere in the event they were not rehired. And it is significant to note in Section IX a corresponding obligation of the faculty member to inform the University if he intends not to return the next year, a provision presumably added to the Handbook in order to insure that the University would not be obligated to search for a replacement at a time after the market has become foreshortened.[5]

It is instructive against this background to look at those facts which are undisputed in the case of Dr. Andress Taylor, a teacher appellant whose situation is not untypical of that of the other such appellants. On March 15, 1967, Dr. Taylor's name was among those recommended by his Dean to be continued as an Assistant Professor of English for a term of two years to run from July 1, 1967 to June 30, 1969. On or about April 1, 1967, Dr. Taylor requested from his department head a leave of absence for the next academic year in order that he might take a position with the Southern Teaching Program.[6] The chairman, however, ruled that Dr. Taylor's services were required at Howard in that period; and Dr. Taylor, in reliance upon this opinion, rejected the offer.

On May 5, 1967, Dr. Taylor received a "good" rating from his department chairman. On May 22, 1967, the chairman assigned him a course for the fall semester and requested that he produce a reading list. On June 2, 1967, the Director of the Summer School wrote to Dr. Taylor that he had been recommended for an appointment to the staff of the 1967 summer session at Howard.

However, on June 20, 1967 Dr. Taylor received a letter, dated June 19, 1967, but apparently postmarked June 20, 1967, from the Dean of his school informing him that, after the automatic termination of his contract on June 30, 1967, he was not to be "reappointed by the University."

It must be clear that, for all practical intents and purposes, Dr. Taylor had been rehired to teach at Howard for a further period. The record here indicates that the University abruptly changed its mind about this reappointment because its unilateral investigation of the campus disturbances implicated Dr. Taylor. But the record also discloses that Dr. Taylor re-

5. Appellants' reliance upon the University's intention to reemploy them was obvious. This provision buttresses that reliance by imposing an obligation on faculty members upon which the University might rely.
6. Dr. Taylor also received another job offer and a second tentative exploratory offer which he declined on the ground that he was committed to Howard.

ceived no opportunity to be heard on the existence or extent of his involvement in the turmoil, either before or after the non-reappointment letter was sent.

It should be pointed out, moreover, that Dr. Taylor and his fellow appellants were relying not only on personal assurances from University officials and on their recognition of the common practice of the University, but also on the written statements of University policy contained in the Faculty Handbook under whose terms they were employed. The Handbook makes clear, in writing, what the appellants knew to be true in practice: a faculty member, if not finally informed by April 15 (with preliminary notice by March 15) that his contract was not to be renewed, had legitimate reason to believe that he could rely on returning to Howard the following semester.

In the District Court, as here, the University does not deny the force of its regulations and practices in respect of appearing to elevate timely notice of non-reappointment to a contractual status. It argues only that what it gave with one hand it took away simultaneously with the other. It takes its stand, as did the District Court, upon the inclusion in Section IX of the Handbook of the words "without contractual obligation to do so" in the affirmative statement of its purpose to give such notice by certain fixed dates. This qualifying clause, so it is said, relieves the University of any and all obligations of any kind with respect to the observance of its regulations, and vests in the University an unfettered discretion to deny reappointment at any time up to midnight of June 30 whether or not earlier notice has been given.

Thus, as noted above, when notice of non-reappointment is withheld beyond the required date, we think some qualifications come into being—qualifications, moreover, which are not to be automatically considered as negated by the disclaimer invoked here, nor which, indeed, are necessarily at odds with it as a matter of rational interpretation of the bargain the parties may be taken to have struck. Contracts are written, and are to be read, by reference to the norms of conduct and expectations founded upon them. This is especially true of contracts in and among a community of scholars, which is what a university is. The readings of the market place are not invariably apt in this non-commercial context.

The employment contracts of appellants here comprehend as essential parts of themselves the hiring policies and practices of the University as embodied in its employment regulations and customs. The very phrase relied upon by the District Court is in a Faculty Handbook which is replete with other provisions in conflict with the spirit of the use of that phrase now sought to be made. Those provisions seem to us to contemplate a hearing before separating from the academic community for alleged misconduct one who, although a non-tenured employee, has acquired a different dimension of relationship because of the expectations inherent in the University's failure to give notice as contemplated by its own regulations.

That new relationship does not at all mean that the University must invariably reappoint whenever it fails to give notice at the specified time. Of course there may be happenings after that time which bear upon the fitness of a particular person to continue as a member of an academic community. But, in the circumstances which are undisputedly shown by this record, and as we construe the contractual undertakings between the University and these appellants, we hold that appellants should have been afforded an opportunity to give their version of the events which led to their non-reappointment because of misconduct. * * *

We think the record as it stands adequately supports our conclusion that the University acted in contravention of its contractual undertakings *vis-a-vis the teacher* appellants, and we see no necessity for further litigation of this issue in the District Court. What remains is the question of what pecuniary damage, if any, the individual teacher appellants have suffered by reason of the University's failure to effect nonreappointment in a manner compatible with its contractual obligations. The legal injury done by that failure could not now be repaired by affording appellants the hearing which they sought and were denied at the time their reappointments were withheld. The breach of contract resides in the failure to give the hearing then, and does not turn upon what the outcome of such a hearing might be now.

Although the denial of injunctive relief presently appealed from is left undisturbed, we remand the case to the District Court for the purpose of permitting any of the faculty appellants to pursue, if he so chooses, a claim for the monetary damage, if any, attributable to the non-reappointment. The District Court will permit such amendment of the complaints as may be sought to this end, and it will otherwise proceed further in a manner consistent herewith.

It is so ordered.

Circuit Judge BURGER did not participate in the foregoing decision.

**Allegations of nontenure professor, without expectancy of
reemployment, is insufficient to show denial of
rights under the Civil Rights Act or the
U. S. Constitution**

JONES v. HOPPER

United States Court of Appeals, Tenth Circuit, 1969.
410 F.2d 1323.

PER CURIAM.

This appeal is from a judgment dismissing with prejudice
the complaint of appellant Jones, an associate professor of
philosophy. The basis of the dismissal was that the complaint
failed to state a claim upon which relief could be granted.
Appellees, who are the President and members of the Board
of Trustees of Southern Colorado State College, filed the motion to dismiss upon which the judgment is based.

The dismissal of the complaint, drawn as a civil rights
pleading, presents the issue of whether a claim is stated under
the Civil Rights Act.[1]

The complaint alleges jurisdictional facts,[2] identity of parties, their residence and citizenship, and the status of the
college.

The complaint alleges the powers of the Board of Trustees
are as follows:

> "The Board of Trustees is vested by [§§ 124-17-1 and
> 124-5-1 Colo.Rev. Stats. (1963)] with the entire control
> and management of the affairs of the College, has gen-
> eral supervision of said College and the control and direc-
> tion of the funds and appropriations made thereto, with
> power to appoint and remove all subordinate officers, pro-
> fessors, associate professors, teachers, assistants, em-
> ployees or agents, in, about, or concerning said College,
> to appoint or employ, discharge and suspend, contract
> and fail to renew contracts of employees and other sub-
> ordinates, and to fix the salaries of each and prescribe
> their several duties. They further have the power and
> authority to prescribe the various books and texts to be
> used in the Colleges, the courses of study and instruction
> and to make all needful rules, regulations and By Laws
> for the good government and management of the same.
> The actions of President Hopper, hereinafter described,

---

1. 42 U.S.C. §§ 1983, 1985, 1986 and 1988.
2. Jurisdiction of the court is invoked under 28 U.S.C. §§ 1331 and 1343,
   as well as under 42 U.S.C. §§ 1983, 1986 and 1988 of the Civil Rights
   Act.

were approved, authorized and ratified by said Board of Trustees, and each of them."

It is further alleged the acts complained of are exercised under color of the statutes, regulations, customs and usages vesting the power above averred.

The complaint further alleges that Jones was given notice that his services would be terminated at the end of the academic year by a letter sent from the President and authorized by the Board * * *.

The complaint then continues with a partial description of the "John Dean case" referred to in the above exhibit.

The *curriculum vitae* of appellant Jones is set forth in the complaint as well as the details of his association and status with Southern Colorado State College. In this description of his status with the college, Jones points out that the duration of each appointment under which he served was one year and that it was at the end of his second appointment that the appellees determined he would not be reappointed.

The allegations then conclude that the reason Jones was not reappointed was because he had exercised his constitutionally protected rights [4] in the following manner:

(a) He objected to the disqualification of an applicant for his department because the applicant was an Oriental.

(b) He attacked an English department textbook in a student newspaper.

(c) He founded an independent faculty-student publication which contained articles criticizing the war in Viet Nam, commenting on labor problems and pacifism, and an article objecting to monitored classrooms.

(d) He supported the student, John Dean, referred to above in Exhibit A, who had been committed to a hospital pursuant to a court order obtained by his parents as a result of the student's attempt to register with his draft board as a conscientious objector.

Jones averred he was a pacifist by religious conviction and that his views expressed orally and by writing on this subject were an exercise of his religious freedom.

He concluded that because of the above conduct and actions an expectancy of continued employment was terminated which was an injury to an interest which the law will protect against invasion by acts in violation of the Civil Rights Act.

---

4. Under the First and Fourteenth Amendments to the United States Constitution.

Jones alleges he was damaged as a result of the failure to renew his teaching contract, and relief is prayed for in the amount of $300,000.00.

The second claim of Jones' complaint by reference adopts the foregoing allegations describing them as a conspiracy to punish him for exercising his constitutional rights granted by the First and Fourteenth Amendments. He further concludes he was denied equal protection under the law.

The basic requirements of a complaint based upon 42 U.S.C. § 1983 are: (1) that the conduct complained of was engaged in under color of state law, and (2) that such conduct subjected the plaintiff to a deprivation of rights, privileges, or immunities secured by the Federal Constitution and laws. The allegations necessary to state such a claim, as in the case of any other civil action in the federal courts, are not to be held insufficient unless it appears beyond doubt that the plaintiff can prove no set of facts in support of his claim which would entitle him to relief.

When we examine the complaint herein in the light of the foregoing rules, we are directed to ask: What guaranteed right, privilege or immunity was denied Jones which is protected under the Constitution and laws?

The complaint alleges the refusal of the appellees to reappoint Jones after the term of his current appointment expired.

Jones contends the appellees, authorized by the Colorado statutes to administer the college, have denied him a right of expectancy to continued employment because he exercised freely his constitutional rights of speech, publication and religion. * * *

The complaint in our case makes no allegation or inference that a contract existed. Jones' complaint expressly concedes that his "termination was not a breach of contract," thereby admitting that a contract did not exist. Accordingly, the interest which Jones seeks to assert cannot be derived from a contract.

We now look to the Federal Constitution and laws for the source of the interest secured.

The Supreme Court has consistently held, "the interest of a government employee in retaining his job, can be summarily denied. It has become a settled principle that government employment, in the absence of legislation, can be revoked at the will of the appointing officer. * * * This principle was reaffirmed quite recently in Vitarelli v. Seaton, 359 U.S. 535, 79

S.Ct. 968, 3 L.Ed.2d 1012." [12] The foregoing must be read in the light of the principle enunciated in Pickering v. Board of Education,[13] which quotes Keyishian v. Board of Regents.[14] The principle stated teaches that public employment may be denied altogether subject, however, to the restriction that unreasonable conditions may not be imposed upon the granting of public employment.[15] There is nothing in the complaint to warrant an inference or conclusion that the Colorado statute nor its application herein went "beyond what might be justified in the exercise of the State's legitimate inquiry into the fitness and competency of its teachers." [16]

As a matter of fact, there are no allegations relating to conditions of employment of professors or assistant professors at Southern Colorado State College. The complaint merely alleges the duties and authority of the administrators. Therefore, we can find no where in the complaint an allegation of any identified interest which is secured by the Federal Constitution or laws.

The complaint alleges a Colorado institution involved, governed by the laws of Colorado identified in the pleading. Appellant was a professor at this institution of learning. "It is clear that a professor is not an officer, but an employee under contract to fill a chair of learning".[17]

The complaint alleges Jones was appointed for an academic year and then reappointed and served the entire second appointment. He was notified he would not be reappointed for a third academic year. The alleged interest deprived was in the appointment for a third year. It is admitted he did not have a tenure privilege either by Colorado law or contract. "Among the most fundamental rules of the law of master and servant is that which recognizes that, absent an applicable statutory or contractual provision to the contrary, an employer enjoys an absolute power of dismissing his employee, with or without cause." [18]

---

12. Cafeteria & Rest. Workers Union, Local 473, A.F.L.-C.I.O. v. McElroy, 367 U.S. 886, 896-897, 81 S.Ct. 1743, 1749, 6 L.Ed.2d 1230 (1961).
13. 391 U.S. 563, 568, 88 S.Ct. 1731, 20 L.Ed.2d 811 (1968).
14. 385 U.S. 589, 605, 87 S.Ct. 675, 17 L. Ed.2d 629 (1967).
15. Shelton v. Tucker, 364 U.S. 479, 81 S. Ct. 247, 5 L.Ed.2d 231 (1960).
16. Id. at 490, 81 S.Ct. at 253.
17. State Board of Agriculture v. Meyers, 20 Colo.App. 139, 77 P. 372, 373 (1904). See also 75 A.L.R. 1352 (1955). "The courts are almost unanimous in holding that the position of a teacher is that of an employee, resting on the contract of employment, and not that of public officer."
18. 51 A.L.R.2d 745, § 2 (1960).

Southern Colorado State College is a state academic institution organized and existing under Colorado law which vests the government and management of its affairs in a board of trustees which has among other vestitures "power to appoint and remove all subordinate officers, professors, associate professors, teachers, assistants, employees or agents, in, or about, or concerning said college, to appoint or employ, discharge and suspend, contract and fail to renew contracts of employees and other subordinates. * * *" (recited in complaint as set forth, supra).

We think this provision precludes Jones from having the relief he seeks in this proceeding. His claimed interest must find its source in his expired appointment which constituted whatever contract existed. The provision above acknowledged became a part of any contract that may have existed between him and the college.

The provision specifically denies an expectancy to continued employment; therefore, absent an expectancy, there could be no interest. "One has no constitutional right to a 'remedy' against the lawful conduct of another."

As demonstrated above the right, privilege or immunity Jones alleges he was deprived of is non-existent.

We believe the appellees herein were exercising a discretion given them by the power vested under the Colorado statute set forth in the complaint. The exercise of this discretion cannot, under the facts alleged in the complaint, become unlawful conduct which would justify its falling within the ambit of the Civil Rights Act.

"Because of the special needs of the university, both public and private, great discretion must be given it in decisions about the renewal of contracts during the probationary period. In deciding whether to rehire or grant tenure, the considerations involved go well beyond a judgment about general teaching competence."

> " 'Will the interests of an institution of learning be promoted by dispensing with the services of a particular professor?' And yet if we assume that the statute of the state is of any virtue, it is just such a question that the plaintiff in error sought to have determined in the Circuit Court. It is a question which, in our opinion, the Legislature intended to commit to the sound judgment of the regents who are selected because of an especial fitness for the performance of such duties, and who, by their experience and their intimate familiarity with the institution, are qualified to exercise that discretion in a far

sounder manner than any court or jury could be qualified by evidence adduced through witnesses. It is elementary that no cause of action can arise from the lawful exercise of a statutory power in the absence of an express provision conferring it. It is also a principle of law as securely founded that an exercise of a power by an administrative board or officer to whose judgment and discretion it is committed is not a proper subject of review by the courts when fraud or conditions equivalent thereto do not exist." [22]

"It would be intolerable for the courts to interject themselves and to require an educational institution to hire or to maintain on its staff a professor or instructor whom it deemed undesirable and did not wish to employ. For the courts to impose such a requirement would be an interference with the operation of institutions of higher learning contrary to established principles of law and to the best traditions of education." [23]

The second claim re-alleges the various acts complained of in the first claim and describes the charge in the nature of a conspiracy to deprive Jones of claimed rights under the Civil Rights Act and the Constitution of the United States. The complaint alleges 42 U.S.C. §§ 1983, 1986 and 1988 in its jurisdictional allegations and 42 U.S.C. § 1985(2) and (3) in its second claim. Combining them we examine what has been alleged in the complaint as a conspiracy on the part of appellees to deprive Jones of the rights claimed.

If one does not rely on the provisions of 42 U.S.C. § 1985(3), relating to going in disguise, the existence of a conspiracy is an essential allegation in the complaint based upon the substantive law of the state.

The complaint is based upon an act established by the Colorado statutes authorizing the exercise of discretion by the appellees. We concluded above there was not an unlawful or a wrongful exercise of the discretion claimed under the facts alleged.

Colorado has stated the rule, "[A]n action for conspiracy can not be successfully maintained unless the purpose to be effected is unlawful or a lawful purpose is accomplished by an unlawful means."

This court has recognized the similar Utah rule regarding whether or not the action complained of is justified.

The trial court concluded that under the Colorado statutes

22. Ward v. Board of Regents, 138 F. 372, 377 (8th Cir. 1905).
23. Greene v. Howard University, 271 F. Supp. 609, 615 (D.D.C. 1967).

the exercise of discretion was authorized and justified. We agree and affirm.

Affirmed.

Terms of written employment contract cannot be changed by parol evidence

KELEHER v. LA SALLE COLLEGE

Supreme Court of Pennsylvania, 1959.
394 Pa. 545, 147 A.2d 835.

BENJAMIN R. JONES, Justice.

This appeal involves a question of the applicability of the parol evidence rule.

James F. Keleher, appellant, taught philosophy and religion at LaSalle College, Philadelphia, from 1948 to 1953. On June 15, 1951, appellant and appellee, the latter acting through its then President, Brother Paul, entered into a written contract of employment, the summarized terms of which are: (1) appellant was employed as a full-time member of appellee's instructional staff with the rank of "Assistant Professor of Philosophy in the Area of Philosophy and Religion" for the academic year 1951-1952; (2) appellant agreed to (a) serve "faithfully, diligently and according to his best ability", (b) to accept at appellee's request certain administrative and non-teaching duties such as student consultation, etc., (c) by his conduct to uphold appellee's ideals and (d) not to engage, directly or indirectly, in any activity detrimental to appellee; (3) appellant was to be paid a salary—for a minimum semester teaching load of 12 semester credit hours and a maximum teaching load of 16 semester credit hours—of $3,950, provided that if the appellee requested a teaching load in excess of 16 semester credit hours per semester, appellant's compensation would be the sum, per hour, which the maximum semester teaching load multiplied by thirty established academic weeks bears to $3,950, multiplied by fifteen established academic weeks for each semester.

On June 15, 1952, appellant and appellee, the latter again through its then President, Brother Paul, entered into another written contract identical with the 1951 contract in all respects except that it covered the academic year 1952-1953 and appellant's salary was fixed at $4,160.

On March 2, 1953 Brother E. Stanislaus, then appellee's

President, wrote appellant to the effect that appellee could not offer him a new contract upon the expiration of the 1952-1953 contract, assigning as the reason therefor the necessity that appellee curtail its expenditures because of rising costs and diminishing enrollment. On March 7, 1953 the appellant wrote Brother Stanislaus questioning his authority to revoke "academic tenure" which appellant stated had been given him in June 1951 by Brother Paul and requesting of Brother Stanislaus an appeal to appellee's Board of Managers. On March 11, 1953 Brother Stanislaus wrote appellant: "* * * Please be advised that, inasmuch as this [academic] tenure was extended to you by authority of the President, it can, likewise, be revoked under the same authority * * *", and since as President of the Board of Managers, Brother Stanislaus, had full authority to act, no question of an appeal to the Board of Managers was involved. In the same letter Brother Stanislaus offered to continue appellant's services until June 1954 subject to the conditions that appellant would not act as head of the Department of Religion and Philosophy and that his salary would be cut to its previous level, which offer, in the absence of an acceptance by appellant, was withdrawn on April 23, 1953.

On September 18, 1953 appellant instituted an assumpsit action against appellee for an alleged breach of an *oral* contract of employment. In this action appellant alleged that in June of 1951,[1] Brother Paul, appellee's President, entered into an *oral* contract with appellant increasing his salary to $4,160, assigning him as "Acting Chairman of the Area of Philosophy and Religion" and giving him "tenure of academic employment", and that the revocation, without cause, of his tenure and employment by appellee, violated and breached this oral contract. Appellee's answer denied the existence of any oral contract and averred that appellant's employment arose solely under the two written contracts of June 15, 1951 and June 15, 1952. * * *

We repeat, the fundamental issue is whether, in view of the written undertaking of June 15, 1952 between the parties, the appellant should be permitted to prove by parol evidence the terms of the alleged oral contract of June 1951.

Walker v. Saricks, 360 Pa. 594, 598, 63 A.2d 9, 10, well states the Pennsylvania Parol Evidence Rule: "This Court

---

1. Whether the alleged oral contract was entered into prior or subsequent to the written contract of June 15, 1951 does not appear clearly from the record.

said in Gianni v. R. Russell & Co., Inc., 281 Pa. 320, 323, 126
A. 791, 792: 'Where parties, without any fraud or mistake,
have deliberately put their engagements in writing, the law
declares the writing to be not only the best, but the only,
evidence of their agreement. Martin v. Berens, 67 Pa. 459,
463; Irvin v. Irvin, 142 Pa. 271, 287, 21 A. 816. All preliminary negotiations, conversations and verbal agreements are
merged in and superseded by the subsequent written contract * * * and unless fraud, accident, or mistake be averred,
the writing constitutes the agreement between the parties,
and its terms cannot be added to nor subtracted from by
parol evidence. * * * In O'Brien v. O'Brien, 362 Pa. 66, 71,
66 A.2d 309, 311, 10 A.L.R.2d 714, we said: "* * * the test
is 'whether parties, situated as were the ones to the contract,
would naturally and normally include the one in the other if
it were made. If they relate to the same subject-matter, and
are so interrelated that both would be executed at the same
time, and in the same contract, the scope of the subsidiary
agreement must be taken to be covered by the writing. This
question must be determined by the court.' "

The written contract of June 15, 1952 is clear and free of
any ambiguity. It purports to encompass all the terms and
conditions of the relationship between appellant and appellee
concerning the former's employment as a teacher during the
academic year 1952-1953. Appellant now seeks to prove an
oral agreement which would clearly alter and vary the terms
of this written contract in a most material instance, to wit,
the length of appellant's employment. The written contract
distinctly and unambiguously sets forth that appellant is employed for the academic year 1952-1953. What appellant wants
to prove is that, as the result of an oral contract, he acquired
"academic tenure" by which we understand permanent tenure. That appellant's oral contract would vary and alter the
written contract is clear beyond any peradventure of doubt.

Appellant neither alleges nor does he seek to prove any
fraud, accident or mistake, but simply contends that the
parol evidence rule is inapplicable because the written contract did not constitute an integration of the alleged oral
contract and that both the oral and the written contract are
co-existent. A comparison of the subject-matter of the written
contract with that of the alleged oral contract clearly indicates an integration of the latter by the former. To allow appellant to prove an oral contract under these circumstances
would violate the parol evidence rule, a rule to which this

Court requires rigid adherence. Both the spirit and the letter of the parol evidence rule enunciated in Gianni v. R. Russell & Co., Inc., 281 Pa. 320, 126 A. 791 and a host of subsequent decisions, compel the rejection of evidence as to any alleged oral contract in June 1951 between the parties.

For the reasons stated, judgment is directed to be entered for the appellee.

CHAPTER 8
CONSTITUTIONAL RIGHTS OF STUDENTS

Student unrest on the nation's campuses in recent years has created a new concern for the role of the university in its relationship with students. One need not be reminded of the newspaper headlines to be aware of the complex legal issues involved in administering an institution of higher education today. College administrators are caught in the vortex of student activity which has spillover effects to the community, state and nation. Many administrative decisions in colleges involve a delicate balance between the individual rights and freedoms of students and the needs and welfare of the institution, people and the state.

STUDENT-UNIVERSITY RELATIONSHIP

The university has two bases for exercising control or disciplinary power over students, "one in connection with safeguarding the university's ideals of scholarship, and the other in connection with safeguarding the university's moral atmosphere." [1] In the regulation of academic standards, the courts have allowed considerable latitude to university officials.

The university is best qualified to determine the content of academic requirements and to assess the scholarly achievements of students; [2] thus reasoning, the courts have been very reluctant to review school actions based on academic grounds. [3] In cases where the courts have intervened, it has been evident that the university's action was arbitrary, capricious, [4] in bad faith or otherwise in abuse of discretion. [5] The United States Court of Appeals, Fifth Circuit, has said:

> * * * we think, that by seeking admission to and obtaining the benefits of attending a college or university the student agrees that he will abide by and obey the rules

---

1. Anthony v. Syracuse University, 224 App. Div. 487, 231 N.Y.S. 435 (1928).

2. Woods v. Simpson, 146 Md. 547, 126 A. 882 (1924).

3. Steven I. Pollack, "The Scope of University Discipline," *Brooklyn Law Review*, Vol. 35, p. 486 (1969).

4. Connelly v. University of Vermont and State Agricultural College, 244 F. Supp. 156 (1965).

5. Barnard v. Inhabitants of Shelburne, 216 Mass. 19, 102 N.E. 1095 (1913); Coffelt v. Nicholson, 224 Ark. 176, 272 S.W.2d 309 (1954).

and regulations promulgated for the orderly operation of that institution and for the effectuation of its purposes. * * *

We know of no case which holds that colleges and universities are subject to the supervision or review of the courts in the uniform application of their academic standards.[6]

Accordingly there is no constitutional right of a student to remain in a public university regardless of his academic performance.

Where student conduct is concerned, outside the realm of academic performance, the university's power is more limited. Courts which have given universities wide authority in controlling student conduct have relied primarily on two theories of the student-university relationship—*in loco parentis* and privilege.

IN LOCO PARENTIS

While predominately a phenomenon of elementary and secondary education, *in loco parentis* has a surprisingly strong legal basis in higher education. The leading higher education case adopting this theory was a 1923 Kentucky case which said: "[C]ollege authorities stand *in loco parentis* concerning the physical and moral welfare and mental training of the pupils, and * * * may make any regulation for * * * betterment of their pupils that a parent could for the same purpose." [7] This theory places the school in the place of the parent and affords school control over students commensurate with that of the parent in all matters pertaining to functions of the school. The influence of this theory in higher education has greatly diminished in recent years and is not generally regarded as having any substantial impact today on court decisions involving college students.

PRIVILEGE

This theory is based on the supposition that to attend school is a privilege and not a right.[8] Although of apparent wide acceptance a few years ago this notion today is in a state of judicial disrepute. The Supreme Court of the United States cast the first effective stone to destroy this theory when it

---

6. Wright v. Texas Southern University, 277 F. Supp. 110 (S.D. Tex. 1967), aff'd, 392 F.2d 728 (5th Cir. 1968).

7. Gott v. Berea College, 156 Ky. 376, 161 S.W. 204 (1913). See also Stetson University v. Hunt, 88 Fla. 510, 102 So. 637 (1924).

8. Board of Trustees v. Waugh, 105 Miss. 623, 62 So. 827 (1913), aff'd, 237 U.S. 589 (1915).

said in *Brown,* in speaking of segregation in elementary and secondary schools:

> Today, education is perhaps the most important function of state and local governments. * * * It is the very foundation of good citizenship. Today it is a principal instrument in awakening the child to cultural values, in preparing him for later professional training, and in helping him to adjust normally to his environment. In these days, it is doubtful that any child may reasonably be expected to succeed in life if he is denied the opportunity of an education. Such an opportunity, where the state has undertaken to provide it, is a *right* which must be made available to all on equal terms.[9] (Emphasis added.)

Even though the Court was not here speaking of college education its words nevertheless have important implications for education at higher levels. Precise application to a college came in 1961 in *Dixon v. Alabama State Board of Education* when the U. S. Court of Appeals for the Fifth Circuit said that "[t]he precise nature of the private interest involved in this case is the *right to remain* at a public institution of higher learning in which the plaintiffs were students in good standing." [10] (Emphasis added.) This court, like the Supreme Court in *Brown,* felt that "education is vital, and indeed, basic to civilized society." [11]

With the decline in the influence of *in loco parentis* and privilege doctrines, the courts are relying increasingly on other legal rationale to explain the student-university relationship. These theories are *contract, trust, fiduciary* and *constitutional.*[12]

Contract

The *contract* theory, apparently rather popular with the courts, is based on traditional contract principles. This theory assumes that the student and the university are parties to a contract, each giving certain benefits and detriments in order to fulfill the agreement. The school in advertising and seeking students, in effect, makes an offer to the student, and the student by registering accepts. The student

---

9. Brown v. Board of Education of Topeka, 347 U.S. 483, 74 S. Ct. 686 (1954).

10. 294 F.2d 150 (5th Cir.), *cert. denied,* 368 U.S. 930 (1961).

11. *Ibid.*

12. Gregory E. Michael, "The Student-School Legal Relationship: Toward a Unitary Theory," *Suffolk University Law Review,* Vol. V, No. 2, pp. 468-486 (1971).

agrees to pay tuition and fees and the school agrees to provide instruction and subsequently a degree, if the student remains in good standing academically and abides by the school's rules and regulations.[13]

However, the contract theory does not apply in all student-university situations. Some courts have drawn a distinction between private and public schools, maintaining that the pure contract theory can apply to private schools, but not to public schools. The public institution's relationship to the student cannot be termed purely contractual because the public school cannot freely choose the party with which it will contract, thus abrogating an essential ingredient of the contractual relationship. In the public institution where attendance is "a right" the trustees cannot deny or arbitrarily refuse a resident student admission as can a private institution.[14] The need for a contract in the public institution, thus, may be substantially mitigated.

Regardless, of whether the contracting school is public or private, the contractual relationship may be materially altered by disclaimers or express statements by the college that no irrevocable contract arises from a student's enrollment and that the school is allowed to change its rules and regulations at any time.[15]

TRUST

Another theory of student-university relationship is that of *trust*. The school is considered the trustee administering a charitable or educational trust, with the student as the beneficiary. This shadowy theory is apparently mentioned in only two cases;[16] and it has the overriding weakness, that normally a trustee does not have the legal power to change beneficiaries as does the university when in its disciplinary function it is forced to expel a student.

FIDUCIARY

The *fiduciary* theory, while less well-known, has been propounded to explain the student-university relationship.[17] The

13. Booker v. Grand Rapids Medical College, 156 Mich. 95, 120 N.W. 589 (1909).

14. Michael, *op. cit.*

15. Robinson v. University of Miami, 100 So. 2d 422 (1958).

16. People *ex rel.* Turkoff v. Northwestern University, 33 Ill. App. 224, 77 N.E.2d 345, *cert. denied*, 335 U.S. 829 (1947); Anthony v. Syracuse University, 224 App. Div. 487, 231 N.Y.S. 435 (1928).

17. Alvin L. Goldman, "The University and the Liberty of its Students—A Fiduciary Theory," *Kentucky Law Review*, Vol. 54, p. 643 (1966).

fiduciary relationship is characterized by "the confidence subsisting between two parties"; where one party reposes confidence in the fidelity and integrity of another, a fiduciary relation is created.[18] In this situation one party can be inferior or superior to the other; if such is the case, the power of the dominent party "is at all times subject to the equitable limitation that it may not be exercised for the aggrandizement, preference, or advantage of the fiduciary to the exclusion or detriment of one *cestuis*." [19] Goldman summarizes the student-university fiduciary relationship in this manner:

> In sum, the university, like any fiduciary, and not the student, should have the burden of demonstrating that any disciplinary action: (a) was reasonably imposed for cause consistent with its function of maintaining an open-minded atmosphere conducive to the acquisition and use of tools for freely inquiring into and exploring ideas; and (b) was imposed in a manner consistent with scholarly integrity and fair process. In addition, as a fiduciary, the university ought to afford the student every opportunity and means of rehabilitation. On the other hand, the university's fiduciary responsibility should not extend beyond those activities in which it acts in a fiduciary capacity with the relation to the students.[20]

CONSTITUTIONAL

The student has certain human or civil rights which he does not abandon when he enters college. This is the premise on which the constitutional approach to the student-university is best described. As mentioned above, it is the opposite of the privilege theory and possesses the soundest legal basis for discussion of any relationship between the individual and the state.

The First, Fourth, Fifth and Fourteenth Amendments provide the substantive base on which the student-university constitutional relationship is generally described. Students' basic freedoms of speech, press, expression, and assembly, along with procedural and substantive "due process" rights, have each been protected by the courts.

---

18. *Ibid.*
19. *Ibid.*
20. *Ibid.*

THE FIRST AMENDMENT AND THE STUDENT

The First Amendment,* while originally pertaining only to *Congress,* was applied to action by states in *Gitlow v. New York* [21] in 1925. The Supreme Court declared "For present purposes we may and do assume that freedom of speech and of the press—which are protected by the First Amendment from abridgment by Congress—are among the fundamental personal rights and 'liberties' protected by the due process clause of the Fourteenth Amendment from impairment by the State." [22] This statement was dictum in *Gitlow,* but became accepted doctrine two years later when the Court invalidated a state law on the ground that it abridged freedom of speech contrary to the due process clause of the Fourteenth Amendment. Application of the Fourteenth Amendment to the other rights safeguarded by the First Amendment were: freedom of the press in 1931,[23] right of peaceable assembly in 1937,[24] and freedom of religion in 1940.[25] Thus, the individual freedoms and liberties of the Constitution guarantee not only protection against infringement by the United States Congress but also provide safeguards against impairment of individual rights by state governments. The state college or university, as an arm, of the state is subject to the same constitutional limitations. In some cases, private colleges and universities have been held to have sufficient "state action" to be subject to constitutional requirements.

These individual freedoms, however, are not without limitation; every act by an individual depends upon the circumstances in which it is done. As Justice Holmes said in his oft quoted analogy, "The most stringent protection of free speech would not protect a man in falsely shouting fire in a theatre and causing panic." [26]

FREEDOM OF SPEECH AND EXPRESSION

The Supreme Court has established a long line of precedents

---

* The First Amendment provides: "Congress shall make no law respecting an establishment of religion, or prohibiting the free exercise thereof; or abridging the freedom of speech, or of the press; or the right of the people peaceably to assemble, and to petition the Government for a redress of grievances."

21. 268 U.S. 652 (1925).
22. *Ibid.,* p. 666.
23. Near v. Minnesota, 283 U.S. 697 (1931).
24. DeJonge v. Oregon, 299 U.S. 353 (1937).
25. Cantwell v. Connecticut, 310 U.S. 296 (1940).
26. Schenck v. United States, 249 U.S. 47 (1919).

which apply the test of "clear and present" danger to state action in attempting to control individual speech or expression. "The rules require that before an utterance can be penalized by government it must, ordinarily, have occurred in such circumstances or have been of such a nature as to create a clear and present danger" that would of itself bring about "substantial evils" within the power of government to prevent.[27] In *Whitney v. California*,[28] Justice Brandeis restated the clear and present danger test to include *intent* to create danger:

> But, although the rights of free speech and assembly are fundamental, they are not in their nature absolute. Their exercise is subject to restriction, if the particular restriction proposed is required in order to protect the State from destruction or from serious injury, political, economic or moral. That the necessity which is essential to a valid restriction does not exist unless speech would produce, or is intended to produce, a clear and imminent danger of some substantive evil which the State constitutionally may seek to prevent has been settled. * * *, no danger flowing from speech can be deemed clear and present, unless the incidence of the evil apprehended is so imminent that it may befall before there is opportunity for full discussion. If there be time to expose through discussion the falsehood and fallacies, to avert the evil by the processes of education, the remedy to be applied is more speech, not enforced silence." [29]

The Supreme Court makes it quite apparent that unfounded perceived dangers or those dangers which are not "present" or "imminent" will not serve to limit basic freedoms. Justice Black has said: "What finally emerges from the 'clear and present danger' cases is a working principle that the substantive evil must be extremely serious and the degree of imminence extremely high before utterances can be punished." [30]

LIMITS OF STUDENT FREEDOM

Where the university is concerned, clear and present dangers have manifested themselves in riots and demonstrations which disrupt or even completely close the doors of the institution. Acts by individuals for the purpose of disruption, interruption or even destruction of the institution are not constitutionally protected.

---

27. *Ibid.*
28. 274 U.S. 357 (1927).
29. *Ibid.*, pp. 373, 377.
30. Bridges v. California, 314 U.S. 252 (1941).

The normal activities of the university can and must be protected and the university is not obliged to tolerate interference with "any lawful mission, process, or function of the institution." [31] The university not only has a mandate to protect the rights and freedoms of the individual, but also has the obligation to protect itself and to accomplish the societal goals and objectives for which it was created. The rights of the individual are not unlimited, and they are subject to governmental restraint if: (1) the government's restraint rationally relates to the enhancement of the public service; (2) the benefits that are denied by the public by the restraint outweighs the resulting impairment of the individuals' constitutional right; and (3) the government has no alternatives at its disposal which are less subversive of the constitutional right.

Wright illustrates an application of the above principles:

> "The rights of free speech and assembly, while fundamental in our democratic society, still do not mean that everyone with opinions or beliefs to express may address a group at any public place and at any time." * * * a rule barring loud discussions in the reading room of the library does not limit "the exercise of a right guaranteed by the Constitution * * * to persons generally," for no one has a constitutional right to speak in a place so clearly inappropriate. The nature of the university, and the pattern of its normal activities, dictate the kinds of regulations of time, place, and manner that are reasonable, but the First Amendment is no bar to reasonable regulations of that kind.[32]

Even though the student does not have unlimited expression on the university campus, there is no reason to believe that the student has two sets of constitutional rights, one for on-campus and another for off-campus. The constitutional rights of the individual and the police power of the public university operate in the same context as do individuals and the government generally. The government, whether it is manifested in a university or some other state agency, has power for justifiable regulation of individual actions.

The Supreme Court of the United States in the famous "armband" case held that the school, to justify prohibition of a particular expression of opinion, must be able to show that the regulation is caused by something more than "a mere

---

31. Buttny v. Smiley, 281 F. Supp. 280 (1968); Jones v. State Board of Education, 279 F. Supp. 190 (1968), aff'd, 407 F.2d 834 (6th Cir. 1969).

32. Charles Alan Wright, "The Constitution on the Campus," *Vanderbilt Law Review*, Vol. 22, No. 5, pp. 1027-1088 (1969).

desire to avoid discomfort and unpleasantness that always accompany an unpopular viewpoint." [33] In this case, the Court held that the wearing of armbands to protest the Vietnam War was not disruptive and did not "materially or substantially interfere" with the requirements of appropriate discipline of the school. In the opinion of the Court, the school officials had promulgated the rule against armbands merely to avoid controversy which is always attendant to the right of free speech.

The Court commented:

> In the absence of a specific showing of constitutionally valid reasons to regulate their speech, students are entitled to freedom of expression of their views. * * * school officials cannot suppress "expressions of feelings with which they do not wish to contend." [34]

In an earlier decision, 1966, which was cited by the Supreme Court in *Tinker,* the U. S. Court of Appeals for the Fifth Circuit held that a high school regulation prohibiting students from wearing "freedom buttons" which had the words "One Man One Vote" and "SNCC" and which did not appear to hamper the school in carrying out its regular scheduled activities, was an arbitrary, unreasonable and unnecessary infringement on the students' freedom of expression.[35] The reasonable exercise of power in making regulations was defined by the Court of Appeals in the following manner:

> Regulations which are essential in maintaining order and discipline on school property are reasonable. Thus, school rules which assign students to a particular class, forbid unnecessary discussion in the classroom and prohibit the exchange of conversation between students are reasonable even though these regulations infringe on such basic rights as freedom of speech and association, because they are necessary for the orderly presentation of classroom activities. Therefore, a reasonable regulation is one which measurably contributes to the maintenance of order and decorum within the educational system.[36]

Student protest can and frequently does, though, extend beyond mere passive protest. Such was the case at the University of Colorado where several students physically blocked the entrance to the campus placement office protesting against

---

33. Tinker v. Des Moines School Independent Community District, 393 U.S. 503 (1969).
34. *Ibid.*
35. Burnside v. Byars, 363 F.2d 744 (1966).
36. *Ibid.*

the United States Central Intelligence Agency which was recruiting on the campus. Students seeking interviews were deprived of entrance to the office. The demonstrators refused to cease the activity upon request by university officials and, after notice, hearing and appeal, were suspended. The federal court held that the action by the university did not violate the students' right of expression and dissent. The right of free speech does not give a student the right to prevent lawful access to campus facilities.[37]

When student protests have reached the tenor of mass demonstrations resulting in disruption or substantial disorder, the courts have generally held that reasonable school restriction does not deprive the students of the basic rights of speech and expression. For example, two students at Central Missouri State College participated in a mass gathering, illegally blocking a public highway and street and destroying school property, and were suspended pursuant to a college regulation prohibiting mass, unruly, and unlawful gatherings of students. The U. S. Court of Appeals for the Eighth Circuit, after finding the student behavior to be disruptive, upheld this regulation concerning mass demonstrations, stating that it "* * * is relevant to the lawful mission of the educational institution." [38]

Similarly, a state disorderly conduct statute has been upheld as constitutional. In Wisconsin, the state legislature enacted a statute providing that whoever in a public or private place engages in violent, abusive, indecent, profane, boisterous, unreasonably loud, or otherwise disorderly conduct under circumstances in which such conduct causes or provokes disturbance shall be guilty of disorderly conduct. Students at the University of Wisconsin were arrested when they "demonstrated" against the interviewing of students by a chemical manufacturer; they blocked doors, were violent and profane. The Supreme Court of Wisconsin held that the statute did not violate the United States Constitution and said:

> Constitutionally protected rights, such as freedom of speech and peaceable assembly, are not the be all and end all. They are not an absolute touchstone. The United States Constitution is not unmindful of other equally important interests such as public order. To recognize the rights of freedom of speech and peaceable assembly as

---

37. Buttny v. Smiley, 281 F. Supp. 280 (D. Colo. 1968).
38. Esteban v. Central Missouri State College, 415 F.2d 1077 (1969).

absolutes would be to recognize the rule of force; the rights of other individuals and of the public would vanish.[39]

Freedom of speech and expression are, therefore, not absolutes but are subject to reasonable regulation by the institution. However, the reasonable exercise of governmental power by the university is subject to a very strong constitutional standard when free speech or expression is restrained. The First Amendment imposes three standards or limitations on the state university, each of which should be carefully examined and scrutinized before promulgation of regulations: (1) Expression cannot be prohibited because of disagreement with or dislike for its contents; (2) expression is subject to reasonable and nondiscriminatory regulations of time, place and manner; (3) expression can be prohibited if it takes the form of action that materially and substantially interferes with the normal activities of the institution or invades the rights of others." [40]

OUTSIDE SPEAKERS

As a general rule the state college or university can, through proper procedural safeguards, regulate the time, place, and manner of speeches by outside speakers, but it cannot regulate the content of such speeches.[41] In order to stay within constitutional boundaries, the university must specifically limit only those speeches which pose a "clear and present" danger resulting in a substantive evil to the university.[42] The regulatory function of the university can be exercised largely in procedure and form rather than in substance.[43] The institution may schedule speaking events and validly provide that no request for a speaker will be honored unless made to the university by a recognized faculty or student group, within reasonable time, setting forth the proposed date, time, location of meeting and expected size of audience. The approving authority of the school should not be allowed unbridled discretion granted by vague regulations, thus, preventing the possibility of censorship or arbitrary decision.

The courts have made it clear that no one has an absolute

39. State v. Zwicker, 164 N.W.2d 512 (Wis. 1969).
40. Wright, *op. cit.*, p. 1043.
41. 5 A.L.R. Fed. 841.
42. Stacy v. Williams, 306 F. Supp. 963, 5 A.L.R. Fed. 814 (1969).
43. Brooks v. Auburn University, 296 F. Supp. 188, *aff'd*, 412 F.2d 1171 (5th Cir. 1969).

right to speak on a college or university campus.[44] The university facilities are dedicated to the specialized function of education and there is no constitutional requirement that the facilities be used to satisfy the "whimsical curiosity" of the students.[45] However, once the school opens its doors to visiting speakers, the school administration cannot accept some speakers while arbitrarily rejecting others. Such discrimination among speakers may violate the equal protection provisions of the Fourteenth Amendment. So long as the campus remains open to some outside speakers other outside speakers cannot be barred despite the orthodoxy or popularity of their political or social views, except where their presence creates a clear and present danger.

The clear and present danger test does not mean that a speaker can be banned simply because "his *presence* alone provokes riotous conduct among the audience." A person's right of free speech cannot be limited because of the audience's reaction to his presence, but only for results which are engendered by that which the speaker does or says.[46] A simple dislike for the speaker by persons on campus is not sufficient to constitutionally deny freedom of speech.

The clear and present danger doctrine allows a university to deny an invitation to a guest speaker if it reasonably appears that in the course of his speech he would advocate:

(1) Violent overthrow of the government of the United States, the state, or any political subdivision thereof;

(2) Willful destruction or seizure of the institution's buildings or other property;

(3) Disruption or impairment, by force, of the institution's regularly scheduled classes or other educational functions;

(4) Physical harm, coercion, intimidation, or other invasion of lawful rights of the institution's officials, faculty members, or students; or

(5) Other campus disorder of a violent nature.[47]

The speaker, however, must not only clearly advocate the above things, but there must also be present a reasonable apprehension of imminent danger to the essential functions and purposes of the institution.[48]

---

44. Stacy v. Williams, *supra.*
45. Dickson v. Sitterson, 280 F. Supp. 486 (1968).
46. Stacy v. Williams, *supra.*
47. Stacy v. Williams, *supra.*
48. 5 A.L.R. Fed. 846.

Freedom of the Press

The historic antecedents to the freedom of press provisions of the First Amendment were summarized by Blackstone in his *Commentaries* published in 1876:

> The liberty of the press is indeed essential to the nature of a free state: but this consists in laying no *previous* restraints upon publication, and not in freedom from censure from criminal matter when published. Every freeman has an undoubted right to lay what sentiments he pleases before the public: to forbid this, is to destroy the freedom of the press: but if he publishes what is improper, mischievous, or illegal, he must take the consequences of his own temerity. To subject the press to the restrictive power of a licenser, as was formerly done, both before and since the Revolution, is to subject all freedom of sentiment to the prejudices of one man, and make him the arbitrary and infallible judge of all controverted points in learning, religion and government. But to punish as the law does at present any dangerous or offensive writings, which, when published shall on a fair and impartial trial be adjudged of a pernicious tendency, is necessary for the preservation of peace and good order, of government and religion, the only solid foundations of civil liberty. Thus, the will of the individuals is still left free: the abuse only of that free will is the object of legal punishment. Neither is any restraint hereby laid upon freedom of thought or inquiry; liberty of private sentiment is still left; the disseminating, or making public, of bad sentiments, destructive to the ends of society, is the crime which society corrects.[49]

In spite of Blackstone's clearcut philosophic base for freedom of press, the application of the principle has been rather difficult to achieve. On occasion, not only colleges and universities, but states and the federal government attempt to exercise limitation and restraint over the press.[50]

The United States Supreme Court in attempting to interpret the First Amendment has said:

> In the First Amendment the Founding Fathers gave the free press the protection it must have to fulfill its essential role in our democracy. The press was to serve the governed, not the governors. The Government's power to censor the press was abolished so that the press would remain forever free to censure the Government.[51]

Coupling this reasoning with that of the Supreme Court in

---

49. Blackstone, *Commentaries*, p. 145 (1876).
50. New York Times Company v. United States, 91 S. Ct. 2140 (1971).
51. *Ibid.*

Tinker, one may extrapolate the attitude of the Supreme Court toward student publications.

As stated by Justice Fortas in *Tinker,* student rights are not subject to restriction except where they "materially and substantially" interfere with the requirements of appropriate discipline of the school.[52] Mere apprehension of disturbance is not enough to overcome the right to freedom of expression, but the school officials must "reasonably forecast substantial disruption or material interference" with school activities.[53]

This standard was applied in what is probably the leading "student press" case. In *Dickey* v. *Alabama State Board of Education,* a federal district court held that a rule resulting in a student editor's expulsion, precluding editorial criticism of the governor or state legislature, was unreasonable.[54] The court said that:

> State school officials cannot infringe on their students' right of free and unrestricted expression as guaranteed by the Constitution of the United States where the exercise of such right does not "materially and substantially interfere with requirements of appropriate discipline in the operation of the school."[55]

The question of censorship arose at the University of Maryland when a student publication was submitted to the printer containing a picture of a burning American flag on the front cover. The Maryland Attorney General advised university officials that they might be subject to criminal prosecution, under a Maryland statute, if they allowed the picture to be published. Publication was stopped when the university informed the printer that it would not pay for the work if the cover were printed. The Maryland Statute pursuant to which the attorney general acted provides:

> No person shall publicly mutilate, defile, defy, trample upon, or by word or act cast contempt upon any such flag, standard, color, ensign or shield [of the United States or of the State of Maryland].[56]

The federal district court held that the Maryland statute was unconstitutionally applied because of a lack of necessary

---

52. Tinker v. Des Moines Independent Community School District, 393 U.S. 503 (1969).

53. Scoville v. Board of Education of Joliet Township, 38 U.S.L.W. 2542 (7th Cir. 1970), *rev'g* 415 F.2d 860 (7th Cir. 1969).

54. 273 F. Supp. 613 (1967).

55. *Ibid.*

56. Md. Code Ann., art. 27, § 83 (1967 Repl. Vol.)

governmental interests. The interests necessary for government to restrict individual expression are (1) prevention of incitement of others to commit unlawful acts, (2) prevention of the utterance of words so inflammatory they provide physical retaliation, (3) protection of the sensibilities of others, and (4) assurance of proper respect for the national emblem.[57]

The court also pointed out that, even though the student press may not enjoy the same freedoms enjoyed by the regular press, there, nevertheless, must be a showing that the suppression of its contents is necessary for the maintenance of order and discipline. The school officials had failed to make such a showing.

The "material and substantial" interference test was applied in a Texas case in granting injunctive relief for students against university prohibition of distribution of a tabloid published by a school-recognized student organization.[58] University regulations prohibited "lewd, indecent or obscene conduct or expression on University-owned-or-controlled property" and "selling and soliciting on the campus with official authorization." The court granted the injunction and barred university disciplinary actions against the students. The court concluded that the "material and substantial" interference test had not been met. There was no showing by the university of disruption, hostility, or infringement on the rights of other students. Mere "uncrystallized apprehension" of disruption or "annoying and inconvenient" language is not sufficient justification for abridgement of First Amendment rights.

College authorities are not required to wait until after the disruption or interference transpires before seeking to suppress the act which causes it. Several students at East Tennessee State University distributed literature on campus urging students to stand up and fight and called university officials "despots" and problem children.[59] The students who distributed the literature were suspended after being afforded notice and a hearing. The U. S. Court of Appeals for the Sixth Circuit upheld the suspensions and termed the literature "an open exhortation to the students to engage in disorderly and destructive activities" calculated to subject the university administration to ridicule and contempt and to "damage the

57. Korn v. Elkins, 317 F. Supp. 138 (1970).
58. The Channing Club v. Board of Regents of Texas Tech. University, 317 F. Supp. 688 (1970).
59. Norton v. Discipline Committee of East Tennessee State University, 419 F.2d 195 (1969). (U.S. Supreme Court *denied certiorari*).

reputation of the University." The court stated that: "It is not required that the college authorities delay action against the inciters until after the riot has been started and buildings have been taken over and damaged. The college authorities had the right to nip such action in the bud and prevent it in its inception."

Conclusions of law are difficult to determine in an area where the law is in its infant stages of development as it is with regard to student freedom of the press. However, one can glean certain legal standards from these cases which may be helpful in policy formulation. These are:

(1) the constitutional presumption is in favor of the student's freedom of press,

(2) restraint, to be valid, must be supported by evidence showing a reasonable forecast of "material and substantive" interference with a legitimate school activity,

(3) mere apprehension of disruption or annoyance is not sufficient to restrict individual freedom,

(4) showing of an intention to incite or disrupt is not sufficient reason for restraint, unless potential for disruption exists,

(5) where acts of students create a "clear and present danger" which would bring about "substantial evils" to the institution or where it can be shown that the students' activities would materially and substantially disrupt the work and discipline of the school, school officials are not required to sit idly by and watch a riot or demonstration destroy school property or school functions.

SEARCH AND SEIZURE

The Fourth Amendment provides in part: "The right of people to be secure in their persons, houses, papers, and effects, against unreasonable searches and seizures, shall not be violated, and no Warrants shall issue, but upon probable cause * * *." The Supreme Court, while not laying down a very clear standard, has definitely held that the fruits of warrantless and unreasonable search and seizure is inadmissible as evidence in the courts.[60] This falls somewhat short of saying that government officials cannot conduct unreasonable searches at all. However, this protection does afford the citizen a protection against involuntary self-incrimination, which is also pro-

---

60. Mapp v. Ohio, 367 U.S. 643 (1961).

tected by the Fifth Amendment.[61] Some recent cases, though, indicate that the courts in the future may consider the Fourth Amendment as a right of privacy and not merely a right against self-incrimination, thereby, protecting the citizen from warrantless searches and preventing police from seizing and holding private property, regardless of whether the goods are used as evidence.[62]

The general benefit of the Fourth Amendment is that it imposes the magistrate between the citizen and the police. The magistrate or judge decides on the propriety of the proposed search according to standards of reasonableness, probable cause, and necessity.[63] Exceptions to this rule are found where the police search is with legitimate consent,[64] where search is incident to lawful arrest,[65] where an emergency exists,[66] or where the searcher is a private party and not the police.[67]

The legal boundaries of search and seizure in colleges and universities are largely unexplored. Students who do not live in college owned and operated dormitories, of course, retain their Fourth Amendment protections as any other citizen. However, to date, the law surrounding search and seizure of goods on campuses is not so clear. The courts in a series of decisions have not required school officials to obtain search warrants for entry into lockers or dormitory rooms. Where lockers are concerned, the courts have reasoned that the student does not have exclusive possession and control. In *State* v. *Stein*,[68] where a principal opened a student's locker for police and found stolen goods, the court said:

> Although a student may have control of his school locker as against fellow students, his possession is not exclusive against the school and its officials. A school does not supply its students with lockers for illicit use in harboring pilfered property or harmful substances. * * *
We believe this right of inspection is inherent in the au-

61. Boyd v. United States, 116 U.S. 616 (1886).

62. Warden v. Hayden, 387 U.S. 294 (1967); United States v. Blok, 188 F.2d 1019 (1951); Katy v. United States, 389 U.S. 347 (1967).

63. Aguilar v. Texas, 378 U.S. 108 (1964). See also "College Searches and Seizures: Privacy and Due Process Problems on Campus," *Georgia Law Review*, Vol. 3, pp. 426-458 (1968).

64. Gouled v. United States, 255 U.S. 298 (1921); Bumper v. North Carolina, 391 U.S. 543 (1968).

65. United States v. Jeffers, 342 U.S. 48 (1951).

66. McDonald v. United States, 335 U.S. 451 (1951).

67. "The Fourth Amendment Right of Privacy: Mapping the Future," *Virginia Law Review*, Vol. 53, p. 1314 (1967).

68. State v. Stein, 203 Kan. 638 (1969).

thority vested in school administrators and that the same must be retained and exercised in the management of our schools if their educational functions are to be maintained and the welfare of the student bodies preserved.[69]

Similarly, courts have not conceded the college student's right to privacy in his dormitory room against search by college officials. In *People* v. *Kelly*,[70] a student at the California Institute of Technology tried to suppress evidence obtained without a warrant from his dormitory room. Police, accompanied by a school official, had searched the room for property alleged to have been stolen during several burglaries. The court upheld the search because the dormitory rules permitted the house master to enter any room in an emergency. The court did not attempt to define emergency but held merely that when a student accepted residence in the dormitory he impliedly promised to respect and abide by all its rules.[71]

These precedents suggest two reasons for the court's denial of regular search and seizure protections to college students; first, it may be contended that the student waives his rights against search and seizure when he enrolls and occupies a room in the college dormitory. This contention, of course, runs counter to the precedent laid down by the Supreme Court in *Tinker* when it said that: "It can hardly be argued that either students or teachers shed their constitutional rights to freedom of speech or expression at the schoolhouse gate" and "students in school as well as out of school are 'persons'" under our Constitution.[72] Although the Supreme Court was speaking of First Amendment rights, there is little reason to believe that the same rationale does not apply to other provisions of the Constitution. The second reason, which is not necessarily exclusive of the first, is that a college has the power and discretion to make reasonable rules and regulations to maintain order and discipline. This reasoning relies

---

69. *Ibid.* See also People v. Overton, 20 N.Y.2d 360, 229 N.E.2d 596 (1967).

70. 195 Cal. App. 2d 669, 16 Cal. Rptr. 177 (1961).

71. This case was somewhat clouded by the use of the word "emergency" and the fact that the student could have been searched incident to an arrest for burglary. It is well settled that a person and his premises, which is in his immediate possession and control, may be searched "incident to arrest." Agnello v. United States, 269 U.S. 20 (1925). However, there is some question as to the extent of such a search and to what precisely constitutes "immediate possession and control." Go-Bart Co. v. United States, 282 U.S. 344 (1931); Harris v. United States, 331 U.S. 145 (1947).

72. 393 U.S. 503 (1969).

on a showing by the institution that the rules and regulations it promulgates are reasonable and promote the appropriate educational environment. To deny an individual right on this basis, it must be shown that the search is made as a result of "reasonable forecast" of material and substantial interference with the activities of the institution. As indicated in other sections of this chapter such a prerequisite may be rather difficult to prove. The third, and probably the strongest argument supporting the institution's right to search lockers and/or rooms, is that the locker or the dormitory room is school property and is merely used by the student, and the student has no right to assume that he can exclude school officials from entering the property. Rationale for this contention is given by the Supreme Court of Kansas in commenting on the search of a student's locker: "Its status in the law is somewhat anomalous; it does not possess all the attributes of a dwelling, a motor vehicle, or a private locker." As to the latter, the possessor's rights of possession is exclusive; it is protected from unwarranted "intrusion as against the world." The school locker does not have these exclusionary attributes, especially where the school official in charge maintains a key, or combinations to locks, and general control and supervision. The student's possession is exclusive only as against other students and not as against the school.[73]

In *People* v. *Overton* [74] the Court of Appeals of New York said it is axiomatic that the protection of the Fourth Amendment is not restricted to dwellings; however, there are conditions where a depository of goods may be in the possession of more than one person. For example, the Supreme Court held that consent to search given by a landlord, who had a key and accepted deliveries on behalf of the tenant, was valid and no warrant was needed.[75] Extending this logic, the court, in *Overton*, held that the principal of a school could give consent for a search by police. The power to give such consent arose out of the "distinct relationship between school authorities and students." [76]

Ironically, two very important cases involving search and seizure in college dormitories have been handed down by one federal district court in Alabama, with the same judge, Judge

73. State v. Stein, 203 Kan. 638 (1969).

74. 20 N.Y.2d 360, 229 N.E.2d 596 (1967).

75. United States v. Botsch, 364 F.2d 542 (2d Cir. 1966), *cert. denied*, 386 U.S. 937.

76. 20 N.Y.2d 360, 229 N.E.2d 596 (1967).

Frank Johnson, writing both opinions. In the first case, *Moore v. Student Affairs Committee of Troy State University*,[77] the court upheld a college regulation, "the college reserves the right to enter rooms for inspection purposes," as reasonable and necessary to the institution's performance of its duty to operate as an educational institution. This court, while maintaining that a student has a right to be free of "unreasonable" search and seizures, held that the college, nevertheless, has an obligation to promulgate and enforce reasonable regulations. To this court, the issue did not pivot on whether the student waived his constitutional right or contracted it away, but rather on whether the regulations were a reasonable exercise of the college's supervisory duty.

A later case [78] by the same court distinguished the factual situation in *Moore* and held a search to be illegal. In *Moore*, the search of a student's room had been conducted by the Dean of Men and two agents of the State of Alabama Health Department, their having reason to believe that marijuana was hidden in the dormitory room. This situation differed factually from *Piazzola*, where the search was instigated by the police and was not based on any reason except that the police "had information."

These two cases emphasize two very important conditions under which students' dormitory rooms can be searched without a warrant. The search must be conducted by the school officials as the primary investigators, with police only secondary; and the search must be done pursuant to reasonable school regulation promulgated and enforced in furtherance of the educational objectives of the institution. Where police initiate the search to obtain evidence to be used in a criminal proceeding, with only passive support of school officials and without relationship to the necessary performance of educational institution, then the search is unconstitutional and evidence obtained is inadmissible in the courts.

Many commentators feel that to allow college or university officials to search dormitory rooms is, in itself, unconstitutional. This point of view gains credence when one considers that the state college or university, as an arm of the state can, as a result of a search, deprive a student of his future right to an education. Doubt is also cast on the constitutional propriety of such a standard when one considers that the evidence obtained in a legal search by school officials can be

---

77. 284 F. Supp. 725 (M.D. Ala. 1968).
78. Piazzola v. Watkins, 316 F. Supp. 624 (M.D. Ala. 1970).

turned over to police and used as evidence in a criminal proceeding against the student.

The assumption that the students' constitutional rights are mitigated by his occupying a college dormitory room was held to be unsupportable by a New York court in 1968.[79] The court in this case said that the "price of a modern education is not the waiver or surrender of Constitutional privileges." In this case police, accompanied by two Hofstra University officials, entered a student's dormitory room without announcing their purpose and without a search warrant. Consent was not given by the student; in fact, no one was in the room at the time so there was no immediate danger that the evidence would be removed. The court held the search to be in violation of the Fourth Amendment. Characterizing the search as a "fishing expedition" to gain evidence for possible arrest and not "incident to arrest," the court said "A search cannot be justified on the basis that it uncovered facts which gave rise to probable cause for arresting a person and then by a process of induction, to suggest the search is justified because it is an incident to an arrest." Commenting on the doctrine that the student waives his constitutional rights and impliedly consents to searches, the court said, "It offends reason and logic to suppose that a student will consent to an entry into his room designed to establish grounds upon which to arrest him." The court, however, did not specifically deny that a student may impliedly consent to search of his room by university officials, but it said that "even if the doctrine of implied consent were imported into this case, the consent is given, not to police officials, but to the University and the latter cannot fragmentize, share or delegate it."

DUE PROCESS OF LAW

No person can be deprived of life, liberty, or property without due process of law. This right is guaranteed by both the Fifth and the Fourteenth Amendments and can be traced back to the Magna Carta where the king promised that "no free man (*nullus liber homo*) shall be taken or imprisoned or deprived of his freehold liberties or free customs, or outlawed or exiled, or in any manner destroyed, nor shall we come upon him or send against him, except by a legal judgment of his peers or by the law of the land (*per legem terrae*)." The first interpretations of the courts in the United States viewed "due

---

79. People v. Cohen, 57 Misc. 2d 366, 292 N.Y.S.2d 706 (1968).

process" as having only "procedural" requirements, or those aspects which guaranteed the individual rights of certain jury procedural process.[80] It was only later, 1923, when the Supreme Court held a minimum wage act in the District of Columbia unconstitutional that due process was applied to "substantive" content of the law.[81] Today, the protection of due process provides for both substantive and procedural rights for the individual.

SUBSTANTIVE DUE PROCESS

Substantive due process has been lucidly described by an Arizona court as follows:

> The phrase "due process of law," when applied to substantive rights, as distinguished from procedural rights, means that the state is without power to deprive a person of life, liberty or property by an act having no reasonable relation to any proper governmental purpose, or which is so far beyond the necessity of case as to be an arbitrary exercise of governmental power.[82]

Substantive due process provides broad protection for individuals against the government's infringement on individual rights. The Supreme Court has relied on such broad application to hold that substantive due process of the Fifth Amendment applies the same restrictions to the federal government as the "equal protection clause" of the Fourteenth Amendment imposes on state government.[83]

The liberties protected under the Fourteenth Amendment pertaining to education have been held as a reaffirmation of the liberty of a teacher to pursue a lawful calling to teach free and clear of arbitrary restraints imposed by a state.[84] Similarly, substantive liberties of parents found to be infringed upon by the state by requiring all children to attend public schools—"unreasonably interferes with the liberty of parents and guardians to direct the upbringing and education of children under their control." [85] On the other hand, the "liberty" of the Fourteenth Amendment does not extend "the

---

80. Hurtado v. California, 110 U.S. 516 (1884); Murray's Lessee v. Hoboken Land and Improvement Co., 18 How. 272 (1856). See also Norman J. Small (ed.), *The Constitution of the United States*, U.S. Government Printing Office, Washington, 1964, p. 960.
81. Adkins v. Children's Hospital, 261 U.S. 525 (1923).
82. Valley Nat. Bank of Phoenix v. Glover, 62 Ariz. 538, 159 P.2d 292 (1945).
83. Bolling v. Sharp, 347 U.S. 497 (1954).
84. Meyer v. Nebraska, 262 U.S. 390 (1923).
85. Pierce v. Society of Sisters, 268 U.S. 510 (1925).

right to be students in the state university free from obligation to take military training as one of the conditions of attendance." [86]

PROCEDURAL DUE PROCESS

Until recently the judiciary has been extremely reluctant to
intervene in review of university disciplinary proceedings.
Procedural due process, while always applicable in judicial
proceedings, was not applied to the administrative quasi-
judicial functions of universities until the landmark case of
Dixon v. Alabama State Board of Education.[87] The *Dixon*
court held that the student has a right to notice and a hearing
in university disciplinary proceedings when the charges
could lead to suspension or expulsion. No rigid procedural
steps were prescribed by the court, but broad guidelines were
established requiring notice and a hearing. "The notice should
contain a statement of the specific charges and grounds which,
if proven, would justify expulsion . . . . The nature of the
hearing should vary depending upon the circumstances of the
particular case." [88] Generally, however, fundamental fairness
should be provided with the hearing amounting to "something
more than an informal interview,"—both sides must be given
an opportunity to present their sides of the story in detail.
The court went on to say that a full scale judicial hearing,
with the right of cross-examination of witnesses, is not required, but nevertheless, the "rudiments of an adversary proceeding may be preserved without encroaching upon the interests of the college." [89] In this regard the court said further:

> In the instant case, the student should be given the
> names of the witnesses against him and an oral or written
> report on the facts to which each witness testifies. He
> should also be given the opportunity to present to the
> Board, or at least to an administrative official of the
> college, his own defense against the charges and to pro-
> duce either oral testimony or written affidavits of wit-
> nesses in his behalf. If the hearing is not before the
> board directly, the results and findings of the hearing
> should be presented in a report open to the student's
> inspection.[90]

Shortly following *Dixon* came a case which provided further
clarification of the procedural due process required of uni-

---

86. Hamilton v. Regents, 293 U.S. 245 (1934).
87. 294 F.2d 150 (5th Cir. 1961).
88. *Ibid.*
89. *Ibid.*
90. *Ibid.*

versities. Some students at Florida A & M University had been convicted in a Florida circuit court for violation of a restraining order issued against student demonstrators.[91] The students were telephoned and advised to appear before the University Discipline Committee. No charges were made against the students until they had presented themselves before the committee. The students made no request to call witnesses or to obtain counsel. The court found that this procedure did not deny "fundamental fairness" and was consistent with the *Dixon* ruling. Concluding that universities must be fair and reasonable in such hearings but are not required to adhere to a strict procedural format, the court stated:

> More specific routines of notice and advisement may be indicated in this regard, but a foisted system of rigid procedure can become so ritualistic, dogmatic, and impractical as to itself be a denial of due process. The touchstones in this area are fairness and reasonableness.[92]

The fairness and reasonableness standard is apparently in keeping with decisions by other courts regarding procedural due process. Justice Frankfurter enunciated the nature of due process as "not a mechanical instrument" but "a process," the general proposition of which is contingent on the factual situation, the available alternatives, the nature of the administrative agency involved, and the "balance of hurt complained of and good accomplished."[93]

Recent decisions have generally required more procedural specification of fairness in the hearing than was indicated in *Due*. In one such case, the court outlined three minimal requirements to apply in case of severe disciplinary action:

> First, the student should be given adequate notice in writing of the specific ground or grounds and the nature of the evidence on which the disciplinary proceedings are based. Second, the student should be given an opportunity for a hearing in which the disciplinary authority provides a fair opportunity for hearing of the student's position, explanations and evidence. The third requirement is that no disciplinary action be taken on grounds which are not supported by any substantial evidence.[94]

---

91. Due v. Florida A & M University, 233 F. Supp. 396 (1963).
92. *Ibid.*
93. Joint Anti-Fascist Refugee Committee v. McGrath, 341 U.S. 123 (1951).
94. Esteban v. Central Missouri State College, 415 F.2d 1077 (1969). See also "General Order on Judicial Standards of Procedure and Substance in Review of Student Discipline in Tax Supported Institutions of Higher Education," 45 F.R.D. 133, 147 (1968); see Notes of this chapter for other information regarding this statement.

Significantly, and consistently with *Dixon* and *Due*, this court said that: "Within limits of due process, institutions must be free to devise various types of disciplinary procedures relevant to their lawful missions, consistent with their varying processes and functions, and not an unreasonable strain on their resources and personnel."

The prevailing view of the courts is that these broad procedural requirements are sufficient to constitutionally safeguard the student. Some courts have, however, recommended more specific procedural steps which tend to allow the university less prerogative in the establishment of hearing procedures. By viewing the various court decisions a list of procedural checkpoints may be developed, and although no one court has recommended all of these steps, they nevertheless are worthy of consideration by university administrators:

(1) *Written notice should be provided the student, allowing him a reasonable amount of time to prepare his defense.* Notice should specify the charges against the student, referring to the specific institutional rule which allegedly has been violated.

(2) *Prior to the hearing the student should be given a list of witnesses and a copy of their statements or complaints, along with other evidence and affidavits which the university intends to submit against him.*

(3) *The university should give the student the opportunity to choose between a public or private hearing.* Choice of type of hearing has not been required [95] by the courts but is recommended by some commentators as a means of maximizing fairness.

(4) *The hearing should be conducted by the appropriate tribunal.* There is no legal requirement that students or faculty be impanelled, but such procedures may tend to insure against claims of arbitrariness. The hearing committee should be empowered to make decisions regarding the disposition of the case.

(5) *The student should be permitted to have counsel present at the hearing and to seek advice during the course of the proceedings.* A university can maximize fairness by allowing the student to have either lawyer, parent, friend or teacher present during the hearing. Recent cases have indicated that the right of representation by a lawyer depends upon the presence or ab-

---

95. Zanders v. Louisiana State Board of Education, 281 F. Supp. 747 (1968).

sence of other safeguards affecting the student's overall ability to defend himself.[96] In *Soglin v. Kauffman* [97] the court drew an analogy between the right to a lawyer in criminal prosecutions and the right in student discipline cases. However, the prevailing view, at this time, is that the right to have a lawyer as guaranteed by the Sixth Amendment does not apply to administrative proceedings involving student discipline.[98]

(6) *The student should be permitted to confront his accusors and to hear all witnesses.* At least one court has upheld the argument against confrontation in student hearings, on the ground that "honorable students do not like to be known as snoopers and informers against their fellows . . . ." [99] Other courts have held that confrontation is an essential element of due process.[100] This view is not new. In one very old decision, 1887, the court held that:

> The student was entitled to know what testimony had been given against him, and by whom it had been delivered, and that the proofs be made openly and in his presence, with a full opportunity to question the witnesses and to call others to explain or contradict their testimony.[101]

(7) *It is fundamental that the hearing should provide the student with the opportunity to present his own case, his version of the facts and any exhibits, affidavits, or witnesses on his behalf.*

(8) *The student should have the right to remain silent to avoid self-incrimination.* To the present, the privilege against self-incrimination has not been extended to the student in a university hearing. The question of self-incrimination is particularly acute where questions posed to a student may produce evidence which can

---

96. Wasson v. Trowbridge, 382 F.2d 807 (2d Cir. 1967). The Sixth Amendment confers upon the defendant in a criminal proceeding the right to have counsel. Gideon v. Wainwright, 372 U.S. 335 (1963).

97. 37 U.S.L.W. 2357 (W.D. Wis. 1968).

98. Buttny v. Smiley, 281 F. Supp. 280 (1968); Barker v. Hardway, 283 F. Supp. 228 (1968); Madera, *op. cit.*

99. State *ex rel.* Sherman v. Hyman, 180 Tenn. 99, 171 S.W.2d 822 (1942).

100. Jones v. Tennessee State Board of Education, 279 F. Supp. 190 (1968); Esteban v. Central Mo. State College, 277 F. Supp. 649 (1967).

101. Commonwealth *ex rel.* Hill v. McCauley, 3 Pa. County Ct. 77 (1887).

be used against him for violation of federal, state and municipal law as well as for violation of university regulation.[102] Even though cases in other areas of administrative activity indicate that this right is becoming an essential element of procedural due process, it seems unlikely that this right will be fully extended to student disciplinary hearings in the immediate future.

(9) *A full and complete record of the hearing should be made.* The right to make a record of the hearing is recognized by the courts as an element of due process,[103] but the courts have not held that the university is bound to provide the record at its own expense. Where the university does not do so, it may be required, as an alternative, to provide a *de novo* hearing in the event of an appeal by the student.[104]

(10) *The student should be given the right of appeal within the administrative structure of the University.* Van Alstyne found in 1962 that 90 percent of the universities he surveyed provided for some type of administrative appeal from the initial determination.[105]

(11) *The student should not be suspended before a hearing.* The law seems to be unsettled as to whether a university can temporarily suspend a student before a full hearing. In two recent cases, the courts upheld a procedure whereby students were given notice that they had been suspended and that they were entitled to a hearing to show cause why disciplinary action should not be taken. The courts decided that there was no greater burden on the student than if the university had postponed the disciplinary action until after formal hearings.[106] Plaintiffs in *Jones v. State*

102. James M. Smart, Jr., "The Fourteenth Amendment and University Disciplinary Procedures," *Missouri Law Review*, Vol. 34, p. 253 (1969).

103. Esteban v. Central Missouri State College, 277 F. Supp. 649 (1967); Wasson v. Trowbridge, 382 F.2d 807 (2d Cir. 1967); Dixon v. Alabama State Bd. of Educ., 294 F.2d 150 (5th Cir. 1961), *cert. denied*, 368 U.S. 930 (1961).

104. Smart, *op. cit.*, p. 254; Zanders v. Louisiana State Board of Educ., 281 F. Supp. 747 (1968).

105. W.W. Van Alstyne, "Procedural Due Process and the State University Student," *U.C.L.A. Law Review*, Vol. 10, p. 368 (1963). See Smart, *op. cit.*

106. Jones v. State Bd. of Educ., 279 F. Supp. 190 (1968); Barker v. Hardway, 283 F. Supp. 228 (1968).

Board of Education attempted to show that an interim suspension, in fact, constituted expulsion without due process. They sought to prove they were expelled by showing that the subsequent hearing was held so they could show cause why they should be "readmitted." They claimed this shifted the burden of proof from the school to the shoulders of the students. In response to this claim the court said:

> This phase of the plaintiffs' argument resolves itself basically into an unfounded argument of semantics brought about by the use of the word "readmit" by the F. A. C. [Faculty Advisory Committee]. In an administrative proceeding the "demands of due process do not require a hearing, at the initial stage or at any particular point or at more than one point * * * so long as the requisite hearing is held before the final order becomes effective." In this case the requisite hearing was held before the final decision of *indefinite* suspension was made. (Emphasis added.)

In another case a university president in Wisconsin *temporarily* suspended a group of students as a result of their allegedly breaking and entering a fraternity house, firing a gun and beating the occupants. The president summoned the students to his office, where they appeared with a lawyer; they were told of the charges and asked for reasons why they should not be suspended and removed from campus until full disciplinary hearings could be held. The students were temporarily suspended after they generally denied the charges, but did not specifically deny having been the invading group. A federal district court in Wisconsin found that temporary suspension could be justified under such circumstances with no violation of the student's constitutional rights.[107]

The American Association of University Professors' "Joint Statement on Rights and Freedoms of Students" recommends:

> Pending action on the charges, the status of the student should not be altered, or his right to be present on the campus and to attend classes suspended, except for reasons relating to his physical or emotional safety and well-being, or for reasons relating to the safety and well-being of students, faculty, or university property.[108]

Quoting this statement a federal district court in Wisconsin has held that a university can temporarily suspend a student

---

107. Buck v. Carter, 308 F. Supp. 1246 (1970).
108. *A.A.U.P. Bulletin*, No. 53, p. 365 (1967).

after a full hearing while the decision relative to the hearing is still pending, if the university authority has reasonable cause to believe that it will be dangerous to permit the student to remain.[109]

EQUAL PROTECTION

The Supreme Court has interpreted the Fourteenth Amendment to mean:

> No instrumentality of the State, and no person, officer or agent exerting the power of the State shall deny equal protection to any person within the jurisdiction of the State. The clause [equal protection] prohibits "discriminating and partial" legislation * * * in favor of particular persons as against others in like condition.[110]

Equal protection does not prevent the state from enacting legislation which classifies people, but it does prevent unreasonable classification.[111]

The "equal protection clause" of the Fourteenth Amendment has been broadly applied by the courts to guarantee student rights. As pointed out previously, one of the primary thrusts of the Fourteenth Amendment has been its use in bridging the constitutional gap between the guarantees of the Bill of Rights and unconstitutional action by state governments. It is the equal protection provision of this Amendment which has had such significant impact in dismantling racial segregation in the United States. But equal protection has also extended to other relationships between individual rights and government action. Such instances are numerous, but notably include pleas by students against unconstitutional classification according to sex and unreasonable regulation of student appearance.

WOMEN'S RIGHTS

The women's liberation movement has doubtlessly contributed to the increase in legal inquiries regarding the treatment of women as equals.[112] One such question was raised regarding the admission of females to the University of Virginia. The University of Virginia, traditionally a school for men only, developed a three-year plan for admission of females to

---

109. Stricklin v. Regents of the University of Wisconsin, 297 F. Supp. 416 (1969).
110. Minneapolis Railway Co. v. Beckwith, 129 U.S. 26 (1889).
111. Watson v. Maryland, 218 U.S. 173 (1910).
112. Abbott v. Mines, 411 F.2d 353 (6th Cir. 1969).

the University,[113] allowing for the gradual admission of women over a period from 1970 through 1972. After the third year women would be admitted on precisely the same basis as men. Four female students brought suit to compel their admission to the University of Virginia. A three-judge federal district court held that denial of admission to female plaintiffs on the basis of sex violated the equal protection clause of the Fourteenth Amendment. The court, however, denied an injunction to force the University to abandon its three-year plan for admission of females, holding that the plan was reasonable since such a change in a university is "bound to take some time."

The opposite result was reached by a three-judge federal court in South Carolina where boys were seeking admission to a state-supported girls' school, Winthrop College.[114] Four boys sued to enjoin enforcement of the statute limiting enrollment to girls, claiming denial of equal protection under the Fourteenth Amendment. The court held that the classification by sex was not unreasonable nor arbitrary, and in this particular instance was not violative of the equal protection clause.

This court distinguished the Winthrop College case from the University of Virginia case by applying just a tinge of the old "separate but equal" standard to sex. The court said:

> There the women plaintiffs were seeking admission to the University of Virginia and it was conceded that the University occupied a preeminence among the State-supported institutions of Virginia and offered a far wider range of curriculum. No such situation exists here. It is not intimated that Winthrop offers a wider range of subject matter or enjoys a position of outstanding prestige over the other State-supported institutions in this state whose admission policies are coeducational.[115]

STUDENT APPEARANCE

Equal protection has also been called into play as a mechanism to protect the student's right to wear his hair and his beard as he pleases. A federal district court in Alabama held that classification of male students according to hair styles violates the equal protection clause of the Fourteenth Amendment when that classification is not based on health, discipline, moral or social reasons.[116] The court said that the reason-

---

113. Kirstein v. The Rector and Visitors of the University of Virginia, 309 F. Supp. 184 (1970).

114. Williams v. McNair, 316 F. Supp. 134 (1970).

115. *Ibid.*

116. Zachry v. Brown, 299 F. Supp. 1360 (1967).

ableness standard applied to classifications of persons could not be justified merely on the college administrators' "personal dislike" of long hair on men students.

A similar conclusion was reached by a federal court in California where a student was indefinitely suspended for wearing a beard in violation of a college regulation.[117] The school was unable to justify the regulation in terms of discipline, health, morals or physical danger or distraction to others. Results bearing the same rationale for justification of constitutional classification have been reached by other courts in recent years.[118] In most cases it has proven quite difficult, if not impossible, to show that long hair, beards, or sideburns or other forms of student appearance or dress constitutionally constitutes a reasonable classification of students.

Rules of discipline for state university must be contained in properly promulgated regulations

SOGLIN v. KAUFFMAN

United States Court of Appeals, Seventh Circuit, 1969.
418 F.2d 163.

CUMMINGS, Circuit Judge.

This is an appeal from a declaratory judgment that disciplinary proceedings of the University of Wisconsin instituted on the basis of alleged "misconduct" are unconstitutional.

The named plaintiffs are ten students at the Madison campus of the University of Wisconsin and the Madison chapter of the Students for a Democratic Society. They brought this suit on October 16, 1967, for themselves and persons similarly situated. The defendants are various officials of the University of Wisconsin, the State of Wisconsin and the City of Madison allegedly involved in disciplinary actions on the Madison campus. The final complaint alleges the following pertinent facts:

On October 18, 1967, plaintiffs and others were protesting the presence of recruiting representatives of the Dow Chemical Corporation on the Madison campus. On the following day, the defendant Dean of Student Affairs wrote two of the plaintiffs and other "members of their class" that they were "sus-

117. Calbillo v. San Jacinto Junior College, 305 F. Supp. 857 (1969).
118. Reichenberg v. Nelson, 310 F. Supp. 248 (1970).

pended from the University pending a hearing before the Administrative Division of the Committee on Student Conduct and Appeals." The ground for the suspension was stated to be violation of Chapter 11.02 of the Laws and Regulations of the University of Wisconsin * * * and the students were informed that a hearing date would be set at a later time. By letter of October 21, 1967, the chairman of the Administrative Division advised them that the hearing would be held on November 2, and that they would be permitted to attend classes and write examinations in the interim.

On November 1, some of the plaintiffs, as well as other individuals, received "Amended Charges" from the chairman of the Administrative Division. These charges specifically described the offensive conduct ascribed to plaintiffs, including the denial of others' rights to job interviews with the Dow Chemical Corporation by physical obstruction of the doorways and corridors of a university building. This behavior was characterized as "misconduct," as well as violative of Chapters 11.02 and 11.15 of the University Policies on the Use of Facilities and Outside Speakers * * *.

The complaint further alleged that some of the defendants had previously expelled two plaintiffs and another member of their class "by application of the doctrine of 'misconduct'," and were threatening to suspend or expel others for "misconduct." This doctrine was alleged to be so vague and overbroad as to violate the rights of plaintiffs under the First and Fourteenth Amendments. The complaint requested a declaratory judgment that the defendants' misconduct doctrine on its face violated the United States Constitution and prayed for an injunction against further application of that doctrine as the basis for disciplinary proceedings.

For their part, defendants answered that the term "misconduct" "as a standard for disciplinary action by the University" did not violate any of the provisions of the federal Constitution.

The district court, in a scholarly opinion, held that the standard of misconduct alone may not serve as the foundation for the expulsion or suspension of students for any significant time. 295 F.Supp. 978. The court concluded that "misconduct," as so used, violates the Due Process Clause of the Fourteenth Amendment by reason of vagueness or, in the alternative, violates the First Amendment (as applied to the states by the Fourteenth Amendment) by reason of vagueness and overbreadth. Injunctive relief, however, was denied so that the University could have a reasonable time to readjust its regulations.[3] * * *

Turning to the merits, defendants contend that the "misconduct" doctrine does not constitute a "standard" of conduct and that it was not employed as such. They argue that "misconduct" represents the inherent power of the University to discipline students and that this power may be exercised without the necessity of relying on a specific rule of conduct. This rationale would justify the *ad hoc* imposition of discipline without reference to any preexisting standards of conduct so long as the objectionable behavior could be called misconduct at some later date. No one disputes the power of the University to protect itself by means of disciplinary action against disruptive students. Power to punish and the rules defining the exercise of that power are not, however, identical. Power alone does not supply the standards needed to determine its application to types of behavior or specific instances of "misconduct." As Professor Fuller has observed: "The first desideratum of a system for subjecting human conduct to the governance of rules is an obvious one: there must be rules." Fuller, Law and Morality, p. 46 (2d printing, 1965). The proposition that government officers, including school administrators, must act in accord with rules in meting out discipline is so fundamental that its validity tends to be assumed by courts engaged in assessing the propriety of specific regulations. * * * The doctrines of vagueness and overbreadth, already applied in academic contexts, presuppose the existence of rules whose coherence and boundaries may be questioned. * * * These same considerations also dictate that the rules embodying standards of discipline be contained in properly promulgated regulations. University administrators are not immune from these requirements of due process in imposing sanctions. Consequently, in the present case, the disciplinary proceedings must fail to the extent that the defendant officials of the University of Wisconsin did not base those proceedings on the students' disregard of university standards of conduct expressed in reasonably clear and narrow rules.

Having specifically charged the students with the offense of "misconduct" * * *, the University may not now claim that misconduct was not employed as a standard. When tested as

---

3. Plaintiffs have not appealed from the denial of the injunctive relief. At the oral argument we were advised that the University has subsequently redrafted its regulations but defendants do not contend that this case has become moot.

such, however, the term is clearly inadequate in view of constitutional requirements. As the Supreme Court recently remarked concerning the use of the term in a jury instruction:

> "If used in a *statute* which imposed forfeitures, punishments or judgments for costs, such loose and unlimiting terms [as 'misconduct' or 'reprehensible conduct'] would certainly cause the statute to fail to measure up to the requirements of the Due Process Clause." Giaccio v. Pennsylvania, 382 U.S. 399, 404, 86 S.Ct. 518, 522, 15 L.Ed.2d 447.

The use of "misconduct" as a standard in imposing the penalties threatened here must therefore fall for vagueness. The inadequacy of the rule is apparent on its face. It contains no clues which could assist a student, an administrator or a reviewing judge in determining whether conduct not transgressing statutes is susceptible to punishment by the University as "misconduct." Since the misconduct standard is invalid on its face, it was unnecessary for the district court to make any findings with respect to plaintiffs' activities on October 18, 1967. * * * To the extent that Esteban v. Central Missouri State College, 290 F.Supp. 622, 630 (W.D.Mo.1968), affirmed, 415 F.2d 1077 (8th Cir. 1969), refuses to apply standards of vagueness and overbreadth required of universities by the Fourteenth Amendment we decline to follow it.

It is not an adequate answer to contend, as do defendants, that the particular conduct which is the object of university discipline might have violated an applicable state or local law or otherwise merited punishment. The issue here is not the character of the student behavior but the validity of the administrative sanctions. Criminal laws carry their own definitions and penalties and are not enacted to enable a university to suspend or expel the wrongdoer absent a breach of a university's own rule. Nor is "misconduct" necessarily confined to disruptive actions covered by criminal codes. The ability to punish "misconduct" *per se* affords no safeguard against the imposition of disciplinary proceedings overreaching permissible limits and penalizing activities which are free from any taint of impropriety. Hence we feel compelled to strike down the University's reliance on the doctrine of misconduct in order to ensure that "reasonable regulation of speech-connected activities [of students remains confined to] carefully restricted circumstances." Tinker v. Des Moines School District, 393 U.S. 503, 513, 89 S.Ct. 733, 740.

Pursuant to appropriate rule or regulation, the University

has the power to maintain order by suspension or expulsion of disruptive students. Requiring that such sanctions be administered in accord with preexisting rules does not place an unwarranted burden upon university administrations. We do not require university codes of conduct to satisfy the same rigorous standards as criminal statutes. We only hold that expulsion and prolonged suspension may not be imposed on students by a university simply on the basis of allegations of "misconduct" without reference to any preexisting rule which supplies an adequate guide. The possibility of the sweeping application of the standard of "misconduct" to protected activities does not comport with the guarantees of the First and Fourteenth Amendments. The desired end must be more narrowly achieved.

Affirmed.

NOTES

1. An officer of a student organization brought suit against the regents of the University of California asserting that his rights of free speech and association under the First and Fourteenth Amendments to the Federal Constitution were being violated by the university's policy of opening to the public the registration statements filed by student organizations. The California Court of Appeals, First District, Division Two, in ruling against the students held: "(1) that the people of the state have the right to know the identity and responsible officers of organizations that are granted the privilege of becoming campus organizations using the public property and facilities of a state university, (2) that such right is sufficient compelling public interest to warrant minimal indirect infringement of the First Amendment rights of such officers, and (3) that the university regulation, in the instant case, under which only the purpose of the organizations and the names of their officers were made available to the public, was well designed to promote their freedom of expression in a manner consistent with the university's interest in insuring the orderly enjoyment of its facilities." Eisen v. The Regents of the University of California, 269 Cal. App. 2d 696, 75 Cal. Rptr. 45, 37 A.L.R.3d 1300 (1969).

2. Recently, the Civil Rights Act of 1871 (42 U.S.C. § 1983) has been relied upon in federal district courts by plaintiffs seeking damages and equitable relief. This act made it possible for persons to obtain relief in the federal courts for denial of individual constitutional rights by state and local government officials. The Act states:

§ 1983 Civil Action for Deprivation of Rights

Every person who, under color of any statute, ordinance, regulation, custom or usage, of any state or territory subjects, or causes to be subjected, any citizen of the United States or other person within the jurisdiction thereof to the deprivation of any rights, privileges, or immunities secured by the Constitution and laws, shall be liable to the injured in an action at law, suit in equity, or other proper proceeding for redress.

3. *FEDERAL AID TO EDUCATION: CAMPUS-UNREST RIDERS**

Prior to 1968 Congress had adhered to a consistent policy against placing federal controls on the use of federal funds by institutions of higher education. But on May 8, 1968, two weeks after the Columbia University disturbances began, Congress broke with its no-control tradition: An amendment added on the floor of the House of Representatives to the appropriation bill for the National Science Foundation called for the termination of federal aid to individuals involved in campus disturbances. That amendment was the first in a long list of similar provisions to be attached to various federal bills and enacted into law. * * *

I. Control by Termination of Federal Aid

A. *Legislative Approach*

In dealing with campus unrest, Congress has restricted itself to legislation providing for the termination of federal aid to individuals involved in disorders. It is not clear why Congress has chosen to use this particular method. The justification most often given is that the federal government should not use its funds to support individuals engaged in illegal activity * * *.

C. *Types of Provisions*

To date Congress has enacted 10 campus-unrest provisions. Since many of them contain similar language, this Note will treat them in three groups.

1. *The school-administered rider.*

The school-administered rider is the most common type of unrest provision; Congress has attached variations of it to

---

* Robert M. Haddock, "Federal Aid to Education: Campus-Unrest Riders," *Stanford Law Review*, Vol. 22, pp. 1094-1101. Copyright 1970 by the Board of Trustees of the Leland Stanford Junior University. (Some footnotes deleted.)

five different acts.[1] Essentially, the rider requires that an institution of higher education terminate an individual's federal aid if it finds that he falls within either of two categories. The first category includes any individual who has been convicted of a crime that involved "the use of (or assistance to others in the use of) force, disruption, or the seizure of property" when "such crime was of a serious nature and contributed to a substantial disruption of the administration of the institution." The second category applies to individuals who have "willfully refused to obey a lawful regulation or order of such institution" when "such refusal was of a serious nature and contributed to a substantial disruption of the administration of such institution." Before an institution can implement either provision, it must afford "notice and opportunity for hearing" to the individual involved.

The school-administered rider presents two difficult interpretative problems. First, although an educational institution must terminate an individual's aid if it determines that his conduct falls within either category, it is not clear whether an institution has the discretion to make no determination. Second, the rider does not delineate the gravity of conduct that would justify termination of aid. Such key phrases as "force," "seizure of property," "substantial disruption," and "of a serious nature" are undefined, leaving the educational institutions with considerable difficulty in interpreting them.

2. *The self-executing rider.*

Congress has attached a self-executing rider to three different appropriation acts.[2] It provides that no individual can re-

---

[1] Higher Education Amendments of 1968, 20 U.S.C. § 1060 (Supp. IV, 1969) (the rider is part of the HEW Authorization); Independent Offices and Department of Housing and Urban Development 1970 Appropriation Act, 83 Stat. 230 (1969) (the rider is part of the 1970 NSF Appropriation); National Science Foundation 1970 Authorization Act § 7, 83 Stat. 203-04 (1969); National Aeronautics and Space Administration 1970 Authorization Act § 7, 83 Stat. 201-02 (1969); Independent Offices and Department of Housing and Urban Development 1969 Appropriation Act, 82 Stat. 946 (1968) (the rider is part of the 1969 NSF Appropriation).

[2] Department of Defense 1970 Appropriation Act § 641, 83 Stat. 486 (1969); Department of Defense 1969 Appropriation Act § 540, 82 Stat. 1136 (1968); Departments of Labor, and Health, Education, and Welfare 1969 Appropriation Act § 411, 82 Stat. 995 (1968). The exact wording of these riders is as follows: "No part of the funds appropriated under this Act shall be used to provide a loan, guarantee of a loan or a grant to any applicant who has been convicted by any court of general jurisdiction of any crime which involves the use of or the assistance to

ceive funds if he "has been convicted . . . of any crime which involves the use of or the assistance to others in the use of force, trespass, or the seizure of property" at an institution of higher education. The self-executing appearance of this rider is deceiving, for the very nature of its prohibitions demands that either the federal agency or the educational institutions implement it. In view of the explicit reference in the school-administered riders to the institution's enforcement role and the absence of such a reference here, the rider arguably requires agency implementation. The agencies have uniformly rejected this interpretation, however, and have delegated responsibility for administering the riders to the educational institutions.

The self-executing rider permits terminating aid for less disruptive conduct than does its counterpart, Part A, in the school-administered rider. While the self-executing rider requires that the individual be convicted of a crime, it does not stipulate, as does Part A, that the crime "be of a serious nature" and have "contributed to a substantial disruption." Since campus conduct that resulted in court conviction for crimes involving force, seizure of property, or trespass would certainly fulfill the self-executing rider's requirements of "force, trespass, or the seizure of property," the schools are spared the interpretative problem that they face with the school-administered rider—they need not determine what gravity of conduct justifies termination of aid.

3. The independent rider.

The independent rider is the least common of the three types; Congress has attached variations of it to only two acts.[3] The rider states that no individual may receive funds if he "has engaged in conduct . . . which involves the use of (or the assistance to others in the use of) force or the threat of force or the seizure of property" at an institution of higher education. This rider embraces a much less specific notion of prohibited conduct than do the other types of riders. The school-administered and self-executing riders punish the fail-

---

others in the use of force, trespass, or the seizure of property under control of any institution of higher education to prevent officials or students at such an institution from engaging in their duties or pursuing their studies."

[3] Departments of Labor, and Health, Education, and Welfare, and Related Agencies 1970 Appropriation Act § 407, 84 Stat. 48 (1970); Departments of State, Justice, and Commerce, the Judiciary, and Related Agencies 1970 Appropriation Act § 706, 83 Stat. 427 (1969).

ure of an individual to obey a prior decree forbidding certain kinds of conduct; an individual's aid is terminated only if his activity violates the criminal law or a lawful regulation or order of an educational institution. The independent rider, however, withdraws aid without reference to such external guides for determining what constitutes forbidden activity. It contains its own definition of prohibited conduct: that "which involves the use of . . . force or the threat of force or the seizure of property."

By defining conduct in this way, the independent rider may punish activity that is not regarded as serious either by the criminal courts or by campus policy. Undoubtedly some schools do not perceive a "threat of force" as a serious offense and would not prohibit it in a campus regulation. Likewise, the occupation of an unused portion of a building as a gesture in support of a curriculum change might be accepted by some schools as an expression of legitimate student concern, but it might still constitute "seizure of property" within the meaning of the independent rider. In such a case an educational institution would have two standards of campus conduct: one for those receiving federal money and a less burdensome one for everyone else.

The independent rider also suffers from two infirmities found in the other types of riders. First, like the self-executing rider, it does not indicate upon whom the burden of its enforcement falls; second, like the school-administered rider, it does not delimit the severity of the misconduct within its prohibitions against "force or the threat of force or the seizure of property" that would justify termination of aid.

Student editor's dismissal held unreasonable

DICKEY v. ALABAMA STATE BOARD OF EDUCATION

United States District Court, M.D. Alabama, N.D., 1967.
273 F. Supp. 613.

ORDER

JOHNSON, Chief Judge.

Gary Clinton Dickey, a citizen of the United States and a resident of this district, was, for the 1966-67 school year, a student in good standing at Troy State College, a state-operated public institution of higher learning located at Troy,

Alabama, which is controlled and supervised by the Alabama State Board of Education. Dickey had earned as of the end of the school year in June, 1967, 147 quarter hours toward a degree in English, which degree requires 192 quarter hours, according to Troy State standards. He made known his wishes to attend Troy State College for the school year 1967-68, commencing September, 1967, by giving written notice as required by the institution. On July 18, 1967, Dickey received "Official Notice of Admission" from the college, admitting him to the undergraduate division of said college for the fall quarter 1967. On August 11, 1967, Dickey received a certified letter from Troy State College, signed by the Dean of Men, advising him that the Student Affairs Committee at said college had voted not to admit him "at this time." * * *

During the early part of the 1966-67 school year, Gary Clinton Dickey, while a full-time student at Troy State College, was chosen as an editor of the Troy State College student newspaper, The Tropolitan. It appears that Dickey was an outstanding student, as he was also chosen as editor-in-chief of the Troy State College literary magazine; was copy editor of the college's annual student yearbook, and was editor-in-chief of the student handbook. He was also a member of a national honorary journalism fraternity.

In early April 1967, Dr. Frank Rose, President of the University of Alabama, came under attack by certain Alabama state legislators for his refusal to censor the University of Alabama student publication, "Emphasis 67, A World in Revolution." "Emphasis 67," as published for the University of Alabama, served as the program for a series of guest speakers and panel discussions held in March at the University of Alabama. The publication contained brief biographical sketches of the participants, which included Secretary of State Dean Rusk, James Reston of The New York Times, and Professor Robert Scalapino, a leading authority on Asian politics. The theme of the "Emphasis" program was a "World in Revolution." In carrying out this theme, "Emphasis" published excerpts from the speeches of Bettina Aptheker, a Communist who gained notoriety at the University of California, and Stokely Carmichael, President of the Student Nonviolent Coordinating Committee and an incendiary advocate of violent revolution. To give a balanced view of a "World in Revolution," "Emphasis" carried articles by leading anti-revolutionaries such as General Earl G. Wheeler, Chairman of the Joint Chiefs of Staff. After public criticism by certain Alabama legislators, Dr. Rose, in the exercise of his judgment as President of the University of Alabama, took a public stand in support of the right of the University students for academic freedom. Criticism of Dr. Rose for this position by certain state legislators became rather intense. The newspapers widely publicized the controversy to a point that it became a matter of public interest throughout the State of Alabama.

Editor Dickey determined that the Troy State College newspaper, The Tropolitan, should be heard on the matter. He prepared and presented to the faculty adviser an editorial supporting the position taken by Dr. Rose. He was instructed by his faculty adviser not to publish such an editorial. Dickey then took the editorial to the head of the English Department at Troy State College. The head of this department approved the publication of Dickey's proposed editorial. Upon returning to the faculty adviser, Dickey was again informed that the editorial could not be published. Dickey then went directly to the president of the college, Ralph Adams, who also determined that the editorial could not be published. It is without controversy in this case that the basis for the denial of Dickey's right to publish his editorial supporting Dr. Rose was a rule that had been invoked at Troy State College to the effect that there could be no editorials written in the school paper which were critical of the Governor of the State of Alabama or the Alabama Legislature. The rule did not prohibit editorials or articles of a laudatory nature concerning the Governor or the Legislature. The rule has been referred to in this case as the "Adams Rule." The theory of the rule, as this Court understands it, is that Troy State College is a public institution owned by the State of Alabama, that the Governor and the legislators are acting for the owner and control the purse strings, and that for that reason neither the Governor nor the Legislature could be criticized. The faculty adviser furnished substitute material concerning "Raising Dogs in North Carolina" to be published in lieu of Dickey's proposed editorial. Upon being furnished the editorial on the North Carolina dogs, Dickey, as editor of The Tropolitan, determined that it was not suitable, and, acting against the specific instructions of his faculty adviser and the president of the college, arranged to have—with the exception of the title, "A Lament for Dr. Rose"—the space ordinarily occupied by the editorial left blank, with the word "Censored" diagonally across the blank space. In addition to this conduct, Dickey mailed the censored editorial to a Montgomery newspaper. All parties in this case concede that the editorial is well written and in good taste. However, the evidence in this case reflects that solely because it violated the "Adams Rule," Dicky's conduct, in acting contrary to the advice of the faculty adviser and of President Adams, was termed "willful and deliberate insubordination." This insubordination is the sole basis for his expulsion and/or suspension.

It is basic in our law in this country that the privilege to communicate concerning a matter of public interest is embraced in the First Amendment right relating to freedom of speech and is constitutionally protected against infringement by state officials. The Fourteenth Amendment to the Constitution protects these First Amendment rights from state infringements, * * * and these First Amendment rights extend to school children and students insofar as unreasonable rules are concerned. * * * Boards of education, presidents of colleges, and faculty advisers are not excepted from the rule that protects students against unreasonable rules and regulations. This Court recognizes that the establishment of an educational program requires certain rules and regulations necessary for maintaining an orderly program and operating the institution in a manner conducive to learning. However, the school and school officials have always been bound by the requirement that the rules and regulations *must be reasonable*. Courts may only consider whether rules and regulations that are imposed by school authorities are a reasonable exercise of the power and discretion vested in those authorities. Regulations and rules which are necessary in maintaining order and discipline are always considered reasonable. In the case now before this Court, it is clear that the maintenance of order and discipline of the students attending Troy State College had nothing to do with the rule that was invoked against Dickey. As a matter of fact, the president of the institution, President Adams, testified that his general policy of not criticizing the Governor or the State Legislature under any circumstances, regardless of how reasonable or justified the criticism might be, was not for the purpose of maintaining order and discipline among the students. On this point, President Adams testified that the reason for the rule was that a newspaper could not criticize its owners, and in the case of a state institution the owners were to be considered as the Governor and the members of the Legislature.

With these basic constitutional principles in mind, the conclusion is compelled that the invocation of such a rule against

Gary Clinton Dickey that resulted in his expulsion and/or suspension from Troy State College was unreasonable. A state cannot force a college student to forfeit his constitutionally protected right of freedom of expression as a condition to his attending a state-supported institution. State school officials cannot infringe on their students' right of free and unrestricted expression as guaranteed by the Constitution of the United States where the exercise of such right does not "materially and substantially interfere with requirements of appropriate discipline in the operation of the school." Burnside v. Byars, 363 F.2d 744 (5 Cir. 1966). The defendants in this case cannot punish Gary Clinton Dickey for his exercise of this constitutionally guaranteed right by cloaking his expulsion or suspension in the robe of "insubordination." The attempt to characterize Dickey's conduct, and the basis for their action in expelling him, as "insubordination" requiring rather severe disciplinary action, does not disguise the basic fact that Dickey was expelled from Troy State College for exercising his constitutionally guaranteed right of academic and/or political expression.

The argument by defendants' counsel that Dickey was attempting to take over the operation of the school newspaper ignores the fact that there was no legal obligation on the school authorities to permit Dickey to continue as one of its editors. As a matter of fact, there was no legal obligation on the school authorities to operate a school newspaper. However, since this state-supported institution did elect to operate The Tropolitan and did authorize Dickey to be one of its editors, they cannot as officials of the State of Alabama, without violating the First and Fourteenth Amendments to the Constitution of the United States, suspend or expel Dickey from this state-supported institution for his conduct as that conduct is reflected by the facts presented in this case. * * *

Defendants' argument that Dickey's readmission will jeopardize the discipline in the institution is superficial and completely ignores the greater damage to college students that will result from the imposition of intellectual restraints such as the "Adams Rule" in this case. The imposition of such a restraint as here sought to be imposed upon Dickey and the other students at Troy State College violates the basic principles of academic and political expression as guaranteed by our Constitution. Dr. Rose recognized the importance of this academic and constitutional principle when he determined that as to the University of Alabama, such freedoms must be permitted to flourish. * * *

In accordance with the foregoing, it is the order, judgment and decree of this Court that the action taken by Troy State College, acting through its Student Affairs Committee, on Friday, August, 25, 1967, which action denies to Gary Clinton Dickey admission to Troy State College beginning with the fall quarter of 1967, be and the same is hereby declared unconstitutional, void, and is rescinded.

It is further ordered that the defendants immediately reinstate Gary Clinton Dickey as a student in Troy State College, commencing September 11, 1967. * * *

It is further ordered that the costs incurred in this proceeding be and they are hereby taxed against the defendants, for which execution may issue.

Action by university president held to be unconstitutional prior restraint

BROOKS v. AUBURN UNIVERSITY

United States Court of Appeals, Fifth Circuit, 1969.
412 F.2d 1171.

BELL, Circuit Judge:

This appeal involves a decree of the district court restraining the president of Auburn University, Dr. Harry M. Philpott, from barring the scheduled appearance and speech on the Auburn campus of the Reverend William Sloan Coffin. The decree also required the payment to Reverend Coffin of an agreed honorarium and travel expenses. We agree with the result reached by the district court and therefore affirm.

The decree, entered on the complaint of plaintiffs who were students and members of the faculty at Auburn, rested on the premise that Dr. Philpott was denying them their First Amendment right to hear the speaker. The First Amendment, applicable to a state university through the Fourteenth Amendment, embraces the right to hear. * * *

The honorarium and expenses were within the range of the custom and practice in such instances at Auburn. The speaker was requested by a student organization, the Human Rights Forum, and the request was approved by the Public Affairs Seminar Board of the university. Dr. Philpott, in exercise of the final authority which was his as president of the university, ruled that the invitation could not be extended to Reverend Coffin and that his fee and expenses would not be paid.

The record demonstrates that Auburn had no rules or regulations governing speaker eligibility. The practice was for the Public Affairs Seminar Board, as officially chartered student-faculty board, to pass on requests from student groups to invite speakers. Funds were allocated to the Board by the university from student fees for use in obtaining speakers. The Human Affairs Forum wrote the Board under date of November 13, 1968 requesting $650.00 needed for honorarium and expense purposes in bringing Reverend Coffin, Chaplain at Yale University, to Auburn for a speaking engagement on February 7, 1969. The Board, at a formal meeting on November 20, 1968, approved the request. The approval was communicated in writing to the chairman of the Human Affairs Forum by letter dated November 21, 1968.

Dr. Philpott then notified the Public Affairs Seminar Board that the Reverend Coffin would not be allowed to speak on the Auburn University campus because he was a convicted felon and because he might advocate breaking the law. These reasons had not previously been invoked at Auburn to bar a speaker.

The district court was of the view that to invoke them under the circumstances here, where the speaker had been requested by a student organization and approved under normal procedures, was in the nature of a prior restraint and in violation of the First Amendment rights of plaintiffs. * * * This holding is fairly sustained by the law and the evidence.

Attributing the highest good faith to Dr. Philpott in his action, it nevertheless is clear under the prior restraint doctrine that the right of a faculty and students to hear a speaker, selected as was the speaker here, cannot be left to the discretion of the university president on a pick and choose basis. As stated, Auburn had no rules or regulations as to who might or might not speak and thus no question of a compliance with or a departure from such rules or regulations is presented. This left the matter as a pure First Amendment question; hence the basis for prior restraint. Such a situation of no rules or regulations may be equated with a licensing system to speak or hear and this has been long prohibited. * * *

It is strenuously urged on behalf of Auburn that the president was authorized in any event to bar a convicted felon or one advocating lawlessness from the campus.[2] This again depends upon the right of the faculty and students to hear.

2. Reverend Coffin's conviction was on appeal at the time but this fact does not bear on our decision.

We do not hold that Dr. Philpott could not bar a speaker under any circumstances. Here there was no claim that the Reverend Coffin's appearance would lead to violence or disorder or that the university would be otherwise disrupted. There is no claim that Dr. Philpott could not regulate the time or place of the speech or the manner in which it was to be delivered. The most recent statement of the applicable rule by the Supreme Court, perhaps its outer limits, is contained in the case of Brandenburg v. Ohio, decided June 9, 1969, 395 U.S. 444, 89 S.Ct. 1827, 23 L.Ed.2d 430:

> "* * * These later decisions have fashioned the principle that the constitutional guarantees of free speech and free press do not permit a State to forbid or proscribe advocacy of the use of force or of law violation except where such advocacy is directed to inciting or producing imminent lawless action and is likely to incite or produce such action. * * *"

There was no claim that the Coffin speech would fall into the category of this exception. * * *

The responsibilities on courts and university presidents in the area of First Amendment rights is heavy indeed. Judge Godbold, in a special concurring opinion in Ferrell v. Dallas Independent School District, 5 Cir., 1968, 392 F.2d 697, 704, put it well when he said:

> "A school may not stifle dissent because the subject matter is out of favor. Free expression is itself a vital part of the educational process. But in measuring the appropriateness and reasonableness of school regulations against the constitutional protections of the First and Fourteenth Amendments the courts must give full credence to the role and purposes of the schools and of the tools with which it is expected that they deal with their problems, and careful recognition to the differences between what are reasonable restraints in the classroom and what are reasonable restraints on the street corner."

And, as Judge Gewin said in writing for the court in Burnside v. Byars, 5 Cir., 1966, 363 F.2d 744, at 749:

> "* * * [School officials] cannot infringe on their students' right[s] * * * as guaranteed to them under the First Amendment to the Constitution, where the exercise of such rights * * * do not materially and substantially interfere with the requirements of appropriate discipline in the operation of the school."

We find no departure from these teachings in the decree which forms the subject matter of this appeal.

Affirmed.

NOTES

Justice Douglas, in 1949, cautioned against limiting freedom of speech because of audience reaction:

> * * * a function of free speech under our system of government is to invite dispute. It may indeed best serve its high purpose when it induces a condition of unrest, creates dissatisfaction with conditions as they are, or even stirs people to anger. Speech is often provocative and challenging. It may strike at prejudices and preconceptions and have profound unsettling effects as it presses for acceptance of an idea. That is why freedom of speech, though not absolute, is nevertheless protected against censorship of punishment, unless shown likely to produce a clear and present danger of a serious substantive evil that arises far above public inconvenience, annoyance, or unrest.

Terminiello v. Chicago, 337 U.S. 1 (1949).

Disciplinary action against students violated neither procedural nor substantive due process

ESTEBAN v. CENTRAL MISSOURI STATE COLLEGE

United States Court of Appeals, Eighth Circuit, 1969.
415 F.2d 1077.

BLACKMUN, Circuit Judge.

Alfredo Esteban and Steve Craig Roberds, students at Central Missouri State College, a tax-supported institution at Warrensburg, Missouri, were suspended on March 31, 1967, for two semesters but with the right thereafter to apply for readmission. The two, by their next friends, instituted the present action for declaratory and injunctive relief. The named defendants are the College, its President, and its Board of Regents. The plaintiffs allege, primarily, first, fifth, and fourteenth amendment violations. Judge Hunter, with a detailed memorandum, denied them relief and dismissed their complaint. Esteban v. Central Missouri State College, 290 F.Supp. 622 (W.D.Mo.1968). The plaintiffs appeal. * * *

The disciplinary action against the plaintiffs arose out of events which took place on or adjacent to the college campus on the nights of March 29 and 30, 1967. At that time Esteban was on scholastic probation and Roberds was on disciplinary probation. Esteban also had been on disciplinary probation over a knifing incident with a fellow student, but his disciplinary probation had expired a short time before.

Both sides in their appellate briefs specifically adopt findings of fact made by Judge Hunter with respect to these March 1967 events. Accordingly, we set forth certain of those findings here:

"* * * These demonstrations took place at the intersection of the public street adjacent to the school campus and State Highway 13 and overflowed onto the sidewalks and campus. On the evening of March 29, some 350 students were present in the mass and on March 30, there were some 600 students included. As a partial result of these two mass demonstrations there was in excess of $600 damages and destruction of college property, including broken school building windows and destroyed shrubbery; eggs were thrown; the Dean of Men, Dr. Chalquist, was hanged in effigy, his 'dummy' torn up and set on fire; traffic was halted and blocked, cars were rocked, and their occupants ordered out into the street. The college president directed a number of his personnel, including Dr. Meverden, to go to the scene to restore order.

"ESTEBAN EVENT:

"* * * The evening of March 29,[2] 1967, around 11:30 p. m., he left his dormitory about the time the 'disturbance' had subsided. Some of the students were proceeding along the street from the mass demonstration to their dormitories. Esteban proceeded down the sidewalk to within about 100 feet of the intersection of the scene of the mass demonstration and stayed there awhile. Dr. Meverden, a faculty member, who was seeking to disperse students standing outside their dorms, approached Esteban and asked him to go inside the dormitory. Instead of complying, Esteban asked why, and on again being requested to go in, again asked why. He told Dr. Meverden that he was not in violation of any state, county, or federal law and that he had a right to be out there. Dr. Meverden asked for his student identification card which by college regulation he was required to have in his possession at all times. Esteban said ('in rough words' according to one witness) he did not have it. Nor did he give his name. Dr. Meverden again requested him to go in the dormitory and get off the street. Esteban argued with Dr. Meverden and questioned his authority, saying there were no rules limiting the time men could stay outside the dorms. Shortly, and with the encouragement of other students present, he went into the dormi-

2. This is an obvious error. The date is March 30 and was so stated in the charge and by the witnesses at the hearing before the president, hereinafter referred to.

tory. Dr. Meverden also went in and asked Gerald Haddock, the resident assistant of Esteban's dormitory, who Esteban was. Haddock was overheard by Esteban telling Dr. Meverden Esteban's name. Esteban, as Dr. Meverden was leaving, called Haddock a prick and a bastard and told him he 'would not be around very long.' According to Esteban's roommate, Esteban then angrily picked up a waste can and emptied the contents on the floor at the feet of Haddock.

"ROBERDS EVENT:

*   *   *   *   *   *

"Throughout both evenings of the mass demonstrations Roberds was present as a part of the crowd. On March 29, 1967, he arrived at the scene of the demonstration about 10:15 p. m. and returned to his dormitory about 10:45 p. m. On March 30, 1967, he arrived at the scene about 9:30 p. m. and remained until about 10:30 p. m. During the first night, while a part of the gathered crowd, he talked to students who were present in it. Roberds testified that the second evening, also while a part of the crowd at the demonstration, that 'I discussed some of the things that were going on, the rocking of the cars and the dummy. At that time I mentioned my disgust with the college, and we talked, as the people I had talked to had the same feeling.' He saw the dummy brought to the scene of the demonstration; saw it hung, torn up and burned by students in the crowd. He saw the cars approached by the students, saw the cars rocked, saw the attempts to take the occupants out of the cars. He returned to his dormitory after the dispersal of the gathering. He stated he was at the demonstrations each evening simply as a 'spectator', not participating in any of the acts of violence or destruction." [Footnote omitted]

Both sides also adopt Judge Hunter's findings as to Roberds' situation prior to the March events:

"Prior to the mass demonstrations, Roberds had been placed on disciplinary probation and furnished a written statement of the terms of that probation. Dean Chalquist also orally explained those terms to him. He and Dean Chalquist conversed relative to his intention to participate in a demonstration. Roberds asked about the possible repercussions of his involvement in (future) demonstrations or disturbances. He was advised 'that any action on your part which may reflect unfavorably upon either you or the institution can be considered grounds for suspension.' Roberds, under date of February 5, 1967, wrote E. J. Cantrell, a Representative from his county in the Missouri Legislature, the following letter:
    '* * * I assure you, I do not stand alone in my disgust with this institution. From suppression of speech and expression to ridiculous, trivial regula-

tions this college has done more to discourage democratic belief than any of the world's tyrants. * * * My comrades and I plan on turning this school into a Berkeley if something isn't done.' "

[Footnotes omitted]

* * *

The college regulations in effect at the time, and to the extent pertinent, provided:

> "The conduct of the individual student is an important indication of character and future usefulness in life. It is therefore important that each student maintain the highest standards of integrity, honesty and morality. All students are expected to conform to ordinary and accepted social customs and to conduct themselves at all times and in all places in a manner befitting a student of Central Missouri State College.
> "All students that enroll at C.M.S.C. assume an obligation to abide by the rules and regulations of the college as well as all local, state and federal laws.
> "When a breach of regulations involves a mixed group, ALL MEMBERS ARE HELD EQUALLY RESPONSIBLE.
> "Conduct unbefitting a student which reflects adversely upon himself or the institution will result in disciplinary action."
> "Mass Gatherings—Participation in mass gatherings which might be considered as unruly or unlawful will subject a student to possible immediate dismissal from the College. Only a few students intentionally get involved in mob misconduct, but many so-called 'spectators' get drawn into a fracas and by their very presence contribute to the dimensions of the problems. It should be understood that the College considers no student to be immune from due process of law enforcement when he is in violation as an individual or as a member of a crowd."

* * *

a. *Esteban.* This plaintiff, by the adoption of the trial court's findings of fact, now concedes that he left his dormitory as other students were proceeding along the street from the mass demonstration; that he proceeded toward the scene of the demonstration and within 100 feet thereof and "stayed there awhile"; that he was requested by Doctor Meverden, a member of the college staff, to go into his dormitory; that Doctor Meverden was seeking to disperse the students; that he, Esteban, did not comply with these directions but asked more than once why he was being told to go in; that he insisted on his right to be out there; that in response to Meverden's request to produce his identification card he used rough language in his negative reply and refused to give his name; that he questioned Meverden's authority; that only with the encouragement of other students did he go in the dormitory; that Meverden then asked the dormitory resident who Esteban was; and that, when this information was given, Esteban responded with gutter language and with a threat and dumped a waste can's contents at the resident's feet.

Esteban's argument is that conduct not included within the charge is not relevant; that the charge of participation in an unlawful mass gathering was supported only by the specification of resisting Meverden's efforts to disperse and not at all by his refusal to identify himself or by the language he used toward the resident; that the evidence shows that Esteban was not involved in the demonstration or at its scene; that he was studying while it took place; that he was standing a half block away peacefully talking with other students when "accosted" by Meverden; and that there was no college rule which gave Meverden the authority to order him into the dormitory.

We are not at all convinced by this attempted dissection of the aggregate facts. Moments before Esteban's purposeful entrance on the scene an unruly mass gathering had been in control at the intersection. The mob extended to the college premises. Destruction of college property had taken place. Innocent and unsuspecting members of the public had been stopped in their automobiles, had had their cars rocked, and had been ordered out by the mob. It was an explosive situation participated in by college students and affecting college property. Meverden was dispatched there in his capacity as a staff member and at the order of the college president in an attempt to restore order and thus to protect the students from further serious trouble. His assignment, obviously, was not the most enviable one. Just as obviously, the dispersal of the students and their return to the dormitories were effective remedies for a situation which had already erupted and which remained eruptive. Meverden's inquiry of Esteban was made with authority and with reason. He was met with the very attributes of the mob: defiance, challenge to his authority to ask people to move on, a refusal to reveal one's name, the language of a bully, and insults. This, it will be remembered, although perhaps not at that moment known to Meverden, was a student then on scholastic probation and only shortly before on disciplinary probation because of a knifing incident. We fail to see, understand, or comprehend Esteban's argument that there was no substantial evidence of misconduct encompassed within the charge against him. His actions, obviously, were in resistance to Meverden's reasonable efforts to disperse the students and to prevent the recurrence or continuance of mob action. In our view, Esteban by his resistance was a participant in the affair even though he may not have been one of those who actually interfered with the travel rights of others and who destroyed college property.

b. *Roberds.* This plaintiff's case differs factually from Esteban's. But, by the adopted findings, Roberds concedes that he had asked the dean about the result which would flow from his involvement in future demonstrations or disturbances; that he was informed, in response to that inquiry on his part, that any action which would reflect unfavorably upon him or the College, could be considered grounds for suspension; that he was "present as a part of the crowd" on both evenings; that he was so present for a half hour on the first night and for an hour on the second night; that he discussed with others some of the things which were going on and expressed his "disgust with the college"; that he returned to his dormitory only after the gathering was dispersed; and that he wrote the letter to the legislator.

Roberds' argument follows Esteban's to the point where it says that two of the three specifications of a charge failed to support that charge. Roberds then urges that his letter to the legislator is a first amendment petition "for a redress of grievances"; that it does not at all support a finding of intent to participate in any unruly demonstration; that, anyway, intent alone is not participation; that he did not tell the dean he intended to participate; that he was not a ringleader and did not participate; that, instead, he was a mere spectator, standing and sitting "on the sidewalk, watching the events"; that observing is not participating; and that observation is not enough.

We observe in this connection that we do not read Roberds' letter to his legislator as a mere petition for redress of grievances which he would have every right to compose and present. The letter specifies no grievance which we can ascertain. It speaks only of disgust and, as we have noted, it contains a flat threat. His right to write is not an issue. His intent and his participation are in issue.

Mere presence, under certain circumstances, has been held insufficiently representative of criminal involvement. * * * Assuming, without deciding, that such criminal cases would afford precedent for a civil situation of the kind which confronts us, we note that the test as to the propriety of the inference to be drawn from presence is that of rational connection between the facts proved and the ultimate fact presumed. * * * That rational connection, we hold, is definitely present here.

Here, again, we are not persuaded as to Roberds' peaceful spectator status or that the court's findings as to him have no substantial support in the record. Roberds was present at, and as a part of, the milling mass on both nights. He was there as "a part of the gathered crowd." He, too, may not have stopped any automobile or rocked it or forced out its occupants or damaged property, but these incidents took place and were caused by the mob and he was a part of that mob. Mob action or, for that matter, the old style lynching action, always presents to the self-proclaimed "spectator" the opportunity to claim that he was merely watching, that he did not participate, and that someone else did the job. But one may participate by being present and "talking it up" as Roberds concededly did. And when this is buttressed by the intent evidenced from his letter's expressions of disgust and tyranny and his "plan on turning this school into a Berkeley if * * *", we have, in our view, substantial and certainly adequate support for the inferences the trial court drew and for its findings.

2. *The First Amendment rights.* Having resolved the issue as to the sufficiency of the evidence against the plaintiffs, we then encounter the constitutional argument. Were their rights of free speech and of free assembly and to petition denied to them?

Obviously, one does not lose his first amendment rights by matriculation at a college. Those rights follow one through the classroom door and, as we have had occasion recently to observe, even, to a great extent, through a penitentiary's doors. * * * And what better or more ideal place is there for free discussion and for the exchange of ideas than academic halls? * * *

Long settled, too, is the principle that the first amendment freedoms of speech and of association are applicable to the states, either by the due process route of the fourteenth amendment or directly under the first amendment. * * *

On this issue, however, we need look no further than a recent decision of the Supreme Court concerning the application of first amendment rights in the academic environment. In Tinker v. Des Moines Ind. School Dist., 393 U.S. 503, 89 S.Ct. 733, 21 L.Ed.2d 731 (1969), a case from this circuit, the Court first observed, * * *

> "In order for the State in the person of school officials to justify prohibition of a particular expression of opinion, it must be able to show that its action was caused by something more than a mere desire to avoid the discomfort and unpleasantness that always accompany an unpopular viewpoint. Certainly where there is no finding and no showing that engaging in the forbidden conduct would 'materially and substantially interfere with the requirements of appropriate discipline in the operation of the school,' the prohibition cannot be sustained. * * *"

That emphasis is on the absence of "actually or potentially disruptive conduct" by the participants; on the need of school officials, consistent with constitutional safeguards, "to prescribe and control conduct in the schools"; on "a silent, passive expression" unaccompanied by any disorder or disturbance; on the absence of evidence of interference with the school's work or with "the rights of other students to be secure and to be let alone"; on the absence of threats or acts of violence on school premises; on the absence of a finding of material interference "with the requirements of appropriate discipline in the operation of the school"; and on the absence of material disruption of classwork or "substantial disorder or invasion of the rights of others." It is obvious that where there is actual or potentially disruptive conduct, or disorder or disturbance by the petitioners, or interference with the work of the school or of the rights of other students, or threats or acts of violence on the school premises, or substantial disorder, then reasonable action by school authorities is constitutionally permitted. There must, however, be more than mere fear and apprehension of possible disturbance. * * *

So it is here. Judge Hunter's findings have been quoted above. We have found them sufficiently supported by the record. They, too, concern an aggressive and violent demonstration and something quite apart from "peaceful, nondisruptive expression." They, too, focus upon "destructive interference with the right of others." They disclose actual or potentially disruptive conduct, aggressive action, disorder and disturbance, and acts of violence and participation therein by these plaintiffs. Their conduct, therefore, was not protected by the first and fourteenth amendments.

3. *The regulations.* These are additionally attacked for vagueness and overbreadth and hence on substantive due process grounds. Some of the loyalty oath cases are cited and it is said that the regulations' word "unlawful" is only a legal conclusion and that their references to "unruly" and "spectators" and "which might be considered" are undefined and possess no standards. The regulations are likened to city ordinances which have been struck down when they lack sufficiency of definition. It is then argued that "young people should be told clearly what is right and what is wrong, as well as the consequences of their acts." * * * Finally, it is said that the regulations impinge and have a chilling effect upon first and fourteenth amendment rights.

The answers to all this, we think, are several. First, the college's regulations, per se, do not appear to us to constitute the fulcrum of the plaintiffs' discomfiture. The charges against Esteban and Roberds did not even refer to the regulations. Roberds was disciplined because he had participated in the demonstrations in the face of specific warning delivered by personal interview with the dean. This was defiance of proper college authority. Esteban was disciplined because of his refusal to comply with an appropriate request by Doctor Meverden and because of his childish behavior and obscenity toward college officials. This, too, was defiance of proper college authority. There was no confusion or unawareness in either case. The exercise of common sense was all that was required. Each plaintiff knew the situation very well, knew what he was doing, and knew the consequences. Each, we might note, had had prior disciplinary experience. Their respective protestations of young and injured innocence have a hollow ring.

Secondly, we agree with Judge Hunter that it is not sound to draw an analogy between student discipline and criminal procedure, that the standard of conduct which a college seeks to impose must be one relevant to "a lawful mission, process or function of the educational institution", and that,

> "* * * Certainly the regulation concerning mass demonstrations, reasonably interpreted, and as interpreted and applied by the college in the instant case to a participant in student mass demonstrations involving unlawful conduct such as the illegal blocking of a public highway and street, and the destruction of school property, is relevant to a lawful mission of the educational institution." 290 F.Supp. at 629. [Footnote omitted]

Thirdly, we do not find the regulation at all difficult to

understand and we are positive the college student, who is appropriately expected to possess some minimum intelligence, would not find it difficult. It asks for the adherence to standards of conduct which befit a student and it warns of the danger of mass involvement. We must assume Esteban and Roberds can read and that they possess some power of comprehension. Their difficulty was that they chose not to read or not to comprehend.

Fourthly, we see little basically or constitutionally wrong with flexibility and reasonable breadth, rather than meticulous specificity, in college regulations relating to conduct. Certainly these regulations are not to be compared with the criminal statute. They are codes of general conduct which those qualified and experienced in the field have characterized not as punishment but as part of the educational process itself and as preferably to be expressed in general rather than in specific terms. * * *

We agree with those courts which have held that a school has inherent authority to maintain order and to discipline students. * * * We further agree that a school has latitude and discretion in its formulation of rules and regulations and of general standards of conduct. * * *

* * * Our attention has been called to the fact that Judge Doyle, in his recent opinion in Soglin v. Kauffman, 295 F.Supp. 978, 990-991 (W.D.Wis.1968), expresses disagreement with the observations of Judge Hunter on this aspect of the case. To the extent that, in this area, Judge Doyle is in disagreement with Judge Hunter, we must respectfully disagree with Judge Doyle.

The appellants argue, to what exact purpose we are not sure, that attendance by a Missouri resident at a publicly supported educational institution of his state is an important right. We are not certain that it is significant whether attendance at such a college, or staying there once one has matriculated, is a right rather than a privilege. Education, of course, is vital and valuable, Brown v. Board of Educ., 347 U.S. 483, 493, 74 S.Ct. 686, 98 L.Ed. 873 (1954), and remaining in college in good standing, much like reputation, is also something of value. Dixon v. Alabama State Bd. of Educ., 294 F.2d 150, 157 (5 Cir.1961), cert. denied, 368 U.S. 930, 82 S.Ct. 368, 7 L.Ed.2d 193. So, too, is one's personal freedom. But one may act so as constitutionally to lose that freedom. And one may act so as constitutionally to lose his right or privilege to attend a college.

College attendance, whether it be a right or a privilege, very definitely entails responsibility. This is fundamental. It rests upon the fact that the student is approaching maturity. His elementary and secondary education is behind him. He already knows, or should know, the basics of decent conduct, of nonviolence, and of respect for the rights of others. He already knows, or should know, that destruction of property, threats to others, frightening passersby, and intrusions upon their rights of travel are unacceptable, if not illegal, and are not worthy of one who would pursue knowledge at the college level.

These plaintiffs are no longer children. While they may have been minors, they were beyond the age of 18. Their days of accomplishing ends and status by force are at an end. It was time they assumed at least the outward appearance of adulthood and of manhood. The mass denial of rights of others is irresponsible and childish. So is the defiance of proper college administrative authority ("I have the right to be here"; "I refuse to identify myself"; gutter abuse of an official; the dumping of a trash can at a resident's feet; "I plan on turning this school into a Berkeley if * * *"; and being a part of the proscribed college peace-disturbing and property-destroying demonstration). One might expect this from the spoiled child of tender years. One rightly does not expect it from the college student who has had two decades of life and who, in theory, is close to being "grown up."

Let there be no misunderstanding as to our precise holding. We do not hold that any college regulation, however loosely framed, is necessarily valid. We do not hold that a school has the authority to require a student to discard any constitutional right when he matriculates. We do hold that a college has the inherent power to promulgate rules and regulations; that it has the inherent power properly to discipline; that it has power appropriately to protect itself and its property; that it may expect that its students adhere to generally accepted standards of conduct; that, as to these, flexibility and elbow room are to be preferred over specificity; that procedural due process must be afforded (as Judge Hunter by his first opinion here specifically required) by way of adequate notice, definite charge, and a hearing with opportunity to present one's own side of the case and with all necessary protective measures; that school regulations are not to be measured by the standards which prevail for the criminal law and for criminal procedure; and that the courts should interfere only where there is a clear case of constitutional infringement.

After all, the test, we feel, is that of reasonableness. Dickey v. Alabama State Bd. of Educ., supra, 273 F.Supp. at 618. On that standard we perceive here no denial of constitutional rights of Esteban or of Roberds. If these two plaintiffs are really serious in what is said to be their protestations of desire to complete their college education, we naturally assume that they will apply for readmission. We are mildly surprised that they have not done this as yet. We also assume, of course, that the College will view their applications, if and when they are ever submitted, with the respect and deferences to which they are entitled.

Affirmed.

NOTES

1. *Standards for Procedural Due Process.* A joint committee comprised of representatives from the American Association of University Professors, U. S. National Student Association, Association of American Colleges, National Association of Student Personnel Administrators, and National Association of Women Deans and Counselors have drafted a Joint Statement on Rights and Freedoms of Students. This statement prescribes the following standards for providing students with procedural due process.

PROCEDURAL STANDARDS IN DISCIPLINARY PROCEEDINGS

* * *

The administration of discipline should guarantee procedural fairness to an accused student. Practices in disciplinary cases may vary in formality with the gravity of the offense and the sanctions which may be applied. They should also take into account the presence or absence of an honor code, and the degree to which the institutional officials have direct acquaintance with student life in general and with the involved student and the circumstances of the case in particular. The jurisdictions of faculty or student judicial bodies, the disciplinary responsibilities of institutional officials and the regular disciplinary procedures, including the student's right to appeal a decision, should be clearly formulated and communicated in advance. Minor penalties may be assessed informally under prescribed procedures.

In all situations, procedural fair play requires that the student be informed of the nature of the charges against him, that he be given a fair opportunity to refute them, that the institution not be arbitrary in its actions, and that there be provision for appeal of a decision. The following are recommended as proper safeguards in such proceedings when there are no honor codes offering comparable guarantees.

A. *Standards of Conduct Expected of Students*

The institution has an obligation to clarify those standards of behavior which it considers essential to its educational mission and its community life. These general behavioral expectations and the resultant specific regulations should represent a reasonable regulation of student conduct, but the student should be as free as possible from imposed limitations that have no direct relevance to his education. Offenses should be as clearly defined as possible and interpreted in a manner consistent with the aforementioned principles of relevancy and reasonableness. Disciplinary proceedings should be instituted only for violations of standards of conduct formulated with significant student participation and published in advance through such means as a student handbook or a generally available body of institutional regulations.

B. *Investigation of Student Conduct*

1. Except under extreme emergency circumstances, premises occupied by students and the personal possessions of students should not be searched unless appropriate authorization has been obtained. For premises such as residence halls controlled by the institution, an appropriate and responsible authority should be designated to whom application should be made before a search is conducted. The application should specify the reasons for the search and the objects or information sought. The student should be present, if possible, during the search. For premises not controlled by the institution, the ordinary requirements for lawful search should be followed.

2. Students detected or arrested in the course of serious violations of institutional regulations, or infractions of ordinary law, should be informed of their rights. No form of harassment should be used by institutional representatives to coerce admissions of guilt or information about conduct of other suspected persons.

C. *Status of Student Pending Final Action*

Pending action on the charges, the status of a student should not be altered, or his right to be present on the campus and to attend classes suspended, except for reasons relating to his physical or emotional safety and well-being, or for reasons relating to the safety and well-being of students, faculty, or university property.

D. *Hearing Committee Procedures*

When the misconduct may result in serious penalties and if the student questions the fairness of disciplinary action taken against him, he should be granted, on request, the privilege of a hearing before a regularly constituted hearing committee. The following suggested hearing committee procedures satisfy the requirements of procedural due process in situations requiring a high degree of formality.

1. The hearing committee should include faculty members or students, or, if regularly included or requested by the accused, both faculty and student members. No member of the hearing committee who is otherwise interested in the particular case should sit in judgment during the proceeding.

2. The student should be informed, in writing, of the reasons for the proposed disciplinary action with sufficient particularity, and in sufficient time, to insure opportunity to prepare for the hearing.

3. The student appearing before the hearing committee should have the right to be assisted in his defense by an adviser of his choice.

4. The burden of proof should rest upon the officials bringing the charge.

5. The student should be given an opportunity to testify and to present evidence and witnesses. He should have an opportunity to hear and question adverse witnesses. In no case should the committee consider statements against him unless he has been advised of their content and of the names of those who made them, and unless he has been given an opportunity to rebut unfavorable inferences which might otherwise be drawn.

6. All matters upon which the decision may be based must be introduced into evidence at the proceeding before the hearing committee. The decision should be based solely upon such matters. Improperly acquired evidence should not be admitted.

7. In the absence of a transcript, there should be both a digest and a verbatim record, such as a tape recording, of the hearing.

8. The decision of the hearing committee should be final, subject only to the student's right of appeal to the president or ultimately to the governing board of the institution.

2. *Judicial Standards for Student Discipline.* One court's view of the legal relationship between the student and the university. The following significant statement regarding the courts, universities and students was made by the United States District Court for the Western District of Missouri sitting en banc (45 F.R.D. 133). The statement was entitled: *General Order on Judicial Standards of Procedure and Substance in Review of Student Discipline in Tax Supported Institutions of Higher Education.*

The hearings leading to this order were prompted by the filing of three major cases before this court which were decided as follows: Esteban v. Central Missouri State College, 277 F. Supp. 649 (1967), claim of procedural due process violation sustained; Scoggin v. Lincoln University, 291 F. Supp. 161 (1968), claim of procedural due process violation sustained; and Esteban v. Central Missouri State College, 290 F. Supp. 622 (1968), claimed violation of substantive due process held with merit.

RELATIONS OF COURTS AND EDUCATION

Achieving the ideal of justice is the highest goal of humanity. Justice is not the concern solely of the courts. Education is equally concerned with the achievement of ideal justice. The administration of justice by the courts in the United States represents the people's best efforts to achieve the ideal of justice in the field of civil and criminal law. It is generally accepted that the courts are necessary to this administration of justice and for the protection of individual liberties. Nevertheless, the contributions of the modern courts in achieving the ideals of justice are primarily the products of higher education. The modern courts are, and will continue to be, greatly indebted to higher education for their personnel, their innovations, their processes, their political support, and their future in the political and social order. Higher education is the primary source of study and support of improvement in the courts. For this reason, among others, the courts should exercise caution when importuned to intervene in the important processes and functions of education. A court should never intervene in the processes of education without understanding the nature of education.

Before undertaking to intervene in the educational processes, and to impose judicial restraints and mandates on the educational community, the courts should acquire a general knowledge of the lawful missions and the continually changing processes, functions, and problems of education. Judicial action without such knowledge would endanger the public interest and be likely to lead to gross injustice.

Education is the living and growing source of our progressive civilization, of our open repository of increasing knowledge, culture and our salutary democratic traditions. As such, education deserves the highest respect and the fullest protection of the courts in the performance of its lawful missions.

There have been, and no doubt in the future there will be, instances of erroneous and unwise misuse of power by those invested with powers of management and teaching in the academic community, as in the case of all human fallible institutions. When such misuse of power is threatened or occurs, our political and social order has made available a wide variety of lawful, non-violent, political, economic, and social means to prevent or end the misuse of power. These same lawful, non-violent, political, economic and social means are available to correct an unwise but lawful choice of educational policy or action by those charged with the powers of management and teaching in the academic community. Only where erroneous and unwise actions in the field of education deprive students of federally protected rights or privileges does a federal court have power to intervene in the educational process.

LAWFUL MISSIONS OF TAX SUPPORTED HIGHER EDUCATION

The lawful missions of tax supported public education in the United States are constantly growing and changing. For the purposes of this analysis, it is sufficient to note some of the widely recognized traditional missions of tax supported higher education in this country. Included in these lawful missions of education are the following:

(1) To maintain, support, critically examine, and to improve the existing social and political system;

(2) To train students and faculty for leadership and superior service in public service, science, agriculture, commerce and industry;

(3) To develop students to well rounded maturity, physically, socially, emotionally, spiritually, intellectually and vocationally;

(4) To develop, refine and teach ethical and cultural values;
(5) To provide fullest possible realization of democracy in every phase of living;
(6) To teach principles of patriotism, civil obligation and respect for the law;
(7) To teach the practice of excellence in thought, behavior and performance;
(8) To develop, cultivate, and stimulate the use of imagination;
(9) To stimulate reasoning and critical faculties of students and to encourage their use in improvement of the existing political and social order;
(10) To develop and teach lawful methods of change and improvement in the existing political and social order;
(11) To provide by study and research for increase of knowledge;
(12) To provide by study and research for development and improvement of technology, production and distribution for increased national production of goods and services desirable for national civilian consumption, for export, for exploration, and for national military purposes;
(13) To teach methods of experiment in meeting the problems of a changing environment;
(14) To promote directly and explicitly international understanding and cooperation;
(15) To provide the knowledge, personnel, and policy for planning and managing the destiny of our society with a maximum of individual freedom; and
(16) To transfer the wealth of knowledge and tradition from one generation to another.

The tax supported educational institution is an agency of the national and state governments. Its missions include, by teaching, research and action, assisting in the declared purposes of government in this nation, namely:

To form a more perfect union,
To establish justice,
To insure domestic tranquility,
To provide for the common defense,
To promote the general welfare, and
To secure the blessing of liberty to ourselves and to posterity.

The nihilist and the anarchist, determined to destroy the

existing political and social order, who direct their primary attacks on the educational institutions, understand fully the missions of education in the United States.

Federal law recognizes the powers of the tax supported institutions to accomplish these missions and has frequently furnished economic assistance for these purposes.

The genius of American education, employing the manifold ideas and works of the great Jefferson, Mann, Dewey and many other living authorities, has made the United States the most powerful nation in history. In so doing, it has in a relatively few years expanded the area of knowledge at a revolutionary rate.

With education the primary force, the means to provide the necessities of life and many luxuries to all our national population, and to many other peoples, has been created. This great progress has been accomplished by the provision to the educational community of general support, accompanied by diminishing interference in educational processes by political agencies outside the academic community.

If it is true, as it well may be, that man is in a race between education and catastrophe, it is imperative that educational institutions not be limited in the performance of their lawful missions by unwarranted judicial interference.

OBLIGATIONS OF A STUDENT

Attendance at a tax supported educational institution of higher learning is not compulsory. The federal constitution protects the equality of opportunity of all qualified persons to attend. Whether this protected opportunity be called a qualified "right" or "privilege" is unimportant. It is optional and voluntary.

The voluntary attendance of a student in such institutions is a voluntary entrance into the academic community. By such voluntary entrance, the student voluntarily assumes obligations of performance and behavior reasonably imposed by the institution of choice relevant to its lawful missions, processes, and functions. These obligations are generally much higher than those imposed on all citizens by the civil and criminal law. So long as there is no invidious discrimination, no deprival of due process, no abridgement of a right protected in the circumstances, and no capricious, clearly unreasonable or unlawful action employed, the institution may discipline students to secure compliance with these higher obligations as a teaching method or to sever the student from the academic community.

No student may, without liability to lawful discipline, intentionally act to impair or prevent the accomplishment of any lawful mission, process, or function of an educational institution.

The Nature of Student Discipline
Compared to Criminal Law

The discipline of students in the educational community is, in all but the case of irrevocable expulsion, a part of the teaching process. In the case of irrevocable expulsion for misconduct, the process is not punitive or deterrent in the criminal law sense, but the process is rather the determination that the student is unqualified to continue as a member of the educational community. Even then, the disciplinary process is not equivalent to the criminal law processes of federal and state criminal law. For, while the expelled student may suffer damaging effects, sometimes irreparable, to his educational, social and economic future, he or she may not be imprisoned, fined, disenfranchised, or subjected to probationary supervision. The attempted analogy of student discipline to criminal proceedings against adults and juveniles is not sound.

In the lesser disciplinary procedures, including but not limited to guidance counseling, reprimand, suspension of social or academic privileges, probation, restriction to campus and dismissal with leave to apply for readmission, the lawful aim of discipline may be teaching in performance of a lawful mission of the institution. The nature and procedures of the disciplinary process in such cases should not be required to conform to federal processes of criminal law, which are far from perfect, and designed for circumstances and ends unrelated to the academic community. By judicial mandate to impose upon the academic community in student discipline the intricate, time consuming, sophisticated procedures, rules and safeguards of criminal law would frustrate the teaching process and render the institutional control impotent.

Student Discipline

A federal court should not intervene to reverse or enjoin disciplinary actions relevant to a lawful mission of an educational institution unless there appears one of the following:

    (1) a deprival of due process, that is, of fundamental concepts of fair play;

(2) invidious discrimination, for example, on account of race or religion;

(3) denial of federal rights, constitutional or statutory, protected in the academic community; or

(4) clearly unreasonable, arbitrary or capricious action.

PROVISIONAL PROCEDURAL AND JURIS- DICTIONAL STANDARDS

In the absence of exceptional circumstances these standards are applicable.

Jurisdiction

1. Under Sections 1343(3), Title 28, and 1983, Title 42, U.S.C., and also in appropriate cases under Sections 2201, 1331(a) or 1332(a), Title 28, U.S.C., the United States District Courts have jurisdiction to entertain and determine actions by students who claim unreasonably discriminatory, arbitrary or capricious actions lacking in due process and depriving a student of admission to or continued attendance at tax supported institutions of higher education.

Nature of Action

2. The action may be

(a) Under Section 1983, an action at law for damages triable by a jury;

(b) Under Section 1983, a suit in equity; or

(c) Under Section 1983 and Section 2201, a declaratory judgment action, which may be legal or equitable in nature depending on the issues therein.

Question of Exhaustion of Remedies

3. In an action at law or equity under Section 1983, Title 42, U.S.C., the doctrine of exhaustion of state judicial remedies is not applicable. The fact that there is an existing state judicial remedy for the alleged wrong is no ground for stay or dismissal.

Ordinarily until the currently available, adequate and effective institutional processes have been exhausted, the disciplinary action is not final and the controversy is not ripe for determination.

Right to Jury Trial

4. In an action at law under Section 1983, the issues are triable by jury and equitable defenses are not available.

Trial of Equitable Actions

5. In an equitable action by a court without a jury under Section 1983, equitable doctrines and defenses are applicable.
   (a) There must be an inadequate remedy at law.
   (b) The plaintiff must be in a position to secure equitable relief under equitable doctrines, for example, must come with "clean hands."

Question of Mootness

6. In an action at law or equity under Section 1983, Title 42, U.S.C., to review severe student disciplinary action, the doctrine of mootness is not applicable when the action is timely filed.

Provisional Substantive Standards in Student Discipline Cases Under Section 1983, Title 42

1. Equal opportunity for admission and attendance by qualified persons at tax supported state educational institutions of higher learning is protected by the equal privileges and immunities, equal protection of laws, and due process clauses of the Fourteenth Amendment to the United States Constitution. It is unimportant whether this protected opportunity is defined as a right or a privilege. The protection of the opportunity is the important thing.

2. In an action under Section 1983, issues to be determined will be limited to determination whether, under color of any statute, ordinance, regulation, custom or usage of a state ("state action"), a student has been deprived of any rights, privileges, or immunities secured by the Constitution and laws of the United States.

3. State constitutional, statutory, and institutional delegation and distribution of disciplinary powers are not ordinarily matters of federal concern. Any such contentions based solely on claims of unlawful distribution and violation of state law in the exercise of state disciplinary powers should be submitted to the state courts. Such contentions do not ordinarily involve a substantial federal question of which the district court has jurisdiction under Section 1983. This rule does not apply, however, to actions based on diversity jurisdiction under Sections 1331, 1332 or 2201, Title 28, U.S.C.

4. Disciplinary action by any institution, institutional agency, or officer will ordinarily be deemed under color of a statute,

ordinance, regulation, custom or usage of a state ("state action") within the meaning of Section 1983, Title 42, U.S.C.

5. In the field of discipline, scholastic and behavioral, an institution may establish any standards reasonably relevant to the lawful missions, processes, and functions of the institution. It is not a lawful mission, process, or function of an institution to prohibit the exercise of a right guaranteed by the Constitution or a law of the United States to a member of the academic community in the circumstances. Therefore, such prohibitions are not reasonably relevant to any lawful mission, process or function of an institution.

6. Standards so established may apply to student behavior on and off the campus when relevant to any lawful mission, process, or function of the institution. By such standards of student conduct the institution may prohibit any action or omission which impairs, interferes with, or obstructs the missions, processes and functions of the institution.

Standards so established may require scholastic attainments higher than the average of the population and may require superior ethical and moral behavior. In establishing standards of behavior, the institution is not limited to the standards or the forms of criminal laws.

7. An institution may establish appropriate standards of conduct (scholastic and behavioral) in any form and manner reasonably calculated to give adequate notice of the scholastic attainments and behavior expected of the student.

The notice of the scholastic and behavioral standards to the students may be written or oral, or partly written and partly oral, but preferably written. The standards may be positive or negative in form.

Different standards, scholastic and behavioral, may be established for different divisions, schools, colleges, and classes of an institution if the differences are reasonably relevant to the missions, processes, and functions of the particular divisions, schools, colleges, and classes concerned.

8. When a challenged standard of student conduct limits or forbids the exercise of a right guaranteed by the Constitution or a law of the United States to persons generally, the institution must demonstrate that the standard is recognized as relevant to a lawful mission of the institution, and is recognized as reasonable by some reputable authority or school of thought in the field of higher education.

This may be determined by expert opinion or by judicial
notice in proper circumstances. It is not necessary that all
authorities and schools of thought agree that the standard
is reasonable.

9. Outstanding educational authorities in the field of higher
   education believe, on the basis of experience, that detailed
   codes of prohibited student conduct are provocative and
   should not be employed in higher education.

   For this reason, general affirmative statements of what is
   expected of a student may in some areas be preferable in
   higher education. Such affirmative standards may be employed, and discipline of students based thereon.

10. The legal doctrine that a prohibitory statute is void if it
    is overly broad or unconstitutionally vague does not, in
    the absence of exceptional circumstances, apply to stan-
    dards of student conduct. The validity of the form of
    standards of student conduct, relevant to the lawful mis-
    sions of higher education, ordinarily should be determined
    by recognized educational standards.

11. In severe cases of student discipline for alleged miscon-
    duct, such as final expulsion, indefinite or long-term
    suspension, dismissal with deferred leave to reapply, the
    institution is obligated to give to the student minimal pro-
    cedural requirements of due process of law. The require-
    ments of due process do not demand an inflexible pro-
    cedure for all such cases. "But 'due process' unlike some
    legal rules, is not a technical conception with a fixed
    content unrelated to time, place and circumstances."
    Three minimal requirements apply in cases of severe dis-
    cipline, growing out of fundamental conceptions of fair-
    ness implicit in procedural due process. First, the student
    should be given adequate notice in writing of the specific
    ground or grounds and the nature of the evidence on
    which the disciplinary proceedings are based. Second, the
    student should be given an opportunity for a hearing in
    which the disciplinary authority provides a fair oppor-
    tunity for hearing of the student's position, explanations
    and evidence. The third requirement is that no disciplinary
    action be taken on grounds which are not supported by
    any substantial evidence. Within limits of due process, in-
    stitutions must be free to devise various types of disci-
    plinary procedures relevant to their lawful missions, con-
    sistent with their varying processes and functions, and
    which do not impose unreasonable strain on their re-
    sources and personnel.

There is no general requirement that procedural due process in student disciplinary cases provide for legal representation, a public hearing, confrontation and cross-examination of witnesses, warnings about privileges, self-incrimination, application of principles of former or double jeopardy, compulsory production of witnesses, or any of the remaining features of federal criminal jurisprudence. Rare and exceptional circumstances, however, may require provision of one or more of these features in a particular case to guarantee the fundamental concepts of fair play.

It is encouraging to note the current unusual efforts of the institutions and the interested organizations which are devising and recommending procedures and policies in student discipline which are based on standards, in many respects far higher than the requirements of due process. See for example the Joint Statement on Rights and Freedoms of Students, 54 A.A.U.P. Bulletin No. 2, Summer 1968, 258, a report of a joint committee of representatives of the U.S. National Students Association, Association of American Colleges, American Association of University Professors, National Association of Student Personnel Administrators, National Association of Women's Deans and Counselors, American Association of Higher Education, Jesuit Education Association, American College Personnel Association, Executive Committee, College and University Department, National Catholic Education Association, Commission on Student Personnel, American Association of Junior Colleges; and the University of Missouri, Provisional Rules of Procedure in Student Disciplinary Matters.

Many of these recommendations and procedures represent wise provisions of policy and procedure far above the minimum requirements of federal law, calculated to ensure the confidence of all concerned with student discipline.

The excellent briefs and arguments, including those of amici curiae, have been of great assistance in the preparation of this memorandum.

**Students who failed to receive notice of hearing because of
their own failure to keep university advised were
not deprived of constitutional rights**

WRIGHT v. TEXAS SOUTHERN UNIVERSITY

United States Court of Appeals, Fifth Circuit, 1968.
392 F.2d 728.

COLEMAN, Circuit Judge:

In Dixon v. Alabama, 5 Cir., 1961, 294 F.2d 150, this Court
held that in matters of disciplinary action a student attending
a tax supported institution of higher learning is entitled to notice that he is charged with misconduct, including a statement of the charges alleged in justification of anticipated action against him. Moreover, the student must be given the
names of the witnesses against him and must be informed of
the nature of their proposed testimony. Lastly, he should be
given *the opportunity* to present his defense, orally or in writing, after which the findings of the disciplinary body should
be presented in a report available for his inspection.

This does not mean that the student is entitled to the formality of a trial, in the usual sense of that term, but simply
requires that he must be given a fair and reasonable opportunity to make his defense to the charges and to receive such
a hearing as meets the requirements of justice, both to the
school and to himself. In short, the student at the tax supported institution cannot be arbitrarily disciplined without
the benefit of the ordinary, well recognized principles of fair
play.

It is equally well settled, we think, that by seeking admission to and obtaining the benefits of attending a college or
university the student agrees that he will abide by and obey
the rules and regulations promulgated for the orderly operation of that institution and for the effectuation of its purposes
* * *.

We know of no case which holds that colleges and universities are subject to the supervision or review of the courts
in the uniform application of their academic standards. Indeed, *Dixon* infers the contrary.

In this context, appellants, eight in number, former students
of Texas Southern University, at Houston, filed suit on September 8, 1967, alleging that they had been denied admission
to that institution at the fall term in violation of their constitutional rights in that the denial was grounded upon their

suspension at the end of the spring term for participating in several peaceable assemblies protected by the First Amendment. It was further asserted that these suspensions were in violation of the due process clause of the Fourteenth Amendment because appellants were not given notice and an opportunity to be heard.

Three days later, the District Court issued a temporary restraining order, commanding appellees to permit appellants to register at the University pending a hearing on the merits. Two days later, including a night session of the court, the hearing was held. At its close, appellees moved for dismissal of the action and dissolution of the temporary restraining order. On September 15, 1967, these motions were granted and this appeal followed. We affirm the action of the District Court.

The trial court found appellants Franklin, Waller, Nichols, Parker, and Freeman to be scholastically ineligible for admission to the fall term. Franklin had failed 12 of the 13 hours for which he had been enrolled; the others failed all courses. Under the rules and regulations of the University, applicable to all students alike, these appellants were thus subject to mandatory suspension until January, 1968. The court significantly noted, "Counsel for Plaintiffs has not contended that suspension on this ground violates Plaintiffs' constitutional rights." In any event, the findings in this regard are supported by the record and there is no rational basis for holding that they were clearly erroneous.

Only Wright, Richards, and Lowe remain for further consideration. As to them, in language we cannot improve upon, the District Court found and concluded as follows:

"Concerning the Plaintiff Wright, Dean Jones testified that on March 27, 1967, it was reported to him that Wright had violated one of the University regulations. On April 18, during a period of serious unrest and turbulence on the campus, Dean Jones stated that he *personally* observed Wright on the campus after curfew hours. He stated that he confronted Wright and a companion and asked them to leave, but that they refused to do so. He then asked Wright to come to his office to talk with him about the incident. Wright never came. Later, Dean Jones made attempts to contact Wright by mail. He could find no mailing address, although each student was required by University regulations to keep the school informed of his mailing address and any changes thereof. Dean Jones also went to Wright's father to inquire about Wright's address, but was told by the father that he did not know himself. Wright voluntarily withdrew from the University on May 2. He was notified by certified mail on or about May 27 that he would not be permitted to re-enter Texas Southern.

"Concerning the Plaintiff Richards, Dean Jones testified that on January 18, 1967, he personally called at the dormitory where Richards resided to request a conference concerning a reported violation of University regulations. A conference with Richards was held, and Richards was told that he would be under observation for the remainder of the semester. On April 30, 1967, Dean Jones *personally* observed Richards exhorting students to block the entrance way to a campus building so as to prevent entry by the faculty and students alike. A letter was then sent to Richards asking that he report to the Dean for a conference, but it was returned undelivered. Although Richards had changed his mailing address, he, like Wright, failed to notify the University. Richards was notified after the close of the spring term that he would not be permitted to re-enter Texas Southern.

"I think this evidence clearly demonstrates that diligence was exercised in attempting to give proper notice to both Wright and Richards. Wright was given personal notice at a time when he was in the act of violating a valid University regulation. Certainly that situation itself should have impressed him with the necessity of compliance with the Dean's command to visit his office. Moreover, written communications were sought to be delivered to both Wright and Richards. Only because of their failure to comply with a valid University regulation was delivery of the communications unsuccessful. The Dean of Students, I am convinced, exercised his best efforts to inform these two students of the nature of the University's complaints against them. *I do not think more is required.* To now order Defendants to reinstate these Plaintiffs subject to holding a hearing on their grounds for suspension would, it seems to me, be tantamount to condoning the irresponsible attitude exhibited by these Plaintiffs. It would be unreasonable indeed for this Court to hold that a University could not take disciplinary action against students who could not be contacted although diligent attempts were made, particularly where their whereabouts were not disclosed to the University in violation of a valid regulation. In a day where the population of some of our State Colleges and Universities now approaches that of small cities, where there is a decided increase in off-campus residency, and where there are in many instances no attendance rules imposed on the students, to require more of University officials than was done here, would in many cases render University officials powerless to command or rebuke the fanatic, the irritant, the malingerer, the rabble rouser.

"Plaintiff Lowe was allowed leave to join as a party plaintiff on September 12. After leave was granted, he joined in the allegations of the other Plaintiffs, thereby limiting the scope of his own cause of action. The undisputed evidence shows that Lowe was given notice to report to Dean Jones' office and that he did. His conduct during the spring semester was discussed with Dean Jones and he was given the opportunity to speak in his own defense. Lowe was then referred by Dean Jones to the office of the President, and Lowe then discussed with the President the University's complaints against him. After this, Dean Jones and the President conferred and arrived at their decision to deny Lowe re-admission to Texas Southern.

"I find no evidence to indicate that the hearing afforded Lowe was inadequate. Lowe has offered no evidence concerning the hearing, and on such a record I do not think that this or any other Court should substitute its judgment for that of the proper University officials. From what appears of record, Lowe was given a fair opportunity to show his innocence and explain his conduct. This was sufficient."

Again, the factual findings, are not clearly erroneous and we find no error in the application of the law. By violation of regulations Wright and Richards simply frustrated the notice and hearing process. They circumvented the rights which they now seek to vindicate. They cannot now be heard to complain of an impossibility which was of their own creation.

Lowe was not summarily or arbitrarily expelled. He was allowed a hearing before both the dean and the president of the University. He offered no evidence to establish the inadequacy of such hearings or to show that he was prejudiced by the lack of more.

In this state of the record we find no justification for further judicial intrusion upon University operations.

Since the District Judge was manifestly right in his disposition of this controversy we consider it unnecessary to discuss the further point, raised by the appellees, that appellants afterwards sought relief in the state courts, failed, and took no appeal.

Affirmed.

NOTES

*Injunctive Relief Against Campus Disorders**

Drawing on well-established principles of equity, courts have made available an effective remedy for college administrators seeking to defuse explosive campus confrontations. To give a troubled campus some protection from destruction and disruption, courts will enjoin a continuing trespass if three elements are present: (1) the probability of irreparable injury; (2) the inadequacy of damages for such injuries as disruption of study and classes; and (3) the inadequacy of a remedy at law to prevent future trespasses. The requirement that these elements be present before an injunction will issue is based on the principle that equity will not act to punish demonstrators, but only to enjoin them from committing harmful acts, whether criminal or not.

The advantages of injunctive relief are significant. It avoids immediate use of police, allows for a cooling-off period, interjects the courts as mediators, is flexible in application, and has consequences that are not unreasonably harsh. But the remedy is not perfect. If a large number of students violate an injunction, it would be difficult to punish all of them because of the problem of proving that each had adequate notice of the injunction and that each violated its terms. Even if such proof could be adduced, the resulting trial would be very time-consuming. The remedy has thus far been effective because contempt proceedings have been brought only against the leaders of disruptions, and because such proceedings are more expeditious than proceedings in criminal courts.

The future success of the remedy will depend on the good faith of those seeking injunctions and the sound discretion of the courts issuing them. * * *

Injunctive relief is not a panacea; it is no more than a sophisticated device to relieve crisis on a campus. The basic problem—dealing effectively with the conditions spawning the turmoil—is not one which our courts alone can solve.

---

* Robert R. Rosenthal, "Injunctive Relief Against Campus Disorders," *University of Pennsylvania Law Review*, Vol. 118, pp. 764-765 (1970) (reprinted with permission).

University regulation reserving right to enter dormitory rooms is reasonable

MOORE v. STUDENT AFFAIRS COMMITTEE OF TROY STATE UNIVERSITY

United States District Court, M.D. Alabama, N.D., 1968.
284 F. Supp. 725.

ORDER

JOHNSON, Chief Judge.

On February 28, 1968, plaintiff, Gregory Gordon Moore, was a student in good standing at Troy State University and resided in a dormitory on the campus which he rented from the school. A search of his room on that day, conducted by the Dean of Men and two agents of the State of Alabama Health Department, Bureau of Primary Prevention, in plaintiff's presence, revealed a substance which, upon analysis, proved to be marijuana. Following a hearing on March 27, 1968, by the Student Affairs Committee of Troy State University, plaintiff was "indefinitely suspended" from that institution on March 28.

This action was commenced on March 30, 1968, seeking reinstatement of plaintiff as a student in good standing. At a hearing in this court conducted on April 26, 1968, it was determined that plaintiff had exhausted his administrative remedies at Troy State University and that he "was denied his right to procedural due process of law in the hearing conducted at Troy State University on March 27, 1968, as a result of which he was indefinitely suspended." On motion of the defendants, jurisdiction of this cause was retained pending remand to the Student Affairs Committee of Troy State University for the purpose of conducting a hearing comporting with procedural due process of law. Pending those proceedings, plaintiff was ordered reinstated.

On May 1, 1968, a second hearing was held before the Student Affairs Committee and plaintiff was again indefinitely suspended. He again challenges, from a procedural point of view, the action taken in suspending him. He does not challenge the underlying substantive basis for the action of the Student Affairs Committee. If plaintiff while a student possessed marijuana in a dormitory on campus in violation of state law, then indefinite suspension from his status as a student is clearly justified.

Plaintiff now seeks relief in this court. First, he seeks readmission as a student at Troy State University on the ground of denial of procedural due process in the proceedings which resulted in his suspension; second, he seeks a declaratory judgment that none of the evidence seized in the search of his room "may be admitted in any criminal proceedings * * *"; and third, he alleges the admission in the University's hearing of the evidence obtained through a search of his dormitory room violates his Fourth Amendment rights prohibiting illegal search and seizure. The second part of the relief sought is clearly unavailable.[2]

On the morning of February 28, 1968, the Dean of Men of Troy State University was called to the office of the Chief of Police of Troy, Alabama, where a conference was held regarding "the possibility of there being marijuana on the campus." Two narcotics agents, the Chief of Police, and two students were present. A second meeting was held later that morning at which a list was procured of the names of students whose rooms the officers desired permission to search. This information came from unnamed but reliable informers. About 1 p. m., the officers received additional information that some of the subjects they were interested in were packing to leave the campus for a break following the end of an examination period. Upon receipt of this information, and fearing a "leak," two narcotics agents, accompanied by the Dean of Men, searched six dormitory rooms in two separate residence halls. The search of the room which plaintiff occupied alone occurred between approximately 2:30 and 2:45 p. m., in his presence, but without his permission.

At the second hearing before the Student Affairs Committee, the following stipulation was entered concerning the search:

> "That no search warrant was obtained in this case, that no consent to search was given by the defendant, that the search was not incidental to a legal arrest, that no other offense was committed by the defendant in the arresting officers' presence, that Troy State University had in force and effect at the time of the search and subsequent arrest of the defendant the following regulation.
>
> " 'The college reserves the right to enter rooms for inspection purposes. If the administration deems it necessary the room may be searched and the occupant

---

2. 28 U.S.C. § 2283; Stefanelli v. Minard, 342 U.S. 117, 72 S.Ct. 118, 96 L.Ed. 138 (1951). See Cleary v. Bolger, 371 U.S. 392, 83 S.Ct. 385, 9 L.Ed.2d 390 (1963); Pugach v. Dollinger, 365 U.S. 458, 81 S.Ct. 650, 5 L.Ed.2d 678 (1961); Wilson v. Schnettler, 365 U.S. 381, 81 S.Ct. 632, 5 L.Ed.2d 620 (1961); Douglas v. City of Jeanette, 319 U.S. 157, 63 S.Ct. 877, 87 L.Ed. 1324 (1943).

required to open his personal baggage and any other personal material which is sealed.'

This language appears in the Troy State College current bulletin of the year 1967-68. The quoted language also appears * * * in the Troy State Bulletin for the year 1967-68. * * * This language also appears in the current publication of the Oracle, which is a student handbook. * * * This language further appears on the reverse side of a leaflet entitled 'Residence Hall Policies' which is also made available to all students of Troy State University.

"It is further stipulated that the defendant's room was searched at the invitation or consent of Troy State University by the law enforcement officials acting under the above quoted regulations."

The search revealed a matchbox containing a small amount of vegetable matter, which a state toxicologist who examined it testified was marijuana. All this testimony was received over plaintiff's objection that the evidence was seized as a result of a search in violation of the Fourth Amendment. He also challenges the constitutionality, facially and as applied, of the regulation under which the search was conducted. * * *

College students who reside in dormitories have a special relationship with the college involved. Insofar as the Fourth Amendment affects that relationship, it does not depend on either a general theory of the right of privacy [4] or on traditional property concepts.[5] The college does not stand, strictly speaking, *in loco parentis* to its students, nor is their relationship purely contractual in the traditional sense. The relationship grows out of the peculiar and sometimes the seemingly competing interests of college and student. A student naturally has the right to be free of unreasonable search and seizures,[7] and a tax-supported public college may not compel a "waiver" of that right as a condition precedent to admission.[8] The college, on the other hand, has an "affirmative obligation" [9] to promulgate and to enforce reasonable regulations designed to protect campus order and discipline and to promote an environment consistent with the educational process. The validity of the regulation authorizing

---

4. Katz v. United States, 389 U.S. 347, 88 S.Ct. 507, 19 L.Ed.2d 576 (1967).

5. Developments in the Law—Academic Freedom, 81 Harv.L.Rev. 1045, 1143—1156 (1968).

7. Cf. In re Gault, 387 U.S. 1, 87 S.Ct. 1428, 18 L.Ed.2d 27 (1967).

8. Dickey v. Alabama State Board of Education, supra 273 F. Supp. at 618.

9. See People v. Overton, 20 N.Y.2d 360, 283 N.Y.S.2d 22, 24, 229 N.E.2d 596, 598 (1967).

search of dormitories thus does not depend on whether a student "waives" his right to Fourth Amendment protection or on whether he has "contracted" it away; rather, its validity is determined by whether the regulation is a reasonable exercise of the college's supervisory duty. In other words, if the regulation—or, in the absence of a regulation, the action of the college authorities—is necessary in aid of the basic responsibility of the institution regarding discipline and the maintenance of an "educational atmosphere," then it will be presumed facially reasonable despite the fact that it may infringe to some extent on the outer bounds of the Fourth Amendment rights of students.

In Englehart v. Serena, 318 Mo. 263, 300 S.W. 268, 271 (1927), a civil action for alleged wrongful expulsion, the Supreme Court of Missouri defined the dormitory student-college relationship in real property terms as follows:

> "One of the grounds on which appellant seeks a recovery of damages is that he was deprived of the 'possession' of the room he was occupying in the dormitory before the expiration of the period for which he had paid 'rent.' He was not, however, a tenant in any sense of the word. He did not have even the full and unrestricted rights of a lodger, because Albert Hall was not an ordinary lodging house. It was an auxiliary of the college, and was maintained and conducted in furtherance of that institution's general purposes. When appellant took up residence there, he impliedly agreed to conform to all reasonable rules and regulations for its government which were then in force or which might thereafter be adopted by the proper authorities."

That definition is equally apt when measuring the relationship of this plaintiff and Troy State University by the Fourth Amendment. The student is subject only to reasonable rules and regulations, but his rights must yield to the extent that they would interfere with the institution's fundamental duty to operate the school *as an educational institution*. A reasonable right of inspection is necessary to the institution's performance of that duty even though it may infringe on the outer boundaries of a dormitory student's Fourth Amendment rights. * * * The regulation of Troy State University in issue here is thus facially reasonable.

The regulation was reasonably applied in this case. The constitutional boundary line between the right of the school authorities to search and the right of a dormitory student to privacy must be based on a reasonable belief on the part of the college authorities that a student is using a dormitory room for a purpose which is illegal or which would otherwise seriously interfere with campus discipline. Upon this submission, it is clear that such a belief existed in this case.[11]

This standard of "reasonable cause to believe" to justify a search by college administrators—even where the sole purpose is to seek evidence of suspected violations of law—is lower than the constitutionally protected criminal law standard of "probable cause." This is true because of the special necessities of the student-college relationship and because college disciplinary proceedings are not criminal proceedings in the constitutional sense. It is clearly settled that due process in college disciplinary proceedings does not require full-blown adversary hearings subject to rules of evidence and all constitutional criminal guaranties. "Such a hearing, with the attending publicity and disturbance of college activities, might be detrimental to the college's educational atmosphere and impractical to carry out." * * *

Assuming that the Fourth Amendment applied to college disciplinary proceedings, the search in this case would not be in violation of it. It is settled law that the Fourth Amendment does not prohibit reasonable searches when the search is conducted by a superior charged with a responsibility of maintaining discipline and order or of maintaining security. A student who lives in a dormitory on campus which he "rents" from the school waives objection to any reasonable searches conducted pursuant to reasonable and necessary regulations such as this one. * * *

In accordance with the foregoing, it is the order, judgment and decree of this Court that plaintiff's claims for relief be and are, in each instance, hereby denied. It is ordered that this cause be and the same is hereby dismissed.

It is further ordered that the costs incurred in these proceedings be and the same are hereby taxed against the plaintiff, for which execution may issue.

---

11. The school authorities in this case not only had information sufficient to form "reasonable cause to believe" plaintiff was using his room in a manner inconsistent with appropriate school discipline, but they also had enough information to amount to probable cause to believe the conduct was criminal.

University regulation authorizing search of dormitory rooms is unconstitutional if used to obtain criminal evidence

PIAZZOLA v. WATKINS

United States Court of Appeals, Fifth Circuit, 1971.
442 F.2d 284.

RIVES, Circuit Judge:

The district court granted habeas corpus to two Alabama prisoners and ordered their release. Piazzola and Marinshaw v. Watkins, M.D.Ala.1970, 316 F. Supp. 624. The appellants advance two contentions for reversal: (1) that the appellees have not exhausted the remedies available in the courts of the State as required by 28 U.S.C. § 2254; and (2) that the search and seizure which the district court found to be violative of appellees' Fourth Amendment rights were made pursuant to a constitutionally reasonable school regulation permitting such searches and seizures. We affirm. * * *

The district court condensed the transcript of testimony into the following findings of fact:

"On the morning of February 28, 1968, the Dean of Men of Troy State University was called to the office of the Chief of Police of Troy, Alabama, to discuss 'the drug problem' at the University. Two State narcotic agents and two student informers from Troy State University were also present. Later on that same day, the Dean of Men was called to the city police station for another meeting; at this time he was informed by the officers that they had sufficient evidence that marijuana was in the dormitory rooms of certain Troy State students and that they desired the cooperation of University officials in searching these rooms. The police officers were advised by the Dean of Men that they would receive the full cooperation of the University officials in searching for the marijuana. The informers, whose identities have not yet been disclosed, provided the police officers with names of students whose rooms were to be searched. Still later on that same day (which was during the week of final examinations at the University and was to be followed by a week-long holiday) the law enforcement officers accompanied by some of the University officials, searched six or seven dormitory rooms located in two separate residence halls. The rooms of both Piazzcla and Marinshaw were searched without search warrants and without their consent. Present during the search of the room occupied by Marinshaw were two State narcotic agents, the University security officer, and a counselor of the residence hall where Marinshaw's room was located. Piazzola's room was searched twice. Present during the first search were two State narcotic agents and a University official; no evidence was found at this time. The second search of Piazzola's room, which disclosed the incriminating evidence, was conducted solely by the State and City police officials.

"At the time of the seizure the University had in effect the following regulation:

> The college reserves the right to enter rooms for inspection purposes. If the administration deems it necessary, the room may be searched and the occupant required to open his personal baggage and any other personal material which is sealed.

Each of the petitioners was familiar with this regulation. After the search of the petitioners' rooms and the discovery of the marijuana, they were arrested, and the State criminal prosecutions and convictions ensued."

316 F.Supp. at 625.

* * *

2. *Validity of Search and Seizure*

The Fourth Amendment protects "the right of the *people* to be secure in their persons, houses, papers, and effects, against *unreasonable* searches and seizures" (emphasis added). The question is whether in the light of all of the facts and circumstances, including the University regulation, the search which disclosed the marijuana was an unreasonable search. The district judge made reasonableness the touchstone of his opinion as to the validity of the search. We find ourselves in agreement with his view that this search was unreasonable. * * *

Another case somewhat in point on the facts is Commonwealth v. McCloskey, Appellant, 1970, 217 Pa.Super. 432, 272 A.2d 271. There the court reversed a student's marijuana conviction because the policemen who entered his dormitory room to execute a search warrant did not knock or announce their presence and purpose before entering. In part, Judge Cercone speaking for the majority of the court said:

> "It was the Commonwealth's position that the Fourth Amendment protections do not apply to a search of a college dormitory room. The test to be used in determining the applicability of the Fourth Amendment protections is whether or not the particular locale is one '* * * in which there was a reasonable expectation of freedom from governmental intrusion': * * * A dormitory room is analogous to an apartment or a hotel room. It certainly offers its occupant a more reasonable expectation of freedom from governmental intrusion than does a public telephone booth. The defendant rented the dormitory

room for a certain period of time, agreeing to abide by the rules established by his lessor, the University. As in most rental situations, the lessor, Bucknell University, reserved the right to check the room for damages, wear and unauthorized appliances. Such right of the lessor, however, does not mean McCloskey was not entitled to have a 'reasonable expectation of freedom from governmental intrusion' or that he gave consent to the police search, or gave the University authority to consent to such search.

In the case of Katz v. United States, 1967, 389 U.S. 347, 88 S.Ct. 507, 19 L.Ed.2d 576, to which Judge Cercone referred, the Court commented at some length on the concept of "constitutionally protected areas":

> "The petitioner has strenuously argued that the booth was a 'constitutionally protected area.' The Government has maintained with equal vigor that it was not. But this effort to decide whether or not a given 'area,' viewed in the abstract, is 'constitutionally protected' deflects attention from the problem presented by this case. For the Fourth Amendment protects people, not places. What a person knowingly exposes to the public, even in his own home or office, is not a subject of Fourth Amendment protection. * * * But what he seeks to preserve as private, even in an area accessible to the public, may be constitutionally protected. * * *
>
> "The Government stresses the fact that the telephone booth from which the petitioner made his calls was constructed partly of glass, so that he was as visible after he entered it as he would have been if he had remained outside. But what he sought to exclude when he entered the booth was not the intruding eye—it was the uninvited ear. He did not shed his right to do so simply because he made his calls from a place where he might be seen. No less than an individual in a business office, in a friend's apartment, or in a taxicab, a person in a telephone booth may rely upon the protection of the Fourth Amendment. * * *"

389 U.S. at 351-352, 88 S.Ct. at 511.

By a similar process of reasoning, we must conclude that a student who occupies a college dormitory room enjoys the protection of the Fourth Amendment. True the University retains broad supervisory powers which permit it to adopt the regulation heretofore quoted, provided that regulation is reasonably construed and is limited in its application to further the University's function as an educational institution.[2] The

---

2. One of the "Residence Hall Policies" of this University provides that "College men are assumed to be mature adults with acceptable and es-

regulation cannot be construed or applied so as to give consent to a search for evidence for the primary purpose of a criminal prosecution. Otherwise, the regulation itself would constitute an unconstitutional attempt to require a student to waive his protection from unreasonable searches and seizures as a condition to his occupancy of a college dormitory room. Compare Tinker v. Des Moines Independent Community School District, 1969, 393 U.S. 503, 506, 89 S.Ct. 733, 21 L.Ed.2d 731. Clearly the University had no authority to consent to or join in a police search for evidence of crime.

The right to privacy is "no less important than any other right carefully and particularly reserved to the people." Mapp v. Ohio, 1961, 367 U.S. 643, 657, 81 S.Ct. 1684, 1692, 6 L.Ed.2d 1081. The results of the search do not prove its reasonableness. This search was an unconstitutional invasion of the privacy both of these appellees and of the students in whose rooms no evidence of marijuana was found. The warrantless search of these students' dormitory rooms cannot be justified. The judgment is therefore

Affirmed.

NOTES

1. A federal district court in Maine upheld a search of a suitcase of a "corpsman" in a Job Corp Center which was conducted without a warrant and not incident to arrest; a bag of marijuana was found. The court concluded that the search and seizure was reasonable and did not infringe on the defendant's Fourth Amendment rights. The search was a constitutional exercise of the administrative officer's authority "to maintain proper standards of conduct and discipline at the Center." "Quite plainly the investigation was conducted solely for the purpose of ensuring proper moral and disciplinary conditions of the Center, an obligation mandated by federal statute." United States v. Coles, 302 F. Supp. 99 (D. Me. 1969).

2. *Double jeopardy.* The courts have not, to date, held that discipline by the university and subsequent prosecution by the city or state constitutes double jeopardy as violative of the Fifth Amendment. The courts have generally concluded that while prosecution may have been for the same offense, it was

tablished habits." Another adjures students, "Keep rooms locked at all times." The University thus recognized that it cannot exercise that strict control of its students which might be permitted in a boys' school where an "in loco parentis" standard would be more appropriate.

not carried out by the same jurisdiction—the university and city or state constituting separate legal jurisdictions.

This distinction may be questionable, however, in view of a recent United States Supreme Court decision [Waller v. State of Florida, 201 So. 2d 554 (Fla. 1967), 221 So. 2d 749 (Fla. 1968), reversed, ——— U.S. ——— 38 U.S.L.W. 4264, April 7, 1970] which held that a man could not be prosecuted for the same criminal offense by both the city and the state. The state defended the actions by claiming that the city was a "sovereign entity" separate and apart from the state in much the same manner as a state is a "sovereign entity" and not a part of the federal government. The Court rejected this argument holding that the state-federal analogy does not extend to the city and state. The Court cited Reynolds v. Sims, 377 U.S. 533 (1964), saying that cities and counties have never been considered sovereign entities, but rather "subordinate governmental instrumentalities created to assist the state in carrying out its functions."

By carrying the Court's logic further, a court in the not-too-distant future could conceivably hold that since the public university is an arm of the state (a "subordinate instrumentality") and not a "sovereign entity," then both university and state prosecution for the same offense may be in fact double jeopardy. See *College Law Bulletin*, United States National Student Association, Vol. II, No. 8, April 1970.

Regulations requiring some students to live and eat meals in college facilities does not deny constitutional rights

PRATZ v. LOUISIANA POLYTECHNIC INSTITUTE

United States District Court, W.D. Louisiana, Monroe Division, 1970. 316 F. Supp. 872, *affirmed*, 91 S. Ct. 1252 (1971).

DAWKINS, Chief District Judge:

The important issue here is whether a State-supported institution of higher education may, through the establishment of reasonable parietal regulations, require students to live and eat their meals in facilities provided by the institution.

Plaintiffs, and the class they represent, are students at Louisiana Polytechnic Institute (hereinafter sometimes referred to as Tech), a four-year, co-educational institution located at Ruston, Louisiana. Tech was created by Article 12, Section 9, of the Constitution of Louisiana and is under the supervision and control of the Louisiana State Board of Education (hereinafter sometimes referred to as Board), an agency of the State created by La.Const. Art. 12, Sec. 4.

Plaintiffs seek to have this Three-Judge Court [1] declare unconstitutional resolutions of the Board (and Tech regulations pursuant to Board resolutions) which require them to live in dormitories while students at Tech. Those resolutions provide in pertinent part:

> Schedule 44
> "A RESOLUTION FURTHER DEFINING THE PURPOSES AND POLICY FOR THE UTILIZATION OF HOUSING, DINING AND STUDENT LIFE FACILITIES IN THE STATE OF LOUISIANA.
> *   *   *   *   *   *
> "Section 2. It is the policy and philosophy of higher education in the State of Louisiana as interpreted by this Board (subject to recognition by this Board of the differences that exist between the several colleges and universities and the need for reasonable flexibility in the administration thereof) that all unmarried full-time undergraduate students, regardless of age or whether or not emancipated, are required to live in on-campus residence halls as long as space is available * * *. Exemptions from on-campus residence requirement may be granted by Proper Officials of each college or university:
> "A. In any case where it appears that a full-time undergraduate student will otherwise suffer significant hardship or because of sufficient financial, medical or other good and sound reasons shown.
> "B. In the case of older students, as, for example, (i) a returning military veteran; (ii) a previously married person where Proper Officials make a finding of fact that such individual is by virtue of age and experience incompatible with the educational objectives and values sought to be provided by on-campus residence herein outlined * * *"

The second resolution is as follows:

> Schedule 45
> "A RESOLUTION PERTAINING TO OFF CAMPUS RESIDENCE OF STUDENTS WHEN SPACE IS NOT AVAILABLE IN ON-CAMPUS RESIDENCE HALLS. [This resolution provides for the granting of additional exemptions "consistent with the objectives and purposes of higher education" and in order to assure "equal treat-

---

1. Our jurisdiction is based on 28 U.S.C. § 1343(3) and 42 U.S.C. § 1981 et seq. This case was submitted on stipulations, briefs, affidavits and oral argument. It was agreed that this Court may take judicial notice of those factors concerning State Universities and Colleges with which all are familiar.

ment and protection to students similarly situated" in order of priority as follows:]

"1. First, undergraduate students living with parents, grandparents, married brother or sister or in supervised sorority or fraternity housing.

"2. Second, seniors.

"3. Third, juniors.

"4. Fourth, sophomores

"5. Fifth, freshmen.

"Within each of the foregoing classifications, the following additional rules of priority shall be applied:

"1. First shall be the students who have resided in off-campus housing for the longest period of time since attending the institution.

"2. Second, in accordance with the order of date of application filed. (A list may be kept of those full-time graduate students indicating a desire to live off-campus, showing the date each application was made.)"

Due to the important constitutional issues involved in this case, both sides have spent a great deal of time and effort presenting their respective positions. They have argued with every conceivable legal weapon which could be used to gain them victory. Out of all the barrages which have been fired, it is now our task to select the truly determinative points and from these to decide the proper outcome.

It is clear that a State Board of Education and a State University are agencies of the State and are subject to control by the State involved. Consequently, the actions of the Board and Tech are State action and students may not be deprived by such action of those bill of rights guarantees to which States have been subjected by the Courts under the Fourteenth Amendment, as well as the protections guaranteed by that Amendment itself. * * *

Because each side has asked us to consider so many issues, we think it best at the outset here to synopsize what we believe to be the main contentions of both parties and then consider the specific allegations separately.

In brief, plaintiffs assert that students are indeed citizens, that by enrolling in a State-supported institution, they do not give up any of their basic constitutional rights they possessed as non-students. They assert that the First Amendment guarantees them the right to move about, among and in the respective States in any manner they see fit, that it allows them to associate, or not to associate, with anyone they may choose, and that they have certain rights of privacy which are violated when made to live in a communal type arrangement.

They further assert that the contested rules deprive them of certain property rights in that it is possible for a student to live at less cost in non-campus housing and eating facilities than it does in those provided by the State. They say the resolutions are unreasonable and capricious and violate the equal protection of laws of the United States and of Louisiana. Further, they contend that the main reason the resolutions were enacted was to insure that a sufficient number of students occupy the dormitories that revenues from such occupancy will be adequate to retire the bonded indebtedness created when the dormitories and eating facilities were constructed.

Defendants strongly refute all of plaintiff's allegations, especially those concerning the bonded indebtedness. Defendants acknowledge that while they are concerned with what the effect would be for us to strike down the resolutions, the bonds are an obligation of each institution which has incurred that sort of indebtedness, and if revenues from dormitory occupancy are insufficient to retire the bonds, such obligations must be borne by all members of the student body as additional tuition cost. Defendants' main argument is that the so-called parietal rules,[2] as embodied in the contested resolu-

---

2. We pause here to put in its proper context the phrase "parietal rules." "Parietal" is derived from the Latin word "paries, parietis"—"a wall." In the United States the meaning pertains to residence within, or pertaining to life within, the buildings of a college or university. See Webster's New Collegiate Dictionary, 2d ed. For example, in 1837 "Orders and Reg. Harvard Univ. 12" stated:

> "The offiders [sic] resident within the college wall shall constitute a permanent standing committee of the faculty to be called the parietal committee. This committee shall have particular cognizance of all offenses against good order and decorum within the walls."

In one of their main thrusts, plaintiffs assert the doctrine of "in loco parentis" is dead. We find a definition of "in loco parentis" in Black's Law Dictionary:

> "In the place of a parent; instead of a parent; charged factitiously with a parent's rights, duties and responsibilities."

Defendants point out that Louisiana educational institutions have never attempted to operate under a theory of "in loco parentis" because of the tort liability which may have attached as a result of such assumption. See La. Civil Code Art. 2318.

We tend to agree with that line of thinking which states that the modern college or university, which has in attendance thousands of students, even if it should, is ill-equipped to regulate the off-campus social and moral lives of its students, thus making futile, and perhaps improper, any attempt to act "in loco parentis." *Zanders, infra,* fn. 3; Buttny v. Smiley, 281 F.Supp. 280 (D.C.Colo.1968); Moore v. Student

tions, are based on the soundest of educational principles and thinking. Numerous authoritative affidavits in the record point out that educators of the highest calibre from throughout the Nation feel that the living and learning concepts espoused by the regulations have the highest educational value and should be enforced as being in the best interest of all students, present and future. Though defendants admit that some individuals may be able to live and eat off-campus at lesser cost than in campus facilities, they are able to do so only by living in a substandard environment and eating food which is deficient in the basic nutritional aspects called for in a healthful diet. Further, defendants point out that a student may choose to attend any school he pleases, as long as he is qualified, therefore his right to move about as he pleases is in no way restricted; that his freedom of association certainly is not restricted; that his right to privacy is in no way affected by parietal rules (in that the Fourth Amendment adequately protects such rights); and that the exemption priorities and hardship rules established by the resolutions certainly prevent any student from being subjected to any undue problems.

We will not enter that thicket of legal brambles concerning whether one possesses a "right" or a "privilege" to attend a State-supported institution.[3] Rather, we are content to acknowledge that students and State-supported institutions form a special relationship with each other, and the interest possessed by the student is entitled to constitutional protection. Thus, a student does not give up any basic constitutional right when he enters a State college or university * * *.

Since the 1920's, when State institutions of higher learning began to take on their modern role and image, the Federal Government has been deeply concerned with the provision of adequate campus housing and eating facilities on terms more favorable than those available in the private market and has made it possible, through loans and guarantees of loans, that such accommodations are provided at rates students as a whole can afford. Congressional concern and action has been continuous, and as late as 1968 we find the following in the legislative history of the Housing Act of 1950, as amended:

Affairs Committee of Troy State University, 284 F. Supp. 725 (D.C. Ala.1968); Breen v. Kahl, 419 F.2d 1034 (7th Cir. 1969).

Thus, when "parietal" is used herein, we and defendants are speaking of those regulations affecting the educational, particularly the living portion, sphere of a university's function.

3. *Cf.* Zanders v. Louisiana State Board of Education, 281 F. Supp. 747 (W.D.La. 1968).

"The committee has found that there is a need for vast increases in student housing to meet future enrollment increases; to alleviate overcrowding resulting from past enrollments; * * * *the lack of adequate housing may be the bottleneck in meeting our growing higher educational needs, since the relative expansion capacity of academic facilities cannot be fully utilized without available student housing at the lowest possible cost to users of the housing facilities.* * * * The need may be even greater than anticipated when returning Vietnam veterans take advantage of their GI educational benefits." 1968 U.S. Code Congressional and Administrative News, pp. 2978, 2979. (Emphasis added.)

All of the legislative history in this field of higher education clearly indicates that private lending institutions should be the normal sources of credit for the construction of such facilities. Because of this, the regulations for the Federal housing programs were written so that the private capital market would be given the first chance to make the loans. Thus, it was necessary for Federal administrators to specify that terms and conditions for Federal loans must conform to current market requirements, and 12 U.S.C. § 1749a[c] [9] provides general authority for the adoption of bond resolutions with parietal rule covenants as necessary security devices:

"[9] Include in any contract or instrument made pursuant to this subchapter such other covenants, conditions, or provisions he (the Commissioner) may deem necessary to assure that the purposes of this subchapter will be achieved."

The administrative practice founded in federal statutory law specifically approved by regulations promulgated by the appropriate agency of the United States Government and successfully followed in the administration of one of the major national objectives—higher education—is entitled to a strong presumption of constitutional validity.

Just as the federal government has deemed adequate housing and dining facilities to be one of the most important parts of a proper system of higher education, so have the legislatures of the respective States, including Louisiana. These bodies have authorized colleges and universities under their jurisdiction to build and equip dormitory, dining and student life facilities, and to pay for them through reasonable rental charges paid by occupants of these buildings:

"It cannot be questioned that proper housing for students is an integral part of the responsibility placed upon the authorities of the University of Oklahoma. The great majority of the students must have a home away from home while attending school at the University, and it is incumbent upon school authorities to see that all precautions are taken to insure that not only adequate but also suitable housing is available." Pyeatte v. Board of Regents of the University of Oklahoma, 102 F.Supp. 407, affirmed 342 U.S. 936, 72 S.Ct. 567, 96 L.Ed. 696 (1952).

Plaintiff Pyeatte, in the case just cited, was the owner of a rooming house who contested the housing regulations of the University of Oklahoma since they prevented her from having as many roomers as she would have liked. There the Court pointed out:

"It would appear that if any right has been violated, it would be the right of the student to contract for a place to live of his own choice and not a right of a person in the position of the plaintiff. Even so, as stated in Alaska Packers Association v. Industrial Accident Commission of California, 294 U.S. 532, 543, 55 S.Ct. 518, 79 L.Ed. 1044 * * *: 'Legislation otherwise within the scope of acknowledged state power, not unreasonably or arbitrarily exercised, cannot be condemned because it curtails the power of the individual to contract.'
"The housing regulations in effect at the University of Oklahoma result in completely depriving a student of freely contracting with whom he pleases for a place to live. If this restriction upon the student is a valid exercise of the power conferred upon the Board of Regents to prescribe rules for admission to the University, it is absurd for the plaintiff to contend that the indirect effect deprives her of her liberty to contract, for the fact that regulatory law enacted under state power imposes hardship in individual cases, due to special circumstances or other factors, does not subject the law to constitutional objections. * * *

The Court pointed out that if there was any discrimination involved, and it refused to pass on that point, that it was against the students and not against the private home-owners such as Mrs. Pyeatte. Therefore, she was not in position to challenge the constitutionality of the statutes or regulations, but the Court did consider the issue of discrimination against Mrs. Pyeatte as a private householder duly approved by the University to keep students. In doing so, the Court found the regulations reasonable and that they did not deny plaintiff equal protection of the laws.

Since *Pyeatte* in 1952, it has been the consensus of State legislatures that college housing, dining and student life projects be paid for by students who benefit and not by the taxpayers of the State. By Act 619 of 1954, the Louisiana Legislature provided that its institutions of higher learning could construct any revenue producing facility, including dormitories, and only revenues from such facilities would be pledged for the payment of bonds given for financing such construction. Said Act, as amended, specifically authorizes the bond resolution to contain parietal rules:

> "[The State could contract with the holder of bonds that it would assure] the maximum percentage of occupancy of a facility, [by] such parietal rules with reference to * * * residence in a facility and other pertinent matters, as may be deemed necessary by the Board, to assure the marketability of said bonds. * * *"

Thus far, we have seen that an effective system of higher education is one of the highest priority projects of both the federal and State governments. We also have seen that adequate housing, dining and student life facilities, for all prospective students, are agreed to be a necessary and most vital component of such an educational system. Thus, we are concerned hereafter only with whether a State's enactment of parietal rules to carry out the mission of higher education is permissible. * * *

While it might be said that some students will gain very little from living under the parietal rules, it is just as certain that a great majority of students will gain incalculable benefits as a result of such rules. When one considers the fully adequate facilities that are provided by such rules and the thousands upon thousands of students throughout the Nation who are able to obtain a higher education only because of such facilities, reasonably priced, and thus the national objective and goal of achieving a better educated society is fulfilled more easily, certainly it cannot be contended seriously that the parietal rules are unreasonable, arbitrary, or capricious.

The foregoing is what may be styled a substantial and vital benefit to be enjoyed by all student generations. Yet, it is no more important than the personal benefit gained by each student who has the advantage of participating in the living and learning center environment made possible by the parietal rules. This is confirmed by the numerous, nationally prominent educators who supplied affidavits to that effect in this case.

Plaintiffs next would have us hold that through the exemption provisions the parietal rules deny students equal protection of the laws. They speak particularly of those provisions

which require married students not living with their spouses
to live in on-campus residence halls while not so requiring
married students living with their spouses. This, plaintiffs
say, is an unreasonable classification. In short answer to this,
we do not believe this "exemption" is a "classification," since
the class to which the rules speak is composed of *all* undergraduate students. Even so, all members of the same class
need not be treated completely equally.

> "Judicial inquiry under the equal protection clause in-
> to areas of unequal treatment under law demands a stan-
> dard of classification which is neither arbitrary nor cre-
> ative of an invidious discrimination but reasonable when
> judged in light of the objectives of the legislation. * * *
> Legislative bodies [and regulatory agencies created and
> empowered by them], however, are given rather wide
> latitude in their judgments as to the reasonableness of
> classifications." Briggs v. Kerrigan, 307 F.Supp. 295, 302
> (E.Mass.1969).

Moreover, the exemption provision is not unreasonable since
the only reason the married students living with spouses are
exempt from the rule is that to have them live together with
their spouses in the dormitory would certainly be unreasonable, given the contemporary method of housing single students in facilities occupied by only one sex. The contribution
that a married person can give to and receive from the living
center and other students is such that if his or her spouse is
not residing with the student at the school's location, that
student may be required to live on the campus.

Plaintiffs also attack the other exemptions listed in the rules
wherein such exemptions from on-campus residence requirement "may be granted by Proper Officials of the university."
Plaintiffs object to the provisions of the resolution which
state that exemptions may be granted to those full-time undergraduate students who would otherwise "suffer significant
hardship or because of sufficient financial, medical, or other
good and sound reasons shown or in the case of older students." As we have pointed out, exemptions due to certain
hardships are certainly reasonable, not arbitrary, and in no
way violate the equal protection clause. * * *

Plaintiffs next attack the resolution's order of priority in
which it is stated certain groups of students are exempt. They
say this is unreasonable and arbitrary favoritism, but we
must disagree. The order of priority established in Schedule
45 of the Board's Resolution is effective only when on-campus
space is not available. Certainly, an all-encompassing rule

must have such exemptions since it is physically impossible for every student of the institution to live in campus housing facilities. The priority is based on academic seniority, with the underlying presumption being that the higher academic standing, i.e., senior, junior, etc., means that a student is more mature, and in his earlier college years, has already had the benefit of a living and learning center and would stand to gain less than those other students who have not had such a benefit. Regarding those students granted the number one priority to live off-campus in that they are residing with a parent or a close relative, this is only a common sense rule. For certainly students residing at home obtain many of the benefits as offered in a living and learning center, since it is recognized that the values sought to be achieved in such a center may be found in the type of atmosphere generated in family type living. Moreover, we would be less than candid if we did not recognize that it is far less costly for a student to live and eat with his family or close relatives than it is for him to live even in low-cost campus facilities. Many students are able to attend college *only* because they live at home. Moreover, as is often the case, a student who may be granted the exemption because he would live with his family and use its eating facilities is entitled to occupy dormitory facilities if he so chooses.

Plaintiffs' contention that the resolution contains a blanket and overbroad permission to school authorities to grant exemptions and is thus too flexible is unwarranted. Since the parietal rules *must* be general in nature, such a provision must be included so that the peculiar situations of each campus may be provided for in the general rule. Further, plaintiffs' assertion that the resolutions are vague and ambiguous is utterly without foundation. The Supreme Court has declared that

> "* * * a statute which either forbids or requires the doing of an act in terms so vague that men of common intelligence must necessarily guess at its meaning and differ as to its application violates the first essential of due process of law." Connally v. General Construction Co., 269 U.S. 385, 391, 46 S.Ct. 126, 127, 70 L.Ed. 322 (1926).

The terms of the contested resolution are not vague at all; neither are they ambiguous; and good faith on the part of educators must be presumed unless the contrary is shown.

Plaintiffs strongly assert that the resolutions violate their right of privacy. We acknowledge that a student living in a communal type atmosphere is not afforded the same type of privacy in his daily living habits that he would be if he lived alone. However, we do not think the Fourth Amendment right of privacy is intended to be carried to the ultimate and such an unreasonable extreme as plaintiffs would have us do here. We are confident that State educational institutions will henceforth guarantee to occupants of dormitories the basic right to be free from unwarranted searches and intrusions into their private areas. In the event the institutions violate this principle, certainly the Courts will see to it that a student is secure in his papers and other private effects. * * *

We are cognizant of those cases which hold that a statutory classification based upon certain "suspect" criteria or which affect "fundamental rights" will be deemed to violate the equal protection clause unless justified by a "compelling" state interest. See, e. g., Shapiro v. Thompson, 394 U.S. 618, 89 S.Ct. 1322, 22 L.Ed.2d 600 (1969). Even assuming that henceforth the stringent criteria enunciated in those cases will be applied when fundamental rights are involved, we do not feel that the complaints of plaintiffs are based on a denial of fundamental rights: * * *

Certainly, virtually any facet of life could be classified as a fundamental thing and subject to the stricter test enunciated in the recent cases. We think the rights asserted by plaintiffs here are subject to the traditional test regarding equal protection standards:

> "A legislative measure will be found to deny equal protection only if 'it is without any reasonable basis, and therefore is purely arbitrary.' Lindsley v. Natural Carbonic Gas Company, 220 U.S. 61, 78 [31 S.Ct. 337, 55 L.Ed. 369] (1911). It is not enough that the measure results incidentally 'in some inequality' or that it is not drawn 'with mathematical nicety,' *ibid;* the statutory classification must instead cause 'different treatment * * * so disparate, relative to the difference in classification, as to be wholly arbitrary.' Walters v. City of St. Louis, 347 U.S. 231, 237 [74 S.Ct. 505, 98 L.Ed. 660] (1954)." *Shapiro, supra,* Mr. Justice Harlan's dissent, 394 U.S. p. 662, 89 S.Ct. p. 1346.

Even assuming, however, that a "fundamental" right is involved, we are confident there is a compelling State interest to assure that its college-age citizens are properly educated, and if housing, eating and student life facilities are a vital part of that process, as we now know they are, we hold there is no violation of the equal protection clause. * * *

Finally, plaintiffs say that the parietal rules violate the basic rights of the family and cite *Griswold, supra,* in support of that contention. In effect, plaintiffs say that if a parent desires that his child not live in dormitories provided by the institution, he should not be made to do so. This is specious. In the first place, where sufficient hardship or compelling reason may be shown by the parent regarding his child and where he should live, a reasonable interpretation of the State's rules would allow such a student to live off-campus. On the other hand, a parent knows which parietal rules are in effect at the college to which he sends his child, and he should not be allowed to say that he wanted some of the benefits of the college or university for his child but not others. The benefits gained from association with the family are continued when that family happens to live in the same area in which the educational institution the child is attending is located near his home, and the student chooses to live with his family. Where the child goes to a distant institution, thereby making living with the family impossible, the family relationship necessarily and student is temporarily suspended, and the family must defer to the wisdom of the educators at the particular institution the child is attending.

In sum, education of its citizens is perhaps a State's most worthwhile and important function. In implementing that duty, the several States should be allowed wide latitude in determining the manner in which they are to operate. It certainly would be improper, indeed foolish, for this Court to say that all States must teach the same courses, that all educational institutions within one State must teach the same courses as the rest of the institutions, that each State must have a certain number of campuses for its students, and, yes, that it is improper for a State to adopt reasonable parietal rules requiring students to live and eat in an institution's facilities. If sound educational policies, as are shown here, dictate that the educational mission of the State is best carried out by providing for the great majority of student citizens of each State adequate housing and eating facilities at a cost which can be afforded by all students seeking entrance into a particular university, then we do not think it is our place to decree otherwise.

Furthermore, and in the final analysis, each State, including Louisiana, has some State-owned educational facilities which have no dormitory accommodations for students. Moreover, some State institutions have fewer dormitory accommodations than others. If, in selecting the institution he wishes to attend, a student chooses one with dormitory and dining facilities, and parietal rules, he knows what he is choosing and may not be heard to complain.

It is argued that the parietal rules which we today uphold require students to live in dormitories *"under the guise* of having students receive a complete education through the 'living and learning experience' of campus communal living." (Emphasis added.)

We simply do not feel the numerous outstanding educators, many of national renown, who submitted affidavits in this case to the effect that the living and learning center concept is a very valuable educational tool would say so unless this indeed was their sound, professional, expert opinion. It is a travesty of a sort even to infer they would be parties to any sort of disguised scheme to protect the interests of bondholders who bought the bonds within parietal covenants to protect their investments.

As already stated, the living and learning center concept was being followed here long prior to promulgation of the contested rules. Generation after generation of students have profited from such an experience. Only recently did this concept, formerly adhered to voluntarily, have to be placed in writing and made mandatory.

That defendants do strenuously defend the security feature of the bonds is only natural and justifiable. However, as pointed out earlier, the bonds are an obligation of each institution, not the taxpayer, and if revenues from its facilities are insufficient to service the debts, *all* students will be required to do so through higher fees or tuition payments, thereby increasing the cost of education for *all*.

Plaintiffs find further fault in the resolutions by saying that all college and university authorities in Louisiana do not consider themselves bound by the rules. This is so because the Board resolutions are permissive, not mandatory. This feature allows educational institutions to achieve characteristics unique from their fellow schools and is only proper. We would not presume to say that all State schools *must* have the same facilities. * * *

We, therefore, grant defendants' motion for summary judgment.

NOTES

The State Action Doctrine

The prohibitions of the Fourteenth Amendment are directed against state action. This limitation has largely prevented its application to the acts of private individuals and private institutions. The departing line between state action and private action is at times vague, creating the danger that unconstitutional state action will be shielded by private immunity.

The status of "state action" doctrine as it relates to private universities is explained below by Hillman.*

Several theories have been advanced to find state action at private universities. The receipt of government funds, the public function of education, and state contacts with educational institutions have all been argued as bases for determining that the actions of private university administrators are subject to constitutional restraints.

The receipt of government funds was considered in *Grossner v. Trustees of Columbia University*.[1] There, student participants in sit-ins at Columbia University sued to enjoin disciplinary proceedings brought against them. They alleged jurisdiction under the Civil Rights Act of 1871 [2] and argued the presence of state action because, among other things, the University received government funds. The court did not accept this argument because the majority of the University's government income was federal; the small amount of money received solely from the state was found to be insufficient to make the University action state action. The court also pointed out that, in any case, receipt of government funds alone was insufficient to constitute state action.

Powe v. Miles [3] also dealt with this issue. There, a demonstration during a ROTC ceremony at Alfred University resulted in the suspension of seven students, four of whom were members of the University's private liberal arts school.[4]

---

* Quoted from Robert A. Hillman, "Admissibility of Evidence Seized by Private University Officials in Violation of Fourth Amendment Standards," *Cornell Law Review*, Vol. 56, pp. 509-513 (1971). *Reprinted with permission* (portions of footnotes have been deleted).

[1] 287 F. Supp. 535 (S.D.N.Y. 1968).

[2] REV. STAT § 1979 (1875), 42 U.S.C. § 1983 (1964).

[3] 407 F.2d 73 (2d Cir. 1968).

[4] The other three students, members of a state college at Alfred, were afforded constitutional protection. *Id.* at 82-83. The courts are unanimous in holding that public universities are subject to constitutional restraints. Note 13 *supra*.

These students, alleging violation of the Civil Rights Act of 1871, sought injunctions ordering Alfred University to reinstate them.[5] The court stated that the small amount of aid to the private college was "a long way from being so dominant as to afford basis for a contention that the state is merely utilizing private trustees to administer a state activity . . ."[6]

Browns v. Mitchell[7] also considered receipt of government funds as a basis for state action. In that case, students were also suspended, and brought class actions alleging that disciplinary action by the University of Denver was under color of state law and therefore must conform to Fourteenth Amendment due process requirements. The court considered the argument that since the University and its income-producing property were not taxed, it received the equivalent of a financial contribution from the state. Nevertheless, the court held that the money could not influence the administration of University affairs, and therefore government aid did not render the University disciplinary action equivalent to state action.

The receipt of government funds argument is weak because it proves too much. Government subsidies to other institutions would also render their activities state action. Thus, the test would result in almost all institutional activity being under color of state or federal law. Also, the amount of aid necessary to find state action would remain unclear if the test were adopted.

The public function of education has also been discussed in cases dealing with state action at private universities. In *Grossner,* the court dismissed the argument as being "without any basis":

> [P]laintiffs are correct in a trivial way when they say education is "impressed with a public interest." Many things are. And it may even be that action in some context or other by such a University as Columbia would be subject to limitations like those confining the State. But nothing supports the thesis that university . . . "education" as such is "state action."[8]

This argument was also rejected in *Powe.* The court rea-

---

[5] Relief was sought under 28 U.S.C. § 1343 (1964).

[6] 407 F.2d at 81.

[7] 409 F.2d 593 (10th Cir. 1969).

[8] 287 F. Supp. at 549. The court added that if the plaintiffs succeeded with this line of reasoning, "the very idea of a parochial school would be unthinkable." *Id.* n. 19.

soned that because the football field where the demonstration took place was not open to the public, but "was open only to persons connected with the University or licensed by it to participate in . . . [University] events," the public function argument was inapplicable.[9]

Such an argument proves too expansive because there are numerous other activities that are impressed with a "public interest." Their performance might have to be considered state action if the public function rationale were accepted.[10] Furthermore, as the *Grossner* court pointed out, if all education were state action, it would be difficult for private parochial schools to continue in existence because religious training at private institutions would be subject to the establishment clause of the first amendment.[11]

The third theory, state contracts with educational institutions, has provided the only approach that the courts have determined may lead to state action. However, the theory has been greatly refined by the courts. Instead of general contracts such as a charter from the state,[12] public officials on the board of trustees [13] or state regulation of educational standards,[14] the *Grossner* court said there must be specific involvement in the activity under constitutional attack.[15] Since, in that case, the state was not specifically involved in the disciplinary proceedings to which the suit was directed, there was no state action.[16]

The *Grossner* court pointed out that in *Burton v. Wilmington Parking Authority*,[17] the case relied upon by the plaintiffs, the critical involvement was in the very discriminatory action under constitutional challenge.[18] Thus, there was in *Burton* " 'that degree of state participation and involvement in discriminatory action which it was the design of the Fourteenth Amendment to condemn.' " [19] The *Grossner* court said,

---

[9] 407 F.2d at 80.

[10] *See* Schubert, *supra* note 14, at 333-34.

[11] *See* note 28 *supra*.

[12] On the question of whether a charter from the state should be sufficient to find state action, *see* Schubert, *supra* note 14, at 334-38.

[13] McLeod v. College of Artesia, 312 F. Supp. 498, 501 (D.N.M. 1970).

[14] Powe v. Miles, 407 F.2d 73, 81 (2d Cir. 1968) ; Schubert, *supra* note 14, at 338-40.

[15] 287 F. Supp. at 548.

[16] *Id.*

[17] 365 U.S. 715 (1961).

[18] 287 F. Supp. at 548.

[19] *Id., quoting* Burton v. Wilmington Parking Authority, 365 U.S. 715, 724 (1961).

however, that the "[p]laintiffs show nothing approximating
the requisite degree of 'state participation and involvement'
in *any* of the University's activities, let alone the specific proceedings in question. . . ." [20]

In *Powe,* the Second Circuit followed *Grossner's* reasoning.
The court said that the state's regulation of educational standards at private colleges and universities did not make Alfred's disciplinary action state action because "the state must
be involved not simply with some activity of the institution alleged to have inflicted injury upon a plaintiff but with the
activity that caused the injury." [21] Following a similar line of
reasoning the Tenth Circuit said in *Browns* that in order to
find state action at private universities, the state must have
" 'so insinuated itself' in the affairs of [the] private [u]ni-
versity as to be judicially 'recognized as a joint participant
in the challenged' disciplinary proceeding." [22]

The strength of the *Grossner* test is that by requiring state
involvement in the challenged activity it avcids the implication that all activity is infected with state action. The weakness of the test is that the degree of involvement necessary
for a finding of state action has not been spelled out by the
courts employing the test; the only indication of degree is
the *Browns* pronouncement that "joint participation" is essential. Nevertheless, the courts have made one aspect of the
test clear by requiring specific involvement in the activity
under attack and by rejecting other approaches.

---

[20] 287 F. Supp. at 549 (emphasis in original).

[21] 407 F.2d at 81.

[22] 409 F.2d at 595, *quoting* Burton v. Wilmington Parking Authority,
365 U.S. 715, 725 (1961). *See* also McLeod v. College of Artesia, 312 F.
Supp. 498 (D.N.M. 1970).

CHAPTER 9

RACIAL SEGREGATION IN HIGHER EDUCATION

The impact of racial segregation on education in the United States is well known. Racial policies discriminating against Negroes led to the creation of not only dual systems of elementary and secondary education but dual colleges and universities as well.

Even before the Constitution was adopted some states had already enacted anti-slavery legislation. The Constitution of Vermont in 1777 included a declaration of rights which provided that "no male person, born in this country, or brought from over sea, ought to be holden by law, to serve any person, as a servant, slave, or apprentice, after he arrives to the age of twenty-one years, nor female, in like manner, after she arrives at the age of eighteen years, unless they are bound by their own consent . . . ." The road from the first states abolition of slavery in 1777 to the integration of education in the 1970's, covers a long and stony path.

The slavery question was one of the many disputes which had to be settled before the thirteen colonies could agree on a Constitution for the United States. As originally adopted, the Constitution left each state to its own options in handling the question of slavery.[1] Unrestrained by the Constitution, each state continued on its chosen path regarding the question of slavery. From this *laissez faire* beginning the tradition and custom surrounding slavery began to develop, resulting in diverse legal precedents.[2] In view of the conditions of the time, the decisions by most courts probably seemed logical and just; today, however, in retrospect we are aware of their oppressive nature.

In the early 1800's, with slavery so prevalent and the issue of actual physical freedom being of primary importance, little attention was given to the educational overtones of the racial situation. Indeed, at that time, the concept of public education was not well established and there was very little sentiment for mass education regardless of race.

---

1. See Harold W. Horowitz and Kenneth L. Karst, *Law, Lawyers, and Social Change*, Bobbs-Merrill, 1969.
2. See Helen T. Catterall, *Judicial Cases Concerning American Slavery and the Negro*, 5 Volumes, Octagon Books, 1968.

SEPARATE BUT EQUAL

It was not until 1850 that the courts were confronted with the question of racial segregation in public education. The case occurred in Massachusetts, with the ironic result that a court in a northern state first propounded the doctrine of "separate but equal." Boston at that time maintained a system of racially segregated public schools. The Negroes in Boston, following a series of public meetings, submitted a petition, in 1844, asking the School Committee of Boston for the abolition of separate schools.[3] After the School Committee, in 1846, rejected another petition, Benjamin F. Roberts, a Negro, attempted to enroll his daughter in a white primary school. The child's enrollment was repeatedly rejected and Roberts retained Charles Sumner, later the fervent abolitionist United States Senator, along with a Negro lawyer to sue the City of Boston school officials.[4] Sumner argued that the separation of children in the public schools of Boston on account of color or race created a caste system and denied equality[5] as guaranteed by the Massachusetts Constitution. He further claimed that although the teachings of both a white and black school are precisely the same they are nevertheless not equivalent. Separate schools "exclusively devoted to one class must differ essentially, in its spirit and character, from that public school known to the law, where all classes meet together in equality."[6] The court, in holding for the defendants and creating the "separate but equal" doctrine, rather significantly said that the broad general principle that all persons are equal before the law suffers defect when applied to the diverse conditions of society. Expounding on this, Justice Shaw in speaking for the court said:

> But when this great principle [equality before the law] comes to be applied to the actual and various conditions of persons in society, it will not warrant the assertion, that men and women are clothed with the same civil and political powers, and that children and adults are legally to have the same functions and be subject to the same treatment; but only that the rights of all, as they are settled and regulated by law, are equally entitled to the paternal consideration and protection of law, for their

3. Quoted in A. Blaustein and R. Zangrando, *Civil Rights and the American Negro—A Documentary History*, pp. 111-112 (1968).

4. Levy and Phillips, "The Roberts Case: Source of the Separate but Equal Doctrine," 56 *Am. Hist. Rev.* 510 (1951).

5. Roberts v. City of Boston, 59 Mass. (5 Cush.) 198 (1850).

6. *Ibid.*

maintenance and security. What those rights are, to which individuals, in the infinite variety of circumstances by which they are surrounded in society, are entitled, must depend on laws adapted to their respective relations and conditions.[7]

In essence, Shaw makes the point that while all people are created equal under the law, because of societal and other reasons there can be reasonable classification of persons which are not violative of constitutional rights. Shaw did not feel that a segregated education was inimical to the individual's constitutional right. At least, he did not consider education to be a right which is essential to the "maintenance and security" of the individual.

The Civil War, the Emancipation Proclamation in 1863, and the Thirteenth Amendment to the Constitution in 1865 laid the groundwork for the all important Fourteenth Amendment. Except for the *Roberts* case in Boston, most of the racial controversy before the war dealt with the abolition of slavery. However, with the passage of the Fourteenth Amendment in 1868, there was established a new legal tool through which racial discrimination and segregation in voting, housing, employment, criminal justice and education could be attacked.

The plight of the Negro was not ended by the mere passage of the Fourteenth Amendment. Segregation by both government and the individual existed. Litwack [8] reviewed the situation:

> While statutes and customs circumscribed the Negro's political and judicial rights, extralegal codes—enforced by public opinion—relegated him to a position of social inferiority and divided northern society into "Brahmins and Pariahs." In virtually every phase of existence, Negroes found themselves systematically separated from whites. They were either excluded from railway cars, omnibuses, stagecoaches, and steamboats or assigned to special "Jim Crow" sections; they sat, when permitted, in secluded and remote corners of theaters and lecture halls; they could not enter most hotels, restaurants, and resorts, except as servants; they prayed in "Negro pews" in the white churches, and if partaking of the sacrament of the Lord's Supper, they waited until the whites had been served the bread and wine. Moreover, they were often educated in segregated schools, punished in segregated

---

7. *Ibid.*
8. L. Litwack, *North of Slavery: The Negro in the Free States 1790-1860*, p. 97 (Phoenix ed. 1965).

prisons, nursed in segregated hospitals, and buried in segregated cemeteries.

While Litwack here was speaking of the north before 1860, the statement is descriptive of the discrimination which occurred in many parts of the United States as late as 1954. The segregation in the north, however, did not end with the Civil War. As a matter of fact, state Supreme Courts in Ohio,[9] California,[10] Indiana,[11] New York,[12] and Missouri [13] upheld segregated schools after the Civil War.

On April 9, 1866, Congress passed a Civil Rights bill, over the veto of President Andrew Johnson, which gave Negroes equal rights in every aspect of the law. Johnson vetoed the bill because he felt the United States Constitution had not delegated the power to Congress to pass such an all encompassing law. The debate [14] over the scope of the constitutional power of Congress lead to the conclusion that the Constitution should be amended for the fourteenth time.[15] The Fourteenth Amendment became law in 1868. Section 1 provides:

> All persons born or naturalized in the United States, and subject to the jurisdiction thereof, are citizens of the United States and of the State wherein they reside. No State shall make or enforce any law which shall abridge the privileges or immunities of citizens of the United States; nor shall any State deprive any persons of life, liberty, or property, without due process of law; nor deny any person within its jurisdiction the equal protection of the laws.

After the Civil War the higher education opportunities for Negroes began to multiply. By 1870, such schools as Shaw University at Raleigh, Morehouse at Atlanta, Howard University at Washington, D. C., and Fisk University at Nashville, Tennessee, had been founded.[16] However, the "separate but equal" doctrine confined most Negroes to a segregated education. Slavery had been abolished, but segregation and discrimination were still very much present.

---

9. State *ex rel.* Garnes v. McCann, 21 Ohio St. 198 (1871).

10. Ward v. Flood, 48 Cal. 36 (1874).

11. Cory v. Carter, 48 Ind. 327 (1874).

12. People *ex rel.* King v. Gallagher, 93 N.Y. 438 (1883).

13. Lehew v. Brummel, 103 Mo. 546 (1890).

14. Alfred Avins (ed.), *The Reconstruction Amendments Debates*, The Legislative History and Contemporary Debates in Congress on the 13th, 14th, and 15th Amendments, Virginia Commission or Constitutional Government, 1967.

15. Horowitz and Karst, *op. cit.*, p. 124.

16. E. Franklin Frazier, *The Negro in the United States*, MacMillan, rev. ed. 1969, p. 452.

Jim Crow laws began to be adopted [17] as a southern back-lash against northern desegregation pressure. It was a result of one of these laws, segregating railroad passengers, that the "separate but equal" doctrine was embraced by the United States Supreme Court in the famous case of *Plessy v. Ferguson*. This decision laid the groundwork for Jim Crow laws which had such great impact, not only on education but on all American society.

> It was only after the *Plessy* decision that Jim Crow legislation was extended to every feature of southern public life; separate telephone booths for Negroes in Oklahoma; separate storage for textbooks used by black school children in North Carolina and Florida; separate elevators for black passengers in Atlanta; separate Bibles for swearing Negro witnesses in Georgia.[18]

In *Plessy v. Ferguson*, the Supreme Court was called upon to determine whether a Louisiana law segregating railroad passengers violated the equal protection clause of the Fourteenth Amendment. The argument reduced itself to essentially the same question as was brought in *Roberts v. City of Boston*, except in that case, only the free and equal provision of the Massachusetts Constitution was at stake. The Supreme Court, in *Plessy*, had in its grasp the factual situation which would set judicial precedent and decide the fate of the Negro for over one-half a century. Justice Brown writing for the majority, saw the case as resting on the question of what constitutes reasonable regulation under the Fourteenth Amendment:

> So far, then, as a conflict with the Fourteenth Amendment is concerned, the case reduces itself to the question whether the statute of Louisiana is a reasonable regulation, and with respect to this, there must necessarily be a large discretion on the part of the legislature. In determining the question of reasonableness it is at liberty to act with reference to the established usages, customs and traditions of the people, and with a view to the promotion of their comfort, and the preservation of the public peace and good order. Gauged by this standard, we cannot say that a law which authorizes or even requires the separation of the two races in public conveyances is unreasonable, or more obnoxious to the Fourteenth Amendment than the acts of Congress requiring separate schools for colored children in the District of Columbia,

17. See Pauli Murray (ed.), *States' Laws on Race and Color*, Woman's Division of Christian Service, The Methodist Church, 1950.
18. Horowitz and Karst, *op. cit.*, p. 130.

the constitutionality of which does not seem to have been
questioned, or the corresponding acts of state legislatures.[19]

Further, Justice Brown cited the *Roberts* case as evidence
that the "separate but equal" doctrine had been established in
states with very liberal attitudes toward the rights of Negroes. The specific interpretation of the meaning of the Fourteenth Amendment and its application to "separate but
equal," the Court resolved in this fashion.

> The object of the amendment was undoubtedly to en-
> force the absolute equality of the two races before the
> law, but in the nature of things it could not have been
> intended to abolish distinctions based upon color, or to
> enforce social, as distinguished from political equality,
> or a commingling of the two races upon terms unsatis-
> factory to either. Laws permitting, and even requiring,
> their separation in places where they are liable to be
> brought into contact do not necessarily imply the infer-
> iority of either race to the other, and have been gen-
> erally, if not universally, recognized as within the com-
> petency of the state legislatures in the exercise of their
> police power. The most common instance of this is con-
> nected with the establishment of separate schools for
> white and colored children, which has been held to be a
> valid exercise of the legislative power even by courts
> of states where the political rights of the colored race
> have been longest and most earnestly enforced.[20]

Mr. Justice Harlan dissented, saying that the very purpose of separate accommodations was to exclude the black
man from association with the white. The white man in the
United States is the dominant race in prestige, achievements,
education, wealth and power, but in the view of the Constitution there is no dominant or ruling class. The Constitution is
"color blind" and will not tolerate the creation of classes or
castes of people. Harlan was aware of the consequences of
the court's decision and predicted, "In my opinion, the judgment this day rendered will, in time, prove to be quite as
pernicious as the decision made by this tribunal in the *Dred
Scott* case." [21]

LITIGATION LEADING TO BROWN

Only three years had passed following *Plessy* when the
Supreme Court was asked to begin clarification of what it

19. Plessy v. Ferguson, 163 U.S. 537 (1896).
20. Plessy v. Ferguson, 163 U.S. 537 (1896).
21. *Ibid.*

meant by "separate but equal" in education. In *Cumming v. Richmond County Board of Education*,[22] Negro parents and taxpayers sued to enjoin the school board of Richmond, Georgia, from maintaining a high school for white children while not maintaining one for Negroes. The board had previously maintained a Negro high school but had, due to a serious shortage of facilities, decided to temporarily convert the Negro high school into four Negro primary schools. The schools were supported from general tax funds supplemented by tuition of ten dollars per year per child for black children and fifteen dollars per year per child for white children. The school board justified its decision to do away with the Negro high school on the grounds that "it would be unwise and unconscionable to keep up a high school for 60 pupils and turn away 300 little Negroes who are asking to be taught their alphabet and to read and write. No part of the funds of this board accrued or accruing and no property appropriated to education of the Negro race has been taken from them."[23] The Georgia Supreme Court ordered the case dismissed. The Negroes appealed to the Supreme Court to enjoin the board from closing the high school and argued denial of equal protection, once again to no avail. The Supreme Court, with Justice Harlan this time writing for the majority did not expand on its interpretation of "separate but equal." The court decided the question on the narrow grounds of the relief sought in the injunction, which in the court's opinion would "either impair the efficiency of the high school provided for white children or compel the board to close it."[24] The Supreme Court took the view that the desired relief would not enhance the position of the Negro school children and would result in educational privileges being taken from white children. The case, therefore, added very little to clarification of the *Plessy* case. It did though, apparently, make very clear that separate meant just that, and a board of education apparently had no duty to increase educational opportunity for the Negro child if it required a reduction in opportunity for the white child or if it meant an equalizing of expenditures between the two.

The *de jure* separatism instituted by legislatures and permitted by the Supreme Court continued and permeated the educational structures of southern and border states. *Plessy*

22. 175 U.S. 528 (1899).
23. *Ibid.*
24. *Ibid.*

and *Cumming* clearly established that public schools could be segregated, but there was no precedent regarding the segregation status of private schools. In 1908 a Kentucky case involving state mandated segregation of a private institution of higher education gained nationwide attention. The 1904 Kentucky legislature enacted the "Day Law" [25] which prohibited the operation of any college, school or institution where both Negroes and whites received instruction. Berea, a private college, was the only college in the state at that time which was integrated; black and white students alike attended and associated in classrooms, dining halls, dormitories and playgrounds. The school had 962 students of which 157 were Negro. President Frost of Berea maintained that the integration policies of Berea as a mixed school was a valuable object lesson to both races.[26] Berea, in the fall of 1904, set up a class of both Negro and white students deliberately violating the law, resulting in a grand jury indictment against the college. Appeals began which would ultimately lead to the Supreme Court. Lawyers for the college maintained that the Legislature of Kentucky exceeded its powers in enacting the law and violated both the First and Fourteenth Amendments of the federal Constitution. The Kentucky Court of Appeals upheld the constitutionality of the law [27] and the College appealed to the United States Supreme Court. In 1907, before the Supreme Court, the college again maintained that the state had exercised "absolute arbitrary power over the lives, liberty and property of the people." [28] The Attorney General of Kentucky defended, claiming the law was a reasonable exercise of the state's police power. The Supreme Court upheld the validity of the law and centered its decision around the rights of the college corporation, not the individual. Justice Brewer commented "A corporation is not entitled to all the immunities to which individuals are entitled, and a state may withhold from its corporations privileges and powers to which it cannot constitutionally deprive individuals." [29]

25. Richard A. Heckman and Betty J. Hall, "Berea College and the Day Law," *The Register*, Kentucky Historical Society, January 1968, pp. 35-52; named the "Day Law" after a Representative Day who introduced the bill.
26. *Ibid.*
27. The court did set aside one provision of the law which prohibited the setting up of a branch of the college within 25 miles of the main campus. This provision had been added by the legislature to prevent establishing white and black campuses in close proximity to each other.
28. *Ibid.*
29. Berea College v. Commonwealth of Kentucky, 211 U.S. 45 (1908).

Justice Harlan, just as he had done in *Plessy*, vigorously dissented, saying that the law was an "arbitrary invasion of the rights of liberty and property guaranteed by the Fourteenth Amendment against hostile state action and is therefore, void." [30]

Harlan, himself a Kentuckian, commented further:

> Have we become so inoculated with prejudice of race that an American government, professedly based on the principles of freedom and charged with the protection of all citizens alike, can make distinctions between such citizens in the manner of their involuntary meeting for innocent purposes simply because of their respective races? [31]

The law remained on the books and was enforced until April 1950, when legislative amendment permitted integration of the private colleges throughout Kentucky.

The separation of races in the United States extended not only to black and white but to yellow, brown and red as well. The segregation cycle was completed in *Gong Lum v. Rice* in 1927,[32] when the United States Supreme Court held that states could segregate children of the Caucasian race from children of not only the black race but yellow and brown races as well. Martha Lum of the Mongolian or yellow race claimed denial of equal protection when she was assigned to a black school in Mississippi. The Supreme Court held that the issue was no different whether the state segregated white from black or white from yellow. The state was not unreasonable in segregating the races and the exercise of this discretion by the state did not violate the "equal protection clause" of the Fourteenth Amendment.

Segregation of the *Gong Lum* type existed in many states, both in and out of the south. It was not until 1947 that a statute in California was repealed which provided for exclusion from school districts of:

> . . . children of filthy or vicious habits, or children suffering from contagious or infectious diseases, and also to establish separate schools for Indian children and for children of Chinese, Japanese or Mongolian parentage . . . .[33]

---

30. *Ibid.*
31. *Ibid.*
32. 275 U.S. 78 (1927).
33. Cal. Stat., 1921, ch. 685, p. 1160; repealed in 1947, Cal. Stat., 1947, ch. 737, p. 1792, § 1. See Westminister School District of Orange County v. Mendez, 161 F.2d 774 (9th Cir. 1947); Horowitz and Karst, *op. cit.*, pp. 161-162.

Although the doctrine was "separate but equal," little was said or done by the courts to establish what in fact constituted "equal." States were generally left to their own devices in interpreting what quality of education was necessary in separate schools to meet constitutional requirements. Most states embracing and following the "separate but equal" course were very careful to "separate" the schools, but paid little if any attention to the "equal" provision of the phrase. Great variations existed in length of school year, expenditures and services available between black and white schools in elementary and secondary as well as higher education.[34]

Most southern states did not provide separate facilities for Negro students at the graduate or professional school level. Instead of providing such opportunities for Negroes within the state, southern legislatures usually made scholarships available to Negro students to attend graduate or professional schools outside the state. Inevitably, the question was to arise as to the constitutionality of this practice. Negro students, in order to receive a desirable education, were forced either to commute long distances to schools in other states or to move their residences. The constitutionality of this method of segregation was met by the Court of Appeals of Maryland in 1936.[35] A Negro student living in Baltimore was denied admission to the University of Maryland Law School which was in Baltimore. The State of Maryland provided scholarships for black students to attend law school outside the state; generally this meant attendance at Howard University in Washington, D. C., some 35 miles distant from Baltimore. Morgan College, the state Negro institution, had no law school. The court observed that to be consistent with the requirements of the Fourteenth Amendment the state cannot defer its responsibility to provide "separate but equal" legal education. Since the Maryland legislature had evidenced no intention to establish a Negro law school within the state, the court had no alternative but to require the lone state law school to admit the Negro applicant. The court said:

> The case as we find it, then, is that the state has undertaken the function of education in the law, but has omitted students of one race from the only adequate provision made for it, and omitted them solely because of

34. L. Harlan, *Separate and Unequal: Public School Campaigns and Racism in the Southern Seaboard States, 1901-1915*, at 208, 257 (rev. ed. 1968); Horowitz and Karst, *op. cit.*, pp. 162-163.

35. Pearson *et al.* v. Murray, 182 A. 590 (1936).

their color. If those students are to be offered equal treatment in the performance of the function, they must, at present, be admitted to the one school provided.

Two years later, in 1938, in the *Gaines* case the United States Supreme Court was brought squarely to face the definition of "equal" as had the Maryland Court. What was the minimum that a state could provide and be in compliance with the "equal" portion of the *Plessy* doctrine? The precise issue arose over whether the University of Missouri could be compelled to accept a Negro into the University's law school.[36] As in Maryland, a Missouri statute provided tuition for Negro students to attend universities in adjacent states if the preferred courses of study were not offered within the state at Lincoln University, the Missouri state university for Negroes. Lincoln University had no law school and a Negro student did not want to attend school in an adjacent state. The state courts denied relief to the plaintiff, but the United States Supreme Court reversed. Justice Hughes writing for the majority acknowledged that the validity of furnishing equal facilities had been sustained by the court; however, he pointed out that no previous decision had permitted states to force students to go beyond the borders of the state in seeking equal education.

> The admissibility of laws separating the races in the enjoyment of privileges by the state rests wholly upon the equality of the privileges which the laws give to the separated groups within the state.

The Supreme Court, therefore, established the minimal parameters that equal facilities must be offered within the state. Reacting to this decision, the legislature of Missouri in its next session enacted a statute making it mandatory that the Curators of Lincoln University organize the university "so that it shall afford to the Negro people of the state opportunity for training up to the standard furnished at the State University of Missouri." [37]

The *Gaines* decision was the first hint that the Supreme Court would not allow states total freedom in deciding the nature and extent of education to be provided Negroes. This case established that there were constitutional boundaries

---

36. Missouri *ex rel.* Gaines v. Canada, 305 U.S. 337 (1938). See also Sipuel v. Board of Regents of University of Oklahoma, 332 U.S. 631, 68 S. Ct. 299 (1948); Fisher v. Hurst, 333 U.S. 147, 68 S. Ct. 389 (1948).

37. Mo. Rev. Stat. § 10774 (1939). See Horowitz and Karst, *op. cit.*, pp. 163-164.

within which a state must operate. However, it was not until 1950 that the true legal tests of segregation began. The need for a higher education had become quite common among whites and blacks alike and it soon became evident, just as it had in the *Gaines* case, that states were not financially equipped to provide Negroes with "separate but equal" education at either the undergraduate or graduate levels.

In Delaware, in 1950, a permanent injunction was granted restraining the Board of Trustees of the University of Delaware from refusing to receive and consider applications from Negroes applying for admission to the undergraduate college of arts and sciences.[38] The state court of chancery rested its decision on the idea that separate facilities must be equal and found from the evidence that there was no Negro state school in Delaware which could provide an education in arts and sciences commensurate with the University of Delaware. In fact, the only state-supported Negro college was so markedly inferior that the court decided the only way to afford the Negroes equal protection was to accept them to the University.

Although the Delaware case did not go to the United States Supreme Court, two other very similar cases reaching the same conclusion were handed down by the Supreme Court in the same year. These cases from Texas and Oklahoma both dealt with the primary question: "To what extent does the Equal Protection Clause of the Fourteenth Amendment limit the power of a state to distinguish between students of different races in professional and graduate education in a state university?" In the Texas case, *Sweatt v. Painter*,[39] the facts were similar to *Gaines* in that the state did not offer "separate but equal" facilities for Negro law students. In *Gaines* there was no law school within the state of Missouri and the court's mandate was met by the state legislature establishing legal training facilities at Lincoln University. Here in *Sweatt*, however, the separate facility was created but the Negro student refused to register in it, claiming the school was not equal to the University of Texas Law School to which he sought admission. The Supreme Court found from the evidence that the University of Texas Law School had sixteen full-time and three part-time professors, some of whom were nationally recognized, a student body of 850, a library containing 65,000 volumes, a law review, moot court facili-

---

38. Parker v. University of Delaware, 31 Del. Ch. 381, 75 A.2d 225 (1950).
39. 339 U.S. 629 (1950).

ties, and scholarship funds. On the other hand, the court found that the hurriedly contrived law school for Negroes had no independent faculty or library. The faculty was comprised of four University of Texas law professors who would teach at both schools. The school was not accredited. The court concluded that there really was no question as to the inequalities between the schools. In holding that the Equal Protection Clause required the student be admitted to the University of Texas Law School, the court said that in determination of "equality" one must look beyond the number of faculty, size of library, availability of a law review and similar activities and examine such qualities as faculty reputation, position and influence of alumni, standing in community, traditions and prestige.[40]

The court had become increasingly aware of the flaws in the doctrine of "separate but equal," and in *Sweatt*, first attempted to define the term "equal." The court now let it be known that it was no longer of the disposition to give the states unrestrained freedom in setting up separate educational programs. Whether the state's action is unreasonable would be determined by the yardstick of equality laid down by the court. With such broad language as position, influence, tradition, and prestige, the court was serving notice that broad perspective would be taken of the "separate but equal" doctrine. This was an important evolutionary step in the court's thinking.

During the same session in the case of *McLaurin v. Oklahoma State Regents for Higher Education*,[41] the Supreme Court expanded equal protection to require equal treatment of Negroes once they were actually enrolled in a white university. The state legislature of Oklahoma had allowed Negroes to attend white universities in the absence of available courses at Negro schools. However, the course of study in the white school, to which the Negro was accepted, must be conducted on a segregated basis. The Supreme Court held that such setting apart of the student violated the equal protection of the Fourteenth Amendment. The reasoning of the court in expanding the rights of the Negro had progressed about as far as possible without contesting the entire "separate but equal" doctrine. The doctrine had run the gamut from little or no judicial intervention with states' exercise

---

40. *Ibid.*
41. 339 U.S. 637 (1950).

of police power in segregating the races to the establishment of rather elaborate criteria of what constituted equal education and equal treatment.

THE BROWN CASE (The End of "Separate but Equal")

As is shown to some extent in the foregoing cases, there was a gradual building up of a collective disenchantment with the entire notion of separate but equal. Studies were made and books were written condemning the position of the courts. At one border state university as early as 1946, only 22 percent of the faculty opposed the removal of all segregating restrictions at the university level.[42] In 1934 the National Association for the Advancement of Colored People began "a campaign of legal action and public education against unequal apportionment of public funds for education . . . ."[43]

One strategy of the NAACP was to encourage taxpayer suits in such numbers, forcing truly equal accommodations, so as to make dual school systems fiscally prohibitive. Short of all-out abrogation of "separate but equal" the NAACP hoped to focus public attention upon the vicious discrimination which existed in the distribution of public funds between white and black schools.[44] Substantial sentiment existed on the part of prominent desegregation proponents that the strategy of the NAACP should be to support an all-out attack on the fundamental concept of "separate but equal." They voted for returning to the original argument of Sumner in *Roberts v. City of Boston* which denied the validity of "separate but equal" altogether. That is, "separate but equal" is inherently unequal. In grasping for legal straws it was claimed that argument could be made, based on *Yick Wo v. Hopkins,*[45] a much earlier case, that segregation coupled with arbitrary administrative power to discriminate, permitted by statute, was a denial of equal protection. However, this specific argument did not significantly materialize until *Sweatt,* where plaintiffs maintained specifically that governmentally imposed segregation was in and of itself a violation of the individual's rights under the Equal Protection Clause.

42. Harry S. Ashmore, *The Negro and the Schools*, Chapel Hill, 1954, pp. 42-43.

43. 1934 *NAACP Annual Report 22.* See J. Greenberg, *Race Relations and American Law*, Columbia University Press, New York, 1959, pp. 35-39.

44. Greenberg, *op. cit.*

45. 118 U.S. 356 (1886).

Greenberg notes that graduate and professional schools first became the target of the NAACP drive for equality.

> The reasoning behind this attack appears to have been that inequality in higher education could be proved with ease. There were virtually no public Negro graduate and professional schools in the South, and judges would readily understand the shortcomings of separate legal education, which some of the cases concerned.[46]

This emphasis on higher education resulted in the precedents established by *Gaines*, *Sweatt*, and *McLaurin*. The NAACP blueprint eventually lead to the precedent shattering *Brown* cases.

In 1952 the precedent which had set the tone of segregation decisions since 1849 was directly confronted. The United States Supreme Court had before it five cases which contested "separate but equal." NAACP lawyers represented the plaintiffs in all but one of the five cases. The NAACP summed up its position in bringing the cases.

> At ultimate stake is the future of the anachronistic system of segregation not only in education but also in all other phases of public life in the nation. We of the NAACP have long maintained that segregation is a divisive and anti-democratic device designed to perpetuate an obsolete caste system which flatly contravenes the basic ethical concepts of our Judaeo-Christian tradition. We have held that segregation *per se* is unconstitutional. Should the Court uphold this point of view it could mean that all laws requiring or permitting racial segregation in schools, transportation, recreation, shelter, and public accommodations generally would ultimately be invalid.
>
> When Thurgood Marshall and the other NAACP lawyers associated with him address the nine justices of the country's highest tribunal . . . they will contend, at least by implication, that integration cannot be a half-way measure. Our nation cannot remain half-integrated and half-segregated today any more than it could continue half-free and half-slave a century ago.[47]

The five cases were first argued before the Supreme Court in December 1952, and one year later the court was still collecting oral and written arguments and documenting its future position. The five cases before the court, from four states and the District of Columbia—*Briggs v. Elliott* (South Caro-

---

46. Greenberg, *op. cit.*
47. Harry Ashmore, *op. cit.*, pp. 95-96.

lina) ; [48] *Brown v. Board of Education of Topeka* (Kansas) ; [49] *Davis v. County School Board of Prince Edward County* (Virginia) ; [50] *Gebhart v. Belton* (Delaware) ; [51] and *Bolling v. Sharp* (District of Columbia) [52]—viewed the basic issue of segregation in slightly different contexts.

Miller describes what transpired: [53]

Loren Miller, The Petitioners 344-46 (1967)

There was more to this carefully stage-managed selection of cases for review than meets the naked eye. The Kansas case concerned grade-school children in a northern state with a permissive segregation statute; the Virginia case involved high-school students in a state having compulsory laws and located in the upper tier of southern states; South Carolina represented the Deep South, and Delaware the border states. The state cases all presented the issue of the application of the equal-protection-of-law clause of the Fourteenth Amendment, and the Court could have reached and decided that question in any one of them, but the wide geographical range gave the anticipated decision a national flavor and would blunt any claim that the South was being made a whipping boy. Moreover, the combination of cases included Kansas with its permissive statute, while other cases concerned the state constitutional provisions as well as statutes with mandatory segregation requirements. Grade-school students were involved in the Kansas case; high-school students in the Virginia case, and all elementary and secondary students in the Delaware and South Carolina cases. The District of Columbia case drew due process of law into the cases as an issue, in distinction to the equal-protection-of-law clause, and also presented an opportunity for inquiry into the congressional power to impose racial segregation. The NAACP had touched all bases.

Initial arguments were made on December 9, 1952, two-and-a-half years after the *Sweatt* decision. But the Court reached no decision on the basis of the first briefs and arguments. On June 8, 1953, it issued an order setting the case for reargument that fall, submitting a series of questions to the litigants, and inviting the United States Attorney General to participate in the arguments.

48. 98 F. Supp. 529 (E.D.S.C. 1951), *vacated and remanded with directions*, 342 U.S. 350, *reaff'd on rehearing*, 103 F. Supp. 920 (E.D.S.C.), *probable jurisdiction noted*, 72 S. Ct. 1078 (1952).

49. 98 F. Supp. 797 (D. Kan. 1951), *probable jurisdiction noted*, 72 S. Ct. 1070 (1952).

50. 103 F. Supp. 337 (E.D. Va.), *probable jurisdiction noted*, 344 U.S. 1 (1952).

51. 91 A.2d 137 (Del.), *cert. granted*, 344 U.S. 891 (1952).

52. No. 11,018 (D.C. Cir.), *cert. granted*, 344 U.S. 873 (1952).

53. Reprinted from Horowitz and Karst, *op. cit.*, pp. 181-182, copyright 1969, by Bobbs-Merrill Company, Inc. Reprinted by permission. All rights reserved.

The Court's first question asked what evidence there was that the Congress which submitted and the states which ratified the Fourteenth Amendment contemplated that the amendments would abolish school segregation. It then asked whether Congress had the power to abolish all school segregation, regardless of whether the framers or ratifying states believed that the amendment required its immediate abolition, and what was the reach of the Court's power under those circumstances. Its third inquiry was the extent of the Court's power to abolish school segregation in the event that the answers to the first two questions were inconclusive. The fourth question was that of whether a decree favoring the Negro plaintiffs would carry with it an order directing their immediate admission to state-supported schools or whether the Court could devise a gradualistic scheme for their enrollment—a very obvious, and very curious, inquiry as to whether the rights of Negro grade-school students to attend public schools were *personal and present* (as all constitutional rights are) or whether their exercise could be delayed until a more propitious time. The fifth question concerned the form the decree should take, if the Court decided on a gradualistic abolition of segregation.

Thurgood Marshall, counsel and director of the NAACP Legal Defense & Educational Fund, convoked sessions of lawyers, law school professors, and historians from all over the nation to help find answers to the Court's questions and to fashion briefs and arguments. The hard-pressed states hired John W. Davis, one-time Democratic candidate for the presidency of the United States and one of the nation's leading constitutional lawyers, to head an imposing array of counsel.

Reargument began on December 8, 1953, and continued for three days. Then the Court took all of the cases under submission for later decision.

Of course, the primary and all important issue was how the Court itself viewed the intent of the Fourteenth Amendment and what position it would take toward the sovereign right of states to set their own policies in such matters. In this matter, the Court was confronted with a lack of precedent. Could the Court summarily pronounce the end of "separate but equal" if all precedent was contrary to such a decision? In addition to these encompassing questions, the Court had several alternatives as to the judicial position it could take.

Alternatives [54] ranged from upholding *Plessy* without change to flatly declaring segregation unconstitutional. The

54. Leflar and Davis in 1954 listed eleven positions the Court might take, but acknowledged that some were highly improbable and that others could be combined. "Segregation in The Public Schools — 1953," 67 *Harvard Law Review* 377, 387-92 (1954).

primary alternatives which were within the realm of possibility were listed by Ashmore.[55]

    1. That there was no need to rule on the constitutionality of segregation *per se,* since each case might be disposed of on other grounds. (The Supreme Court had repeatedly declared that it would not rule on questions of a constitutional nature if a case could be decided by any other means.)

    2. That the "separate but equal" doctrine was still the law, and when the separate facilities were unequal the Court would allow a reasonable period for the facilities to be made equal in fact.

    3. That the "separate but equal" doctrine was still the law, but when separate facilities were unequal the Court would require immediate admission of Negroes to the white schools pending the achievement of actual equality of facilities.

    4. That the "separate but equal" doctrine was still the law, but the Court might require non-segregation in certain phases of public education which it deemed impossible of equality within the separate framework. (In other words, the Court might conceivably hold that a particular course or activity could not be provided equally under segregation, as it had at least implied in the higher education cases.)

    5. That whether segregation in a given case was a denial of equal protection of the laws was a question of fact, to be decided as are other questions of fact in the lower trial court.

    6. That segregation was unconstitutional; the Court recognized the need for orderly progress of transition to non-segregation; but the Court would limit itself to minimum personal relief of the plaintiffs, leaving to Congress the job of legislating detailed rules for implementing desegregation in the schools generally. (This would be in keeping with the idea that the administration of local school systems involves a "political question.")

    7. That "separate but equal" was a clear denial of equal protection of the laws and thus unconstitutional; but the Court would permit a gradual change-over to a non-segregated system under the supervision of the District Courts, or under the direction of a master appointed by the Supreme Court itself.

    8. That "separate but equal" was unconstitutional and must be ended immediately; Negro plaintiffs in the cases before the Court must be admitted at once to the white schools.

Everyone is aware how the Court decided, "We conclude that in the field of public education the doctrine of 'separate

---

55. Harry S. Ashmore, *op. cit.,* pp. 107-108.

but equal' has no place. Separate educational facilities are inherently unequal." [56]

Pollak [57] commented on the decision: "Except for waging and winning the Civil War and World Wars I and II, the decision in the *School Segregation Cases* was probably the most important American governmental act of any kind since the Emancipation Proclamation." Without exaggeration, the decision has had more impact on public education in the United States than any other development in American history.

The decision was immediately and jointly attacked by ninety-six southern Congressmen: ". . . The decision of the Supreme Court in the school cases . . . [is] clear abuse of judicial power. . . . The Original Constitution does not mention education. Neither does the Fourteenth Amendment or any other amendment . . . ." [58]

Charges that the Court had exceeded its judicial authority, by legislating instead of adjudicating, were lodged and are still maintained. There is little doubt that this decision was the watershed on which the Warren Court became famous as the "activist court." The Court did, in fact, forge ahead and assume the responsibility for establishing desirable social as well as judicial precedent. In the absence of favorable judicial precedent, the court relied on sociology, psychology and what it intuitively considered to be the appropriate standard of moral human behavior to justify its conclusion.

> The Court was simply making a judgment about the dominant moral values of the American community, values which have altered in substantial measure since *Plessy* was decided in 1896. Weighing such moral values is an accredited, indeed essential, part of constitutional adjudication.[59]

DESEGREGATION OF HIGHER EDUCATION AFTER BROWN

As pointed out above, one of the primary questions facing the Court was how to make desegregation work. Should the Court permit gradual desegregation rather than immediate

56. Brown v. Board of Education, 347 U.S. 483 (1954).

57. Louis H. Pollak, *The Constitution and the Supreme Court, A Documentary History*, Vol. II, The World Publishing Company, 1966, p. 266.

58. James Morton Smith and Paul L. Murphy (eds.), *Liberty and Justice: A Historical Record of American Constitutional Development*, Knopf, New York, 1958, p. 562.

59. Pollak, *op. cit.*, pp. 266-267.

changeover in states which exercised dual enrollment laws. The Court resolved this question in the second *Brown* case [60] in 1955 which produced the famous "all deliberate speed" criterion for desegregation.

The long road of defining and redefining the intent of the Court began immediately. Several states announced intentions to defy the Court, and the courts, especially in the south, began to wage an inch by inch battle to enforce the mandate of the Court. The speed with which desegregation was accomplished was certainly not "all deliberate" in elementary, secondary or higher education.

The series of confrontations began almost immediately with an appeal from Autherine J. Lucy, a young Negro woman who sought to enter the University of Alabama. She had been refused admission in 1952 and now sought a court order admitting her to the University. In 1955, the University was ordered to admit her and she began school on February 1, 1956. Miss Lucy had no more begun school than disturbances broke out protesting her admission, and much publicity ensued. After a few days, the Board of Trustees required her to withdraw from school on the grounds that her continued presence would endanger herself and other students. She filed a motion with the federal district court asking that the University officials be held in contempt of court. Her petition stated that her suspension was a "cunning stratagem for denying her right to attend and pursue courses of study at the University of Alabama." The Court denied the petition and found that "the action which the Trustees and officials took to protect her and others from bodily harm was not taken in defiance of the court's injunction, but was taken in good faith." Following the court test, the Board of Trustees of Alabama adopted a resolution to permanently expel Autherine Lucy for her "defamatory, impertinent and scandalous charges" against University authorities and trustees.[61]

Other decisions shortly followed which illustrated the resistance to which desegregation would be confronted in years to come. The University of North Carolina had to be compelled to accept Negro students to undergraduate programs. In the Spring of 1955, three Negro youths were denied admission to the University, the policy of the school being to accept qualified Negroes to only graduate and professional courses. The

---

60. Brown v. Board of Education, 349 U.S. 294 (1955).

61. Lucy v. Adams, 134 F. Supp. 235 (N.D. Ala. 1955), *aff'd*, 228 F.2d 619 (3d Cir. 1955), *cert. denied*, 351 U.S. 931 (1956).

students appealed to the courts and a federal district court ordered the University to admit the students.[62] The Board of Trustees of the University appealed to the United States Supreme Court maintaining that the *Brown* decision did not apply to higher education. The basis of the Trustees' argument was that the *Brown* case mandated desegregation because of the tendency of segregation to retard the educational and mental development of Negro children *not adults*.[63] The Supreme Court did not agree with this contention and affirmed the federal district court decision admitting the students.[64]

The College of Law of the University of Florida denied admission to Negroes before *Brown* and continued to resist afterwards. In 1949, Virgil D. Hawkins first applied for admission to law school at the University of Florida in Gainesville, but was denied admission by the Florida Supreme Court pending the establishment of "separate but equal" law facility at Florida Agricultural and Mechanical University at Tallahassee.[65]

Since the Florida Supreme Court retained jurisdiction to determine if the facility at Florida A. and M. was to be equal, the United States Supreme Court denied *certiorari* "for want of a final judgment." Justices Douglas and Black dissented.[66]

Hawkins tried again by appealing for an original writ of *mandamus* to compel his admission and again the Florida Supreme Court gave him no relief, finding no evidence was offered as to the equality of the Florida A. and M. Law School. By this time the judicial picture had changed and the *Brown* case had been decided. The United States Supreme Court now granted *certiorari*, vacated the judgment of the Florida court, and remanded the case "for consideration in the light of the segregation cases and the conditions that now prevail." [67]

Reacting to the order of the Supreme Court, the Florida Supreme Court appointed a commissioner to take testimony on the University's defense and report to the court within four months. For the third time, appeal was made to the

---

62. Frasier v. Board of Trustees, 134 F. Supp. 589 (M.D.N.C. 1955).
63. See Thomas E. Blackwell, *College Law*, American Council on Education, 1961, p. 114.
64. Board of Trustees v. Frasier, 350 U.S. 979 (1956).
65. State *ex rel.* Hawkins v. Board of Control of Florida, 47 So. 2d 608 (1950).
66. 53 So. 2d 116 (Fla. 1951), *cert. denied*, 342 U.S. 877, 72 S. Ct. 166, 96 L. Ed. 659 (1951).
67. 60 So. 2d 162 (Fla. 1952), *vacated and remanded*, 347 U.S. 971, 74 S. Ct. 783, 98 L. Ed. 1112 (May 24, 1954).

United States Supreme Court. This time the Court recalled and vacated its previous mandate to the lower court "to consider in light of segregation cases." The Court said:

> On May 24, 1954, we issued a mandate in this case to the Supreme Court of Florida. We directed that the case be reconsidered in light of our decision in the Segregation Cases. . . . In doing so, we did not imply that decrees involving graduate study present the problems of public elementary and secondary schools. We had theretofore, in three cases, ordered the admission of Negro applicants to graduate schools without discrimination because of color. *Sweatt v. Painter*, 329, U.S. 629; *Sipuel v. Board of Regents of the University of Oklahoma*, 332 U.S. 631; *McLaurin v. Oklahoma State Regents for Higher Education*, 339 U.S. 637. Thus, our second decision in the *Brown* case, 349 U.S. 294 [Brown II, 1955, "all deliberate speed" case], which implemented the earlier one, had no application to a case involving a Negro applying for admission to a state law school. Accordingly, the mandate of May 25, 1954, is recalled and is vacated. In lieu thereof, the following order is entered: . . . As this case involves the admission of a Negro to a graduate professional school, there is no reason for delay. He is entitled to prompt admission under the rules and regulations applicable to other qualified candidates.[68]

The United States Supreme Court had thus reconsidered its earlier decision and changed its mind. It was now clear that higher education would not be viewed in the same light as elementary and secondary schools. The time delays and transitional benefits afforded by the "all deliberate speed" provision would not be generally applicable to colleges and universities. However, the Florida Supreme Court was not yet to the end of its string of legal devices and, in the next round, it denied Hawkins' peremptory writ, without prejudice, allowing petitioner the right to renew his motion when he was able to show that his admission to the University would not cause "great public mischief." [69] The court was relying on the supposition, as did the Alabama court in *Lucy*,[70] that denial of admission was not unconstitutional if admitting the student would impair the safety of the individual and the University. Justices Thomas and Drew of the Florida court dissented, with Drew saying "Justice delayed is justice denied." This time the United States Supreme Court denied

---

68. Florida *ex rel.* Hawkins v. Board of Control of Florida, 350 U.S. 413 (March 12, 1956).
69. 93 So. 2d 354 (Fla. 1957).
70. Lucy v. Adams, *supra.*

certiorari, without prejudice to the plaintiffs seeking redress in a federal district court." [71]

Finally on June 18, 1958, the long drawn-out affair was in the United States District Court in Tallahassee, Florida, where Judge DeVane held that the University could be enjoined from arbitrarily denying admission to a Negro, but the prospective student could not be admitted unless he furnished evidence of his eligibility.[72] A check of the records indicates that Hawkins was never admitted to the University of Florida Law School. His admission was denied purportedly for reasons other than race. The same year, however, the University of Florida Law School accepted another Negro student in its freshman class.

In spite of cases with unhappy endings such as *Lucy* and *Hawkins,* new inroads were made and discriminatory practices of universities were methodically terminated during the the 1950's and 1960's.[73] As was typical of most southern states, Louisiana in 1956 enacted legislation designed to restrict the impact of the *Segregation Cases.* The statute provided for admission to college of students only after filing of a certificate with a state institution of higher education; the certificate attested to the eligibility and good moral character of the student and had to be signed by the local school superintendent and principal of the high school from which the applicant had graduated. Evidence existed that this was merely a segregation device since Negro high school principals were given only certificates addressed to Negro colleges.[74] Two companion cases were brought to enjoin colleges from rejecting applicants who could not file the required certificate. A federal district court held the statute void and granted injunctive relief.[75] The circuit court of appeals af-

---

71. 355 U.S. 839, 78 S. Ct. 20, 2 L. Ed. 2d 49 (1957), *cert. denied without prejudice.*

72. Hawkins v. Board of Control of Florida, 162 F. Supp. 851 (N.D. Fla. 1958).

73. See M.M. Chambers, *The Colleges and the Courts Since 1950,* The Interstate, 1964; pp. 35-51. Also see M.M. Chambers, *The Colleges and the Courts 1962-1966,* The Interstate, 1967, pp. 41-53.

74. M.M. Chambers, *The Colleges and the Courts Since 1950,* The Interstate, 1964, pp. 43-44.

75. Ludley v. Board of Supervisors of Louisiana State University, and Lark v. Louisiana State Board of Education, 150 F. Supp. 900 (E.D. La. 1957).

firmed the decision [76] and the United States Supreme Court refused to review.[77]

In another case, where Negro enrollment was delayed in an evidently good faith attempt to make a smooth transition to integrated status, the Tennessee State Board of Education devised a plan for the gradual desegregation of six state colleges in Tennessee. The plan provided for desegregation of graduate schools in 1956-57, desegregation of graduate students and seniors in 1957-58 and so on until the freshman class was desegregated. Five Negro students sought admission as freshmen in 1956-57. When denied admission, they appealed to the federal district court in Memphis. The federal court held the state plan to be reasonable; however, on appeal, the Circuit Court of Appeals, found that the five applicants were denied admission solely because they were Negro and the delay of five years for admission of freshmen constituted "a clear discrimination between the races." [78]

FORCIBLE DESEGREGATION

The courtroom was not always the stage on which the desegregation play was rehearsed and acted out. Most notable examples took place in Arkansas, Mississippi and Alabama, the latter two involving the desegregation of institutions of higher education. In Little Rock, Arkansas, the board of education on May 23, 1954, established that it would comply with federal constitutional requirements; [79] however, the state government of Arkansas was not so inclined. Resentment stirred and by November 1956, the Arkansas Constitution was amended mandating that the state's legislature oppose in every "Constitutional manner the Unconstitutional desegregation decisions" (*Brown* cases). Later, on September 2, 1957, the Governor of Arkansas ordered the Arkansas National Guard to Central High School in Little Rock to prevent the enrollment of Negro students. The Governor's action caused the board of education to ask that Negro students not attend school "until the dilemma was solved." The school board petitioned the federal district court for instructions and the court

76. 252 F.2d 372 (5th Cir. 1958).

77. 358 U.S. 819, 79 S. Ct. 31, 3 L. Ed. 2d 61 (1958) and 358 U.S. 820, 79 S. Ct. 32, 3 L. Ed. 2d 61 (1958), *cert. denied.*

78. Booker v. State of Tennessee Board of Education, 240 F.2d 689 (6th Cir. 1957). See also Hunt v. Arnold, 172 F. Supp. 847 (N.D. Ga. 1959).

79. Pollak, *op. cit.,* p. 268; Aaron v. Cooper, 143 F. Supp. 855 (1956), *aff'd,* 243 F.2d 361 (1957).

ordered the board to proceed with its desegregation plan.[80] Agitation by the Governor persisted throughout the month of September, resulting in a federal district court enjoining the Governor and members of the Arkansas National Guard from preventing the attendance of Negro children at Central High School. On September 23, the children entered the school, but were removed by officials of the Little Rock Police Department and the Arkansas State Police when they had difficulty controlling a large, demonstrating crowd.[81] The tempestuous September in Little Rock ended with the President of the United States dispatching federal troops to Central High School to effect the admission of the Negro students. Federal troops remained in the high school with only eight Negro students throughout the academic year of 1957-58. The Little Rock Board of Education and the Superintendent, on February 20, 1958, filed a petition to postpone the desegregation plan, claiming that "chaos, bedlam, turmoil and violence" accompanied the integration attempt, and the threat of such disorder continued. Repeated incidents of "more or less serious violence" were directed at the Negro children. The federal district court granted the relief requested by the school board. However, the federal court of appeals reversed and the case was appealed to the United States Supreme Court. The Court said:

> One may sympathize with the position of the Board in face of frustrating conditions which have confronted it, but regardless of the Board's good faith, the actions of the other state agencies responsible for those conditions compel us to reject the Board's legal position. * * * The constitutional rights of respondents are not to be sacrificed or yielded to violence and disorder which have followed upon the actions of the Governor and Legislature.
>
> * * * It is urged that this proposed segregation will promote the public peace by preventing race conflicts. Desirable as this is, and as important as is the preservation of the public peace, this aim cannot be accomplished by laws or ordinances which deny rights created or protected by the Federal Constitution. * * * Thus, law and order are not here to be preserved by depriving the Negro children of their constitutional rights.[82]

The Mississippi and Alabama cases were similar except the

---

80. Aaron v. Cooper, 156 F. Supp. 220 (1957).
81. 163 F. Supp. at 16.
82. Cooper v. Aaron, 358 U. S. 1 (1958). The Supreme Court said later (May 27, 1963), "The best guarantee of civil peace is adherence to, and respect for, the law." Watson v. Memphis, 373 U.S. 526 (1963).

confrontations between state and federal officials took place on the steps of the state universities rather than a high school. In Mississippi, James Meredith, a twenty-nine year old Negro, attempted to enter the University of Mississippi. Meredith had served in the Air Force and while in the service had earned academic credits from the University of Kansas, Washburn University in Topeka, and from correspondence courses with the United States Armed Forces Institute; in addition, from 1958 to 1960 he had earned thirty-four semester hours from the Far Eastern Division of the University of Maryland. He had good to superior grades in his work. Meredith had returned to Mississippi and attended Jackson State for one year, after which he applied for admission to the University of Mississippi at Oxford. His application was denied and he appealed to the federal district court, which court refused to enjoin the University to admit Meredith. On appeal to the U.S. Court of Appeals, the court declined to reverse the lower court, holding that a full trial on the merits was needed to clear the "muddy" record. The record did not show whether there was nondiscriminatory grounds on which the plaintiff could be excluded from the university. The court did, however, hold that the university's policy of requiring alumni certificates as a criterion for entrance effectively denied Negro candidates equal protection of the laws.[83]

Upon re-establishment and clarification of the record the case once again went to the court of appeals, resulting this time in a decision for Meredith.[84] Justice Wisdom, writing for the court, held the record indicated that Meredith had been denied admission solely because he was a Negro and the reasons given for his rejection, such as alumni certificates, "insufficiency" of credits, alleged false voting registration and an averment that he was a trouble-maker were without substance and were not valid nondiscriminatory reasons for rejection.

The University then appealed and Circuit Judge Cameron issued stays pending final judgment by the Supreme Court. Justice Black of the Supreme Court vacated the stays on September 10, 1962,[85] and a short time later the Supreme Court denied a review of the case.[86]

---

83. Meredith v. Fair, 298 F.2d 696 (1962).

84. Meredith v. Fair, 305 F.2d 343 (1962).

85. 371 U.S. 828, 83 S. Ct. 10, 9 L. Ed. 2d 66, (1962). See Procedural explanation, Pollak, *op. cit.*, p. 280.

86. *Certiorari denied*, 371 U.S. 828, 83 S. Ct. 49 (1962).

With the decision of the Supreme Court the conflict did not abate, but increased in magnitude and became extra-judicial. Governor Ross Barnett, on September 24, issued a proclamation which called for the arrest of any federal official who tried to arrest and fine a state official in the performance of his official duties. Barnett personally refused to enroll Meredith for the fall term. The President of the United States responded and issued a proclamation asserting the supremacy of federal law, stating that "all persons engaged in such obstructions of justice cease and desist . . . ." The President took command of the Mississippi National Guard and authorized and directed the Secretary of Defense to "remove all obstructions of justice" in Mississippi.[87] Meredith was taken to the Ole Miss Campus, rioting ensued, but when the smoke cleared Meredith was enrolled at the University of Mississippi. The federal government had prevailed in its enforcement of desegregation, but probably just as important a new chapter had been written in the book of federal-state legal relations. It was clearly established that a state could not interpose itself between the individual's rights and the federal government's enforcement of those rights.

In a similarly dramatic but less violent episode, the Governor of Alabama stood in the doorway of the University of Alabama and blocked the entrance of two Negro students. As previously mentioned, the federal district court in *Lucy*[88] in 1955 had permanently enjoined the dean of admissions of the University of Alabama from denying admission to qualified Negro applicants. Federal District Judge H. H. Grooms, on May 16, 1963, declared the injunction to be in continuing effect and applicable to admission requests of the two qualified Negroes. The members of the board of trustees of the University of Alabama sought delay of the order, claiming prevailing racial unrest in the community. On May 21, 1963, Judge Grooms denied the motion by the board of trustees, whereby Governor George C. Wallace announced he would personally "bar the door." The district court issued a temporary injunction restraining the Governor from impeding the enrollment of the students.[89] Judge Lynne of the district court viewed the situation this way:

Thoughtful people, if they can free themselves from

---

87. Pollak, *op. cit.*, p. 282.

88. Lucy v. Adams, 134 F. Supp. 235 (1955), *aff'd*, 228 F.2d 619 (1955), *cert. denied*, 351 U.S. 931, 76 S. Ct. 790, 100 L. Ed. 1460 (1956).

89. See M.M. Chambers, *The Colleges and the Courts 1962-66*, The Interstate, 1967, pp. 43-44.

tensions produced by established principles with which they violently disagree must concede that the governor of a sovereign state has no authority to obstruct or prevent the execution of the lawful orders of a court of the United States. No legalistic formula is required to express the craving of honest, hardworking, God-fearing citizens for a moral order logically supported,—an attitude long ago expressed when Coke informed King James that there was a law above the King.[90]

The students were enrolled with the help of the office of the Attorney General of the United States.

For all practical purposes this ended the overt opposition to the desegregation at southern universities. The rule of law was clear, a qualified student could not be denied admission to a state university for reason of race. There was no distinction among professional, graduate or undergradate programs; a qualified Negro student could and would be permitted to enroll.

INTEGRATION VERSUS DESEGREGATION

It is well established that laws, rules, or regulations governing public colleges and universities which segregate the races violate the Fourteenth Amendment. This constitutional standard is clear and unmistakable. The precise definition of desegregation, however, is not clear. Desegregation has been interpreted to mean everything from a simple lowering of segregation barriers [91] to an affirmative duty to effectuate racial mix.[92] Arguments persisted and intensified as public school facilities were desegregated on paper but remained, in fact, largely segregated. The Supreme Court's intent by the word desegregation in the first *Brown* case has been widely interpreted. One decision closely following *Brown* held:

---

90. United States v. Wallace, Governor, 218 F. Supp. 290 (1963). See case materials: Gnatt v. Clemson Agricultural College of South Carolina, 320 F.2d 611 (1963), *reversing and remanding* 213 F. Supp. 103 (1962), *cert. denied*, 375 U.S. 814, 84 S. Ct. 46, 11 L. Ed. 2d 49 (1963).

91. Briggs v. Elliott, 132 F. Supp. 776 (E.D.S.C. 1955); Stell v. Savannah—Chatham County Bd. of Educ., 333 F.2d 55 (5th Cir.), *cert. denied*, 379 U.S. 933 (1964); Kelley v. Board of Education, 270 F.2d 209 (6th Cir.), *cert. denied*, 361 U.S. 924 (1959); Avery v. Wichita Falls Independent School Dist., 241 F.2d 230 (5th Cir.), *cert. denied*, 353 U.S. 938 (1957).

92. Green v. County School Board of New Kent County, 391 U.S. 430 (1968); Bowman v. County School Board, 382 F.2d 326 (4th Cir. 1967); United States v. Jefferson County Bd. of Educ., 372 F.2d 836, *aff'd en banc*, 380 F.2d 385 (1967). See also J. Skelly Wright, "Public School Desegregation: Legal Remedies for De Facto Segregation," *Western Review Law Review*, Vol. 16, p. 478 (May 1965).

>[A]ll that is decided, is that a state may not deny to any person on account of race the right to attend any school that it maintains. . . . The Constitution, in other words, does not require integration. It merely forbids segregation.[93]

The efficacy of this definition was not always substantiated in practice, especially where constitutional rights were measured in terms of the black and white mix in the schools. It soon became quite clear, that in some school districts in the south it would take more to desegregate than merely a policy against discrimination. "Freedom of choice," the formal plan or procedure first required by the courts to desegregate, was not always effective, resulting in continued segregation. As it developed from this judicial experimentation, a double standard was adopted—one for the north and one for the south. In the north, federal courts [94] held no affirmative duty existed on the part of school boards to integrate.

>We hold that there is no constitutional duty on the part of the board to bus Negro or white children out of their neighborhoods or to transfer classes for the sole purpose of alleviating racial imbalance . . . .[95]

On the other hand, in the south, the United States Court of Appeals, Fifth Circuit, held that there is an affirmative duty to integrate where dual enrollment had once been the legal condition of the state.[96] This court said that the "initiative in achieving desegregation of the public schools must come from school authorities." The court distinguished *de facto* segregation, segregation caused by housing patterns, of the north from the *de jure*, governmentally promulgated and enforced, segregation in the south.

The United States Supreme Court in a later Virginia case arrived at essentially the same conclusion; that school districts have an affirmative duty to overcome segregation.[97] In this case the constitutionality of "freedom of choice" provisions was contested. The plaintiffs claimed that a formerly segre-

---

93. Briggs v. Elliott, *supra.*
94. Bell v. School City, 324 F.2d 209 (7th Cir. 1964), *cert. denied,* 377 U.S. 924 (1964); Deal v. Cincinnati Bd. of Educ., 369 F.2d 55 (6th Cir. 1966), *cert. denied,* 389 U.S. 847 (1967).
95. Deal v. Cincinnati, *supra.* See also David W. Beggs and Kern Alexander, *Integration and Education,* Rand McNally, 1969, pp. 107-120.
96. United States v. Jefferson County Board of Education, 372 F.2d 836 (1966).
97. Green v. County School Board of New Kent County, Virginia, 391 U.S. 430, 88 S. Ct. 1689, 20 L. Ed. 2d 716 (1968).

gated school district had the duty to take steps, other than offering "freedom of choice," to integrate the schools. The Supreme Court agreed with the plaintiffs saying: "The school officials have the continuing duty to take whatever action may be necessary to create a unitary, nonracial system." [98]

Questions of desegregation versus integration in elementary and secondary schools were answered in this decision at least as far as *de jure* segregation is concerned. School officials must create a unitary system and as far as the court is concerned desegregation and integration are synonymous. However, the Supreme Court has not yet ruled on the constitutionality of *de facto* segregation. The Supreme Court only goes so far as to say that where the state created segregation, it must correct it. Where the segregation is due to housing patterns or social and economic phenomena not created by state action there is no affirmative duty to integrate.

President Nixon summarized the status of the court decisions thusly:

> There is a fundamental distinction between so-called "de jure" and "de facto" segregation: de jure segregation arises by law or by the deliberate act of school officials and is unconstitutional; de facto segregation results from residential housing patterns and does not violate the Constitution.[99]

The above precedents pertain only to elementary and secondary schools and their application to higher education can only be conjectured. Whether an institution of higher education must take affirmative action to overcome racial imbalance will undoubtedly be the source of much litigation in the future. One can make the argument that if a college or university does not have a racial quota or ratio the same as the population it serves, discrimination exists. However, the historical nature of higher education, having academically selective standards and the absence of compulsory attendance statutes as in elementary and secondary education, indicates that the courts will have more difficulty in identifying discrimination in higher education than at lower levels of education. If latent discrimination cannot. be identified the courts will have a difficult time in justifying the enforcement of enrollment policies which require affirmative steps to balance the races. The Supreme Court's mandate of an affirmative duty on the

---

98. *Ibid.*

99. President Richard M. Nixon, television statement on legal status of school desegregation and federal policy, March 24, 1970.

part of school districts to overcome racial imbalance was predicated on evidence that "freedom of choice" did not work.[100] Analogously, for the courts to rule that colleges must take affirmative steps to integrate, there first must be evidence to conclude that the "open door" or "nondiscriminatory admission standards" are not sufficient to overcome the influence of previous policies of racial segregation.

Cases, to date, clarify the issue very little. One federal district court found that racial discrimination in higher education in Tennessee existed because Tennessee A. & I., a formerly Negro university, had ninety-nine percent black enrollment while the formerly white state universities had ninety-three percent white enrollment.[101] This court held that Tennessee must submit a plan to desegregate the state's higher education system; the state had an affirmative duty to dismantle the dual system of education.

Taking the opposite position in another federal jurisdiction in Alabama, a federal district court held that while the state was under an affirmative duty to dismantle its dual enrollment system at the elementary and secondary level, it was under no such obligation in higher education.[102] The court found that the Supreme Court's decision in *Green*[103] was inapplicable at the college level, since "[f]reedom to choose where one will attend college unlike choosing one's elementary or secondary public school, has a long tradition and helps to perform an important function, *viz.*, fitting the right school to the right student."[104]

On appeal, the Supreme Court, affirmed this decision with Justices Douglas and Harlan dissenting. Justice Douglas queried:

> Can we say in 1969 that a State has no duty to disestablish a dual system of higher education based upon race? * * * The inference is that if this were an elementary school, the result would be different.[105]

In spite of the Supreme Court's affirming the Alabama decision, one may expect an increasing number of cases con-

100. Green v. County School Board of New Kent County, Virginia, *supra*.

101. Sanders v. Ellington, 288 F. Supp. 937 (M.D. Tenn. 1968).

102. Alabama State Teachers Association v. Alabama Public School & College Authority, 289 F. Supp. 784 (M.D. Ala. 1968).

103. Green v. County School Board of New Kent County, *supra*.

104. 289 F. Supp. 784 (M.D. Ala. 1968), *aff'd per curiam*, 393 U.S. 400, 89 S. Ct. 681 (1969).

105. *Ibid.*

testing higher education "open door" policies. If the courts, in the not-too-distant future, observe the higher education scene and discover that in large measure Negro students still attend predominately Negro colleges and faculties remain segregated, one can expect the courts to substitute judicial integration remedies for college administrative policies.

DESEGREGATION OF PRIVATE UNIVERSITIES

The "Equal Protection" provision of the Fourteenth Amendment makes it unlawful for public universities to discriminate on account of race. The situation, however, becomes more complicated with discrimination in private universities. The Fourteenth Amendment specifically forbids deprivation of certain individual rights by the *state*; no mention is made of private individuals or institutions.

The status of the law today indicates that racial segregation by a private school does not violate the equal protection provision unless the school's governance is so entwined with the state, through either financial or other assistance, that the school is effectively performing a state function. Fundamentally, "state action" can be established either by (1) significant state involvement in private activities or (2) performance of a public function by a private entity.[106] As both state and federal assistance to private colleges and universities increases, the argument for application of the equal protection provision to private education gains strength.

In order to receive governmental subsidies, private schools often claim that they are serving a "public purpose" beneficial to the people and the state. Where the public purpose philosophy is accepted and governmental subventions are provided for private school use, the courts will not sit idly by and allow private institutions to discriminate. It is quite clear that a school will not be allowed to operate with public assistance while at the same time claiming immunity from constitutional constraints.

While the precedents are few, the courts have made some comments concerning private schools, the implications of which are applicable here. The Supreme Court of the United States has held unconstitutional a scheme whereby a state could establish and maintain segregated private schools at

---

106. See Eaton v. Grubbs, 329 F.2d 710 (4th Cir. 1964); Simkins v. Moses H. Cone Memorial Hospital, 323 F.2d 959 (4th Cir. 1963), *cert. denied*, 84 S. Ct. 793 (1964).

the exclusion of public desegregated schools. In *Griffin v. County School Board of Prince Edward County*,[107] the Supreme Court said:

> Prince Edward children must go to a private school or none at all; all other Virginia children can go to public schools. Closing Prince Edward's schools bears more heavily on Negro children in Prince Edward County since white children there have accredited private schools which they can attend. . . . [T]he result is that Prince Edward County school children, if they go to school in their own county, must go to racially segregated schools which, although designated as private, are beneficiaries of county and state support. A state, of course, has a wide discretion in deciding whether laws shall operate statewide or shall operate only in certain counties. . . . But the record in the present case could not be clearer that Prince Edward's public schools were closed and private schools operated in their place with state and county assistance, for one reason, and one reason only: to ensure, through measures taken by the county and the state, that white and colored children in Prince Edward County would not, under any circumstances, go to the same school. Whatever nonracial grounds might support a state's allowing a county to abandon public schools, the object must be a constitutional one, and grounds of race and opposition to desegregation do not qualify as constitutional.[108]

Here the Supreme Court well establishes that state action to segregate through the use of private schools will not be tolerated.

Subsequent to the Supreme Court decision, another state attempt to desegregate through the use of private schools was struck down in the *Poindexter* case.[109] The Louisiana legislature devised an individual grant program whereby tuition was paid for children who desired to attend private schools. The court, in holding the act unconstitutional, found that public payment of tuition grants constituted "state action" falling under the Fourteenth Amendment, that the funds were a stimulus for establishing "quasi-public" segregated schools, and that the segregation resulting from such a financing plan deprived Negro children of equal protection. The court saw that this state-supported system of private schools would tend to drain students, teachers, and fiscal re-

107. 377 U.S. 218 (1964).
108. *Ibid.*
109. Poindexter v. Louisiana Financial Assistance Commission, 36 U.S.L.W. 2150 (5th Cir. 1967).

sources away from the public schools, thus perpetuating the aparthied. It was maintained by defendants that in order to apply constitutional constraints to private schools, the school must be "operated wholly or predominantly from and through the use of governmental funds." [110]

Apparently, the implication was that if public support of a private institution was less than "predominant," then segregation was not subject to constitutional attack. The court refused to be confined by the test of "predominant" support and held instead that "any amount of state support to help found segregated schools or to help maintain such schools is sufficient to give standing to Negro school children." [111]

The court condemned the "predominant" support test as allowing for half-way discrimination, saying, "Any affirmative and purposeful aid promoting private discrimination violates the equal protection clause. There is no such thing as the state's legitimately being just a little bit discriminatory." [112]

If the proportion or level of state support is unimportant then one can assume that private schools which receive *any* state support at all cannot segregate. Dorsen maintains:

> The "support" necessary to fulfill the constitutional test of the *Poindexter* case can be found in the financial aid now provided private schools through many federal programs . . . . Likewise, at least in some jurisdictions, there is much state aid to independent schools. If the test is "any support" there would seem ample basis for a judicial decision that private schools are subject to the Fourteenth Amendment.[113]

As mentioned above, many private schools justify their receipt of public funds on the grounds that they serve a "public purpose." In many states no public funds can be expended for other than a public purpose. Where this contention is maintained, trends in judicial logic indicate that the performance of a public function makes constitutional standards applicable. Dorsen gives the basis for such a legal determination:

> . . . where private individuals are allowed to perform a function ordinarily undertaken by the state, they are to be treated as agents of the state for constitutional

110. This defense was built on the wording of the Civil Rights Act of 1964, § 401 (c).

111. 258 F. Supp. 164.

112. Poindexter, *supra*. See also Simkins v. Moses H. Cone Memorial Hospital, 323 F.2d 959 (4th Cir. 1963), *cert. denied*, 376 U.S. 938 (1964).

113. Norman Dorsen, "Racial Discrimination in 'Private' Schools," *William and Mary Law Review*, Vol. 9, No. 1, p. 49 (1967).

purposes, and their discriminatory acts therefore prohibited. This theory has been applied where private bodies conducted a primary election, administered a company town, or operated a park.[114]

In a case in 1962 involving segregation at private Tulane University, which was later overturned on procedural grounds, Judge J. Skelly Wright said:

> . . . one may question whether any school or college can ever be so "private" as to escape the reach of the Fourteenth Amendment . . . . [I]nstitutions of learning are not things of purely private concern . . . . Clearly the administrators of a private college are performing a public function. They do the work of the state, often in the place of the state. Does it not follow that they stand in the state's shoes? And, if so, are they not agents of the state, subject to the constraints on governmental action, to the same extent as private persons who govern a company town . . . or control a political party . . . Reason and authority strongly suggest that the Constitution never sanctions racial discrimination in our schools and colleges, no matter how "private" they may claim to be.[115]

Under this rather extreme position, even though a private university receives no governmental support at all it is subject to the same constitutional regulation as is a state supported university. While this is not now the prevailing judicial view, it is nevertheless a logical judicial extension of constitutional freedom applied in the context of the "public purpose" theory.

In attempting to reconcile the precedents it is only safe to say that the constitutional rights and restraints on private institutions lie somewhere between that of the individual and that of the state. The Supreme Court in 1961 said:

> It is clear, as it always has been since the *Civil Rights Cases,* . . . that "individual invasion of individual rights is not subject matter of the amendment," . . . and that private conduct abridging individual rights does no violence to the Equal Protection Clause unless to some significant extent the state in any of its manifestations has been found to have become involved in it.[116]

The Court has, therefore, not attempted to provide a defini-

---

114. *Ibid.* See Terry v. Adams, 345 F.2d 461 (1953); Marsh v. Alabama, 326 U.S. 501 (1946); Evans v. Newton, 382 U.S. 296 (1966).

115. Guillory v. Administrators of Tulane University, 203 F. Supp. 855 (E.D. La. 1962).

116. Burton v. Wilmington Parking Authority, 365 U.S. 715 (1961). See also Shelley v. Kraemer, 334 U.S. 1 (1948).

tive formula of what constitutes state action or state involvement. What is meant by "significant extent" is the key to the entire question. The Court has noted that to provide a precise formula is an "impossible task" which "this court has never attempted." [117] In way of an advisory comment, the Court said that: "Only by sifting facts and weighing circumstances can the nonobvious involvement of the state in private conduct be attributed its true significance." [118]

Sengstock [119] has expressed the feelings of many who prefer more concise judicial tests for determining "significant" involvement.

> Significant involvement has produced dissatisfaction for those seeking to fix upon a test whereby the presence of state action could be identified. The dissatisfaction is due to the fact that significant involvement is not a test of state action. When used, it is a conclusion that state action is present. It reveals nothing of the reasons inducing the conclusion . . . . Significant involvement requires a weighing of correlative facts. The Court does not tell what facts are to be weighed or what the rationality of the scale should be . . . . A new test for ascertaining state action is badly needed.

By "sifting" the facts to determine the extent of state involvement in private universities one federal court in Puerto Rico held in 1969 that although a private junior college received certain grants and loans from the federal and Puerto Rican governments for plant development, operation and student scholarships, evidence was not sufficient to hold that the college was acting under color of state or federal authority.[120]

In another recent decision, the United States Court of Appeal, Tenth Circuit, held that the fact that the University of Denver received specific tax exemption not enjoyed by other like corporations did not place it under "color of state law" [121] within the meaning of the federal Civil Rights Act.[122]

---

117. Kotch v. Pilot, 330 U.S. 552 (1947).

118. Burton v. Wilmington Parking Authority, *supra*. See also Evans v. Newton, 382 U.S. 296 (1966).

119. Frank S. Sengstock and Mary C. Sengstock, "Discrimination: A Constitutional Dilemma," *William and Mary Law Review*, Vol. 9, p. 59 (1968).

120. Torres v. Puerto Rico Junior College, 298 F. Supp. 458 (D. Puerto Rico 1969). See also Hammond v. University of Tampa, 344 F.2d 951 (1965).

121. Browns v. Mitchell, 409 F.2d 593 (10th Cir. 1969).

122. 42 U.S.C.A. § 1983 (Civil Rights Act of 1871).

One of the best known cases interpreting the extent of involvement of the state in discriminatory practices transpired in Pennsylvania in the *Girard College* case.[123] Litigation in this case extended over several years and contested the extent of involvement of the state in attempting to enforce an 1830 will creating a segregated school for "white male orphans" and placed the funds for the college in trust to the "Mayor, Aldermen and citizens of Philadelphia." The dispute began in 1954 when two Negro students were rejected admission solely because of race.

The United States Supreme Court in 1958 held that this trust arrangement, whereby a board of directors appointed by the City of Philadelphia operated the school, constituted state action. The board was in fact an agency of the state. Subsequently, the board was changed in an attempt by the City to maintain control but at the same time remove Girard College from constitutional equal protection restrictions.

In 1968 the United States Court of Appeals held that segregation under this arrangement was likewise unconstitutional and significantly involved the state in private discriminations. The details of this case are given in the case material below.

From these cases, we can say that the exact nature of "state action" has not been judicially determined. The Supreme Court has left substantial leeway for "shifting" of facts and deciding each case on its merits. What constitutes significant involvement of the state in one jurisdiction may not apply in another; it is sufficient to say that, based on today's precedents in both federal and state courts, a trend exists which will tend to increase the constitutional constraints on private institutions as these schools seek and obtain greater federal and state fiscal assistance. Such aid will, in the future, in a large measure establish "sufficient state involvement."

Predictably, the second ground for establishing state action, that of private school performing public functions, will likewise serve to restrict the prerogative of the private institution. As pointed out above, the private institution will relinquish its independence as its functions and fiscal resources become more public.

STATE ENFORCEMENT OF PRIVATE SEGREGATION

If individuals can segregate against each other and not

---

123. Commonwealth of Pennsylvania v. Brown, 392 F.2d 120 (3d Cir. 1968), *cert. denied*, 391 U.S. 921, 88 S. Ct. 1811 (May 20, 1968).

violate the federal constitution, the question then arises as to whether a state can enforce segregation requirements of a covenant between two private individuals or between an individual and a private college. With particular application to private colleges, this means, can a state enforce wills, grants, trusts, charters, or other covenants between the college and an individual, which contain racially discriminatory features? This is a slightly different situation than was posed in the *Berea College* case.[124] In that instance the state passed legislation to force segregation in private colleges. Here the question is, whether the state can enforce private agreements which call for segregation of private colleges. This question was resolved in Virginia [125] and Texas [126] cases, each involving a trust provision providing for segregated education.

In the *Sweet Briar* case, the college brought suit in a state circuit court, seeking a declaratory judgment to determine whether the provisions of a trust which endowed and established the college would permit acceptance of non-white students. The state court found that the trust fund provision stating, "for the education of white girls and young women," was not ambiguous and declined to issue a declaratory judgment. The college then brought suit in a federal district court seeking an injunction to prevent the Attorney General of Virginia and the Amherst County Attorney from bringing suit in the state courts to force the school to comply with the racially restrictive language of the trust as required by the state code. The federal court issued a temporary restraining order against the defendants until a three-judge court could rule on whether or not to issue an injunction against the defendants. The defendants, thereafter, submitted a motion to the three-judge federal court seeking abstention of further proceedings until the case was carried through the state courts. A jurisdictional dispute ensued over whether the federal court should abstain; the argument was made by defendants that the doctrine of comity "forcefully directs" that a federal court abstain in favor of the state court which had first jurisdiction. The three-judge federal court finally adopted this argument and abstained from rendering a decision until remedies were exhausted in the state courts. On appeal, the United States Supreme Court, reversed and remanded the decision for consideration on its merits.

---

124. Berea College v. Commonwealth of Kentucky, *supra*.
125. Sweet Briar Institute v. Button, 280 F. Supp. 312 (1967).
126. Coffee v. William Marsh Rice University, 408 S.W.2d 269 (1966).

On remand, the lower federal court held that a state cannot require compliance with a provision in the founder's will restricting the college's enrollment to white persons. Such action is barred in the Fourteenth Amendment. A permanent injunction was entered preventing the state from enforcing the racially restrictive provision in the will.[127]

The Texas case [128] involved the enforcement of a restriction in an original trust and charter to Rice University which prohibited the school from charging tuition and admitting Negroes. The original action was brought by Rice University against the Attorney General of Texas seeking a judgment authorizing the school to depart from the trust and charter provisions. The trial court held that it had now become impractical to carry out the tuition and segregation provisions and the school could legally disregard the restrictions. After more litigation, where individuals, friends and alumni appealed and sued for enforcement, the appellate court held that the individuals did not have standing to sue since the state Attorney General was not a party to the appeal. The Texas Supreme Court reversed this judgment and remanded the case to the Court of Civil Appeals for a decision based on the merits of the case. The Court of Civil Appeals observed that the charter provision must be construed in the light in which it is written and noted that it restrained the charging of tuition and also contained a segregation aspect. Nevertheless, the appellate court found, as did the trial court, that a court could depart from the specific terms of a trust in order to allow fulfillment of the dominant intent of the donor, and the dominant intent of the donor was to establish a first class, high quality institution. Since a segregated institution cannot retain first class stature, nor can it properly maintain itself without some tuition charges, the court affirmed the trial court's decision, allowing the university to admit students without regard to color or race and to disregard the charter provision against charging of tuition.[129]

---

127. See *Race Relations Law Reporter*, Vol. 12, No. 1-2, pp. 85-97 and Vol. 12, No. 3-4, pp. 1188-1189, Vanderbilt University School of Law, 1967.
128. Coffee v. William Marsh Rice University, *supra*.
129. See *Race Relations Law Reporter*, Vol. 12, No. 1-2, pp. 70-71. Vanderbilt University School of Law, 1967.

**If State provides separate facilities they must
be truly equal**

SWEATT v. PAINTER

Supreme Court of the United States, 1950.
339 U.S. 629.

MR. CHIEF JUSTICE VINSON delivered the opinion of the
Court.

This case and McLaurin v. Oklahoma State Regents present different aspects of this general question: To what extent does the Equal Protection Clause of the Fourteenth Amendment limit the power of a state to distinguish between students of different races in professional and graduate education in a state university? Broader issues have been urged for our consideration, but we adhere to the principle of deciding constitutional questions only in the context of the particular case before the Court. We have frequently reiterated that this Court will decide constitutional questions only when necessary to the disposition of the case at hand, and that such decisions will be drawn as narrowly as possible. * * *

In the instant case, petitioner filed an application for admission to the University of Texas Law School for the February, 1946 term. His application was rejected solely because he is a Negro.[4] Petitioner thereupon brought this suit for mandamus against the appropriate school officials, respondents here, to compel his admission. At that time, there was no law school in Texas which admitted Negroes.

The state trial court recognized that the action of the State in denying petitioner the opportunity to gain a legal education while granting it to others deprived him of the equal protection of the laws guaranteed by the Fourteenth Amendment. The court did not grant the relief requested, however, but continued the case for six months to allow the State to supply substantially equal facilities. At the expiration of the six months, in December, 1946, the court denied the writ on the showing that the authorized university officials had adopted an order calling for the opening of a law school for Negroes the following February. While petitioner's appeal was pending, such a school was made available, but petitioner refused

---

4. It appears that the University has been restricted to white students, in accordance with the State law. See Tex. Const., Art. VII, §§ 7, 14; Tex.Rev.Civ.Stat. (Vernon, 1925), Arts. 2643b (Supp. 1949), 2719, 2900.

to register therein. The Texas Court of Civil Appeals set aside the trial court's judgment and ordered the cause "remanded generally to the trial court for further proceedings without prejudice to the rights of any party to this suit."

On remand, a hearing was held on the issue of the equality of the educational facilities at the newly established school as compared with the University of Texas Law School. Finding that the new school offered petitioner "privileges, advantages, and opportunities for the study of law substantially equivalent to those offered by the State to white students at the University of Texas," the trial court denied mandamus. The Court of Civil Appeals affirmed. 210 S.W.2d 442 (1948). Petitioner's application for a writ of error was denied by the Texas Supreme Court. We granted certiorari, 338 U.S. 865, 70 S.Ct. 139 (1949), because of the manifest importance of the constitutional issues involved.

The University of Texas Law School, from which petitioner was excluded, was staffed by a faculty of sixteen full-time and three part-time professors, some of whom are nationally recognized authorities in their field. Its student body numbered 850. The library contained over 65,000 volumes. Among the other facilities available to the students were a law review, moot court facilities, scholarship funds, and Order of the Coif affiliation. The school's alumni occupy the most distinguished positions in the private practice of the law and in the public life of the State. It may properly be considered one of the nation's ranking law schools.

The law school for Negroes which was to have opened in February, 1947, would have had no independent faculty or library. The teaching was to be carried on by four members of the University of Texas Law School faculty, who were to maintain their offices at the University of Texas while teaching at both institutions. Few of the 10,000 volumes ordered for the library had arrived; [5] nor was there any full-time librarian. The school lacked accreditation.

Since the trial of this case, respondents report the opening of a law school at the Texas State University for Negroes. It

5. "Students of the interim School of Law of the Texas State University for Negroes [located in Austin, whereas the permanent School was to be located at Houston] shall have use of the State Law Library in the Capitol Building. * * *" Tex.Laws 1947, c. 20, § 11, Tex.Rev.Civ.Stat. (Vernon, 1949 Supp.), note to Art. 2643b. It is not clear that this privilege was anything more than was extended to all citizens of the State.

is apparently on the road to full accreditation. It has a faculty
of five full-time professors; a student body of 23; a library
of some 16,500 volumes serviced by a full-time staff; a practice court and legal aid association; and one alumnus who has
become a member of the Texas Bar.

Whether the University of Texas Law School is compared
with the original or the new law school for Negroes, we cannot find substantial equality in the educational opportunities
offered white and Negro law students by the State. In terms
of number of the faculty, variety of courses and opportunity
for specialization, size of the student body, scope of the library,
availability of law review and similar activities, the University
of Texas Law School is superior. What is more important, the
University of Texas Law School possesses to a far greater
degree those qualities which are incapable of objective measurement but which make for greatness in a law school. Such
qualities, to name but a few, include reputation of the faculty,
experience of the administration, position and influence of
the alumni, standing in the community, traditions and prestige. It is difficult to believe that one who had a free choice
between these law schools would consider the question close.

Moreover, although the law is a highly learned profession,
we are well aware that it is an intensely practical one. The
law school, the proving ground for legal learning and practice, cannot be effective in isolation from the individuals and
institutions with which the law interacts. Few students and
no one who has practiced law would choose to study in an
academic vacuum, removed from the interplay of ideas and
the exchange of views with which the law is concerned. The
law school to which Texas is willing to admit petitioner excludes from its student body members of the racial groups
which number 85% of the population of the State and include most of the lawyers, witnesses, jurors, judges and other
officials with whom petitioner will inevitably be dealing when
he becomes a member of the Texas Bar. With such a substantial and significant segment of society excluded, we cannot
conclude that the education offered petitioner is substantially
equal to that which he would receive if admitted to the University of Texas Law School.

It may be argued that excluding petitioner from that school
is no different from excluding white students from the new
law school. This contention overlooks realities. It is unlikely
that a member of a group so decisively in the majority, attending a school with rich traditions and prestige which

only a history of consistently maintained excellence could command, would claim that the opportunities afforded him for legal education were unequal to those held open to petitioner. That such a claim, if made, would be dishonored by the State, is no answer. "Equal protection of the laws is not achieved through indiscriminate imposition of inequalities." Shelley v. Kraemer, 334 U.S. 1, 22, 68 S.Ct. 836, 846 (1948).

It is fundamental that these cases concern rights which are personal and present. This Court has stated unanimously that "The State must provide [legal education] for [petitioner] in conformity with the equal protection clause of the Fourteenth Amendment and provide it as soon as it does for applicants of any other group." Sipuel v. Board of Regents, 332 U.S. 631, 633, 68 S.Ct. 299 (1948). That case "did not present the issue whether a state might not satisfy the equal protection clause of the Fourteenth Amendment by establishing a separate law school for Negroes." Fisher v. Hurst, 333 U.S. 147, 150, 68 S.Ct. 389, 390 (1948). In Missouri ex rel. Gaines v. Canada, 305 U.S. 337, 351, 59 S.Ct. 232, 237 (1938), the Court, speaking through Chief Justice Hughes, declared that "petitioner's right was a personal one. It was as an individual that he was entitled to the equal protection of the laws, and the State was bound to furnish him within its borders facilities for legal education substantially equal to those which the State there afforded for persons of the white race, whether or not other negroes sought the same opportunity." These are the only cases in this Court which present the issue of the constitutional validity of race distinctions in state-supported graduate and professional education.

In accordance with these cases, petitioner may claim his full constitutional right: legal education equivalent to that offered by the State to students of other races. Such education is not available to him in a separate law school as offered by the State. We cannot, therefore, agree with respondents that the doctrine of Plessy v. Ferguson, 163 U.S. 537, 16 S.Ct. 1138 (1896), requires affirmance of the judgment below. Nor need we reach petitioner's contention that Plessy v. Ferguson should be reexamined in the light of contemporary knowledge respecting the purposes of the Fourteenth Amendment and the effects of racial segregation.

We hold that the Equal Protection Clause of the Fourteenth Amendment requires that petitioner be admitted to the University of Texas Law School. The judgment is reversed and the cause is remanded for proceedings not inconsistent with this opinion.

Reversed.

Negro students must be treated as other students when attending desegregated university

McLAURIN v. OKLAHOMA STATE REGENTS

Supreme Court of the United States, 1950.
339 U.S. 637.

MR. CHIEF JUSTICE VINSON delivered the opinion of the Court.

In this case, we are faced with the question whether a state may, after admitting a student to graduate instruction in its state university, afford him different treatment from other students solely because of his race. We decide only this issue; . . . .

Appellant is a Negro citizen of Oklahoma. Possessing a Master's Degree, he applied for admission to the University of Oklahoma in order to pursue studies and courses leading to a Doctorate in Education. At that time, his application was denied, solely because of his race. The school authorities were required to exclude him by the Oklahoma statutes, . . . which made it a misdemeanor to maintain or operate, teach or attend a school at which both whites and Negroes are enrolled or taught. Appellant filed a complaint requesting injunctive relief, alleging that the action of the school authorities and the statutes upon which their action was based were unconstitutional and deprived him of the equal protection of the laws. Citing our decisions in *Missouri ex rel. Gaines v. Canada*, 305 U.S. 337 (1938), . . . a statutory three-judge District Court held that the State had a Constitutional duty to provide him with the education he sought as soon as it provided that education for applicants of any other group. It further held that to the extent the Oklahoma statutes denied him admission they were unconstitutional and void. On the assumption, however, that the State would follow the constitutional mandate, the court refused to grant the injunction, retaining jurisdiction of the cause with full power to issue any necessary and proper orders to secure McLaurin the equal protection of the laws. . . .

Following this decision, the Oklahoma legislature amended these statutes to permit the admission of Negroes to institutions of higher learning attended by white students, in cases where such institutions offered courses not available in the Negro schools. The amendment provided, however, that in such cases the program of instruction "shall be given at such colleges or institutions of higher education upon a segregated basis." [1] Appellant was thereupon admitted to the University of Oklahoma Graduate School. In apparent conformity with the amendment, his admission was made subject to "such rules and regulations as to segregation as the President of the University shall consider to afford to Mr. G.W. McLaurin substantially equal educational opportunities as are afforded to other persons seeking the same education in the Graduate College," a condition which does not appear to have been withdrawn. Thus he was required to sit apart at a designated desk in an anteroom adjoining the classroom; to sit at a designated desk on the mezzanine floor of the library, but not to use the desks in the regular reading room; and to sit at a designated table and to eat at a different time from the other students in the school cafeteria.

To remove these conditions, appellant filed a motion to modify the order and judgment of the District Court. That court held that such treatment did not violate the provisions of the Fourteenth Amendment and denied the motion. . . . This appeal followed.

In the interval between the decision of the court below and the hearing in this Court, the treatment afforded appellant was altered. For some time, the section of the classroom in which appellant sat was surrounded by a rail on which there was a sign stating, "Reserved For Colored," but these have been removed. He is now assigned to a seat in the classroom in a row specified for colored students; he is assigned to a

---

[1] The amendment adds the following proviso to each of the sections relating to mixed schools: "Provided, that the provisions of this Section shall not apply to programs of instruction leading to a particular degree given at State owned or operated colleges or institutions of higher education of this State established for and/or used by the white race, where such programs of instruction leading to a particular degree are not given at colleges or institutions of higher education of this State established for and/or used by the colored race; provided further, that said programs of instruction leading to a particular degree shall be given at such colleges or institutions of higher education upon a segregated basis." . . . Segregated basis is defined as "classroom instruction given in separate classrooms, or at separate times." . . .

table in the library on the main floor; and he is permitted to eat at the same time in the cafeteria as other students, although here again he is assigned to a special table.

It is said that the separations imposed by the State in this case are in form merely nominal. McLaurin uses the same classroom, library and cafeteria as students of other races; there is no indication that the seats to which he is assigned in these rooms have any disadvantage of location. He may wait in line in the cafeteria and there stand and talk with his fellow students, but while he eats he must remain apart.

These restrictions were obviously imposed in order to comply, as nearly as could be, with the statutory requirements of Oklahoma. But they signify that the State, in administering the facilities it affords for professional and graduate study, sets McLaurin apart from the other students. The result is that appellant is handicapped in his pursuit of effective graduate instruction. Such restrictions impair and inhibit his ability to study, to engage in discussions and exchange views with other students, and, in general, to learn his profession.

Our society grows increasingly complex, and our need for trained leaders increases correspondingly. Appellant's case represents, perhaps, the epitome of that need, for he is attempting to obtain an advanced degree in education, to become, by definition, a leader and trainer of others. Those who will come under his guidance and influence must be directly affected by the education he receives. Their own education and development will necessarily suffer to the extent that his training is unequal to that of his classmates. State-imposed restrictions which produce such inequalities cannot be sustained.

It may be argued that appellant will be in no better position when these restrictions are removed, for he may still be set apart by his fellow students. This we think irrelevant. There is a vast difference—a Constitutional difference—between restrictions imposed by the state which prohibit the intellectual commingling of students, and the refusal of individuals to commingle where the state presents no such bar. . . . The removal of the state restrictions will not necessarily abate individual and group predilections, prejudices and choices. But at the very least, the state will not be depriving appellant of the opportunity to secure acceptance by his fellow students on his own merits.

We conclude that the conditions under which this appellant is required to receive his education deprive him of his personal and present right to the equal protection of the laws. . . . We hold that under these circumstances the Fourteenth Amendment precludes differences in treatment by the state based upon race. Appellant, having been admitted to a state-supported graduate school, must receive the same treatment at the hands of the state as students of other races. The judgment is   *Reversed.*

NOTES

1. The impact of the *Sweatt* and *McLaurin* cases was demonstrated in many cases. One particularly noteworthy decision was handed down in 1951. Here four qualified Negro students applied for admission to the school of Law of the University of North Carolina and were rejected, solely on the basis of race and color. The court thoroughly examined the quality of separate facilities at the all Negro North Carolina College Law School and found substantial inequality. The court went into such depth as to compare the number, reputation, salaries, and scholarly research of the faculties; in addition the court counted and compared the courses taught by both schools, facilities, libraries, and expenditure per pupil. The court concluded from this analysis that the schools although separate were not equal. An important aspect of the court's decision was to observe that it was extremely difficult and expensive for a state to establish two equivalent quality institutions in the "higher reaches of the educational field." This, of course, reflected the strategy of Negro groups who were endeavoring to force states to desegregate if for no other than economic reasons. McKissick v. Carmichael, 187 F.2d 949 (1951).

2. In 1954 a federal court held that the Louisiana system of "separate but equal" in higher education violated the Fourteenth Amendment because it established a regional college for white students but did not do the same for Negroes. It was found that white students could attend Southwestern Louisiana Institute in Lafayette Parish while Negro students were forced to drive 89 miles to receive an equivalent education. The court held for the plaintiffs and stated:

> In this case, that facility is the privilege given to the white people in the area of Lafayette and denied the Negro citizens in the area of Lafayette, namely, going to college at home—together with its economic advantages. White persons, thousands of them, have received college education solely because of this privilege. . . . The state

is under no compulsion to establish these colleges, yet if they establish them, the rights of white and Negro alike must be measured by the test of equality of privileges and opportunities. The right of the individual student to the privilege of public instruction equivalent to that given by the State to the individual student of another race is a personal one. . . . "The question cannot be decided by averaging the facilities provided for the two classes of pupils throughout the country and comparing one with the other, since the rights created by the Fourteenth Amendment are individual and personal and the prohibitions of the Amendment are observed only when the same or equivalent treatment is accorded to persons of different races similarly situated."

Constantine v. Southwestern Louisiana Institute, 120 F. Supp. 417 (1954).

Racial segregation by the state is unconstitutional

BROWN v. BOARD OF EDUCATION OF TOPEKA

Supreme Court of the United States, 1954.
347 U.S. 483.

MR. CHIEF JUSTICE WARREN delivered the opinion of the Court.

These cases come to us from the States of Kansas, South Carolina, Virginia, and Delaware. They are premised on different facts and different local conditions, but a common legal question justifies their consideration together in this consolidated opinion.

In each of the cases, minors of the Negro race, through their legal representatives, seek the aid of the courts in obtaining admission to the public schools of their community on a nonsegregated basis. In each instance, they have been denied admission to schools attended by white children under laws requiring or permitting segregation according to race. This segregation was alleged to deprive the plaintiffs of the equal protection of the laws under the Fourteenth Amendment. In each of the cases other than the Delaware case, a three-judge federal district court denied relief to the plaintiffs on the so-called "separate but equal" doctrine announced by this Court in Plessy v. Ferguson, 163 U.S. 537, 16 S.Ct. 1138, 41 L.Ed. 256. Under that doctrine, equality of treatment is accorded when the races are provided substantially equal facilities, even though these facilities be separate. In the Delaware case, the Supreme Court of Delaware adhered to that doctrine, but ordered that the plaintiffs be admitted to the white schools because of their superiority to the Negro schools.

The plaintiffs contend that segregated public schools are not "equal" and cannot be made "equal," and that hence they are deprived of the equal protection of the laws. Because of the obvious importance of the question presented, the Court took jurisdiction. Argument was heard in the 1952 Term, and reargument was heard this Term on certain questions propounded by the Court. * * *

In the first cases in this Court constructing the Fourteenth Amendment, decided shortly after its adoption, the Court interpreted it as proscribing all state-imposed discriminations against the Negro race. The doctrine of "separate but equal" did not make its appearance in this Court until 1896 in the case of Plessy v. Ferguson, supra, involving not education but transportation. American courts have since labored with the doctrine for over half a century. In this Court, there have been six cases involving the "separate but equal" doctrine in the field of public education. In Cumming v. Board of Education of Richmond County, 175 U.S. 528, 20 S.Ct. 197, 44 L.Ed. 262, and Gong Lum v. Rice, 275 U.S. 78, 48 S.Ct. 91, 72 L.Ed. 172, the validity of the doctrine itself was not challenged. In more recent cases, all on the graduate school level, inequality was found in that specific benefits enjoyed by white students were denied to Negro students of the same educational qualifications. State of Missouri ex rel. Gaines v. Canada, 305 U.S. 337, 59 S.Ct. 232, 83 L.Ed. 208; Sipuel v. Board of Regents of University of Oklahoma, 332 U.S. 631, 68 S.Ct. 299, 92 L.Ed. 247; Sweatt v. Painter, 339 U.S. 629, 70 S.Ct. 848, 94 L.Ed. 1114; McLaurin v. Oklahoma State Regents, 339 U.S. 637, 70 S.Ct. 851, 94 L.Ed. 1149. In none of these cases was it necessary to reexamine the doctrine to grant relief to the Negro plaintiff. And in Sweatt v. Painter, supra, the Court expressly reserved decision on the question whether Plessy v. Ferguson should be held inapplicable to public education.

In the instant cases, that question is directly presented. Here, unlike Sweatt v. Painter, there are findings below that the Negro and white schools involved have been equalized, or are being equalized, with respect to buildings, curricula, qualifications and salaries of teachers, and other "tangible" factors. Our decision, therefore, cannot turn on merely a comparison of these tangible factors in the Negro and white schools involved in each of the cases. We must look instead to the effect of segregation itself on public education.

In approaching this problem, we cannot turn the clock back to 1868 when the Amendment was adopted, or even to 1896 when Plessy v. Ferguson was written. We must consider public education in the light of its full development and its present place in American life throughout the Nation. Only in this way can it be determined if segregation in public schools deprives these plaintiffs of the equal protection of the laws.

Today, education is perhaps the most important function of state and local governments. Compulsory school attendance laws and the great expenditures for education both demonstrate our recognition of the importance of education to our democratic society. It is required in the performance of our most basic public responsibilities, even service in the armed forces. It is the very foundation of good citizenship. Today it is a principal instrument in awakening the child to cultural values, in preparing him for later professional training, and in helping him to adjust normally to his environment. In these days, it is doubtful that any child may reasonably be expected to succeed in life if he is denied the opportunity of an education. Such an opportunity, where the state has undertaken to provide it, is a right which must be made available to all on equal terms.

We come then to the question presented: Does segregation of children in public schools solely on the basis of race, even though the physical facilities and other "tangible" factors may be equal, deprive the children of the minority group of equal educational opportunities? We believe that it does.

In Sweatt v. Painter, supra [339 U.S. 629, 70 S.Ct. 850], in finding that a segregated law school for Negroes could not provide them equal educational opportunities, this Court relied in large part on "those qualities which are incapable of objective measurement but which make for greatness in a law school." In McLaurin v. Oklahoma State Regents, supra [339 U.S. 637, 70 S.Ct. 853], the Court, in requiring that a Negro admitted to a white graduate school be treated like all other students, again resorted to intangible considerations: "* * * his ability to study, to engage in discussions and exchange views with other students, and, in general, to learn his profession." Such considerations apply with added force to children in grade and high schools. To separate them from others of similar age and qualifications solely because of their race generates a feeling of inferiority as to their status in the community that may affect their hearts and minds in a way unlikely ever to be undone. The effect of this separation on their educational opportunities was well stated by a finding in the Kansas case by a court which nevertheless felt compelled to rule against the Negro plaintiffs:

> "Segregation of white and colored children in public schools has a detrimental effect upon the colored children. The impact is greater when it has the sanction of the law; for the policy of separating the races is usually interpreted as denoting the inferiority of the Negro group. A sense of inferiority affects the motivation of a child to learn. Segregation with the sanction of law, therefore, has a tendency to [retard] the educational and mental development of Negro children and to deprive them of some of the benefits they would receive in a racial[ly] integrated school system."

Whatever may have been the extent of psychological knowledge at the time of Plessy v. Ferguson, this finding is amply supported by modern authority. Any language in Plessy v. Ferguson contrary to this finding is rejected.

We conclude that in the field of public education the doctrine of "separate but equal" has no place. Separate educational facilities are inherently unequal. Therefore, we hold that the plaintiffs and others similarly situated for whom the actions have been brought are, by reason of the segregation complained of, deprived of the equal protection of the laws guaranteed by the Fourteenth Amendment. This disposition makes unnecessary any discussion whether such segregation also violates the Due Process Clause of the Fourteenth Amendment.

Because these are class actions, because of the wide applicability of this decision, and because of the great variety of local conditions, the formulation of decrees in these cases presents problems of considerable complexity. On reargument, the consideration of appropriate relief was necessarily subordinated to the primary question—the constitutionality of segregation in public education. We have now announced that such segregation is a denial of the equal protection of the laws. In order that we may have the full assistance of the parties in formulating decrees, the cases will be restored to the docket, and the parties are requested to present further argument on Questions 4 and 5 previously propounded by the Court for the reargument this Term. The Attorney General of the United States is again invited to participate. The Attorneys General of the states requiring or permitting segregation in public education will also be permitted to appear as *amici curiae* upon request to do so by September 15, 1954, and submission of briefs by October 1, 1954.

It is so ordered.

Appointment of trustees by state court to carry out testamentary racial exclusion is unconstitutional state action

COMMONWEALTH OF PENNSYLVANIA v. BROWN

United States Court of Appeals, Third Circuit, 1968.
392 F.2d 120.

GERALD McLAUGHLIN, Circuit Judge.

The problem here arises from the will of Stephen Girard, a Philadelphia, Pennsylvania resident who died in 1831. In his will, dated 1830, he laid down his fundamental thesis that he had "been for a long time impressed with the importance of educating the poor, and of placing them by the early cultivation of their minds and the development of their moral principles, above the many temptations, to which, through poverty and ignorance they are exposed; * * *." Continuing, he said "* * * I am particularly desirous to provide for such a number of poor male white orphan children, as can be trained in one institution, a better education as well as a more comfortable maintenance than they usually receive from the application of public funds." * * * The will went into considerable particulars regarding the Girard Philadelphia and Kentucky property. Concerning a personal estate bequest of two million dollars for the College the will outlined at length where it would be located and in great detail the exact construction of the College and outbuildings, etc. * * *

Mr. Girard stated specifically in his will:

> "In relation to the organization of the college and its appendages, I leave, necessarily, many details to the Mayor, Aldermen and citizens of Philadelphia and their successors; and I do so, with the more confidence, as, from the nature of my bequests and the benefit to result from them, I trust that my fellow citizens of Philadelphia, will observe and evince especial care and anxiety in selecting members of their City Councils, and other agents * * *."

He provided that the College accounts be kept separately so that they could be examined by a committee of the Pennsylvania legislature and that an account of same be rendered annually to said legislature together with a report of the state of the College. Philadelphia accepted the bequests and by ordinance set up a plan to administer the College by a Trusts Board. In 1833 a building committee of the City Council was appointed, a president of the College was chosen under an ordinance created for that purpose and the cornerstone of the main building laid. Construction was concluded in 1847 and the College opened the first of the following year. Down to 1869 the City Council operated the College directly, first by way of the trustees until 1851 when the latter offices were abolished, and the Council again took over direct management. In 1869 the Commonwealth enacted a law which gave Philadelphia a local Board of Trusts to take over the control of Girard College. From that date the Board of City Trusts remained in charge of the College until 1958. Broadly summing up the Commonwealth and City's intimate association with Girard College, the District Court, with full justification in the record, found as fact that:

> "Beginning in 1831 and continuing to date, the Commonwealth of Pennsylvania and the City of Philadelphia, by the enactment of statutes and ordinances, by the use and supervision of public officials, appointed by legislative and judicial bodies, by rendering services and providing tax exemptions, perpetual existence and exemption from tort liability have given aid, assistance, direction and involvement to the construction, maintenance, operation and policies of Girard College." * * *

In 1954 two applicants requested admission to the College. They were fully qualified but were refused because they were Negroes. They brought their cause to the United States Supreme Court which held in that suit, titled Commonwealth of Pennsylvania et al. v. Board of Directors of City Trusts of City of Philadelphia, 353 U.S. 230, 231, 77 S.Ct. 806, 807, 1 L.Ed.2d 792 (1958):

> "The Board which operates Girard College is an agency of the State of Pennsylvania. Therefore, even though the Board was acting as a trustee, its refusal to admit Foust and Felder to the college because they were Negroes was discrimination by the State. Such discrimination is forbidden by the Fourteenth Amendment. Brown v. Board of Education of Topeka, 347 U.S. 483, 74 S.Ct. 686, 98 L.Ed. 873. Accordingly, the judgment of the Supreme Court of Pennsylvania is reversed and the cause is remanded for further proceedings not inconsistent with this opinion."

The Supreme Court of Pennsylvania on remand took none of the plainly indicated proceedings called for by the United States Supreme Court. It simply remanded the litigation to the Orphans' Court of Philadelphia County.[1] That court, without notice or opportunity for the plaintiffs to do anything and with no request from the City or other source whatsoever, on its own initiative ousted Philadelphia as trustee and installed in place of the City Board, persons of its own choosing. * * *

The Philadelphia City Trustees took no appeal from their ouster. The children plaintiffs did. The Pennsylvania Supreme Court found that the Orphans' Court action was not inconsistent with the mandate of the United States Supreme Court or the Fourteenth Amendment or the Girard will. Application for certiorari was denied by the United States Supreme Court, 357 U.S. 570, 78 S.Ct. 1383, 2 L.Ed.2d 1546 (1958).

The present litigation was instituted in the United States District Court for the Eastern District of Pennslyvania. The trial judge originally passed solely upon the question of whether Girard College was within the jurisdiction of the Pennsylvania Public Accommodations Act of June 11, 1935, P.L. 297, as amended by the Act of June 24, 1939, P.L. 872. The Court held it was within Sections (a) and (c) of the Act and not within the proviso of Section (d). This Court reversed that finding and returned the suit to the District Court for trial on the merits of Count 1 of the complaint which charges that "The refusal of the trustees of Girard College to admit applicants without regard to race violates the Constitution of the United States of America and applicable Federal statutes."

Appellants argue that they have not violated the equal pro-

---

1. As rightly found by the District Court:
   "In 1959, after the decision of the United States Supreme Court in [Commonwealth of] Pennsylvania v. Board of Directors [etc.] 353 U.S. 230 [77 S.Ct. 806, 1 L.Ed.2d 792] (1957), the Legislature of Pennsylvania enacted a statute granting the Orphans' Court the power and the duty to appoint substitute trustees for the property of minors, when a previous trustee which was a political subdivision is removed 'in the public interest,' and authorized a substitute trustee to invest such property of minors committed to their custody. The Act also contained other enabling legislation, without which the present defendants would be unable to carry out their duties. Act of November, 19, 1959, P.L. 1526 (Exh. P-51 (10)). The Legislature Journal of the Senate of the Commonwealth of Pennsylvania shows that this statute was passed specifically as enabling legislation in aid of Girard College (Exh. P-51 (10))."

tection clause of the Fourteenth Amendment by denying admission to individuals because of their color. In support of this they cite some Pennsylvania decisions including the State Supreme Court Girard College opinion on the remand of the United States Supreme Court to that State Court "for further proceedings not inconsistent with this opinion." What the State Court did was turn the matter over to its Orphans' Court which eliminated the City as trustee and installed its own group, sworn to uphold the literal language of the Girard will, a move effectively continuing the very segregation which had been condemned by the United States Supreme Court. True, the latter had denied the application for certiorari. Times without number that Court has plainly ruled that there is no inference permissible from its denial of application for certiorari, favorable or unfavorable to either side of a litigation. Certainly in the whole muddy situation flowing from the State excision of the City Board, thereby taking away the linchpin of the Girard will, the then existing state litigation picture did not bring into the necessary sharp focus, the set piece maneuver which had completely circumvented the Supreme Court's directive. We, however, as above seen, do have all of that amazing effort to maintain Girard's discriminatory status before us in its true perspective.

Even in the above short résumé of the conception, creation and functioning of Girard College, the close, indispensable relationship between the College, the City of Philadelphia and the Commonwealth of Pennsylvania intended by Mr. Girard, meticulously set out in his will and faithfully followed for one hundred and twenty-seven years is self evident. * * *

On the whole vital Commonwealth and City relationship to Girard College shown we must agree with Judge Lord in the District Court, that the facts in Evans v. Newton, 382 U.S. 296, 301, 302, 86 S.Ct. 486, 15 L.Ed.2d 373 (1966) are fairly comparable to those in this appeal and that the decision of the Supreme Court therein governs the issue before us. In Evans a tract of land was willed to the Mayor and City Council of Macon, Georgia, as a park for white people, to be controlled by a white Board of Managers. The city desegregated the park and the managers thereafter sued the city and the trustees of the residuary beneficiaries, asking for the city's removal as trustee and the appointment of private trustees to enforce the racial limitations of the will. The Court accepted the city's resignation and appointed three new trustees. The State Supreme Court upheld the terms of the will and the appointment of the new trustees. The United States Supreme Court reversed. Mr. Justice Douglas for the Court in the opinion said as to the park in issue:

> "The momentum it acquired as a public facility is certainly not dissipated ipso facto by the appointment of 'private' trustees. So far as this record shows, there has been no change in municipal maintenance and concern over this facility. Whether these public characteristics will in time be dissipated is wholly conjectural. If the municipality remains entwined in the management or control of the park, it remains subject to the restraints of the Fourteenth Amendment * * *.
>
>   *   *   *   *   *   *
>
> "Under the circumstances of this case, we cannot but conclude that the public character of this park requires that it be treated as a public institution subject to the command of the Fourteenth Amendment, regardless of who now has title under state law." * * *

Girard's definitive position in this period of more than ever being operated by an agency of the state does not simply emanate from the momentum of the Commonwealth and City legitimate participation in the establishment of Girard and its institutional life from its beginning to the present moment. It is in addition, as we hold, the obvious net consequence of the displacement of the City Board by the Commonwealth's agent and the filling of the Girard Trusteeships with persons selected by the Commonwealth and committed to upholding the letter of the will. Those radical changes pushed the College right back into its old and ugly unconstitutional position. Had the City Trustees been left undisturbed it is inconceivable that this bitter dispute before us would not have been long ago lawfully and justly terminated. It is inconceivable that those City Trustees would not have with goodwill opened the College to all qualified children. Given everything we know of Mr. Girard, it is inconceivable that in this changed world he would not be quietly happy that his cherished project had raised its sights with the times and joyfully recognized that all human beings are created equal.

We do not consider the move of the state court in disposing of the City Trustees and installing its own appointees to be a non obvious involvement of the State as mentioned in the test outlined in Burton v. Wilmington Parking Authority, 365 U.S. 715, 722, 81 S. Ct. 856, 6 L.Ed.2d 45 (1961). The action in this instance and its motivation are to put it mildly, conspicuous. And what happened to Girard does "* * * signifi-

cantly encourage and involve the State in private discriminations." Reitman v. Mulkey, 387 U.S. 369, 381, 87 S. Ct. 1627,
1634, 18 L.Ed.2d 830 (1967). As the Court there said by Mr.
Justice White, "We have been presented with no persuasive
considerations indicating that these judgments should be
overturned."

The judgment of the District Court will be affirmed.

KALODNER, Circuit Judge (concurring in the result).

NOTES

The United States Court of Appeals for the Fourth Circuit held in 1964 that a private hospital performing a state
function as a chosen instrument of the state was bound by the
Fourteenth Amendment to refrain from racial discrimination
and could not deny admission to staff memberships and treatment facilities on racially discriminatory basis. This court
pointed out that the right of tax exemption and the power
of eminent domain granted a private hospital were facts
which must be considered in determining state participation
or state action. Eaton v. Grubbs, 329 F.2d 710 (1964) ; see
also Simkins v. Moses H. Cone Memorial Hospital, 323 F.2d
959 (4th Cir. 1963), *cert. denied*, 84 S. Ct. 793 (March 3,
1964).

Good faith actions by state satisfies obligations
to dismantle segregation at college level

ALABAMA STATE TEACHERS ASSOCIATION
v. ALABAMA PUBLIC SCHOOL AND
COLLEGE AUTHORITY

United States District Court, M.D. Alabama, N.D., 1968.
289 F. Supp. 784.

FRANK M. JOHNSON, Jr., District Judge:

The plaintiffs in this class action seek to prevent the State
of Alabama from constructing and operating a four-year, degree-granting extension of Auburn University in the City of
Montgomery, Alabama. Plaintiffs originally sought a declaratory judgment as to the invalidity of and an injunction against
any action under or pursuant to Alabama Act No. 243 of 1965
and Alabama Act No. 403 of 1967. * * *

Plaintiffs primary attack on Act No. 403 may be stated as

a syllogism: Alabama historically has had a dual system of higher education by law; although no longer supported by law, the dual system in fact remains largely intact; this Court and the Fifth Circuit recognize in the elementary and secondary education area an affirmative duty to dismantle the dual system, * * * that duty is equally applicable to higher education; that duty requires officials to utilize new construction or expansion of facilities as an opportunity to dismantle the dual system; the history and operation of Acts Nos. 243 and 403 indicate that in planning the construction of the Auburn branch at Montgomery defendants did not maximize desegregation; therefore, their action is unconstitutional and should be enjoined.

At the outset it should be noted that this argument presents a case of first impression. To our knowledge, no court in dealing with desegregation of institutions in the higher education area has gone farther than ordering nondiscriminatory admissions. That is also as far as Congress went in the 1964 Civil Rights Act.[2] The Department of Health, Education and Welfare has also largely limited its concern to admissions policies in administering Title 6 of the 1964 Civil Rights Act.[3]

We too are reluctant at this time to go much beyond preventing discriminatory admissions. Although much of plaintiffs' argument is valid, several faulty premises lead us to reject the conclusion they urge upon us. * * *

Plaintiffs fail to take account of some significant differences between the elementary and secondary public schools and institutions of higher education and of some related differences concerning the role the courts should play in dismantling the dual systems. Public elementary and secondary schools are traditionally free and compulsory. Prior to "freedom of choice," children were assigned to their respective schools. This could be done with equanimity because, in principle at least, one school for a given grade level is substantially similar to another in terms of goals, facilities, course offerings, teacher training and salaries, and so forth. * * *

Higher education is neither free nor compulsory. Students

---

2. 42 U.S.C. § 2000c-4(a) (2). Compare subsection (2) with subsection (1), which seems to authorize a wider range of civil action by the Attorney General in the elementary and secondary school area.

3. 45 C.F.R. § 80.4(d). Compare subsection (d) with subsection (c) which for elementary and secondary schools requires a plan for desegregation. Pursuant to this, H.E.W. has compiled an elaborate set of guidelines. See 45 C.F.R. § 181 (1967).

choose which, if any, institution they will attend. In making that choice they face the full range of diversity in goals, facilities, equipment, course offerings, teacher training and salaries, and living arrangements, perhaps only to mention a few. From where legislators sit, of course, the system must be viewed on a statewide basis. In deciding to open a new institution or build a branch or expand an existing institution, and in deciding where to locate it, the legislature must consider a very complicated pattern of demand for and availability of the above-listed variables, including, also, impact on the dual system. We conclude that in reviewing such a decision to determine whether it maximized desegregation we would necessarily be involved, consciously or by default, in a wide range of educational policy decisions in which courts should not become involved. * * *

At the present time there are four institutions of higher learning in Montgomery: two private—Huntingdon College and Alabama Christian College—and two public—Alabama State College and the University of Alabama Montgomery Extension Center. The Center does not grant degrees; its offerings are similar to those of a junior college. Alabama State is a predominately Negro four-year liberal arts college with an emphasis on education of teachers. * * *

Plaintiffs make a number of contentions * * *. They maintain that the reason for having a new college in Montgomery was to provide for white students in the area. To the extent that this may mean "to provide for white students only," the record does not bear them out. Plaintiffs rely heavily upon testimony that 137 students commuted from Montgomery County for the purpose of attending the Alexander City State Junior College located at Alexander City, Alabama, although Montgomery County is not supposed to be in that school's geographic area. However, it is noted that 12 of those 137 students are Negroes, and there is nothing in the record now before this Court to indicate that those Negroes, if they so desire, will not be absorbed into the new Auburn branch in Montgomery along with other Negroes and whites.

Plaintiffs further contend that inadequate consideration was given to how the proposed Auburn branch might be operated so as to eliminate the dual school system and that, because of this, the new college has become and will continue to be an identifiably "white" institution. * * * But this argument overlooks the fact that Alabama State is at least as identifiably "black" as Auburn is identifiably "white." In terms of eliminating the dual school system, one label is no more preferable than the other.

We thus reject plaintiffs' conclusion that, when the new college is put into operation, Montgomery will have two colleges —one Negro, one white. As plaintiffs themselves indicate: "In terms of anything heretofore existing in Montgomery, the Auburn branch will be for all practical purposes a 'new institution.' " It is certainly as reasonable to conclude that a new institution will not be a white school or a Negro school, but just a school, as it is to believe that Alabama State would so evolve. * * *

Auburn University has been ordered by this Court to admit all qualified Negroes on terms consistent with the equal protection clause of the Fourteenth Amendment. * * * It would appear that Auburn has abided and will continue to abide by that order in good faith. Testimony indicated that it has recruited and is continuing to recruit more Negro faculty members.

We conclude, therefore, that as long as the State and a particular institution are dealing with admissions, faculty and staff in good faith the basic requirement of the affirmative duty to dismantle the dual school system on the college level, to the extent that the system may be based upon racial considerations, is satisfied.

This is not to suggest that we view the problem as merely personal rather than systematic. As plaintiffs indicated, nondiscriminatory admissions in higher education are analogous to a freedom-of-choice plan in the elementary and secondary public schools. We are also cognizant that recent Supreme Court decisions [4] have cast doubt on the continued viability of freedom of choice in the public schools. But we do not interpret those decisions as applying to the operation of an education system on a college level. Freedom to choose where one will attend college, unlike choosing one's elementary or secondary public school, has a long tradition and helps to perform an important function, viz., fitting the right school to the right student.

We believe that an effective beginning has been made at Auburn to dismantle the racial characteristics of that school system and that, as effective desegregation plans are developed in the elementary and secondary public schools, the problem

4. Green v. County School Board of New Kent County, Virginia, 391 U.S. 430, 88 S.Ct. 1689, 20 L.Ed.2d 716 (U.S. May 27, 1968) * * *.

will probably resolve itself in the case of higher education. If the Auburn branch at Montgomery is administered as "just a school," as we are assured it will be and as we are confident it will be, our conclusions as herein outlined will receive significant confirmation.

Accordingly, it is the order, judgment and decree of this Court that the challenged statute, Alabama Act No. 403, 1967 Legislature, is not unconstitutional on its face or as applied to plaintiffs; it is further ordered that the relief herein sought by plaintiffs be and the same is hereby denied.

It is further ordered that the costs in this proceeding be and they are hereby taxed against the plaintiffs, for which execution may issue.

Affirmative steps to integrate may be required if "open door" policy does not effectuate desegregation

SANDERS v. ELLINGTON

United States District Court, M.D. Tennessee, Nashville Division, 1968.
288 F. Supp. 937.

FRANK GRAY, Jr., District Judge.

This action was brought in an effort to prevent the University of Tennessee from constructing a new facility for expanding its program at the Nashville Center. * * *

By its complaint in intervention the United States seeks not only an injunction to prevent the construction of the new facility, but also asks that this court order the State defendants to present a plan calculated to produce meaningful desegregation of the public universities of Tennessee.

In considering this case it is necessary, in my opinion, to put the present situation in perspective. The history of public educational opportunities for Negroes in Tennessee is not a pretty one. Prior to the Supreme Court decision in Brown v. Board of Education in 1954 [347 U.S. 483, 74 S.Ct. 686, 98 L.Ed. 873] the public educational system of Tennessee operated under one-half of the decision of the Supreme Court in Plessy v. Ferguson of 1896 [163 U.S. 537, 16 S.Ct. 1138, 41 L.Ed. 256]. The races were certainly kept separate in the schools, but I would assume that no one would argue in good faith that the schools were equal.

The lone institution for so-called higher learning operated by the State of Tennessee for Negroes was the institution now designated as Tennessee Agricultural and Industrial State University. One of its chief functions was, according to the statutory history, the training of teachers. * * *

The record does show, however, that now all institutions of higher learning are at this time pursuing an open-door policy.

Complaint is made here that the dual education system admittedly heretofore established by law in Tennessee has not been dismantled and, to support this allegation, figures have been introduced showing that the historically white institutions still have overwhelmingly white enrollments, and the Tennessee A & I State University still has an overwhelmingly Negro enrollment.

Figures introduced at this hearing indicate that some 57,000 students attend the State's public universities, of whom slightly over 6,000 are Negroes, or approximately 11 percent of the total.

In the individual traditionally white institutions the percentage of Negro enrollment ranges from six-tenths of one percent to a high of about 7 percent at Memphis State University. Incidentally, Memphis State University's percentage is not closely approached by any of the other schools.

On the other hand, Tennessee A & I State University continues substantially all Negro with a Negro enrollment in excess of 99 percent.

Based on the foregoing, the court finds that the dual system of education created originally by law has not been effectively dismantled. It appears, with the possible exception of Memphis State University, that progress toward desegregating these institutions in the eight years of the open-door policy has been slow. The reasons for this slow progress are, as I view the record, many and diverse.

I do not find, however, that the defendant Board of Trustees for the University of Tennessee or its administrative officials or the State Board of Education operating the other Tennessee public institutions of higher learning or its administrative officials are now or have been in the recent past, and I emphasize recent, guilty of any constitutionally impermissible acts in the administration of the institutions. Rather, it appears to the court clearly evident that the present situation is the result of mistakes and inequities in the past. * * *

The University of Tennessee Nashville Center was established some twenty years ago to provide evening courses for employed persons who could not attend regularly scheduled classes at ordinary day institutions. The record indicated that the University made this step in Nashville at the request of Nashville citizens when other schools located in Nashville discontinued evening offerings. The Nashville Center remains primarily an evening program. The enrollment has steadily grown and the number of course offerings has gradually increased to the point that students can now complete their requirements for a degree at the Nashville Center.

In addition to its evening program the Nashville Center operates the graduate school of social work for the University of Tennessee. At the request of Nashville Metropolitan Board of Hospitals, the Center has just begun to offer a two-year day program leading to the degree of Associate of Arts in Nursing.

From the record it appears that the University of Tennessee plans to construct a new building for the Nashville Center to provide more adequate space and facilities for the constantly growing programs mentioned above. In addition, the University seeks to provide for use of the new facility by other programs. The Government-Industry-Law Center of the University of Tennessee has planned to use the facilities of the new building for its Center for Training and Career Development. This program, which was begun in June of last year, is designed to provide continuous in-service training and career development for state and local government employees.

Further, the record indicates that the new facility is designed to provide space for statewide or regional conferences, seminars and workshops which are held in conjunction with the University's continuing education program.

Comparable programs at A & I consist of a nursing course and a limited evening program begun in recent years.

There is nothing in the record to indicate that the University of Tennessee has any intention to make the Nashville Center a degree-granting day institution. On the contrary, the record clearly indicates and the court finds that, in its expansion program for the Nashville Center, the University of Tennessee seeks only to provide a quality continuing education and public service center for Nashville and Middle Tennessee with overwhelming emphasis being placed upon the provision of educational opportunity for employed persons of all races who must seek their education at night.

I do not find that the proposed construction and operation of the University of Tennessee Nashville Center will necessarily perpetuate a dual system of higher education. It may well be that, under the provisions of what I shall say later on in this opinion, this additional educational facility in the Nashville area may play a part in the furthering of a unitary system.

I specifically point out that, in reaching this decision that injunctive relief should be denied, I have not grounded it on the recent case of Alabama State Teachers Association v. Alabama Public School and College Authority, 289 F. Supp. 784 (M.D.Ala., July 26, 1968), involving the construction in Montgomery, Alabama, by Auburn University, a historically white institution, of a facility completely duplicating a historically Negro public college in that City.

Having said as I did earlier that many of the problems facing the responsible authorities in attempting desegregation of the public universities are not of their making does not mean that thereby they are relieved of the responsibility of achieving a desegregated system of higher education.

Upon consideration of the relevant precedents, particularly the decision of the Supreme Court in Green v. County School Board of New Kent County, 391 U.S. 430, 88 S.Ct. 1689, 20 L.Ed.2d 716 (1968), and its companion cases, the court is convinced that there is an affirmative duty imposed upon the State by the Fourteenth Amendment to the Constitution of the United States to dismantle the dual system of higher education which presently exists in Tennessee.

The next question is whether the State is discharging this duty or has indicated that it has any plan to discharge this duty. In resolving this question the court has not attempted to fashion a comprehensive definition of what the duty requires. The court has, on the other hand, examined the record carefully in an attempt to determine what steps, if any, have been taken by the State of Tennessee through its higher educational institutions to disestablish the dual system.

From this examination the court has come to the conclusion that the University of Tennessee and the historically white institutions under the Tennessee Board of Education have made at least some good faith efforts to bring about desegregation of their institutions. I cannot say that I find any indication from the record, incomplete as it is, that the individual school administrators at these institutions are failing to do what is within their individual powers to do to desegregate their institutions.

Insofar as these historically white institutions are concerned, when everything is considered, including the geographic location of the various institutions, the quality of secondary schools surrounding them and the number of available Negro students who are qualified for admission, it appears that genuine progress is being made.

However, the court does not find it necessary to decide whether these efforts have fulfilled the duty of the individual institutions, because the fact remains that nothing has been done to dismantle effectively the dual system so graphically illustrated by the enrollment at Tennessee A & I State University.

Nothing has been shown in the record to indicate that any plan has been proposed, devised or considered to lead to the desegregation of that University except the naked fact of an open-door policy. The court is convinced that this policy alone does not discharge the affirmative duty imposed upon the State by the constitution where, under the policy, there is no genuine progress toward desegregation and no genuine prospect of progress.

Therefore, the court will enter an order requiring the defendants to submit to the court a plan designed to effect such desegregation of the higher educational institutions of Tennessee, with particular attention to Tennessee A & I State University, as to indicate the dismantling of the dual system now existing. * * *

I will provide that the plan to be submitted shall be submitted on or before April 1, 1969.

I will ask counsel to prepare an appropriate order in which the two salient factors of this decision will be set forth; that is, the denial of relief insofar as the prevention of the expansion of the University of Tennessee's program for its Nashville Center, and the provision for the submission of a plan.

NOTES

INTEGRATION OF HIGHER EDUCATION IN THE SOUTH*

[Critique of Court's position in Alabama case]

The court gave three arguments in support of its approach. It felt that higher education, unlike primary and secondary

* *Columbia Law Review*, Vol. 69, pp. 118-120 (1969); *reprinted with permission.*

education, involved policy considerations beyond the competence of the judiciary and consequently called for a much nar-
rower scope of review. It further distinguished higher from
primary and secondary education by noting that universities
are neither compulsory nor free and that there is a tradition
of choosing one's own college. Finally, although the court
found that a nondiscriminatory admissions policy on the college level is analogous to freedom-of-choice plans at lower levels, it refused to apply decisions which cast doubt on the constitutionality of such plans. It felt that the traditional freedom of choice in selecting a college served an important educational function: fitting the right school to the right student.

The court's reasoning suffers from several infirmities. First,
the noncompulsory character of attendance at a state university should be of no constitutional significance. The presence of compulsory attendance in primary schools has been a
relevant or critical factor in cases dealing with de facto segregation in the North. This was because the compulsion to attend
a particular school established the required state action.[41]
However, as previously noted, this problem is not relevant in
the case of an education system that was originally segregated
as a matter of law.[42]

Furthermore, the court almost certainly both overstates the
extent to which college integration poses harder policy questions than high school integration and understates the willingness of courts to override reasonable educational policy in
order to achieve integration at the primary and secondary
level. Where to locate a new high school may be every bit as
difficult a decision as where to locate a new college. The neighborhood school is a sound and traditional educational policy,
but the courts have required that this concept be adapted to
achieve integration.[43] If a Southern state made admission to
some high schools competitive, the courts would most likely
review this policy if it served to maintain the dual system.
Such review has occurred where Northern schools divide
classes on the basis of ability because this otherwise sound

41. See note 30 supra.
42. See note 23 supra.
43. Many courts while accepting the principle of neighborhood schools,
have closely scrutinized its effects on racial imbalance and have required
school boards to redraw district lines when the existing districts were
found to be unacceptable, e.g., Branche v. Board of Educ., 204 F. Supp.
150 (E.D.N.Y. 1962); Jackson v. Pasadena City School Dist., 59 Cal. 2d
876, 382 P.2d 878, 31 Cal. Rptr. 606 (1963).

educational policy serves to maintain a racial imbalance within a particular classroom.[44]

But more basically, the court's reluctance to question freedom of choice and the policy of state officials in the higher education context stems from a misconception of its constitutional role in achieving integration, especially where segregation has previously been imposed by law. * * *

The Alabama court, * * * failed even to suggest that it had power to demand that school officials consider racial factors. Other courts have often gone further and required close judicial surveillance and review of political judgments which adversely affect the interests of racial or impoverished minorities. Although all courts are reluctant to review closely those decisions which they believe to be within the discretion and expertise of school boards or other administrative agencies,[49] the increasing importance of higher education in general,[50] and public higher education specifically,[51] combined with recent evidence of the continuing inequality of educational resources and opportunities available to minorities,[52] suggests the need for an active judicial role.

---

44. *See* Hobson v. Hansen, 269 F. Supp. 401 (D.D.C. 1967). The argument employed by school officials in defense of the use of ability groupings at the primary school level, although it perpetuates the dual system, is strikingly similar to that forwarded in the *Alabama State* decision. In Hobson v. Hansen, *id.*, the district court, facing such an argument, acknowledged the fact that such groupings are an accepted educational practice designed "to fit the right program to the right student." Nevertheless, that court rejected this justification for the resulting racial imbalance, pointing out that "where disadvantaged children, primarily negro, are relegated to lower tracts . . . such disadvantaged children are denied equal educational opportunity." 269 F. Supp. at 415.

49. *See e.g.*, Pitts v. Board of Trustees, 84 F. Supp. 975, 988 (E.D. Ark. 1949).

50. The need for higher education and the duty of the state to provide it as part of a public educational system, are part of the democratic faith of most of our states.
West Virginia State Bd. of Educ. v. Barnette, 319 U.S. 624, 656 (1943) (Frankfurter, J., dissenting).

51. *Id.*

52. *See* REPORT OF THE NATIONAL ADVISORY COMMISSION ON CIVIL DISORDERS 424-40 (1968).

STATE'S AFFIRMATIVE DUTY TO DESEGREGATE HIGHER EDUCATIONAL FACILITIES NOT DISCHARGED BY GOOD FAITH BUT UN- SUCCESSFUL "OPEN DOOR" POLICY*

[Is the affirmative duty rationale in elementary and secondary education applicable to higher education?]

Doctrinal considerations indeed may warrant a complete abandonment of the affirmative duty concept on the college level. The imposition of a duty to integrate must rest on a judgment that the present system treats students unequally. It is arguable that no such inequality exists in a free choice situation since all students are accorded an equal right to choose the school they will attend. *Green* rejected this argument in the context of lower education, but distinctions can be drawn between higher and and lower education.

Conceivably, physical and economic threats by whites which coerce black students toward choosing a separate school, regarded by some as a major cause of the failure of free choice plans to undo primary school segregation,[10] have diminished effect on a college level. However, *Green* does not rest on the theory that the black children were coerced into attending a black school. The Court acknowledged existence of the view that "free choice" in the South is not really free, but expressly refused either to adopt or reject it,[11] apparently considering the issue irrelevant to the basic concern: whether the plan did or did not, for whatever reason, disestablish the dual system.

Absent the rationale of coercion, *Green's* necessary determination that free choice treats students unequally must rest on an implicit assumption that racially separate education is inherently debilitating and therefore that states which are under an affirmative duty to provide equality cannot merely furnish an opportunity to avoid the inferior educational environment but must actually prevent the student from being placed in it. On an elementary school level, where a child can be presumed incompetent to judge his own interests, the

* *Harvard Law Review*, Vol. 82, pp. 1759-1761 (1969); *reprinted with permission*.

10 See UNITED STATES COMMISSION ON CIVIL RIGHTS, SOUTHERN SCHOOL DESEGREGATION 1966-67, at 47-65 (1967). For an example of the effect community hostility can have on the operation of a free choice program, see Coppedge v. Franklin County Bd. of Educ., 273 F. Supp. 289 (E.D.N.C. 1967).

11 391 U.S. at 440 n.5. The view was that of the United States Commission on Civil Rights.

Court may be warranted in imposing this view and rejecting a parent's choice of school, as the law often does in other contexts where important interests of the child are deemed to need protection.[12] But the rationale of protecting the child disappears when the reference is to higher education. Though racial separation still has its harms at this level,[13] one is dealing here with students of college age who are presumed mature enough to choose whether to attend college at all. Such persons ought to be able to choose between an integrated and a predominantly black college, weighing for themselves the harms against the particular educational, social, or cultural benefits they seek.

Of course, one may argue that black students in the South have been so conditioned by the southern caste system that their choice of a black school in any "free choice" situation is preordained and that the courts should nudge them toward integration. It is highly questionable, however, whether the courts ought thus to place themselves in the patronizing position of overruling the expressed preferences of college-age blacks and substituting a "superior" judicial insight. The courts ought particularly to be wary of so interfering unless that interference can be predicated upon principles which command the respect of diverse elements of society. Given the present difference of opinion as to whether immediate integration or separate cultural development will best achieve equality for blacks in America, it may behoove the courts to leave the resolution of this question to the mature blacks whose lives will be affected by it.[14] There is a difficulty of

---

[12] For example, courts have ordered blood transfusions for minors where necessary to save their lives despite expressed opposition from the parents on religious grounds. *See* People *ex rel.* Wallace v. Labrenz, 411 Ill. 618, 104 N.E.2d 769 (1952); *cf.* Battaglia v. Battaglia, 9 Misc. 2d 1067, 172 N.Y.S.2d 361 (Sup. Ct. 1958) ("Petitioner . . . may practice the religious faith of her choice without interference. She has not, however, the right to impose upon an innocent child the hazards to it flowing from her own religious convictions"). *See also* Prince v. Massachusetts, 321 U.S. 158 (1944).

[13] *See* Fiss, *Racial Imbalance in the Public Schools: The Constitutional Concepts*, 78 HARV. L. REV. 564, 570 (1965); *cf.* Pettigrew, *A Social Psychological View of the Predominantly Negro College*, 36 J. NEGRO EDUC. 274, 282 (1967).

[14] *Cf. Developments in the Law—Equal Protection*, 82 HARV. L. REV. 1065, 1113-15. Conceivably, even on an elementary school level the courts may, in response to pressure from advocates of black separatism, distinguish *Green* as controlling in only those cases where no black litigants intervene to voice opposition to forced integration.

course in determining when choice of a black school is made out of racial pride and a desire for cultural enrichment and when because of qualms about leaving a comfortable and secure segregated milieu to venture into an alien, predominantly white environment.[15] But this problem disappears if one is willing to allow that a choice made for either reason is equally valid. Although undoubtedly some benefit is gained from integrated education in terms of learning to live and work with those of other races,[16] for some students social and academic adjustment may be hindered by the insecurity and sense of being "on display" that can result from integration.[17] Provided that nondiscriminatory access to all state institutions, access free from retaliation or harassment, can be assured for those blacks interested in an integrated education,[18] and as long as all are made fully aware of the opportunities available,[19] a court should not insist that other black college students abandon an environment that, for whatever reason, they prefer.

Even if in principle, however, one is willing to allow the imposition of an affirmative duty, there may be valid educational considerations, as Judge Johnson pointed out in *Alabama State Teachers,* which argue for maintenance of the free choice system. At the elementary school level, equal educational opportunity might require that all schools be basically fungible. At the college level, however, differences in courses, programs, living arrangements, and faculty strength in particular subjects may be educationally justifiable and in any event unavoidable. Self-selection therefore becomes important in assuring that the school fits the student's academic predilections.[20] * * *

---

[15] *See* Wiggins, *Dilemmas in Desegregation in Higher Education,* 35 J. NEGRO EDUC. 430, 433 (1966); Jencks & Riesman, *The American Negro College,* 37 HARV. EDUC. REV. 3, 37-38 (1967).

[16] *Cf.* Sweatt v. Painter, 339 U.S. 629 (1950).

[17] *See* NEWSWEEK, Feb. 10, 1969, at 55.

[18] The problem, in terms of a barrier to absolute free choice, that might be presented were black students unable to obtain admission to white institutions on academic grounds, does not arise in Tennessee where several of the predominantly-white state universities have admissions requirements virtually identical to those of A.&I. *See* AMERICAN COUNCIL ON EDUCATION, AMERICAN UNIVERSITIES & COLLEGES 1418, 1428, 1436 (10th ed. 1968) (requirements for admission to East Tennessee State, Memphis State, and Tennessee A.&I. State Universities).

[19] The importance of making the existence of available opportunities known to prospective students cannot be gainsaid. *See* Jencks & Riesman, *supra* note 15, at 36.

[20] This was admitted by the plaintiff-intervenor in *Sanders. See* Trial Brief for the United States at 5-6.

University resolution prohibiting racially discriminatory policy of fraternity is not unconstitutional

SIGMA CHI FRATERNITY v. REGENTS OF THE UNIVERSITY OF COLORADO

United States District Court, D. Colorado, 1966.
258 F. Supp. 515.

DOYLE, District Judge.

This is an action in which the plaintiffs seek injunctive relief against the defendant, The Regents of the University of Colorado, primarily based on two actions of the defendant, a resolution which was passed in 1956 and an enforcement order directed to the defendant Beta Mu Chapter of Sigma Chi issued on May 29, 1965. A third but less important claim is based on a resolution adopted by the Regents in December, 1965. It is alleged that the Regents acted contrary to the Constitution and laws of the United States in the actions which they took. The 1965 enforcement action gave immediate rise to the present court action. On that occasion the regents adoped a resolution placing the Beta Mu Chapter of Sigma Chi on probation with loss of rushing and pledging privileges "until it can fully comply with the University policy resolution of March 19, 1956." This came about following receipt by the Regents of information that Sigma Chi had suspended its Stanford University chapter purportedly as a result of the pledging by that chapter of a Negro student. The complaint further alleges that Beta Mu chapter is affiliated with the international fraternity Sigma Chi, hereinafter referred to as the "national" organization; that it is required to abide by the rules of the national fraternity; that as an affiliated chapter it may pledge any person it wishes but that the national fraternity must approve a pledge in order for him to be initiated. Beta Mu House Corporation, an association of alumni of Beta Mu chapter, owns the chapter house at Boulder, Colorado.

In addition to injunctive relief, plaintiffs seek a declaratory judgment that "the actions of defendant complained of be declared to be in excess of defendant's jurisdiction, arbitrary and capricious, unconstitutional and void and of no force or effect." It is prayed that an injunction be issued prohibiting defendant from enforcing or attempting to enforce against plaintiff(s) * * * the resolutions and threats herein complained of." * * *

The parties have entered into a stipulation as to the issues which are before the court as follows:

"The only issues before the court are whether the actions of the defendant are constitutionally valid * * *.

The 1956 resolution of the Regents is the center of plaintiffs' attack. They contend that this resolution, subjecting to probation any student group "compelled by its constitution, rituals or government to deny membership to any person because of his race, color or religion," constitutes an interference with a federally-protected right—the right of freedom of association—and is therefore unconstitutional. They claim that this right has received recognition as a part of the freedoms guaranteed by the First Amendment and incorporated in the due process clause of the Fourteenth Amendment as a restriction on state action such as here complained of. * * *

It will be helpful to reexamine the contentions so as to place them in better perspective. As to the plaintiffs, it would be an exaggeration to say that they are seeking the recognition of the right to discriminate if they choose to do so on the basis of race or creed, and to be able to do it with impunity. A more apt description of the plaintiffs' contention is in terms of their seeking recognition of a right of association which grants to them freedom to select members free of state regulation. They contend that this right is of such a nature that any official interference, and particularly the present resolution, amounts to constitutional infringement. The Regents, on the other hand, are not forcing plaintiffs to take members who belong to any particular group. The extent and degree of the attempted regulation would be more accurately described as an effort to eliminate from the charters and rituals of the organizations affected a provision which *compels* discrimination on the basis of race, color or creed.

Turning now to the background facts that we consider important to this decision, we point out first the admitted conclusion that the Board of Regents has broad powers to regulate the affairs of the University of Colorado. Constitution of Colorado, Article IX, sections 12 to 14; 1963 C.R.S. 124-2-10. Counsel for defendants maintain that the Regents stand in a paternal relationship toward social organizations on the campus. While we need not adopt this characterization, it is clear nevertheless that the University, and the Regents as its governing board, can validly impose a wide variety of regulations.

A university, in the promotion of its educational objectives, has in some instances abolished fraternities altogether and such legislation has been upheld by the courts. Waugh v. Board of Trustees, 237 U.S. 589, * * *. In *Waugh*, supra, a statute was passed *prohibiting* the existence of Greek letter fraternities and similar societies in the state's educational institutions. The statute also deprived members (persons who joined) of the right to receive or compete for diplomas, class honors, prizes, or medals. It required existing members of Greek letter fraternities to renounce allegiance to and affiliation with such fraternities. This statute was upheld against the contention that it constituted a denial of due process, equal protection and privileges and immunities of citizens.* * *

Another factor which cannot be overlooked is that the interest which the Board of Regents was advancing in passing the 1956 resolution was not an inherently invalid interest. Indeed, the Supreme Court of the United States has in recent years recognized the importance cf elimination of racial discrimination in educational institutions. * * * It can be said that the policy which the Regents were promoting constituted implementation of the substantive rights guaranteed by the Fourteenth Amendment.

Finally, the resolution itself is, as compared with that approved in *Waugh*, supra, a mild regulatory measure. It seeks to promote the principle of racial and religious equality, but there is nothing in it that can be regarded as an excessive exercise of power.

Therefore, we need not base our decision on the proposition that the right of association as recognized by the cases is not a right which has had prior recognition. Instead, we hold that if the right exists it is a relative one. Thus the plaintiffs can not insist on immunity from state regulation. We further hold that the particular relationship before us renders the plaintiffs susceptible to regulation of the kind here questioned. We further conclude that the purpose of the resolution is valid and clearly within the powers of the Board. Thus plaintiffs' contention that the resolution of 1956 violates their constitutional right is without merit and must be rejected. * * *

For the reasons stated, it is

Ordered that judgment be entered in favor of the defendant and against the plaintiffs; * * *.

NOTES

RACIAL DISCRIMINATION IN FRATERNITIES AND SORORITIES—STATE ACTION? *

John P. Jacoby, *Illinois Law Forum*,
Fall 1964, pp. 631-645
(*reprinted with permission*).

The thought has been correctly expressed that there is a law which brings men together in groups; it acts like the law of gravity, and regardless of what is done to divert it, it holds true. Thus we have the college fraternity.[1]

That such a law exists is substantiated by the fact that 3,500,000 men and women have organized themselves into 7,500 collegiate chapters of American social fraternities and sororities.[2]

Voluntary associations have generally been held to have a right to impose conditions for membership in their organizations, no matter how arbitrary the conditions may be.[3] Fraternities and sororities, as voluntary associations, have assumed that the right to impose conditions for membership, including those of racial qualification, extends to them. Existing in a society in which racial separation has been the rule rather than the exception—in education, housing, and other areas of social relationships—fraternities and sororities are especially likely to reflect discriminatory practices in their membership selection. The very words "fraternity" and "sorority" envision the creation of particularly intimate social relationships.[4] Such racial restrictions may be expressly imposed upon each collegiate chapter of a national fraternity by the express terms of its constitution.[5] But a racial restriction of equal force may arise through the "blackball" procedure, whereby one or two members of the chapter may arbitrarily reject any applicant. It is the existence of a constitutional prohibition of racial discrimination by fraternity or sorority chapters located at state educational institutions—

---

* Some footnotes are deleted.

[1] Myers, "The Legal Rights of College Fraternities and Sororities," *The Fraternity Month*, Oct. 1960, p. 46.

[2] Baird, *Manual of American College Fraternities* X (17th ed. 1963).

[3] Trautwein v. Harbourt, 40 N.J. Super. 247, 123 A.2d 30 (1956). *Cf.* Grand Lodge Order Hermann's Sons v. Schuetz, 36 Tex. Civ. App. 539, 83 S.W. 241 (1904).

[4] Webster, *International Dictionary* (3d ed. 1961) defines "fraternity:" "2a: the quality or state of being a brother or being brothers. . . " "Sorority" is correspondingly defined.

[5] Delta, Oct. 1960, pp. 84-103 (publication of Sigmu Nu Fraternity).

the applicability of the "state action" concept of the Fourteenth Amendment—which is the subject of this paper. * * *

The concept of state action is elusive because the degree of relationship between private act and state involvement which will trigger the Fourteenth Amendment prohibition has been made to depend upon the particular facts of each case. Moreover, although recent cases have "typically reaffirmed both the theoretical distinction and the holding of the Civil Rights Cases," they are also expanding by interpretation the latitude of private acts which will be brought within the amendment's prohibition. * * *

Fraternities and Sororities as State "Agents"

In order to apply these principles of "state action" to a fraternity or sorority located at a state educational institution, an "arm" of the state itself,[75] the functions of the organization and its relationship with the institution must be understood. Broadly speaking, a fraternal organization provides an educational opportunity beyond that of the regular course work. That this function is not within the exclusive realm of an educational institution appears clear. While the "liberal university" emphasizes "humane values and the personal development of the student and scholar," [76] the expressed educational function of the fraternity,[77] there exist "multi-versities," or aggregations of educational research, and service instrumentalities," which assume "that values and dedication are a man's own business." [78] Moreover, fraternal organizations which further their educational function by undertaking the housing function have not encroached an activity which, because of the public interest, is thought to be exclusively within the realm of the state. At state universities the idea of housing students is a relatively new and developing concept.[79] Finally, not only are the functions of a fraternity or sorority not the exclusive functions of the educational institution, but the function of higher education itself is not an exclusive state function.* * *

---

[75] Missouri ex rel. Gaines v. Canada, 305 U.S. 337, 343, 59 Sup. Ct. 232, 234 (1938).

[76] Brown, "The Squeeze on the Liberal University," Atlantic, May, 1964, p. 85.

[77] Baird, Manual of American College Fraternities 1-49 (16th ed. 1957); 48 National Interfraternity Conference Yearbook 84 (1956); 47 National Interfraternity Conference Yearbook 19-20 (1955).

[78] Brown, supra note 76.

[79] Crane, "Residence Halls as 'Academic' Communities" (1963) (unpublished article on file in Law Forum office).

The leasehold cases, however, point to a different result at certain campuses. Some state colleges and universities have undertaken to provide housing for fraternities and sororities. By constructing student residences, the state institution has undertaken the performance of the housing function, and so far as the particular facility is concerned, its operation is a governmental function. So long as an interest in the residence is maintained by the state, the fraternity or sorority which operates it would appear to be held to the commands of the Fourteenth Amendment.

It would seem clear that under the present boundaries of the state action concept, the Fourteenth Amendment would not be rendered applicable through the "assistance" analysis. The benefits conferred by the institution to a fraternal organization vary from campus to campus, but at a maximum they include the use of the name of the institution, the occasional use of facilities such as a union building or classroom space, the use of a "university depository" for the organization's . funds, advice from members of the collegiate staff, the availability of an intra-mural athletic program, the availability of financial aid, the use of the institution's publicity outlets, and a voice in the general student government. In addition, the organization may receive a property tax exemption directly from the state.[90] It is difficult to see that the existence of the organization is dependent upon the continuance of any part of this assistance or all of it taken together. Use of the institution's name appears to be a mere token advantage. Although use of facilities might be a convenience for the organization, a fraternity or sorority could certainly find non-institutional facilities when the necessity arises, which, it is submitted, is a relatively infrequent occurrence. The use of a depository for funds is also a convenience, but at colleges and universities where this convenience is not available, the students have proved adequate in managing their own finances. Intra-mural athletic competition is a small phase of fraternity's activities, and minute in the case of sororities. Athletic competition seems another function which could be left to the resources of the organization itself. While advice and cooperation from

---

[90] Such a tax exemption however, would be an exception to the general rule, "With few exceptions the courts have held that college fraternities and sororities are not exempt from taxation, because they exist primarily for the convenience of their members, and are mainly concerned with providing them with board, lodging, and recreation, while any educational, charitable and benevolent purposes are of secondary importance." Annot., A.L.R.2d 904-05 (1959).

staff members in conducting the organization's affairs may facilitate its operations, to say that the organization is dependent upon such assistance would be to deny excessively the intelligence of the college student. Only the rendering of financial aid appears as a possibility for finding state action through assistance, unless the requisites for the applicability of the state action concept are relaxed so as to require something less than dependence upon the assistance by the private party. It would seem that such a relaxation could occur if a court were faced with the question of whether a fraternal organization which receives many of the enumerated benefits is an "agent" of the "donor state."

The "control" analysis could also be the source of Fourteenth Amendment vulnerability of fraternities and sororities. While recognition of fraternities and sororities, universally required for such organizations to operate on a college campus, has been suggested to be a benefit without which the organization could not continue to exist,[91] it is submitted that recognition, like licensing, is a control device, whereby the licensor may prescribe standards of conduct, and, to a certain extent, control the activities of the licensee.

Controls exercised over a collegiate fraternity or sorority pursuant to recognition are numerous. Where the organization provides housing, the institution imposes regulations which force the organization's housing to conform to the physical standards which the institution deems acceptable for student living. Social activities are controlled, not only by requirements for registration and chaperoning, but by regulations prescribing permissible activities, the times at which they may be conducted, the places at which they may be held, and standards of student conduct. The organization may be placed on a probationary status if it breaches the institution's regulations. State colleges and universities have shown their interest in the broad educational purpose of fraternities and sororities, not only through their imposition of controls over the recreational activities and housing facilities, but through controls over other phases of the organization's activities. It may be required to obtain a permanent faculty adviser. The elected leaders may be required to maintain a specified scholastic achievement. And the organization may be required to

---

[91] Horowitz, "Discriminatory Fraternities at State Universities — A Violation of the Fourteenth Amendment?" *25 So. Cal. L. Rev.* 289 (1952). Portland College sororities, however, upon being suspended for discrimination, have continued to exist "off-campus." Letter from Mark Howard, Director of Public Services, to the *Law Forum*, March 24, 1964.

keep in close communication with the institution by filing reports on its financial standing, membership, and general progress.

But it appears that the controls must reach the very conduct which is the cause of the deprivation of rights in order for the Fourteenth Amendment to apply. Thus, it is the control over selection of members, indicating a public interest in this activity of the organization, which is determinative. Regulations over the process of selecting members include restrictions on the time periods during which persons may join the organization,[99] and restrictions upon eligibility for membership based upon scholastic record and "student status." Further, many institutions have in recent years adopted regulations requiring local chapters to select their members without regard to race. The reaction from some fraternities and sororities has been a contention that such regulations deprive the organizations of their freedom of assembly. But that there is no such constitutional freedom in the case of fraternities and sororities existing at state educational institutions appears clear. "A state may adopt such measures, including the outlawing of certain social organizations, as it deems necessary to its duty of supervision and control of its educational institutions." [104]

Where the institution has not taken the step of requiring the local chapters to select members without regard to race, it would appear that the Fourteenth Amendment would not preclude the chapter from excluding a person on racial basis. Although the institution has prescribed a group which is eligible for membership in the organization, it has made no regulation concerning selection from persons within the group. In the absence of such regulation, there is an absence of existing control over the selection process. Where the institution has taken the additional step of prohibiting the fraternity or sorority from the discriminating on the basis of race, it does exert control over the process of selection. Presumably, if the organization proceeds to violate the institution's regulation, the latter would take some corrective measure.[105] This con-

---

[99] *E.g.*, University of Utah, *Handbook for Student Organizations* 15-16 (1963).

[104] Webb v. State University, 125 F. Supp. 910, 912 (N.D.N.Y.), *appeal dismissed*, "(for the want of a substantial federal question," 348 U.V. 867, 75 Sup. Ct. 113 (1954).

[105] Sororities at Portland State College were suspended when two Negro girls were dropped during rush by all six sororities. Letter from Mark Howard, *supra* note 102.

trol over the process of selection by the state would seem to impose upon the organization, subject to the control, the commands of the Fourteenth Amendment. The applicability of the amendment in one situation and not in the other results in the anomalous conclusion that dual protection is available where the state has undertaken to provide protection, but none is available where the state has declined to provide protection.

The *present confines* of the state action concept, therefore, indicate that fraternities which are provided housing from a state educational institution are subject to the commands of the Fourteenth Amendment. In the absence of extraordinary assistance from the state, the only other chapters of fraternities and sororities subject to the amendment's commands are those where the state institution has undertaken to guarantee to persons the equal opportunity to become members of the organization, regardless of race. With increased attention towards discriminatory practices in fraternities and sororities and the subsequently increased controls, more and more chapters may be brought within the state action concept through the increased regulations of their institutions.

Moreover, if a court were faced with a plaintiff complaining of discrimination by a fraternal organization at a state institution, the close relationship of assistance and control between the state and the organization could cause an expansion of the present boundaries of the state action concept. Ironically, however, the passage of the federal civil rights legislation (which does not cover fraternal organizations) may stifle further expansion of the state action concept. Pressure for the recent trend may have been induced by the fact that "liberal-thinking" courts have possessed no means other than "state action" for effecting civil rights. This vacuum no longer exists.

CHAPTER 10

TORT LIABILITY

DEFINITION OF TORT

Tort is an elusive term which legal scholars have had great difficulty in defining. So difficult is it to describe that one writer commented that it is doubtful whether any textbook has ever successfully introduced all of the dimensions of the term.[1] However, for the purpose of this book, the term may be defined as a group of civil wrongs, other than breach of contract, for which a court will provide a remedy in the form of damages. Tort actions are brought to compensate individuals for harm to them caused by unreasonable conduct of others. Social norms and custom provide the basis for legal precedent in the determination of that which is considered unacceptable or unreasonable conduct.

The socially and legally acceptable relationship between two persons may be breached when, by either an act or an omission to act, one party causes injury to the other party. The word tort is derived from the Latin word "tortus" meaning twisted.[2] In personal relationships, the term "twisted" applies to activity which in some way deviates from a normally acceptable pattern of behavior. Speaking negatively, tort is not a crime, nor a breach of contract, nor concerned with property; nor is it a problem generally falling within the legal realm of governmental operations.

A civil action for tort is initiated and maintained by the injured party for the purpose of obtaining compensation for an injury he has suffered, whereas in a criminal proceeding the action is brought by the state to protect the public from actions of a wrongdoer. In a criminal prosecution the state prosecutes not to compensate the injured person, but rather to protect the public from further wrongful acts. Since criminal law does not and was never intended to compensate an injured individual, social justice demanded the birth of the action in tort.

GROUNDS FOR ACTIONS

Grounds for actions in tort may be divided into three categories: (1) intentional interference with an individual, (2)

---

1. William L. Prosser, *Law of Torts*, West Publishing Co., St. Paul Minnesota, p. 1.
    2. *Ibid.*, p. 2.

strict liability, and (3) negligence. These three divisions of tort actions are described below.

Intentional Interference

An individual may be liable in tort for an intentional act from which injury results to another. Here it is not necessary for the wrongdoer to be hostile or desire to do harm to the injured party. An intentional tort, may result from an intended act whether accompanied by enmity, antagonism, maliciousness or by no more than a good-natured practical joke.[3] Even where a person does not plan to injure another but proceeds intentionally to act in a way which invades the rights of another, he commits an intentional tort. Intent exists when a person realizes with substantial certainty that his act will create a specific result. In other words, a person must know the results of his intended act in order to have committed an intentional tort. If he does not know with substantial certainty the result of his act, then it is no longer an intentional tort but instead constitutes negligence.

Assault. An intentional tort may be committed even if no physical "touching" takes place. Such a tort may be couched in the term "assault" by the court. In order for an assault to exist there must be an "overt act or an attempt, or the unequivocal appearance of an attempt, to do some immediate physical injury to the person of another." [4] The overt act must be a display of force or menace of violence of such nature as to cause reasonable apprehension of immediate bodily harm. For example, when a man said "Were you not an old man, I would knock you down," [5] the court held there was no assault. There was no assault because the old man had no reason to expect immediate harm. On the other hand, assault was adjudged when a man in striking distance of another, with fist clenched and arm bent, said, "I have a great mind to strike you." [6] Such words and acts were sufficient to put the plaintiff in immediate apprehension of imminent harm and there was apparent and present ability of the defendant to effectuate the harm.

Therefore an intentional tort may transpire by an act

---

3. Reynolds v. Pierson, 29 Ind. App. 273, 64 N.E. 484 (1902); State v. Monroe, 121 N.C. 677, 28 S.E. 547 (1897).

4. State v. Ingram, 237 N.C. 197, 74 S.E.2d 532 (1953).

5. State v. Crow, 1 Ired. L. (N.C.), 375; Seavey, Keeton, Keeton, *Law of Torts*, West Publishing Co., St. Paul, Minnesota, p. 7.

6. State v. Hampton, 63 N.C. 13 (1868).

which, while not involving physical contact, places a person in immediate fear of physical attack.

Battery. Battery constitutes another type of intentional tort.[7] Battery comes about through physical contact while, as pointed out above, assault is the mere apprehension of physical contact. While "assault" is the attempt and threat to do violence, "battery" is the unlawful commission or execution of such violence.[8] Prosser points out that it is battery to injure a man in his sleep, even though he does not discover the injury until later; while it is an assault to shoot at him while he is awake, and frighten but miss him.[9] In both cases a person's interests are invaded and violated by another. If a wrongdoer swings a bottle intending to strike the plaintiff, and the plaintiff sees the movement and is apprehensive for his own safety, at this point there is assault. If the attack is consummated and the blow is actually landed, a battery is committed.

In a very old English case involving the meeting of two individuals in a narrow passageway, the judge explained assault and battery in this fashion. "First, the least touching of another in anger is a battery. Second, if two or more meet in a narrow passage, and without any violence or design of harm, the one touches the other gently, it will be no battery. Thirdly, if any of them use violence against the other, to force his way in a rude inordinate manner, it will be a battery; or any struggle about the passage to that degree as may do hurt will be a battery." [10]

Both assault and battery may be criminal wrongs as well as tort or civil wrongs. While "assault" and "battery" as a criminal offense has in some instances been dealt with in common law, the courts usually rely on statutes more in criminal cases than in civil cases. In most jurisdictions, assault and battery is not a crime unless it is declared so by statute.[11]

Statutes usually define "assault" and "battery" in much the same language as have the courts in common law. It is a general rule of law that if a legislature fails to properly define

7. 6 Am. Jur. 2d § 40.

8. Marker v. Hanratty, 6 Boyce (Del.) 217, 97 A. 904 (1916).

9. Prosser, *op. cit.*, p. 37.

10. Cole v. Turner, at Nisi Prius, coram, Holt, C.J., 6 Mod. 149 (1704). (*Nisi Prius* courts are those held for the trial of issues of fact before a jury and one presiding judge. *Black's Law Dictionary*, West Publishing Co.)

11. 6 Am. Jur. 2d § 9, p. 16.

the terms "assault" and "battery," they are to be understood in their common law meaning.[12]

The judicial view prevails that a teacher has a "privilege" against assault and battery in the moderate and reasonable exercise of disciplinary authority over students. This view has been accepted in a long series of cases involving the student-teacher relationship at the elementary and secondary level of education. The common law principle still prevails today that a parent may chastise his child and a school master may chastise his scholar.[13] While the courts have not made a clear cut distinction in this area between elementary-secondary and higher education, it would be safe to assume that a teacher's privilege in a college or university is much less pervasive. This is due primarily to the fact that most college students have reached or are about to reach the age of majority by the time they enter college and are not considered to be chastiseable children.[14]

Interference With Peace of Mind. A third type of intentional interference which has been used by the courts with more frequency in recent years involves the mental and emotional state of the plaintiff. In keeping with the theory that every man who is injured should have recompense, modern courts have had a tendency to recognize as a separate tort the infliction of mental or emotional anguish. The primary problem with these cases is the difficulty in proving mental suffering. Some evident and convincing injury which the plaintiff can prove must exist. The courts have also had difficulty in drawing the line between real injury and what is considered everyday rough language or other interpersonal relationships which hurt one's feelings yet are not severe enough to be a cause sufficient for a tort action. The courts have said an individual cannot recover simply because he has had his feelings hurt.[15]

Courts have held that if an act is malicious, as distinguished from being merely negligent, there may be recovery for mental anguish, even though no physical injury results.[16] However, cases involving actions for mental anguish and suffering are easier to prove before a jury if the emotional distress has produced some visible or identifiable physical harm.

12. State v. Lehman, 131 Minn. 427, 155 N.W. 399 (1915).
13. Donnelley v. Territory, 5 Ariz. 291, 52 P. 368 (1898).
14. State v. Mizner, 50 Iowa 145 (1878).
15. Wallace v. Shoreham Hotel Corp., 49 A.2d 81 (1946).
16. Barnett v. Collection Service Co., 214 Iowa 1303, 242 N.W. 25 (1932).

False Imprisonment. Another kindred intentional tort is false imprisonment. This tort is sometimes called false arrest. Relatively few cases have occurred in this area, but the general rule is that an unauthorized person cannot detain or physically restrain the movements of another.

STRICT LIABILITY

Located somewhere outside the periphery of the intentional interference tort and the negligence tort is a third type, that of strict liability. Generally, liability for tort has been imposed with regard to "fault" on the part of the defendant. Both intentional interference and negligence are based on the supposition that someone was injured at the fault of another party. However, cases have arisen where a person has been injured through no fault of anyone. Such cases have forced some courts to hand down damage awards based on strict liability of the defendant. This is to say that in certain cases a person may be liable for damages even if he is not at fault for another's injury. The courts have adopted this strict liability philosophy in order to place the liability on the person best able to bear the burden. In these cases, the defendant's acts are not so important as the injury and suffering of the injured person. Underlying this type of decision is the older social justice reasoning that requires that "he who breaks must pay" regardless of whether the damage is knowingly or negligently caused.[17]

While fault is not a prerequisite to liability in these cases, the courts do generally require that the defendant has caused some unusual hazard to exist. The defendant's activity must be one which involves abnormal danger to others. The concept of strict liability is not usually related to activities which are performed within the scope of higher education operation. But for the sake of illustration, let us assume that a biology professor took students to a zoo where monkeys and other animals were kept. Through no fault of the teacher or the zoo keepers, one of the monkeys bit a student. The court in such a case may very likely assess damages against the owner of the zoo by relying on the doctrine of strict liability.[18]

The reasoning of the court is that "strict responsibility is placed on those who, even with proper care, expose the community to risk of a very dangerous thing." [19] In this case, for

---

17. Prosser, *op. cit.,* p. 315.
18. May v. Burdett, 9 Q.B. 101, 16 L.J.Q.B. 64 (1846).
19. Prosser, *op. cit.,* p. 322.

an unusual hazard to exist, the animal inflicting the injury had to be what is normally considered a "dangerous" animal. Generally, household and farm animals are not considered dangerous by nature, and keeping such animals does not impose strict responsibility on the part of the owner. Generally, today in the United States, strict liability will not be imposed unless the activity or thing is classified as hazardous or even "ultrahazardous." [20]

While strict liability cases reported by appellate courts involving activities in colleges and universities are very scarce, the possibility of such actions nevertheless, exists. The hazards in colleges created by laboratory experiments,[21] shop activity, or even field trips, present possibilities of actions involving strict liability.

NEGLIGENCE

Negligence is conduct falling below an established standard which results in injury to another person. It involves an unreasonably great risk which causes damage or harm to others. Negligence differs from an intentional tort in that negligent acts are neither expected nor intended; an intentional tort may be both anticipated and intended. While negligent acts are neither expected nor intended, a reasonable man in the position of the actor could have anticipated the harmful results.

An accident which is unavoidable and could not have been prevented by reasonable care does not constitute negligence. No liability exists for an unavoidable accident. Many times what first appears to be an accident can be traced to someone's negligence; however, instances of pure accident do occur where someone is injured and no one is actually negligent. For example, it is an accident when a baseball player loses control of the ball and hits a person standing nearby. Numerous instances of pure accidents arise each year on school campuses. In such cases, the actor is not liable in damages for negligence.

A negligent act in one situation may not be negligence under a different set of circumstances. No definite rules apply to what constitutes negligence. The standard of conduct of the actor is the key to the determination of negligence. The conditions embracing a negligent act have been described in this fashion:

---

20. *Restatement of Torts*, pp. 519-520.
21. Hamburger v. Cornell University, 240 N.Y. 328, 148 N.E. 539 (1925).

It is fundamental that the standard of conduct which is the basis of the law of negligence is determined by balancing the risk, in the light of the social value of the interest threatened, and the probability and extent of the harm, against the value of the interest which the actor is seeking to protect, and the expedience of the course pursued.[22]

In order for the court to strike a balance between the threatened harm and the utility of the actor's conduct,[23] the court must establish a judicially manageable standard by which the activity can be measured. In attempting to set boundaries for negligent acts committed under different factual situations, courts developed the reasonableness theory. An injury must have been sustained as a result of an "unreasonable risk" taken by another person. The courts have personified the reasonableness test in the "reasonable man."

The Reasonable Man. The reasonable man is a hypothetical person, a community ideal of human behavior, whose conduct under the same or similar circumstances is regarded as the measure of reasonable behavior, "a fictitious person who never has existed on land or sea." [24] The reasonable man has been described by different courts as a prudent man, a man of average prudence, a man of ordinary sense using ordinary care [25] and skill, and as a reasonably prudent man. He is an ideal, a model of conduct, and a community standard. Herbert humorously portrayed him as "this excellent but odious character [who] stands like a monument in our courts of justice, vainly appealing to his fellow-citizens to order their lives after his own example." [26] The model of the rea-

---

22. Terry, "Negligence," 29 *Harvard Law Review* 40 (1915). See also *Restatement of Torts*, pp. 291-293.

23. Prosser, *op. cit.*, p. 123.

24. *Ibid.*, p. 124.

25. *Ibid.*, p. 124.

26. A.P. Herbert, *Misleading Cases in Common Law*, 1930, pp. 12-16 (cited in Prosser, *op. cit.*, p. 125). "He is an ideal, a standard, the embodiment of all those qualities which we demand of a good citizen. * * * He is one who invariably looks where he is going, and is careful to examine the immediate foreground before he executes a leap or a bound; who neither star gazes nor is lost in meditation when approaching trapdoors or the margin of a dock; * * * who never mounts a moving omnibus and does not alight from any car while the train is in motion * * * and will inform himself of the history and habits of a dog before administering a caress; * * * who never drives his ball until those in front of him have definitely vacated the putting-green which is his own objective; who never from one year's end to another makes excessive demand upon his wife, his neighbors, his servants, his ox or his ass; * * * who never

sonable man, although a community ideal, varies in every case. His characteristics are: (1) the physical attributes of the defendant himself; (2) normal intelligence; (3) normal perception and memory with a minimum level of information and experience common to the community, and (4) such superior skill and knowledge as the actor has or holds himself out as having.[27] While this standard of behavior provides a uniform framework for the theory of negligence, the precise formula varies with each case. As can be seen from the measures given above, the reasonable man formula changes with different factual situations because of the attributes or deficiencies of the defendant himself and because of peculiarities of beliefs, values and customs of the individual community.

The reasonable man then has the same physical characteristics as the actor himself and the acts in question are measured accordingly. Correspondingly, the man who is crippled is not held to the same standard as the man with no physical infirmities. The courts have also made allowances for the weaknesses or attributes connected with the sex [28] and age [29] of the individual. Courts have not, however, been so lenient with individuals who have mental deficiencies. The courts have traditionally held that a man with less mental ability than an average person must adjust and conform to the rules of society. He is not given an allowance by the courts for his mental deficiencies. Where a man is actually insane, a more convincing argument can be made for allowing for his particular incapacity.

Courts have held that where a person is temporarily ill and loses control of his faculties, he may not be held strictly accountable for his actions. This is true only, however, where the illness is caused by circumstances beyond the control of the actor. Prosser has said that the general rule seems to be that "one who intentionally or negligently becomes intoxicated, is held to the same standard of conduct as if he were sober." [30]

---

swears, gambles or loses his temper; who uses nothing except in moderation, and even while he flogs his child is meditating only on the golden mean. * * * In all that mass of authorities which bears upon this branch of the law, there is no single mention of a reasonable woman."

27. *Ibid.*

28. Hassenger v. Michigan Cent. R. Co., 48 Mich. 205, 12 N.W. 155 (1882).

29. Johnson v. St. Paul City R. Co., 67 Minn. 260, 69 N.W. 900, 36 A.L.R. 586 (1897); Kitsap Co. Transp. Co. v. Harvey, 15 F.2d 166, 48 A.L.R. 1420 (1927).

30. Prosser, *op. cit.*, p. 127.

ELEMENTS OF NEGLIGENCE

In order to have a valid cause of action for negligence, certain prerequisite conditions must exist. The necessary elements are frequently summarized into four categories: (1) a *duty* on the part of the actor to protect others against unreasonable risks; (2) a failure on the part of the actor to exercise a *standard of care* commensurate with the risks involved; (3) the conduct of the actor must be the *proximate cause* or *legal cause* of the injury—a causal connection must exist between the act and the resulting injury; (4) *injury, actual loss or damage* must result from the act.

DUTY

In a society as dependent on interpersonal relationships as exists today, individuals constantly rely upon the reasonable acts of others for their own protection. The normal routine of everyday life creates situations where people cause risks and incur obligations for the safety of others. In negligence cases a person has a duty to abide by a standard of reasonable conduct in the face of apparent risks.

The courts generally hold that no duty exists where the defendant could not have reasonably foreseen the danger or risk involved. A duty owed by one person to another may well intensify as the risk increases. In other words, the duty to protect another is proportional to the risk or hazard of a particular activity. In educational functions where risks are greater to students, a teacher has an increased level of obligation or duty. For example, whenever an instructor has a student perform a dangerous experiment, he has a greater obligation for the student's safety than when he is merely lecturing to a class. One judge has explained the duty requirement in this way:

> Every person is negligent when, without intending any wrong, he does such an act or omits to take such a precaution that under the circumstances he, as an ordinary prudent person, ought reasonably to foresee that he will thereby expose the interest of another to an unreasonable risk of harm. In determining whether his conduct will subject the interest of another to an unreasonable risk of harm, a person is required to take into account such of the surrounding circumstances as would be taken into account by a reasonably prudent person and possess such knowledge as is possessed by an ordinary reasonable person and to use such judgment and discretion as is exercised by persons of reasonable intelligence under the same or similar circumstance.[31]

---

31. Osborne v. Montgomery, 203 Wis. 223, 235 N.W. 372 (1931).

A person is negligent when he injures another by an affirmative act. However, the question often arises as to whether a person can be liable for failure to act at all? Generally the law holds that a person is not liable for an omission to act where there is not some definite relationship or duty owed between the parties. No general duty exists to aid a person in danger. Even though a moral duty is present, no legal duty requires a bystander to aid a drowning person. If a person takes an affirmative act to assist a person in peril, however, he assumes a duty to the person and all his subsequent acts must be performed reasonably. Because of this requirement, passersby in many situations will not assist an injured person. Some states, in order to encourage more humanitarian responses and to protect well-meaning rescuers, have enacted laws which protect such "good Samaritans" from liability.

A teacher has no more of a duty than anyone else to be a "good Samaritan" to the general public, but he may have the obligation to help a student under his jurisdiction when injured at school. A teacher has an inherent duty to a student and generally must take affirmative actions to protect him. Because of the teacher-student relationship, a teacher may be liable for an omission to act as well as for an affirmative act. In such a case, though, the teacher is only required to provide such assistance as a man with his training and experience in similar circumstances could reasonably provide.[32]

STANDARD OF CARE

A legally recognized duty or obligation requires the actor to conform to a certain standard of conduct or care. As the foreseeable risk involved in an act increases, the standard of care required of the actor likewise increases. The standard of care owed to students by a lab instructor experimenting with dangerous chemicals is greater than that of the college librarian. This is, of course, true because the risk of injury involved is much greater than the risk of being injured while reading a book.

The standard of care required to avoid liability is not uniform among all persons. Children and aged persons have generally been given substantially more leeway in their activities than is allowed a normal adult. While both children and aged persons are liable for their torts, they are not held to the

---

32. Bogust v. Iverson, 10 Wis. 2d 129, 102 N.W.2d 228 (1960).

same standard as are others without impairments of age. While it is difficult to pinpoint precise standards to determine the reasonableness of a child because of the great variations in age, maturity and capacity, the courts nevertheless have established a rough standard as a guideline. This subjective test for negligence in children is ". . . what it is reasonable to expect of children of like age, intelligence and experience."[33] As the age,[34] intelligence and experience of the child increases, a commensurate increase in the standard of care is required of the child. A child is generally held to a standard of care of a reasonable child of the same age, intelligence, and experience in the same or similar circumstances.

While most courts appear to follow the above criteria for determination of negligence of children, some courts have applied criminal law standards which specifically prescribe age criteria for purposes of liability; however this does not appear to be the prevailing view.[35]

PROXIMATE OR LEGAL CAUSE

"Proximate cause" or "legal cause" is the sequential connection between the actor's negligent conduct and the resultant injury to another person. The *Restatement of Torts* explains the necessity of adequate causal relation in this way:

> In order that a negligent actor shall be liable for another's harm, it is necessary not only that the actor's conduct be negligent toward the other, but also that the negligence of the actor be a legal cause of the other's harm.[36]

In order for proximate or legal cause to exist, there must first be a duty or obligation on the part of the actor to maintain a reasonable standard of conduct. In such cases the courts require that the defendant's conduct be the legal or proximate cause of the injury. In most negligence cases, however, the courts will not refer to proximate cause but will rely solely on the duty or obligation of the defendant and the standard of conduct required to avoid liability. Proximate cause as

---

33. Prosser, *op. cit.*, p. 128.

34. The *Restatement of Torts* § 464 states that: "Age is only one of the elements to be considered, along with experience and judgment, the latter involving discretion and power of self control, being predominant."

35. This is sometimes referred to as the Illinois Rule since the nonliability of children under seven is provided for in that state. (Howard C. Leibee, *Tort Liability for Injuries to Pupils*, Campus Publishers, Ann Arbor, Michigan, 1965, p. 11.)

36. *Restatement (Second) of Torts* § 430.

a criterion of liability has been used most often where some doubt is present as to whether the injured person was within the zone of obvious danger.[37]

In these cases the courts require that the negligence of the defendant must be the "substantial" cause of the harm to the plaintiff. In other words, the cause must be substantial enough to lead reasonable men to conclude it is indeed the cause of injury. If the negligence is not a substantial factor in producing the harm, then no liability is present. The following considerations are important in determining whether the specific negligence is the substantial factor in bringing about the injury:

(a) Other factors which contribute in producing the harm and their effect in producing it.

(b) Whether the actor's conduct has created a force or series of forces which are in continuous and active operation up to the time of the harm.

(c) Lapse of time.[38]

The other factors antecedent to the harm must not be of such importance that they dilute the actor's negligence; if this happens, the defendant is not liable. The actor's negligent act must be a continuous and active force up to the actual harm and the lapse of time must not be so great that contributing causes and intervening factors render the original negligent act to be an unsubstantial or insignificant force in the harm.

Therefore, a teacher or student may be relieved of liability for negligent conduct if some intervening act is sufficient to break the causal connection between the act and the injury.

The intervening act must legally supersede the original negligent act in order to break the chain of events causing injury.[39] This rule found application in a case where a student was cleaning a power saw in a shop class and another student turned on the switch starting the machine in violation of safety rules. The court in this instance held that the board's negligence in not having a guard over the beltdrive was not the legal cause of injury, but instead the injury was attributable to the intervening act of the other student.[40]

37. Prosser, *op. cit.*, p. 252.
38. *Restatement (Second) of Torts* § 433.
39. Miller v. Baumgartner, 152 N.W.2d 732 (Minn. 1967).
40. Meyer v. Board of Education, Middletown Twp., 86 A.2d (N.J. 1952).

INJURY OR ACTUAL LOSS

A defendant is not liable unless he has in fact caused the injury. The plaintiff therefore must show that he has actually suffered an injury or shows loss or damages resulting from the act. Nominal damages cannot be obtained where no actual loss can be shown or has occurred.

Damages for an injury may be assessed against one or more persons. If the harm suffered was caused by more than one person, then damages may be apportioned among the tortfeasors. Also, if more than one harm is present and the harms and damages can be distinguished, there will be apportionment of damages.

DEFENSES FOR NEGLIGENCE

Whenever an action is brought against a teacher for negligence, several defenses or legal arguments are present on which the teacher's lawyer may base a defense. In all cases involving negligence the defendant may attempt to show that he is not negligent because the injury was a mere accident, that his act was not the legal cause of injury, or that some other act intervened and was responsible for the injury. However, aside from these essentials of a tort claim, there are other rejoinders against negligence which are classified as defenses. The more common of these are generally classified into four categories: (1) contributory negligence; (2) comparative negligence; (3) assumption of risk, and (4) immunity.

Of all of these defenses, contributory negligence and assumption of risk are the most prevalent in education cases. Immunity as a defense is most often used by public institutions in states where common or statutory law provides for sovereign immunity. Each of these concepts is briefly explained below.

CONTRIBUTORY NEGLIGENCE

Contributory negligence involves some fault or breach of duty on the part of the injured person, or failure on his part to exercise the required standard of care for his own safety.

The injured party through his own negligence and fault contributes to his injury. One court explained contributory negligence as conduct on the part of the injured party which caused or contributed to the injury and which would not have been done by a person exercising ordinary prudence under the circumstances.[41] The *Restatement of Torts* defines contributory negligence in much the same manner:

> . . . conduct on the part of the plaintiff which falls below the standard to which he should conform for his own protection, and which is legally contributing cause co-operating with the negligence of the defendant in bringing about the plaintiff's harm.[42]

If an injured student is himself negligent and his negligence contributes to his harm, then a defendant teacher, who is also negligent, may be absolved from liability.

When a plaintiff's negligence or fault contributes to his injury, the court will bar him from recovery of any damages at all. Some courts have held that complete barring of all damages because of contributory fault is perhaps a little drastic and have therefore endeavored to prorate damages for comparative negligence, which is discussed in more detail later.

The doctrine of "last clear chance" is sometimes considered to be a type of contributory negligence. Indeed the concept does supplement and modify the defense of contributory negligence. What the doctrine of "last clear chance" does in effect is to shift the fault or legal cause of an injury from a contributorily negligent plaintiff back to the negligent defendant. If the defendant has a "last clear chance" to avoid the harm and does not, then the plaintiff's negligence is not the legal cause of the result. Therefore, the "last clear chance" concept can probably best be explained as a counterattack against the defense of contributory negligence.

Most courts will allow the use of the "last clear chance" doctrine where the plaintiff is either helpless or inattentive and the defendant discovers the peril in time to avoid it but does not. Prosser points out that "last clear chance" was first used in 1842; in this case the plaintiff left his ass tied in a highway and the defendant drove into it. The court observed that the plaintiff could recover, notwithstanding his own negligence, if he could show that the defendant had a last clear chance to avoid injuring the animal. Prosser says that as a result of this case, the "last clear chance" rule is sometimes referred to as the "jackass doctrine," with whatever implications that nickname may carry.[43]

---

41. Walsh v. West Coast Coal Mines, 31 Wash. 2d 396, 197 P.2d 233 (1948).

42. *Restatement (Second) of Torts* § 463.

43. Prosser, *op. cit.*, pp. 290-291.

COMPARATIVE NEGLIGENCE

As previously pointed out, if contributory negligence on the part of the plaintiff is shown, the defendant is often absolved from any liability at all. This, some courts and legislatures have felt, works a hardship on the negligent plaintiff who suffers injury but can recover nothing from the negligent defendant. This concern for the injured party has led legislatures in some states to enact statutes to determine degrees of negligence and allow recovery based on the relative degree of fault. While the specific provisions of "comparative negligence" statutes vary from state to state, the concept works this way: If the plaintiff's fault is found to be about equal to the defendant's, then the plaintiff will recover one-half the damages and must bear the remainder of the loss himself. If the plaintiff's negligence amounted to one-third of the fault and the defendant's two-thirds, then the plaintiff could recover two-thirds of the damages. In all states with "comparative negligence" statutes, the idea is carried forth that the plaintiff, even though he is partly to blame for his own harm, will not be totally barred from recovery.

ASSUMPTION OF RISK

Another defense against negligence is assumption of risk. The theory here is that the plaintiff in some manner consents to relieve the defendant of his duty or obligation of conduct. He who consents cannot receive an injury (*volenti non fit injuria*). In other words, the plaintiff by expressed or implied agreement assumes the risk of the danger and thereby absolves the defendant of responsibility. The plaintiff with knowledge of the danger voluntarily enters into a relationship with the defendant, and by so doing agrees to take his own chances.[44] The defendant is simply not under any legal duty to protect the plaintiff.

Essential to the doctrine of assumption of risk is that the plaintiff have knowledge of the risks; if he is ignorant of the conditions and dangers, he does not assume the risk. For example, a boy playing basketball was injured when his arm went through a glass pane in a door immediately behind the basketball backboard. The court later said that the boy had not assumed the risk of such an injury. The boy did not know the glass in the door was not shatterproof.[45] However, another court held that a boy had assumed the risk when he

44. Prosser, *op. cit.*, p. 303.
45. Stevens v. Central School District No. 1, 270 N.Y.S.2d 23 (1966).

suffered an injury by colliding with a doorjamb in a brick wall while playing as a voluntary member of a team in a school gymnasium. The boy had played in the gym previously and knew the location of the basket, door and wall and therefore was aware of the danger involved in voluntarily playing in this particular gymnasium.[46] In a case where a batter in a softball game struck a classmate who was sitting on the third base line, the court said the student who was struck either assumed the risk or was contributorily negligent.[47]

The courts have generally established that the participant in athletic events, whether intramural or interscholastic, assumes the risk of the normal hazards of the game when he participates. This rule also applies to spectators attending sports and amusement activities. Spectators assume all the obvious or normal risks of being hurt by flying balls,[48] fireworks explosions,[49] or the struggles of combatants.[50]

Even if the injured party does not take reasonable precautions to determine the hazards involved, the courts will hold he has assumed the risk. However, neither a participant nor a spectator assumes the risk for negligence or willful or wanton conduct of others. For example, a spectator at an athletic contest does not assume the risk of the stands falling at a football game nor does he assume that by attending a baseball game, a player will intentionally throw a bat into the stands and injure him. He assumes only those hazards or risks normally associated with the activity.

IMMUNITY

Immunity from tort liability is used in different contexts. Immunity is generally conferred on (1) national[51] and state governments unless abrogated by statute, (2) public officials performing judicial, quasi-judicial, or discretionary functions,[52] (3) charitable organizations granted immunity in

---

46. Maltz v. Board of Education of New York City, 114 N.Y.S.2d 856 (1952).

47. Benedetto v. Travelers Ins. Co., 172 So. 2d 354 (La. 1965).

48. Brisson v. Minneapolis Baseball and Athletic Association, 185 Minn. 507, 240 N.W. 903 (1932); Kavafiam v. Seattle Baseball Club Assoc., 105 Wash. 215, 177 P. 776 (1919).

49. Scanlon v. Wedger, 156 Mass. 462, 31 N.E. 642 (1892).

50. Dusckiewicz v. Carter, 115 Vt. 89, 52 A.2d 419 (1947).

51. The United States government has surrendered immunity to the extent of liability allowed by the Federal Tort Claims Act.

52. See "Defenses Against Liability for Defamation," *infra* in this chapter.

606   COLLEGE AND UNIVERSITY LAW

some states, (4) infants under certain conditions, and in some cases insane persons.[53]

The defense of immunity is usually employed to protect the public college or university against liability. This governmental or sovereign immunity is a historical and common law precedent which protects a state agency against liability for its torts. Because of the importance of this concept and its frequent applicability in education tort cases, governmental immunity is treated separately in the following chapter.

DEFAMATION

The role of the educator is performed in a highly sensitive area of personal relationships. The professor or administrator is constantly engaging in activities which if conducted recklessly may cause permanent damage to a student's future. One of the legal areas of potential harm is that of defamation of character.

DEFAMATION DEFINED

Defamation is communication to others which diminishes the good name of a person. It tends to injure a person's reputation and to do damage to the esteem, respect, and confidence in him.[54] One case defined defamation as being:

> [W]ords which tend to expose one to public hatred, shame, obloquy, contumely, odium, contempt, ridicule, aversion, ostracism, degradation or disgrace, or to induce an evil opinion of one in the minds of right-thinking persons, and to deprive one of their confidence and friendly intercourse in society.[55]

The twin torts of libel and slander constitute defamation. If a person is defamed by written communication, it is libel; if by word of mouth, it is slander. Early Anglo-Saxon law seemed a little uncertain as to the appropriate punishment for slanderers, with extremes ranging from excision of the tongue to making the offender hold his nose and call himself a liar.[56] Slander was recognized as an offense worthy of statu-

---

53. See "Standard of Care," *supra* in this chapter.
54. Prosser, *op. cit.*, p. 574.
55. Kimmerle v. New York Evening Journal, 262 N.Y. 99, 186 N.E. 217 (1933).
56. Theodore F. T. Plucknett, *A Concise History of the Common Law*, 5th ed., Little, Brown, and Co., Boston, 1956, pp. 483; III Edgar, 4 (c. 946-c. 961); II Canute, 16 (c. 1027-c. 1034).

tory remedy as early as 1275 when the statute *scandalum magnatum* was enacted.[57] This statute protected the king and his nobles from false news and slander. Slander at this time was a political device designed primarily to protect the king from either warranted or unwarranted criticism. The law of slander did not allow damages in civil actions until the middle sixteenth century.[58]

The offense of libel made its debut as a legal wrong much later than slander. The Star Chamber in 1559 laid down the general proposition that "libelling and calumniation is an offence against the law of God." At this point in history (1635), the relationship between libel and slander was somewhat obscure, but it was generally held that libel was a crime, while slander was merely a civil wrong. It was reasoned that libel was more serious since writing constituted a more deliberate act, while slander or word of mouth was more spontaneous, subject to whim or heat of the moment and many times could be safely ignored.[59] These early distinctions supplemented the law of slander with the law of libel, thus beginning the development of the civil wrong of defamation as we know it today. The tort of defamation can be described as having three aspects: (1) a false statement concerning another which is published or communicated; (2) the statement brought hatred, disgrace, ridicule, contempt, or in some way diminished a person; (3) damages resulted from the statement.[60]

It is interesting to note that the courts are not necessarily concerned with the method or mode by which defamation is conveyed. If a communication is in fact defamatory, it does not matter how artful its disguise or how clever its assertion.[61] A defamatory charge may be made directly or indirectly. Mere insinuation, sarcasm, or inquisitory remarks may constitute defamation as well as positive and overt declarations or assertion.[62]

"Criticism" is not necessarily "defamation," the distinction being that criticism deals only with those things which invite public attention and call for public comment, but does not

57. Westminster I (1275), c. 34; Plucknett, *op. cit.*, pp. 485-486.
58. *Ibid.*
59. *Ibid.*, pp. 490, 497.
60. Kern Alexander, Ray Corns, Walter McCann, *Public School Law*, West Publishing Co., 1969, p. 325.
61. Lauder v. Jones, 13 N.D. 525, 101 N.W. 907 (1904).
62. *Ibid.*

follow a man into his private life, or pry into his domestic concern. Criticism never attacks the man, but only his works.[63]

Defenses Against Liability for Defamation

The two primary defenses against an action for defamation are "privilege" and "truth."

Privilege. The defense of "privilege" is an appropriate and well established means of protecting certain legal rights. A "privilege" invests a person with a peculiar benefit or legal power to do something, or negatively it may grant immunity from attack or harm. Privileges may be enjoyed by persons or classes of persons. The granting of privilege is restricted by constitutional limitations providing that "no citizen or class of citizens shall be granted privileges or immunities which upon the same terms shall not be granted to all citizens." [64] However, classifications for "privileged communication" such as legislators, teachers, and physicians possess are not unconstitutional classifications.

A privilege for communication is extended to professors and college administrators by virtue of the fact they are performing a service, the nature of which necessitates the communication, handling and analysis of personal information without which the educational function could not operate.

Immunity for privileged communications are generally divided into two categories, absolute and conditional or qualified privileges. Absolute privileges are provided to persons who are acting in a capacity which furthers a public or private interest recognized by law.

The operation of government is given a privileged position in defamation cases. Individuals performing vital governmental services are given enough latitude to adequately perform their essential duties. Governmental functions involving judicial proceedings, legislative proceedings, and certain executive proceedings are given absolute privilege.

In cases involving the judiciary, absolute privilege protects only the particular statements which are relevant or pertinent to the issue of the case.[65] In legislative proceedings, legislators have absolute immunity when their statements are

63. Schwimmer v. Commercial Newspaper Co., 131 Misc. 552, 228 N.Y.S. 220 (1928); Triggo v. Sun Printing, 179 N.Y. 144, 71 N.E. 739 (1904).

64. California, Constitution Art. 1, § 21; Daigh v. Schaffer, 23 Cal. App. 2d 449, 73 P.2d 927 (1937).

65. Prosser, *op. cit.*, p. 609.

made in the course of debate, voting, reports or work in committees.[66] Witnesses making statements in legislative hearings are, likewise, given absolute immunity.[67] Officers in executive positions have absolute immunity for communications made in connection with the performance of their official duties. The tendency has been in recent years for the courts to be more lenient with public servants and to extend absolute immunity not only to officers but also to some employees as well.[68]

The question of absolute privilege arose in an education case in Nebraska in which the state superintendent was the defendant. The superintendent of public instruction of Nebraska was sued when, in his official capacity, he wrote to a county supervisor accusing the plaintiff of playing poker and drinking liquor. The court held that the state superintendent had an absolute privilege.[69] In an Oklahoma case, a college president made defamatory remarks about the college librarian at a meeting of the board of regents. The court held that the president had an absolute privilege based upon a directive by the board of regents commanding the president to report to the board any irregularities and misconduct on the part of teachers or employees.[70] An Illinois court held that communications between public officials regarding their duties in conducting public business is necessarily absolutely privileged.[71]

Teachers are generally considered to hold qualified privileges. As pointed out above, the qualified privilege requires that the person conveying information do so for reasons which protect the interest of the public, third parties or one's self. Most jurisdictions provide for qualified immunity where misinformation is given but the conveyor honestly believed the information to be reliable, and the information was given to advance a legitimate interest. However, a qualified privilege will not be allowed where the defendant conveyed false defamatory information which he does not believe nor has reasonable grounds to believe is the truth.[72]

---

66. Coffin v. Coffin, 4 Mass. 1, 3 Am. Dec. 189 (1808).

67. Prosser, *op. cit.*, p. 611. Absolute privileges may also be granted where statements are made (1) with the consent of the plaintiff and (2) for communications between husband and wife.

68. Public officers are distinguished from public employees in that officers usually hold statutorily or constitutionally created positions and such positions are usually said to possess a portion of sovereignty.

69. DeBolt v. McBrien, 92 Neb. 237, 147 N.W. 462 (1914).

70. Hughes v. Bizzel, 189 Okla. 473, 117 P.2d 763 (1941).

71. Haskell v. Perkins, 165 Ill. App. 144 (1911).

72. Reynolds C. Seitz, "The Law of Privileged Communications as it

Truth as a Defense. In some states truth is a defense for a defamation action. In such jurisdictions it is not necessary to show that the statement is the literal truth, but it is adequate to show that the imputation is only substantially true.

In a Texas case, the president of a commercial college was asked for information concerning a former student. He replied that the man had been a student at the institution but had not graduated. He related, in fact, that the student had been dismissed from school for stealing a typewriter and had been placed in jail. The student sued for damages. The president could not show that the statement was even substantially true. The student showed that the statement was untrue, and the case was decided for the student.[73]

While some states still use truth as a defense, the more modern concept is that even if an utterance is the truth, it must be made with good intentions and for justifiable reasons. There is little justification for a teacher to make statements concerning students for reasons other than being of some benefit to the pupil.

STUDENT RECORDS AND INFORMATION

Teachers, professors, counselors and administrators are charged with the responsibility of gathering, processing, and analyzing information concerning ability, achievement and general conduct of pupils. Such information, while valuable in assisting in the educational process, constitutes a potential source of liability if handled wrongly. Professors are generally involved in the release of student information and records to other teachers, professional personnel within the school, prospective employers outside the school, or to other educational institutions to which students may be applying for entrance. Considering this information flow, the following rules should be followed. First, information should not be related to other professors or administrators unless the motive and purpose is to assist and enhance the educational opportunities of the student. Transmittal should be made in the proper channels and to persons assigned the responsibility for the relevant educational function. Gossip or careless talk among teachers which is not calculated to help the student is not protected by the cloak of qualified privilege. Second, student information should be transmitted to prospective employers only upon re-

---

Affects the Work and Responsibility of the Principal," *Law and the School Principal*, The W. H. Anderson Co., 1961, p. 155.

73. Tyler v. Lattimore, 24 S.W.2d 361 (1930).

quest by the student. This protects the teacher from the presumption that the transmittal was made with malice.[74] A qualified privilege has been upheld where a communicator responded to a questionnaire and only gave answers to specific questions.[75] Third, records should be released to other institutions only if there are statutory or regulatory requirements for the transmittals or if the student himself requests the transmittal. Outside of legally prescribed areas, it may be hazardous to release pupil information without the pupil's consent. The student may, of course, indirectly request the transfer of his records by allowing the institution to which he is a prospective student request his grades, scores and records for him.

While the potential of liability for defamation is always present, it is interesting to note that there is a paucity of cases where students have instituted actions against teachers or administrators for defamation. This can possibly be attributed to the careful handling of student records and information, or may be due to limited knowledge of parents and students as to their common law rights against libel and slander by college personnel.

In one of the cases which did find its way to an appellate court and which holds implications for college law, a student sued a school principal because he had informed the board of education that rumors about the plaintiff were circulating among students and teachers. The court held that the principal in this communication was protected by a qualified privilege and was free from liability. There was no evidence that the principal had acted with malice or with wanton and reckless disregard for the student's rights.[76]

In another case where a college teacher was talking to a student, and the conversation was allegedly overheard by a second teacher, the student sued claiming slander. The court found against the student, holding that in order to have slander there must be publication.[77] Here there was no evidence that the third party had overheard the remarks. The court went on in dicta to say:

> This case cannot be justly decided if the fact that it involves the relationship, standards and duties of a col-

74. Salow v. General Motors Truck Co., 64 F.2d 105 (1933).
75. Hoff v. Pure Oil, 147 Minn. 195, 179 N.W. 891 (1920).
76. Forsythe v. Durham, 270 N.Y. 141, 200 N.E. 674 (1936).
77. "Publication" is the actual communication of the imputation to another person.

lege faculty and the students is lost sight of. Does a father slander his child when he accuses it of wrong in the presence of its mother? The parent-child relationship very closely parallels that of a college faculty and students on matters of discipline, discovering misconduct and punishing therefore. Any legal restraint of either parent or faculty in the reasonable discharge of duty not only would not be beneficial to the child or student but might well be disasterous to them. Neither the home nor the school can properly and successfully function if faculty or parental authority to control and discipline is withheld. * * * There is neither law nor good sense for denying or fettering such powers.[78]

While this opinion is obviously going to great extent to protect the teacher, the court, nevertheless, seems to be saying that the communication indulged in on the part of the faculty must be reasonable and calculated to help the student.

In a similar case,[79] a college dismissed a boy for indecent exposure. The president wrote two letters to the father of the boy, delicately explaining the reason for the dismissal of the boy. The father sued the president for libel. The court said the sole basis for determination was the question of whether there was a privilege or whether there was malice on the part of the president in writing the letters? The court found no malice on the part of the college president; therefore, he was not liable.

In this case, as in *Walter v. Davidson*,[80] the court placed the college official in the place of the parent (*in loco parentis*) in his relationship with the student. Not only did both courts uphold the action of the college officials, but they indicated that the actions taken were a part of their responsibility to parent and student. But in both cases the courts pointed out that the officials acted reasonably and for the best interest of the student.

In another case,[81] which bears relevance here, a college dismissed a girl for not living right and having a venereal infection. The school wrote letters to the parent of the child stating the reasons for dismissal. Subsequently, an action was brought claiming libel. The court found that the school official, in this case the dean, had a conditional privilege. The court in explaining the conditional privilege said:

When words are conditionally privileged, "the law sim-

---

78. Walter v. Davidson, 214 Ga. 187, 104 S.E.2d 113 (1958).
79. Baskett v. Crossfield, 190 Ky. 751, 228 S.W. 673 (1921).
80. 214 Ga. 187, 104 S.E.2d 113 (1958).
81. Kenney v. Gurley, 208 Ala. 623, 95 So. 34 (1923).

ply withdraws the legal inference of malice," * * * the
burden of proof being * * * upon the plaintiff in respect
of the establishment of the presence of such malice.

The court also said that a mere mistake innocently made
through excusable error is not evidence of malice. The court,
after defining conditional privilege and its relationship to malice, finally held that the communication, the letter, from the
dean to the parent was a "privileged occasion." The letters
were not evidence of actual or express malice. On the contrary, the letters indicated a "sympathetic and friendly" concern for the girl.[82]

LIABILITY OF COLLEGE ADMINISTRATORS AND OFFICERS

While there is some conflict in precedents, the general view
prevails that a public officer is not liable for negligence committed in the exercise of discretionary functions. This American view is contradictory to the more ancient and more English concept that "every official, from the Prime Minister
down to a constable or a collector of taxes, is under the same
responsibility for every act done without legal justification as
any other citizen." [83]

The general feeling that judges should be immune from liability is the basis for conferring immunity for discretionary
acts on administrative public officers. The principle supporting this rule maintains that a public officer should be free
from the harassment of private suits in order for him to fear-
lessly pursue public administration as prescribed by law.[84]
The Supreme Court of the United States used this logic as
early as 1845 and declared that "A public officer is not liable
to an action if he falls into error in a case where the act to
be done is not merely a ministerial act, but is one in relation
to which it is his duty to exercise judgment and discretion;
even [though] an individual may suffer by his mistake. A
contrary principle would indeed be pregnant with the greatest mischiefs." [85]

In decisions involving liability of public officers, the courts
are careful to draw the line between discretionary acts and
ministerial acts. The courts recognize that public officials are

---

82. *Ibid.*

83. Dicey, *The Law of the Constitution*, 8th ed. 1915, p. 189.

84. Kenneth Culp Davis, *Administrative Law Treatise*, West Publishing Co., p. 508.

85. Kendall v. Stokes, 44 U.S. 87, 11 L. Ed. 506 (1845).

in the unique position of performing judicial, legislative and executive functions, most of which require some discretion. In the performance of these duties the public official is protected against liabilities which may accrue from errors in judgment. "The general principle is established by an almost uniform course of decisions, that a public officer, when acting in good faith, is never to be held liable for an erroneous judgment in a matter submitted to his determination." [86] "The rule is certainly a reasonable one. * * * Any other rule might work great hardship to honest men who, with the best of motives, have faithfully endeavored to perform the duties of [public] officers." [87]

On the other hand, a public official may not perform only discretionary functions; he usually will, in the course of his duties, also perform ministerial functions. If someone is injured by the officers' failure to properly perform a ministerial duty, then the official may be liable.

While a public officer may perform some ministerial functions, such duties are usually accomplished by an "employee." The factor distinguishing a "public officer" from an "employee" is whether any sovereign function of government is conferred on the individual, to be exercised by him for the benefit of the public, largely independent of control of others.[88]

In other words, does the individual have vested in him a portion of the sovereignty of the state; if he does, then he is an officer.[89] One court has listed five indispensable elements which are required to make a public office. These are: "(1) It must be created by the Constitution or by the Legislature or created by a municipality or other body through authority conferred by the Legislature; (2) it must possess a delegation of a portion of the sovereign power of government, to be exercised for the benefit of the public; (3) the powers conferred, and the duties to be discharged, must be defined, directly or impliedly, by the Legislature or through legislative authority; (4) the duties must be performed independently and without control of a superior power, other than the law, unless they be those of an inferior or subordinate office, created or authorized by the Legislature, and by it placed under the general control of a superior officer of body; (5) it

---

86. Donahoe v. Richards, 38 Me. 379, 61 Am. Dec. 256.
87. McCormick v. Burt, 95 Ill. 263, 35 Am. Rep. 163.
88. Aldine Independent School District v. Standley, 154 Tex. 547, 280 S.W.2d 578.
89. State *ex rel.* Milburn v. Pethtel, 153 Ohio St. 1, 90 N.E.2d 686.

must have some permanency and continuity, and not be only temporary or occasional. In addition, an officer must take and file an official oath, hold a commission or other written authority, and give an official bond, if the latter be required by proper authority." [90]

Courts are somewhat divided, to say the least, on the precise line distinguishing college employees from college public officers, but at least one court has held that state university professors elected by the board of regents are not "public officers." In the same case the court also held that the fact that the state university president was an ex officio member of the state board of regents did not make him a "public officer." [91] Likewise a physician in a state university hospital is an employee, does not have immunity of a public officer, and may be liable for negligence.[92] However, the "public officer" immunity has on occasion been extended down to levels below that of dean in the university hierarchy. Utilizing the public officer rule, one court has held that the dean, assistant dean, and physicians of a state university were not suable in tort by a student. In this case the deans had ordered the student off campus and the physicians had given out information about the student's mental condition. The court felt that these acts were performed in carrying out the university's duty to police its grounds and protect its students from improper influences.[93]

Members of an incorporated board of regents of a state university who were expressly declared by statute to be public officers have been held not to be individually liable to a person injured by fallen telegraph wires which were allegedly negligently maintained.[94] Similarly, it has been held that members of a board of administration of a state college were not liable personally for exercising their quasi-judicial powers in an alleged malicious dismissal of a professor.[95]

In keeping with the general rule of immunity of "public officers," courts have held that administrative officers of a pri-

90. Gibson v. Fernandez, 40 N.M. 288, 58 P.2d 1197 (1936).

91. Martin v. Smith, 239 Wis. 314, 1 N.W.2d 163, 140 A.L.R. 1063 (1941).

92. Davie v. University of California, 66 Cal. App. 689, 227 P. 247 (1924).

93. Morris v. Nowoty, 323 S.W.2d 301, *cert. denied*, 361 U.S. 889, 4 L. Ed. 2d 124, 80 S. Ct. 164, *rehearing denied*, 361 U.S. 921, 4 L. Ed. 2d 189, 80 S. Ct. 264.

94. Lundy v. Delmas, 104 Cal. 655, 38 P. 445 (1894).

95. Gottschalck v. Sheppard, 65 N.D. 544, 260 N.W. 573 (1935).

vate college are not responsible in damages for a mere mistake in judgment in respect to government of the institution.[96] To protect an official from personal liability the courts will generally attempt to find a rational connection between the act and the discretionary duties of the official's job. If a discretionary duty is imposed on a public board, failure to perform the duty has been held to render the board liable, but not the members of the board as individuals.[97] In one case in which a teacher sued a board of trustees for injuries sustained from stepping in a hole in the floor of a schoolroom, the court held the trustees not personally liable saying:

> But it is not seen how a member of a corporate body, upon which body a duty rests, can be held individually liable for neglect of its duty by that body. There is no duty upon him to act individually. His duty is as a corporator, and it is to act in the corporation in the way prescribed for its action, and by the use of its powers and meanings. And if there is neglect to exert its powers or all its means, it is the neglect of the body and not of the individuals composing it.[98]

Board members are not liable personally for improvident but good faith judicial or discretionary acts.[99]

State is liable for failure of physical education instructor to provide reasonable care and supervision in conducting physical fitness tests

BRITTAN v. STATE

Court of Claims of New York, 1951.
103 N.Y.S.2d 485.

GORMAN, Judge.

The present claim arises out of an accident which occurred on April 5, 1946, at Cortland State Teachers College while claimant was undergoing a series of physical fitness tests to determine her eligibility for admission as a student to the college.

Cortland State Teachers College is a college owned and operated by the State of New York to prepare and train

---

96. John B. Stetson University v. Hunt, 88 Fla. 510, 102 So. 637 (1924).
97. Lundy v. Delmas, 104 Cal. 655, 38 P. 445 (1894); Bronaugh v. Murray, 294 Ky. 715, 172 S.W.2d 591 (1943).
98. Bassett v. Fish, 75 N.Y. 303.
99. Lemon v. Girardot, 100 Colo. 45, 65 P.2d 1427 (1936).

students as elementary school teachers and as physical education instructors in elementary and secondary schools.

Claimant, an 18 year old high school senior at Van Etten High School, Van Etten, N. Y., sought admission to the college as a student in the physical education program. As a prerequisite for admission, certain mental and physical tests were administered to the applicants. These tests included physical fitness index tests, known as P.F.I. tests, designed to measure the fitness of the body as a whole through a test of physical strength. The battery of strength tests consisted of seven tests, the first five of which, namely, the height and weight, lung capacity, grip test, back lift and leg lift, were taken in the foyer, and the last two, push ups and pull ups, were taken in the gymnasium itself.

Professor T. Fred Holloway, a physical education instructor at the college, was in charge of the administration of these tests. At the time of the claimant's accident, he was not present in the foyer. Each test was administered by one senior student, while another recorded the results. While performing the fifth test in this series, the leg lift test, claimant received a serious injury to her left knee. * * *

The leg lift test was administered to claimant by one Charles Patrick, a senior physical education student at Cortland State Teachers College. This was his first assignment in an official capacity. Patrick had, the previous semester, completed a course in tests and measurements during which students were instructed in the administration of this test. It also appears that several days before these tests, Patrick and the other student assistants had been given general group instruction in the administration of the various components of the physical fitness index tests.

The record is not clear as to the instructions given to claimant by Patrick as she prepared to undergo the leg lift test, but it appears that they were not too comprehensive, and the terminology used by him in his testimony regarding the instructions he gave did not accord closely with that used by the experts. Claimant testified that she began lifting and had about reached her maximum, but Patrick encouraged her to continue and she therefore kept pulling. She then started to weave a little bit, and there was a sudden snap, followed by a sharp pain in her left knee causing her to stagger and fall forward in a faint. * * *

The battery of strength tests * * * has been advantageously used in many colleges and secondary schools throughout the United States. Testimony of witnesses for both the claimant and the State indicates that the tests are not dangerous if properly administered. Strain and injury may result if the proper procedure is not followed. * * * Patrick testified that he had never been taught that there was a possibility of injury to the cartilages and ligaments of the knees from the leg lift test.

It is widely conceded that experience is necessary to render one an adequate tester, at least from the standpoint of securing accurate statistical results from the various components of the strength test. Admittedly, the leg lift and the back lift tests are the most difficult to administer. The same lack of experience which may result in erroneous scoring of the tests may also result in injury to the subject in the administration of the test. We believe that if the leg lift test had been administered to claimant by or under the direct supervision of a qualified and experienced tester the accident would not have occurred. * * *

The State of New York, through its agents, the staff of Cortland State Teachers College, owed to the claimant the duty of reasonable care in the conduct of the tests to which she was required to submit in order for her application for admission to the college to be considered. That duty embraced the proper administration and supervision of these tests. An adequate degree of supervision is provided by furnishing an experienced and competent man. * * * The New York State Board of Regents requires that in order to teach physical education a teacher "must have completed a four-year approved high school course followed by four years of academic and professional training leading to a degree or its equivalent as approved by the Commissioner of Education." A similar standard of care, competence and supervision should be required in the administration of the physical fitness index tests. There is no persuasive proof that Patrick had himself received sufficient instructions in the administration of the leg lift test, that he was aware that the test could be dangerous, or that he had sufficient experience to anticipate or recognize any evidence of strain, over-exertion or erroneous technique on the part of the person to be tested. It is extremely doubtful that the claimant received proper instructions from Patrick on how to take the test. She was not instructed to do any warm up exercises prior to taking the test, a procedure recommended by the experts.

Allowing a physical education class to be conducted by a

student physical education instructor in the absence of a qualified instructor has been held to constitute negligence. * * * In order to establish negligence, plaintiff is not required to exclude or eliminate every other possible cause. * * * Under all the circumstances disclosed by the record, we conclude that the mishap was within the reasonable apprehension of the State and that the State was negligent.

Claimant at the time of the accident was an extremely healthy and athletic girl. * * *

As a result of the accident, claimant sustained a torn anterior cruciate ligament of the left knee which condition is permanent. * * * Medical testimony indicates that while for normal pursuits, claimant's knee will give little trouble, she will be unable to engage in any personal contact sports and has been unable to pursue a career as a physical education instructor.

Judgment is accordingly directed in favor of the claimant and against the State of New York, in the amount of $7,500. The foregoing constitutes the written and signed decision upon which judgment may be entered.

NOTES

A college was held not to be liable where a girl was injured when she slipped on an unknown sticky substance on the floor during physical education class activities. The court found that the evidence was insufficient to show that the college was responsible for the presence of the unknown substance on the floor. Cumberland College v. Gaines, 432 S.W.2d 650 (Ky. 1968).

State is not liable for injury to student in wrestling class

REYNOLDS v. STATE

Court of Claims of New York, 1955.
207 Misc. 963, 141 N.Y.S. 615.

MAJOR, Judge.

These claims were filed to recover damages for injuries sustained by the above-named infant at Milne High School, Albany, New York, and alleged to have been caused by the negligence of the State through improper instruction and supervision of a wrestling class.

Unlike most high schools, Milne High School is a part of the University of the State of New York.

On April 14, 1953, John E. Reynolds, age 16, while receiving instructions in a particular wrestling maneuver as part of the physical education course at Milne High School, sustained a comminuted fracture of his left clavicle. The class consisted of thirty students, paired off for the instructions. The maneuver known as the "heel block and rear take down", was executed with another student, Robert Keller, blocking claimant's heels with his foot, pulling claimant over backwards to a sitting position, and rolling him to the mat. Claimant and Keller were close friends and had chosen each other. Keller weighed about ten pounds more than claimant, but claimant was slightly taller than Keller. The instructor approved the voluntary matching of these boys after making a mental comparison of their weights and watching them throughout the maneuver. Claimant, a sophomore, had received instructions in the simpler movements of wrestling in the 7th, 8th, 9th and 10th grades. In addition, both claimant and Keller had received instructions and taken part in substantially the same maneuver during their freshman year. Just before the accident, claimant had gone through the fall movement and had taken Keller to the mat first. Then when Keller took claimant to the mat, the accident happened. The progressive method, used at the school, is an accepted method. A proper and sufficient mat was furnished and used. The class instructor was experienced, qualified and competent.

Physical education is covered by a syllabus issued by the New York State Education Department, and such syllabus states: "the list of physical education activities included in this syllabus is suggestive rather than exhaustive". It describes numerous exercises and acrobatic feats and, at page 141, includes a "take down" as one of the wrestling exercises to be taught in high school. Considerable discretion is given to the instructor.

The State was not the insurer of claimant's safety. It is common knowledge, and experience has shown, that competitive contests, athletic events and gymnasium exercises, like most other activities of life, have certain dangers and hazards, and injuries are sustained therefrom on many occasions despite the use of necessary care, regulations and safety appliances. Wrestling is in this category. It is a form of sport or athletics in which many individuals of all ages voluntarily partake at one time or another, regardless of size, weight, supervision or equipment, and usually no liability attaches thereto. However, in colleges, schools and similar institutions certain standards of safety are required. The State has conformed to such standards.

By employing an experienced and competent instructor, the State has provided an adequate degree of supervision. * * *

Such instructor, supervisor or teacher has the duty of reasonable care in the prevention of injury, and must use the judgment of a qualified prudent person under similar circumstances. The question is resolved into whether such supervisor, as a reasonably prudent man before the occurrence of the accident had been apprehensive that, in the situation presented, there lurked the possibility of serious injury to anyone participating in the exercise. * * * There is no evidence that the supervisor had or had reason to have, such apprehension or anticipation of the happening of this accident.

It cannot justifiably be said that the keeping, or the failure to keep, records of weights, ages, height or other statistics, caused or contributed to this accident. The supervisor, experienced, trained and well-acquainted with these students was able to judge the strength and potentialities of the members of his class without reference to records or statistics. It appears very improbable in a class of thirty to pair off any exact match. In addition to size and weight, the supervisor, in this type of sport, must consider the muscular, nervous and mental reactions and the capabilities of the participants. The supervisor and instructor used the judgment of a prudent man and committed no act of negligence.

No permanent disability resulted from the accident.

The Court finds that the State has fulfilled its duty of reasonable care and is not chargeable with negligence.

The claim of John E. Reynolds, an infant, by Madelyn G. Reynolds, his guardian ad litem, is dismissed.

The claim of John S. Reynolds, being contingent on the outcome of the claim of John E. Reynolds, is also dismissed. * * *

Let separate judgments be entered accordingly.

**Student was contributorily negligent for injuries
sustained when she fell on college grounds**

RUE v. STATE OF NEW YORK

Court of Claims of New York, 1958.
174 N.Y.S.2d 556.

This is a claim for damages for personal injuries sustained
by claimant as a result of the alleged negligence of the State
of New York properly to maintain the paved concrete walks
and pathways on the grounds of the Long Island Agriculture
and Technical Institute at Farmingdale, New York. * * *

The testimony indicates that on January 3, 1956, at approximately 8:30 A.M. the claimant Mary Edith Rue, a student at
the Institute, was walking on the sidewalk immediately in
front of the building known as Number 18. She was proceeding toward her physiology class in another building and fell on
the sidewalk, sustaining an injury to her right ankle, described as "an oblique fracture through the distal end of the
lateral malleolus." * * *

The claimant stated that at the time it was cold and that
there was a drizzling rain with some snow mixed in it. She
stated further that she noticed there was some ice on the sidewalk. * * *

The claimant also introduced into evidence three photographs, Claimant's Exhibits 3, 4 and 5 in evidence which were
taken in July, 1956 and on which she marked with a red circle
the spot where she said she fell. At the location where the
claimant says she fell, there is plain evidence of deterioration
and breakdown of the sidewalk flags. The photographs indicate an uneven level between the flag where she fell and the
one next to it, and in addition an obvious abnormal opening
of some 2 inches between the flags. The photographs were
taken during the summer when there was indication of crab
grass growing between the flags which no doubt was not there
in January. The State offered no contradictory evidence concerning the condition of the flags but it rested on the claimant's case.

The claimant also stated that at the time of the accident she
was wearing saddle shoes with rubber soles and heels, the
latter being ¾" high, and that she was carrying her books and
her pocketbook as she was walking along the concrete path.
She said that she knew the condition of the sidewalk since
she was a freshman in school and had been traversing it for

the months past. She said that when she fell she noticed the sidewalk was cracked and jagged when she looked around. She said further: "When I fell, I was walking and looking straight ahead." After the accident, she was helped upon her feet by two boys whom she did not know and who carried her to her class, which she attended. * * *

The only testimony offered on behalf of the claimant herein was that of the claimant herself. She said that as she was walking to class she fell. No proof was offered that she fell as a result of the alleged deteriorated and broken condition of the walk or as a result of the presence or accumulation of snow and ice. There was no evidence that she caught her shoe or a part thereof on the sidewalk or that she slipped upon any snow which may have been present thereon. The Court may not assume that her fall was caused by either of these situations.

Further, although the claimant had been using the sidewalk for some months prior to the date of the accident, she testified that at the time she fell, she was walking and looking straight ahead. If she had seen the alleged condition of the sidewalk prior to the date of the accident, as she must have, and if in addition there was ice and snow upon the sidewalk at the time of her fall, then she should have looked where she was walking and certainly should have kept her eyes upon the walk, at least intermittently. Her failure to do so constitutes contributory negligence on her part.

A municipality's liability depends on whether or not, having in mind the circumstances of each case, it has neglected and failed to keep its public thoroughfares * * * whether the sidewalk of a street or the pathway in a park * * * in a condition reasonably safe for pedestrians. * * *

The Court finds that under all of the circumstances of this case, the State has not been negligent in its maintenance of the sidewalk. No proof has been submitted by the claimant to indicate that the alleged injuries sustained by her were the result of the negligence of the State.

The motions to dismiss made by the State, upon which decision was reserved, are hereby granted.

The claim is dismissed.

NOTES

1. In keeping with the general rule of reasonable care, a university, through its agents and employees, must exercise reasonable care to protect students involved in hazardous

school activities. In a case in which a student was injured when a block of wood was kicked out by the blades of a jointer in a woodshop, the court held it was the obligation of the university to exercise reasonable care.

A court in Connecticut found that the absence of a push block necessary to operate a jointer in a woodshop subjected a student to greater danger when operating the machine. The court said it was the obligation of the university to exercise reasonable care not only to instruct and warn students in the safe and proper operation of machines, but also to furnish and have available such appliances as would be reasonably necessary for the safe and proper use of the machines. Kirchner v. Yale University (Conn.), 192 A.2d 641 (1963).

2. Where a student at New York State Teachers College, New Paltz, New York, was injured when he collided with a flag pole while playing right field in a baseball game, the court directed a verdict for the student. The flag pole was 10 to 15 feet within the foul line, and baseball was a school activity directed by a regularly employed coach. The state defended by claiming the boy was contributorily negligent because he had played right field on previous occasions. The court, however, did not agree with the defendant and in rendering a $12,000 judgment against the state said that "it could reasonably have been foreseen by a reasonably prudent person that a baseball player, especially an outfielder, running to catch a long fly would direct his primary attention to the ball in the air and would be unaware of obstructions in his path, although the location of such obstructions was actually known to him." Scott v. State, 158 N.Y.S.2d 617 (1956).

Fatal injury in basketball game was hazard of game, instructor and board not liable

KAUFMAN v. CITY OF NEW YORK

Supreme Court, Kings County, 1961.
214 N.Y.S.2d 767.

J. IRWIN SHAPIRO, Justice.

When this case was called for trial, both sides agreed to waive a trial by jury and to have the Court decide all issues of law and fact.

The plaintiff is the father of the deceased, Alan Kaufman, and the administrator of his estate.

He brings this action against the City of New York and The Board of Higher Education to recover damages for the death of his son, caused, he contends, by the negligence of the defendants. * * *

The deceased, nineteen years of age, was a student in his fourth term at Brooklyn College.

On November 18, 1954, between 1:00 and 2:00 p. m. he was engaged in what has been described as a three-man basketball game in the third-floor gymnasium of the college.

Plaintiff's proof establishes that this three-man basketball game is played by three men on each side. It was being played in one of the sections of the gymnasium, and the accident occurred when one Charles Kochenski, playing guard opposite the deceased, jumped for the basketball at the same time that the deceased did; they were going up for a jump-shot, and in the process they bumped their heads together.

It is conceded that as a result of that occurrence the deceased immediately became unconscious, never regained consciousness, and that his death ensued therefrom.

Giving the plaintiff the benefit of every doubt on the uncontradicted facts in the case, the Court must conclude that the plaintiff has failed to make out a cause of action as a matter of law. There is no contention in this case of improper construction of the gymnasium, or that the premises were otherwise maintained in an unsafe or improper condition. The sole complaint is the alleged failure to properly supervise the playing of this three-man basketball game.

Even if it be assumed that there were no instructors present at the time, and the plaintiff's proof is deficient in this respect, for his witness to the occurrence merely testified that he did not know or recall whether any instructor was present at the time that the game was being played, and the examination before trial, offered in evidence by the plaintiff, contains a sworn statement by an instructor, that he and another instructor were in fact present in the gymnasium at the time of the occurrence, there is no legal causal connection between the alleged failure of an instructor to be present and the injury and consequent death of the decedent.

If the instructor were present and watching and supervising the game, he could not have stopped the boys from bumping their heads together; that is one of the natural and normal possible consequences or occurrences in a game of this sort which cannot be prevented no matter how adequate the supervision. As the Court said in the oft-cited case of Ohman

v. Board of Education of City of New York, 300 N.Y. 306, 310, 90 N.E.2d 474, 475.

> "This is one of those events which could occur equally as well in the presence of the teacher as during her absence."

If it may be said that the absence of a supervisor or instructor, under the circumstances, was negligence, still such lack of supervision was not the proximate cause of the accident.

Therefore, assuming that there was here the absence of a supervisor or instructor and that such absence constituted negligence, still, under the circumstances, such lack of supervision was not the proximate cause of the accident. * * *

In Frazier v. Young Men's Christian Ass'n of Little Falls, 286 App. Div. 464, 144 N.Y.S.2d 448, 449, affirmed 1 N.Y.2d 904, 154 N.Y.S.2d 963, the Appellate Division, Fourth Department reversed a judgment for the plaintiff and dismissed the complaint in a case where the infant plaintiff was injured when "One of the boys was 'dribbling' a basketball toward a basket. The plaintiff was 'guarding' him. The other boy jumped up and they collided. The dribbler's knee hit the plaintiff's eye."

Even though the boys there were of the tender age of eight to eleven and not as in this case, mature college boys, the Court said:

> "In any event, there is no causal relation between the absence of a supervisor and the accident. Bodily contact is inherent in the game. There is no evidence which indicates that the 'dribbling' and the 'guarding' were done in any but the usual manner of the sport. The boy whose knee hit the plaintiff testified he did not mean to strike him. It does not appear how the presence of a supervisor during the play would have prevented the accident. It happened without warning and in the course of the play. The hazard of an accident resulting in injury is inherent in a game such as basketball."

If there was no liability in that case to an immature age group in leaving them unattended while playing a game of basketball, because supervision could not have prevented the contact which caused the injury, how much more so must that be the conclusion in this case where the Court is dealing with a college student and not an elementary school boy.

The presence or absence of the instructors in this case had nothing to do with the occurrence. Their presence would not have prevented the guard on the opposite side from attempting to wrest the basketball from the deceased; that was part of the game and was to be expected. Under such circumstances the plaintiff does not make out a case merely because there was an absence of supervision. * * *

It follows as a consequence that the plaintiff's complaint must be dismissed as a matter of law and the Clerk is directed to enter judgment accordingly. The plaintiff may have a thirty days stay of execution and sixty days within which to make a case upon appeal. Proceed accordingly.

College authorities violated no duty when student sustained an injury in pushball game

RUBTCHINSKY v. STATE UNIVERSITY OF NEW YORK AT ALBANY

Court of Claims of New York, 1965.
46 Misc. 2d 679, 260 N.Y.S.2d 256.

The claimant, Ira Rubtchinsky, entered the State University College at Albany in the fall of 1961 as a freshman. As part of the orientation program of the college he was issued a college handbook, Exhibit 9, which among other things set forth information relative to a "competitive period of contests and fun between the freshman and sophomore classes" called "Rivalry". This competitive program had been in effect, with minor changes, since 1923 and was conducted under the aegis of the Student Association of the college. There is no question that the college authorities strongly recommended participation in the "Rivalry" program as a means of building up the *esprit de corps* of the college. Part of the Rivalry program was participation in the game of pushball. * * * It is a rough physical game * * * on the style of football or rugby. * * * Claimant Ira Rubtchinsky chose the game of pushball. He appeared at the college field set aside for the pushball game at a few minutes before 10:00 A.M. on November 11, 1961. No special equipment was provided for the game which was conducted under the guidance of upper-classmen. There were four student referees, all upperclassmen, in charge of the game. He was given rudimentary instructions in the game and watched the game being played for four or five minutes before he was sent into the game by the freshman leader as a member of the defensive team. He participated as a defensive player for one play in which he did what he could to keep the sophomore offensive player to whom he was assigned away from the ball. Ira was then shifted to the offensive team. On the next play he got away from the man who was against him and then was hit from behind at or below the knees, which would be considered clipping in football, and was propelled to the ground. He stretched out his hands to break his fall and in so doing sustained a severe and painful gross posterolateral dislocation of the proximal ulna and proximal radius relative to the distal right humerus, together with an associated comminuted fracture of the radial head. The State did not dispute the diagnosis, medical treatment, and prognosis testified to at the trial. * * *

Claimant's counsel has very persuasively argued that this 17 year old, young man was compelled, if not by edict by moral suasion, to participate in this game. We do not so find. Ira impressed us as a self-reliant young man with a mind of his own. He was in part working his way through school which we believe tends to increase the self reliance and independence of the college student. He could have participated in many different events (Exhibit 9) but voluntarily chose to participate in pushball, perhaps because being 6 feet tall and 200 pounds he believed such would be his forte. He watched the game being played and entered the play knowing it was a rough game. In our opinion he voluntarily assumed the risks of the game.

Although the State College had control over Student Association activities, we do not find that it is required to provide supervision for organized extracurricular activities of students on or off school grounds, unless such activities are so inherently dangerous that the College authorities are under actual or constructive notice that injuries may result to students.

Pushball had been a part of the "Rivalry" program since 1923 and in the 38 year period prior to this incident there apparently was no serious injury; or, if there was such, it was not presented to the Court at the trial. Certainly the College authorities were not under notice that serious injury would result from participation in this game.

Even if we found that the College should have supervised this activity we would not find liability against the State.

There was no allegation that the playing field used by the students was in defective condition. Therefore, we must assume the College provided a safe area for the conduct of this game. As stated previously four upperclassmen refereed this game. There was no proof that these referees did not adequately and properly supervise said game. Certainly, even in professionally refereed games such as football, and pushball is in that category, there are isolated instances of violations such as clipping with resulting injury. It is entirely possible that even if the State College had provided referees from its own staff that this incident might have occurred. We do not believe the State should be made the insurer of the safety of those who participate in this type sport. * * *

We grant the State's motions to dismiss made at the end of claimant's case and at the end of the entire case.

Professor of education not liable for damages in suicide of counselee

BOGUST v. IVERSON

Supreme Court of Wisconsin, 1960.
10 Wis. 2d 129, 102 N.W.2d 228.

MARTIN, Chief Justice.

Defendant is "an educator by profession." Jeannie Bogust was born May 3, 1939. At the times referred to in the complaint she was a pupil at Stout State College where defendant was employed as a full time director of student personnel services and professor of education with a Ph.D. degree. It is alleged that in such capacity the defendant was "charged with the maintenance of a counseling and testing center for personal, vocational, educational, scholastic, or other problems, including those students torn by conflicting feelings which cause worry and social ineffectiveness."

The complaint states that commencing in November 1957 Jeannie, as a student of the college, was under the direct guidance and supervision of the defendant; that defendant administered to her aptitude and personality tests and he was familiar with her personal, social and educational problems and her conflicting feelings, environment and social ineffectiveness; that he was well aware of her emotional disturbances, social conflicts, scholastic difficulties and personal problems during the period of November 11, 1957 through April 15, 1958; and

"* * * that although said student was constantly in need of professional guidance after April 15th, 1958, said defendant suggested termination of future interviews regarding her problems; that as a result of the failure of proper guidance by said defendant as aforesaid, she suffered psychological and emotional injuries and disturbances depriving her of her own volition and resulting in death by her own hand on May 27th, 1958."

It is alleged:

"That said defendant negligently and carelessly failed to perform his duties as such Director in the following:

"(a) That he failed to secure or attempt to secure emergency psychiatric treatment after he was aware or should have been aware of her inability to care for the safety of herself.

"(b) That he failed at all times to advise the said parents of Jeannie Bogust or contact them concerning the true mental and emotional state of their said daughter, thus preventing them from securing proper medical care for her.

"(c) That he failed to provide proper student guidance."

For the purposes of this decision we can assume the truth of only such allegations as are material statements of fact. Statements which are conclusions are not admitted by demurrer. Mitchell v. City of Horicon, 1953, 264 Wis. 350, 59 N.W.2d 469.

"A demurrer to a complaint admits all the facts therein well pleaded, but it does not admit erroneous conclusions drawn from such facts by the pleader even though the conclusions bear the semblance of statements of fact." . . .

The first question presented on appeal is whether there is a legal duty on the part of the defendant of such nature as will sustain this action. As pointed out by the trial court, before liability can attach there must be found a duty resting upon the person against whom recovery is sought and then a breach of that duty. . . .

Defendant is not a person qualified as a medical doctor or a specialist in mental disorders. It is alleged that he is an "educator by profession," a professor of education with a doctor of philosophy degree. Admitting that a teacher is not an insurer of the health, welfare and safety of his students, . . . , plaintiffs argue that he does have the duty to use reasonable care, ...

"b. Helplessness of other. * * * So too, a child while in school is deprived of the protection of his parents or guardian. Therefore, the actor who takes custody of * * * a child is properly required to give him the protection which the custody or the manner in which it is taken has deprived him. * * *

"*d. Duty to anticipate danger.* One who has taken custody of another may not only be required to exercise reasonable care for the other's protection when he knows or has reason to know that the other is in immediate need thereof, but also to make careful preparations to enable him to give effective protection when the need arises, and to exercise reasonable vigilance to ascertain the need of giving it. * * *"

The three acts of negligence with which the defendant is charged in the complaint are grounded on the theory that he had such a familiarity with and knowledge of Jeannie's problems and her "emotional disturbances, social conflicts, scholastic difficulties" that in the exercise of reasonable intelligence and judgment he should have realized her need for psychiatric treatment and acted accordingly—in securing such treatment, in advising her parents, and in providing proper guidance.

The trial court held:

"To hold that a teacher who has had no training, education or experience in medical fields is required to recognize in a student a condition the diagnosis of which is in a specialized and technical medical field, would require a duty beyond reason." * * *

The first act of negligence alleged is that the defendant failed to secure psychiatric treatment for Jeannie "after he was aware or should have been aware of her inability to care for the safety of herself." This clearly implies that he should have known she had suicidal tendencies. But there is no allegation of fact that would have apprised the defendant, as a reasonably prudent man, that she had such tendencies. The statement is merely a conclusion. The same comment applies to the second act of negligence alleged, that of failing to advise the parents "thus preventing them from securing proper medical care for her." The duty of advising her parents could arise only from facts establishing knowledge on the part of defendant of a mental or emotional state which required medical care; and no such facts are alleged.

The allegation that defendant failed to provide proper student guidance apparently refers to the fact that he "suggested termination of future interviews regarding her problems."

Jeannie was suffering from emotional disturbances and social conflicts before she came under defendant's guidance. Plaintiffs rely on the "further harm" doctrine defined in Restatement of the Law of Torts, Vol. II, sec. 322, where it is stated, in part (Comment *d*, p. 872):

"The liability which this Section recognizes is not imposed as a penalty for the actor's original misconduct, but for a breach of a separate duty to aid and protect the other after his helpless condition caused by the actor's misconduct is or should be known."

There is no allegation that the interviews between the defendant and Jeannie benefited her or that there was a duty on his part to continue them or that their termination caused the injury or placed her in a worse position than she was when they were begun. . . .

"One who gratuitously renders services to another, otherwise than by taking charge of him when helpless, is not subject to liability for discontinuing the services if he does not thereby leave the other in a worse position than he was in when the services were begun."

Jeannie had various problems before the interviews were undertaken, but was she "helpless" in that she was unable to look after her own safety? There is no allegation of such a fact, as pointed out above. Nor is there any allegation that she became so "helpless" during the time the interviews were carried on or that, if she did, she exhibited such manifestations as would charge the defendant with knowledge thereof.

The allegation in point is that although the deceased was in need of professional guidance after April 15, 1958, the defendant suggested termination of the interviews and that:

"* * * as a result of the failure of proper guidance by said defendant as aforesaid, she suffered psychological and emotional injuries and disturbances depriving her of her own volition and resulting in death by her own hand on May 27th, 1958."

We may assume the interviews were terminated, although the act complained of is the *suggestion* that they be terminated. There is no allegation that defendant's counseling caused injury. The only question is whether, at the time he suggested the interviews be terminated, he should reasonably have foreseen, acting as an ordinarily prudent and intelligent person, that as a consequence thereof Jeannie would do harm to herself, i.e., commit suicide.

In Dahlberg v. Jones, 1939, 232 Wis. 6, 11, 12, 285 N.W. 841, 843, it was held that where a mental patient was under the care of a doctor in a private hospital, the degree of care owed such patient "should be in proportion to the physical and mental ailments of the patient rendering him unable to look after his own safety." In that case such a patient suffered injuries as the result of escaping from the hospital, and this court held there was no liability on the hospital where there was no evidence to support the conclusion that the doctor or the hospital staff had reasonable grounds to anticipate or to take precautions against suicide or escape. . . .

"There was no evidence introduced tending to show that the deceased was possessed of suicidal mania, or mania of any kind, for that matter, at most that he was insane at intervals, but no indication whatever, prior to the fatal leap, that he intended to do himself or any one else any personal harm. In the absence of such showing there was no evidence tending to show that the defendant had any reason to anticipate that the deceased contemplated self-destruction."

Paraphrasing the above, in this case we can substitute for evidence or proof the fact that the complaint contains no allegation of a suidical tendency or mania or any indication that Jeannie showed any disposition to injure herself.

If a hospital for the treatment of mental disorders cannot be held liable for self-injury of a patient where there is no evidence (allegation) that the patient would injure herself if not restrained, certainly the mere allegation of an awareness by a teacher of emotional disturbance and personal problems of a student is insufficient to support an action for death by suicide.

The suicide took place almost six weeks after defendant suggested terminating the interviews. The complaint alleges that Jeannie's loss of volition occurred after the interviews terminated. To hold that the termination was a negligent act, it must be alleged that defendant knew or should have known that Jeannie would commit suicide.

This is an action for wrongful death . . . . The basic theory of plaintiff's complaint and their argument on appeal is the foreseeability of Jeannie's suicide as the proximate result of defendant's acts and omissions. . . .

"Where an action is brought under a wrongful death statute the general rule is that suicide constitutes an intervening force which breaks the line of causation from the wrongful act to the death and therefore the wrongful act does not render defendant civilly liable." * * *

Plaintiffs plead that as the result of defendant's suggestion that the interviews be terminated Jeannie suffered mental injury depriving her of her own volition and resulting in her death. * * * There are no facts alleged which, if proved, would establish a cause-effect relationship between the alleged

634   COLLEGE AND UNIVERSITY LAW

nonfeasance of the defendant and the suicide of the deceased.
* * *

"As a general rule a person will not be relieved of liability
by an intervening force which could reasonably have been
foreseen, nor by one which is a normal incident of the risk
created. However, if such intervening force takes the form of
suicide the practically unanimous rule is that such act is a
new and independent agency which does not come within and
complete a line of causation from the wrongful act to the
death and therefore does not render defendant liable for the
suicide." * * *

The peculiar difficulty encountered in proving causation in
a case of this kind is largely due to the nature of the subject
matter. The fact that the deceased, before she came under the
defendant's counsel, may already have been afflicted with a
condition which would account for her suicide further compli-
cates the issue. In discussing the reluctance of courts to extend
any doctrine of recovery for mental distress alone to a situation where the defendant is charged with ordinary negligence, it is said . . . :

"The contention that because of the nature of the evidentiary problems involved, the judicial process if not well
adapted to distinguishing valid from fraudulent claims in this
area, has been recognized as probably the most substantial of
the reasons advanced for denying recovery for mental distress
or its physical consequences."

A further difficulty is present in this case. Defendant is
charged with three acts of negligence. Even assuming he had
secured psychiatric treatment for Jeannie or that he had
advised her parents of her emotional condition or that he had
not suggested termination of the interviews—it would require
speculation for a jury to conclude that under such circumstances she would not have taken her life.

Order affirmed.

**Coach is not liable for injuries sustained by school
soccer player while riding in school car**

ADAMS v. KLINE

Superior Court of Delaware, 1968.
239 A.2d 230.

Plaintiff, Gary Adams, has sued Loren Kline and the University of Delaware, alleging that he suffered injury as a result of their negligence. * * *

The accident occurred on November 13, 1964. At the time, plaintiff was 19 years old, a student at the University of Delaware, and a member of its soccer team. On that date, the team was to play in a soccer game against Temple University in Philadelphia. The team departed from the University in two vehicles, the leading car being driven by defendant Kline, the coach. The second vehicle was a University-owned Ford Econoline Van driven by the plaintiff. The Econoline carried six other players and their equipment. The Kline vehicle carried the remainder of the players.

After leaving the campus, the vehicles proceeded along the Kirkwood Highway with Kline's vehicle in the lead. When the vehicles approached the Milltown Road intersection, the light turned amber and the Kline vehicle stopped suddenly. The plaintiff then applied the brakes of the Econoline. According to him, the brakes were ineffective to stop the vehicle and to prevent it from crashing into the Kline vehicle. As a result of the ensuing crash, the plaintiff suffered injuries. * * *

The complaint alleges among other things that the defendants (1) provided the plaintiff with a vehicle which they knew or should have known had defective brakes, and (2) allowed him to overload the vehicle when they knew or should have known that the overloading would prevent stopping of the vehicle within a safe distance.

These allegations, if proved, constitute a valid claim against the University which had a duty to exercise due care under all the circumstances.

If proved, the foregoing allegations also state a valid personal claim against Kline. In his role as teacher, Kline had a duty to exercise reasonable care under the circumstances. * * * Kline would be negligent if in fact he allowed the vehicle to be overloaded and could foresee that overloading would cause the brakes to malfunction. Likewise, if he knowingly allowed plaintiff to use a vehicle having defective brakes, this would be actionable.

However, Kline's duty of due care did not include that of inspecting the brakes, nor was he required to test the vehicle provided by the University. A team coach who does not own, and is not assigned the duty of inspecting, the vehicle cannot be held liable for failure to inspect or test. He may be charged only with that knowledge of defects which he in fact possessed and of defects which were apparent. Kline by un-

636   COLLEGE AND UNIVERSITY LAW

contradicted affidavit attests to having had no knowledge of a defect and no defect was apparent. There is no evidence on which a finding could be based that Kline knew or should have known by exercising due care, that the brakes were defective. Summary judgment will be granted with respect to his alleged negligence in allowing plaintiff to use a vehicle with defective brakes.

With respect to the alleged defective brakes, summary judgment must also be granted on behalf of the University. * * * The record is devoid of evidence which shows that any brake defect was known or could have been discovered by reasonable inspection. * * * The evidence is that the brakes operated properly until they failed immediately before the accident. Since the plaintiff has not made a prima facie case as to this aspect of the alleged brake defect and because the University has attested by uncontradicted affidavit that it had no actual knowledge of any braking defect, summary judgment for the University will be granted on this issue.

Plaintiff further alleges that the defendants negligently allowed the car to become overloaded and that this caused the brakes to fail. The record indicates that the Econoline was carrying up to 400 pounds over what is pictured as the normal carrying load. From this fact, a jury might reasonably infer that the vehicle was so overloaded as to cause the brakes to stop the car less effectively under the added strain. The record does not show that such a possibility was totally unforeseeable. The Court declines to hold as a matter of law that the defendants' behavior in this respect was not negligent. Defendants' motion for summary judgment will be denied as to allegations based on overloading the vehicle.

The gist of the remaining allegations is that defendants Kline and the University of Delaware were negligent in:

1) failing to determine whether the plaintiff was a competent driver,

2) failing to instruct the plaintiff in the correct operation of the vehicle,* * *

It would be difficult indeed for plaintiff to recover under * * * these allegations since it was he himself who elected to drive the vehicle.* * *

In any event [neither] of these allegations is legally sufficient because in view of the undisputed facts of the case [neither] of the alleged violations can be shown to be the proximate cause of the accident.

Defendants' failure to determine whether the plaintiff was

a competent driver cannot be said to have proximately caused the accident. The record shows that any inquiry made into the plaintiff's driving competence would only have revealed that the plaintiff was a competent driver. Furthermore, plaintiff cannot allege that his own lack of competence was the cause of the accident.

Similar reasoning applies to the allegation that the defendants failed to instruct the plaintiff in the proper use of the vehicle. The record shows that the plaintiff had driven the vehicle on a previous occasion, and had also driven the vehicle for some distance prior to the accident. Moreover, the record contains no evidence tending to show that the plaintiff did not know how to drive it. On the contrary the only reasonable conclusion to be drawn is that the plaintiff knew how to drive the vehicle properly. There is no evidentiary basis to support a contention that lack of instruction caused the accident or that instruction in the operation of the vehicle would have prevented the accident. * * *

The defendants argue that, as to all the allegations contained in the complaint, summary judgment should be granted on the ground that the record shows that plaintiff was contributorily negligent as a matter of law. Contributory negligence is ordinarily a question of fact for the jury unless but one conclusion can be drawn or inferred from the facts. * * * Since the evidence in the record permits more than one conclusion as to contributory negligence, summary judgment will not be granted on the remaining issues raised by the defense of contributory negligence. * * *

NOTES

1. *Transportation in private vehicles*. Transportation of pupils by private automobile is a very common practice in the colleges today. Most of such transportation occurs in interscholastic competition where small numbers of participants represent opposing schools. Baseball, basketball, tennis, golf, and debate teams, to name a few, may be transported in private vehicles. It is well known that loaning a car or using it to transport pupils is a hazardous undertaking and should be avoided when possible.

The courts have held that "the owner of the car is liable for negligence, whether he drives the car himself or not. This rule is based on the presumption that the person driving the car is acting as an agent of the owner." Gorton v. Doty, 69 P.2d 136 (Idaho 1937).

Under the "dangerous instrumentality" rule, which is applicable in Florida, the owner of an automobile is liable for negligent acts of any person operating an automobile with the owner's knowledge or consent. American Fire & Casualty Co. v. Blanton, 182 So. 2d 36 (1966).

Under Iowa law, an owner's liability may be predicated upon driving with his consent regardless of whether there is an employer-employee relationship. Accola v. Fletcher, 216 F. Supp. 202 (1963).

Where an automobile owner's permission to drive is restricted as to time, purpose or area of travel, permission is considered terminated only where there has been substantial violation of such restrictions. It is a question of fact whether restrictions have been substantially violated prior to occurrence of an accident so as to vitiate owner's permission and thus absolve him from statutory vicarious liability. Peterson v. Grieger, Inc., 17 Cal. Rptr. 828, 367 P.2d 420 (1961).

Owner is not liable for injuries inflicted by automobile while being negligently operated by another, unless the person driving it was an agent of the owner or unless the owner entrusted the auto to the driver while knowing the driver to be incompetent or reckless, or unless the automobile had some mechanical defect. Young v. Kickliter, 96 S.E.2d 605 (1957).

2. *Guests.* Whether a person is a "guest" is very important to court determination in private vehicle cases. The standard of care of the driver is lower where a passenger is a "guest." If passengers are "guests," then the driver of the car must generally be guilty of wilful or wanton negligence in order to be held liable. If passengers are not "guests," mere negligence will generally make the driver liable.

A "guest" in an automobile is one who takes a ride in an automobile driven by another person, merely for his own pleasure or on his own business, and without making any return or conferring any benefit on the automobile driver. Elliott v. Camper, 194 A. 130 (1937).

Delaware has a statute which provides that guests injured in an automobile accident shall not have a cause of action against the driver unless the driver acted with wanton or wilful disregard of the rights of others. The question arose in Delaware as to whether a student transported by a teacher at the parent's request was a "guest." The court held that though the teacher did not receive any monetary compensation he was still compensated because he was performing duties in furtherance of his professional duties as a teacher and was earning a salary. Because he was compensated in this indirect way, the injured pupil was not considered a guest and was allowed recovery. Fruitt v. Gaines, 317 F.2d 461 (Del. 1963). See also Kitzel v. Atkeson, 245 P.2d 170 (Kan. 1952); Fessenden v. Smith, 124 N.W.2d 554 (Iowa 1964).

Communication between university president and parent is privileged

BASKETT v. CROSSFIELD

Court of Appeals of Kentucky, 1921.
190 Ky. 751, 228 S.W. 673.

Appeal from Circuit Court, Henderson County.

Action by Oscar R. Baskett and another against R. H. Crossfield and another. From judgment for plaintiffs against the named defendant, giving him insufficient relief, plaintiffs appeal, and named defendant cross-appeals. Affirmed.

SAMPSON, J. Transylvania University is a coeducational institution regularly incorporated, with a board of trustees, located at Lexington, Ky., and R. H. Crossfield is and has been for several years its president. Appellant Oscar R. Baskett matriculated as a student in the University in September, 1918, and with another young man from Henderson was assigned to a room on the second floor of a boys' dormitory on the campus, facing one of the principal thoroughfares of the city of Lexington. One or more windows of the room looked out upon the street. About two weeks after the arrival of young Baskett at the university, complaint was made to President Crossfield that he (Baskett) had and was then indecently exposing his person at the open window of his room in such way as persons traveling the street saw his nude form and were embarrassed thereby. Some of the college faculty immediately set about to investigate the charge, and on entering Baskett's room found him in absolutely nude condition with the window shades partly up. Baskett was directed to report at the office of President Crossfield, which he did within a short time thereafter, and an investigation was had, resulting in President Crossfield suggesting to young Baskett that he immediately withdraw from the school, and leave on the afternoon train for his home in Henderson. Baskett called up his mother over the telephone and told her that he was leaving the school because some women had reported that he had been exposing his person; thereupon his mother called up a member of the faculty of the university to inquire the reason of the exclusion of her son. That day President Crossfield wrote the father of Baskett a letter. It was dated October 1st. A further investigation being later made, Crossfield again wrote the father another letter, dated October 4th, and these two letters are the basis of an action against the University and President Crossfield to recover damages for libel. They read as follows:

"Transylvania College, Lexington, Ky.,
"Office of the President.

"October 1, 1918.

"Dear Mr. Baskett: I am greatly grieved to be put to the necessity of asking your son to withdraw from our campus. It is always a source of great distress to us to have a case of any sort of discipline. The object of the institution is to train men rather than to discipline them, but sometimes situations arise that make it impossible for a student to remain upon the campus.

"The report came to me yesterday morning that your son had been observed by a number of people indecently exposing himself from the window of his room. I think there can be no sort of question as to the act. I was perfectly sure of my ground before I called the boy into my office. He denied the act very strongly. However, in order to save mortification to him, and possibly arrest, for feeling was running pretty high against him, both on the part of the students and others, I told him he should withdraw at once. Our treasurer refunded him the money that he paid with the exception of the proportionate amount for the two weeks. I instructed him to see Mrs. Perkins, and to have her refund the board money he had not used.

"Assuring you of the deep humiliation that it causes me to be compelled to write you in this fashion, and hoping the boy may take this as a serious lesson for all of his life, and develop into useful manhood, I am

"Sincerely yours,   R. H. Crossfield."

"Mr. Thomas Baskett, 724 Center Street, Henderson, Ky.,"

"Transylvania College, Lexington, Ky.,
"Office of the President.

"October 4, 1918.

"Dear Mr. Baskett: Mr. Hall, of your community, came to see me night before last, and he and I talked over the situation, with respect to your son, at length. I told him just how we felt about the whole matter that it was a source of the greatest measure of pain and sorrow to us to be compelled to advise a young man to return to his home, and that we undertook to act in the place of a parent to all those who come to us for instruction. I told Mr. Hall that I would come home, further investigate the case, and report the results. I said to him that the evidence that your son was guilty of most serious misconduct was overwhelming, and that the charge that he had exposed himself from his room window was positive and thoroughly confirmed. I told him that one of the professors of the college, who was in charge of the dormitory and the inspector of the dormitory went to the room of your son, and found him lying upon the bed in an entirely nude condition, the curtains being sufficiently raised to allow him to be seen from the street. I said, furthermore, that women, not members of the college community, who claimed that they had seen your son in a nude condition on Sunday and Monday morning, were so indignant that it was not really wise for your boy to remain on the campus, and that my advice to him to go home was as much an act of kindness to him as a matter of discipline.

"I have returned from Richmond, and have gone into the case again. I am very sorry to state that a second investigation seems to make the case against your boy more damaging than the first investigation. Under no circumstances would he be permitted to live in the dormitory, and Professor Kuykendall would not in any way advise that he be permitted to board out in town. Every one of us feels that it would not be wise for the boy to return, and that his denying the statement attested by so many witnesses makes him an utterly impossible student for our student body.

"I told Mr. Hall that had the boy manifested any sense of shame and mortification and penitence there would have been no question about his having a second chance, but that coupled with the offense was his utter disclaimer, and that the kind thing to do under the circumstances was not to make it a matter of faculty action, nor to allow the police to take hold of it, but to advise the young man in the strongest terms to withdraw immediately from the campus and from the city.

"I am exceedingly sorry, both on the young man's account and that of his mother. We were in no wise responsible for the occurrence, and feel that the least severe discipline possible has been administered. Had this been brought before the faculty, his expulsion would have been practically certain. Had it gotten to the officers of the law, his arrest would have been certain.

"I regret more than I can tell you to be put under the necessity of writing you the above statement, but after going into the matter that morning I find that the evidence is even more damaging than the statements as they came to me last Monday.

"It is my sincerest hope that the young man may learn the lesson that he may develop into a useful and successful man of the highest type. We shall want to help him whenever possible.

"Cordially yours,   R. H. Crossfield.

"Mr. Thos. Baskett, 724 Center Street, Henderson, Ky."

The answer contained a plea averring (1) the truth of the statements contained in the two letters; (2) a statement of facts showing the communications privileged. On a trial the jury returned a verdict for the university, and found for the plaintiff Baskett the sum of $100 against the defendant and appellee Crossfield. The case was tried in the Henderson circuit court, and the appeal by Baskett is from that court. Crossfield prosecuted a cross-appeal.

Without reviewing the evidence at great length, it will be sufficient to say that there was such conflict in it as would have warranted the trial court in submitting the case to the jury on the question of whether the young man did or did not indecently expose his person from a window of his room. But we have, for reasons hereinafter pointed out reached the conclusion that the judgment in so far as it affects the university must be affirmed and reversed on the cross-appeal.

The gist of an action for libel is the injury to the character.

A writing is libelous if it subjects the person referred to to odium or ridicule or tends to subject him to obloquy.

To render words actionable, unless special damages are

shown, they must import that the person to whom they are spoken is guilty of a felony, or some crime of such turpitude as to render him liable on an indictment.

In an action for libel the truth is always a complete defense, although the publication may be inspired by malice or an ill will and be libelous per se.

If a communication comes within the class denominated absolute privileged or qualifiedly privileged, no recovery can be had. Privileged communications are divided and defined as follows:

"(1) That the communication was made by the defendant in good faith, without malice, not voluntarily, but in answer to an inquiry, and in the reasonable protection of his own interest or performance of a duty to society; (2) that the defendant must honestly believe the communication to be true; (3) there must have been reasonable or probable grounds known to him for the suspicion; (4) that the communication, if made in answer to an inquiry, must not go further than to truly state the facts upon which the suspicion was grounded, and to satisfy the inquirer that there were reasons for the suspicion."

Under that definition, not only must the communication be made in good faith, without malice, upon reasonable grounds and in answer to an inquiry, but in addition thereto it must be made by the defendant either in the protection of his own interest or the performance of a duty to society.

A privileged communication has been defined as one made upon a proper occasion, from a proper motive, in a proper manner, and based upon reasonable or probable cause. In such cases there is no prima facie presumption of malice from the publication. There must be some evidence beyond the mere fact of publication.

A qualifiedly privileged communication takes place when the circumstances are held to preclude any presumptions of malice but still leave the party responsible for both falsehood and malice if affirmatively shown.

Where a party makes a communication and such a communication is prompted by a duty owed either to the public or to a third party, or the communication is one in which the party has an interest and is made to another having a corresponding interest, the communication is privileged if made in good faith and without actual malice.

The sole inquiry necessary for us to consider on this appeal is, were the two letters of which complaint is made privileged or qualifiedly privileged communications? If they were, no action for libel is maintainable by Baskett; if they were not, or if the letters were only qualifiedly privileged and there was actual malice on the part of President Crossfield, then the defendants were liable.

What was the duty of President Crossfield to the father of young Baskett under all the circumstances as they existed on October 1 and 4, 1918, at the date of the writing of the two letters? The president of the school was *in loco parentis* to young Baskett as a student. There was a relation of trust and confidence between the two and between the president of the school and the father of the pupil; and the president of the school, being in charge of the student body, owed a duty to the father and family of young Baskett, which he could not discharge except by faithfully, fully, and accurately reporting to the father and family the progress and deportment of the student. In the performance of this duty the president of the university had the right to act, write, and say of and concerning the dismissed student what a reasonably prudent and considerate official of a college would under like circumstances have done and said. If he had done and said less than is shown by the letters, he would have been remiss [in] the duty; if he had done more, he would have subjected himself to the charge of being actuated by malice. In this case Dr. Crossfield appears to have done only what his duty required of him. He gently and rather apologetically wrote and sent to the father of the student the two letters of which complaint is made. That these letters were written in the utmost good faith and for the good of the father and the dismissed student is beyond cavil. There is a total absence of evidence tending in the slightest degree to show malice on the part of President Crossfield towards young Baskett or his father. They were not even acquainted, and the president did not know the boy by sight, for he had only been in the school two weeks, and there was a large number of students in attendance on the school. Under the state of pleadings—the answer pleading privileged communications—the burden was upon the plaintiff Baskett to show actual malice on the part of President Crossfield and the University, which he was unable to do. In so failing he surrendered his right of recovery, and the trial court should have sustained both the motion of the university and President Crossfield for a directed verdict in their favor, made at the conclusion of all the evidence. Had President Crossfield, after hearing the complaint against young Baskett and the evidence in support thereof, failed to communicate these facts to the father of young Baskett, he would not have been worthy of the presidency of a great educational institution. Having acted in the line of his duty both to the school and community, young Baskett, and his father, he as well as the university are blameless, and no recovery can be had by Baskett. President Crossfield has entered a motion in this court for a cross-appeal, but he cannot have such relief in a common-law action, unless he had filed motion and grounds for a new trial in the court below.

For the reasons indicated the judgment is affirmed.

Judgment affirmed.

NOTES

1. *Absolute privilege* is restricted "to cases in which it is so much to the public interest that the defendant should speak out his mind fully and freely that all actions in respect to the words used are absolutely forbidden, even though it be alleged that they were used falsely, knowingly, and with express malice. This complete immunity obtains only where the public service or the due administration of justice requires it; *e.g.*, words used in debate in Congress and the state legislatures, reports of military or other officers to their superiors in the line of their duty, everything said by a judge on the bench, by a witness in the box, and the like. In these cases the action is absolutely barred."

Conditional or qualified privilege. "[W]here the public interest does not require such absolute immunity, the plaintiff will recover in spite of the privilege, if he can prove that the words were not used *bona fide*, but that the defendant used the privileged occasion artfully and knowingly to falsely defame the plaintiff. In this class of cases, an action will lie only where the party is guilty of falsehood and express malice." Ramsey v. Cheek, 109 N.C. 270, 13 S.E. 775 (1891).

2. *Malice.* By claiming "privileged communication" the defendant effectively rebuts the prima facie claim of malice and forces the plaintiff to prove there was malice in fact. Such proof must show that the defendant was actuated by motives of personal spite or ill will, independent of the occasion on which the communication was made. Wright v. Woodgate, 2 Cromp., M. & R. 577.

"The word 'privileged,' when applied to the law of libel, simply means that the circumstances under which the alleged libelous communication was made were such as to repel the legal inference of malice, and throw on the plaintiff the burden of proving it by extrinsic evidence." Hinman v. Hare, 5 N.Y. St. Rep. 504 (1887).

"A 'privileged communication' means nothing more than that the occasion of making it rebuts the prima facie inference of malice arising from the publication of matter prejudicial to the character of the plaintiff, and throws upon him the onus of proving malice in fact, but not of proving it by extrinsic evidence only." National Cash Register Co. v. Salling, 97 C.C.A. 334, 173 Fed. 22.

3. A written communication between private persons involving their private affairs is prima facie privileged. Moore v. Manufacturer's National Bank of Troy, 51 Hun. 472, 4 N.Y.S. 378 (1889).

4. A "privileged communication" is one made by a person who has an interest in the subject-matter and stands in such a relationship to the other person that it is proper for the writer or speaker to give the information, or is one of his reasonable duties. Hall v. Rice, 117 Neb. 813, 223 N.W. 4 (1929).

5. Where a teacher published in a newspaper that a student teacher "by her conduct in class, by her behavior in and around the building, and by her spirit, as exhibited in numberless personal interviews, has shown herself tricky and unreliable, and almost destitute of those womanly and honorable characteristics that should be the first requisites in a teacher," the court held the words to be libelous. In an action for libel, the plaintiff does not have to prove that the publication was not privileged; the defense must show an absence of legal malice in the publication. Dixon v. Allen, 69 Cal. 527, 11 P. 179 (1886).

6. In a case where a college president was sued for slander because he informed the landlady of a female student that the girl was crazy and should not be allowed to continue living in the rooming house, the court held for the president and said: "In the instant case we have a defendant who is head of a great institution of learning, who is expected, and whose duty it is, so far as he is able, to look after the students attending the school, and to look after their environment. He has relations, too, with the keepers of the rooming houses in which these students find temporary homes. If the defendant * * * had not conferred with those ladies [owners of the rooming house], he would have been derelict in his duty. The occasion was privileged." Everest v. McKenny, 195 Mich. 649, 162 N.W. 277 (1917).

7. We have established that public officials are protected by "privilege" from being liable for defamatory communications made in the course of their public service. However, these "public officials" have correspondingly less redress against communications made about them. The courts have held that in the absence of malice, "the First and Fourteenth Amendments afford a privilege to public discussion of official conduct even though it has some factually erroneous or defamatory content." In the same vein the courts have held that a person who casts himself into the "vortex of public controversy" and seeks to shape and influence public opinion is not protected from derogatory statements, unless these are made with malice. One court said: "* * * therefore, that if such a person seeks to realize upon his capacity to guide public policy and in the process is criticized, he should have no greater remedy than does his counterpart in public office." Pauling v. Globe-Democrat Publishing Company, 362 F.2d 188 (1966).

8. Notation made in a register by a teacher saying that a student was "ruined by tobacco and whiskey" was defamatory and did not constitute a "privileged communication." It was shown that the student had good habits, never drank whiskey, and seldom used tobacco. Dawkins v. Billingsley, 69 Okla. 259, 172 P. 69 (1918).

9. A communication from parents of female students to a school superintendent, alleging a boy student used degrading language and displayed unbecoming conduct, was qualifiedly privileged. There was no evidence of actual malice. The court said "Wide latitude should be allowed to the father of young girls in protection of their morals. The county superintendent was a proper person to whom to make a report as to such occurrences * * *." Hansen v. Hansen, 126 Minn. 426, 148 N.W. 457 (1914).

CHAPTER 11

GOVERNMENTAL AND CHARITABLE IMMUNITY

HISTORICAL BACKGROUND

Historically, in the United States, both public and private institutions of higher education have been immune from tort liability. In more recent years there have been numerous instances where courts have pierced the armor of immunity and allowed injured parties to recover from both public governmental agencies and private charitable institutions. The trend today is definitely away from immunity for both the public and the private sector. Many courts and legislatures [1] in evaluating the merits of the doctrine are finding that it is neither logically nor morally acceptable for dealing with problems of liability in modern society.

The historical development of governmental immunity in Europe and its subsequent transmittal to the United States is somewhat difficult to follow both chronologically and philosophically. It appears that throughout time rulers have had certain legal immunities bestowed upon them by virtue of their exalted positions. Of course, these rulers were usually the law givers, and it became a relatively simple matter to bestow immunity upon themselves. The origin of immunity in Anglo-American law has been traced to a date prior to the signing of the Magna Charta, the era of ultimate power and authority of the king. We know that a judgment in the king's court of England in 1234 proclaimed: "Our lord the king cannot be summoned or receive a command from anyone." [2]

The argument over the power and immunities of the king waxed and waned through several centuries of English history. A law dictionary, *The Interpreter,* published in 1607 proclaimed that the king was "above the law by his absolute power." In fact, as King James declared in 1607, the king was the supreme judge of England and all courts were under him. It was declared that God himself had ordained kings and had given them power to make laws; *rex est lex loquens* (the king

---

1. The federal government abrogates immunity within definable limits of damages through the Federal Tort Claims Act, 28 U.S.C.A. §§ 1346, 2671-2680.

2. Quoted by Pollock & Maitland, *History of English Law,* 2d ed. 1923, p. 516.

is the law speaking).[3] Under these conditions it is not difficult to see how the doctrine of sovereign immunity prevailed. The much-quoted phrase "The King can do no wrong" was made by Blackstone in 1765.[4] By this time, the doctrine was so firmly established that Blackstone was prompted to report that "The king, moreover, is not only incapable of doing wrong, but even of thinking wrong; he can never mean to do an improper thing: in him is no folly or weakness." [5] The king's courts of England had no jurisdiction to hear claims made against the king. The Court of Exchequer was the sole arbiter of claims for equitable relief against the crown. Such claims were filed in the form of a Petition of Right which could be barred by the king's prerogative.[6] If permission to sue the king was granted, the king would write "Let right be done" across the petition, thereby allowing himself to be sued the same as any commoner, but the matter was solely within the king's discretion.[7]

The incorporation of the concept of sovereign immunity into American law has been called "one of the mysteries of legal evolution." [8] It is difficult to comprehend why in the United States, where there was such great fear of tyranny of kings, this doctrine was unquestionably adopted so wholeheartedly. It would have been reasonable to assume that in the absence of sheer oversight by the framers of the constitution, immunity of the government would have been denied or at least carefully circumscribed.

The exact documentation of the transatlantic migration of the doctrine of immunity is not entirely certain; however, it would have been relatively simple for the immunity doctrine to become Americanized since all of the early law books used in the United States were printed in England and were based on English law. As early as 1788, Alexander Hamilton in commenting on the new Constitution said:

It is inherent in the nature of the sovereignty not to be

3. Leonard W. Levy, *Origins of The Fifth Amendment*, Oxford University Press, 1968, pp. 242-243.

4. Blackstone, *Commentaries* (10th ed. 1887).

5. *Ibid.*; see also, Kenneth Culp Davis, *Administrative Law Treatise*, West Publishing Company, § 25.01, p. 436.

6. Verne Lawyer, "Birth and Death of Governmental Immunity," *Cleveland-Marshall Law Review*, Vol. 15, No. 1. pp. 529-530 (1966).

7. See Alexander Wollcott, "The Archer-Shee Case," *Law in Action*, Bonanza Books, New York, pp. 167-176.

8. Edwin Borchard, "Government Liability in Tort," *Yale Law Journal*, Vol. 34, p. 4 (1924).

amenable to the suit of an individual without its consent. This is the general sense, and the general practice of mankind; and the exemption, as one of the attributes of sovereignty, is now enjoyed by the government of every state of the Union. Unless, therefore, there is a surrender of this immunity in the plan of the convention, it will remain with the states. The contracts between a nation and individuals are only binding on the conscience of the sovereign and have no pretension of compulsive force. They confer no right of action, independent of the sovereign will.[9]

The sovereign immunity of the king was simply replaced by the sovereign immunity of the state. In attempting to explain the transition of immunity from the king to the state, Garber [10] has identified two interesting old cases. One of these cases, *Russell v. The Men Dwelling in the County of Devon,* took place in 1788.[11] Here, the plaintiff sued the Men of Devon for damage done to his wagon as a consequence of a bridge being out of repair. It was claimed that the bridge should have been kept in good repair by the men in the county. The court in holding for the defendants, vaguely enunciated four primary reasons for denying recovery:

(1) the lack of a common treasury from which to pay damages; (2) allowing recovery would open the door to an infinity of such actions; this the judges considered to be bad public policy; (3) it was better for an individual to suffer an injury than for the public an inconvenience; and (4) there was no precedent for such a suit; such a suit could be maintained only with the express permission of the legislature.

The key reason, apparently, was the last mentioned above, which found there was no precedent for such an action; for such to exist, the Parliament must render a description of the men who would be liable in such an action. Parliament had not done this; therefore, there was no liability. This court was convinced that if an action were permitted it must be done by statute enacted by the legislative branch of government. The common law precedent simply had not in the past allowed a civil action in tort against a governmental body.

Although Hamilton and others had proclaimed the doctrine of sovereign immunity, there apparently was no case invoking

---

9. *The Federalist* No. 81, at 374 (Hallowell ed. 1842) (Hamilton).

10. Lee O. Garber, *Origin of the Governmental Immunity From Tort Doctrine,* The Interstate Printers and Publishers.

11. Russell v. The Men Dwelling in the County of Devon, 100 Eng. Rep. 359, 2 T.R. 667 (1788).

it in America until an 1812 Massachusetts case.[12] In this case, a stagecoach operator's horse was killed when it stepped in a hole on a bridge in the town of Leicester. The plaintiffs claimed that the town of Leicester was responsible for the condition of the bridge and that the injury was caused by neglect of this responsibility. The plaintiffs pointed out that here in the town of Leicester there was a common treasury out of which damages might be paid. The court denied relief and said that it is well settled that common law provides for no such action. No liability for neglect can be maintained unless a statute gives authority for a quasi-corporation to be sued in the civil action of tort.

It seems that the philosophic foundation for the doctrine was never fully examined, and the courts apparently proceeded with the surface assumption that immunity was in the best interest of good government. Marshall, the great Chief Justice of the United States Supreme Court, gave no reason or logic for his conclusion of 1821 when he said, "The universally received opinion is, that no suit can be commenced or prosecuted against the United States; that the judiciary act does not authorize such suits." [13] By mid-eighteenth century, the precedent was so well established that the Supreme Court said, "No maxim is thought to be better established or more universally assented to, than that which ordains that a sovereign, or a government representing the sovereign, cannot *ex delicto* be amenable to its own creatures or agents employed under its own authority for the fulfillment merely of its own legitimate ends." [14]

Shortly thereafter, in 1857, the Supreme Court reaffirmed its view of sovereign immunity, once again stating: "It is an established principle of jurisprudence in all civilized nations that a sovereign cannot be sued in its own courts, or in any other, without its consent and permission." [15]

Not until more recent times was there evidence of profound philosophical questioning of the doctrine, and arguments both for and against the doctrine began to be waged. Probably the chief proponent of sovereign immunity was Justice Holmes; this is evidenced by a Supreme Court opinion in 1907 and later by a 1926 letter to Laski. Holmes, in writing for a unanimous

---

12. Ephraim Mower v. The Inhabitants of Leicester, 9 Mass. 247 (1812).

13. Cohens v. Virginia, 19 U.S. (6 Wheat.) 264, 5 L. Ed. 257 (1821).

14. Hill v. United States, 50 U.S. (9 How.) 386 (1850).

15. Beers v. Arkansas, 61 U.S. (20 How.) 527 (1857).

court, said: "A sovereign is exempt from suit, not because of any formal conception or obsolete theory, but on the logical and practical ground that there can be no legal right as against the authority that makes the law on which the right depends." [16]

By the early nineteen hundreds, scholars began seeking more extensive explanation and logic for the doctrine, to such an extent that in 1926 Holmes was prompted to expound on support of his position in a letter to Laski: "Do you know I really am bothered by the old difference between us, if there is one, as to sovereignty, because as I understand the question, it seems to me one that does not admit of argument . . . . If you should say that the Courts ought in these days to assume a consent of the U.S. to be sued, or to be liable in tort on the same principles as those governing private persons, I should have my reason for thinking you wrong, but should not care, as that would be an intelligible point of difference. But what I can't understand is the suggestion that the United States is bound by law even though it does not assent. What I mean by law in this connection is that which is or should be enforced by the Courts and I can't understand how anyone should think that an instrumentality established by the United States to carry out its will, and that it can depose upon a failure to do so, should undertake to enforce something that ex hypothesis is against its will. It seems to me like shaking one's fist at the sky, when the sky furnishes the energy that enables one to raise the fist." [17]

Gradually, opposition to the concept began to emerge. The blind adoption of the principle was no more acceptable. Borchard, in a three-part law review article in 1924, laid the ground work for today's trend toward abolition of immunity: [18]

> . . . there is no reason why the most flagrant of the injuries wrongfully sustained by the citizen, those arising from the torts of officers, should be allowed to rest, as they now generally do, in practice if not in theory, at the door of the unfortunate citizen alone. . . . this hardship becomes the more incongruous when it is realized that it is greatest in countries like Great Britain and the United States, where democracy is assumed to have

16. Kawananakoa v. Polyblank, 205 U.S. 349, 27 S. Ct. 526, 51 L. Ed. 834 (1907).

17. 2 Holmes-Laski Letters 822 (1953); Kenneth Culp Davis, *Administrative Law Treatise*, West Publishing Co., § 2501, pp. 437-438.

18. Borchard, *op. cit.*, p. 129.

placed the individual on the highest plane of political freedom and individual justice. . . . It was Lord Macaulay who remarked that "the primary end of government is the protection of the persons and property of men." [19]

Borchard's attack had little immediate effect, but it did create a watershed from which a gradual shifting of legal philosophy took place.

IMMUNITY OF PUBLIC COLLEGES AND UNIVERSITIES

Since the state is generally immune from tort liability, a public college, university or other institution of higher learning under state control is also immune.[20] It has been held that even if the legislature has consented to allow the state to be sued, this does not necessarily mean that the state is liable for acts or omissions committed in connection with public colleges or universities.[21] The cloak of immunity inherited from the state which protects the institution is not removed by general legislation which does not apply specifically to the public colleges and universities of a state.[22]

In keeping with the immunity doctrine, the state institution is not liable for the acts of its officers or employees. *Respondeat superior*, that is, the master is liable for the acts of his servant, does not generally apply. The general rule prevails that the officials or governing boards of state institutions are merely agents or instrumentalities of the state and accordingly are immune from tort liability.[23]

Immunity is granted public colleges and universities, "since in performing governmental functions they merely act for the benefit of the state and of the public generally in the process of government." [24]

Applications of sovereign immunity to higher education are numerous. In an Ohio case, a child receiving treatment in the

---

19. *Ibid.*

20. Holzworth v. State, 238 Wis. 63, 298 N.W. 163 (1941); Public colleges, universities, or other institutions of higher education, or their governing boards, have generally been treated by the courts, like school districts and school boards, as mere agencies of the state engaged in governmental functions. (160 A.L.R. 66.)

21. Commonwealth v. Madison, 269 Ky. 571, 108 S.W.2d 519 (1937); Daniel v. Hoofnel, 287 Ky. 834, 155 S.W.2d 469 (1941).

22. Bacon v. Harris, 221 Ore. 553, 352 P.2d 472 (1960).

23. Davie v. Board of Regents, University of California, 66 Cal. App. 693, 227 P. 243, 160 A.L.R. 53 (1924).

24. 86 A.L.R.2d 511, § 8.

Ohio State University Hospital punctured her hand on a spindle on the nurse's desk and was immediately given an anti-tetanus inoculation, even though she protested that she was allergic to it. She sued the university alleging she had suffered serious injury from the reaction. The Supreme Court of Ohio upheld the immunity of the University on the ground that "The board of trustees of the state university cannot be held liable in tort for any claimed negligence of employees of the state university hospital which is operated by the board of trustees," since no statute authorizes such a tort action.[25]

In an excellent discussion of the merits and fallacies of governmental immunity, the Supreme Court of Michigan upheld the immunity doctrine on the grounds that to change the doctrine is a legislative responsibility upon which the court should not encroach.[26] The court of Michigan had for some years reflected its dislike for sovereign immunity; however, the legislature was not willing to abolish immunity and had so reflected by allowing suits in very specific and narrowly prescribed instances. This was indication to the court that the legislature did not wish to totally abrogate immunity. The primary question as the court saw it was not the propriety of governmental immunity, but whether the court had the authority to intervene and impose its will on the legislature and the people:

> If such a fundamental change of our present system is thought to be desirable, it should be brought about through legislative action, and after the general public, through its representatives in the Legislature, has had an opportunity to consider the wisdom thereof, and its effect upon the agencies involved.[27]

An early case held the Board of Regents of the University of California not liable for malpractice of a physician in the university hospital.[28] The case rested on the conclusion that the health responsibilities of the university hospital were a part of the educational responsibility of the university and was, therefore, a governmental function which was protected by immunity. The court acknowledged that such a rule of law may work a hardship on the plaintiff, but abided by the rule

25. Wolf v. Ohio State University Hospital *et al.*, 170 Ohio St. 49, 162 N.E.2d 475 (1959).

26. Williams v. City of Detroit, 364 Mich. 231, 111 N.W.2d 1 (1961).

27. Williams v. City of Detroit, *supra*; Hayes v. Town of Cedar Grove, 126 W. Va. 828, 30 S.E.2d 726, 156 A.L.R. 702.

28. Davie v. Board of Regents, Univ. of California, 66 Cal. App. 693, 227 P. 243 (1924).

of immunity and *respondeat superior*. However, the court in a companion case held the physician personally liable and thereby provided recompense for the plaintiff's injuries.[29]

A Maryland court recently commented that immunity "is too firmly established and has been too long unchanged by the legislature in the face of repeated reminders of its role in the matter in the opinions of the courts * * * to be changed judicially."[30]

In a 1967 case,[31] the Kentucky Court of Appeals refused to render school districts liable for tort claims. This same court had shortly before set precedent in that state by abolishing the immunity of municipalities.[32] The court in taking what appeared to be a contradictory position said:

> It is a fundamental concept of our form of government that the members of the legislative branch of government are elected from time to time to reflect the feeling of the people and to enact laws to meet their needs. When the people of this Commonwealth want sovereign immunity waived as to counties or county boards of education, their elected legislative representatives will be charged with this responsibility.

EXCEPTIONS TO IMMUNITY RULE

Despite these pro-immunity decisions, some states have directly abrogated immunity by either court edict or legislative mandate. Most states have gradually chipped away at the immunity doctrine until today it is doubtful if any state is wholly and absolutely immune from liability for all its governmental functions. Davis makes the flat pronouncement that "Of all deserving tort claims against federal, state, and local governmental units, probably far more are paid today than are unpaid * * *."[33]

LEGAL DEVICES TO BY-PASS IMMUNITY

Various devices have been used to give relief to injured parties who have legitimate claims. These are: (1) general statutes exemplified by one Federal Tort Claims Act, (2) pri-

---

29. *Ibid.*
30. Weisner v. Board of Education, 206 A.2d 560 (Md. 1965).
31. Cullinan v. Jefferson County, 418 S.W.2d 407 (Ky. 1967).
32. Haney v. City of Lexington, 386 S.W.2d 738, 10 A.L.R.3d 1362 (1964).
33. Kenneth Culp Davis, *Administrative Law Treatise*, § 25.01, West Publishing Co., p. 434.

vate laws and special or limited public legislation,[34] (3) liability imposed for performance of nongovernmental or proprietary functions, (4) nuisance or trespass doctrine used to circumvent immunity from tort, and (5) indirect liability such as subsumed by the government under insurance programs.

GOVERNMENTAL AND PROPRIETARY FUNCTIONS

Since courts have been reluctant to totally abrogate immunity, they have sought ways to avoid directly confronting the issue. In order to do this, courts have settled some tort actions on the basis of the activity or function which is being performed at the time of the injury. Colleges and universities operate in a dual capacity, performing functions which are purely governmental the majority of the time, but at times performing proprietary functions which could be discharged by a private corporation. However, the courts in all jurisdictions have not made this distinction. In these jurisdictions it is maintained that any function relative to the avowed purpose of the university is governmental and is therefore immune from liability.[35] These courts have noted that although a school may participate in proprietary functions the court will not distinguish them and will maintain strict sovereign immunity. In doing this, one court stated:

> We are aware of a modern tendency for many school[s] * * * to engage in commercial enterprises and proprietary functions only remotely related to public education. * * * However, in view of the formidable precedent established by the foregoing authorities, which have established a uniform rule of governmental immunity from all tort liability with respect to all involuntary units of government, * * * we are persuaded that the modification of so firmly an established principle with its broad consequences in public affairs presents a matter for general restatement of public policy by legislative enactment.[36]

In the same vein, a court in Tennessee denied that a school district could perform any functions other than those governmental. The court reasoned that since the legislature limited the duties of a board of education to those required to operate

---

34. An example is the Texas City disaster, where Congress, without amending the Federal Tort Claims Act, provided for payment of claims. Pub. Law 378, 84th Congress, 1st Sess., approved August 12, 1955. See Davis, *op. cit.*, p. 435.

35. Holzworth v. State, 238 Wis. 63, 298 N.W. 163 (1941).

36. Bragg v. Board of Public Instruction, 160 Fla. 590, 36 So. 2d 222 (1948).

the schools, "Therefore, in legal contemplation there is no such thing as such a Board acting in a proprietary capacity for private gain." [37]

Even with this general philosophy prevailing, a number of courts have relied on the proprietary versus governmental distinction to hold public agencies liable in tort. The courts in Pennsylvania are probably the best example of the transition from total nonliability to liability for proprietary functions.[38] The court in 1949 abandoned unqualified immunity and held that a school district was performing a proprietary function by charging fees to a football game. The court noted that the distinction between governmental and proprietary functions had long been in a state of confusion. The court said that the only rational distinction was that of necessity, that is, a governmental function is one performed in "pursuance of the duty of government to provide for the safety, health, and welfare of its citizens." On the other hand, proprietary functions were those performed for the "convenience or comfort of the persons served" which could just as well be performed by private individuals.[39]

Subsequent Pennsylvania decisions held that ownership of an apartment house by a school district was a proprietary function,[40] as was a summer recreation program which was open to the general public on payment of certain charges.[41]

A Texas court found that a state college, in operating an agricultural experimental station, was engaged in a "governmental function." [42] When an employee was injured as a result of the station superintendent's failure to provide him with safe equipment, the court held the college not liable. The court said, "The state is not liable for the torts or negligence of its officers, agents, or servants engaged in the performance of a governmental function, unless it has expressly assumed liability." [43]

The controlling feature of a proprietary function is not whether admission is charged or a profit is made; instead, the

37. Reed v. Rhea County, 189 Tenn. 247, 225 S.W.2d 49 (1949).

38. Hoffman v. Scranton School District, 67 Pa. D. & C. 301, 51 Lack Jur. 25, 41 Munic. L.R. 21 (1949).

39. *Ibid.*

40. Pintek v. Allegheny County, 186 Pa. Super. 366, 142 A.2d 296 (1958).

41. Morris v. School Dist. of Mt. Lebanon, 393 Pa. 633, 144 A.2d 737 (1958).

42. State *et al.* v. Morgan, 170 S.W.2d 652 (1943).

43. *Ibid.*

courts seem to be in general agreement that the true test is whether the activity is carried on for the use and benefit of the general public.[44]

In this regard, other courts have defined proprietary functions as those things not normally required by law or things not governmental in nature. Generally, it may be said that if a function is within the scope of the college's or university's operation, as expressed or implied by statute, then the function is governmental and not proprietary. The Supreme Court in Oregon has laid down this test for distinguishing proprietary from governmental functions: "The underlying test is whether the act is for the common good of all without the element of special corporate benefit or pecuniary profit." [45]

NUISANCE

A number of jurisdictions have held that agencies such as public colleges and universities may be liable for personal injuries and death resulting from the creation or maintenance of a nuisance regardless of whether the agency is performing a proprietary or governmental function.[46] These courts have recognized that the general rules pertaining to governmental immunity do not extend to the creation of a nuisance by the governmental instrumentality.

A "nuisance" has been defined as "the existence or creation of a dangerous, unsafe, or offensive condition which is likely to cause injury, harm, or inconvenience to others." [47] A more complete definition has been given by a Connecticut court:

> * * * to constitute a nuisance there must have arisen a condition the natural tendency of which is to create danger or inflict injury upon person or property, * * * there must be more than an act or failure to act on the part of the defendant, * * * the danger created must have been a continuing one * * *.[48]

Nuisance in any one case depends on many things, the type of neighborhood, the nature of the wrong complained of, the proximity of the injured party and damage, the frequency,

---

44. Shoemaker v. City of Parsons, 154 Kan. 387, 118 P.2d 508.
45. Rankin v. School District No. 9, 23 P.2d 132 (Ore. 1933).
46. Bush v. Norwalk, 122 Conn. 426, 189 A. 608 (1937); Jones v. Kansas City, 176 Kan. 406, 271 P.2d 803 (1954); Molinari v. Boston, 333 Mass. 394, 130 N.E.2d 925 (1955); Michael v. School Dist. of Lancaster, 391 Pa. 209, 137 A.2d 456 (1958).
47. National Educational Association, op. cit., p. 21.
48. Bush v. City of Norwalk, 189 A. 608 (Conn. 1937).

continuity of duration, and the damage or annoyance resulting.[49]

A leading case in which a school was held to have created a nuisance was in Michigan. In this case snow had fallen from the roof of a school building onto adjacent property. The snow and ice damaged the property and the owner of the property was injured when he fell on the ice. The court held that in this case there was both nuisance and trespass. The court said:

> The plaintiff had the right to the exclusive use and enjoyment of his property, and the defendant had no right to erect a building in such a manner that the ice and snow would inevitably slide from the roof, and be precipitated upon the plaintiff's premises, than it would have to accumulate water upon its own premises, and then permit it to flow in a body upon his premises * * *.[50]

In keeping with the legal definition of "nuisance," a dangerous condition must have been created before the college can be liable. Of course, if the school or governmental unit does not create the nuisance then it is not liable. In a case in which students threw wet paper towels on a lavatory floor and a student slipped and was injured, the court held for the school. The court said the school did not create the nuisance and therefore was not liable.[51]

In other similar cases, a school district was held liable when a pupil was injured falling from a junk pile which was on school grounds.[52] In another case, students playing baseball on a school ground broke windows and destroyed an adjacent homeowner's garden. The court ordered the school district to pay $300 in damages for creating a nuisance.[53] Liability was likewise adjudged where night baseball games created a nuisance for surrounding homeowners.[54]

In a case in which a college erected a dike to protect school property from a river, the embankment so narrowed the channel of the river that the water washed away and destroyed fertile bottom land on the other side of the river. The plaintiff landowner claimed that a nuisance was created and the college

49. Rose v. Board of Education, 184 Kan. 486, 337 P.2d 652 (1959).

50. Ferris v. Board of Education of Detroit, 81 N.W. 98 (Mich. 1899).

51. Jones v. Kansas City, 271 P.2d 803 (Kan. 1954).

52. Popow v. Central School District No. 1, 13 N.E.2d 463 (N.Y. 1938).

53. Ness v. Independent School District of Sioux City, 230 Iowa 771, 298 N.W. 855 (1941).

54. Hansen v. Independent School Dist. No. 1, 98 P.2d 959 (Idaho 1940).

had in effect taken his property without due process of law. The court held that the college could not avail itself of the state's governmental immunity, and since it built the dike for its own proprietary and corporate purposes it is liable to the opposite riparian owner for damaging and taking his property without due process.[55]

While "nuisance" as demonstrated by these cases is a remedial approach to averting the immunity doctrine, the courts will not always allow relief on such bases. A Tennessee court refused to allow a claim of nuisance to avert immunity regarding a student who was injured when he fell down a stairwell.[56] Other courts have denied damages on the basis of a nuisance claim: one involving a student who died from inhaling sewer gas [57] and another involving a student who was killed by a swing on the school playground.[58]

ABROGATION OF IMMUNITY

While most jurisdictions have attacked sovereign immunity only on a piecemeal basis, some states have by either legislative mandate or by court decision abolished it. These states have ignored the 1868 United States Supreme Court proposition which admonished: "It is obvious that the public service would be hindered, and the public safety endangered, if the supreme authority could be subjected to suit at the instance of every citizen, * * *." Davis, in commenting on state actions to abolish immunity, said, "Not only is this proposition not obvious, but the opposite of the proposition is rapidly becoming obvious." [59] The states allowing such suits have not experienced hindrance to governmental processes, nor have they found that services to individual citizens of the state were in any way diminished. New York was the first state to abrogate immunity and has done so more completely than any other jurisdiction in America, including the federal government.[60]

Illinois is probably the best example of total repudiation of

---

55. Hopkins v. Clemson Agriculture College, 221 U.S. 636, 31 S. Ct. 654, 55 L. Ed. 890 (1911).

56. Barnett v. City of Memphis, 196 Tenn. 590, 269 S.W.2d 906 (1954).

57. Folk v. City of Milwaukee, 84 N.W. 420 (Wis. 1900).

58. Anderson v. Board of Education, 190 N.W. 807 (N.D 1922).

59. Kenneth Culp Davis, op. cit., § 25.01, pp. 438-439.

60. Stanley Mosk, "The Many Problems of Sovereign Immunity," San Diego Law Review, Vol. 3, p. 9 (Jan. 1966).

the doctrine of immunity.[61] One important aspect of this case is that the abrogation of immunity was carried out by the court and not the legislature. Such a precedent doubtlessly provided momentum and credence for the abrogation of immunity through the vehicle of common law. The case was of great importance, also because of its all encompassing language which indicated the court's intention to totally abrogate sovereign immunity in Illinois and not confine abolishment to parts and portions of governmental operation. In this regard the *American Law Reports* state, "The language of the opinion leaves little doubt that the court did not intend to limit recognition of tort liability to school districts but expects to extend it to other governmental entities." [62] The court did limit recovery to only "future occurrences," disallowing claims for injuries which arose before the date of *Molitor*.[63] The legislature of Illinois reacted to the *Molitor* case by enacting legislation limiting tort liability recoveries to $10,000 for "each separate cause of action." [64]

California, like New York and Illinois, has waged a broadside attack on the doctrine of sovereign immunity. In 1961, the Supreme Court of California handed down a decision [65] which followed in the footsteps of the *Molitor* case. In this case the court rejected the entire notion of governmental immunity. The court gave little creditability to the argument that the legislature should be the only branch of government to abrogate immunity. The court pointed out that the doctrine of governmental immunity was originally instigated by the court, and the court could take it away. The court said that the legislature, by waiving immunity for selected areas of governmental operation, was thereby sanctioning immunity for the areas not waived.[66] The court said: "Nor are we faced with a comprehensive legislative enactment designed to cover a field. What is before us is a series of sporadic statutes, each

---

61. Molitor v. Kaneland Community Unit District No. 302, 18 Ill. 2d 11, 163 N.E.2d 89, 86 A.L.R.2d 469, *cert. denied*, 362 U.S. 968, 80 S. Ct. 955 (1959).

62. 86 A.L.R.2d 526.

63. Bergman v. Board of Education, 30 Ill. App. 2d 65, 173 N.E.2d 565 (1961); Garrison v. Community Consolidated School Dist., 34 Ill. App. 2d 322, 181 N.E.2d 360 (1962).

64. Ill. Rev. Stat., Ch. 122, §§ 821-831 (1959).

65. Muskopf v. Corning Hospital District, 55 Cal. 2d 211, 11 Cal. Rptr. 89, 359 P.2d 457 (1961).

66. Gov't Code, § 53051 (dangerous and defective public property defined).

operating on a separate area of governmental immunity where
its evil was felt most.* * * We read the statutes as meaning
only what they say: that in the areas indicated there shall be
no governmental immunity. They leave to the court whether
it should adhere to its own rule of immunity in other areas." [67]
In a later decision,[68] suit was brought against the Regents of
the University of California for injury sustained as a result
of negligence by physicians in treatment at the university hospital. While there was no direct claim of governmental immunity and the issue was somewhat clouded by the fact that
the hospital claimed it was a charitable institution, the court
did not hesitate to rule for the plaintiff. Significantly, the
court's opinion stated:

> The integrated and specialized society of today, struc-
> tured upon mutual dependency, cannot rigidly narrow the
> concept of the public interest. From the observance of
> simple standards of due care in the driving of a car to the
> performance of the high standards of hospital practice,
> the individual citizen must be completely dependent upon
> the responsibility of others.
> The fabric of this pattern is so closely woven that the
> snarling of a single thread affects the whole. We cannot
> lightly accept a sought immunity from careless failure to
> provide the hospital service upon which many must de-
> pend.[69]

In 1963, the legislature of California in following the "sporadic" pattern of legislative elimination of immunity abolished
sovereign immunity for medical, health, and public health activities.[70]

Pursuant to the education code [71] making school districts
liable, a long series of cases have held school districts in California liable in tort actions. Junior colleges in California, unlike most states, are a part of the local school district. As such,
the San Mateo Junior College was held to be within the stat-

---

67. *Ibid.*

68. Tunkl v. Regents of University of California, 60 Cal. 2d 92, 32
Cal. Rptr. 33, 383 P.2d 441 (1963), *vacating* 23 Cal. Rptr. 328 (1962).

69. *Ibid.*

70. Cal. Gov't Code, Div. 3.6, §§ 854-856.4. See M.M. Chambers, *The
Colleges and The Courts, 1962-1966*, Interstate Publishers, p. 269.

71. Educ. Code, § 903. Section 903 was later repealed and replaced by
Government Code § 815.2, West's Annotated California Codes. The new
section imposes liability upon public entities for tortious conduct by employees. It makes clear, however, that a public entity cannot be held liable for an employee's act or omission where the employee himself
would be immune. An employee is immune for discretionary acts within
the scope of his employment.

ute rendering a school district liable for injuries arising out of negligence of the district, its officers or employees.[72]

The philosophy of these newer precedents is contrary to the 1924 case of *Davie v. Regents of University of California,*[73] cited above, which rested on the conclusion that the University is immune from liability when it is performing a governmental function. If the *Davie* case were appealed to the California Supreme Court today, it is highly unlikely that the same decision would be reached.

Several other states have indicated disenchantment with the doctrine of immunity in recent years. Florida and Nebraska abrogated immunity by statute in 1969. Florida's abrogation, however, was for only one year and was not reenacted in the 1970 legislative session. The enactment of the Florida abrogation statute was given impetus by an incident at the University of Florida where a small child climbed and fell from the coaching tower on the football practice field.

The Supreme Court of Arizona, in 1963, examined the governmental question and apparently totally rejected the doctrine.[74] The Arizona court remarked that, "This doctrine of the English Common Law seems to have been windblown across the Atlantic as were the Pilgrims on the Mayflower and landed as if by chance on Plymouth Rock." [75]

In view of the changing status of the law in this area, it would not be worthwhile to try to enumerate the states which have partially, substantially, or completely abrogated immunity. However, the best information available indicates that less than twenty states have done so and in most of these the abrogation was applied to municipalities and school districts and not necessarily institutions of higher education. As pointed out previously, it may be precarious to assume that rulings on the immunity of school districts apply to institutions of higher education. This is illustrated by a situation which transpired in Oregon, where the state legislature enacted legislation to abolish immunity for certain types of public corporations.[76] One of the public corporations mentioned in the statute was school districts.[77] A girl fell on a stairway at

---

72. Grover v. San Mateo Junior College District of San Mateo County, 146 Cal. App. 2d 86, 303 P.2d 602 (1956).
73. *Supra.*
74. Stone v. Arizona Highway Commission, 381 P.2d 107 (1963).
75. *Ibid.*
76. O.R.S. § 30.320.
77. O.R.S. § 30.10.

the University of Oregon, was injured, and sued the State Department of Higher Education and the State Board of Higher Education for damages.[78] The court concluded that the term "public corporation" used in the statute did not apply to higher education in the state; therefore, there could be no liability. However, since this decision, the Oregon legislature has passed the "Tort Actions Against Public Bodies Act" which allows suit against public bodies.[79] Public body is defined in the new act as including boards or commissions of the state.

TORT LIABILITY OF PRIVATE COLLEGES

A college or university, just as any other institution or person, may be liable for its tortious acts. This general statement, however, is modified by the rule of law in some jurisdictions which provides that nongovernmental charitable organizations and institutions are immune from tort liability. Because of the charitable nature of the tort-feasor, some courts have given them a preferred position which protects them from liability. The application of this doctrine, in fact, means that an injured party must suffer the loss and cannot recover simply because of the tort-feasor's charitable nature.

HISTORICAL DEVELOPMENT

Historically, the rule of charitable immunity is based on very shaky precedent. The rule derives from an 1846 English case [80] which did not involve tort liability nor governmental institutions, but was brought by the plaintiff charging wrongful exclusion from the benefits of a governmental charitable hospital. In this case Heriot's Hospital had been willed to the town of Edinburgh for the "maintenance, relief, bringing up, and education" [81] of poor fatherless boys. The plaintiff was denied admission and he sued for damages, claiming that he was from Edinburgh, poor, and fatherless. The court in searching for precedent relied on *Duncan v. Findlater*,[82] a case involving liability for negligence under a public road act. Dictum in *Duncan* was relied on by Lord Cottenham in the *Heriot's Hospital* case, where he stated:

---

78. Bacon v. Harris, 221 Ore. 553, 352 P.2d 472 (1960).
79. O.R.S. §§ 30.260 to 30.300.
80. The Feoffees of Heriot's Hospital v. Ross, 12 Clark & F. 507, 8 Eng. Rep. 1508 (1846).
81. *Ibid.*
82. 6 Clark & F. 894, 7 Eng. Rep. 934 (1839).

The question then comes to this,—whether by the law of Scotland a person who claims damages from those who are managers of a trust fund, in respect of their management of that fund, can make it liable in payment. It is obvious that it would be a direct violation, in all cases of the purposes of a trust, if this could be done; for there is not any person who ever created a trust fund that provided for payment out of it damages to be recovered from those who had the management of the fund. No such provision has been made here. There is a trust, and there are persons intended to manage it for the benefit of those who are to be the objects of the charity. To give damages out of a trust fund would not be to apply it to those objects whom the author of the fund had in view, but would be to divert it to a completely different purpose.[83]

This precedent was followed in *Holliday v. St. Leonard* [84] in 1861, but here it ended. In 1866, in *Mersey Daks v. Gibbs*,[85] the court pointed out that Lord Cottenham's opinion in the case of *Heriot's Hospital* could lead to very mischievous and unreasonable consequences "to deny injured persons the right to seek a remedy from the body authorizing the injurious acts." It is much more reasonable, in such a case, that the trust or corporate property should be amenable to the individual injured, because there is then no failure of justice, seeing that the beneficiary will always have his right of complaint * * *."

By 1871 the immunity precedent had been totally overruled.[86] Five years hence, the courts in the United States being evidently unaware of the overruling of these precedents, pronounced that charities were immune from liability in this country.[87] The Massachusetts court held that the funds of a charitable hospital could not be diverted to pay a charity patient's claim for damages. Subsequently, a Maryland case [88] in 1885 relied on the *Heriot's Hospital* case in deciding that funds could not be used to compensate an inmate for an assault on him committed by officers of an institution. Both this court and the Massachusetts court were apparently unaware that the precedent they were citing had been overruled.

The court in Rhode Island, unlike Massachusetts and Maryland, refused to establish the charitable immunity doctrine in

---

83. The Feoffees of Heriot's Hospital v. Ross, *supra.*

84. 11 C.B. N.S. 192, 142 Eng. Rep. 769 (1861).

85. 11 H.L. Cas. 686, 11 Eng. Rep. 1500 (1866).

86. Foreman v. Canterbury Corp., (Eng.) L.R., 6 Q.B. 214 (1871).

87. McDonald v. Massachusetts General Hospital, 120 Mass. 432, 21 Am. Rep. 529 (1876).

88. Perry v. House of Refuge, 63 Md. 20, 52 Am. Rep. 495 (1885).

that state;[89] however, the legislature subsequently repudiated the court's decision and statutorily established immunity.

Since 1876 the history of the charitable immunity doctrine can only be distinguished by its contradictions. Several states have adopted it totally, others partially, some have repudiated the doctrine,[90] and three states [91] have neither accepted nor rejected the doctrine.[92]

Prior to 1942 only six states considered charities to have full liability status.[93] In that year Justice Rutledge in a pervasive opinion reviewed the bases for charitable immunity and logically destroyed them all.[94]

In recent years several states have abrogated immunity of charities and the trend is definitely toward treating a charity as any other business organization.

The courts which have granted immunity to charities have generally based their judgments on one of four theories: (1) the trust fund theory; (2) the theory that the doctrine of *respondeat superior* does not apply to charities; (3) the theory that a beneficiary of a charity has waived his claim; and (4) the public policy theory.

TRUST FUND THEORY

This theory dates back to the *Heriot's Hospital* case, where the court decided that charitable funds held in trust could not be diverted to pay damages. Down through the years the courts have reasoned that to allow the payment of damages may impair the usefulness of the charity,[95] thereby thwarting the intent of the donor.

The courts have also held that the trustees of a fund do not

---

89. Glavin v. Rhode Island, 12 R.I. 411, 34 Am. Rep. 675 (1879).

90. Charles Glidden Johnson, "Charitable Immunity: A Diminishing Doctrine," *Washington and Lee Law Review*, Vol. XXIII, p. 109, (1966).

91. The question of charitable immunity has not been raised in Hawaii, New Mexico and South Dakota. Charles Glidden Johnson, *op. cit.*

92. See Notes, this chapter, for listing of states and their charitable immunity status.

93. Charles Glidden Johnson, *op. cit.*

94. Prosser said that Rutledge "reviewed all of the arguments in favor of the immunity and demolished them so completely as to change the course of the law." William Prosser, *Law of Torts*, West Publishing Co., 2d ed. 1955, p. 787.

95. Ettlinger v. Trustees of Randolph-Macon College (Va.), 31 F.2d 869 (4th Cir. 1929); Parks v. Northwestern Univ., 218 Ill. 381, 75 N.E. 991 (1905); Southern Methodist Univ. v. Clayton, 142 Tex. 179, 176 S.W.2d 749 (1943); Vermillion v. Woman's College, 104 S.C. 197, 88 S.E. 649 (1916).

have the power to divert funds from their intended purpose,[96] and that the funds, being set aside for a specific purpose, cannot be subject to execution.[97] In following this theory, no liability exists regardless of whether the injured person is a recipient of benefits, an employee, or a stranger. It is immaterial whether the injury was caused through the fault of an employee or the employer.

Critics of the trust fund theory maintain that as a general rule of trust law other trust funds are not exempt from liability for torts committed in administering the trust. They also say that the trust funds are not exempt in the hands of the donor, so why should they be conferred exemption by the donor's turning them over to a charitable trust fund. A third argument against the trust fund theory, is that donations to charities have not diminished in jurisdictions where immunity has been abolished.[98] This third argument strikes at the heart of the tort immunity protection of charities.[99] There is little rationale for the courts to protect a charity at the expense of an injured person, if, in fact, the protection does not enhance or deter the financial position of the charity. Charities still exist in states without immunity and appear to be just as prevalent as in states abiding by the immunity doctrine. There is, however, apparently very little statistical data either supporting or rejecting this argument. It is difficult to determine whether the charities in states without immunity would have expanded to an even greater extent if they had been immune.[100]

RESPONDEAT SUPERIOR THEORY

The view is taken in some jurisdictions that because of the nature of the charity it is exempt from the doctrine of *respondeat superior*. The doctrine of *respondeat superior* means that the master or employer is liable for the torts of his servants or employees committed in the course of employment.

---

96. Parks v. Northwestern, *supra;* Downes v. Harper Hospital, 101 Mich. 555, 60 N.W. 42 (1894).

97. St. Mary's Academy v. Solomon, 77 Colo. 463, 238 P. 22 (1925); Moore v. Moyle, 405 Ill. 555, 92 N.E.2d 81 (1950); Anderson v. Armstrong, 180 Tenn. 56, 171 S.W.2d 401 (1943).

98. Gregory v. Salem General Hospital, 175 Ore. 464, 153 P.2d 837 (1944); Christini v. Griffin Hospital, 134 Conn. 282, 57 A.2d 262 (1948).

99. Cohen v. General Hospital, 113 Conn. 188, 154 A. 435 (1931); Bond v. City of Pittsburgh, 368 Pa. 404, 84 A.2d 328 (1951).

100. Schulte v. Missionaries of LaSalette Corp. of Mo., 352 S.W.2d 636 (Mo. 1961).

This is not unlike sovereign immunity in the public sector, which generally holds that *respondeat superior* does not apply. This theory, when followed in either the public or private sector, places the burden of liability on the employee; the employer or organization will not assume the liability for torts of employees.

The logic supporting the inapplicability of *respondeat superior* is derived from the notion that the charity does not derive any benefits or profits from the services of its employees.[101] The doctrine of *respondeat superior* is said to be based on the assumption that where the employer or master derives a financial benefit it is only just that he should answer for the torts of his servants.[102]

The question of whether the charity derives a profit is critical to this theory of immunity. This theory ignores the nature of the modern charity which, regardless of what its earnings are called, does profit and benefit from the activities of its employees.[103] The position is also frequently taken that immunity from *respondeat superior* is inconsistent with other theories supporting immunity. If the derivation of a profit or benefit is crucial to whether an institution is immune, then different standards may exist for paying or nonpaying patients in hospitals or paying or nonpaying or scholarship students in college. An Arizona court has pointed out the fallacy of this argument:

> If based upon the theory that the doctrine of *respondeat superior* does not apply because the defendant is a nonprofit institution, then it can make no difference whatever whether the patient pays or does not pay or whether the claimant is or is not a stranger. Its character as a nonprofit organization is not changed or affected by the fact that an injured patient pays or does not pay for the care he receives nor by the fact that the injured person is a stranger. It reduces itself to an absurdity to say that the doctrine does apply to strangers and paying patients but does not apply to nonpaying patients.[104]

The lack of applicability of tort liability under *respondeat*

101. Williams' Adm'x v. Church Home for Females, 223 Ky. 355, 3 S.W.2d 753 (1928); Wilcox v. Idaho Falls Latter Day Saints Hosp., 59 Idaho 350, 82 P.2d 849 (1938); Hearns v. Waterbury Hospital, 66 Conn. 98, 33 A. 595 (1895); Morrison v. Henke, 165 Wis. 166, 160 N.W. 173 (1917); Backman v. Y.W.C.A., 179 Wis. 178, 191 N.W. 751 (1922).

102. Schumacher v. Evangelical Deaconess Society, 218 Wis. 169, 260 N.W. 476 (1935).

103. Charles Glidden Johnson, *op. cit.*

104. Ray v. Tucson Medical Center, 72 Ariz. 22, 230 P.2d 220 (1951).

superior has also been objected to on the grounds that liability should not be exempted on the grounds of whether the master profits, but should be predicated on the relationship between master and servant and on the authority and control the master exercises.[105]

Philosophically, it has been suggested, that if in the nature of things a master employs servants he is simply responsible for their acts.[106] Looking at the argument from the position of an injured person, it is easy to see that a charity administers its functions the same as any other corporation and it harms and benefits third parties exactly as they are harmed and benefited by noncharities.[107]

IMPLIED WAIVER THEORY

This theory rests on the grounds that a person who avails himself of the benefits of a charity impliedly waives his right to recover for injury.[108] In effect, some courts have held that the beneficiary assumes the risk of negligence and therefore cannot recover.[109]

Implied waiver is probably the least logical of the theories of charitable immunity. The question arises: Can an injured, unconscious person or a newborn baby waive his right of recovery or assume the risk for injury?[110]

Waiver is generally defined as a voluntary and intentioned relinquishment of a known right.[111] Johnson observed [112] that many times people enter charitable hospitals for treatment simply because there are no other hospitals available to them; in such circumstances the lack of voluntariness negates the implication of waiver or assumption of risk. One court said in commenting on the waiver, "The theory of implied waiver

---

105. Lichty v. Carbon County Agriculture Assoc., 31 F. Supp. 809 (D.C. Pa. 1940); Kellogg v. Church Charity Foundation, 128 App. Div. 214, 112 N.Y.S. 566 (1908).
106. Tucker v. Mobile Infirmary Assoc., 191 Ala. 572, 68 So. 4 (1915); Wendt v. Servite Fathers, 332 Ill. App. 618, 76 N.E.2d 342 (1947).
107. Mulliner v. Evangelischer Diakonniessenverein, 144 Minn. 392, 175 N.W. 699 (1920).
108. Williams v. Church Home for Females, 223 Ky. 355, 3 S.W.2d 753 (1928); Adams v. University Hospital, 122 Mo. App. 675, 99 S.W. 453 (1907).
109. Weston v. Hospital of St. Vincent, 131 Va. 587, 107 S.E. 785 (1921).
110. Vanderbilt Univ. v. Henderson, 23 Tenn. App. 135, 127 S.W.2d 284 (1938); Gamble v. Vanderbilt Univ., 138 Tenn. 616, 200 S.W. 510 (1918).
111. Phillips v. Buffalo General Hospital, 239 N.Y. 188, 146 N.E. 199 (1924).
112. Charles Glidden Johnson, *op. cit.*

. . . is so thorougly illogical that it is difficult to understand how it has gained the approval of any court. It not only denies the very individual for whom the charity was intended the benefit of the charity, but it makes it compulsory upon him, if injured by the negligence of an employee, to donate to charity the amount he would otherwise be entitled to recover for his injuries." [113]

Treating the implied waiver as an implied contract between the patient and the hospital, or the student and the college, ignores other factors which should be considered any time an agreement is inferred between two parties. This seems to be especially true where a person pays for the services rendered him. A court in Mississippi held that there was no implied waiver where a paying patient was injured in a hospital, since there was no consideration given by the hospital in exchange for the waiver.[114]

The implied waiver theory is at best a device through which the courts have rationalized a desired result. The courts in upholding this theory ignore the intention of the parties involved and assume that they have agreed on waiver by simply becoming beneficiaries of the charity. Since it is nearly always impossible to determine if the patient has knowingly waived any claim for negligence, the courts find themselves in the position of implying an agreement which never really existed.[115]

Public Policy Theory

Courts at times feel competent to assess and enunciate what public policy dictates in regard to certain matters, the position of the courts being that the good of the public as a whole takes precedence over the good of an individual. With regard to charitable immunity, some courts have relied on the justification of public policy to uphold immunity. "Public policy" encompasses the three previously discussed theories and incorporates in them the idea that the benefits of the charity to the public outweigh the detriments and injuries to an individual. The rights of the individual must be subordinate to the public good.[116] The question that inevitably arises is "Why is it good

---

113. Ray v. Tucson Medical Center, 72 Ariz. 22, 230 P.2d 220 (1951).

114. Mississippi Baptist Hospital v. Holmes, 55 So. 2d 142 (Miss. 1951).

115. Nicholson v. Good Samaritan Hospital, 145 Fla. 360, 199 So. 344 (1940).

116. Vermillion v. Woman's College of Due West, 104 S.C. 197, 88 S.E. 649 (1916).

public policy to protect a charity and not good public policy to protect an injured individual?" Public policy could indeed demand that as a member of the public, the injured party is entitled to protection. One writer commented: "It seems anomalous that a person should enter a hospital for treatment, sustain an injury while there, and finally have to pay for his original treatment and for treatment for the new injury." [117] It might be said also that it is in the interest of good public policy to require that charitable institutions perform their duties in a manner which will not harm the health and well-being of citizens.[118]

The public policy rule, in the absence of specific legislation, allows the courts to interpret what is good public policy. Good public policy as it relates to charitable immunity is a question of considerable disagreement among the courts. In fact, one may wonder if the courts are in fact capable of determining public policy when the various courts take so many diverse and inconsistent positions on a matter of policy. The various jurisdictions in the United States have held that public policy requires the granting of complete immunity, granting exemption of the charity's trust property from execution in a suit, granting many kinds of qualifications and limitations, and denying any immunity [119] whatsoever. Good public policy in one state is not good public policy in another. There is apparently a trend away from immunity, and in view of the nature of today's charities and the expectations of the public there will continue to be an eroding away of the charitable immunity rule. One commentator has said:

> Present social conditions, the interests of justice and the need for clarification of the law combine to require the judiciary and legislatures of those jurisdictions which still adhere to this incongruity to relinquish their wavering hold on this theory and to respond to the needs and economic realities of our twentieth century society by discarding all remnants of this crumbling anachronism.[120]

---

117. Charles Glidden Johnson, *op. cit.*; Vanderbilt Univ. v. Henderson, 23 App. 135, 127 S.W.2d 284 (1938); Gamble v. Vanderbilt Univ., 138 Tenn. 616, 200 S.W. 510 (1917).

118. Nicholson v. Good Samaritan Hospital, 145 Fla. 360, 199 So. 344 (1940).

119. 25 A.L.R.2d 71.

120. Edith L. Fisch, "Charitable Liability for Tort," *Villanova Law Review*, Vol. 10, p. 91 (Fall 1964).

University of Missouri as a "public corporation" is not liable in suit for negligence

TODD v. CURATORS OF UNIVERSITY OF MISSOURI

Supreme Court of Missouri, Division No. 1, 1941.
147 S.W.2d 1063.

CLARK, Judge.

Plaintiff sued to recover for personal injuries alleging that defendant is a corporation, created by law as an educational institution, with power to contract and sue and be sued; that it conducts the State University and has control of the campus and buildings thereon; that it employed plaintiff to make certain repairs on one of said buildings; that under the law it was the duty of defendant to furnish plaintiff a safe place to work; that defendant negligently furnished plaintiff an insecure scaffold (described) upon which to work; that said scaffold fell with plaintiff and he suffered certain injuries.

Defendant filed a demurrer stating "that it appears upon the face of plaintiff's amended petition that the petition does not state facts sufficient to constitute a cause of action in favor of plaintiff and against defendant, Curators of the University of Missouri."

The court sustained the demurrer and plaintiff has appealed.

Appellant cites our statute and certain decisions on the allegations required to properly charge negligence in providing a defective scaffold. It is unnecessary to discuss them. This case must turn upon one point, to wit: may this defendant be sued in tort for negligence; if not, does the demurrer properly raise this objection?

There is no doubt that this defendant has the right to sue and is liable to be sued in some kinds of action. That right and that liability are expressly provided by statute and said defendant has frequently sued and been sued in the courts of this state. * * *

The defendant, the Curators of the University of Missouri, is a public corporation. § 10783, Revised Statutes Missouri 1939, Mo.St.Ann., § 9626, p. 7330; * * *

In the absence of express statutory provision, a public corporation or quasi corporation, performing governmental functions, is not liable in a suit for negligence. * * *

A statutory provision that such a public corporation "may sue and be sued" does not authorize a suit against it for negligence. "* * * But the waiver by the state for itself or its officers or agents of immunity from an action is one thing. Waiver of immunity from liability for the torts of the officers or agents of the state is quite another thing." * * *

The cases heretofore cited are mainly based upon the principle that a public corporation, performing governmental functions, is an agency or arm of the State and entitled to the same immunity as the State itself, in the absence of express statutory provision to the contrary. Another reason for immunity of public educational institutions, not organized for profit, from suits for negligence rests upon the public policy which has existed in this state from its beginning. The funds of the State University, whether raised by taxation, endowments or tuition fees, are dedicated to the beneficent purpose of education. It has no funds, nor means of raising funds, for the purpose of paying damages for tort nor is its property subject to execution for such purpose. Courts should maintain such public policy unless and until it be changed by positive legislative enactment. * * *

We hold that the demurrer interposed by the defendant properly raised the defense of its immunity from the alleged cause of action stated in the petition. On its face, the petition shows the nature of defendant as a public educational corporation and seeks to recover damages for its alleged negligence.

The judgment is affirmed.

All concur.

School district tort immunity is abolished in Illinois

MOLITOR v. KANELAND

Supreme Court of Illinois, 1959.
18 Ill. 2d 11, 163 N.E.2d 89.

KLINGBIEL, JUSTICE.

Plaintiff, Thomas Molitor, a minor, by Peter his father and next friend, brought this action against Kaneland Community Unit School District for personal injuries sustained by plaintiff when the school bus in which he was riding left the road, allegedly as a result of the driver's negligence, hit a culvert, exploded and burned.

The complaint alleged, in substance, the negligence of the School District, through its agent and servant, the driver of the school bus; that plaintiff was in the exercise of such ordinary care for his own safety as could be reasonably expected of a boy of his age, intelligence, mental capacity and experience; that plaintiff sustained permanent and severe burns and injuries as a proximate result of defendant's negligence, and prayed for judgment in the amount of $56,000. Plaintiff further alleged that defendant is a voluntary unit school district organized and existing under the provisions of sections 8-9 to 8-13 of the School Code and operates school buses within the district pursuant to section 29-5. Ill.Rev.-Stat.1957, chap. 122, pars. 8-9 to 8-13 and par. 29-5.

The complaint contained no allegation of the existence of insurance or other non-public funds out of which a judgment against defendant could be satisfied. Although plaintiff's abstract of the record shows that defendant school district did carry public liability insurance with limits of $20,000 for each person injured and $100,000 for each occurrence, plaintiff states that he purposely omitted such an allegation from his complaint.

Defendant's motion to dismiss the complaint on the ground that a school district is immune from liability for tort was sustained by the trial court, and a judgment was entered in favor of defendant. Plaintiff elected to stand on his complaint and sought a direct appeal to this court on the ground that the dismissal of his action would violate his constitutional rights. At that time we held that no fairly debatable constitutional question was presented so as to give this court jurisdiction on direct appeal, and accordingly the cause was transferred to the Appellate Court for the Second District. The Appellate Court affirmed the decision of the trial court and the case is now before us again on a certificate of importance.

In his brief, plaintiff recognizes the rule, established by this court in 1898, that a school district is immune from tort liability, and frankly asks this court either to abolish the rule *in toto* * * *

Thus we are squarely faced with the highly important question—in the light of modern developments, should a school district be immune from liability for tortiously inflicted personal injury to a pupil thereof arising out of the operation of a school bus owned and operated by said district?

It appears that while adhering to the old immunity rule, this court has not reconsidered and re-evaluated the doctrine of immunity of school districts for over fifty years. During these years, however, this subject has received exhaustive consideration by legal writers and scholars in articles and texts, almost unanimously condemning the immunity doctrine. * * *

Historically we find that the doctrine of the sovereign immunity of the state, the theory that "the King can do no wrong," was first extended to a subdivision of the state in 1788 in Russell v. Men of Devon, 2 Term Rep. 671, 100 Eng.-Rep. 359. As pointed out by Dean Prosser (Prosser on Torts, p. 1066), the idea of the municipal corporate entity was still in a nebulous state at that time. The action was brought against the entire population of the county and the decision that the county was immune was based chiefly on the fact that there were no corporate funds in Devonshire out of which satisfaction could be obtained, plus a fear of multiplicity of suits and resulting inconvenience to the public.

It should be noted that the Russell case was later overruled by the English courts, and that in 1890 it was definitely established that in England a school board or school district is subject to suit in tort for personal injuries on the same basis as a private individual or corporation. * * *

The immunity doctrine of Russell v. Men of Devon was adopted in Illinois with reference to towns and counties in 1870 in Town of Waltham v. Kemper, 55 Ill. 346. Then, in 1898, eight years after the English courts had refused to apply the Russell doctrine to schools, the Illinois court extended the immunity rule to school districts in the leading case of Kinnare v. City of Chicago, 171 Ill. 332, 49 N.E. 536, where it was held that the Chicago Board of Education was immune from liability for the death of a laborer resulting from a fall from the roof of a school building, allegedly due to the negligence of the Board in failing to provide scaffolding and safeguards. That opinion reasoned that since the State is not subject to suit nor liable for the torts or negligence of its agents, likewise a school district, as a governmental agency of the State, is also "exempted from the obligation to respond in damages, as master, for negligent acts of its servants to the same extent as is the State itself." Later decisions following the Kinnare doctrine have sought to advance additional explanations such as the protection of public funds and public property, and to prevent the diversion of tax moneys to the payment of damage claims. Leviton v. Board of Education, 374 Ill. 594, 30 N.E.2d 497; Thomas v. Broadlands Community Consolidated School Dist., 348 Ill.App. 567, 109 N.E.2d 636.

Surveying the whole picture of governmental tort law as

it stands in Illinois today, the following broad outlines may be observed. The General Assembly has frequently indicated its dissatisfaction with the doctrine of sovereign immunity upon which the Kinnare case was based. Governmental units, including school districts, are now subject to liability under the Workmen's Compensation and Occupational Disease Acts. * * * The State itself is liable, under the 1945 Court of Claims Act, for damages in tort up to $7,500 for the negligence of its officers, agents or employees. (Ill.Rev.Stat. 1957, chap. 37, pars. 439.1-439.24.) Cities and villages have been made directly liable for injuries caused by the negligent operation of fire department vehicles, and for actionable wrong in the removal or destruction of unsafe or unsanitary buildings. (Ill.Rev.Stat.1957, chap. 24, pars. 1-13, 1-16.) Cities and villages, and the Chicago Park District, have also been made responsible, by way of indemnification, for the nonwilful misconduct of policemen. * * * In addition to the tort liability thus legislatively imposed upon governmental units, the courts have classified local units of government as "quasi-municipal corporations" and "municipal corporations." And the activities of the latter class have been categorized as "governmental" and "proprietary," with full liability in tort imposed if the function is classified as "proprietary." The incongruities that have resulted from attempts to fit particular conduct into one or the other of these categories have been the subject of frequent comment. * * *

Of all of the anomalies that have resulted from legislative and judicial efforts to alleviate the injustice of the results that have flowed from the doctrine of sovereign immunity, the one most immediately pertinent to this case is the following provision of the Illinois School Code: "Any school district, including any non-high school district, which provides transportation for pupils may insure against any loss or liability of such district, its agents or employees, resulting from or incident to the ownership, maintenance or use of any school bus. Such insurance shall be carried only in companies duly licensed and authorized to write such coverage in this state. Every policy for such insurance coverage issued to a school district shall provide, or be endorsed to provide, that the company issuing such policy waives any right to refuse payment or to deny liability thereunder within the limits of said policy, by reason of the non-liability of the insured school district for the wrongful or negligent acts of its agents and employees, and, its immunity from suit, as an agency of the state performing governmental functions." Ill.Rev.Stat. 1957, c. 122, § 29-11a.

Thus, under this statute, a person injured by an insured school district bus may recover to the extent of such insurance, whereas, under the Kinnare doctrine, a person injured by an uninsured school district bus can recover nothing at all.

Defendant contends that the quoted provision of the School Code constitutes a legislative determination that the public policy of this State requires that school districts be immune from tort liability. We can read no such legislative intent into the statute. Rather, we interpret that section as expressing dissatisfaction with the court-created doctrine of governmental immunity and an attempt to cut down that immunity where insurance is involved. The difficulty with this legislative effort to curtail the judicial doctrine is that it allows each school district to determine for itself whether, and to what extent, it will be financially responsible for the wrongs inflicted by it.

Coming down to the precise issue at hand, it is clear that if the above rules and precedents are strictly applied to the instant case, plaintiff's complaint, containing no allegation as to the existence of insurance, was properly dismissed. On the other hand, the complaint may be held to state a good cause of action on either one of two theories, (1) application of the doctrine of Moore v. Moyle, 405 Ill. 555, 92 N.E.2d 81, or (2) abolition of the rule that a school district is immune from tort liability.

As to the doctrine of Moore v. Moyle, that case involved an action for personal injuries against Bradley University, a charitable educational institution. Traditionally, charitable and educational institutions have enjoyed the same immunity from tort liability as have governmental agencies in Illinois. * * * The trial court dismissed the complaint on the ground that Bradley was immune to tort liability. The Supreme Court reversed, holding that the complaint should not have been dismissed since it alleged that Bradley was fully insured. Unfortunately, we must admit that the opinion in that case does not make the basis of the result entirely clear. However, the court there said, 405 Ill. at page 564, 92 N.E.2d at page 86: "* * * the question of insurance in no way affects the liability of the institution, but would only go to the question of the manner of collecting any judgment which might be obtained, without interfering with, or subjecting the trust funds or trust-held property to, the judgment. The question as to whether or not the institution is insured in no way affects its liability any more than whether a charitable institution holding private nontrust property or funds would affect its liability. These questions would only be of importance at the proper time, when the question arose as to the collection of any judgment out of nontrust property or assets. * * * Judgments may be obtained, but the question of collection of the judgment is a different matter." If we were to literally apply this reasoning to the present school district case, we would conclude that it was unnecessary that the complaint contain an allegation of the existence of insurance or other nonpublic funds. Plaintiff's complaint was sufficient as it stood without any reference to insurance, and plaintiff would be entitled to prosecute his action to judgment. Only at that time, in case of a judgment for plaintiff, would the question of insurance arise, the possession of nonpublic funds being an execution rather than a liability question. It cannot be overlooked, however, that some doubt is cast on this approach by the last paragraph of the Moore opinion, where the court said: "It appears that the trust funds of Bradley will not be impaired or depleted by the prosecution of the complaint, and therefore it was error to dismiss it." These words imply that if from the complaint it did not appear that the trust funds would not be impaired, the complaint should have been dismissed. If that is the true holding in the case, then liability itself, not merely the collectability of the judgment, depends on the presence of nontrust assets, as was pointed out by Justice Crampton in his dissenting opinion. The doctrine of Moore v. Moyle does not, in our opinion, offer a satisfactory solution. Like the provision of the School Code above quoted, it would allow the wrongdoer to determine its own liability.

It is a basic concept underlying the whole law of torts today that liability follows negligence, and that individuals and corporations are responsible for the negligence of their agents and employees acting in the course of their employment. The doctrine of governmental immunity runs directly counter to that basic concept. What reasons, then, are so impelling as to allow a school district, as a quasi-municipal corporation, to commit wrongdoing without any responsibility to its victims, while any individual or private corporation would be called to task in court for such tortious conduct?

The original basis of the immunity rule has been called a "survival of the medieval idea that the sovereign can do no wrong," or that "the King can do no wrong." (38 Am.Jur.,

Mun.Corps., sec. 573, p. 266.) In Kinnare v. City of Chicago, 171 Ill. 332, 49 N.E. 536, 537, the first Illinois case announcing the tort immunity of school districts, the court said: "The state acts in its sovereign capacity, and does not submit its action to the judgment of courts, and is not liable for the torts or negligence of its agents, and a corporation created by the state as a mere agency for the more efficient exercise of governmental functions is likewise exempted from the obligation to respond in damages, as master, for negligent acts of its servants to the same extent as is the state itself, unless such liability is expressly provided by the statute creating such agency." This was nothing more nor less than an extension of the theory of sovereign immunity. Professor Borchard has said that how immunity ever came to be applied in the United States of America is one of the mysteries of legal evolution. (Borchard, Government Liability in Tort, 34 Yale L.J. 1, 6.) And how it was then infiltrated into the law controlling the liability of local governmental units has been described as one of the amazing chapters of American common-law jurisprudence. * * *

We are of the opinion that school district immunity cannot be justified on this theory. As was stated by one court, "The whole doctrine of governmental immunity from liability for tort rests upon a rotten foundation. It is almost incredible that in this modern age of comparative sociological enlightenment, and in a republic, the medieval absolutism supposed to be implicit in the maxim, 'the King can do no wrong,' should exempt the various branches of the government from liability for their torts, and that the entire burden of damage resulting from the wrongful acts of the government should be imposed upon the single individual who suffers the injury, rather than distributed among the entire community constituting the government, where it could be borne without hardship upon any individual, and where it justly belongs." Barker v. City of Santa Fe, 47 N.M. 85, 136 P.2d 480, 482. Likewise, we agree with the Supreme Court of Florida that in preserving the sovereign immunity theory, courts have overlooked the fact that the Revolutionary War was fought to abolish that "divine right of kings" on which the theory is based.

The other chief reason advanced in support of the immunity rule in the more recent cases is the protection of public funds and public property. This corresponds to the "no fund" or "trust fund" theory upon which charitable immunity is based. This rationale was relied on in Thomas v. Broadlands Community Consolidated School Dist., 348 Ill.App. 567, 109 N.E.2d 636, 640, where the court stated that the reason for the immunity rule is "that it is the public policy to protect public funds and public property, to prevent the diversion of tax moneys, in this case school funds, to the payment of damage claims." This reasoning seems to follow the line that it is better for the individual to suffer than for the public to be inconvenienced. From it proceeds defendant's argument that school districts would be bankrupted and education impeded if said districts were called upon to compensate children tortiously injured by the negligence of those districts' agents and employees.

We do not believe that in this present day and age, when public education constitutes one of the biggest businesses in the country, that school immunity can be justified on the protection-of-public funds theory.

In the first place, analysis of the theory shows that it is based on the idea that payment of damage claims is a diversion of educational funds to an improper purpose. As many writers have pointed out, the fallacy in this argument is that it assumes the very point which is sought to be proved, i. e., that payment of damage claims is not a proper purpose. "Logically, the 'no fund' or 'trust fund' theory is without merit because it is of value only after a determination of what is a proper school expenditure. To predicate immunity upon the theory of a trust fund is merely to argue in a circle, since it assumes an answer to the very question at issue, to wit, what is an educational purpose? Many disagree with the 'no-fund' doctrine to the extent of ruling that the payment of funds for judgments resulting from accidents or injuries in schools is an educational purpose. Nor can it be properly argued that as a result of the abandonment of the common-law rule the district would be completely bankrupt. California, Tennessee, New York, Washington and other states have not been compelled to shut down their schools." (Rosenfield, Governmental Immunity from Liability for Tort in School Accidents, 5 Legal Notes on Local Government, 376-377.) Moreover, this argument is even more fallacious when viewed in the light of the Illinois School Code, which authorizes appropriations for "transportation purposes" * * * and authorizes expenditures of school tax funds for liability insurance covering school bus operations. * * * It seems to us that the payment of damage claims incurred as an adjunct to transportation is as much a "transportation purpose" and therefore a proper authorized purpose as are payments of other expenses involved in operating school buses. If tax funds can properly be spent to pay premiums on liability insurance, there seems to be no good reason why they cannot be spent to pay the liability itself in the absence of insurance.

Neither are we impressed with defendant's plea that the abolition of immunity would create grave and unpredictable problems of school finance and administration. We are in accord with Dean Green when he disposed of this problem as follows: "There is considerable talk in the opinions about the tremendous financial burdens tort liability would cast upon the taxpayer. In some opinions it is stated that this factor is sufficient to warrant the courts in protecting the taxpayer through the immunity which they have thrown around municipal corporations. While this factor may have had compulsion on some of the earlier courts, I seriously doubt that it has any great weight with the courts in recent years. In the first place, taxation is not the subject matter of judicial concern where justice to the individual citizen is involved. It is the business of other departments of government to provide the funds required to pay the damages assessed against them by the courts. Moreover, the same policy that would protect governmental corporations from the payment of damages for the injuries they bring upon others would be equally pertinent to a like immunity to protect private corporations, for conceivably many essential private concerns could also be put out of business by the damages they could incur under tort liability. But as a matter of fact, this argument has no practical basis. Private concerns have rarely been greatly embarrassed, and in no instance, even where immunity is not recognized, has a municipality been seriously handicapped by tort liability. This argument is like so many of the horribles paraded in the early tort cases when courts were fashioning the boundaries of tort law. It has been thrown in simply because there was nothing better at hand. The public's willingness to stand up and pay the cost of its enterprises carried out through municipal corporations is no less than its insistence that individuals and groups pay the cost of their enterprises. Tort liability is in fact a very small item in the budget of any well organized enterprise." Green, Freedom of Litigation, 38 Ill.L.Rev. 355, 378.

We are of the opinion that none of the reasons advanced in support of school district immunity have any true validity today. Further we believe that abolition of such immunity may tend to decrease the frequency of school bus accidents by coupling the power to transport pupils with the responsibility of exercising care in the selection and supervision of the drivers. As Dean Harno said: "A municipal corporation today is an active and virile creature capable of inflicting much harm. Its civil responsibility should be co-extensive. The municipal corporation looms up definitely and emphatically in our law, and what is more, it can and does commit wrongs. This being so, it must assume the responsibilities of the position it occupies in society." (Harno, Tort Immunity of Municipal Corporations, 4 Ill.L.Q. 28, 42.) School districts will be encouraged to exercise greater care in the matter of transporting pupils and also to carry adequate insurance covering that transportation, thus spreading the risk of accident, just as the other costs of education are spread over the entire district. At least some school authorities themselves have recognized the need for the vital change which we are making. See Editorial, 100 American School Board Journal 55, Issue No. 6, June, 1940.

"The nation's largest business is operating on a blueprint prepared a hundred, if not a thousand years ago. The public school system in the United States, which constitutes the largest single business in the country, is still under the domination of a legal principle which in great measure continued unchanged since the Middle Ages, to the effect that a person has no financial recourse for injuries sustained as a result of the performance of the State's functions * * *. That such a gigantic system, involving so large an appropriation of public funds and so tremendous a proportion of the people of the United States, should operate under the principles of a rule of law so old and so outmoded would seem impossible were it not actually true." Rosenfield, Governmental Immunity from Liability for Tort in School Accidents, 9 Law and Contemporary Problems 358, 359.

We conclude that the rule of school district tort immunity is unjust, unsupported by any valid reason, and has no rightful place in modern day society.

Defendant strongly urges that if said immunity is to be abolished, it should be done by the legislature, not by this court. With this contention we must disagree. The doctrine of school district immunity was created by this court alone. Having found that doctrine to be unsound and unjust under present conditions, we consider that we have not only the power, but the duty, to abolish that immunity. "We closed our courtroom doors without legislative help, and we can likewise open them." Pierce v. Yakima Valley Memorial Hospital Ass'n, 43 Wash.2d 162, 260 P.2d 765, 774.

* * *

For the reasons herein expressed, we accordingly hold that in this case the school district is liable in tort for the negligence of its employee, and all prior decisions to the contrary are hereby overruled.

The judgment of the Appellate Court sustaining the dismissal of plaintiff's complaint is reversed and the cause is remanded to the circuit court of Kane County with instructions to set aside the order dismissing the complaint, and to proceed in conformity with the views expressed in this opinion.

Reversed and remanded, with directions.

University may be liable for injury to invitee

SANDOVAL v. THE BOARD OF REGENTS OF NEW MEXICO STATE UNIVERSITY

Supreme Court of New Mexico, 1965.
75 N.M. 261, 403 P.2d 699.

CARMODY, Chief Justice.

The trial court having sustained a motion for summary judgment, the plaintiff appeals.

The plaintiff, in connection with her work as a case worker for the Department of Public Welfare, went to the campus of the defendant university to visit with a blind student concerning his welfare assistance. The walk leading to the dormitory in which the student lived was a ramp-type walk, in that it was, in part, sloping. The plaintiff entered the building by this walkway, visited the student, and upon leaving the residence hall, slipped and fell at a point on the walkway where it sloped into a downgrade.

The record is not clear as to the cause of the fall, but, actually, the case must turn upon whether or not there was a controverted question of fact as to the construction and maintenance of the walk; whether or not the walk was hazardous to pedestrian traffic; and the resolution of the question of notice and knowledge of the dangerous condition if it existed. However, the status of the plaintiff must first be determined, i. e., whether she was a business visitor (often termed invitee), or a licensee, because, depending upon the character of her relationship rests the degree of care and legal liability of the defendant university.

We believe that, under the facts now before us, there can be no question but that the plaintiff was a business visitor or an invitee. 2 Restatement of the Law, Torts, § 332, defines a business visitor as follows:

> "A business visitor is a person who is invited or permitted to enter or remain on land in the possession of another for a purpose directly or indirectly connected with business dealings between them."

The student occupied the position of a lessee of the university, and certainly the plaintiff's business was in furtherance of a benefit to the student, thereby coming within that class of persons discussed under Comment h of § 332. Compare City of Madisonville v. Poole, (Ky.Ct.App.1952), 249 S.W.2d 133. However, our determination that the plaintiff was a business visitor does not solve the problem—it merely determines, from a legal standpoint, the degree of care resting upon the defendant.

In Crenshaw v. Firestone Tire & Rubber Co., 1963, 72 N.M. 84, 380 P.2d 828, we quoted with approval the duty of a possessor of land to business visitors as set out in 2 Restatement of the Law of Torts, § 343, and the same definition is applicable here. Nevertheless, each case must rest upon its own peculiar facts, and the facts here require a different result than that announced in Crenshaw.

The trial court had before it evidence, which was, in some respects, directly contradictory. There was the affidavit and deposition of the director of the university's physical plant, who testified that the ramp-type walk was not a smooth-troweled surface, but, contrariwise, was rough. This witness testified that the walk was in substantially the same condition on the day of the accident as it had been at the time it was built some eleven years earlier. He stated that it was not slippery and that his office had no record of anyone else having fallen upon the walk, even though, by his estimate, it had been utilized by perhaps a hundred thousand people. Contrary to this testimony was the affidavit of a civil engineer, with a degree in traffic engineering, to the effect that he had examined the walk and that, in his opinion, it was smoothly troweled, sloping, and extremely slippery and dangerous to pedestrian traffic. The plaintiff's deposition also discloses that, after the fall, it appeared to her that the walk had a smooth, slippery surface. Each of these witnesses testified as to other matters, which are not material to our decision; but, from what is stated above, it should be quite apparent that there was a substantial conflict as to the nature of the surface and the relative safety to pedestrian travel.

The university, fully realizing that there is a conflict in the testimony, attempts to discount the affidavit of the engineer, because it was opinion evidence and that there are not set forth sufficient facts to show that the opinion would be admissible in evidence. Admittedly, portions of the affidavit cannot be considered upon a motion for summary judgment, and we would point out that, similarly, portions of the affidavit and deposition of the defendant's witness are subject to a like criticism. Nevertheless, eliminating opinion and hearsay statements, a substantial issue of material fact is raised. There is evidence in the plaintiff's deposition, taken together with the affidavit of the engineer, that the walkway was sloping and had a smoothly troweled finish which presented a dangerous hazard to pedestrian traffic. Our determination of the presence of an issue of material fact is strengthened when the deposition of the defendant's witness is considered, inasmuch as it contains the reluctant concession that if the sloping walkway had a smoothly troweled finish, it would present a dangerous hazard to pedestrian traffic. Thus, without regard to the testimony objected to by the defendant contained in the plaintiff's deposition and the engineer's affidavit, it appears that a doubt is raised with respect to the condition of the sidewalk, which the university knew, or in the exercise of reasonable care should have known, would involve an unreasonable risk to the plaintiff and possibly not apparent to her. Under the rules applicable to motions for summary judgment, entitling the party against whom the motion is directed to have all reasonable inferences construed in his favor, the motion should have been denied. Hewitt-Robins, Inc., etc. v. Lea County Sand & Gravel, Inc., 1962, 70 N.M. 144, 371 P.2d 795. See also Coca v. Arceo, 1962, 71 N.M. 186, 376 P.2d 790, and the cases therein cited. Compare Linton v. Mauer-Neuer Meat Packers, 1963, 71 N.M. 305, 378 P.2d 126.

As we said in Coca, we mean no implication that a case of negligence has been made out by the plaintiff, only that she is entitled to present the merits of her case to the fact finder. Also, without repeating in its entirety the quotation appearing in Coca from Pierce v. Ford Motor Co. (4th Cir. 1951), 190 F.2d 910, we would again say:

"* * * Even in cases where the judge is of opinion

that he will have to direct a verdict for one party or the other on the issues that have been raised, he should ordinarily hear the evidence and direct the verdict rather than attempt to try the case in advance on a motion for summary judgment, * * *."

The judgment will be reversed and the case remanded to the trial court with direction to set aside its summary judgment and proceed in a manner not inconsistent herewith. It is so ordered.

CHAVEZ and MOISE, JJ., concur.

NOTES

Safe Place Statutes

Some states have enacted "safe place" statutes which require public agencies to provide employees with a safe place to work.[1] The Wisconsin "safe place" statute reads: "Every owner of * * * a public building now or hereafter constructed shall so construct, repair, or maintain such * * * public building * * * and to render the same safe."[2] The courts in Wisconsin have defined the word "safe" to mean "freedom from danger to life, health, safety, or welfare of employees or frequenters or the public."[3] A "frequenter" entitled to recover is now anyone other than a trespasser.[4]

In defining what constituted a building where safe conditions were required, the court held that the school district was not liable where a pupil was killed by a falling flagpole.[5] The court said that neither the school grounds, the sidewalk area surrounding the pole, nor the pole itself came within the meaning of the statute.

The California law, unlike Wisconsin's, is not limited to buildings. The California law makes public agencies liable for torts resulting from defective condition of public property. Public property is defined to include buildings, grounds, and property.[6]

The Colorado Safe Place and Safe Appliance statute provides:

---

1. A search of the literature indicates that three states currently have safe place statutes: Colorado, California, Wisconsin.
2. Wis. Stat., Ch. 101, § 101.06 (1933).
3. *Ibid.*, § 101.01 (11).
4. Schaerer, Robert W., "The Liability Status of Indiana Public Schools," *Indiana School Boards Association*, 1959, p. 12.
5. Lawyer v. Joint School Dist., 228 N.W. 192 (Wis. 1939).
6. Cal. Gov't Code, §§ 53050, 53051.

>Any person, firm, corporation, or association operating a * * * school house * * * or place of public assemblage, or any kind of establishment wherein laborers are employed or machinery used * * * shall provide safeguards * * * and if machinery is not safeguarded as provided by this act, the use thereof is prohibited.[7]

The law further provides that in order to establish liability the plaintiff need only prove that the defendant school district failed to provide the safeguards required by statute.[8]

Court reviews theory of charitable immunity

ETTLINGER v. RANDOLPH-MACON COLLEGE

Circuit Court of Appeals, Fourth Circuit, 1929.
31 F.2d 869.

PARKER, Circuit Judge. This action was instituted in the court below in behalf of one Reginald Ettlinger, hereafter called the plaintiff, against the Trustees of Randolph-Macon College, Inc., as defendant, to recover damages for personal injuries sustained by him when the Randolph-Macon Military Academy at Front Royal, Va., was destroyed by fire. The academy was owned by the defendant, and plaintiff was a student therein. He alleges that defendant was negligent in not maintaining the electric wiring and fixtures in the academy in proper condition, in not providing that building with adequate fire escapes, and in not maintaining a night watchman on the premises. The trial judge directed a verdict for defendant, and from a judgment thereon plaintiff has appealed.

The defendant is a nonstock corporation chartered and organized at the instance of the Conference of the Methodist Episcopal Church of Virginia, for the purpose of carrying on the work of education. It operates a system of schools and colleges, not for the sake of profit, but for the education and enlightenment of the people. Its property has come to it through charitable gifts and bequests, and this together with what is received from tuition is used for the purpose of education. It makes special rates to sons of ministers and young men studying for the ministry and loans to needy and deserving students. A charge is made for board and tuition, but the amount realized therefrom does not by any means equal the

---

7. School Laws of the State of Colorado, Ch. XI, § 539 (1941).
8. *Ibid.*

688   COLLEGE AND UNIVERSITY LAW

cost of the work which is being carried on. The Military
Academy at Front Royal was one of the schools operated by
defendant, and plaintiff was attending it as a regular paying
student.

On the 10th day of January, 1927, early in the morning,
the academy building was destroyed by fire. Plaintiff was
sleeping on the third floor, and when he awoke the fire had
gained such headway, and the hall into which his room opened
was so filled with smoke, that he could not reach a fire escape and was unable even to go from his room into the hall.
He accordingly jumped from the window of his room to a
blanket which was being held for him in the yard below, and
in doing so received the injuries of which he complains. Verdict was directed on the ground that, being an eleemosynary
institution, defendant was not liable for the negligence alleged.

We have reviewed the evidence carefully; and, even if we
lay to one side the fact that defendant is an eleemosynary institution, we think that the verdict was properly directed, as
the evidence failed to establish that plaintiff's injury was due
to the negligence of the defendant or its employees. It was
shown without contradiction that the defects in the electrical
wiring and fixtures upon which plaintiff relied had been repaired prior to the fire. There was no evidence upon which
a jury could have found that there was a duty on the part
of the defendant to maintain a night watchman in the building or that the presence of such a watchman would have
prevented plaintiff's injury. And it was shown that the building was equipped with fire escapes, approved by the proper
public authorities, and that there were other means of escape
from the third floor, which plaintiff could have utilized had
it not been for the blinding smoke in the hallway. As he could
not get beyond the door of his room on account of the smoke,
additional fire escapes would have been as useless to him as
those which existed, and their absence could not possibly be
said to have been the proximate cause of his injury.

But we think, also, that the learned trial judge was correct
in holding that the defendant was an eleemosynary institution and as such was not liable to plaintiff on account of the
negligence of its officers, agents, or servants. "The eleemosynary sort of corporations," says Blackstone, "are such as
are constituted for the perpetual distributions of the free
alms or bounty of the founder of them, to such persons as he
has directed. Of this are all hospitals for the maintenance of

the poor, sick and impotent; and all colleges both in our universities and out of them." . . . It is clear that a corporation is to be deemed eleemosynary or charitable where its property is derived from charitable gifts or bequests and is administered, not for the purpose of gain, but in the interest of humanity; and an educational institution, established and endowed by private charity, falls clearly within the classification . . . . Parks v. Northwestern University, 218 Ill. 381, 75 N.E. 991, 2 L. R. A. (N. S.) 556, 4 Ann. Cas. 103; McDonald v. Massachusetts General Hospital, 120 Mass. 432, 21 Am. Rep. 529.

And it is equally clear both that the eleemosynary or charitable nature of an educational institution is not destroyed by the fact that it makes a charge for tuition, and that the payment of tuition by its students does not prevent their being considered beneficiaries of the charity. The evidence in this case is that the charges made by defendant cover only a part of the cost of carrying on its work; and it is a matter of general and common knowledge that the tuition and other charges of public educational institutions and those which are privately endowed are much lower than would be required to pay even their running expenses, being purposely made low so that education may be placed within the reach of those who need it. In a very direct and practical sense, therefore, not only are such institutions engaged in a work of charity, but the pay student as well as others is a beneficiary thereof. And, apart from the fact that what such a student pays does not equal the cost of his education, he is a beneficiary of the charity for the reason that but for the charitable gifts made to the institution and the charitable work which it is carrying on, it would not exist to serve him. . . .

Since, therefore, it appears not only that the defendant is an eleemosynary institution, but also that plaintiff was a beneficiary of the charity which it administers, we think there can be no question that defendant could not be held liable to him for the negligence alleged. "The courts are practically agreed that a charitable institution is not responsible to those who avail themselves of its benefits for any injuries they may sustain through the negligence or torts of its managers, agents and servants." . . .

* * *

As stated above, the courts are practically agreed upon the rule of law applicable here; but they are by no means agreed upon the reason for the rule, and this disagreement has given rise to much discussion on the part of the courts themselves and of textwriters and annotators, as will be readily seen by reference to the above notes and authorities. We do not deem it necessary to choose between the conflicting theories or to enter into the rather inviting field of theoretical discussion. Some courts have based the rule upon the theory that the funds of eleemosynary institutions are held in trust for charitable purposes and may not be diverted to the payment of damages on account of wrongs committed by those who administer them. Other courts base it upon the theory that the doctrine respondeat superior, being itself based upon the theory that the principal derives a benefit from the services of the employee or agent for whose negligence he is held liable, has no application where the service of the employee is for the benefit of humanity and not for the gain of the institution which employs him. Others base it upon broad grounds of public policy, holding that, as the institution is engaged in work highly beneficial to the state and to humanity, its funds ought not be diverted from this important purpose to the payment of private claims for damages. And still others base it upon the theory of an implied agreement on the part of one accepting the benefits of a charity not to hold it liable for injuries which he may receive at the hands of its servants.

All of these theories have to a greater or less extent entered into the formulation of the rule of law which has now become too well settled to be questioned or overturned. Underlying all of them is the matter of public policy, and it is upon this that the rule may be said finally to rest. The theory that trust funds are not to be taken under execution for the torts of those who administer them rests, in the last analysis, upon considerations of public policy, as does the holding that the rule respondeat superior shall not apply to the agents and servants of a charity. So also, the theory of implied agreement can be sustained only if the agreement be conceived of as implied in law as a matter of public policy. But, resting upon public policy, the rule rests upon a sufficiently firm foundation. A policy of the law which prevents him who accepts the benefit of a charity from suing it for the torts of its agents and servants, and thus taking for his private use the funds which have been given for the benefit of humanity, which shields gifts made to charity from "the hungry maw of litigation" and conserves them for purposes of the highest importance to the state, carries on its face its own justification, and, without the aid of metaphysical reasoning, commends itself to the wisdom of mankind. It is significant that almost without exception the courts, while giving different reasons for the rule, have not hestitated to apply it where the one seeking to enforce liability against a charitable institution is one who has accepted benefits from it. In Rhode Island the Supreme Court refused to follow the rule, but the succeeding Legislature proceeded to establish it by statute. There is quite a conflict of authority as to the liability of a charitable corporation to employees or strangers; but we need not consider these cases, as they have no application here.

Counsel for plaintiff attempt to distinguish the case at bar from the many other cases against charitable institutions, on the ground that the negligence here alleged is not the careless act of a nurse or other employee, but the negligence of the managers of the corporation themselves in failing to maintain the academy building in a safe condition. We do not think, however, that this is a valid distinction. If there had been negligence in the respects claimed, it would have been the negligence of those who were carrying on the charitable work in which the corporation was engaged; and we see no more reason for diverting the funds of the charity on account of their negligence than there would be if the negligence had been that of any minor employee, but from the principle that the funds of a charity ought not be diverted from the purpose for which they have been given to pay damages to a beneficiary on account of the wrongs or negligence of those who administer the charity. It is true that many of the cases have stated the rule to be that a charitable corporation is not liable for the torts of its agents where due care is used in selecting them. This, however, is a correct statement of the rule properly applicable in the case of ordinary private corporations who employ physicians and surgeons to treat their injured employees. . . . We do not think that it is properly applicable in the case of charitable corporations. The subject was thoroughly considered by Chief Justice Rugg . . . , and we agree with the conclusion which he reached. . . . Said he:

"There is no sound distinction in reason between the liability of a hospital for the negligence of its inferior agents and its liability for the carelessness of its managers. The conduct of both relates to the execution of the charity. The inferior agents usually work for pay, while the managing officers as matter of common knowledge generally undertake the administration of the public charity without compensation, solely out of public spirit in a desire to serve the general welfare. If the hospital is held responsible for their acts of negligence, the funds devoted to the relief of suffering humanity must be diverted in the one instance to the same extent and manner as in the other to the payment of claims wholly foreign to the purposes of the public trust."

* * *

After careful consideration of the briefs and arguments of counsel, and the authorities upon which they rely, we are of opinion, for the reasons stated, that verdict was properly directed for defendant; and the judgment thereon is accordingly affirmed.

Affirmed.

NOTES

1. "A charitable corporation is not liable for negligence in the course of activities within its corporate powers carried on to accomplish directly its charitable purposes. This is true even though such activities incidently yield revenue. On the other hand, there is liability for negligence in the course of activities incidental to the corporate powers but primarily commercial in character, though carried on to obtain revenue to be used for the charitable purposes of the corporation." Reavey v. Guild of St. Agnes, 284 Mass. 300, 187 N.E. 557 (1933).

2. The general rule in Georgia is that charitable trust funds are not to be depleted by subjection of charitable organization to liability for negligence. Butler v. Berry School, 27 Ga. App. 560, 109 S.E. 544 (1921). However, a charitable organization upon taking a liability insurance policy waives its immunity to the amount of the policy. Cox v. DeJarnette, 104 Ga. App. 664, 123 S.E.2d 16 (1961).

3. *Status of charitable immunity.*

Arkansas: Helton v. Sisters of Mercy of St. Joseph's Hosp., 234 Ark. 76, 351 S.W.2d 129 (1961) ; *Connecticut:* Haliburton v. General Hosp. Soc'y, 133 Conn. 61, 48 A.2d 261 (1946) (selection of employee) ; Cohen v. General Hosp. Soc'y, 113 Conn. 188, 154 Atl. 435 (1931) (stranger) ; *Georgia:* Morton v. Savannah Hosp., 148 Ga. 438, 96 S.E. 887 (1918) (selection of employee) (liability to paying patient) ; *Indiana:* St. Vincent's Hosp. v. Stine, 195 Ind. 350, 144 N.E. 537 (1924) (selection of employee) ; *Louisiana:* Jurjevich v. Hotel Dieu, 11 So. 2d 632 (La. Ct. App. 1943) (selection of employee) ; Bougon v. Volunteers of America, 151 So. 797 (La. Ct. App. 1934) (stranger) ; *Maine:* Jensen v. Maine Eye & Ear Infirmary, 107 Me. 408, 78 Atl. 898 (1910) ; *Maryland:* Perry v. House of Refuge, 63 Md. 20, 52 Am. Rep. 495 (1885) ; *Massachusetts:* McDonald v. Massachusetts Gen. Hosp., supra note 1; *Missouri:* Dille v. St. Luke's Hosp., 355 Mo. 436, 196 S.W.2d 615 (1946) ; *Nebraska:* Marble v. Nicholas Senn Hosp. Ass'n, 102 Neb. 343, 167 N.W. 208 (1918) (stranger) ; *Nevada:* Bruce v. Y.M.C.A., 51 Nev. 372, 277 Pac. 798 (1929) ; *North Carolina:* Barden v. Atlantic Coast Line R.R., 152 N.C. 318, 67 S.E. 971 (1910) (selection of employee) ; *Rhode Island:* R.I. Gen. Laws Ann. § 7-1-22 (1956) ; *South Carolina:* Caughman v. Columbia Y.M.C.A., 212 S.C. 337, 47 S.E.2d 788 (1948) ; *Texas:* Southern Methodist Univ. v. Clayton, 142 Tex. 179, 176 S.W.2d 749 (1943) (selection of employee) ; *Virginia:* Weston's Adm'x v. Hospital of St. Vincent of Paul, 131 Va. 587, 107 S.E. 785 (1921) (selection of employee) ; Hospital of St. Vincent of Paul v. Thompson, 116 Va. 101, 81 S.E. 13 (1914) (stranger) ; *Wyoming:* Bishop Randall Hosp. v. Hartley, 24 Wyo. 408, 160 Pac. 385 (1916) (selection of employee).

The following states have refused to grant immunity to charities. *Alabama:* Tucker v. Mobile Infirmary Ass'n, 191 Ala. 572, 68 So. 4 (1915) ; *Alaska:* Tuengel v. City of Sitka, 118 F. Supp. 399 (D.C. Alaska 1954) ; *Arizona:* Ray v. Tucson Medical Center, 72 Ariz. 22, 230 P.2d 220 (1951) ; *California:* Silva v. Providence Hosp., 14 Cal. 2d 762, 97 P.2d 798 (1939) ; *Colorado:* St. Mary's Academy v. Solomon, 77 Colo. 463, 238 Pac. 22 (1925) ; *Delaware:* Durney v. St. Francis Hosp., Inc., 46 Del. 350, 83 A.2d 753 (Super. Ct. 1951) ; *Florida:* Nicholson v. Good Samaritan Hosp., 145 Fla. 360, 199 So. 344 (1940) ; *Illinois:* Marabia v. Mary Thompson Hosp., 309 Ill. 147, 140 N.E. 836 (1923) ; *Iowa:* Haynes v. Presbyterian Hosp. Ass'n, 241 Iowa 1269, 45 N.W.2d 151 (1950) ; *Minnesota:* Mulliner v. Evangelischer Diakonniessenverein, 144 Minn. 392, 175 N.W. 699 (1920) ; *Mississippi:* Mississippi Baptist Hosp. v. Holmes, 214 Miss. 906, 55 So. 2d 142 (1951) ; *Montana:* Howard v. Sisters of Charity, 193 F. Supp. 191 (D.C. Mont. 1961) ; *New Hampshire:* Kardulas v. City of Dover, 99 N.H. 359, 111 A.2d 327 (1955) ; *New York:* Bing v. Thunig, 2 N.Y.2d 656, 143 N.E.2d 3, 163 N.Y.S.2d 3 (1957) ; *North Dakota:* Rickbeil v. Grafton Deaconess Hosp., 74 N.D.

525, 23 N.W.2d 247 (1946); *Oklahoma:* Gable v. Salvation Army, 186 Okla. 687, 100 P.2d 244 (1940); *Tennessee:* Baptist Memorial Hosp. v. Couillens, 176 Tenn. 300, 140 S.W.2d 1088 (1940); *Utah:* Sessions v. Thomas D. Dee Memorial Hosp. Ass'n, 94 Utah 460, 78 P.2d 645 (1938); *Vermont:* Foster v. Roman Catholic Diocese, 116 Vt. 124, 70 A.2d 230 (1950).

The following states have recently abrogated immunity doctrines. *Idaho:* Wheat v. Idaho Falls Latter Day Saints Hosp., 78 Idaho 60, 297 P.2d 1041 (1956); *Kansas:* Noel v. Menninger Foundation, 175 Kan. 751, 267 P.2d 934 (1954); *Kentucky:* Mullikin v. Jewish Hosp. Ass'n, 348 S.W.2d 930 (Ky. 1961); *Michigan:* Parker v. Port Huron Hosp., 361 Mich 1, 105 N.W.2d 1 (1960); *New Jersey:* Dalton v. St. Luke's Catholic Church, 27 N.J. 22, 141 A.2d 273 (1958); *Ohio:* Avellone v. St. John's Hosp., 165 Ohio St. 467, 135 N.E.2d 410 (1956); *Oregon:* Hungerford v. Portland Sanitarium & Benevolent Ass'n, 235 Ore. 412, 384 P.2d 1009 (1963); *Pennsylvania:* Flagiello v. Pennsylvania Hosp., 417 Pa. 486, 208 A.2d 193 (1965); *Washington:* Pierce v. Yakima Valley Memorial Hosp. Ass'n, 43 Wash. 2d 162, 260 P.2d 765 (1953); *West Virginia:* Adkins v. St. Francis Hosp., infra note 6; *Wisconsin:* Kojis v. Doctors Hosp., 12 Wis. 2d 367, 107 N.W.2d 131 (1961). Charles Glidden Johnson, "Charitable Immunity: A Diminishing Doctrine," *Washington and Lee Law Review,* Vol. XXIII, 1966, pp. 109-111.

University has charitable immunity, regardless of whether it requires student tuition

PARKS v. NORTHWESTERN UNIVERSITY

Supreme Court of Illinois, 1905.
218 Ill. 381, 75 N.E. 991.

BOGGS, J. The declaration in this case, after alleging that the appellee undertook for hire to teach the appellant the science of dentistry, dental surgery, etc., charged that the appellant received injuries resulting in the loss of an eye through the negligence of one of the professors employed by the appellee while the appellant was in his charge as a student in a classroom or laboratory of the appellee. A demurrer was sustained to the declaration by the superior court of Cook county, and the cause dismissed; and this is an appeal from the judgment of the Appellate Court for the First District, affirming the judgment entered in said superior court.

The ground of the demurrer was that the appellee university is a charitable institution organized for the purpose of disseminating education and professional learning, and that the doctrine that the employer shall be liable to respond for the negligent act of the employé has no application to it. * * * The appellee university was created by a special charter granted to its trustees by the Legislature of the state of Illinois (Priv. Laws 1851, p. 20), and is being operated under that charter and the amendments thereto passed in 1855, 1861, and 1867. * * *

It is clear from the reading of this charter that the appellee's entire funds, whether from tuition fees received from students or other sources, must be used solely for educational purposes. The appellee corporation has no capital stock, it cannot declare dividends or share profits, and everything that it has is held in trust to be applied in such manner as to best accomplish the purpose for which it was created, viz., the diffusion of knowledge and learning. In the statute of charitable uses (St. 43 Eliz. c. 4), which is a part of the common law of this state (Heuser v. Harris, 42 Ill. 425; Andrews v. Andrews, 110 Ill. 223), "schools of learning, free schools," etc., are mentioned as charitable objects, and the fact that the appellee requires its students to pay tuition does not change its character as a charitable institution. * * *

The appellee university is a private corporation, but is organized for purely charitable purposes. It declares no dividends, and has no power to do so. It depends upon the income from its property and the endowments and gifts of benevolent persons for funds to carry out the sole object for which it was created—the dissemination of learning. Its charter secures to all persons of good moral character who have made sufficient preliminary advancement the benefits of the university, and all of its funds and property, from whatever source derived, are held in trust by it, to be applied in furtherance of the purpose of its organization and increasing its benefits to the public. The funds and property thus acquired are held in trust, and cannot be diverted to the purpose of paying damages for injuries caused by the negligent or wrongful acts of its servants and employés to persons who are enjoying the benefit of the charity. An institution of this character, doing charitable work of great benefit to the public without profit, and depending upon gifts, donations, legacies, and bequests made by charitable persons for the successful accomplishment of its beneficial purposes, is not to be hampered in the acquisition of property and funds from those wishing to contribute and assist in the charitable work by any doubt that might arise in the minds of such intending donors as to whether the funds supplied by them will be applied to the purposes for which they intended to devote them, or diverted to the entirely different purpose of satisfying judgments recovered against the donee because of the negligent acts of those employed to carry the beneficent purpose into execution.

That the appellee, though a private, and not a public, corporation, being a purely charitable institution, is not answerable for the negligent acts of its employés, is held but with little diversity of opinion. * * *

The ruling of the superior court of Cook county in sustaining the demurrer to appellant's declaration was correct. The judgment of the Appellate Court must be, and is, affirmed.

Judgment affirmed.

Charitable corporation is immune from liability for tort of its agents, provided no negligence exists in the employment of the agent

SOUTHERN METHODIST UNIVERSITY v. CLAYTON

Supreme Court of Texas, 1944.
176 S.W.2d 749.

BREWSTER, Commissioner.

During a football game between the teams of petitioner, Southern Methodist University, and Texas A. & M. College, at Dallas, on November 9, 1940, a temporary bleacher collapsed. This is a suit by respondent, J. B. Clayton, to recover damages for injuries sustained by his wife, who was seated in the bleacher when it fell. After Clayton rested his case the trial court sustained the university's motion for an instructed verdict. That action was reversed by the Court of Civil Appeals and the cause was remanded for a new trial. 172 S.W.2d 197.

There is no dispute as to the material facts. Southern Methodist University is incorporated under the laws of Texas as an institution of higher education. It is owned and maintained by the Methodist Church and is governed by a board of trustees elected by subordinate bodies of the church. It has no capital stock and nobody can receive any pecuniary profit from its operation. In addition to a college of arts and sciences, it conducts schools of theology, law, engineering, music, business and the like. It also has a department of athletics, supervised by a professor of physical education, and every student is required to take some form of physical training. Football is one of them, but it is not self-sustaining. Over a period of fifteen years this department showed a net loss of $55,000 to the university's general fund. Besides moneys received from athletic contests, this general fund is constituted by tuition and fees collected from students and by income realized from gifts and endowments. From it all expenses of the university's operation are paid.

One L. B. Morgan had been employed by the university for about fifteen years with the duty, among others, of supervising the football field. That included the erection of temporary bleachers when it was expected that the permanent stands would not seat the spectators. The stand that fell and injured Mrs. Clayton was finished about five days before the game in question. Morgan directed the work.

Clayton alleged that the university was negligent (1) in permitting this stand to be crowded beyond its normal capacity; (2) in failing sufficiently to brace it; and (3) in constructing it of old and defective material. He alleged, further, that it was negligent in keeping Morgan in its employ, on the theory that he was incompetent. However, during the trial Clayton formally waived this last issue. Hence, the trial court's action in instructing a verdict was a holding that the other three acts of negligence charged, if true, did not render the university liable for Mrs. Clayton's injuries.

Because it is devoted to public education without private gain, the university is a charitable institution, despite the fact that it is under the control of a religious denomination and charges tuition. * * * There is a divergence of opinion in our several American jurisdictions as to the tort liability of such an institution to its beneficiaries or to strangers. Some extend absolute immunity, others recognize a limited liability, while a few hold to the doctrine of respondeat superior. * * * Since the limitation generally is based on the theory that it is better that the injured individual go without his damages than that the assets of the charity be dissipated to pay them, it is sometimes held that liability exists but that it cannot be enforced by levy of execution on property exclusively devoted to charity purposes. Obviously this holding is to permit the injured party to get the benefit of indemnity insurance carried by the charity. * * *

It seems definitely established in this state that a charity corporation is liable to an employee for injuries proximately caused by the negligence of its officers, vice principals or agents. * * * On the other hand, it is equally well settled that it is not liable for such injuries to beneficiaries of the charity, provided it is not negligent in hiring or keeping the agent whose negligence proximately causes the injuries. The principle has been applied in several cases where injuries were received by patients in charity hospitals because of the alleged negligence of nurses. * * *

Whether this rule is to be extended to strangers to the charity is the question we have to decide. It is contended that since the Claytons were on the university's campus as guests paying to watch a football game, they were strangers to the university's charitable purpose of promoting education and are entitled to damages for the injuries sustained by Mrs. Clayton. Or, as respondent puts it in his brief, "If J. B. Clayton had been a student at the University at the time of the injury, the University would have been liable in damages only if it had been negligent in the hiring of L. B. Morgan. But since it is patently clear that Clayton was not a student and was a stranger to the charities of the institution, its negligence in hiring Morgan becomes of no consequence, if the institution is otherwise found to have been negligent." We do not believe there is any solid ground for such a distinction. * * *

To hold the university liable in damages to Clayton would unquestionably take from it, to the extent of the judgment, funds which would otherwise be devoted to its charity purpose. It would, to that extent, deprive the public of the benefit of the charity. The principle of respondeat superior, if applied to situations like that presented in this case, could result in impairing or destroying the university, in the face of a clear public policy demand that it be preserved. * * *

Public policy considerations have long been heeded by our courts. * * * Therefore, we think sound public policy demands that charity corporations be held immune from liability for the torts of their agents, in the absence of negligence in employing or keeping the latter, whether the injured party be a beneficiary of the trust or a stranger to it, since the result to the charity would be the same in either case.

It would serve no good purpose to extend this opinion in a

discussion of the authorities holding contrary to our conclusion. We simply do not follow them.

The judgment of the Court of Civil Appeals is reversed and that of the district court is affirmed.

Opinion adopted by the Supreme Court.

NOTES

1. The Supreme Court of South Carolina held that a private woman's college was not liable for an invited paying guest (stranger), who was killed while attending a function in the college's auditorium. This court held that a charity is not only immune from liability for injuries suffered by beneficiaries of the charity, but it is also immune from liability for injuries to strangers or paying guests. The court said:

> * * * the exemption of public charities from liability in actions for damages for tort rests not upon the relation of the injured person to the charity, but upon grounds of public policy, which forbids the crippling or destruction of charities which are established for the benefit of the whole public to compensate one or more individual members of the public from injuries inflicted by the negligence of the corporation itself, or of its superior officers or agents, or of its servants or employees. The principle is that, in organized society, the rights of the individual must, in some instances, be subordinated to the public good. It is better for the individual to suffer injury without compensation than for the public to be deprived of the benefit of the charity. * * * Questions of public policy must be determined upon consideration of what on the whole will best promote the general welfare.

Vermillion v. Woman's College of Due West, 104 S.C. 197, 88 S.E. 649 (1916).

2. New Jersey courts have made the liability of charitable institutions dependent on whether the person harmed was a "beneficiary" or a "stranger." The theory being that an injured party waives his right of recovery from a charity if he benefits from the charities services. Collopy v. Newark Eye and Ear Infirmary, 27 N.J. 29, 141 A.2d 276 (1958).

3. The Supreme Court of Missouri has said that the "beneficiary" theory is a rather illogical distinction and refused to follow it.

The court in Missouri identified the predominate themes which have provided the rationale for the overthrow of charitable immunity by most courts.

Running predominantly through the opinions refusing

> all charitable immunity, are such statements as the fol-
> lowing: that liability insurance is available and is usually
> carried; that the courts are "not informed" that hard-
> ships or calamities have ensued where liability is recog-
> nized; that today's hospitals are quite different from
> those of prior years, with wide community support, many
> employees and business-like operations; and also that
> the trend is to shift the burden from innocent victims
> to the community at large.

The court then rejected these arguments by restating its adherence to the principle of judicial restraint and maintaining that the legislature is the appropriate governmental branch
to overturn the immunity doctrine. The court further said,

> that many charities have not availed themselves of in-
> surance and that in any event, the existence of insurance
> (in the absence of statute) should make no difference in
> *liability*; and that the courts which refer to the lack of
> hardship in states refusing immunity have no evidence
> or statistics to support the statement, are not in position
> to know, and are merely speculating.

Schulte v. Missionaries of La Salette Corp. of Mo., 352 S.W.2d
636 (Mo. 1961).

Charitable institution is liable for its wrong doing

PRESIDENT AND DIRECTORS OF GEORGETOWN UNIVERSITY v. HUGHES

United States Court of Appeals for the District of Columbia, 1942.
130 F.2d 810.

RUTLEDGE, Associate Justice.

The appeal brings here for the first time the question
whether a charitable corporation is liable for injury negligently caused by an employee acting in the course of duty.
Issues of negligence and contributory negligence also are
raised.

The plaintiff had judgment on a verdict with special inter-
rogatories. Defendant's motions for a directed verdict and to
set aside the verdict were denied. . . . We affirm the judgment.

* * *

I. Negligence and Contributory Negligence

On both issues the evidence was sufficient to go to the jury.
Hence its findings for the plaintiff must be sustained.

Defendant conducts Georgetown Hospital. Plaintiff, a special nurse on duty, was struck in the back by a door hinged to swing both in and out and located between a ward and the corridor along which she was passing. The door was pushed open suddenly and violently by a student nurse coming out from the ward. The corridor ran east and west. It was a little more than six feet wide. The ward and the door were on the north. Nurses were instructed to keep to the right of the center line and to be cautious about the door. Plaintiff was walking westwardly, to the right of the center, and had already passed the door, when it was pushed open and struck her. She was thrown violently to the floor, and incurred the injuries which have permanently disabled her. There is no issue concerning the character of the injury or the amount of the damages.

The evidence to show negligence is, in part, that the student nurse and several others, in company with the head instructor, Miss Sandmaier, entered the ward just prior to the injury for an hour's work. Miss Sandmaier found some needed article was lacking and sent the student nurse for it. The latter turned and went hurriedly, not running, but walking very fast. Her own and other testimony describes her as rushing, not stopping at the door "because it was a swinging door," not looking through the wire mesh at the bottom to see if anyone were outside, not slowing or slackening her speed as she approached the door, pushing it, meeting an obstacle which fell, pushing it open again after it had swung back toward her, and finding the plaintiff lying on the floor. The testimony also showed that the morning was unusually busy, the article was needed quickly—"the work had to be done in an hour"—and the student nurse habitually rushed and hurried about her work. More need not be related.

At times things happen fast, and have to, in hospitals. When they do accidents may occur which the law must classify as negligence. The student nurse made things move. Ordinarily this would be commendable. Unfortunately that cannot relieve her act here of negligent quality. It was careless, because thoughtless and hasty. We cannot say that the jury could not find it was unreasonably dangerous to others.

The claim of contributory negligence is that plaintiff walked too closely to the door and failed to take due care regarding it, with full knowledge of the danger. The evidence, however, was not so one-sided as to require the case to be kept from the jury. The corridor was not a one-way street. It was only a few inches over six feet wide. Nurses were instructed to walk to the right of the center line. Plaintiff followed the instructions. She was told also to be cautious about the door. The distance from the center to the right side was only about three feet. Nothing shows that plaintiff was not keeping proper lookout for the door as she approached and passed it. She passed in safety. Only after she had gone by was she struck. Whatever might be true if this had taken place before she passed the door, we cannot say as a matter of law that she was bound to anticipate it would be pushed open with such violence as to strike her from behind after she had passed and throw her more than eight feet across the hall. Busy as the period was, it cannot be ruled she was required at her peril to keep her head turned or turning toward the door over her shoulder and backward to guard against so sudden, violent and wide an opening. Nor can it be said certainly that the danger to herself or others would have been greater or less, had she followed a path nearer the center or nearer the wall. There was not much leeway either way, and clearly she was not required to step beyond the center each time in passing the door. Her instructions required the contrary.

* * *

II. Liability of Charitable Corporations

* * *

A few further facts pertinent to this issue should be stated, in view of the trial court's finding that plaintiff was a stranger to the charity, and the importance the finding has assumed on appeal. She was a special nurse. She was called to duty and assigned to the case by the hospital's superintendent of nurses. The patient was a paying one, who also paid plaintiff and paid the hospital for her meals. The hospital furnished her working facilities. The arrangement was the usual one for special nurses.

Paradoxes of principle, fictional assumptions of fact and consequence, and confused results characterize judicial disposition of these claims. From full immunity, through varied but inconsistent qualifications to general responsibility is the gamut of decision. The cases are almost riotous with dissent. Reasons are even more varied than results. These are earmarks of law in flux. They indicate something wrong at the beginning or that something has become wrong since then. They also show that correction, though in process, is incomplete.

On the other hand, scholarly treatment outside the courts is almost uniform. There is general agreement of such opinion in support of liability and against immunity. Legal scholarship finds an important function not only in research and instruction, but as the most effective agency for constructive criticism of judicial thought and action. Great names in law rest on this foundation, some as revered as any made so by the judicial function itself. One may mention among others in the common law, Blackstone, Wigmore, Mechem. A few have combined the two functions, each adding luster to the other, for example, Kent, Story, Cooley, Holmes and Stone, in addition to the great Commentator. Therefore, when opinion among scholars who are not judges is uniform or nearly so and that among judges is in high confusion, the former gives direction to the law of the future, while the latter points presently in all directions. In such circumstances scholarly opinion has more than merely persuasive effect. It is the safest guide for jurisdictions where the question has never been determined.

A. Underlying Principles

We start with general principles. For negligent or tortious conduct liability is the rule. Immunity is the exception. Human beings ordinarily are responsible for their own legally careless action. They respond also for negligent harms inflicted by their agents and employees. So do business corporations. Likewise trustees and other fiduciaries generally are liable for their own negligence in administration and operation of the business or property committed to their control. Respondeat superior more and more has made them, as it has private corporations, responsible for wrongs done by their inferior functionaries.

Generally also charity is no defense to tort. For wrong done, it is no answer ordinarily to say, "He did not pay and was not bound to pay for the service. I gave it to him." One who undertakes to aid another must do so with due care. Whether the Good Samaritan rides an ass, a Cadillac, or picks up hitchhikers in a Model T, he must ride with forethought and caution. He is not relieved because it is his driver rather than himself who lapses into carelessness. Nor does it matter that the doer of good is a corporation, if the act of gratuitous service is fairly incidental to the business. Railroad companies, through their employees, may and often do undertake to do more for the passenger than the strict bargain or duty of carriage requires. But if they depart from normal conduct in doing it, they pay for the deviation. Charity and gratuity generally go to motive, not to duty. The automobile guest statutes show that legislation has been required to modify the common-law rule, though even in this application they do not entirely abolish it. Charity suffereth long and is kind, but in the common law it cannot be careless. When it is, it ceases to be kindness and becomes actionable wrongdoing.

*   *   *

It is a strange distinction, between a charitable institution and a charitable individual, relieving the one, holding the other, for like service and like lapse in like circumstances. The hospital may maim or kill the charity patient by negligence, yet the member of its medical staff, operating or attending without pay or thought of it, dare not lapse in a tired or hurried moment. . . . . The institution goes free. The physician pays. Yet they render a common service, which the hospital could not furnish without him. The physician cannot incorporate. He cannot shield himself behind a trust. He cannot escape respondeat superior. . . . . So it is with the lawyer.

The basis of the distinction cannot be charity. It cannot be habit or continuity in charity. If it were either, individuals would be free upon proof of the fact, or institutions would be liable upon proof of the contrary in the particular instance. The distinction reverses the general trend of responsibility in a risk-sharing and distributing age. Institutions have a survival value no individual possesses. They withstand vicissitudes individuals cannot meet. It is probable that charitable ones resist demise more stoutly than business ones. Certainly they incur no greater risks. If charity should exempt either institutions or individuals, it should be the latter. But there should be no distinction. Unless motive is to replace duty, both should be liable and liable alike.[14] Institutions should

---

14 ". . . under the common law . . . an individual is bound to make compensation for his negligent acts causing damage to others, whether his motives be charitable or otherwise. He is also obliged to compensate the recipient of his charity for an injury received in its negligent performance. If he undertakes to act through others, his employees, the situation is not changed: 'Qui facet per alium facit per se.' Nor is the situation altered by the organization of a corporation for the carrying out of his purpose." . . .

"What possible rational basis could the court have for distinguishing . . . between a charitable institution and a charitably disposed individual? . . . . If the policy of the law is to encourage donations to charity, the same policy would seem to favor and foster other individual acts of

shoulder the responsibilities all other citizens bear. They should minister as others do, within the obligation not to injure through carelessness.

Nor should the legal form in which the charitable institution is cast create immunity. It is not altogether clear that it does, except possibly when the corporate form is used. Unless the normal law of trusts is modified, the trustee must go down in his pocket as other trustees do, though he cannot dip into the fund. But when the charity is incorporated, somehow charity plus incorporation creates a certainty of immunity neither can attain apart from the other. Because the directors do not hold the legal title to the corporate property and therefore are not "principals" as trustees are, though they have all the latters' control and more, there is no personal liability of the ultimately responsible management except when its members participate personally in the negligent action. When charity is incorporated, therefore, it takes on a cloak of immunity not granted it in other guises, and not granted in that guise to other activities.

B. Historical Background

* * *

E. The So-Called "Stranger-Beneficiary" Distinction

We think it does not matter whether the plaintiff is stranger or beneficiary. Whether the one or the other is denied recovery, the distinction is without justice or legal justification. To give it to a stranger but not to a beneficiary makes the latter accept succor at the risk of greater harm. When it occurs he bears a burden which should fall on all alike, not on him alone. On the other hand, no one has the right to have cure or care at the cost of harm inflicted upon another. To allow recovery to the beneficiary, but deny it to the stranger, would unload on the latter in some part not only the cost of care and cure, but the cost of injury to the former.

* * *

In hospitals, for instance, the stranger group generally includes all except patients, in some states all except nonpaying patients. Physicians, nurses, including special ones, those regularly employed and others in training, orderlies, laboratory technicians and assistants, business officers and office em-

---

kindness and helpfulness; yet the courts do not hestitate to hold an individual 'good Samaritan' liable for his failure to exercise due care."

ployees, maids, janitors, kitchen and cleaning help, all who
render aid to the patient directly or indirectly, make their
livelihoods doing so, and carry on the work of the institution, are within the "stranger" class. So is the minister or
priest who comes to give comfort or administer the last
sacrament. Likewise the relative, friend or stranger who
visits the sick. Delivery men and others who have business
to do on the premises may recover if they are injured. The
ambulance driver or operator of the hospital's truck is protected, as is the person he negligently runs down on the
street. . . . .

* * *

F. Summary

We think, therefore, the trial court was right in allowing
plaintiff to recover. But this is not, as it held, because she was
a stranger to the charity. We do not undertake to say whether
she was stranger or beneficiary. She was trained in the hospital. She worked there many years. When she did, it was at
the hospital's summons and she was, partially, at least, under
its control. In a sense she was beneficiary more than most patients. We think she should recover because she was injured
by the negligence of the hospital's employee while the latter
was discharging its business in the course of her employment.

We return therefore to the starting point. The law's emphasis ordinarily is on liability, not immunity, for wrongdoing. Respondeat superior has widened it in an institu-
tionally, and to a large extent corporately, organized community. Charity is generally no defense. When it has been
organized as a trust or corporation, emphasis has shifted
from liability to immunity. The conditions of law and of fact
which created the shift have changed. The rule of immunity
is out of step with the general trend of legislative and judicial
policy in distributing losses incurred by individuals through
the operation of an enterprise among all who benefit by it
rather than in leaving them wholly to be borne by those who
sustain them. The rule of immunity itself has given way
gradually but steadily through widening, though not too well
or consistently reasoned, modifications. It is disintegrating.
Each modification has the justification that it is a step in
result, if not in reason, from the original error toward even-
tual correction. As more and more steps are taken, correction
becomes more complete. The process is nearing the end. This
leaves the steps untaken standing out as the more anomalous.

In taking this view we are not unmindful that charitable institutions perform a high service in the community. In days when the state was less mindful of individual need, they gave a helping hand not otherwise held out to large numbers of people. They still do so. They recently have faced, and still face grave problems. Purse strings no longer are loose, as they were before world wars and world-wide depressions. But individuals and business institutions face similar uncertainties. It does not recompense injured persons that the loss is inflicted by charitable institutions, nor should they alone bear it because all together face a hard future. For reasons already stated we do not believe the survival of charities will turn on whether or not they must answer for their wrongs to persons they are formed to help. There may be some added expense of operation. It may be no more than the cost of litigating these claims over and over, for the issue will not down. Insurance must be carried to guard against liability to strangers. Adding beneficiaries cannot greatly increase the risk or the premium. This slight additional expense cannot have the consequences so frequently feared in judicial circles, but so little realized in experience. To offset the expense will be the gains of eliminating another area of what has been called "protected negligence" and the anomaly that the institutional doer of good asks exemption from responsibility for its wrong, though all others must pay. The incorporated charity should respond as do private individuals, business corporations and others, when it does good in the wrong way.

The judgment is affirmed.

NOTES

1. The *charitable enterprise today* is in a much different financial situation than it was when the charitable immunity doctrine was first promulgated. Universities, hospitals and religious organizations have extensive assets, rich endowments, valuable property and many times operate businesses which rival any competitors. The reasons originally expounded for charitable immunity do not exist today. The change in the social and economic status of the charity was commented on by Justice Musmanno in overruling the doctrine of charitable immunity in Pennsylvania in 1965. He said:

Whatever the law may have been regarding charitable institutions in the past, it does not meet the conditions of today. Charitable enterprises are no longer housed in ramshackly wooden structures. They are not mere storm shelters to succor the traveler and temporarily refuge those stricken in a common disaster. Hospitals today are growing into mighty edifices in brick, stone, glass and marble. Many of them maintain large staffs, they use the best equipment that science can devise, they utilize the most modern methods in devoting themselves to the noblest purpose of man, that of helping one's stricken brother. But they do all this on a business basis, submitting invoices for services rendered—and properly so.

Flagiello v. The Pennsylvania Hospital, 417 Pa. 486, 208 A.2d 193 (1965), overruling Michael v. Hahnemann Medical College and Hospital, 404 Pa. 424, 172 A.2d 769 (1961).

2. *Charity* is defined in Webster's dictionary as: "Whatever is bestowed gratuitously on the needy or suffering for their relief." "Acts of benevolence to the poor." Flagiello v. The Pennsylvania Hospital, 417 Pa. 486, 208 A.2d 193 (1965).

3. The Supreme Court of Michigan in 1960 ruled that there is no longer any justification for charitable immunity:

It is our conclusion that there is today no factual justification for immunity in a case such as this, and that principles of law, logic and intrinsic justice demand that the mantle of immunity be withdrawn. The almost unanimous view expressed in the recent decisions of our sister states is that insofar as the rule of immunity was ever justified, changed conditions have rendered the rule no longer necessary.

Parker v. Port Huron Hospital, 361 Mich. 1, 105 N.W.2d 1 (1960).

Charitable institution operating commercial businesses liable for injury

RHODES ET AL. v. MILLSAPS COLLEGE

Supreme Court of Mississippi, Division B, 1937.
179 Miss. 596, 176 So. 253.

ETHRIDGE, P.J., delivered the opinion of the court.

Mrs. Myrtle Rhodes, G.C. Rhodes, adults, and their minor children, Mary, Robert, and Rudine, by their mother and next friend, brought suit against Millsaps College, appellee, for the death of Grover Evans Rhodes, the twelve year old son of G.C. Rhodes and Mrs. Myrtle Rhodes, said Grover

Evans Rhodes having been killed on August 17, 1936, by the elevator in the Millsaps Building, owned by appellee.

The declaration alleges that Millsaps College is a corporation operating an institution of learning in Jackson, Miss., and owning certain real estate among which is the building on the corner of Capitol and Roach streets, which it rents to tenants for office space and business purposes, and, for the accommodation of its tenants, it operates therein an elevator by electrical power, which elevator is operated by employees of appellee; that in the operation it is caused to travel up and down on ropes and pulleys, and in its construction there are heavy weights so placed as to operate in reverse order to the elevator, and there are windows, for the purpose of giving light and air, opening out of the elevator shaft onto the roof of the adjoining one-story building, which also belongs to appellee. It was also alleged in the declaration that for a long time prior to August 17, 1936, appellee left open the window from the second-story building out onto the roof of the one-story building, and also the window from the elevator shaft onto the roof of said one-story building, and had knowingly permitted small children to crawl through the window from the stairway onto the roof of the adjoining one-story building and to play thereon. It was also alleged that it was the custom of the tenants of said two-story building to throw wrappings and tin foil from cigars and cigarettes and chewing gum out of the windows, and that children of tender years were known to be accustomed to crawl out on said roof to gather this up and that appellee negligently left open the window from the stairway to the roof of the adjoining one-story building, well knowing the habits and disposition of small children, and allowed them to look into the elevator shaft to watch the elevator go up and down. The declaration also alleged that this open window was, in effect, an invitation to all children, a challenge to their natural curiosity, and that it did actually attract Grover Evans Rhodes, deceased, who, on August 17, 1936, was playing in and about the building above mentioned, having crawled through the window on the stairway, and, while so engaged in play, said Grover Evans Rhodes suddenly put his head into the window opening at the time the heavy weight came down; his head was caught between the window sill and the heavy weight, and was, by the counter weight of the elevator, completely severed from his body. It was further alleged in the declaration that the death of Grover Evans Rhodes was due solely because of the fact that appellee maintained and operated an elevator with the window open at such a height as to become an attraction to small children, and judgment was demanded against appellee.

The appellee pleaded the general issue with notice thereunder setting up facts substantially the same as those in the special plea to be hereinafter noted. There was a motion to strike the notice under the general issue plea, but thereafter a special plea was filed; demurrer was filed thereto, which demurrer was overruled, and, plaintiffs declining to plead further, final judgment was rendered dismissing the suit.

The special plea alleged: (1) That plaintiffs ought not to recover because appellee is a charitable institution, having been created under an act of the Legislature approved February 21, 1890 (Laws 1890, c. 379), as shown by a copy thereof made an exhibit to the plea; (2) that appellee is not incorporated for profit, pays no dividends, has no capital stock, and that all its property was acquired by private donation and is held in trust for charitable purposes; (3) that it does not now, nor did it on August 17, 1936, operate for profit, but that all of its resources, including all donations, legacies, and receipts from students, or otherwise are devoted solely and exclusively to charitable and benevolent purposes; (4) that the building on the corner of Roach and Capitol streets, in Jackson, Miss., and the lot on which it is located, were donated to appellee by R.W. Millsaps, as a result of whose benevolence said appellee was instituted; that said building constitutes a part of the endowment of appellee; that all revenues therefrom are devoted solely and exclusively to appellee's charitable and benevolent purposes, and all revenues constitute a trust fund devoted to the charitable purposes of appellee, and cannot be diverted from the purpose to which the same has been dedicated; that appellee has, at all times, since its creation, been solely engaged in the operation of a college for the education of the youth, and, while it is denied that the injury and death resulted from any negligence on the part of the appellee, nevertheless, by reason of the foregoing facts, said appellee cannot be held to be liable to appellants in any manner whatsoever.

This special plea was demurred to: (1) Because it was alleged that it did not state a cause of defense; (2) that the building in question is owned by Millsaps College, and is operated as an office building for hire, and therefore said appellee would not be exempt from suit on tort; (3) that, the operation of the building being for hire, appellee would be liable in tort; (4) that no benevolent institution could be exempt from liability for tort when it occurred in the operation of a business separate and apart therefrom, for profit, even though the profit received is used exclusively for said benevolent institution; and (5) that there is no legal defense set up in said special plea.

The charter of appellee granted in 1890 provides that R.W. Millsaps and certain other persons were a body corporate and politic under the name of "Millsaps College," and thereby they and their successors could sue and be sued, contract and be contracted with, have common seal and break same at pleasure, and could accept donations of real and personal property for the benefit of the college, and do and perform all other acts for its benefit that were not repugnant to the Constitution and laws of the state or the United States; that said college could confer degrees and certificates, and should keep down the cost of education. It was also provided in said charter that said college could own grounds, not to exceed 100 acres, for its building and campus, and could accept donations or grants of land for the site of said institution, and should be exempt from all state, county, and municipal taxation so long as said college should be kept open and maintained for the purposes contemplated. And the said college was to be under the supervision of the conferences of the Methodist Church in Mississippi.

It will be seen from a careful reading of the special plea that appellee claims complete immunity from liability for negligence of its servants on the ground that it is a charitable institution. It is not alleged in this special plea how the servants placed in charge of the building were selected, nor their experience or qualification.

This court has not heretofore passed upon the question as to whether or not a charitable institution which conducts a business separate and apart from its charity, said business being a commercial venture, is liable for torts of agents in the operation of said separate business, where the funds derived from this business are applied to the charitable purposes of this institution. We have decided that as to the operation of its charity, as such, there is no liability, where it has exercised care and caution in the selection of its servants, for an injury. . . . . .

Our court has never been committed to the doctrine that a charitable institution has full immunity from suit, and that trust funds may not be diverted from that use. In these cases it is recognized there is liability where there is negligence in selecting its agents. While we have no case directly in point to the effect that where a charitable institution engages in a commercial venture, apart from its charity, it is subject to liability as other persons or corporations for injuries, yet in other cases from this court we think the reasoning is analogous, and that the principles of liability there should be announced in the case at bar. . . .

There is considerable confusion in the different states as to the basis of liability or immunity therefrom, but it seems to us that where a charitable corporation enters into business apart from its charity, although with the purpose of securing revenue to be used in its charity, it is liable in tort to the same extent as a private corporation.

* * *

In Gamble v. Vanderbilt University, 138 Tenn. 616, 200 S.W. 510, . . . it was held that to the extent of income derived from an office building operated largely for profit, and separate from its educational plant, though occupied, in part, by its law school and library, Vanderbilt University was liable to a tenant's representatives for his death in an elevator due to negligence, although the university was a charity, and the general rule is that charitable trust funds are not to be depleted by subjection to liability for negligence. There is valuable discussion in this case, but we will not quote therefrom in order to not unduly lengthen this opinion. The majority of the courts of the country hold that a person injured by the negligence of some industry not connected with a charity may recover for such injury.

We are thoroughly of the opinion that where a charitable institution, or corporation, goes into an independent business, apart from its charity not to be operated for any of its charitable purposes, but to be operated solely for profit, or to secure funds for its charitable purposes, it is liable for injuries as other corporations. It will be noted from the charter of appellee in the case at bar that no specific power is given thereby to operate a building which was donated to it subsequent to the granting of the charter. It could, of course, sell the building and apply the proceeds to its charity; it could lease the building to be operated by the lessee, or, by the grace of the sovereign, it could operate the building itself, but its charter, per se, did not give it the power to operate a business disconnected with its charity, consequently it is subject to the general law as to such operation.

We decide this question solely on the sufficiency of the special plea, but we do not decide whether the appellee was liable for the death involved, as we do not know what the facts would be when finally developed.

It follows that the judgment of the court below must be reversed, and the demurrer to the special plea sustained.

Reversed and remanded.

NOTES

1. *Nontrust property.* In jurisdictions having immunity, the courts have usually held that the charity's immunity extends only to trust property. Nontrust property can be taken on execution of a judgment rendered against the charity in a tort action. St. Mary's Academy v. Solomon, 77 Colo. 463, 238 P. 22 (1925); McLeod v. St. Thomas Hospital, 170 Tenn. 423, 95 S.W.2d 917 (1936); Vanderbilt Univ. v. Henderson, 23 Tenn. App. 135, 127 S.W.2d 284 (1938); Moore v. Moyle, 405 Ill. 555, 92 N.E.2d 81 (1950).

2. *Liability insurance.* Liability insurance is generally considered by the courts to be nontrust property. In such instances, liability insurance may be appropriated to satisfy a judgment in tort. Moore v. Moyle, 405 Ill. 555, 92 N.E.2d 81 (1950); Wendt v. Servite Fathers, 332 Ill. App. 618, 76 N.E.2d 342 (1947); Baptist Memorial Hospital v. Couillens, 176 Tenn. 300, 140 S.W.2d 1088 (1940).

3. *Workmen's compensation acts.* Workmen's compensation acts provide for payment of benefits to injured persons regardless of fault. The primary questions to be answered in workmen's compensation cases is whether the injured person and the institution are covered by the specific state's workmen compensation acts. Some states expressly include charities in their coverage—others do not. The Massachusetts act covers "laborers, workmen and mechanics employed by religious, charitable or educational institutions." (Mass. Ann. Laws, Ch. 152, § 1(4) (1958).)

This statute has been interpreted to apply to a student nurse who paid tuition to a charitable hospital but worked at the hospital for room and board. *In re* Brewer's Case, 141 N.E.2d 281 (Mass. 1957). On the other hand, New York's statute excludes persons working for charitable organizations. The act excepts persons "engaged in a professional or teaching capacity in or for a religious, charitable or educational institution." This act excepts "volunteers in or for a religious, charitable or educational institution, or persons participating in and receiving rehabilitative service in a sheltered workshop" or recipients of charitable aid or those who work for aid. (N.Y. Workmen's Comp. Law, § 201 (5) (1963).)

In Georgia and Arkansas, institutions operated as public charities are excluded from coverage (Ga. Code Ann., § 114.07 (1956); Ark. Stat. Ann., § 81-1302 (1960)). In Idaho, coverage is optional with the employer (Idaho Code, § 72-105A (1959).) In instances where charities are not mentioned at all by statute, the courts have held that there was implication that they be included. Hartford Acc. & Ins. Co. v. Dept. of Ind. Relations, 139 Cal. App. 632, 34 P.2d 826 (1934); Schneider v. Salvation Army, 217 Minn. 448, 14 N.W.2d 467 (1944); Gardner v. Trustees of Main Street Methodist E. Church, 217 Iowa, 1390, 250 N.W. 740 (1933). Courts in Tennessee and Pennsylvania have held that if the legislature had intended to exclude charities from coverage, the statute would have expressly said so. Smith v. Lincoln Memorial Univ., 304 S.W.2d 70 (Tenn. 1957); Schreckengost v. Gospel Tabernacle, 188 Pa. Super. 652, 149 A.2d 542 (1959).

In states where charities are not liable in tort for negligence, the courts have generally held that exclusion of coverage from the statute is implication that the legislature did not intend that charities be covered. Caughman v. Columbia Y.M.C.A., 212 S.C. 337, 47 S.E.2d 788 (1948); Thurston County Chapter, American Red Cross v. Dept. of Labor, 166 Wash. 488, 7 P.2d 577 (1932).

4. The Supreme Court of Tennessee has held that members of a board of trustees of a private college cannot be held individually liable for injuries sustained by a student as a result of lack of adequate fire escapes and accumulations of trash in a dormitory. There was no showing that the defendant trustees had knowledge of the condition, nor was there any showing that the trustees had been negligent in the selection of minor employees who maintained the building. Scott v. Burton, 173 Tenn. 147, 114 S.W.2d 956.

CHAPTER 12
OTHER RELATED LEGAL MATTERS

The following legal issues regarding accreditation, copyright and collective bargaining were not among the topics heretofore discussed, but are important to any treatment of college and university law. The first case presented involves a private profit-making college's efforts to invoke constitutional protections against a regional accrediting association. Although ultimately unsuccessful, the plea of the plaintiffs is of legal significance because it illustrates the potential for future cases broadening the application of current constitutional principles. The second case discusses the age-old issue of copyright protection for works of scholars. Though the field of copyright law is quite broad and beyond the scope of this book, it is nevertheless of sufficient importance to college professors to merit case reference. The third case given, along with the subsequent notes, deals with the emerging issues of teacher collective bargaining in institutions of higher education.

ACCREDITATION

Accreditation restriction by regional college accreditation association held to have reasonable basis

MARJORIE WEBSTER JUNIOR COLLEGE v. MIDDLE STATES ASSOCIATION OF COLLEGES AND SECONDARY SCHOOLS

United States Court of Appeals, District of Columbia Circuit, 1970.
Certiorari Denied, 91 S. Ct. 367, 1970.

BAZELON, Chief Judge:

Middle States Association of Colleges and Secondary Schools, Inc., is a voluntary nonprofit educational corporation, the successor to an unincorporated association of the same name established in 1887. Its general purposes are to aid and encourage the development of quality in secondary schools and institutions of higher education located within its geographical domain (New York, New Jersey, Pennsylvania, Delaware, Maryland, and the District of Columbia) or outside of the continental United States. Chief among its activities is that of accrediting member institutions and applicants for membership.[1] Marjorie Webster Junior College, Inc., is a proprietary junior college for women located in the District of Columbia. In 1966, it applied to Middle States for accreditation. Relying upon a policy statement of the Federation of Regional Accrediting Commissions of Higher Education,[2] and upon its own past practice,[3] Middle States refused to consider Marjorie Webster for accreditation because the latter was not "a nonprofit organization with a governing board representing the public interest." Following this refusal, Marjorie Webster brought suit to compel its consideration for accreditation without regard to its proprietary character. The District Court found Middle States' refusal to consider proprietary institutions of higher education for accreditation a violation of § 3 of the Sherman Act [4] and of the developing common law regarding exclusion from membership in private associations; in addition, it found that Middle States' activities in the field of accreditation were sufficiently under the aegis of the Federal Government as to make applicable the limitations of the Due Process Clause; and that to deny accreditation to all proprietary institutions solely by reason of their proprietary character was arbitrary and unreasonable, in violation of the Fifth Amendment. Concluding, finally, that continued denial of consideration for accreditation would result in irreparable injury to Marjorie Webster, the District Court enjoined Middle States from denying Marjorie Webster accreditation solely because of its proprietary character, and ordered it to accredit Marjorie Webster if it should otherwise qualify for accreditation under Middle States' standards.[5] On the application of Middle States, we stayed the District Court's order pending our determination of this appeal. For the reasons hereafter set forth, we conclude that the Sherman Act is not applicable to Middle States' conduct as indicated by the pres-

1. Accreditation by Middle States is concomitant with membership.
2. The Federation, which is made up of Middle States and the five other regional liberal arts accrediting associations, was established in 1964 to coordinate the policies of the six associations, to speak for them in matters of common interest, and to exchange information, experience, and personnel.
3. Middle States has never accredited or evaluated a proprietary institution of higher education. This restriction has been explicit since at least 1928. Middle States has, however, accredited three proprietary secondary schools and continues to do so.
4. 15. U.S.C. § 3 (1964).
5. Marjorie Webster Junior College, Inc., v. Middle States Ass'n of Colleges & Secondary Schools, Inc., 302 F.Supp. 459 (D.D.C. 1969).

ent record; that the circumstances are not such as to warrant judicial interference with the accreditation and membership policies of Middle States; and that, assuming the Due Process Clause to be applicable, Marjorie Webster has not sustained its burden of showing the irrationality of the policy in question as applied to bar consideration of Marjorie Webster for accreditation. Accordingly, we reverse the judgment of the District Court.

I.

Appellee strongly urges, and the court below concluded, that once it be determined that appellee is engaging in "trade," restraint of that "trade" by appellant's conduct is subject to the limitations of the Sherman Act. If this were the ordinary case of a trade association alleged to have transgressed the bounds of reasonable regulation designed to mitigate the evils afflicting a particular industry, this reasoning might be conclusive. But in our view, the character of the defendant association, and the nature of the activities that it regulates, require a finer analysis.

Despite the broad wording of the Sherman Act, it has long been settled that not every form of combination or conspiracy that restrains trade falls within its ambit. For the language of the Act, although broad, is also vague; and in consequence of that vagueness, "perhaps not uncalculated, the courts have been left to give content to the statute, and in the performance of that function it is appropriate that courts should interpret its word in light of its legislative history and of the particular evils at which the legislation was aimed. The Act was a product of the era of "trusts" and of "combinations" of businesses and of capital organized and directed to control of the market by suppression of competition in the marketing of goods and services, the monopolistic tendency of which had become a matter of public concern. Apex Hosiery Co. v. Leader, 310 U.S. 469, 492-493, 60 S.Ct. 982, 84 L.Ed. 1311 (1940). "The Court in *Apex* recognized that the Act is aimed primarily at combinations having commercial objectives and is applied only to a very limited extent to organizations, like labor unions, which normally have other objectives."

That appellant's objectives, both in its formation and in the development and application of the restriction here at issue, are not commercial is not in dispute. Of course, when a given activity falls within the scope of the Sherman Act, a lack of predatory intent is not conclusive on the question of its legality. But the proscriptions of the Sherman Act were "tailored

* * * for the business world," not for the noncommercial aspects of the liberal arts and the learned professions. In these contexts, an incidental restraint of trade, absent an intent or purpose to affect the commercial aspects of the profession, is not sufficient to warrant application of the antitrust laws.

We are fortified in this conclusion by the historic reluctance of Congress to exercise control in educational matters. We need not suggest that this reluctance is of such depth as to immunize any conceivable activity of appellant from regulation under the antitrust laws. It is possible to conceive of restrictions on eligibility for accreditation that could have little other than a commercial motive; and as such, antitrust policy would presumably be applicable.[21] Absent such motives, however, the process of accreditation is an activity distinct from the sphere of commerce; it goes rather to the heart of the concept of education itself. We do not believe that Congress intended this concept to be molded by the policies underlying the Sherman Act.

II.

* * *

The extent of judicial power to regulate the standards set by private professional associations, however, must be related to the necessity for intervention. Particularly when, as here, judicial action is predicated not upon a legislative test but upon the developing doctrines of the common law, general propositions must not be allowed to obscure the specific relevant facts of each individual case. In particular, the extent to which deference is due to the professional judgment of the association will vary both with the subject matter at issue and with the degree of harm resulting from the association's action.

With these factors in mind, we turn to consider the harm appellee will suffer by virtue of the challenged exclusion. We note in this regard that denial of accreditation by Middle States is not tantamount to exclusion of appellee from operating successfully as a junior college. It has been, and without regard to accreditation by appellant will remain, accredited by the District of Columbia Board of Education, and licensed to award the Associate in Arts degree. The record indicates

---

21. For example, if accreditation were denied any institution purchasing textbooks from a supplier who did not provide special discounts for association members, it would be hard to imagine other than a commercial motive for the action.

that appellee's listing in the major publications available for use by high school guidance counsellors (and often, by students and their families) does not depend upon its accreditation by appellant. Appellee's lack of accreditation does not appear to render it, or its students, ineligible to receive federal aid. Appellee's students seeking to transfer to four-year colleges at the completion of their programs are not necessarily barred from obtaining credit for their studies because of the unaccredited status of the institution. We recognize, as the trial court found, that lack of accreditation may be a not insignificant handicap to appellee both in the effect that such lack may have on students considering application for admission, and in the loss of the substantial benefits that the accreditation process itself has upon the institution under study. But appellee has operated successfully as a junior college since 1947. Although it suffered a decline in applications for admission in the years immediately preceding the instant suit, this decline was shared by the other woman's institutions in the District of Columbia. In the last year for which figures were introduced, it received over 100 more applications than Mount Vernon Junior College, the institution receiving the second highest number. We do not believe, therefore, that the record supports the conclusion that appellee will be unable to operate successfully as a junior college unless it is considered for accreditation by appellant.

Accordingly, we believe that judicial review of appellant's standards should accord substantial deference to appellant's judgment regarding the ends that it serves and the means most appropriate to those ends. Accreditation, as carried out by appellant, is as involved with educational philosophy as with yardsticks to measure the "quality" of education provided. As found by the trial court,

> whether an institution has clearly defined appropriate objectives, whether it has established conditions under which it can reasonably be expected to obtain them, and whether it appears to be obtaining them. Under this criteria [sic], Middle States, in its publication, The Nature of a Middle States Evaluation, notes that "Organization, administration, facilities, and resources are not important in themselves." Accreditation means that the institution has achieved quality within the context of its own aims and program—not that such institution is more qualified than any other accredited or unaccredited institution.[36]

---

36. 302 F.Supp. at 474.

Appellee does not challenge this view of the accreditation process as improper. And given this view, we cannot say that appellant's refusal to consider proprietary institutions is an unreasonable means of seeking to reach the ends sought. Of course no institution, no matter how well endowed, can afford to entirely ignore the balance sheet. But when the institution itself is responsible in large part for setting the measure by which it is to be judged, we do not think it has been shown to be unreasonable for appellant to conclude that the desire for personal profit might influence educational goals in subtle ways difficult to detect but destructive, in the long run, of that atmosphere of academic inquiry which, perhaps even more than any quantitative measure of educational quality, appellant's standards for accreditation seek to foster. Likewise, we may recognize that, even in nonprofit institutions, the battle for academic freedom and control of educational policy is still sporadically waged; but this factor would seem to strengthen, rather than weaken, the reasonableness of appellant's judgment that motives of personal profit should not be allowed to influence the outcome. Finally, we need not say that appellant's views of the proper measure for accreditation of an educational institution are the only, the best, or even particularly well chosen ones. The core of appellant's argument is not that proprietary institutions are unworthy of accreditation, but rather that they, like many trade and professional schools, should properly be measured by standards different from those used by appellant, and which appellant is possessed of no special competence or experience in using. In this regard appellee is unlike the individual denied membership in or certification by a professional society. Rarely, if ever, could it be said that such an individual could realistically be expected to combine with others excluded on the same grounds to form his own association. Appellee, however, is free to join with other proprietary institutions in setting up an association for the accreditation of institutions of such character; and such an association, if recognized, could obtain for its members all the benefits of accreditation by appellant save, perhaps, prestige. Appellee has made no attempt to show that any such course has ever been attempted. In these circumstances, we do not think that appellant's refusal to consider appellee for accreditation as a proprietary institution lacks sufficient basis in reason to warrant judicial intervention.

In reaching this conclusion, we need neither disregard nor

disbelieve the extensive testimony introduced by appellee below regarding the values and benefits, both for the educational process and for the country as a whole, that flow from proprietary educational institutions. We do not conclude, nor does appellant even suggest, that competition from proprietary institutions is anything but wholesome for the nonprofit educational establishment. We merely find that, so far as can be discerned from the present record, appellant does not wield such monopoly power over the operation of educational institutions that its standards for accreditation may be subject to plenary judicial review; and that in light of the substantial latitude that must accordingly be allowed appellant in setting its criteria for accreditation, appellee's exclusion solely on the basis of its proprietary character is not beyond the bounds of appellant's allowable discretion.

III.

What has been said above should also dispose of so much of appellee's argument as is based upon the Due Process Clause. We may assume, without deciding, that either the nature of appellant's activities or the federal recognition which they are awarded renders them state action subject to the limitations of the Fifth Amendment. If so, however, the burden remains with appellee to show the unreasonableness of the restriction, not simply in the abstract but as applied specifically to it. We need not decide here the precise limits of those circumstances under which governmental action may restrict or injure the activities of proprietary educational institutions. For the reasons already discussed, we conclude that appellee has failed to show that the present restriction was without reasonable basis. Accordingly, it must be upheld.

Reversed.

COPYRIGHT

Teacher, rather than university, owns common-law copyright to his lectures

WILLIAMS v. WEISSER

Court of Appeals, Second District, Division 5, 1969.
79 Cal. Rptr. 542.

KAUS, Presiding Justice.

Defendant Weisser, who does business under the fictitious

name of Class Notes, appeals from a judgment which enjoins him from copying, publishing and selling notes of lectures delivered by plaintiff in his capacity as an Assistant Professor of Anthropology at the University of California at Los Angeles ("UCLA"). The judgment also awards plaintiff $1,000.00 in compensatory and $500.00 in exemplary damages.

A joint pretrial restatement described the nature of the case as follows: "Plaintiff is Assistant Professor at UCLA in the Anthropology Department. Defendant does business in Westwood, California as Class Notes selling outlines for various courses given at UCLA. In 1965, defendant paid Karen Allen, a UCLA student, to attend plaintiff's class in Anthropology 1 to take notes from the letters, and to type up the notes. Allen delivered the typed notes to defendant and defendant placed a copyright notice thereon in defendant's name, reproduced the typed notes, and sold and offered them for sale. Plaintiff objected. Defendant did not cease these activities until served with summons, complaint and temporary restraining order. Plaintiff seeks a permanent injunction, general damages, and punitive damages."

At the pretrial it was agreed that: "Defendant has used plaintiff's name in selling the publications here in question."

The judgment in plaintiff's favor was based on two grounds: 1. defendant infringed plaintiff's common law copyright in his lectures; and 2. defendant invaded plaintiff's privacy by the use of plaintiff's name. * * *

On appeal defendant advances the following points:

1. The common law copyright in plaintiff's lectures presumptively belonged to UCLA. Defendant's efforts at the trial to show that a purported assignment of the rights of the university to plaintiff was not intended to be an assignment or, if it was, that it was made under a mistake of law, were erroneously cut off by a peremptory ruling that plaintiff was the owner of the copyright.

2. Even if plaintiff was the owner of the copyright the "general and unrestricted publication" of the "organization and content" of the lectures constituted a divestment of any such right.

3. Defendant's use of the notes was "a fair use and did not constitute a wrongful trading on, or actionable commercial abuse of, plaintiff's personality or reputation."

4. The evidence does not support the award of damages, compensatory or exemplary. * * *

Ownership Of Copyright

Plaintiff became employed by UCLA starting in July 1965. Defendant's relations with the university started in 1948 when he began to publish and sell to students what purported to be notes of various courses. In 1963 defendant and the university authorities agreed on certain ground rules as a condition to advertising in the Daily Bruin, the student newspaper. Friction arose between defendant and the administration. The matter culminated in a memorandum dated November 19, 1964, addressed to all members of the faculty. It is copied in the footnote.[1]

At the trial Vice Chancellor Sherwood of UCLA appeared as one of plaintiff's witnesses. He testified, among other matters, to the following: He had served for eight years as a member of the faculty committee charged with the responsibility of approving manuscripts for publication by the University of California Press. If a professor's manuscript was thought to have commercial value, the university would sign a regular publisher's contract with the author, under which contract the professor would receive royalties at commercial rates.

---

1. "MEMBERS OF THE FACULTY: As many of you know there is now a business firm operating in Westwood Village offering for sale lecture notes on current UCLA courses. This company, CLASS LECTURE NOTES, publishes notes taken by its agents who attend classes either as auditors or, occasionally, as enrolled students. The notes are marketed to students who, for a variety of reasons, believe they need an additional study aid.

"Many instructors object to this procedure. Others apparently do not. We believe, however, that all should be aware of the instructor's rights regarding use of notes taken on his lectures.

"First, regarding the attendance of auditors, whatever their purposes may be (except for Summer Session) it is the policy of the University to defer entirely to the wishes of the individual faculty member. Any faculty member has the right to deny the attendance of auditors if he so desires.

"Secondly, regarding the faculty member's right to control distribution of notes taken in classroom lecture, it appears quite clear that under California's recognition of common law copyright, the lecturer retains a property right to his words spoken before a limited audience. Any unauthorized duplication and distribution of these words, either verbatim or in the form of notes may therefore constitute an infringement of this right. It is emphasized that the common law copyright in a lecture is the property of the lecturer rather than of the University, and therefore any legal actions for the infringement of such right must be brought in the name of the aggrieved faculty member.

"Charles E. Young
Vice Chancellor"

This was, to his knowledge, the practice throughout the United States.

In 1964 Vice Chancellor Sherwood and Vice Chancellor Young drafted the memorandum of November 19, 1964. This was done after a discussion with Mr. John Sparrow, counsel representing the university. The court's peremptory ruling to the effect that plaintiff, rather than the university, was the owner of the copyright came right after Sherwood, on cross-examination, had perhaps admitted that if it were the law of California that the copyright in a professor's lectures belongs to the university that might have somehow affected the November 19, 1964, memorandum. He did, however, point out that if such were the law, it would simplify his job immensely, since "a faculty member would not be able to leave the university for the university would have a right to his lectures and he could only go to another institution if he were in a position to turn his attention to a new subject."

During the argument that followed the ruling, counsel, although he perhaps was not required to do so * * * stated: "* * * I believe he would testify, and I offer by way of offer of proof, that this witness will further testify if allowed to do so that this letter was nothing more than a statement of his and Chancellor Young's understanding of California common-law."

After this offer of proof the court asked a few questions of the witness: "* * * I will just ask one more question on this subject, Dr. Sherwood. Whether it was rightly or wrongly the expression of the opinion of counsel, is this the policy that was followed by the university with respect to these lecture notes? THE WITNESS: It is. THE COURT: And that is what you intended? THE WITNESS: And that is what we intended."

If it were the law that, in the absence of evidence one way or another, UCLA rather than plaintiff is presumed to be the owner of the copyright to plaintiff's lectures or if the record contained any evidence that plaintiff had assigned his copyright to the university, the trial court's ruling would have been premature. For what it was worth, defendant was still developing his theory that the November 19 memorandum did not effectively transfer the university's copyright to plaintiff.

We are, however convinced that in the absence of evidence the teacher, rather than the university, owns the common law copyright to his lectures. Since there was no evidence that plaintiff had assigned his copyright to the university, the entire question of whether the university had quitclaimed something it did not own was beside the point. Defendant was therefore not prejudiced by the ruling.

Defendant claims that the opposite is the law. His sole statutory authority is section 2860 of the Labor Code which reads as follows: "Everything which an employee acquires by virtue of his employment, except the compensation which is due to him from his employer, belongs to the employer, whether acquired lawfully or unlawfully, or during or after the expiration of the term of his employment."

It is obvious that a literal application of that section does not cover the present situation. The code speaks of things which the employee "acquires," not matters which he creates. In Burns v. Clark, 133 Cal. 634, 639, 66 P. 12, 14, the Supreme Court said that the section, then section 1985 of the Civil Code, was to be construed as "but an expression of the familiar principle that forbids an agent or trustee from using the trust property or powers conferred upon him for his own benefit, and which, in case of his doing so, requires him to account for the profits. * * *." * * * Thus the section has been applied principally, though not exclusively, to unfair competition carried on by former employees with the use of trade secrets and the like. Even so it has been narrowly employed. (Aetna Bldg. Maintenance Co. v. West, 39 Cal.2d 198, 204, 246 P.2d 11.) We do not believe it applies here.

Defendant also claims that plaintiff is in the position of an employee for hire whose employment calls for the creation of a copyrightable work, or, perhaps, of an independent contractor who has been so commissioned. (Nimmer on Copyright §§ 62, 63.) In such cases it is usually presumed that, unless a different intention is shown, the employer or commissioner is the owner of the copyright. * * *

This contention calls for some understanding of the purpose for which a university hires a professor and what rights it may reasonably expect to retain after the services have been rendered. A university's obligation to its students is to make the subject matter covered by a course available for study by various methods, including classroom presentation. It is not obligated to present the subject by means of any particular expression. As far as the teacher is concerned, neither the record in this case nor any custom known to us suggests that the university can prescribe his way of expressing the ideas he puts before his students. Yet expression is what this lawsuit is all about. No reason has been suggested why a university would want to retain the ownership in a professor's expression. Such retention would be useless except possibly for making a little profit from a publication and for making it difficult for the teacher to give the same lectures, should he change jobs.

Indeed the undesirable consequences which would follow from a holding that a university owns the copyright to the lectures of its professors are such as to compel a holding that it does not. Professors are a peripatetic lot, moving from campus to campus. The courses they teach begin to take shape at one institution and are developed and embellished at others. That, as a matter of fact, was the case here. Plaintiff testified that the notes on which his lectures were based were derived from a similar course which he had given at another university. If defendant is correct, there must be some rights of that school which were infringed at UCLA. Further, should plaintiff leave UCLA and give a substantially similar course at his next post, UCLA would be able to enjoin him from using the material, which according to defendant, it owns.

No one but defendant, an outsider as far as the relationship between plaintiff and UCLA is concerned, suggests that such a state of the law is desirable.

Another strange consequence which would follow from equating university lectures with other products of the mind which an employee is hired to create is, that in order to determine just what it is getting, the university would have to find out the precise extent to which a professor's lectures have taken concrete shape when he first comes to work. Not even defendant suggests that a contract for employment implies an assignment to the university of any common law copyright which the professor already owns.

The many cases cited by defendant for the general rule probably reach desirable results that are in accord with common understanding in their respective areas, but a rule of law developed in one context should not be blindly applied in another where it violates the intention of the parties and creates undesirable consequences. University lectures are *sui generis*. Absent compulsion by statute or precedent, they should not be blindly thrown into the same legal hopper with valve designs * * *, motion picture background music * * *, commercial drawings * * *, mosaics designed for the Congressional Library in Washington, D.C. * * *, high school murals * * *, song stylings * * *, radio scripts * * *, commercial jingles * * *, lists of courses taught by a correspondence school * * *, treatises on the use of ozone * * * or on larceny and homicide * * *.

On the other hand, there is a short but sturdy line of authorities dealing with lectures. Though none of the cases have as their protagonists the teacher opposed by the institution, the latter's position is at least tangentially discussed in some. The fact that none of the defendants—pirates all—ever thought that the question of the institution's rights, as such, was worth raising is surely not without significance.

The first and leading case is Abernethy v. Hutchinson, 3 L.J. (Ch. 209 (1825), 1 H. & T. 28 (1825). If in point it is controlling authority. (Civ.Code § 22.2); Cole v. Rush, 45 Cal.2d 345, 355-356, 289 P.2d 450, 54 A.L.R.2d 1137.

Doctor Abernethy was a surgeon who had delivered lectures on surgery to students and others at Saint Bartholomews Hospital in London. His lectures were based on notes, but he did not read from or refer to them during the lectures. Defendant had published Abernethy's lectures in its periodical "The Lancet." After much soul-searching Lord Eldon granted an injunction. Near the end of his opinion he states: "One question had been, whether Mr. Abernethy, from the peculiar situation which he filled in the hospital, was precluded from publishing his own lectures for his profit: *but there was no evidence before the Court, that he had not such right.* Therefore the defendants must be enjoined in future." (3 L.J. at 219. Italics added.) Earlier in the opinion the court had likened Doctor Abernethy's position to that of a university professor.[7] From our point of view, the significance of the quoted passage is that in the absence of positive evidence to the contrary the Chancellor assumed as a matter of course

---

7. One of the reasons why Lord Eldon assumed that professors have a common law copyright in their lectures was the historical fact that Blackstone had published the Vinerian Lectures under copyright: "Now, if a professor be appointed, he is appointed for the purpose of giving information to all the students who attend him, and it is his duty to do that; but I have never yet heard that anybody could publish his lectures; nor can I conceive on what ground Sir William Blackstone had the copyright in his lectures for twenty years, if there had been such a right as that; we used to take notes at his lectures; at Sir Robert Chamber's lectures also the students used to take notes; but it never was understood that those lectures could be published;—and so with respect to any other lectures in the university, it was the duty of certain persons to give those lectures; but it never was understood, that the lectures were capable of being published by any of the persons who heard them." (3 L.J. at 215.)

that the copyright was with the lecturer and not with the hospital. *A fortiori* it would not belong to a university.

The case which is factually closest in point is Caird v. Sime (1887) 12 A.C. 326 (H.L.). There the House of Lords had before it a case coming from Scotland. There is, however, no suggestion that Scottish law differed from that of England in respect to the issues involved. Caird, the "pursuer," was a professor of moral philosophy at the University of Glasgow. Sime, the "defender," had published pamphlets of lectures given by Caird. The pamphlets were based on shorthand notes taken by one of Caird's students. There was a substantial question whether Sime's pamphlets were in fact reproductions of Caird's lectures. It was contended that in certain particulars they were "blundering and unsuccessful" copies of the lectures "with ignorant or foolish additions." This, the court said, did not matter. In law the case turned on the question whether Caird had lost his common law copyright because as a professor in a public university it was his obligation "to receive into his class all comers having the requisite qualification." Therefore, it was argued, "his lectures are really addressed to the public." In answer to this point the court noted that it was a "fact that professors and their representatives have been in frequent use to publish lectures which had been annually delivered for years before such publication, and have enjoyed, without objection or challenge, the privilege of copyright." Sime's point did not prevail.

While at this point in our discussion we are not concerned with any possible divestment of plaintiff's copyright by the giving of his lectures, we think it is of some significance to the question of his ownership of the copyright vis-a-vis the university, that Caird's position as a professor at a public university was used as an argument in Caird v. Sime and found not to be an obstacle to recovery.

Caird v. Sime is also significant in that it lays to rest an argument made by the defendant in this court, namely that Abernethy v. Hutchinson, *supra*, had been overruled. The House of Lords took note of the fact that its records showed that within a few months after the injunction in that case was issued, it was dissolved on motion by the defendant; however "no trace had been found of the affidavit on which the motion was made, so that the recall of the injunction may have been the result of an arrangement between the parties, and at all events it cannot detract from the weight of Lord Eldon's deliberate judgment causa cognita."

The plaintiff in Nichols v. Pitman, 26 Ch. Div. 374 (1884) had composed a lecture entitled "The Dog as the Friend of Man," which he delivered at a working men's college. Defendant attended the lecture, wrote it down in shorthand and published it in his publication "The Phonographic Lecturer." Relying chiefly on Abernethy v. Hutchinson, *supra*, a perpetual injunction was granted.

Crossing the Atlantic we find Sherrill v. Grieves, 57 Wash.-L.R. 286, 20 C.O.Bull. 675, decided by the Supreme Court of the District of Columbia in 1929. Sherrill was an instructor at the postgraduate school for officers of the United States Army at Fort Leavenworth. He found that no suitable text existed on military sketching, map reading and surveying. During his leisure time, not as an incident to his work as instructor, he prepared material for and worked on a book designed to fill the gap. Before the book was actually published he permitted the authorities at Leavenworth to print a pamphlet containing the part relating to military sketching. Sherrill obtained a statutory copyright on the pamphlet. It was claimed by defendants, who had published an infringing work, that they could freely do so because Sherrill's pamphlet was a "publication of the United States Government." (17 U.S.C. § 8.) Discussing that claim the court said: "The evidence shows that the authorities at Leavenworth responsible for the printing asked permission to print the pamphlet for a limited use because it was thought that to do so would facilitate the giving of instruction to the students. Counsel for defendant say that it may be conceded arguendo that it was no part of the plaintiff's duty to print the instructions in military sketching, either at his own or at Government expense, but that it was his legal contract duty to the Government to give to the student officer the identical instruction contained in the pamphlet if that was the best treatment of the subject of which he was capable, and that when he adopted as a means of performing his duty written instructions and had them printed at Government expense in a Government printery the court must assume that he had the consent of the superior officers at the school to discharge his duty in that way. But the evidence shows that the plaintiff did not have the pamphlet printed; it was his superior officer who did so. The plaintiff at the time was employed to give instruction just as a professor in an institution of learning is employed. *The court does not know of any authority holding that such a professor is obliged to reduce his lectures to writing or if he* *does so that they become the property of the institution employing him.* * * * The fact is that officers do write such books which are copyrighted and used in Government schools with the approval of the military establishment, and such books are found in the libraries of those establishments. See Callaghan v. Myers, 128 U.S. 617, 9 S.Ct. 177, 32 L.Ed. 547, which interprets Wheaton v. Peters, 8 Pet. 591, 8 L.Ed. 1055, as holding that even though a reporter of the Supreme Court of the United States is paid by the Government a salary for such reports, he may have copyright in his original notes and other original matter in the reports." (Sherrill v. Grieves, 20 C.O.Bull. 675, 687-688. Italics added.)

There is, of course, a possible distinction between Sherrill v. Grieves and the case at bar: the report does state that the material was prepared in Sherrill's "leisure time, not as an incident to his work as instructor."

The distinction is illusory. If the employing institution has any rights at all, they stem from the fact that the teacher, when preparing his lectures, is only doing that which he is hired to do. Since it is not customary for a college to prescribe the hours of the day when a teacher is to prepare for class, it follows that the time when he does so automatically ceases to be leisure time.

In any event, it is quite arguable that plaintiff prepared his notes in his "leisure time" if that concept has any validity. The evidence below showed that he signed his contract with UCLA early in 1965, was put on a salary in July of that year and started to teach in September. Before arriving at UCLA he had accumulated notes over a period of years. He prepared the notes from which he eventually delivered his lectures during the summer.

There is therefore no real difference between Sherrill and plaintiff. Neither was under a duty to make notes, neither was under a duty to prepare for his lectures during any fixed hours, but the notes that each made did directly relate to the subjects taught.

The parties make much over the protracted Rickover litigation. In Public Affairs Associates, Inc. v. Rickover, D.C., 177 F.Supp. 601, 604, the trial court held that Admiral Rickover could legally copyright speeches "that have some bearing on, or that arise out of his official actions, although writing the book or delivering the address in question, is no part of his official duties." The speeches in question were prepared by the Admiral after normal working hours or while traveling.

The court held that such works, which fall somewhere between copyrightable products which an employee is hired to write and writings which have no connection whatever with his official activities, did not constitute publications of the United States Government. (17 U.S.C. § 8.) It also held that the delivery of the speeches and the distribution of a limited number of copies was not an abandonment of the literary property or a dedication to the public. On this latter point the trial court was reversed in Public Affairs Associates, Inc. v. Rickover, 109 U.S.App.D.C. 128, 284 F.2d 262. The Court of Appeals agreed that the speeches were not government publications, but held that because of the wide distribution of the speeches to the press and others, there had been a divestive publication before Admiral Rickover had registered his claim to copyright in twenty-two of the speeches involved. With respect to the balance of the speeches the court remanded the case to the District Court for further evidence. The Supreme Court granted certiorari, but later vacated the judgment of the Court of Appeal for lack of a sufficient record. (369 U.S. 111, 82 S.Ct. 580, 7 L.Ed.2d 604). The matter was eventually retired (Public Affairs Associates, Inc. v. Rickover, D.C., 268 F.Supp. 444), but only with respect to two speeches given after the Admiral had obtained a statutory copyright. He again prevailed.

To whatever extent the *Rickover* cases are in point and persuasive, they do not hurt plaintiff's case. Mention of the fact that the Admiral prepared his speeches after normal working hours or while traveling has already been shown to be beside the point. A person in Admiral Rickover's position —"Assistant Director for Naval Reactors, Division of Reactor Development, Atomic Energy Commission, and Assistant Chief of the Bureau of Ships for Nuclear Propulsion, United States Navy"—has no normal working hours any more than a university professor. Whatever distinctions between "on" and "off-duty" hours might be appropriate in the case of an hourly employee who punches a clock, they are quite out of place in cases such as *Rickover* and the one at bar. * * *

It is thus apparent that no authority supports the argument that the copyright to plaintiff's notes is in the university. The indications from the authorities are the other way and so is common sense.

Divestive Publication

Little needs to be said on the point of divestive publication. The question of what manner of publication divests a com-

mon law copyright to a lecture is extensively discussed in
D. E. Harding, Copyright in Lectures, Sermons, and Speeches
(1966) 14 Ascap, Copyright Law Symposium 270, 291-324.
The author there points out that the authorities approach
the problem in two ways. Professor Nimmer's view is that
no divestive publication occurs unless there is a distribution
of tangible copies of the work. (Nimmer on Copyright §§ 49,
52; Nimmer, Copyright Publication, 56 Colum.L.R. 184, 197.)
In other words the doctrine of Ferris v. Frohman, 223 U.S.
424, 32 S.Ct. 263, 56 L.Ed. 492, that performance does not
dedicate, applies. Other authorities make the distinction between "limited" and "general" publication. * * * Under either
view the oral delivery of the lectures did not divest plaintiff
of his common law copyright to his lectures. Nothing tangible
was delivered to the students and every case that has considered the problem of divestment from the limited versus
general publication point of view has reached the conclusion
that the giving of a lecture is not a general publication. (Abernethy v. Hutchinson, *supra;* Caird v. Sime, *supra;* Nichols
v. Pitman, *supra;* Bartlett v. Crittenden, 2 Fed.Cas. p. 981,
No. 1,082; Nutt v. National Institute Inc. for the Imp. of
Memory, *supra;* Sherrill v. Grieves, *supra.*) As the court said
in Caird v. Sime, holding that the publication of the plaintiff's lecture was only limited: " * * * The principle which
pervades the whole of that reasoning is, that where the persons present at a lecture are not the general public, but a limited class of the public, selected and admitted for the sole and
special purpose of receiving individual instruction, they may
make any use they can of the lecture, to the extent of taking
it down in shorthand, for their own information and improvement, but cannot publish it * * *." (12 A.C. at 347-348.)

Privacy

Although defendant speaks of "fair use," the context of
his argument shows that he is not relying on the defense of
fair use as known in the law of copyright. (Nimmer on Copyright § 145.) Rather he claims a defense to the alternative
basis on which the court found in plaintiff's favor, that is
to say, invasion of privacy.

Liability on that theory was predicated on defendant's use
of plaintiff's name in connection with the publication, distribution and sale of the notes. It is defendant's position that,
copyright aside, he was privileged to publish the notes and to
use plaintiff's name in connection with such publication be-

cause "[p]laintiff intentionally placed himself in the public eye when he undertook his employment as an instructor * * *." * * *

Leaving aside the extent to which a person thrusts himself upon the public eye by giving a course at UCLA, defendant forgets to mention certain aspects of this particular case which bring it into the field of actionable privacy.

An author who owns the common law copyright to his work can determine whether he wants to publish it and, if so, under what circumstances. Plaintiff had prepared his notes for a specific purpose—as an outline to lectures to be delivered to a class of students. Though he apparently considered them adequate for that purpose, he did not desire a commercial distribution with which his name was associated. Right or wrong, he felt that his professional standing could be jeopardized. There is evidence that other teachers at UCLA did not object to representatives of Class Notes being in the classroom, indeed some cooperated with defendant in revising the product of the note takers. Plaintiff considered the Anthropology 1 notes sold by defendant as defective in several respects, chiefly because of certain omissions. Any person aware of the cooperation given by other faculty members could reasonably believe that plaintiff had assisted in the final product. We think that these considerations easily bring the case within the ambit of Fairfield v. American Photocopy, etc., Co., 138 Cal.App.2d 82, 291 P.2d 194. There the defendant used the plaintiff's name in advertising a certain product. He was said to be one of the many satisfied users of the product. He had been a user, but had returned the product to the defendant. The court held that defendant's conduct was "an unauthorized and unwarranted appropriation of plaintiff's personality as a lawyer for pecuniary gain and profit." (138 Cal.App.2d at 87, 291 P.2d at 197.) We think that the Fairfield case is indistinguishable from the one at bar.

* * *

Taking the evidence as a whole, the trial court was amply justified in concluding that defendant was not an innocent layman, caught in the complexities of the law, but a businessman who, for personal profit, was determined to pursue a certain course of action even if it meant riding roughshod over the rights of others.

The judgment is affirmed.

COLLEGE FACULTIES AND COLLECTIVE
BARGAINING

Whether collective bargaining will become a primary vehicle for faculty participation in the decisions of higher education in the future remains to be seen, but there is little doubt that the role of collective bargaining between faculty and administrators will attain much greater relative importance and power in the years ahead. Recent developments in the law indicate a changing attitude toward the status of collective bargaining in institutions of higher education, especially private colleges and universities. Ronald C. Brown provides in an exhaustive report an excellent statement on the status of professors and unions. Excerpts from Brown follow:[1]

Collective bargaining is a legal relationship between a faculty and its administration; therefore, those faculties which choose it as their means of faculty governance should understand which laws, if any, will govern their relationship with the administration. Depending on whether the institution is public or private, the nature of that relationship will be prescribed by federal or state laws. These laws and the potential problems of collective bargaining in higher education are examined below.

A. Role of Federal Law

Since state educational institutions are excluded from jurisdictional coverage by the National Labor Relations Act (NLRA), and private colleges until recently had not had NLRB jurisdiction exercised over them, college and university administrators have not had to deal with the operations of the Act nor follow its legal developments.[199] However, it is increasingly evident that this legislation "has made a terrific impact on all employer-employee-union relations, including colleges and universities."

1. Private Institutions

In a landmark decision involving Syracuse and Cornell Universities on June 12, 1970, the National Labor Relations Board asserted jurisdiction over non-profit colleges and universities

---

1. Ronald C. Brown, "Professors and Unions: The Faculty Senate: An Effective Alternative to Collecting Bargaining in Higher Education," *William and Mary Law Review*, Vol. 12, No. 2, 1970, pp. 302-308 (some footnotes have been omitted).

199. *See* National Labor Relations Act, 29 U.S.C.A. § 151 (1947).

which meet its jurisdictional standards.[201] In asserting jurisdiction, the NLRB overruled the leading case of *Trustees of Columbia University* in which the Board in 1951 declined to assert its jurisdiction over a ". . . non-profit, educational institution where the activities involved are non-commercial in nature and intimately connected with charitable and educational activities of the institution." [202]

The NLRB prefaced its holding by noting that union organization by both non-professional and academic employees on college campuses is growing and ". . . as advancing waves of organization swell . . . it is unreasonable to assume that . . . disputes will not continue to occur in the future." [203] The Board then justified its assertion of jurisdiction by observing that since 1959, after Congress passed Section 14(c) of the National Labor Relations Act [204] which allowed states to exercise jurisdiction when the Board declined to do so, only fifteen states had established labor laws to meet the needs of employees who were denied federal relief.[205] Consequently, the Board stated, jurisdiction is asserted "to insure the orderly, effective and uniform application of the national labor policy." [206]

In deciding that a state-wide bargaining unit was appropriate, the NLRB applied the tests used in the industrial sector. Noting its inexperience in the educational area, the Board stated that it could reliably analogize that situation with those experienced in the industrial sector.

> We are mindful that we are entering into a hitherto unchartered area. Nevertheless, we regard the above principles as reliable guides to organization in the educational context as they have been in the industrial, and will apply them to the circumstances of the instant case.[207]

It appears that when faculties designate a union, they will be placed in an industrial relations context, rather than receive

---

201. Cornell University, 183 NLRB No. 41, 74 L.R.R.M. 1269 (1970).

202. 97 NLRB No. 424, 29 L.R.R.M. 1098 (1951).

203. Cornell University, 183 NLRB No. 41, 74 L.R.R.M. 1269, 1275 (1970).

204. National Labor Relations Act § 14(c), *added by* 73 Stat. 541 (1959), 29 U.S.C. § 164(c) (Supp. 1963).

205. Of the states having labor laws to meet the needs of NLRB—excluded employees, only eight states have legislation expressly covering employees of private educational institutions.

206. Cornell University, 183 NLRB No. 41, 74 L.R.R.M. 1269, 1274-75 (1970).

207. *Id.* at 1276.

special considerations that some argue are appropriate to the educational area.

The immediate effect of the *Cornell University* decision on private colleges and universities is that they, as well as their faculties, will have NLRB procedures and remedies available to them should a collective bargaining agent be designated. The long range effect of this decision raises significant questions for higher education in general: (1) Since strikes are permitted under federal law, what impact will this have on public employee collective bargaining where the strike is prohibited by state law? (2) Will these new rights and remedies for private colleges and their faculties (*e.g.*, the right to strike, and remedies against unfair labor practices by either the union or the employer) create a demand for equal rights and remedies by public colleges and their faculties? (3) What would be the effect on public educational institutions if private sector concepts were applied in labor relations matters?

2. Public Institutions

State colleges and universities have been expressly excluded from coverage by the federal law: "The term 'employer' . . . shall not include any state or political subdivision thereof . . . ." [209] Neither are their employees "employees" within the meaning of the Act.[210]   Therefore, the significance of labor legislation on the operations of public institutions is necessarily indirect, but it is very real.

3. Impact of Federal Law on Public Colleges and Universities

Although federal law is inapplicable to public colleges and universities, its statutory and decisional principles have long been emulated by state agencies. Typically, industrial relations concepts are reflected in state public employee legislation which most frequently is modeled after the NLRA. Although state agencies often point out that they are not bound by NLRB decisions, they consistently look to NLRB and court interpretations of the federal law as guidelines in defining the state law.

In view of the recent *Cornell University* decision, there will

---

209. National Labor Relations Act, 29 U.S.C.A. § 152(2) (1964).

210. In the following cases, NLRB Regional Directors dismissed representation petitions on that basis: Board of Regents, The University of Michigan, Case No. 7-RC-1208 (1951, unpublished); Louisiana State University, Case No. 15-RC-3329 (1966, unpublished); and University of Rhode Island (Motor Vessel Trident), Case No. 1-RC-7773 (1964, unpublished).

undoubtedly develop a body of decisional law relative to private educational institutions. One can safely predict that state administrative agencies and courts will look to these decisions when faced with similar situations in cases involving public colleges and universities. The author suspects that in the future, should collective bargaining gain favor on the public campuses without coextensive state legislative rights and remedies for public employees and employers, then the same justifications for NLRB jurisdiction will exist as in the *Cornell University* case. Public employers and employees alike may seek legislative changes to allow coverage under the NLRA. Regardless of whether it is by new legislation or by state application of present legislation, it would appear that federal private industrial relations concepts will be used in the public employee sector including the college campus setting, notwithstanding the fact that federal law presently does not apply to public institutions.

B. State Labor Legislation

As public employees are excluded from coverage under federal labor law, state labor laws and state judicial decisions govern the legality of union organization and strikes. Presently there is no state public employee labor legislation which distinguishes between employees in higher education and those in elementary or secondary education. In fact, very few states distinguish between public employees in the area of education versus those employed in other areas. Moreover, few states have established different administrative agencies to administer public sector law and private sector law, which suggests why there is rarely any difference in approach or concept between the two.

1. Anti-Strike Legislation

In recent years, a number of states have enacted legislation providing collective bargaining rights for public employees, including those employed in education.[216] Thus, by legislation or judicial decision, all states but Alabama appear to have provided for bare unionization of public employees.[217] However, with the exception of Vermont,[218] the states have invariably

---

216. *See* note 213 *supra*.

217. *See* International U. of Op. Eng., Local 312 v. Waterworks Bd. of City of Birmingham, 276 Ala. 462, 163 So. 2d 619 (1964).

218. Vermont has recognized a right to strike for situations in which the exercise of such right does not endanger the public health, welfare

reaffirmed the traditional prohibition against strikes by these same public employees.[219] The anti-strike statutes usually provide for fines, discharge, and loss of employment rights for those participating in a strike. * * *

---

and safety. VT. STAT. ANN. tit. 21, § 1704 (Supp. 1968). *See also* Smith, *supra* note 77, at 910, for a similar proposal.

219. *See, e.g.*, State Bd. of Regents v. United Packing House Food and Allied Workers, Local 1258, — Iowa —, 175 N.W.2d 110 (1970).

INDEX

A

ACCREDITATION.
Colleges and universities, p. 715.

ACTIONS.
Procedure of courts.
Commencement of actions.
Catching the defendant, pp. 15, 16.
Picking court, p. 15.
Stating the claim, p. 16.

ADMINISTRATORS AND OFFICERS.
Basketball.
Fatal injury is hazard of game, p. 624.
Collective bargaining.
See Collective Bargaining.
Governmental and charitable immunity.
See Governmental and Charitable Immunity.
Physical fitness tests.
State is liable for failure to provide reasonable care and supervision,
p. 616.
Pushball game.
No duty violated when students sustain injury, p. 627.
Tort liability.
Generally, pp. 613 to 616.

ADMISSIONS TAX.
See Taxation.

AGENCIES.
Charitable corporations.
Liability for tort of agents.
Corporation may be immune, p. 696.
State university as a subordinate agency.
See State Universities.

APPEARANCE.
Students.
Equal protection, pp. 439, 440.

APPELLATE REVIEW.
Procedure of courts.
Generally, pp. 18, 19.

ASSAULT.
Intentional interference, pp. 591, 592.

ASSUMPTION OF RISK.
Negligence.
Defenses for negligence, pp. 604, 605.

ATHLETICS.
Basketball game.
Fatal injury is hazard of game, p. 624.
Coach.
Liability for injuries sustained by player while riding in school car,
p. 634.

R

DATE DUE

MY 2 8 '75		
NO 1 8 '75		
OC 2 5 '76		
NO 21 '76		
AUG 11 '77		
MY 7 '79		
JUN 9 1980		
DEC 5 1983		
AUG 2 2 1984		
MAY 2 5 '87		
MAY 3 1 '93		
		PRINTED IN U.S.A.